*Critical Issues in Education*

# Critical Issues in Education

## Dialogues and Dialectics

### FOURTH EDITION

**Jack L. Nelson**
*Rutgers University*

**Stuart B. Palonsky**
*University of Missouri*

**Kenneth Carlson**
*Rutgers University*

*Foreword*
*Nel Noddings*

Boston   Burr Ridge, IL   Dubuque, IA   Madison, WI   New York
San Francisco   St. Louis   Bangkok   Bogotá   Caracas   Lisbon   London
Madrid   Mexico City   Milan   New Delhi   Seoul   Singapore   Sydney
Taipei   Toronto

# McGraw-Hill Higher Education

*A Division of The **McGraw-Hill** Companies*

CRITICAL ISSUES IN EDUCATION: DIALOGUES AND DIALECTICS,
FOURTH EDITION

This book is printed on acid-free paper.

1 2 3 4 5 6 7 8 9 0 DOC/DOC 0 9 8 7 6 5 4 3 2 1 0

ISBN 0–07–228661–X

Editorial director: *Jane E. Vaicunas*
Sponsoring editor: *Beth Kaufman*
Editorial coordinator: *Teresa Wise*
Marketing manager: *Daniel M. Loch*
Project manager: *Vicki Krug*
Production supervisor: *Enboge Chong*
Coordinator of freelance design: *Rick Noel*
Compositor: *Precision Graphics*
Typeface: *10/12 Palatino*
Printer: *R. R. Donnelley & Sons Company/Crawfordsville, IN*

Cover designer: *Chris Reese*
Cover image © *Harald Sund/The Image Bank*

**Library of Congress Cataloging-in-Publication Data**

Nelson, Jack L.
  Critical issues in education : dialogues and dialectics / Jack L.
Nelson, Kenneth Carlson, Stuart B. Palonsky.— 4th ed.
    p.   cm.
  Includes bibliographical references and index.
  ISBN 0–07–228661–X
  1. Education—United States.   2. Teaching—United States.
3. Educational evaluation—United States.   4. Critical thinking–
–United States.   I. Carlson, Kenneth.   II. Palonsky, Stuart B.
III. Title.
LA217.2.N45     2000
370'.973—dc21                                                    99–32995
                                                                      CIP

www.mhhe.com

# Brief Contents

## Part Three
## HOW SHOULD SCHOOLS BE ORGANIZED AND OPERATED?

# Contents

Part Two
WHAT SHOULD BE TAUGHT?

# *Foreword*

We all know that reasonable people differ on matters of great importance in education and, more generally, on issues concerning the public good. However, in the crush of demands, teacher educators often bypass critical issues in favor of meeting the pressing need to prepare teachers for their instructional and managerial roles in classrooms. We expect them to help their students learn how to think critically, but we sometimes assume that they already engage in such thinking themselves. *Critical Issues in Education* presents educators-in-training with the opportunity to consider opposing arguments on almost two dozen vital issues.

In this fourth edition of their popular text, Jack Nelson, Stuart Palonsky, and Kenneth Carlson bring these important issues up to date. They offer persuasive arguments, pro and con, on vouchers, affirmative action, whole language, multicultural studies, standardized testing, increased academic freedom for teachers, and many other contemporary issues. In most cases, the arguments, although they are presented dialectically, are not posed at the extremes. Indeed, readers may want to search out and defend even stronger arguments on one side or the other. I found myself reacting to several of the arguments with some emotion, thinking, "Oh, this could be argued more strongly!" or "This should be protested more vigorously!" That reaction says something about both the salience of the issues and the power of the presentations.

Most people interested in education have opinions on the topics in *Critical Issues,* but their opinions are often highly emotional and unsupported by careful argument. Because opinions are so frequently founded on strong feelings, educators have endorsed critical thinking as an essential aim of education in liberal democracies. We want our students to hold their beliefs evidentially, to support their opinions with arguments that others cannot brush aside as mere feeling. To understand our own positions, however, we need to understand the positions of those who oppose us. John Stuart Mill (1859/1993) was eloquent on this:

> The greatest orator, save one, of antiquity, has left it on record that he always studied his adversary's case with as great, if not with still greater, intensity than even his own. What Cicero practised as the means of forensic success, requires

to be imitated by all who study any subject in order to arrive at the truth. He who knows only his own side of the case, knows little of that. His reasons may be good, and no one may have been able to refute them. But if he is equally unable to refute the reasons on the opposite side; if he does not so much as know what they are, he has no ground for preferring either opinion. (p. 43)

But Mill would have us encourage our students to go beyond the arguments presented in *Critical Issues,* and this is good advice:

Nor is it enough, that he should hear the arguments of adversaries from his teachers, presented as they state them, and accompanied by what they offer as refutations. . . . He must be able to hear them from persons who actually believe them; who defend them in earnest, and do their very utmost for them. (p. 43)

This is the invitation *Critical Issues* offers. Nelson, Palonsky, and Carlson do not claim to present comprehensive opposing arguments, nor do they suggest that there are only two sides to the crucial issues discussed. The dialectical mode should spark reaction (as it did in me), and lead students to investigate more deeply and, perhaps, to construct alternatives.

One reason for studying the opposing side carefully is, as Mill pointed out, to understand our own position more thoroughly. But another reason, too often neglected, is the possibility that we may achieve a genuine appreciation for the other side. We may be persuaded; thinking reflectively, we may change our minds. But even when we become more deeply committed to our own position, we may arrive at a more genuine respect for our adversary. As a result, we may work actively and honestly toward a compromise that will not do serious damage to our basic commitments.

An example may help here. In the past few years, I have had conversations—some written, some oral—with members of the Christian right. We disagree on many issues. At a symposium of the American Educational Research Association, an evangelical intellectual spoke eloquently about "his" values. They included honesty, courage, compassion, loyalty, and the like. Annoyed, I responded (to heartening applause from the audience) that these were not just "his" values but, rather, values that most of us, including humanists, accept and cherish. My adversary answered in a way I will never forget. He admitted that we might share important values, but he said that the values—important as they are—are secondary. Of primary importance is the worldview in which they arise. In his worldview, God is the source of value; in mine, human beings in interaction with one another construct value. How can we create a program of moral education if we must start with a worldview?

I am still struggling with this problem, and I believe that secular educators must find a way to accommodate religious worldviews in public school curricula. It is likely that no suggestion we can make will entirely satisfy fundamentalists, because they believe honestly that only one view is right, and they will condemn our attempts to include their view along with others as "relativism." Here, my own view seems clearly better: After all, I am willing to include theirs, whereas they stubbornly label mine wrong. But if I swallow my feeling of liberal superiority, I can see that my willingness to include all views is, in a sense, an insistence on my own. That, at bottom, *is* my worldview—that there are many reasonable, interesting competing views we should hear and allow to live side by side. In a way, if I can get agreement on this, I've won.

My adversary has a much tougher problem, and working together is incredibly difficult. Still, I think we must try. Many of the fundamentalist's points are well taken. Schools pay far too little attention to the great existential questions, and they are afraid even to consider discussing religious answers to these questions. If a compromise can be achieved, we may all gain from it.

A third reason for attending to current conflicts is to acquire educational literacy. Even if we are personally uninterested in some of these problems, we should recognize that others find them intensely interesting. As professionals, we need to know what arouses such interest and how it is likely to play out politically.

One more reason for studying opposing views is to get a better understanding of what it means to be reasonable. We sometimes consider a heartfelt sentiment expressed by someone we like as reasonable without examination. And sometimes we allow the possibility that an outrageous opinion is reasonable because we want to show our own tolerance or sophistication. However, unreasonable positions do exist, and students must learn how to assess them and how to deal with the people who express them. They have to learn how to evaluate their own arguments for reasonability, too. At a certain stage, well-educated people are prone to say of unreasonable people, "You can't talk to those people." They even consider it morally questionable to talk to "those people." Thus, the world, in the hands of "reasonable" people, deteriorates into physical and psychological violence. When others are unreasonable, perhaps the best strategy is to change the subject so that a relationship of care and trust can be established or maintained. When it is clear that both sides find it unthinkable to do real harm to one another, they can return to the questions that separate them. It is ultimately reasonable to offer and to elicit caring responses without denying reality and truth.

The educational contribution of *Critical Issues* goes well beyond helping students achieve literacy on current issues. It should help them to understand their own positions more fully, to gain an appreciation for the motives and predicaments of others, and to increase their understanding of what it means to be reasonable. This is no mean contribution.

NEL NODDINGS
STANFORD UNIVERSITY
TEACHERS COLLEGE, COLUMBIA UNIVERSITY

## *Reference*

MILL, J. S. (1859/1993). *On Liberty* and *Utilitarianism*. New York: Bantam Books.

# *Preface*

Welcome to the great debates about schools in society.

Schools , at the beginning of the twenty-first century, are still among the most important and most controversial social institutions. For over three hundred years, people on this continent have agreed on the importance of education, but have disagreed over how it should be controlled, financed, organized, conducted, and evaluated. Two centuries ago, a very young United States was debating the establishment of free and compulsory education, arguing over who should be educated, who should pay, and what should be taught. We have mass education now, but some of these same arguments continue about schools in society. Of course, controversies about important issues are inevitable and, we argue, healthy in a democratic society.

A century ago John Dewey published "My Pedagogic Creed," 1897, calling the school the "fundamental" means for progress and reform of society. His book, *School and Society*, which he published in 1900, laid out some basic social premises for progressive education. Those progressive premises remain under attack in the first decade of the twenty-first century. Social reformer Jane Addams, speaking at the National Education Association meeting of 1897, noted the social purposes of education and the need for schools to provide improved education to "foreign-born children," a precursor to current battles over multicultural education. Susan B. Anthony, cofounder of the National Womans Suffrage Association, argued, also in 1897, that schools then closed to women should open their doors to equality. Race, class, and gender discrimination remain educational issues a century later. Many other school controversies have arisen over the course of time, but pervasive issues survive, often different in patterns and details.

Persistent school issues reflect basic human disagreements. Ideological differences in politics, economics, and social values undergird the battles over schools. The issues and competing ideologies deserve critical examination. It is informative to study schooling by reading newspaper or magazine reports of test scores, finance, and school activities. But the media often ignore or gloss over basic social or ideological conflicts, and they can sterilize issues by presenting only one view; few media provide alternative views of an issue. The implication that there is one correct view obscures the historical, political, and social contexts that surround school controversies.

Our effort, in this book, is to explore a collection of pervasive and critical school issues by providing divergent views on each. The issues presented are dynamic; by presenting them in the form of opposing essays, we intend to show how provocative and complex they are. That does not mean they are unsolvable problems; it does suggest that good solutions rely upon engaged and informed debate. We see the terrain of education as rugged and rocky, with few clear paths and many conflicting road signs.

## The Book's Organization

The introductory chapter presents a background for examining reform efforts and debates in education.

The three following sections are each devoted to a major question about schooling and are introduced with background material to provide a context:

Part One—What interests should schools serve?

Part Two—What should be taught?

Part Three—How should schools be organized and operated?

Each part contains chapters on specific critical issues, and each chapter contains two essays expressing divergent positions on that issue. Obviously, these do not exhaust all the possible positions; they do provide at least two views on the issue, and references are provided in each chapter to encourage further exploration. At the end of each chapter are a few questions to consider and a brief sample of related data.

On the one hand, the public views American education as being in deep trouble and getting worse; on the other hand, they view their local schools as remarkably good, with excellent teachers and high-quality programs. If we had a third hand, we could add another view. New views emerge as debates over education stimulate us to rethink our positions.

The authors took initial responsibility for different parts of this volume. For Nelson this included: Introduction to Part II and chapters 1, 7, 11, 12, 15, 17, and 19; for Carlson: Introduction to Part I and chapters 2, 3, 4, 5, 6, and 10; and for Palonsky: Introduction Part III and chapters 8, 9, 12, 14, 16, and 18.

## Acknowledgments

We received valuable suggestions from a variety of faculty members and students who have used this book in the three previous editions. For this edition, we revised and updated all chapters and replaced some topics that appeared in older editions with new chapters on current educational issues-debates over approaches to: reading instruction, gender, and the inclusion and mainstreaming of exceptional children in schools.

We owe great intellectual debts to people who examine the relation of education to society, and who express divergent ideas in the extensive literature available. That group includes a variety of both widely known and relatively obscure theorists and critics, as well as a corps of practitioners. We are also indebted to students, colleagues, and others who provided specific criticism and assistance as we worked through the various topics. In particular, we express appreciation to Beth Kaufman, our encouraging editor at McGraw-Hill, to Vicki Krug, our project manager, and to Gwen, Karen, and Nancy for support, enthusiasm, and criticism when needed.

We especially appreciate the contributions of many colleagues who reviewed the manuscript, criticized the work in progress, or provided provocative ideas to challenge us. Among these are: David Blacker, The University of Delaware; Pat Benne, Wittenberg University; David Cauble, Western Nebraska Community College; James Daly, Seton Hall University; Emily de la Cruz, Portland State University; Russell Dennis, Bucknell University; Annette Digby, The University of Arkansas; Gloria Earl, Indiana Wesleyan University; Herbert Edwards, attorney, Harbor Springs, Michigan; Paul Edwards, attorney, Colorado Springs, Colorado; Dean Kenneth Eltis, University of Sydney, Australia; William Fernekes, Hunterdon, New Jersey, Central High School; Karen Graves, Denison University; Kevin Laws, University of Sydney, Australia; Dean Steven Lilley, California State University, San Marcos; Joseph McCarthy, Suffolk University; Wally Moroz, Edith Cowan University, Perth, Australia; Nel Noddings, Stanford University; Valerie Pang, San Diego State University; Bonnie Rose, Riverside City Schools, California; Dean William Stanley, University of Colorado; Rocco Tomazic, Doctoral Student at Rutgers; Doris Terr, City Schools of New York; David Tyack, Stanford University; Jackie Thousand, California State University, San Marcos; Atilano Valencia, California State University, Fresno; Dorothy Watson, University of Missouri; and Burt Weltman, William Paterson College.

We further dedicate this effort to Megan, Jordan, Jonathan, Kirsten, Tom, Melanie, Chris, Mike, Barbara, Mark, Steven, Tory, and others of the generation of students and teachers who will be at the core of education in the twenty-first century.

# CHAPTER 1

# Introduction: Critical Issues and Critical Thinking

A number of questions face schools for the twenty-first century:

**On Purposes and Expectations**

Why isn't everyone happy with our schools?

What is a good school, a good teacher, a good curriculum, a good society?

Who should be going to school, for how long, at whose cost, and what should be taught to them?

Why don't we know, by now, what works best in education?

Whose interests should schools serve?

**On Preparing**

How should schools change to meet changing social conditions and expectations? How should they change to meet the challenges of increasing technology? expanding knowledge? climbing school expenses?

Where will we get the financial and human resources we need to provide high-quality schooling?

How should we prepare our teachers, and what should they expect in terms of salary, class size, academic freedom, and professional respect?

**On Deciding**

What evidence supports one view or another of school quality and school reform? Who can we trust to provide answers to schooling issues?

Why are arguments about schools so extended and deep-seated?

Why do we seem clueless about the best education? Aren't these the same questions we might have asked in the first decade of the twentieth century?

## EDUCATION AND SCHOOLING

These questions do not challenge the basic idea of education. Rare is the person who questions the value of education. The debates arise instead over the proper nature, form, and process of education, not on its fundamental virtues. If anything, the debates are more strident because of the pervasive agreement on the benefits of education. If it were an inconsequential activity, education would not be worthy of the intensity and longevity of the disputes.

Education is important to all. We support education and want to be educated, but we disagree over what education should be and how we should organize and operate the educational system. So we argue about education, and about how schools should run.

Schooling, of course, is not the only way to organize and operate education. Education actually occurs in many settings, including the home, the workplace, religious institutions, the media, libraries, friendships, coffee shops, or just sitting and thinking. In Colonial America, most people received their educations outside of schools (Bailyn, 1960). Some of today's reluctant students might prefer that alternative to their life in school, but that is not an option available to many.

In this first decade of the twenty-first century, the school remains the most common approach to education around the world. Schools for small, elite groups of students have existed since ancient times, but mass education in schools is a relatively recent global phenomenon. Though it is essentially a twentieth-century development, schooling has become a dominant social institution worldwide. Public and private schools are the social institutions organized to provide formal education in modern nations. Schools increasingly involve nearly all the student-age populations of most nations. Wealthier nations provide schooling for the largest proportion of children for the longest period of time, but less wealthy nations have rapidly increased primary school education and are moving to expand secondary and higher education opportunities for more students. Figure 1.1 shows the global effort to educate.

The schools of the world now employ 57 million teachers, who comprise the largest professional occupation. Finding adequate resources to support these teachers is becoming a major global issue. Schools in the poorest nations face serious shortages of basic requirements, from electricity and water to textbooks. Many schools in all parts of the world are in poor physical condition and are getting worse. Significant numbers of schools are ill-prepared, in equipment, staff, and resources, to provide the technological knowledge needed to handle contemporary world affairs, increasing the separation between the rich and the poor nations. And teachers' income and status have "stagnated or even declined" (*UNESCO World Education Report, 1998*).

Schooling also involves large numbers—of people, dollars, and locations—in the United States. The number of school districts approaches 15,000. These districts have individual schools, student enrollments, numbers of teachers, and costs that indicate the enormity of the schooling enterprise today. Table 1.1

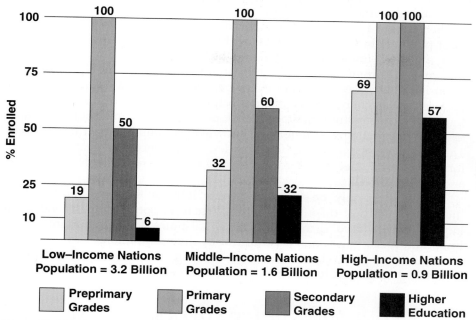

Source: World Development Indicators 1998. Washington, D.C.: The World Bank.

FIGURE 1.1

**TABLE 1.1  School Enrollments and Public School Expenditures, Projected 1985 to 2005**

| YEAR | Enrollments (in millions of students) | | | Expenditures | |
| | PUBLIC | PRIVATE | TOTAL | TOTAL COSTS (IN BILLIONS OF CONSTANT 1995 DOLLARS) | PER PUPIL COST |
|---|---|---|---|---|---|
| 1985 | 39.4 | 5.5 | 44.9 | $184.6 | $5,071 |
| 1990 | 41.2 | 5.2 | 46.4 | 229.1 | 6,060 |
| 1995 | 44.8 | 5.7 | 50.5 | 250.5 | 6,151 |
| 2000 | 47.4 | 6.0 | 53.4 | 294.6 | 6,742 |
| 2005 | 48.3 | 6.1 | 54.4 | 326.6 | 7,306 |

Source: *Projections of Educational Statistics to 2008*. U.S. Department of Education, 1996.

summarizes U.S. school enrollments for public and private schools and the expenditures of the public schools.

Schools are a focus of criticism and reform because schools are among the most public of institutions, are one of the most common experiences people have, and are of immense importance to the lifeblood and future of societies. In the smallest community and the largest city, schools are highly visible and extensively discussed. Virtually every person spends long periods of life in schools; teachers may spend a lifetime. Schools carry significant social trust for transmitting the cultural heritage, developing economic and political competence, and providing inspiration and knowledge to improve the future society. The nature and form of that heritage, that competence, and that knowledge form constant battlegrounds for different views of what schools ought to be and ought to be doing.

School is not only the subject of dispute, it is also the logical place for the thoughtful study of disputes. A setting where reasoned thought and open inquiry are practiced is most suitable for disputes about important issues. Important social issues are characterized by diverse opinions. Critical issues, those of the greatest significance, are subject to the most intense disputes. Indeed, debate is basic to the very definition of the word *issue.*

## CONTINUING DEBATES OVER SCHOOLING

Earlier human groups in simpler times argued about what knowledge children should learn, how they should behave, and who should teach them. Evidence from ancient civilizations shows that schooling was an important topic of concern. In the contemporary world, abundant material in newspapers and magazines shows that debates about schooling have not been resolved. Education is a vital subject of sometimes shrill discussion in families, neighborhoods, regions, and societies around the globe. Ask a variety of people what they think of schools in their area and in the nation; you can expect a variety of strongly held opinions.

Conservative economist Thomas Sowell (1993) argues that American schools are low in quality and are deteriorating even further as a result of educators' deceptive tactics, the "shockingly low" caliber of teachers and professors of education, dogma about student "self-esteem," teacher tenure, and multicultural diversity, and "classroom brainwashing" designed to change the values of students. Sowell states: "The brutal reality is that the American system of education is bankrupt . . . That bankruptcy is both in institutions and in attitudes" (pp. 285–286).

Educational researchers David Berliner and Bruce Biddle (1995) present an opposite view. Based on their examination of test scores, international school finance data, and various other indicators of achievement and support, they conclude that school critics are mistaken or uninformed. They discount the critics' assertions that student achievement and teacher quality have declined and that schools are failing the society. Berliner and Biddle summarize their analysis with the response that "these assertions are errant nonsense" (p.13), and they conclude that "American education has recently been subjected to an unwarranted, vigorous, and damaging attack—a Manufactured Crisis . . . the major claims of the attack turn out to have been myths; the Manufactured Crisis was revealed as a Big Lie" (p. 343).

For a variety of reasons, schools continue to be one of the most critical issues of the twenty-first century. Education represents the continuation of the past and the direction of the future for all societies. As the world becomes more complex and as knowledge expands, education increases in importance. More and more people need to know more and more about more and more subjects. Ironically, education is one reason for the increasing complexity of life as well as one of the main means for dealing with that complexity.

Through the search for knowledge, we develop faster and more comprehensive systems of communication, travel, and research—which then require faster and more comprehensive systems of education to comprehend and extend that knowledge. The economics and the politics of this change in technology has not been lost in education battles. Doheny-Farina (1996), discussing the coming of virtual society and virtual schools, cites the argument that "Distance education will become the norm, the least expensive way to deliver the educational product, while face-to-face teaching will be only for the well-to-do"(p. 108). He concludes, however, that "most of those [distance learning] materials will be in the form of prescribed packages, which over time will tend to centralize expertise . . ." and that "the virtualization of school removes it from the fabric of the local community" (pp. 110, 116, 117). That scenario is a serious threat to many and deserves debate. Educational theorist Michael Apple (1994) claims that distance learning de-skills teachers, making them switch-turners and simple conduits for other people's ideas and procedures. That will destroy the central characteristic of democratic education: the freedom to learn and to teach.

## THE POLITICAL CONTEXT OF SCHOOLING

The public has lofty expectations for education, giving schools the responsibility for much of their children's welfare, values, skills, and knowledge. One expectation is that schools can correct social ills like crime and slovenliness. Individuals also expect schools to provide self-fulfillment, ranging from employment skills to personal happiness. Meeting those diverse expectations is extraordinarily difficult; many expectations result in many interpretations of what schools should be doing and what they are doing well or badly.

Schools, then, are seen as a source of both problems and solutions. Problems include wasted tax money as well as students with poor skills, low test scores, and rude behavior. Proposed solutions to social problems include programs in drug and sex education, moral training, and crime prevention.

Schooling issues are complex topics of crucial individual and social importance. That is why education has emerged again as one of the most highly charged areas in political contests. Candidates tend to offer clean, neat, and simple answers to long-term school problems. Most candidates for President, state governor, or the U.S. Congress have high-profile, albeit often inconsistent, messages about schools:

- Cut class size, but cut school expenses.
- Repair buildings, but lower taxes.
- Allow more local control, but impose more national standards and support.
- Have schools educate against violence and drug abuse, but have schools teach only the basics.
- Improve sex education, but do not teach values in school.
- Make teachers more accountable, but give teachers more freedom and responsibility.
- Increase distance learning by computers, but increase schooltime and the school year.
- Increase school competition for grades and awards, but make schools more collaborative, inclusive, and supportive.

There are reasons for the often schizophrenic quality of school debates. As Theodore Sizer said, "Everybody is for high test scores till their kids get low test scores" (Bronner, 1998). Also, it is easy to claim that our own education was vastly superior to what students are now getting in school, and to advocate a return to the good old days. But how many would actually want their children to return to the reality and the limitations of yesterday's schools?

Arguments fly about the quality and value of shifts in schooling. These arguments are worthy of attention because they involve ideological, political, and personal interests. School reforms are subject to intense political pressure as politicians struggle to position themselves as saviors of education. It is not surprising that schools are not only the subject of public dispute but also of partisan political interest. Schools are, among other things, both political agencies and handy targets from every side of party politics. Schools consume more local budget money than any other social agency, and they are among the top consumers of state funds. Schools are a major responsibility under state legislation and local control, subjecting them to political pressures both from those in office and those vying to be.

The national level has seen a rekindling of political interest in education since 1975. The Department of Education became a pulpit for strong views on schools when William Bennett was Secretary, even though one of the goals of President Reagan's party was the abolition of the Department. Presidential politics now include a strong focus on schools, and most candidates want to be your Education President.

## DEMOCRATIC VITALITY AND EDUCATIONAL CRITICISM

Critics of schools are easy to find. People are not bashful about noting school problems, but there is disagreement over what is wrong, who is responsible, and what should be done to change schools. Criticism of schools is fully consistent with open democracy. Of all social institutions, the school should be the most ready for examination; education rests upon critical assessment and reassessment. That does not mean that all criticism is justified, or even useful. Some of it is simplistic, mean-spirited, or wrong-headedly arrogant. But much of it is thoughtful and cogent. Although some unjustified criticism can be detrimental to education in a democracy, open debate can permit the best ideas to be developed and revised.

Over the long haul, schooling has improved, and civilization has been served by the debates over education. More people get more education of a better quality across the world now than in previous generations. Despite lapses and declines, the debates force us to reconsider ideas about schooling and increase our sophistication about schools and society.

Democratic vitality and educational criticism are good companions. Democracy, as Thomas Jefferson so wisely noted, requires an enlightened public and free dissent. Education is the primary means to enlightenment and to thoughtful dissent. It follows that schools would be among those fundamental social institutions under continuing public criticism in a society striving to improve democracy.

Dewey (1916) put schools at the center of democracy:

> The devotion of democracy to education is a familiar fact. . . . Since a democratic society repudiates the principle of external authority, it must find a substitute in voluntary disposition and interest; these can only be created by education. (p. 87)

Bertrand Russell (1928) also noted that education is basic to democracy:

> . . . it is in itself desirable to be able to read and write . . . an ignorant population is a disgrace to a civilized country, and . . . democracy is impossible without education. (p. 128)

Democratic vitality and educational criticism both require the open expression of diverse ideas, and yet both are based upon an optimistic sense of unity of purpose. Diverse ideas and criticism provide necessary tests of our ideas. Criticism can easily appear to be negative, pessimistic, or cynical, but these are not its only forms. Informed skepticism, the purpose for this book, offers a more optimistic view without becoming like Pollyanna. Diverse ideas are sought because we think, optimistically, that education can be improved. Unity of purpose suggests that there is a bedrock of agreement on basic values, the criteria against which to judge diverse ideas. Without diverse ideas, there is no vitality and opportunity for progress; without unity of purpose, diverse ideas can be chaotic and irrational.

## THE CHANGING FOCUS OF DEBATES

In the last two decades of the twentieth century, public debates over education changed significantly from a focus on crisis, hand-wringing, and derisive blame to arguments over which political candidate could offer more financial support, smaller classes, and better facilities and teachers to schools. The 1980s competition to bash schools and teachers has been replaced by a public affirmation that the future of schools and of society are intertwined. Serious disagreements, of course, continue on such topics as affirmative action, access to schooling, multi- or monocultural emphasis, school choice, tracking, curriculum, morals and values education, privatization and public financing, uses of standardized testing, gender, race, and/or class discrimination, violence, and other topics. The tenor of the debates, however, has shifted from castigation and condemnation to diverse proposals for cash infusions, accountability, and specific corrective action.

Harsh criticisms of schools and teachers spiked during the 1980s. Governmental reports claimed that schools, floating on a rising tide of mediocrity, had put the nation at risk and were responsible for declining American values and economic competitiveness. More reasoned analyses of the data indicate that schools were not as bad as they had been portrayed to the public (Bracey, 1992, 1994, 1995, 1997, 1998; Berliner, 1993; Berliner and Biddle, 1995).

Evidence even exists that the government suppressed for two years a major government-sponsored study that showed that U.S. schools were better than the Bush administration wanted to divulge (Tanner, 1993). In 1990, the government contracted Sandia National Laboratories, a widely respected research agency, to conduct a thorough study of American education (Carson, Huelskamp, and Woodall, 1992). The Sandia Report, submitted to the Department of Energy in 1991, showed that U.S. schools were far better than the government and influential media had been reporting and that government-heralded school reforms were based on misinterpretations of the data.

The main findings of the Sandia Report include the facts that: (1) scores on SAT tests for comparable students have remained the same or increased over time, but many more students from the lower half of a class now take the test, causing the average score to decline; (2) nonwhite ethnic and racial groups have maintained or improved their SAT test scores since the late 1970s; (3) scores on National Assessment of Educational Progress tests have improved; (4) the United States has the highest college enrollment rates in the world, and the highest percentage of women and minorities who earn degrees; at the same time, scores on the Graduate Record Exam have actually risen significantly; (5) high school dropout rates for all groups except Hispanics have decreased, and the Hispanic group included a high proportion of immigrants who had dropped out of school before they came to the United States; (6) teachers' beginning salaries, after adjusting for inflation, were essentially the same in 1990 as they were in the 1970s; and (7) school expenditures for all except special education students have stagnated, in constant dollars, for over two decades (Huelskamp, 1993; Tanner, 1993, p. 293).

Among its conclusions, the Sandia Report notes: "Much of the 'crisis' commentary today claims total system-wide failure in education. Our research shows that this is simply not true" (Carson, Huelskamp, and Woodall, 1992, p. 99).

Findings of the Sandia Report did not support the idea that U.S. schools had declined precipitously, an idea fostered by government educational policy and prominently featured in news reports. In an apparent effort to change or suppress the Report, government agencies subjected it to extensive delays and revisions. These changes did not refute the major conclusion that the public schools were actually doing pretty well in educating our youth. Delays and revisions did, however, effectively suppress the Report from public view for over two years (Tanner, p. 292), placing it among the ten most censored stories of 1994 (Jensen, 1994).

Obviously, recent arguments over the best means for improving buildings, providing more and better prepared teachers, and increasing school budgets are far more pleasant to school people than the accusations fired at them in the latest era of dissatisfaction. Although fundamental differences may arise in educational viewpoint, it is much nicer to argue over how to spend an increased budget than to face critics who denounce and seek to demolish schools.

Wholesale shifts in the public view, however, are cyclical. One can predict that the early twenty-first century will find schools again the focus of blame for a variety of social ills. Educators should not be complacent about the contemporary and more positive arguments over who has the best idea for supporting schooling; negative critics are standing by.

## *PUBLIC RATINGS OF SCHOOLS*

Even with negative publicity about schools, survey evidence shows that the public rating of *local* public schools has actually been positive, and often increasingly so, for over a quarter-century. The Annual Phi Delta Kappa/ Gallup Poll has surveyed the public since 1974. In 1992, the poll showed the largest one-year increase in the grades people give to their local public schools in almost two decades, from 40 percent grading their schools A or B in 1992 to 47 percent rating them that high in 1993 (Elam, 1993). In 1998, the annual poll showed that 46 percent of all respondents gave their local schools an A or B, and 52 percent of public school parents gave their children's schools an A or B grade (Rose and Gallup, 1998).

Ironically, people rate local schools significantly higher than they rate unknown schools across the nation (only 18 percent give the nation's schools an A or B). When members of the public grade the school that their oldest children attended, the rating is very high (about 65 percent rating them A or B). Gallup interpreted these data to suggest that the more the public knows about actual practices in schools, the better they rate them. The data also indicate that negative political and media treatment of schooling influences the way people grade the schools they know the least, not those they know well.

The decreasing stridency in negative criticism of schools might suggest that school reforms in the past fifteen years have been successful, but that would be a misreading. No clear evidence exists about the reforms and their consequences;

the outcomes are still in dispute. Although many claims surround specific reforms, few comprehensive studies show that any school is significantly better or worse now as a result of the 1980s reforms. Since recent evidence shows that the schools were never as bad as the government and the media reported, one could make the case that some of the reforms hindered school progress by improperly blaming and alienating teachers and by forcing more testing and governmental intervention in school requirements and operations.

The national Goals 2000 campaign and legislation presses the schools to meet a strange mix of externally determined standards that are vague (students will come to school ready to learn) or unrealistic (American students will score highest in international mathematics tests). This reflects a political view based on unsupported assumptions that the schools have failed and government has to interfere (Clinchy, 1995; Resnick and Nolan, 1995). Goals 2000 does not meet the concerns of educational thinkers who propose a qualitatively different idea of progress for schools, one where caring, ethics, critical thinking, and creative imagination are worthy conditions for a liberal education (Noddings, 1995; Greene, 1995). Perhaps a different program under the title Goals 2015 or 2025 will have more success.

Even though local schools are well-received, schooling remains one of the most controversial topics in society. The evidence that schools are better than reported should not lead to complacency since schools benefit from good criticism, but the suppressed evidence should suggest that we should maintain a level of skepticism about news media reports and political statements about schools. The political nature of educational issues suggests the importance of schooling in contemporary society as well as ideological differences over the direction society and its schools should take.

Obviously, it is not difficult to find an argument about schools. We as a society share an interest in good schools, but we hold strongly felt, diverse views of what makes schools good or bad. These views are shaped by differing visions of the good society and how new generations should be prepared for it. In the United States, we are reform-minded about all aspects of society and, as in our views on schools, we hold widely disparate views on what societal changes we need to make. Historian David Tyack (1991), discussing the intertwining of school reform with social reform, says, "For over a century and a half, Americans have translated their cultural anxieties and hopes into demands for educational reform" (p. 1).

## IDEOLOGICAL ROOTS OF SCHOOL CRITICISM

Schools are directly engaged in developing the individuals and society of the future. People care a great deal about what kind of individuals and society will develop. Apple (1990) states:

> . . . the conflicts over what should be taught are sharp and deep. It is not "only" an educational issue, but one that is inherently ideological and political. (p. vii)

Ideologies are sets of beliefs which enable people to explain and justify the society they would prefer. An ideology includes assumptions about the nature and purpose of society and the related nature of individuals (Shils, 1968); it provides criteria against which one can judge human life and society (Lane, 1962); and it provides a means for self-identification (Erikson, 1960). Ideologies are basic rationales for divergent educational views that want to either sustain, alter, or overthrow the contemporary school (Christenson, et al., 1971). Each ideology also provides unity around its beliefs.

Thus, traditionalists share a general view that schools ought to follow time-honored ideas, practices, and authorities from a previous golden age of education. Progressivists share a different view—that schools must be flexible, child-centered, and future-oriented. Radical educational ideologies from the right include the views of libertarians (get government off our backs and out of our schools); abolitionists (abolish public schooling); and extreme elitists (schooling for the best only). Radical left wing views include those of liberationists (liberate students from school oppression); reconstructionists (use schools to criticize and remake society); and extreme egalitarians (abolish all privilege). Each ideology provides different views of schooling, from advocating the abolition of public schools to using public schools for social criticism and the overthrow of oppression.

Divergent views of schooling and politics can be understood in terms of an ideological continuum: from elitist positions on the extreme right to egalitarian positions on the extreme left, with mainstream conservative and liberal positions in the center (see figure 1.2).

Radical views are important because they present stark and clearly defined differences between egalitarian and elitistic ideologies. However, mainstream conservative and liberal ideas govern most reform movements because of their general popularity and their immense influence over the media and government. Liberals, conservatives, and radicals differ in their views of which mainstream position has the schools in its grip (Aronowitz and Giroux, 1993).

FIGURE 1.2

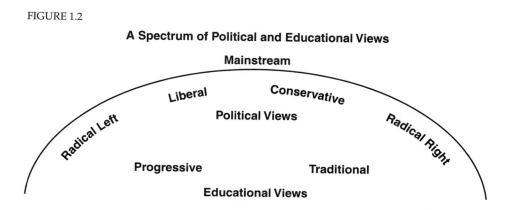

**A Spectrum of Political and Educational Views**

## Plato, Dewey, and Counts: Three Positions

The importance of education in society is reflected in the controversies surrounding divergent ideological positions. Plato, along with significant philosophers of every time period, considered education one of the most important social activities. Despite some progressive ideas for his time, Plato remains a prime example of the conservative ideology identified as traditionalism or essentialism in education. Traditionalism usually holds that

- There is a specific body of essential or traditional knowledge that students must learn.
- Authority rests on tradition.
- Precise standards should be expected and enforced.
- "Wrong" ideas could be subject to censorship.
- The cultural heritage should be exalted and taught.

Although traditionalist education has been portrayed as dull and pedantic, we doubt that either Plato or current traditionalist thinkers would like joyless schools run by stern teachers who do not permit deviation from the lesson, where rote memorization and recitation of useless information are the standard, and where such measures as SAT scores are considered the prime indicators of learning. We can't blame traditionalists for all bad school practices, but uncritical traditionalist ideology can lead to dull and lifeless schools, repetitive drill, and memorization of trivial information to pass tests or to meet externally imposed standards.

John Dewey, whose views represent the liberal, progressive side of the ideological continuum, also clearly recognized the power and importance of education in society. Dewey's *Democracy and Education* (1916) challenges Plato's concept of a fixed ideal for school and for society, arguing that society is dynamic and change is necessary. Dewey argued strongly against Plato's idea that knowledge comes from outside the students' experience and that students should only learn what previous generations learned. Dewey's view of learning involves reconstruction, where students are actively involved in learning, constantly reconstructing and reorganizing their experiences to gain better understanding of life as it is happening. Dewey makes a case for individual differences and active participation in experiences and learning. He also makes a powerful case for strong teachers who are sensitive to student needs and who can guide students well. Dewey, however, would not condone some things which go on in today's schools under the progressive label. We doubt that Dewey would support acquiescent teachers, chaos, and complete permissiveness in classrooms. Progressives, like traditionalists, are not to blame for all the ills in schools, but unthoughtful progressivist ideology can lead to a lack of standards, freeform learning, and teacher irresponsibility.

George Counts extended Dewey's reconstructionism idea to a more radical view of schooling. Dewey's reconstructionism refers to individual learning that results as students mentally reorganize experiences. Counts argued that the purpose of schools is to reconstruct society, not just to reflect and transmit the cultural heritage. The Reconstructionist view holds that schools are the best place for teachers and students to engage in social criticism aimed to change and improve society (Counts, 1932; Brameld, 1956; Stanley, 1992). This view places schools at the center of social change, criticizing the existing problems in society and involving students in social action to correct, or reconstruct, society. Clearly, this is a radical position, given the tradition of schools as agents of social stability and preservation—and the long-held expectation of student apathy.

Those who have power under the status quo, whether traditionalist or progressive, are not likely to be enamored of reconstructionist ideas for schools. Reconstructionism is highly controversial, but very interesting because it recognizes the potential power of schools. Reconstructionism attracted some thoughtful advocates and remains an intriguing reform idea, but few have attempted practicing these ideas in schools (Stanley, 1992).

Plato, Dewey, and Counts illustrate that wise thinkers can have thoughtful but divergent views on society and schools. Their conservative, liberal, and radical positions are historic examples of divergent views on educational issues. Each of these views makes different assumptions about the nature of students, knowledge, and society. And each suggests a different kind of school, a different kind of teacher, a different society.

## CONTEMPORARY CONSERVATIVE, LIBERAL, AND RADICAL VIEWS

Definitions of "conservative" and "liberal" may be slippery, but these terms are commonly applied and widely understood to refer to two distinct groups of ideas and people in any time period. Liberal ideas in one time period may be considered conservative in another, and vice-versa. Neoconservative and neoliberal views are a rethinking of conservative or liberal ideas (Steinfels, 1979; Rothenberg, 1984).

Radical positions from the right and left provide highly polarized answers to pervasive educational issues. Radical critiques influence the general debate by providing extremes that allow liberals and conservatives to take more popular positions in the center. Radical ideas tend to have limited credibility in mainstream discussions, but liberals and conservatives draw from those ideas in proposing reforms.

More deeply discordant ideological roots run beyond the mainstream liberal-conservative dialogue. These include a variety of radical positions on what a society and its schools should be. Critical positions often appear first in the radical literature, then filter into the liberal and conservative rhetoric (Nelson, Carlson, and Linton, 1972). Those mainstream views sound much more reasonable as bases for reform, but the radical ideas contain the seeds for longer-term and more significant change. In the age when kings and queens were presumed to rule by divine right, democracy was a radical view. In a dictatorship, individual freedom is radical.

Radical right wing ideas about schooling are not uniform; they come from different special interest groups. Some promote the teaching of fundamentalist religious dogma. Some seek to censor all teaching materials that deal with sex, socialism, atheism, or anything they think is "anti-American." And some want to undercut publicly supported schools in favor of elite schooling for a select group of students. Right wing groups have attacked "secular humanism," feminism, abortion rights, sex education, global education, and values education in schools (Kaplan, 1994).

The radical left wing also offers a disparate view of schools. Some see education as the way for the masses to uncover the evils of capitalism and the corporate state. Some advocate free schools, where students may study whatever they want. And some propose education as the means for revolution, opening all the institutions of society to criticism. Left wing groups have attacked business-sponsored teaching materials, religious dogma in the public schools, and education on patriotic obedience.

Conservative, liberal, and radical views of society and education provide different rationales for criticism of schools and different proposals for reform. They are general frameworks which underlie individual and group discontent with schools. We would like to include in this volume all viewpoints on each educational issue, but that is an obvious impossibility. We have therefore limited the views to those that illustrate issues in current society; some draw from liberal-progressive ideas, some from conservative-traditional, and some from radical critiques. Additional references to conservative, liberal, and radical literature are included, and we encourage students to explore these highly divergent views.

## *A TRADITION OF SCHOOL CRITICISM AND REFORM*

Criticism and reform in education are not new phenomena. We have had educational reform advocates for so long that it is impossible to identify their beginnings. Perhaps the first educational reformer, a member of some prehistoric group, rose up to protest that children in the group were not learning the basic skills, as he had. Another member may have come up with a radical new plan to improve children's hunting and gathering skills. Some of the bashed skulls lying about prehistoric sites are probably the results of arguments over education!

From the intensity and vigor of the public debate over schooling, a debate that has continued in Western society at least since the time of Socrates, one would expect either dramatic changes in schools or their abolition in favor of an alternative structure. At least one critic has argued to abolish schools (Illich, 1971), and some have proposed very significant changes in schooling (Sinclair, 1924; Rafferty, 1968; Apple, 1990). Most of the changes have been moderate, however, and no serious abolition attempts have occurred.

Our written records contain considerable evidence of efforts to use education to alter society and, thus, the recognition that ideas about education can be very controversial. One of the two accusations leveled against Socrates in the indictment that brought him to trial and sent him to his death by taking hemlock, was "corruption of the young" through schooling. Socrates may have paid the ultimate price for being an educational reformer in a political setting that was not ready for his reforms.

Some school purposes are commonly accepted, such as distributing knowledge and providing opportunity, but controversies arise over what knowledge we should distribute, which children should get which opportunities, and who should be making these decisions. For more than three thousand years, human societies have recognized the value of education—and have argued about what the goal of schooling should be and how to achieve it (Ulich, 1954). For about three hundred years, Americans have agreed that education is one of the most significant social topics, but they have engaged in arguments over what schools should be.

Shifts in criticism and efforts at reform are common in U.S. educational history (Cremin, 1961; Welter, 1962; Tyack, 1967; Karier, 1967; Katz, 1971), but the schools actually change only modestly. Traditional and progressive agendas differ, but schools seem to respond to them by moving very gradually in the direction proposed, with a few widely publicized examples of reform, and then to await the next movement. Kaestle (1985) notes, "[The] real school system is more like a huge tanker going down the middle of a channel, rocking a bit from side to side as it attends to one slight current and then to another" (p. 423). Purpel (1989) considered the highly visible school reforms of the 1980s to be relatively inconsequential, a trivialization of the important educational issues of the times.

## SCHOOL REFORM IN EARLY TWENTIETH CENTURY AMERICA

The United States has a long tradition of innovation in education, stemming from its pioneer role in providing popular education to large numbers of students at public expense. There are some major failures in this history, most notably in the lack of equal educational opportunities for African Americans, Native Americans, women, immigrants, and those of the lower classes. We have, however, expanded our view of education as a major means for developing democracy and for offering some social mobility. We may not realize these ambitions, and our real intentions may be less altruistic (Katz, 1968). But the idealization of democratic reform through education is in the traditional American rhetoric.

American schools, from the nineteenth century, were expected to blend immigrants into the American mainstream. They were to accomplish this through compulsory education with an emphasis on such subjects as English, American history, and civics. A history of racism, sexism, and ethnic prejudice was commonly ignored in American social life and schools, while we labored under the idea that everyone shared a happy society made up of people who should all talk, think, and form values the same way. Schools were understood to be a primary social agency to meld students from divergent cultural backgrounds into the American ideal, which, not unsurprisingly, exhibited European, white, male characteristics and values. Standard use of English language and belief in the superiority of western literature, history, politics, and economics dominated the schools. Schools were expected to be key institutions in "Americanizing" generations of immigrants.

In the early twentieth century, compulsory education laws became a primary reform agenda for schools, which were a part of a larger social reform movement. Urbanization and industrialization had created the need for different forms of school services. Large numbers of children from the working classes were now in schools in urban areas, and many criticized the traditional classical curriculum, teaching methods, and leisure-class approach to school.

Graham (1967) identifies the extensive development of vocational and technical courses as the most dominant change in schooling before World War I, as school activities broadened to include medical exams, health instruction, free lunch programs, schools open during vacation periods for working parents, and other community services. These reforms fit with the evolving sense of social progressivism.

The progressive education movement, from about 1920 to World War II, incorporated severe criticisms of traditional schooling ideas and practices. These traditional practices included corporal punishment, rigid discipline, rote memorization and drill, stress on the classics, and high failure rates.

Progressives offered a positive program involving students in deciding what was to be studied, engaging in practical experiences and projects and in community activities, opening up the study of opposing opinions on controversial topics, practicing democracy in the schools, and organizing the school as an embryonic society. Schools became more open to students of all classes, and the curriculum moved from more esoteric studies to courses with social applications, such as driver education, home economics, business and vocational education, current events, health, sociology, sex education, and consumer math.

Sporadic and severe criticisms of progressive thought cropped up throughout that time, but a major reform movement from the right gained more public interest near the end of the Depression and again following the war. Graham, summarizing the shift, states:

> Sometime between 1919 and 1955 the phrase "progressive education" shifted from a term of praise to one of opprobrium. To the American public of 1919, progressive education meant all that was good in education; thirty-five years later nearly all the ills in American education were blamed on it. (1967, p. 145)

Gurney Chambers (1948) notes that after the 1929 stock market crash, education came under attack: "Teachers were rebuked for their complacency and inertia, and the schools, surprisingly enough, were blamed for the increasing crime and divorce rates and political corruption" (pp. 142–143).

# RECENT CYCLES OF EDUCATIONAL REFORM

Attacks on the schools increased in intensity and frequency during the late 1940s and 1950s. The great school debates of this time involved many issues that extend into the twenty-first century.

Church-state issues, including school prayer and the use of public funds for religious school busing and other school services, gained significance. Racial issues, with the implications of the landmark Supreme Court decision in Brown vs. The Board of Education of Topeka (1954) and forced busing, became another focus of school controversy. Rapidly increasing tax burdens, to pay for the new schools and teachers required by the baby boom, aroused protests from many school critics. Rising expectations for education, driven by the thousands of "non-college-prep" veterans who went to college on the GI Bill, were applied to the lower schools. Curricular issues, including disputes over the most effective way to teach reading and over test scores that showed students did not know enough history or math or science or English, filled the popular press. The McCarthy "Red Scare" produced rampant public fear of a creeping Communistic influence in American life and created suspicions that schools were breeding grounds for "communal" and progressive thought. These, and other factors, led to renewed criticism of the schools. For many, there was simply a lingering sense that the schools were not doing their job.

Two books illustrate the criticisms of this period: Albert Lynd's *Quackery in the Public Schools* (1950, p. 53) and Arthur Bestor's *Educational Wastelands* (1953). Each attacked progressive education, and the "educationists" who advocated it, for turning schools away from traditional discipline and subject knowledge and toward the "felt needs" of children. As historian Clarence Karier notes in his discussion of the impact of Bestor's book, ". . . the educationist who spoke out for 'progressive education' and 'life adjustment education' appeared increasingly out of place in the postwar, cold war period" (1985, p. 238).

Major foundations began to examine America's schools. The Ford Foundation stated that education had emerged as the focal point of its work. Grants were made to the Educational Testing Service to improve measures of student performance. The Carnegie Foundation asked James Bryant Conant, former President of Harvard and U.S. Ambassador to West Germany, to conduct a series of studies of public education. There was much public criticism of the academic failures of American schools. Then came the Soviet launch of Sputnik in 1957, ahead of the United States, and a new focus for educational reform. The Sputnik launch was a highly visible catalyst for conservative critics, illustrating a lack of American competitiveness they attributed to progressive reforms in schools during the pre-World War II period. These critics blamed the "permissive" atmosphere in schools for this deficiency.

## *Excellence and Discontents*

Post-Sputnik reform included a reinstitution of rigor, discipline, traditional subject teaching, and standards. They added up to the theme, to be repeated in the 1980s, of "Excellence." In fact, there are some remarkable similarities in the language and rationales used in the earlier reform movement and those used in the 1980s efforts to return schools to traditional work. International competition, advancing technology, and the needs of business are rationales cited in the literature of both periods.

*Excellence*, ill-defined and excessively used, is a cue word that shows up in many reports and statements from both periods. John Gardner's prominent document for the Rockefeller Brothers Fund, *The Pursuit of Excellence: Education and the Future of America* (1958), is one illustration. Another term common to both periods is *mediocrity*, a threat suggested in the title of Mortimer Smith's book, *The Diminished Mind: A Study of Planned Mediocrity in Our Public Schools* (1954). The Conant Report, *The American High School Today* (1958), was a moderate book which proposed a standard secondary school curriculum, tracking by ability group, special courses for gifted students, improvements in English composition, better counseling, and other recommendations. It became a guide for many schools.

Federal funds for reform were dramatically increased in the late 1950s and early 1960s. The National Defense Education Act (NDEA) responded to pleas that the schools were key to providing "national defense," and that Sputnik showed that the United States was militarily vulnerable. Funds were provided to improve teaching in science and math, foreign languages, social studies, and English. These curricular projects primarily sought to encourage university scholars in each field to determine better ways to convey the subject matter; many projects attempted to make the curriculum "teacherproof" (as in foolproof) to prevent classroom teachers from teaching it incorrectly. Teacher education came in for its share of criticism, with blasts at the teachers' colleges, the progressive techniques they advocated, and the quality of students going into teaching. All of this sounds hauntingly familiar to those who read current educational criticism.

As the trend toward conservative educational ideas gained support and school practice turned back to standards and "rigor," criticism from the left began to emerge. This liberal criticism was a response to the rote memorization, excessive testing, lock-step schooling, and increased school dropout and failure rates that began to characterize schools. A number of writers, including Paul Goodman, George Dennison, Edgar Z. Friedenberg, A. S. Neill in England, Nat Hentoff, John Holt, Herbert Kohl, and Jonathan Kozol, attacked the schools for their sterility, bureaucracy, boredom, lack of creativity, rigidity, powerlessness of students and teachers, and inadequacy in educating disadvantaged youth. Holt (1964) stated:

> Most children in school fail . . . They fail because they are afraid, bored, and confused . . . bored because the things they are given and told to do in school are so trivial, so dull, and make such limited and narrow demands on the wide

spectrum of their intelligence, capabilities, and talents . . . Schools should be a place where children learn what they want to know, instead of what we think they ought to know. (pp. xiii, xiv, 174)

This 1960s left-wing reform rebelled against conservative authoritarianism and the dehumanization of schools. Reforms included open education, non-graded schools, more student freedom, more electives, less reliance on standardized tests, abolition of dress codes and rigid rules, and more teacher-student equality. The Vietnam War and demonstrations spurred the politics that stimulated much of the late 1960s educational reform literature.

Multicultural education was not on the educational agenda in early America because the main purpose of school was to produce a melting pot where various cultural strands were blended into the "new American." Consistent with ideas emerging from the civil rights movement in the 1950s and 1960s, at a time of great social transition toward equality of opportunity for minorities, the melting pot thesis about American society was judged to be a myth. This led to other approaches to the issue of diversity and unity in society and schools. One was the advocacy of separatism, where each major subcultural group would go its own way with separate social and school structures. Another was an effort to reconstitute a form of the melting pot idea by enforcing integration in such institutions as housing, restaurants, and schools. Integration often led to resegregation by white flight and the establishment of private all-white academies. Multicultural education, which aimed to recognize the positive contributions of a variety of national, racial, ethnic, gender, and other groups to American life, developed as a way to recognize both diversity and unity.

The multicultural effort was to correct a century of schooling which featured white male American or European heroes from the middle and upper social classes. African American, Latino, and women authors showed up on the lists of standard readings in English classes. The societal contributions of Native Americans, blacks, Chicanos, and females were added to history and civics books. Equal physical education opportunities for boys and girls, compensatory education for the disadvantaged, and programs featuring minority and women role models were developed.

## CONSERVATISM REVISITED: THE 1980S AND 1990S

In the early 1980s, reports of falling SAT and ACT scores, drug abuse, vandalism, and chaos in schools increased the public receptivity to reform. Nervousness about international competition, the resurgence of business and technology as dominant features of society, and questions about shifting morality and values provided a political setting that could blame the schools for inadequacies. The presidentially appointed National Commission on Excellence in Education published a highly political document, *A Nation at Risk* (1983), which claimed that there was a "rising tide of mediocrity" in the schools. The ensuing public debate produced a flurry of legislation to develop "excellence" and raise the quality of schools. The key term, *excellence,* suggests the competitive nature of schooling and the demand for increased standards.

Student protests of the 1960s had died and a negative reaction set in. "Yuppies" (Young Upwardly Mobile Professionals) emerged as role models for student style in the 1980s, embracing careerism and corporate fashion. There was an increasing perception of disarray in the American family, and a return to religion for many. The recurrence, under President Reagan, of open confrontation with Communism subsided as the Iron Curtain collapsed in the late 1980s. Anti-communism, a major influence on conservative educational reform since the 1920s, seemed to be replaced by the Drug War and character education. Schools were blamed for social ills and challenges to traditional values, and they were expected to respond to these strains by suddenly becoming academically excellent and moralistic.

Foundations and individual critics again undertook the study of schools, publishing their findings. These include generally conservative reports from the Twentieth Century Fund (1983), the College Entrance Examination Board (1983), and the National Science Foundation (1983), as well as Mortimer Adler's *The Paideia Proposal* (1982). The more liberal works included John Goodlad's *A Place Called School* (1983) and Theodore Sizer's *Horace's Compromise* (1984). Ernest Boyer's moderate *High School* (1983) for the Carnegie Foundation was also popular.

States pumped up school financing until the 1990s recession, and state officials, having enacted myriad new regulations governing school matters, began claiming some credit for educational change (*Results in Education 1990; The Education Reform Decade,* 1990; Webster and McMillin, 1991). In the main, jawboning by the federal government and increased regulatory activity in the states produced little in the way of dramatic change, but many adjustments were undertaken. Most of the underlying social problems—for example, poverty, family disruption, discrimination, and economic imbalance—worsened during the 1980s, and schools suffer the continuing effects. In the 1990s, the focus of educational criticism and reform shifted from state regulation and test score worries to more diverse views of the national influence on schools, school choice, curriculum control, at-risk students, restructuring schools to lead to more school-based management, teacher empowerment, parental involvement, interagency collaboration for community services, school district reorganization, and shared decision making. These ideas are potentially conflicting, some leading to increased centralization while others lead to increased decentralization. The core disputes over unity and diversity remain.

The idea of replacing the traditional canons of literature and social thought with modern multicultural material engendered other unity-diversity battles. Finn (1990a) and Ravitch (1990), high officials of the U.S. Department of Education under former Secretary of Education William Bennett, argue for teaching traditional content that emphasizes unified American views rather than diverse views from segments of the society. The Organization of American Historians, however, supports the teaching of non-Western culture and diversity in the schools (Winkler, 1991). Camille Paglia, arguing against feminist positions, states that her book "accepts the canonical Western tradition and rejects the modernist idea that culture has collapsed into meaningless fragments" (1990, p. xii). Unity and diversity in educational content also engaged in battle when Stanford University's faculty debated whether to substitute modern literature for traditional in its basic course, when New York state social studies curriculum revision stirred the New York governor to be "wary," and when English-only resolutions passed in state legislatures.

## Evaluation of the Reforms

There is general agreement that the results of the multiple reform efforts have been mixed. No clear evidence indicates that the reforms have significantly changed educational practice. Analyses of the decade of well-publicized school reform show great diversity in view (Giroux, 1989; Finn, 1990b; Darling-Hammond, 1990; US News and World Report, 1990; Fiske, 1991; Safire, 1991; Moynihan, 1991; New York Times, 1992). Ideological chasms appear among the analysts as they try to explain why the reforms did not seem to work and what should be done now. Stories about drugs, shootings, and gang violence around schools compete with news articles stating that American students can't read, are ignorant in math and science, and fail tests of common knowledge in history and geography (Business Week, 1990; Hawley, 1990; McEvoy, 1990; Novak, 1990; Holt, 1989; Newsweek, 1989). The premise is that drastic changes need to be made in schooling.

One solution is to make school much tougher, requiring and testing for higher standards and expelling school deviants. More discipline, emphasis on basic skills, training in moral behavior, longer school days and school years, and nationally standardized curriculum and testing are advocated to correct school problems.

From another view, schools are defective because they are too standardized, excessively competitive, and too factorylike. Students are measured and sorted in an assembly-line atmosphere where social class, gender, and race determine which students get which treatments. Teachers are deprofessionalized, treated as servile workers. Critical thinking is punished; one kind of curriculum or classroom instruction fits all. Creativity and joy are excluded from the school lexicon because education is supposed to be hard, dreary, boring work (Nathan, 1991; Fisher, 1991; McLaren, 1989; Purpel, 1989). The need for drastic action to correct these defects is apparent. A proposed answer is to liberate schools, teachers, and students from the oppression of standardized tests, uncritical knowledge, and dehumanizing school operations. Making schools active, pleasant, student-oriented, and sensitive to social problems is the reform advocated.

Critics (Bastian, et al., 1985; Presseisen, 1985; Giroux, 1988b) charge that the 1980s school reform movement was dominated by mainstream conservative thought. This conservative agenda includes standardization, more testing, more rigor in school, a return to basics, more implanting of patriotic values, increased regulation of schools, more homework for students, fewer electives, less student freedom, renewed emphasis on dress codes and socially accept-able behavior for students and teachers, stricter discipline, and teacher accountability. This conservative agenda enhanced changes already underway in schools in response to declining student test scores and a sense that the young had lost respect for authority.

Conservative school reform has recently been the main influence on schooling in the United States, but liberal and radical ideas have not disap-peared. Teacher empowerment, academic freedom, student rights, human knowledge, and social participation are liberal ideas percolating in school reform to come. Reconstructionist ideas that place schools at the center of social change have not been entirely forgotten in the current surge of literature on schools and reform. William Stanley (1992) presents a rethinking of social reconstructionism and examines key ideas from the critical pedagogy move-ment in an intriguing book on educational possibilities for the twenty-first cen-tury. His focus is on practical reasoning, which provides critical examination of social issues and stimulates positive social action. His book proposes a liberat-ing role for schools in society, based on careful analysis of educational theory and practice.

Recent public arguments have also arisen over multicultural education and politically correct speech in schools (*National Review,* 1990; Kinsley, 1991; *The Progressive,* 1991; D'Souza, 1991; Winkler, 1991; Banks, 1995). This conflict involves questions about knowledge and process, including: Should the schools emphasize the positive influences of divergent minority cultures and women, or should they stress the traditional unifying themes from a Eurocentric, white, male-dominated curriculum? Should they restrict racist, sexist, or other bigoted comments, or does that conflict with free speech?

"Politically correct" (PC) speech, defined as speech which does not deni-grate any minority group, gender, or sexual preference, attracts protest because it is equivalent to censorship, stifling free expression. The effort to make schools more civil places by controlling statements that could be offensive to some groups was met by a storm of protest. PC became a lightning-rod issue for schools at all levels. Protecting civil rights to free speech appeared to be at odds with protecting the civility of schools and protecting the "multiculturally diverse" from enduring negative comments. The argument against PC is that the free marketplace of ideas requires free speech, not courteous speech, and that the best response to epithets and slurs is reasoned argument and public disapproval. Although there are few who are open advocates of politically cor-rect regulations in schools, there are many who would like to find a way to limit racist and sexist comments and graffiti.

There is no shortage of current school critics and reformers. They present a bewildering array of educational ideas, from left-wing, right-wing, moderate, and radical positions. Some want schools to emphasize classical white, male, upper-class knowledge. Others would have schools focus on multicultural and contemporary ideas. Some would separate students into tracks and provide special treatment for academically gifted students, while others want students of all abilities and talents mixed. Some would allow students to determine much of their own education, while others would mandate substantial material for all to master. Some would target social problems that schooling should solve, while others would keep social problems separate from school affairs. Some expect schools to emancipate students from the oppressive aspects of society and economics, while others would have schools be training grounds for working in industry and developing national patriotism.

Although polls continue to show general public support of local schools, most of us can identify one or more areas that need correction. Impatient or burned-out teachers, cloddish administrators, frazzled counselors, and outdated textbooks and curriculum are examples. Most of us know the virtues as well as the warts and blemishes of schools from our direct personal experience. Some critics propose quick and simplistic reforms to improve schools. Fortunately, most people understand that change in schooling is more complex, and that the potential consequences of change need more thought.

Schools are controversial. Nearly everyone can find some fault in the way schools are organized and operated. Education, along with sex, religion, and politics, is one of the most debated topics in society. School, in fact, is the focus of much of the public debate over sex, religion, and politics. Sex education, religious study in schools, and "anti-American" teaching materials are among the many controversial issues which swirl about schools. Should we provide condom distribution and abortion clinic information in schools, use sexually explicit films, examine issues of date-rape and sexual abuse, or teach that homosexuality is a legitimate lifestyle? Should we allow prayer in school and public financing of religious schools? Should we suspend students who refuse to salute the flag, censor school books which contain criticisms of the United States, and require more patriotic exercises in schools? Should we change the canon of required literature to ensure that women and minority authors are represented, and require multicultural education?

Reformers see schools as either the cause of some problem or part of the cure. We are led to believe that schools can solve major social problems such as racism, sexism, automobile accidents, AIDS, teenage pregnancy, and drugs.

Although few advocate keeping schools exactly as they are, many are relatively content with the way schools work. Their suggestions for change are very moderate. They may propose adding to the curriculum to enhance computer skills, increasing the time spent in school, cutting back on extracurricular activities, or giving more homework to students. Modest though these proposals may be in reforming education, they can be items of intense debate in communities and they represent another set of views of the schools. And some who accept the status quo believe that schools cannot change significantly because schools are actually marginal institutions, with little power and no independence.

## UNITY AND DIVERSITY

Among the conditions of human civilization is the tension between unifying and diverse ideas. We want to share a vision of the good life with others, yet we recognize that human improvement depends upon new ideas that may conflict with that vision. Unity provides a focus, but also complacency; diversity provides stimulation, but also dissension. Both comfort and discontent thus reside in unity and diversity. This tension occurs in all parts of life, and it is most evident in important matters such as schooling.

However, diverse ideas combined in a unified purpose is an ideal, not easily and perhaps not ever attained. Diversity and unity are more commonly seen as contradictory. Some diverse ideas are too radical, too preposterous, or too challenging to deeply held beliefs for some people. Fundamental religions expect unity and do not accept diversity; criticism of religious dogma is considered heretical and sacrilegious. For those religions, just as for some people who believe they have the only truth, unity of belief is sacrosanct.

On the other hand, some question unity. One argument is that unity of purpose or values is a myth perpetuated by those in power to stay in power. Hard work, frugality, and acceptance of authority are seen as fictional values that are part of an effort by the powerful class to hide their oppressive actions and to maintain the social order and enslave docile workers.

Thus, diversity and unity can be seen as adversarial positions, bound in opposition. Those on the side of unity believe that diverse ideas can be censored, ignored, or disdained; those arguing for diversity consider unity to be a facade hiding the basic conflicts in society. It is also possible to understand diversity and unity as collateral positions, supporting and energizing. There is even diverse opinion about the relation of diversity to unity. It is this tension between diversity and unity, multiple views and common principles, that informs this book about schools. Among the current critical issues in education, the debates about the purposes and practices of schooling, are such matters as school choice, finance, racism, sexism, child welfare, privatization, curriculum, business orientations, academic freedom, unionism, and testing. These issues reflect deeper social and political tensions between unity and diversity, liberty and equality, rights and responsibilities, consensus and conflict, and individual and social development.

## A LACK OF ANSWERS AMIDST LOTS OF ANSWERS: CRITICAL THINKING

Questions about schooling stimulate a variety of potential and often competing answers, but there is no single set of clear and uncontested resolutions. Life would be easier, although less interesting, if we had singular and simple answers to all our problems. But critical social issues are usually too complex to be adequately resolved by easy or absolute solutions. In fact, simple answers often create new problems, or cause the problems they were supposed to solve to merely rise again.

Quick, easy, and absolute resolutions to a variety of social issues are readily available in contemporary society. Radio talk shows, letters to the editor, syndicated columnists, political brochures, interest group newsletters, and coffee shops are among the places where we can find lots of clear and forceful answers to most of our problems, including educational issues. These answers may well be simple, clear, and forceful—but they will often be contradictory, competing, or inconsistent. Significant debates over complicated human issues such as politics, international relations, economics, religion, sex, friendship, healthcare, and the environment are engaging partly because they usually are not subject to quick and easy resolution. However, that fact does not diminish the many efforts to provide answers to social and educational issues.

Clearly, some of the quick answers to school problems are good ideas, but virtually all have been advocated or adopted in various places over a long period of time and we still have spirited and passionate arguments about schools. That is a good thing; the debates are worth it. Progress depends on thinking through competing ideas about important matters.

Emphatically worded and precise answers to school and social questions are enticing, but a proper skepticism and critical thinking are the friends of wisdom. Critical thinking, the main process and goal of education, involves at least:

- recognition that an important issue deserves considered judgment,
- thoughtful formulation of good questions,
- a search for possible answers and pertinent evidence,
- consideration of alternative views, and
- drawing of tentative conclusions that are acceptable until another question or a better answer arises.

Critical thinking is far more difficult, and significantly more important, than just finding answers. The search for knowledge goes well beyond puzzle pages with answers printed upside down at the bottom, quiz items with answers at the end of a book, or reporting back to a teacher what an encyclopedia says.

Rather than present a single answer to each school question, we offer divergent answers based on different views of what is good. Because schools and schooling are such critical issues for contemporary society, our goal is to provide a framework for examining a number of contemporary school issues, presenting illustrative arguments and evidence which represent some of the diverse opinions on educational issues. The continuing examination of various arguments assists in the search for better answers—and better schools.

## The Dialogues: A Dialectic Approach

Critical issues deserve dialogue, an approach to reasoning that encourages disputes and divergent opinions in an attempt to arrive at a better idea—similar to the idea of dialectic reasoning. The dialectic occurs when you pit one argument (thesis) against another (antithesis) in an effort to develop a synthesis superior to either. It is an inquiry into important issues that identifies the main points, important evidence, and logical arguments used by each of at least two divergent views on an issue. This requires critical examination of the evidence and the arguments on each side of a dispute, granting each side some credibility in order to understand and criticize it. Dialogues, as a dialectic approach, are dynamic. A synthesis from one level of reasoning can become a new thesis at a more sophisticated level, and the process of inquiry continues to spiral (Adler, 1927; Cooper, 1967; Rychlak, 1976).

The purpose of a dialogue between competing ideas is not to defeat one and accept the other, but to search for an improved idea. In this sense, the approach is optimistic—it assumes that there are better ideas for improving society and that examining diverse ideas is a productive way to develop them. Roth (1989) notes that dialectical study of educational issues can offer enlightenment for social improvement and support for reflective teachers.

As in any form of human discourse, dialogues don't necessarily lead to truth; they can merely repeat errors and bias. Thus, we also advocate a healthy skepticism in examining these disputes. In the ancient Greek tradition, exercising skepticism meant to examine or to consider—to raise questions about reasons, evidence, and arguments. Skepticism is not simply doubt, despair, or cynicism. Without skepticism, we can easily fall into "complacent self-deception and dogmatism"; with it, we can "effectively advance the frontiers of inquiry and knowledge," applying this knowledge to "practical life, ethics, and politics" (Kurtz, 1992, p. 9). Dialogues on educational issues, with prudent skepticism, are a thoughtful form of inquiry.

This book presents two differing views on each topic in each chapter. The views expressed aren't always exactly opposing views, but they represent publicly expressed and divergent ideas about how schooling could be improved. Contrasting these views in terms of the evidence presented and the logic of each argument offered can stimulate a realistic dialogue, offering an opportunity to examine the issues as they occur in human discourse. You should note that divergent essays will sometimes use the same data or the same published works to make opposite cases, but they will usually offer evidence from widely separate literatures. The search for improvement in society and in schooling is a unifying purpose; dialogues require diversity.

The last years of the twentieth century and the first decade of the twenty-first may be placid for schools, a period of recuperation from the latest reforms. Even in placidity, however, educational issues are sure to arise, cause alarm, and inflame passions. Some of these issues will spawn elements of new school reforms; nearly all will be disputed. Welcome to this exchange of ideas.

## *References*

ADLER, M. (1927). *Dialectic.* New York: Harcourt, Brace.
ADLER, M. (1982). *The Paideia Proposal.* New York: Macmillan.
APPLE, M. (1990). *Ideology and Curriculum.* 2nd Ed. London: Routledge.

APPLE, M., AND WEIS, L., eds. (1983). *Ideology and Practice in Schooling.* Philadelphia: Temple University Press.

APPLE, M. (1994). "Computers and the Deskilling of Teachers." *CPSR Newsletter* 12(2):3.

ARONOWITZ, S., & GIROUX, H. (1983). *Education Under Siege: The Conservative, Liberal, and Radical Debate over Schooling.* South Hadley, MA: Bergin & Garvey. (2nd ed. 1993)

BAILYN, B. (1960). *Education in the Forming of American Society.* Chapel Hill: University of North Carolina Press.

BANKS, J. A. (1995). "The Historical Reconstruction of Knowledge About Race: Implications for Transformative Teaching." *Educational Researcher* 24:15–25.

BASTIAN, A., ET AL. (1985). *Choosing Equality: The Case for Democratic Schooling.* San Francisco: New World Foundation.

BERLINER, D. (1993). "Mythology and the American System of Education." *Kappan* 74:632+.

BERLINER, D., AND BIDDLE, B. J. (1995). *The Manufactured Crisis: Myths, Fraud, and the Attack on America's Public Schools.* Reading, MA: Addison-Wesley.

BESAG, F., AND NELSON, J. (1984). *The Foundations of Education: Stasis and Change.* New York: Random House.

BESTOR, A. (1953). *Educational Wastelands.* Urbana: University of Illinois Press. (2nd ed. 1985)

BOYER, E. (1983). *High School.* New York: Harper & Row.

BRACEY, G. (1992). "The Second Bracey Report on the Condition of Public Education." *Kappan* 74:104–108+.

BRACEY, G. (1994). "The Fourth Bracey Report on the Condition of Public Education." *Kappan* 76:115–127.

BRACEY, G. (1995). "Stedman's Myths Miss the Mark." *Educational Leadership* 52:75–78.

BRACEY, G. (1997). *The Truth About America's Schools: The Bracey Reports, 1991–1997.* Bloomington: IN: Phi Delta Kappan.

BRACEY, G. (1998). "The Eighth Bracey Report on the Condition of Public Education." Phi Delta Kappan. 80(2), 112–131.

BRAMELD, THEODORE. (1956). *Toward a Reconstructed Philosophy of Education.* New York: Holt, Rinehart & Winston.

BRONNER, E. (1998). "Candidates Latch onto Education Issue." *San Diego Union-Tribune.* Sept. 20, A10.

BROWN, S. (1991). "Free Speech Undermined." *Civil Liberties* 373:1,4.

Brown v. Board of Education of Topeka, Shawnee County, Kansas, et al. (1954). 74 Sup. Ct. 686.

*Business Week.* (1990). "Using Flash Cards and Grit to Defeat a Secret Shame." July 16, pp. 22, 23.

CARSON, C. C., HUELSKAMP, R. M., AND WOODALL, T. D. (1992). "Perspectives on Education in America." Final Draft, April. Albuquerque, NM: Sandia National Laboratories.

CHAMBERS, G. (1948). "Educational Essentialism Thirty Years After." In R. Hahn and D. Bidna, eds., *Secondary Education: Origins and Directions.* New York: Macmillan, 1970.

CHRISTENSON, R. M., ET AL. (1971). *Ideologies and Modern Politics.* New York: Dodd, Mead.

CLINCHY, B. MC. (1995). "Goals 2000: The Student as Object." *Kappan* 76:383–385.

College Entrance Examination Board. (1983). *Academic Preparation for College.* New York: The College Board.

CONANT, J. B. (1959). *The American High School Today.* New York: McGraw-Hill.

*The Condition of Education, 1996.* (1996). National Center for Educational Statistics. Washington, DC: U.S. Department of Education.

COOPER, D. ed. (1967). *To Free A Generation: The Dialectics of Liberalism.* New York: Collier.

COUNTS, G. S. (1932). *Dare the Schools Build a New Social Order?* New York: John Day Co.

CREMIN, L. (1961). *The Transformation of the School.* New York: Random House.

CREMIN, L. (1965). *The Genius of American Education.* New York: Random House.

DARLING-HAMMOND, L. (1991). "Achieving Our Goals: Superficial or Structural Reforms?" *Kappan* 72:286–295.

DE RUGIERRO, G. (1959). *The History of European Liberalism.* R. G. Collingwood, translator. Boston: Beacon Press.

DENNISON, G. (1969). *The Lives of Children.* New York: Random House.

DEWEY, J. (1916). *Democracy and Education.* New York: Macmillan.

DEWEY, J. (1933). *How We Think.* Boston: D.C. Heath.

D'SOUZA, D. (1991). *Illiberal Education: The Politics of Race and Sex on Campus.* New York: Free Press.

DOHENY-FARINA, S. (1996). *The Wired Neighborhood.* New Haven: Yale University Press.

*The Education Reform Decade.* (1990). Policy Information Report. Princeton: Educational Testing Service.

ELAM, S., ET AL. (1993). "25th Annual PDK–Gallup Poll." *Phi Delta Kappan,* 75. September.

ERIKSON, E. H. (1960). *Childhood and Society.* New York: W. W. Norton.

FINN, C. (1990a). "Why Can't our Colleges Convey our Diverse Culture's Unifying Themes?" *The Chronicle of Higher Education* 36:40,41.

FINN, C. (1990b). "The Biggest Reform of All." *Kappan* 71:584–593.

FISHER, E. (1991). "What Really Counts in Schools." *Educational Leadership* 48:10–15.

FISKE, E. B. (1991). *Smart Schools, Smart Kids.* New York: Simon & Schuster.

FRIEDENBERG, E. Z. (1965). *Coming of Age in America.* New York: Random House.

FREIRE, P. (1973). *Education for Critical Consciousness.* New York: Continuum.

FULLAN, F., AND HARGREAVES, A. (1992). *Teacher Development and Educational Change.* London: The Falmer Press.

GARDNER, J. (1958). *The Pursuit of Excellence: Education and the Future of America.* New York: Rockefeller Brothers Fund.

GIROUX, H. (1988a). *Teachers as Intellectuals: Toward a Critical Pedagogy of Learning.* Granby, MA: Bergin & Garvey.

GIROUX, H. (1988b). *Schooling and the Struggle for Public Life.* Granby, MA: Bergin & Garvey.

GIROUX, H. (1989). "Rethinking Educational Reform in the Age of George Bush." *Kappan* 70:728–730.

GOODLAD, J. I. (1983). *A Place Called School: Prospects for the Future.* New York: McGraw-Hill.

GOODMAN, P. (1964). *Compulsory Miseducation.* New York: Horizon Press.

GOULDNER, A. (1970). *The Coming Crisis of Western Sociology.* New York: Basic Books.

GRAHAM, P.A. (1967). *Progressive Education: From Arcady to Academe.* New York: Teachers College Press.

GREENE, M. (1995). "Art and Imagination: Reclaiming the Sense of Possibility." *Kappan* 76:378–382.

GURR, T. (1970). *Why Men Rebel.* Princeton, NJ: Princeton University Press.

HAHN, R., AND BIDNA, D., eds. (1970). *Secondary Education: Origins and Directions.* New York: Macmillan.

HAWLEY, R. A. (1990). "The Bumpy Road to Drug-Free Schools." *Phi Delta Kappan* 72:310–314.

HENTOFF, N. (1977). *Does Anybody Give a Damn?* New York: Alfred Knopf.

HENTOFF, N. (1998). "God's Place in the Public Schools." *San Diego Union-Tribune.* Aug. 18, B7.

HOLT, J. (1964). *How Children Fail.* New York: Pitman.

HOLT, R. (1989)."Can we Make our Schools Safe?" *NEA Today* 8:4–6.

HUELSKAMP, R. (1993). "Perspectives on Education in America." *Phi Delta Kappan* 74:717–720.

ILLICH, I. (1971). *Deschooling Society.* New York: Harper & Row.

*International Education Indicators.* (1997). National Center for Educational Statistics. Washington, DC: U.S. Department of Education.

JENSEN, C. (1994). *Censored: The News that Didn't Make the News—and Why.* New York: Four Walls Eight Windows Press.

JOHNSON, C. (1966). *Revolutionary Change.* Boston: Little, Brown.

KAESTLE, C. F. (1985). "Education Reform and the Swinging Pendulum." *Kappan* 66: 410–415.

KAPLAN, G. R. (1994). "Shotgun Wedding: Notes on Public Education's Encounter with the New Christian Right." *Kappan* 75:K1–K12.

KARIER, C. (1967). *Man, Society and Education.* Chicago: Scott, Foresman.

KARIER, C. (1985). "Retrospective One." In A. Bestor. *Educational Wastelands.* 2nd ed. Urbana: University of Illinois Press, 1985.

KATZ, M. (1968). *The Irony of Early School Reform.* Cambridge: Harvard University Press.

KATZ, M. (1971). *Class, Bureaucracy, and Schools: The Illusion of Educational Change in America.* New York: Praeger.

KERLINGER, F. (1984). *Liberalism and Conservatism.* Hillsdale, NJ: Erlbaum.

KINSLEY, M. (1991). "P.C.B.S." *The New Republic* 204:8,9.

KOHL, H. (1967). *36 Children.* New York: New American Library.

KOHLBERG, L. (1981). *The Meaning and Measurement of Moral Development.* Worcester, MA: Clark University Press.

KOHLBERG, L., AND R. DEVRIES. (1987). *Child Psychology and Childhood Education.* New York: Longmans.

KOZOL, J. (1967). *Death at an Early Age.* Boston: Houghton Mifflin.

KRISTOL, I. (1983). *Reflections of a Neoconservative.* New York: Basic Books.

KURTZ, P. (1992) *The New Skepticism.* Buffalo, NY: Prometheus Books.

LANE, R. E. (1962). *Political Ideology.* New York: The Free Press of Glencoe.

LLOYD, T. (1988). *In Defense of Liberalism.* Oxford: Basil Blackwell.

LYND, A. (1950). *Quackery in the Public Schools.* Boston: Little, Brown.

MARSHALL, C. (1997). *Feminist Critical Policy Analysis I: A Perspective from Primary and Secondary Schooling.* London: The Falmer Press.

MARTIN, J. R. (1994). *Changing the Educational Landscape: Philosophy, Women, and Curriculum.* New York: Routledge.

MCEVOY, A. (1991)."Combating Gang Activities in Schools." *Education Digest* 56:31–34.

MCLAREN, P. (1989). *Life in Schools.* New York: Longman.

MOYNIHAN, D. P. (1991). "Educational Goals and Political Plans." *The Public Interest* Winter, pp. 32–49.

NATHAN, J. (1991). "Toward Educational Change and Economic Justice: An Interview with Herbert Kohl." *Phi Delta Kappan* 72:678–681.

National Commission on Excellence in Education. (1983). *A Nation at Risk.* Washington, DC: U.S. Government Printing Office.

*National Review.* (1990). "Academic Watch." 42:18.

National Science Foundation. (1983). *Educating Americans for the 21st Century.* Washington, DC: National Science Foundation.

NEILL, A. S. (1966). *Summerhill: A Radical Approach to Child Rearing.* New York: Hart.

NELSON, J. L., CARLSON, K., AND LINTON, T. L. (1972). *Radical Ideas and the Schools.* New York: Holt, Rinehart & Winston.

*Newsweek.* (1989). "Kids: Deadly Force." 111:18–20.

*New York Times.* (1992). "Education Life" special supplement. January 5, Section 4A, pp. 1–60.

NODDINGS, N. (1984a). *Awakening the Inner Eye: Intuition and Education.* New York: Teachers College Press.

NODDINGS, N. (1984b). *Caring: A Feminine Approach to Ethics and Moral Education.* Berkeley: University of California Press.

NODDINGS, N. (1995). "A Morally Defensible Mission for Schools in the 21st Century." *Kappan* 76:365–368.

NOVAK, M. (1990). "Scaring our Children." *Forbes* 144:167.

PAGLIA, CAMILLE. (1990). *Sexual Personae.* New Haven: Yale Press.

PIAGET, J. (1950). *The Psychology of Intelligence.* London: Routledge & Kegan Paul.

PIERCE, R. K. (1993). *What are We Trying to Teach Them, Anyway?* San Francisco: Center for Self-Governance.

PLATO. (1930). *The Works of Plato.* Irwin Erdman, ed. New York: Modern Library.

PRESSEISEN, B. (1985). *Unlearned Lessons.* Philadelphia: Falmer Press.

PRICE, H. B. (1990). "The Bottom Line for School Reform." *Kappan* 72:242–245.

*The Progressive.* (1991). "The PC Monster." 55:9.

*Projections of Education Statistics to 2008.* (1996). National Center for Educational Statistics. Washington, DC: U.S. Department of Education.

PURPEL, D. (1989). *The Moral and Spiritual Crisis in Education: A Curriculum for Justice and Compassion in Education.* Granby, MA: Bergin & Garvey.

RAFFERTY, M. (1968). *Max Rafferty on Education.* New York: Devon Adair Co.

RASPBERRY, W. (1998). "Public Schools Bad for Education." *San Diego News-Tribune.* Aug. 18, B6.

RAVITCH, D. (1990). "Multiculturalism: E Pluribus Plures." *American Scholar* 59:337–354.

RESNICK, L., AND NOLAN, K. (1995). "Where in the World are World Class Standards?" *Educational Leadership* 52:6–11.

*Results in Education: 1990.* (1990). The Governors' 1991 Report on Education. Washington, DC: National Governors' Association.

RICKOVER, H. (1959). *Education and Freedom.* New York: E. P. Dutton.

ROSE, L. C., AND GALLUP, A. M. (1998). "The 30th Phi Delta Kappa/Gallup Poll of the Public's Attitudes Toward the Public Schools." *Phi Delta Kappan* 80(1), 41–56.

ROTH, R. A. (1989). "Preparing Reflective Practitioners." *Journal of Teacher Education* 40, 31–35.

ROTHENBERG, R. (1984). *The Neoliberals.* New York: Simon & Schuster.

RUSSELL, B. (1928). *Sceptical Essays.* London: George Allen & Unwin.

RYCHLAK, J. F. ed. (1976). *Dialectic.* Basil, Switzerland: Karger.

SAFIRE, W. (1991). "Abandon the Pony Express." *New York Times* April 25, 140, A17.

SHILS, E. (1968). "The Concept of Ideology." In *The International Encyclopedia of the Social Sciences.* D. Sills, ed. New York: Macmillan and Free Press.

SINCLAIR, U. (1924). *The Goslings.* Pasadena: Sinclair.

SIZER, T. (1984). *Horace's Compromise: The Dilemma of the American High School.* Boston: Houghton Mifflin.

SOWELL, T. (1993). *Inside American Education: The Decline, the Deception, the Dogmas.* New York: The Free Press.

SMELSER, N. (1962). *Theory of Collective Behavior.* New York: Free Press.

SMITH, M. (1954). *The Diminished Mind.* New York: Regnery.

STANLEY, W. (1981). "Toward a Reconstruction of Social Education." *Theory and Research in Social Education* 9:67–89.

STANLEY, W. (1992). *Education for Utopia: Social Reconstructionism and Critical Pedagogy in the Postmodern Era.* Albany: SUNY Press.

STEINFELS, P. (1979). *The Neoconservatives.* New York: Simon & Schuster.

STERNBERG, R. J. (1985). *Beyond I.Q.: A Triarchic Theory of Human Intelligence.* New York: Cambridge University Press.

TANNER, D. (1993). "A Nation Truly at Risk." *Kappan* 75:288–297.

TAWNEY, R. H. (1964). *The Radical Tradition.* London: George Allen & Unwin.

TOCH, T. (1991). *In the Name of Excellence.* New York: Oxford University Press.

TOWNS, E. L. (1974). *Have the Public Schools "Had It"?* New York: Thos. Nelson, Inc.

TREND, D. (1995). *The Crisis of Meaning in Culture and Education.* Minneapolis: University of Minnesota Press.

TWENTIETH-CENTURY FUND. (1983). *Making the Grade.* New York: Twentieth-Century Fund.

TYACK, D. (1967). *Turning Points in American Educational History.* Waltham, MA: Blaisdell.

TYACK, D. (1991). "Public School Reform: Policy Talk and Institutional Practice." *American Journal of Education* 100:1–19.

*US News and World Report.* (1990). "The Keys to School Reform." Feb. 26: 108,50+.

ULICH, R. (1954). *Three Thousand Years of Educational Wisdom.* 2nd ed. Cambridge, MA: Harvard University Press.

USEEM, M. (1975). *Protest Movements in America.* Indianapolis: Bobbs-Merrill.

WATT, J. (1985). *The Courage of a Conservative.* New York: Simon & Schuster.

WEBSTER, W. E., AND MCMILLIN, J. D. (1991). "A Report on Calls for Secondary School Reform in the United States." *NASSP Bulletin* 75:77–83.

WELTER, R. (1962). *Popular Education and Democratic Thought in America.* New York: Columbia University Press.

WINKLER, K. (1991). "Organization of American Historians Backs Teaching of non-Western Culture and Diversity in Schools." *The Chronicle of Higher Education* 37:5–8.

*UNESCO World Education Report, 1998.* (1998). Paris: UNESCO.

# What Interests Should Schools Serve?

Part I presents opposing viewpoints on the general theme of liberty versus equality.

You may think it strange to see these two values cast in competition. After all, aren't they both basic American values? Liberty and equality were clarion calls of the American Revolution. The colonists felt that the British government was not treating them in a manner equal to that it afforded its citizens in England, because it placed greater restraints on the colonists' liberty. Thus, liberty and equality are the values on which our nation was founded. The U.S. Constitution says that our government was formed to "promote the general Welfare, and secure the blessings of Liberty." Ask almost any American whether he or she believes in liberty, and you will get a positive answer. Even children like to remind each other

that "it's a free country." Ask the same people whether they believe in equality, and you will hear, "Of course." Better yet, ask yourself these questions.

The difficulty is that liberty and equality lie along the same continuum. At one end is total liberty, and at the other, complete equality. Very few people wish to go all the way out on either of these limbs. They try to have it both ways by venturing back and forth from the center of the line.

Those whose steps take them more often toward the liberty (or right) end of the continuum are called "Republicans," "conservatives," or "libertarians," in order of their distance from the center, with libertarians the most distant. Sometimes the people in these categories are identified with the generic label "right-wingers." Persons who incline more often to the equality (or left) side of the continuum are "Democrats," "liberals," "egalitarians," with the egalitarians the farthest out. The generic label for these groups is "left-wingers."

Presidential elections are reminders of how skittish politicians can be about these terms, since most people pride themselves on their moderation and don't want to seem too far out in either direction. And the labels really are misleading, since most of us are an amalgam of conflicting urges: sometimes right-leaning, sometimes left, pendulumlike, depending on the particular issue or the context, or just the mood we are in at the moment. That explains why we can use seemingly oxymoronic terms as "liberal Republican" and "conservative Democrat." These terms indicate that a lot of presidential aspirants have concluded it is electorally wise to be in the middle of the road.

The reason why right- and left-wingers get into such bitter wrangles is that each wing believes its values are imperiled by the other side's efforts to promote its own beliefs. Right-wingers see liberty weakened with each increase in equality among Americans. That happens, in their view, because equality—even equality of opportunity—is imposed by government actions that reduce our individual freedoms and may hinder us from rising above the herd. Left-wingers, on the other hand, believe liberty diminishes equality—including equality of opportunity—when individual freedoms allow some people to exploit and oppress others. Fortunately, right- and left-wingers do hold some values in common, such as family stability and job opportunity. The disagreement is about whether the government is an effective agency for promoting those values (Kuttner, 1991).

Education is a good place to observe the liberty-equality battle. Education involves us all and has momentous consequences for our lives. Its pervasive influence commands the attention of people on all points of the political spectrum. Much is at stake, depending on whether government makes education and educational opportunity more equal for students of different backgrounds or whether government leaves education to the varying fortunes of students' families. Because the stakes are so high, both the left and the right try to steer the government's education policies in their direction.

## THE "LIBERTY" POSITION

In general, the right subscribes to the notion that less government is better. Parents should be free to find or develop the kind of education they want for their children. Parents can do this in cooperation with others who share their views, and most often they do so by living in communities with people who are like themselves. The government's role is to *allow* this to happen, to guarantee this freedom.

The right echoes its position on education in its attitude toward all the other areas of social policy. It fuels the centuries-old fervor about the extent to which government should interfere in people's lives to promote the welfare of the less fortunate. Those on the right argue that the government's attempts to help the disadvantaged do more harm than good to the very people who are supposed to benefit. The handouts these people receive, whether in the form of educational benefits, welfare benefits, or some other kind of benefit, sap initiative. As Irving Kristol (1978) put it, "Dependency tends to corrupt and absolute dependency corrupts absolutely" (p. 242). Ira Glasser (1978), a liberal and the executive director of the American Civil Liberties Union, examined the way well-intentioned government officials end up imprisoning the people they set out to help. He concluded: "Because their motives were benevolent, their ends good, and their purpose caring, *they assumed the posture of parents* toward the recipients of their largesse. . . . As a result, they infantilized those they intended to help, and denied them their rights" (p. 107). Charles Murray (1991, 1994a) argued that welfare benefits and the way they were apportioned encouraged lower-class women to stay single but still have children, and that this was the primary cause of family disintegration among America's poor. Lawrence Mead said that "no real progress in welfare is imaginable until government obligates needy adults to assume greater responsibility for their condition" (1988, p. 52). When the federal government dramatically overhauled the welfare system in 1996 by putting a time limit on benefits and allowing the states to try Draconian experiments to reduce the welfare rolls even further, the right rejoiced. They were convinced that the get-tough approach would force welfare recipients to take responsibility for their lives. The generally robust economy has enabled many welfare recipients to find jobs, allowing the right to claim credit for the wisdom of their counsel.

The right is well-aware that the handouts the government provides do not materialize from thin air. They are pried from the pockets of hard-working, productive people, and that discourages these people in their industriousness. "The egalitarian seeks a collective equality, not of opportunity, but of *results*. He wishes to wrest the rewards away from those who have earned them and give them to those who have not" (Simon, 1978, p. 200). One of the rewards that the right believes people in our society earn is the wherewithal to give their children a good education. If children cannot benefit from their parents' effort, or can benefit no more than other people's children, parents lose a powerful work incentive.

Those on the right are therefore declaring the signal advantage of inequality: that it makes us all work harder and realize ourselves more fully. When we do so, we not only help ourselves, but we automatically advance the whole of society. This is the "invisible hand" Adam Smith, the eighteenth-century Scottish economist, described (1776/1976):

> As every individual, therefore, endeavours as much as he can both to employ his capital in the support of domestic industry, and so to direct that industry that its produce may be of the greatest value; every individual necessarily labours to render the annual revenue of the society as great as he can. . . . He intends only his own gain, and he is in this, as in many other cases, led by an invisible hand to promote an end which was no part of his intention. (p. 477)

Mickey Kaus accepts the harsh reality behind this:

> You cannot decide to keep all the nice parts and get rid of all the

nasty ones. You cannot have capitalism without "selfishness," or even "greed," because they are what make the system work. You can't have capitalism and material equality, because capitalism is constantly generating extremes of inequality as some individuals strike it rich . . . while others fail and fall on hard times. (Quoted by Bluestone, 1994, p. 92)

Thus, each of us, by our own labors, helps those less fortunate simply by the sum we add to the *national* welfare. Those who help the most are the rich because they have money to invest in job-creating industries. George Gilder (1981) went so far as to say that this is *the* function of the rich: "fostering opportunities for the classes below them in the continuing drama of the creation of wealth and progress" (p. 82). Indeed, Gilder asserted that in order for the poor to get richer, the rich must first get richer so they will have more to invest in opportunities for the poor (p. 86). The general public seems to accept this argument; only 21 percent think the country would be better off if there were no rich people (Samuelson, 1998). "Do-gooders" dismiss the argument too easily, says Milton Friedman, the foremost conservative economist of our time. The do-gooders prefer simple, emotional arguments for collectivism to subtle, rational ones for individualism (Friedman, 1994).

A single paragraph written in 1835 by Alexis de Tocqueville, the French statesman and author famous for his insightful analyses of American society, captured a subtle and rational argument for individualism:

Any permanent, regular, administrative system whose aim will be to provide for the needs of the poor will breed more miseries than it can cure, will deprave the population that it wants to help and comfort, will in time reduce the rich to being no more than the tenant-farmers of the poor, will dry up the sources of savings, will stop the accumulation of capital, will retard the development of trade, will benumb human industry and activity, and will culminate in bringing about a violent revolution in the State, when the number of those who receive alms will have become as large as those who give it, and the indigent, no longer being able to take from the impoverished rich the means of providing for his needs, will find it easier to plunder them of all their property at one stroke than to ask for their help. (1835/1968, p. 25)

This quote echoes a common concern of today's conservatives: that assistance to the poor becomes a bottomless sinkhole. The assistance is a magnet that attracts more and more people into dependency, and the level of assistance is never adequate to restore them to independence. A look at the price tags that liberals put on their pet programs can cause disbelief and alarm. The Committee for Economic Development (CED) called for an annual outlay of $19.53 billion just for programs for poor kids under the age of 5 (*The Unfinished Agenda*, 1991). At that rate, the so-called peace dividend could be diverted entirely to the poor, with no investment in America's productive capacity or in keeping international order. If earlier investments in the poor had yielded better results, we might view additional expenditures as wise investments in human capital. Indeed, if the earlier investments had yielded better results, additional expenditures might not be necessary. The disappointing results may explain why the CED, in its 1994 report, had almost nothing to say about increased expenditures and much to say about more effective management of existing resources (*Putting Learning First*, 1994).

Moreover, conservatives worry because liberals are demanding additional expenditures not just for children, but also for able-bodied adults who refuse to work. These are the passive poor who are content to watch while immigrants exploit job opportunities. The passive poor have been resistant to attempts to put them to work, and cutting them from the welfare rolls victimizes their hapless children. Society must find a way to make the passive poor assume the work ethic of their fellow citizens (Murray, 1991, 1994b). The state of Connecticut, by putting a 21-month time limit on welfare benefits, compelled hundreds of welfare-dependent people to find jobs, and they did (Rabinovitz, 1997). Other states have also undertaken to transform people from welfare-dependents to work-dependents. The right-wingers' faith in this transformation is hardened by the fact that so many of them grew up poor. They are their own best evidence that it is possible to escape poverty.

## THE "EQUALITY" POSITION

Those on the left do not want a hands-off government content merely to guarantee the freedom of the powerful. They demand a government that will guarantee that children every-where have equally good schooling, regardless of their parents' circumstances. This means taking power away from parents and giving it to the government, allowing it to act as a benevolent parent to all our children (Keniston and the Carnegie Council on Children, 1977, p. 204).

The purpose of government, as far as those on the left are concerned, was expressed eloquently by Abraham Lincoln in his first annual message to the Congress: "To lift artificial weights from all shoulders; to clear the paths of laudable pursuit; to afford all an unfettered start, and a fair chance in the race of life" (quoted in Grant Foundation Commission, 1988, p. 118).

This, of course, is a classic exhortation to equality of *opportunity*. As such, it invokes the approval of those on the right as well as those on the left. However, those on the right disagree about the extent to which equality of opportunity is synonymous with equality of *condition*. To those on the left, being poor means having little opportunity. It means suffering poor prenatal and neonatal care, poor early childhood development, poor homes, poor schools, and ultimately poor jobs or no jobs at all. Conversely, "the children of the rich [tend] to grow up rich and powerful far more often than mere talent or energy or morality could have guaranteed. . . . Power, privilege and prosperity [are] transmitted not only by the direct inheritance of wealth but also by the subtler route of acquired manners, learned skills, and influential friends" (Keniston and the Carnegie Council on Children, 1977, p. 40). "If we Americans wish children to reap the equality of opportunity that is so honored a goal of our society, we must address an issue that has, ironically, been obscured by our focus on equality of opportunity; we must attempt to create greater equality of social condition directly, not indirectly through children" (deLone, 1979, p. 25). In short, the distinction between opportunity and condition is not nearly as clear to those on the left as it is to those on the right. Fischer et al. (1996) devote an entire book to demonstrating how a child's environment and education predict his future socioeconomic status, and how deliberate public policies determine the kinds of environments and education different children will experience.

Furthermore, the left sees governmental attempts to give the poor more opportunity as much too feeble. Ever since modern welfare reforms began in the sixteenth century, the purpose has been to keep the poor just content enough to remain dependent on the niggardliness of employers to improve their condition beyond the subsistence level. "Efforts to shape relief arrangements so they would not intrude on market relations virtually define the history of social welfare. . . ." (Block et al., 1987, p. 12). Equal opportunity is not provided to the poor, but only continuing vulnerability to exploitation. The only reason governmental relief is offered at all is to keep the poor from rioting, according to analysts on the left. Welfare is "a mechanism of social control, designed to pacify the poor and [serve] the interests of the business elite" (Block et al., 1987, p. 168). The Personal Responsibility and Work Opportunity Reconciliation Act that President Clinton signed into law in 1996 caused many in his own administration to quit in disgust because they believed it would leave the poor worse off.

Moreover, liberals point out, there are two welfare systems: one for the poor and the other for the rich and the middle class. The first consists of such programs as Temporary Aid for Needy Families (TANF) and Food Stamps. It cost $117 billion in 1990. The second includes Social Security payments and tax breaks. It cost $1,265 billion (Huff, 1992, p. 38). Even the conservative columnist William Safire grants that the U.S. budget deficits were "caused far less by helping the poor than by the aged and elderly of all incomes ripping off the young and middle aged" (Safire, 1995, p. A27). Bartlett and Steele (1994) say that "America's most expensive social welfare program ever" was the $200 billion in federal income tax money that Congress decided to return to the nation's most affluent individuals and families" between 1987 and 1994 (p. 17). In 1998, *Time* magazine commissioned Bartlett and Steele to do a special report on corporate welfare. They concluded that the government subsidization of corporate America costs every working person two weeks' pay per annum. The $125 billion in corporate welfare equals all the taxes paid by 60 million individuals and families (Bartlett and Steele, 1998).

Those on the left disagree that redistributing the wealth in America to improve the living and educational conditions of the disadvantaged will backfire. They see the desperate situation of the poor as such social dynamite that more, not less, redistribution is imperative to defuse it. Naturally, they would like to see the redistribution schemes administered more wisely so that the intended beneficiaries do not suffer unintended consequences. The left also believes that equalizing the educational *condition* of children from different social classes is a good public investment. "Our primary concern should be with the acute failure to provide a vast number of low-income and minority students with decent schools and skills" (Bastian et al., 1985, p. 117).

Finally, people on the left are not persuaded that the rich always invest their money in ways that benefit the rest of society. In recent years especially, tremendous wealth has been invested in stock speculation and corporate takeovers that have benefited rich insiders at the expense of everyone else (Bruck, 1988). How much the insiders gained is demonstrated by the fact that one brokerage house, Drexel Burnham Lambert, could afford to pay a $650 million fine for its confessed felonies (Cowan, 1992). That whopping amount was soon topped by a $700 million fine assessed against Prudential Securities for its Wall Street shenanigans (Eichenwald, 1994). Moreover, Americans have become wise to the fact that the chief executive officers (CEOs) of corporations keep getting fatter compensation packages at a time when their employees are forced to take wage cuts or endure layoffs. In 1996, Bill Gates, the head of Microsoft, made so much money that it would have taken the median U.S. household earning $35,000 a year 600,000 years to make as much (Ivins, 1997). At the same time, Gates was engaging in practices that caused the U.S. Department of Justice to charge him with violating the antitrust laws. Corporations try to conceal these exorbitant deals by packaging some of the money not in salaries, but instead in bonuses and stock options (Hass and Nayyar, 1994). As Derek Bok, former president of Harvard University and a labor economist, complains, these extravagant levels of compensation are not tied to the CEOs' productivity, but to an insider network of boards of directors that allows CEOs on each other's boards to protect each other (Bok, 1994).

This practice causes part of the generally widening gap between the rich and the rest of America. The wealth gap in the United States is wider than that in any other Western nation, making America the most economically stratified of industrialized nations. Kevin Phillips, a former Republican consultant, argues at book length that the *upward* redistribution of America's wealth was engineered by policymakers in the Reagan administration. Reaganomics coupled a reduction of government services to the poor with a reduction in taxes and regulations on the rich. It was the test of Gilder's theory that if the rich got richer, benefits would trickle down to the poor. The theory has not been proved by the facts (Phillips, 1990). Statistics from the U.S. Bureau of the Census show the widest rich-poor gap since the Bureau began collecting this information in 1947. Top-fifth families now take in almost 50 percent of U.S. income, compared with less than 5 percent for the bottom fifth (Bernstein, 1994). Young children are especially hard hit by this inequality. Between 1979 to 1983 and 1992 to 1996, the national poverty rate among young children increased by 12 percent, from 22.0 to 24.7 percent ("Child Poverty in Many States . . .," 1998). Economist James Galbraith has analyzed this growing inequality and attributes it primarily to the actions of the Federal Reserve Board, which keeps interest rates so high that chronic unemployment results, obviously hurting those on the bottom but also helping the stockholders and bankers at the top (Galbraith, 1998). Lawrence Mischel (1997) calculates the loss in wages to the American worker as a 3.6 percent reduction annually. As *The New York Times* put it in an editorial aptly titled "The Tide Is Not Lifting Everyone" (1997, p. A18), "median income, adjusted for inflation, for the poorest 20 percent of families *fell* last year, even though the economy was zipping along . . . the chilling lesson from the census data is that even a healthy economy leaves the poor firmly in a depressing place." Compounding the plight of the poor is the inaccessibility of good medical care, with 41 million Americans still uninsured (Pear, 1998a), and health maintenance organizations (HMOs) continuing to cut off Medicare patients (Pear, 1998b).

Perhaps the most significant difference between the right and the left lies in their *psychological* needs. Karl Marx always maintained that socialism could not come about until a technology of abundance existed to take care of our *material* needs. Such a technology is "an absolutely necessary practical precondition [of socialism], for without it one can only generalize *want*, and with such pressing needs, the struggle for necessities would begin again and all the old crap would come back again" (quoted by Harrington, 1973, p. 33). The United States now has a technology of abundance capable of satisfying everyone's basic material needs. The difficulty is that some people have a psychological need for more material goods than their neighbors

have. This is often referred to as "conspicuous consumption," the practice of acquiring and flaunting material possessions. This psychological dynamic can be observed even in the kinds of schools that parents "purchase" for their children, and it resists equalization (Thurow, 1980, p. 198).

Of late it has become popular to talk about an emerging two-class society: those with education, technical skills, and good job opportunities; and those without. Conservatives like Herrnstein and Murray (1994) are pessimistic about tempering this trend, but liberals like former U.S. Secretary of Labor Robert Reich keep insisting that it is an imperative task of American education to prevent the development of a permanent underclass.

Let us now get a preliminary sense of how the theme of liberty versus equality is played out in the chapters of this section.

## CHOICE OR COMMON SCHOOLS

Chapter 2 presents arguments for and against allowing parents to pick the schools their children will attend. The traditional American pattern has been for a child to attend the school in his or her neighborhood. Where you live determines where you will be educated.

Giving parents choices beyond this traditional nonoption approach certainly enhances their liberty. The choices can be made possible in a variety of ways. Parents could have a choice among all schools—public, private, and parochial—in a large geographic area, perhaps the size of a county. Or the choice could be limited to public schools, or still further to the public schools in an existing school district. Districts can create "magnet" or "theme" schools that children and their parents can choose from. The choice might even be restricted to minischools within the same building, sometimes known as "schools-within-schools." The more limited the number and kinds of schools people can choose from, the less liberty there is, but limited-choice plans have the advantage of being easier to administrate.

A recent variation on these possibilities is the "charter" school—a public school a group of parents and teachers or other interested people are authorized to set up relatively free of the bureaucratic requirements for other public schools in the area. If the local district itself is the authorizing body, it may be resistant to freeing anyone from its requirements. In Colorado, the state board of education had to order Denver to allow the establishment of a charter school (Stevens, 1994). A judge in Michigan has ruled that only the state board of education has the authority to charter schools (Walsh, 1994). In New Jersey, the state board of education grants the charter, and the local school district in which the charter school is to be located can only make a recommendation for or against. By September 1997, thirty states had passed charter school laws and twenty-four states had charter schools in operation, with a total of 693 schools and a combined enrollment reaching 110,122 (Berman et al., 1998).

President Reagan's administration gave rhetorical support to the idea of choice in education, but did nothing significant to bring this about. President-elect Bush, in the days before his inauguration, came out strongly in support of choice. He asserted that "choice has worked," and that he intended "to provide every feasible assistance to the states and districts interested in further experimentation with choice plans" (Weinraub, 1989, p. B28). After becoming president, Bush asked Congress to appropriate $100 million for magnet schools in order to increase parental choice (Cohen, 1989). In 1986, the National Governors' Association (NGA) went on record in favor of choice within the public school sector (*Time for Results*, 1986, p. 13).

A leading member of the NGA at that time was Governor Clinton of Arkansas, As President Clinton, he still voices support for choice within the public school sector, but fostering it has not been a priority of his administration. The state that has gone the furthest in this regard is Minnesota, which allows interdistrict choice of schools for all students (*Choice in Public Education*, 1988).

Cities also can create choice plans. Milwaukee has a plan whereby 15 percent of public school students can receive money to use to attend private and parochial schools. The inclusion of parochial schools provoked a court case under the First Amendment separation of church and state clause, and that case wended its way to the U.S. Supreme Court. However, since the court declined to hear the case, the ruling of the Wisconsin Supreme Court upholding the choice to attend parochial schools was allowed to stand (Walsh, 1998). Other cities have had choice plans for some time that provide a choice among the "magnet" or theme schools, so that students can focus on their particular interests in schools that center on those interests. Even one of the community school districts in New York City—District 4, in the area commonly known as Spanish Harlem—has had a magnet school plan, with fifty-three different schools operating in twenty-two school buildings. These include a bilingual school, a music academy, an environmental science school, and a communication arts school (Fliegel, 1993; Kirp, 1992; Meier, 1991).

In Jersey City, the mayor fought to get the state legislature to permit a plan that will make public school students eligible for vouchers they can use to pay tuition at the city's many private schools. The mayor sees this as triply beneficial: it will give students an opportunity to transfer out of the public schools, it will thereby relieve the pressure on the public schools, and it will reduce the cost of education to the taxpayers (Schundler, 1994). The state legislature and the governor both ducked this plan as too politically volatile because it slapped too directly at the public schools.

All of this should suggest that "choice" is an idea that has taken firm root in education and will sprout lots of shoots for the foreseeable future. This can be attributed to the way choice plans invoke the value of liberty. Their relation to the value of equality is not so clear-cut, however. Choice plans can increase equality, but they can also decrease it.

Equality is increased when people who previously had no choice are given some say about the school in which their children are to be educated. In this way, choice plans make these people more equal to those who can afford to send their children to private schools or who can afford to live in communities that have good public schools. Whether these people really achieve equality depends, of course, on how large a voucher they are given to pay the tuition at nonpublic schools, or whether they can attend nonpublic schools at all. As Jonathan Kozol puts it:

> The advocates for vouchers nowadays pose the issue in a clever, but I think dishonest, manner. They say something like this: "The rich have always had the opportunity to send their kids to private school. Why shouldn't we give poor people the same opportunity?" But when you ask them what kind of vouchers they have in mind, the amount of money they propose varies from about $1,000 to at most the amount that is spent on an inner-city public school, maybe $5,000. None of them are suggesting the $10,000 or $15,000 voucher that it would take to send these kids to the prep schools the rich children attend. (Quoted by Kemper, 1993, pp. 25–26)

Kozol's opponents would obviously reply that this is still $1,000 or $5,000 more equality than the poor students had previously.

Equality is decreased if a choice plan gives the same amount of benefit to both the rich and the poor, thereby augmenting the advantage the rich already have. For example, if both rich and poor families are guaranteed a modest amount of government financial support to seek out schools to their liking, the rich can add this amount to what they already spend on good private schools and find even better ones, while the poor might only be able to afford the kind of schools they are attending under the no-choice system. Voucher proposals like that of the Friedmans (1980), which would give the same amount to all families regardless of wealth, threaten to have this *disequalizing* effect. So, too, do tuition tax credit plans that grant all families the same tax credit for tuition they pay for their children's schooling. Only parents who can afford to pay tuition in the first place are eligible for the tax credit. Even more disequalizing would be a plan that gave parents a tax credit in the amount they actually paid for tuition, since the wealthiest people tend to send their children to the schools that charge the highest tuitions.

The disequalizing potential was a major reason for the overwhelming defeats of the voucher proposals in Oregon in 1990, in Colorado in 1992, and in California in 1993. In California, for example, the proposal would have given a flat $2,600 to each student to spend on private school tuition, including students who were already attending expensive private schools. Many voters viewed this as a $2,600 subsidy for the rich and a virtually useless pittance for the poor. Moreover, the $2,600 each private school student would receive would have come out of money that would otherwise go to the public schools (Schorr, 1993).

Choice plans can also reduce equality if schools are allowed to refuse certain kinds of pupils. The "choice" in this situation is only the choice to try to get into a desired school, and could result in no real choice but the kind of school one had been attending previously. Former Secretary of Education Lamar Alexander said that private and religious schools were intended to be part of the Bush administration's choice plan, eligible for federal anti-poverty funds, and that these schools could still deny children the opportu-

nity to enroll (Pitsch, 1991; Shanker, 1991). Democrats, such as President Clinton, are generally unwilling to include private and parochial schools in publicly supported choice plans, or to allow "choice" schools many justifications for rejecting applicants. But even when a student does get into a desired school, he or she can be segregated into a *program* that is much like the one in his or her old school. Some magnet schools segregate pupils according to ability, and the low-ability youngsters participate in less attractive programs (Moran, 1987).

Christopher Jencks and his colleagues at Harvard once designed a choice system that had safeguards against such inequalities (Jencks, 1970). For instance, poor families would get larger amounts of money than rich families; schools could not demand more in tuition than the amount of money a family received from the government; and schools would be limited in their latitude to refuse admission to applicants.

Ironically, Jencks's kind of system provokes claims of another kind of inequality. If the poor are guaranteed as much choice as the rich, they have been given as much liberty as the rich. That means that the rich have lost in terms of *relative* equality. Their hard-earned wealth no longer entitles them to purchase greater benefits than the poor can enjoy. By being made more equal to the poor, the rich are made less equal to their previous status.

Myron Lieberman (1994) has made an insightful comment on this, and it is worth keeping in mind for every chapter in this section:

> For a century or more, two concepts of freedom have dominated political debate. One is

that freedom consists of absence of government restraint. . . . The other understanding of freedom is that it consists of the power to do something. The first concept implies a minimal government and is the one most often embraced by conservatives. The latter concept is usually associated with activist and interventionist government. . . . This concept is very much in keeping with the philosophy of the left in the Democratic Party.

School choice has turned this political and intellectual line-up upside down. On this issue, it is conservatives who are asserting that the legal freedom to attend a private school is insufficient; government should provide "real freedom," that is, the same means that are available for the affluent. Meanwhile, liberals are insisting that the legal freedom to attend private schools is all that government should provide. . . . Whatever the political outcome, the philosophical winner is clearly Vilfredo Pareto, the Italian sociologist who observed that men find it easy to convert their interests into principles. (p. 34)

## SCHOOL FINANCE EQUITY

The longstanding practice in America has been for the public schools to obtain their financial support from their communities. The schools in Chicago are supported by the people of Chicago; the schools in suburban Winnetka, Illinois, by the people in Winnetka. The most common means the local residents have used to pay for their public schools is a tax on

property (Goertz et al., 1982, pp. 9, 44). In 1994, Michigan became a dramatic exception to this practice when its citizens voted to replace the historical reliance on property taxes with a reliance on state sales and cigarette taxes (Celis, 1994). Since the sales tax is not as stable a source of revenue as the property tax, Michigan may have traded one set of problems for another. Furthermore, the connection between property wealth and local school district revenue still remained strong three years after Michigan enacted its "reform" (Prince, 1997). And nationally, it is the local property tax that causes funding disparities among school districts.

Over time, the reliance on local property taxes has led to two kinds of disparities. The first is that low-income people in poor communities bear a heavier tax burden than people in rich communities. A larger proportion of their income goes to pay property taxes than is true for wealthier people. Since poor people don't have much income to begin with, this hits them especially hard. The second disparity is that even when poor people make the extra effort to support their schools, they come up with less money per pupil than do people in wealthier communities. The amount spent on each public school child in a poor community may be only half as much as the amount spent per pupil in a wealthy community (Slavin, 1997–1998).

States have reduced these spending gaps by giving more aid to poor communities than to richer ones. For some poor communities, the state actually covers 75 percent or more of the school budget, since the local residents cannot afford to pay for more than a small portion. But even with this state assistance, the poor communities still spend less per student than do richer communities elsewhere in the state. And this continues to be true even after federal aid is added to the picture, belying the assumption among federal officials that the poor districts they are giving aid to have some initial spending equality with rich districts (Taylor and Piche, 1991).

Two further wrinkles complicate this picture: educational overburden and municipal overburden. Educational overburden exists when a school has an unusually high number of students who require special services. These are students who are handicapped or disadvantaged in some way. City schools typically have educational overburden, while suburban schools typically do not. Municipal overburden occurs when taxpayers have to support a lot of other public services in addition to the schools—services such as police and fire departments, welfare offices, and housing authorities (Jordan and McKeown, 1980, p. 81: Levine and Havighurst, 1989, p. 302). Cities are much more likely to experience municipal overburden than suburbs are. Thus, cities in America, especially the large cities, have high educational costs but not good revenue bases. And even when states try to help, the children in poor communities get a less expensive education than the children in rich communities.

The observable consequences of this situation in the cities are large class sizes, run-down buildings, beat-up and outdated textbooks, inexperienced and emergency-certificated teachers, and inadequate supplies and space. As scandalous as these conditions may sound at first, they beg a very basic question: How bad must things be before the government

and its citizens have a legal obligation to do something? How large a class size is too large? When is a beat-up textbook too beat-up? How inexperienced and unqualified is it permissible for teachers to be? When does inadequate become unacceptable? To put the questions another way, how identical must the schools of poor students and rich students be?

These questions have been brought before state and federal courts in a rash of litigation over the past quarter century. The answers have been wide-ranging. Originally, the courts declined to deal with the questions in terms of specific school components. Judges do not feel competent to rule on such specifics as class size, textbook quality, and teacher qualifications. Moreover, the educational experts, who appear before the courts contradict each other, and this leaves the judges even less inclined to get into these thickets. When they do, as Judge Skelly Wright did in *Hobson v. Hansen,* they often must withstand a barrage of criticism accusing them of going beyond their ability to comprehend the issues (Spring, 1988, pp. 161–166). Instead, the courts tended to construe the issue in the simplest possible terms: dollars. That is, how equal is the amount of money one school district spends per pupil to the amount another district spends? Is the difference too large to be legally permissible?

The California Supreme Court ruled that the amount spent on a student could *not* be based on the wealth of the student's family or of the community in which the student lives. This meant there had to be statewide equalization in California (*Serrano v. Priest,* 1971). It did not mean that the same amount had to be spent on every pupil, but only that the education tax base had to be the same for all school districts. A district had some say about how much it wanted to draw on this base; it could determine the amount it was willing to tax itself. The New Jersey Supreme Court ruled, by contrast, that there did not have to be complete tax-base equalization, but rather a large reduction in inequality (*Robinson v. Cahill*, 1973). Seventeen years later, the New Jersey Court found it necessary to rehear the issues, since the gap between rich and poor districts had actually widened. It ruled that the amount spent per pupil in the 28 poorest districts had to be substantially equivalent to that spent in the state's richest districts (*Abbott v. Burke*, 1990). It later ruled that supplemental programs for the poor had to be identified and funded (*Abbott v. Burke*, 1998). The Georgia Supreme Court decided that the disparities in Georgia were not in violation of that state's constitution, so nothing had to be changed (*Thomas v. Stewart*, 1981). In 1997, the New Hampshire Supreme Court ruled that the local property tax used to support schools was, in fact, a state tax because education was a state responsibility. The local property tax had to be equalized across school districts (*Claremont School District v. Governor*, 1997). In the same year, and right next door, the Vermont Supreme Court came to the same conclusion (Sack, 1998). Both states have been forced by their courts to find ways of equalizing the education in school districts of different wealth. As of the spring of 1996, there were seventeen states in which the courts had ruled against the funding systems and in favor of greater equity, and twenty-two states where the funding system had been upheld in state

court (Reed, 1996). Interestingly, some of the state supreme courts have managed to rule on both sides of the issue over time. Because the court decisions have been so divided, no national pattern has developed. However, in those states where the funding formulas have been declared illegal most recently, a pattern has emerged in court decisions. The decisions show a willingness on the part of the courts to define equity more broadly than in minimum dollar terms. Equity is coming to mean *equality* between the richest and poorest districts, as well as the *adequacy of funding* to provide a *quality* education (Verstegen, 1994).

In 1973, a case was brought before the U.S. Supreme Court on the basis of the U.S. Constitution. The Supreme Court ruled that the spending inequalities in the state of Texas did not violate the "equal protection" guarantee of the Fourteenth Amendment to the Constitution. This ruling obviously implied that such inequalities are constitutionally tolerable in other states as well, which is why the challenges to the inequalities are being brought in state courts under state constitutions. However, this did not mean that the justices of the U.S. Supreme Court approved of the inequalities, but only that they could find no justification in the Constitution for acting against them. Justice Potter Stewart wrote in his concurring opinion that the inequalities were "chaotic and unjust," but not illegal (*San Antonio Independent School District v. Rodriguez*, 1973). Since there was no U.S. Supreme Court ruling against the inequalities, each state, through its judicial and legislative branches, will continue to decide how much inequality it will permit. Texas itself tried several different finance formulas before fashioning one that the state Supreme Court found constitutional.

Even if a state decides it will not tolerate differences in the taxable wealth available per pupil, it still has to decide whether it will allow the taxpayers in different communities to tax themselves so differently that one community raises a lot of money for its schools and another raises very little. In other words, states still have to decide how equal they want *spending* to be. The state of Hawaii contains one single school district, so it does not have this problem. A problem it does have in common with other states, however, is deciding how much additional money should be spent on students in each special category. For example, how much extra is needed for the education of a blind student, or a mentally retarded student, or a socially maladjusted student?

We hope that the foregoing overview of school finance issues has given you a good sense of how the values of liberty and equality come into play. If complete liberty were to exist for each school district, the rich districts could raise large amounts of money and have lavish education programs. Poor districts might have the theoretical liberty to do so, but they would not have the practical liberty because they simply cannot raise much money from their limited resources. This places limitations on their liberty to provide all kinds of programs and services:

> The shortage of funds in some districts actually minimizes local discretion in programming and in the ability to compete for the services of good teachers. School boards in poor districts cannot opt to institute special services

when their budgets do not include adequate funds even for essentials. In this sense local control is illusory. It is control for the wealthy, not for the poor. (*Robinson v. Cahill*, 1972, p. 64)

A state can increase the liberty of a poor school district by equalizing its resources up to the level of richer districts. The more it does so, the more it will cost the state. That means that the state will have to collect taxes in rich communities and give funds to poor communities. This brings equality to the poor at the expense of the rich; there is no other way. The rich can then claim correctly that the state has intruded on their liberty by confiscating their wealth, denying them the freedom to spend it as they see fit.

The major public policy question in school finance is: How much dollar liberty should be reserved for the rich, and how much dollar equality should be conferred on the poor?

## INTEGRATION: COMPULSORY OR VOLUNTARY

One of the truly epochal events in American judicial history was the 1954 decision of the U.S. Supreme Court in the case of *Brown v. the Board of Education of Topeka, Shawnee County, Kansas.* That decision began the long, turbulent, and still unfinished dismantling of racial segregation in America. It said that the government no longer could require that the education of blacks and whites take place in separate schools. Richard Kluger (1976), in his definitives history of the *Brown* decision, described its significance:

At a moment when the country had just begun to sense the magnitude of its global ideological conquest with Communist authoritarianism and was quick to measure its own worth in megaton power, the opinion of the Court said that the United States still stood for something more than material abundance, still moved to an inner spirit, however deeply it had been submerged by fear and envy and mindless hate. (p. 710)

Most of you who are now reading this are likely to have been born long after 1954 and to have come of age after government segregation ceased to be taken for granted as part of the American way of life. Thus, it may be difficult for you to understand how the land of the free could ever have been officially racist. It may help to trace the judicial history of desegregation since 1954.

Some people were so determined to maintain a segregated society that there was not just one *Brown* decision, but another that came to be known as *Brown II*. This decision, issued a year after the first one, directed local governments to eliminate their segregated schools "with all deliberate speed" (*Brown v. Board of Education*, 1955). There had been no movement after the first *Brown* decision, and the Court's vague exhortation hardly sped things up at all. The vast majority of black students in the south continued to attend all-black schools.

For thirteen years after *Brown II*, southern school districts found ways to continue segregation while appearing to comply with the Court's directive. The most common way was to set up "schools of choice," whereby black and white students were free to attend whatever school they wanted. Predictably, the black students stayed in their black schools and the white students in their white schools. In 1968, the Supreme Court declared that the time for "all deliberate speed" had run out (*Green v. County School Board of New Kent County*, 1968). Three years later, the Court began allowing lower federal courts to impose remedies to rid the south of segregation, with the most controversial remedy being forced busing (*Swann v. Charlotte-Mecklenburg Board of Education*, 1971).

After that, the Court turned its attention to northern school districts. It found that even though these systems had not been explicitly segregated by law, they had, in fact, been segregated through the deliberate actions of local officials (*Keyes v. School District No. 1, Denver, Colorado*, 1973).

The Supreme Court decision most directly related to the chapter you will be reading was issued in 1974. This decision said, in effect, that the suburbs of Detroit did not have to participate in a desegregation plan with the city of Detroit since it could not be shown that the racial segregation practiced within the Detroit city limits caused segregation throughout the whole metropolitan area. Detroit would have to desegregate its schools without the suburbs' help (*Milliken v. Bradley*, 1974). "The *Milliken* decision is surely the basic reason why Illinois, New York, Boston, Michigan, and New Jersey, each of which has a much lower share of African American students than many Southern states, have been the most segregated states for black students for more than a decade" (Orfield, 1993, p. 2). "The goal of genuinely integrated schooling suffered a tragic setback in 1974 when the Supreme Court, in a case from Michigan, allowed the city line across which many whites had fled to set the boundaries of Detroit's efforts to desegregate its schools" ("Forty Years and Still Struggling," 1994, p. A22).

When Detroit and other northern cities tried to desegregate their schools, they provoked a "white flight" to the suburbs, leaving the city to desegregate a system that had become mostly black. (White flight was inhibited in the south by the fact that many southern school districts are countywide and include both a city and its suburbs.) The rapid growth of northern suburbs was in large part propelled by people intent on living in segregated white communities.

In several cases in the north, the lower federal courts found that state housing policies had deliberately segregated an entire metropolitan region. The first such case was in the Wilmington, Delaware, area (*Evans v. Buchanan,* 1977). In these cases, the courts ordered desegregation plans that involved both the cities and their suburbs.

One of the most bitter and protracted cases of court-ordered school desegregation took place in the cradle of American liberty, Boston. It pitted the working-class Irish, who were intent on preserving their ethnic enclaves in South Boston and Charlestown, against the blacks in Roxbury, who wanted schools that would give their children a chance to escape the ghetto. When the federal court tried to impose cross-neighborhood busing when school opened in 1974, years of violence began. Some children stayed out of school for as long as three years (Wilkinson, 1979, p. 208). There was

even an ironic sidelight: School officials from Boston traveled to Charlotte, North Carolina, for advice on how to handle racial integration. And now there is the melancholy postscript so common in these cases: *resegregation.* A system that once had 85,000 students, 49 percent of whom were white, in 1995 had about 63,000 students, 18 percent of whom were white (*Digest of Education Statistics,* 1997).

J. Harvie Wilkinson traced five stages in the desegregation of America: absolute defiance, token compliance, modest integration, massive integration, and resegregation (Wilkinson, 1979, p. 78). We are well into the last stage now. The proportion of the minority population in large cities grows daily, and many large cities are now overwhelmingly minority in population. The public schools of these cities are even more racially isolated than the cities themselves.

In 1991, the Supreme Court gave a qualified endorsement to resegregation. It ruled that the Oklahoma City school district could discontinue busing, even though the discontinuance would mean a return to racially segregated neighborhood schools. The Court said this would be allowable if Oklahoma City had taken all "practicable" steps to eliminate the "vestiges" of past discrimination, and the case was referred to a lower court for a finding of fact as to whether this condition was met (*Board of Education of Oklahoma City v. Dowell,* 1991). In 1992, the Court ruled in the Georgia case of *Freeman v. Pitts* that once a school district had made a good faith effort to comply with a desegregation order, it could be freed from further court control. If it had complied with only part of the order, it could still be released from court control over that aspect of its operations (*Freeman v. Pitts*, 1992).

In 1993, the Supreme Court upheld a lower court ruling that the schools of Topeka, Kansas, still had not desegregated. This was the school district at issue in the original *Brown* decision of 1954. That case was brought on behalf of a little schoolgirl, Linda Brown, who is now a grandmother in her sixties (Turner, 1994). In 1995, the U.S. Supreme Court decided a case from Kansas City, Missouri. Improving the segregated schools of Kansas City so that they might attract white students from the suburbs and provide better education had cost $1.3 billion, most of which the Court had ordered the state of Missouri to pay. The state then asked the Court to agree that it had done all it could to desegregate the Kansas City schools and make up for the past segregation. Kansas City school officials argued that the state had not done all it could until students' test scores had improved. The Court agreed with the state (*Missouri v. Jenkins*, 1995). Although the district judge still refused to rule that the state of Missouri had done all that it could to desegregate the Kansas City schools, he did agree that the state was no longer obliged to support the desegregation plan with an annual subsidy of $100 million (Hendrie, 1997). Elsewhere, federal courts continue to rule that *everything* has been done to rid certain districts of segregation, and those districts are now deemed to be "unitary," meaning single, nonsegregated districts. A recent ruling came in Nashville, Tennessee (Manzo, 1998).

The Supreme Court has also ruled on the matter of college segregation. Nineteen southern states historically had dual college systems, and while black students can now apply to the historically white colleges (and vice versa), the Court has said that the states must produce more deliberate desegregation *and equalization* of these two sets of colleges. State officials say they are not sure what it will take to satisfy the Court, and the black colleges worry that they might lose their identity altogether (Jaschik, 1992). As a result, the lower federal courts are regularly being asked to apply the Supreme Court ruling to a particular set of colleges, and one of the requests may well lead to a new Supreme Court ruling.

Even while resegregation is taking place in many cities, there are still attempts at desegregation elsewhere in the nation. In a very dramatic case over school desegregation in the city of Yonkers, New York, the federal court ruled that Yonkers officials had enacted policies with the clear but unannounced intention of segregating both schools and city housing. Yonkers was therefore ordered to desegregate its housing as well as its schools. When city officials refused to comply, the judge assessed fines that would soon have brought the city to bankruptcy. This move induced years of foot-dragging compliance. The Yonkers crisis also had the school officials of a northern city going to the south for advice on successful integration (Foderaro, 1988; Belkin, 1999).

In 1994, the Commonwealth Court of Pennsylvania ordered the desegregation of the Philadelphia schools. School officials contend that since 75 percent of the 191,000 students are black or Hispanic, desegregation is possible only if a metropolitan plan is created that includes suburban school districts. Since the case was brought under a state law and not the U.S.

Constitution, the *Milliken* decision did not apply, and the court could order desegregation across the entire metropolitan region (Hinds, 1994). However, in 1996, the state Supreme Court said that the state of Pennsylvania did not have an obligation to spend millions of dollars to promote desegregation programs even *within* the city of Philadelphia ("Philadelphia Loses Round in Court Ruling," 1997).

New Jersey is a prime example of how intractable desegregation can be. The state supreme court directed the state education department to find a way to integrate an Englewood high school with white students in the surrounding towns. After many tumultuous town meetings and expensive reports, the state board of education threw up their hands and directed the people in Englewood to find a way of attracting white students from other communities to their high school. They are back in court.

Once the court and public battles end and integrated schools are established in an area, scholars try to measure the effects of the integration. Their main concern is with the consequences of integration for the children involved. How has it affected their academic performance? How has it affected their attitudes?

Unfortunately, the answers to these question are not clear-cut or consistent. For example, Nancy St. John, in reviewing the relevant studies, found that the students whose academic performance was most enhanced by integration were the middle-class younger black students. She also found, however, that integration had a negative effect on the self-esteem and aspirations of black students generally (St. John, 1975).

Laurence and Gifford Bradley reviewed twenty-nine desegregation studies and found that all of them had methodological weaknesses, limiting the faith one could put in their findings. The better-designed studies were divided between those that showed improved academic performance for black students and those that did not (Bradley and Bradley, 1977).

In a major study for the National Institute of Education, David Armor (1984) reached this conclusion:

> The very best studies available demonstrate no significant and consistent effects of desegregation on black achievement. There is virtually no effect whatsoever for math achievement, and for reading achievement the very best that can be said is that only a handful of grade levels from the 19 best available studies show substantial positive effects, while the large majority of grade levels show small and inconsistent effects that average out to about 0. (See also Armor, 1995.)

An important statement on this question, signed by fifty-eight scholars, summarizes the research of the 1970s and 1980s. The conclusions are: (1) school desegregation can positively influence residential desegregation; (2) integration is associated with moderate academic gains for minority students and does no harm to white students; (3) integration works best when the mechanism includes as many grades and as large a geographic area as possible, and when the plan includes clearly defined goals; and (4) integration is most effective when linked to other types of educational reform (Coughlin, 1991).

An analysis by Wells and Crain (1994) assesses studies of the long-term effects of school desegregation on the life chances of African American students. As they conclude: "There is a strong possibility . . . that when occupational attainment is dependent on knowing the right people and being in the right place at the right time, school desegregation assists black students in gaining access to traditionally 'white' jobs" (p. 552).

One of the most interesting studies, in terms of attitude toward integration, was done by Leroy McCloud. He was the black principal of a black school in Englewood, New Jersey, when the Englewood schools were integrated in 1963. At the time, he opposed the integration. In the late 1970s, McCloud contacted his former pupils to assess the impact integration had had on them and to learn their current opinions about integration. He hypothesized that both the impact and the opinions would be negative, given the turmoil and acrimony of the integration process. His findings clearly showed the opposite to be true. His former students, who had since become young adults, overwhelmingly considered the integration experience to have been worth the pain and disruption that had marked its beginning. They said they felt they were much better equipped to survive and thrive in a multiracial world than they would have been if their education had remained segregated (McCloud, 1980). It is ironic that twenty years later, Englewood is again embroiled in a desegregation battle.

Those who believe that integration has positive effects for blacks, in terms either of academic gains or of improved attitudes, and either in the short-term or over the long-term, are willing to intrude on the liberty of its opponents to bring these benefits about. They are convinced that blacks deserve this equalization even if it has to be forced on an unwilling white community by court edict. To the extent that blacks themselves are reluctant to have their schools integrated, the court edict can be seen as a violation of their liberty, too. People who see integration as necessary for a more just society believe that the advantages that black children reap from integration not only make them more equal, but give them resources to be used in the exercise of their liberty. Greater equality means greater liberty for those who are brought up to equalization. Alas, one person's gain is another person's loss in a competitive society with a finite number of opportunities. This reality is what pits caring parents against each other in the matter of school integration.

## GENDER

Chapter 5 is new for this edition of *Critical Issues in Education*. The chapter is on gender, certainly a controversial topic. Sex has always been a controversial social topic, and any term, like *gender*, that stands for sex is likely to be subject to strong debate. In previous editions, we covered a variety of topics about women, women's rights, sexism, and gender in parts of different chapters. But we decided to create a separate chapter on gender in this edition because reviewers and readers recommended it, and it is a topic of continuing interest for educators.

Additionally, the contemporary battles over feminism and the women's movement create some interesting and perplexing problems for schools. There are no easy, clear, and generally accepted views of how gender issues should be resolved, and of how schools should handle them. Sexism and discrimination against women are generally frowned upon in modern society, as we frown upon discrimination by race, creed, age, or disability, but gender differences pose more complex issues. These disputes relate to fundamental disagreements about nature and nurture, social roles and deviancy, cultural tradition and change, and human rights. These, of course, are also issues of liberty and equality.

A crucial caveat is in order when discussing gender. Some people believe the term *gender* should be reserved for parts of speech and not living things. They would use the term *sex* when referring to organisms. "Masculine" and "feminine" characteristics are distributed along continua, and the continuum for masculine traits overlaps with that for feminine traits. When we talk about gender, then, we are referring to averages, to typicalities. The average for the male or female gender may be considerably off the mark for any given man or woman. A specific man may be further along the feminine continuum than a particular woman, just as the woman may be more "masculine" than the man. We are placed into a gender category on the basis of surface physical features, but all the subsidiary characteristics that are supposed to flow from our gender identities do so to a greater or lesser degree for each individual. Moreover, the cultural and subcultural context sets a variety of expectations for each of the genders. There is pressure to behave, and support for behaving, like a "woman" or "man" according to generalized patterns of behavior.

The sciences thrive on generalization and categories, but individuals must be understood on their own unique terms. How idiosyncratic individuals can be is dramatized by the emergence of the transgender movement. Transgendered individuals, unlike homosexuals, believe that their essential selves are trapped in the bodies of the opposite sex. A "man" who feels like a woman and wishes to behave as one is transgendered. Such individuals devise their own coping mechanisms, and more are resorting to sex-change surgery with chemical augmentation. The politically organized members of the transgendered community are now demanding public acceptance and the accommodation of their sexual status.

Gender questions extend from the earliest human writings to the most recent. Cave paintings communicate gender differences in roles and power. Plato, and many other Western philosophers, accepted the separation of the genders as natural; they laid out rules of society and government which prohibited women from participating in the affairs of state, but sometimes gave them special authority over the affairs of the household. For some, women were no more than slaves or property. Major religious tracts, including the Bible, have differentiated the genders and have been interpreted as demonstrating the superiority of one gender over the other. The literature, politics, and economics of all societies include issues which stem from the relation between the genders.

The lack of voting rights for women at the time the U.S. Constitution was written stands as a stark example of a gender issue in our national history. Schools also offer many examples of gender-based issues in American society. The earliest American secondary schools were for boys only; teaching has long been perceived as a profession dominated by women; girls and boys have experienced differing treatment, expectations, support, and rejection in schools. Resistance and reform movements have arisen to redress the most egregious products of the gender wars—egregious in terms of the ideals of democracy, equality, and justice. Those who spurred these movements have had many titles, including suffragettes and feminists, but they have shared a common interest in equality and liberty—the theme of this section.

Modern feminism in America can be traced to The "First Wave" of feminism, the nineteenth-century struggle for political and educational equality. This highly controversial movement, after some bitter and vicious battles, won voting rights and better educational opportunities for females. After World War II, women's rights emerged again as an important social issue. The United Nations recognized the change, asking only that nations gauge the status of women. Simone de Beauvoir published *The Second Sex* in 1949, heralding a renewed look at that status. Eleanor Roosevelt, appointed by President Kennedy in 1961, headed the President's Commission on the Status of Women.

The advent of the "Second Wave" of feminism is generally tied to the publication of Betty Friedan's *The Feminine Mystique* in 1963, the year that Congress passed the Equal Pay Act. Discrimination based on sex was legally proscribed in the Civil Rights Act of 1964, and the National Organization for Women (NOW) was established in 1966. Publications, political activism, legislation, and court cases furthered the women's movement during the 1970s and beyond. Reactions to these activities have run the gamut from wild applause to fierce resistance from members of both genders. Some advocate radical feminism, some accommodation, some moderation, and some vehement opposition.

The feminist movement is obviously about equity: Are the two sexes treated equitably in every sphere of society? The answer may seem to be just as obvious: no. However, the debate is often about whether equitable should mean "the same." Many feminists think it should, and allow for few, if any, exceptions. Those who disagree see more exceptions—some see many more. Even avowed feminists disagree as to the number of situations in which males and females can legitimately be treated differently. And even men are feminists if they support feminist goals, which is why NOW is the National Organization *for* Women, not *of* Women.

For many feminists, there may be just one basic difference between women and men: the ability to bear children, which includes the menstrual cycle and lactation. All the other presumed differences are cultural overlays on that biological fact, and what culture giveth, culture can take away. Moreover, the task of changing cultural expectation does not require the evolutionary time spans that nature needs to alter biology. Women and men are pretty much the same, according to many feminists, and the cultural differentiation that now exists between them tends to be invidious for the women and self-serving for the men.

The nonfeminists and antifeminists believe nature is implicated in many of the so-called cultural differences between the sexes. Indeed, nature explains how these distinctions came about. And to the extent that the cultural differences are "natural," that is, expressions of biology, they are not readily amenable to change. We are what we are; pretending otherwise creates strain and artificiality. You can't fool Mother Nature. Similarly, long traditions hold weight nearly as strong as nature: girls have always needed protection; boys have always needed discipline.

Gender issues are fought in the arena of politics. The most divisive gender issue is abortion, with feminists asserting a woman's right to choose whether to abort a fetus. The Democratic Party endorses this right, and feminists generally find Democrats to be more supportive than Republicans. Differing interpretations of gender differences, natural and cultural, undergird differences in treatment, expectations, schooling, and power, often creating inequality and discrimination. Some consider the inequalities justified; others consider them unjust.

The educational implications of gender are enormous. How are schools to teach about this topic, if at all? How are schools to treat male and female students? Schools cannot avoid making choices in these matters, and the choices they make will offend some people as much as they give comfort to others. The choices will greatly influence the beliefs and attitudes future generations of Americans hold.

# AFFIRMATIVE ACTION

*Affirmative action* has become a highly charged term in the thirty-some years since its introduction. President Kennedy's 1961 Executive Order 10925 directed companies doing business with the government to take "affirmative action" to overcome racial, religious, and ethnic discrimination. The order did not spell out exactly what these federal contractors were expected to do, but it was clear that they had to do something positive and not just desist from discriminatory practices. Since colleges, universities, and school districts receive significant amounts of federal money, they were included in Kennedy's order.

President Johnson's Executive Orders 11246 and 11375 were more explicit. Federal contractors were required to make attempts to recruit, hire, and promote minorities and women. Johnson believed that knocking down racial barriers was not enough. "You do not take a person who, for years, has been hobbled by chains and liberate him, bring him to the starting line of a race and then say, `You are free to compete with all others' and still justly believe you have been completely fair" (quoted by Mills, 1994, p. 7). But even Johnson's orders were not much more specific than Kennedy's. It was President Nixon who ordered federal contractors to come up with goals stating the number of minorities and women they would hire and setting deadlines for meeting the goals. The government had authority to approve and monitor the goals and timetables. It was Nixon, then, who introduced the era of goals and good faith.

Terms such as *goals* and *good faith* raised skepticism among minorities and women. If a school district set goals and said it was making a good faith effort to hire more minorities and women, but, in fact, it consistently fell short of its goals, suspicion arose that perhaps the district was playing a game. In this situation, the government's Equal Employment Opportunity Commission could charge the district with discrimination and take it to court. Major corporations, such as AT&T and the Bank of America, and educational institutions such as Brown University were so charged, and they consented to hire more minorities and women.

This pressure from the government caused some people to say that the goals had turned into quotas. Once the government set an example with big fish like AT&T, Bank of America, and Brown University, everyone else knew the game was serious and became intent on avoiding a similar fate. The only way a company could guarantee that it would stay in the government's good graces was by meeting its own goals, and that effectively made the goals quotas. U.S. Attorney General Edward Levi acknowledged this when he stated that the goals were "said with great profoundness not to be the setting of quotas. But it is the setting of quotas . . . [even though] we will call quotas goals" ("In Job-Bias Test, Colleges Get Passing Grades," 1975, p. 73).

Opponents of affirmative action saw a danger: In order to meet quotas, companies and government agencies would hire minorities and women even if they were not qualified to do the job. This would hurt the productivity of the enterprise and the American economy overall. Rather than going down this slope, the opponents urge us to rely instead on Title VII of the 1964 Civil Rights Act. This law forbids discrimination based on "race, color, sex, or national origin." A woman or a member of a minority group who believed that he or she was denied a job because of discrimination could take legal action against the employer. Title VII is designed to ensure that all *individuals* have equal opportunity; affirmative action calls for preferential treatment to ensure that *groups* who were historically denied equal opportunity are brought into full economic and educational citizenship.

Affirmative action has led to some landmark Supreme Court decisions. The first involved Allan Bakke. Bakke, a white man, was denied admission to the medical school at the University of California, Davis. He charged that he had a higher score on the Medical College Admissions Test than the sixteen minority students the University admitted. A deeply divided Supreme Court ruled that the medical school could not have a strict minority quota, but it could take an applicant's minority status into consideration (*Regents of the University of California v. Bakke*, 1978). Bakke had been excluded because of a minority quota, so the medical school was ordered to admit him. He is now a physician.

The second case was brought by Brian Weber, a white steelworker who was excluded from a company training program that would have upgraded his skills. He had more seniority than any of the black workers who got into the program. The Supreme Court ruled against Weber on the grounds that his situation was sufficiently different from Bakke's that it did not constitute illegal discrimination. The training program from which Weber was excluded had been established jointly by the United Steelworkers union and Kaiser Aluminum Corporation for the specific purpose of allowing blacks to qualify for the skilled craft positions they traditionally had been barred from. Moreover, the Court said that Title VII did not prohibit "private employers and unions from voluntarily agreeing upon bona fide affirmative action plans" (*United Steelworkers of America v. Weber*, 1979).

In *Fullilove v. Klutznik* (1980), the Court ruled that Congress had acted properly in legislating that 10 percent of federal funds for public works projects had to be spent with minority-owned businesses. This is known as the minority set-aside program.

When President Reagan succeeded in giving the Supreme Court a majority of conservative justices, a series of rulings began against affirmative action plans. In *Richmond v. A. J. Crosson Co.* (1989), the Court decided that the city of Richmond, Virginia, had created its minority set-aside program too broadly and without sufficient evidence that discrimination had existed prior to the program. In *Martin v. Wilks* (1989), the Court ruled that white firefighters in Birmingham, Alabama, could bring a case of reverse discrimination caused by an affirmative action plan that gave jobs and promotions to black firefighters. In the *Adarand Constructors v. Pena* case, the Court dealt another blow to affirmative action, ruling that Federal programs classifying people by race were presumably unconstitutional without a "compelling governmental interest" (Greenhouse, 1995).

Three major cases came to the federal courts during the Clinton adminis-

tration. In the first of these, *Taxman v. Board of Education of Piscataway* (1993), the Clinton Justice Department actually reversed the position of the Bush Justice Department. The Bush officials agreed with Taxman that she had been wrongly dismissed as a teacher so that an African American teacher with the same length of service could be kept on. The Clinton officials argued that the dismissal was justified on the grounds that it allowed the Piscataway High School business department to maintain racial diversity. The federal district court and the appeals court agreed with Taxman that she had been impermissibly dismissed. When the case got to the U.S. Supreme Court, Piscataway threw in the towel and agreed to a financial settlement with Taxman. Very significantly, a civil rights group paid for part of the settlement because the civil rights community saw the Taxman case as a weak one that could seriously set back the cause of affirmative action.

The second case, *Hopwood v. Texas*, was filed against the University of Texas School of Law. The complaint was that the law school admitted African American and Latino students whose Law School Admission Test (LSAT) scores were well below those of rejected white applicants. The federal district court found that the law school did, indeed, violate the Fourteenth Amendment to the Constitution, which guarantees equal opportunity (Rossow and Parkinson, 1994). The Hopwood case was won by a public interest law firm called the Center for Individual Rights, and it has since sued the University of Michigan on the same grounds (Lederman, 1997). That suit applies to the entire university, not just its law school.

The third case, *Podberesky v. the University of Maryland*, was brought by a white student who objected to the university's policy of targeting some of its scholarships for black students only. The Supreme Court has upheld the federal appeals court in siding with the student plaintiff (Jaschik, 1995).

These three cases taken together, plus the fact that the state of California passed its Civil Rights Initiative barring preferential treatment in all government agencies, suggest that affirmative action may be losing favor in the judicial and higher education circles that once supported it. Before jumping to that conclusion, however, note that the people of Houston voted decisively to continue affirmative action (Verhovek, 1997). Pundits have speculated that the rejection of affirmative action in California and its retention in Houston both had to do with the way the question was put to the voters. Ballot questions are often worded in a "Mom and Apple Pie" fashion, making the unwary voter all too ready to endorse the position of the people who got to frame the question.

All of the foregoing court cases illustrate the way in which the values of liberty and equality are involved in every affirmative action case. On the one hand, an employer or an educational institution should have the liberty to decide who comes through the door or who gets promoted. On the other hand, the minority or female applicant should have the right to equal opportunity. Affirmative action complicates the conflict between these rights even further because a third party becomes involved: a

white person, such as Bakke, Weber, Taxman, Hopwood, or Podberesky, who feels that his or her right to equal opportunity has been sacrificed so that society can make up for denying this right to minorities in the past.

The complexity of affirmative action is reflected in poll results. When asked whether companies should be required to hire about the same proportion of blacks and other minorities as live in the surrounding community, the respondents were almost evenly divided, with 45 percent saying Yes and 50 percent saying No ("Racial Quotas in the Workplace," 1991). But when other respondents were asked whether women and minorities should be given preferential treatment in getting jobs and enrolling in college, or whether their ability, as determined by test scores, should be the major consideration, only 10 percent favored preferential treatment, with 84 percent choosing ability. The latter results continue a trend that began in 1977 (Colasanto, 1989). The overall conclusion we can draw from these poll results is that Americans do not support the idea of enforced racial proportionality in the workplace, and they are especially opposed to preferential treatment for either minorities or women. Unfortunately for race relations, such feelings of disapproval are restricted to whites, 58 percent of whom decry racial preferences in hiring even when past discrimination has taken place. By contrast, 66 percent of blacks think that preferential treatment is in order ("Views on Race: Progress Made, Needed," 1993).

Affirmative action cases are also good examples of the unintended consequences that can arise when the government attempts to right a wrong. In a situation where two sets of rights and three parties are involved, the government is in the unenviable position of trying to strike a balance. Schools are one of the arenas in which this drama is frequently played out. The school setting adds an important new value to the struggle between liberty and equality: the value that cultural diversity has in the education of young people in a democracy. Increasingly, white parents are going to court to reject this value when it excludes their child from a school or a school program (Lewin, 1998).

## References

*Abbot v. Burke.* (1998). Sup. Ct. N.J., Case A155, May 21.

———— (1990). Sup. Ct. N.J., Case A61, June 5.

ARMOR, D. (1995). *Forced Justice.* New York: Oxford University Press.

———— (1984). *The Evidence on Desegregation and Black Achievement.* Washington, DC: National Institute of Education.

BARTLETT, D., AND STEELE, J. (1998). "Corporate Welfare." *Time,* November 9, pp. 36–52.

———— (1994). *America: Who Really Pays the Taxes.* New York: Simon & Schuster.

BASTIAN, A., ET AL. (1985). *Choosing Equality: The Case for Democratic Schooling.* New York: New World Foundation.

BELKIN, L. (1999). *Show Me a Hero* Boston: Little, Brown.

BERMAN, P., ET AL. (1998). *A National Study of Charter Schools.* Washington, DC: U.S. Department of Education.

BERNSTEIN, A. (1994). "Inequality: How the Gap Between Rich and Poor Hurts the Economy." *Business Week,* August 15, pp. 78–83.

BLOCK, F., ET AL. (1987). *The Mean Season: The Attack on the Welfare State.* New York: Pantheon.

BLUESTONE, B. (1994). "The Inequality Express." *The American Prospect,* Winter, pp. 81–93.

*Board of Education of Oklahoma City v. Dowell.* (1991). 111 S. Ct. 630.

BOK, D. (1994). *The Cost of Talent: How Executives and Professionals Are Paid and How It Affects America.* New York: Free Press.

BRADLEY, L., AND BRADLEY, G. (1977). "Academic Achievement of Black Students." *Review of Educational Research* 47, 399–449.

*Brown v. Board of Education of Topeka, Shawnee County, Kansas et al.* (1954). 74 Sup. Ct. 686.

*Brown v. Board of Education* (1955), 349 U.S. 294.

BRUCK, C. (1988). *The Predators' Ball.* New York: Simon & Schuster.

CELIS, W. (1994). "Michigan Votes for Revolution in Financing Its Public Schools." *The New York Times,* March 17, pp. 1, 21.

"Child Poverty in Many States Takes a Turn (Mostly for the Worse)." (1998). *News and Issues* (a publication of the National Center for Children in Poverty) 8(2), 1–2.

*Child Poverty Up Nationally and in 33 States.* (1992). Washington, DC: Children's Defense Fund.

*Choice in Public Education.* (1988). New Brunswick, NJ: Eagleton Institute of Politics.

*Claremont School District v. Governor.* (1997). The Supreme Court of New Hampshire, Merrimack No. 97-001.

COHEN, D. (1994). "Making the Connection." *Education Week* 13(31), 1–15.

COHEN, R. (1989). "Bush Details 7-Point Program for 'Educational Excellence.'" *Newark Star-Ledger,* April 6, pp. 1, 6.

COLASANTO, D. (1989). "Public Wants Civil Rights Widened for Some Groups, Not for Others." *The Gallup Poll Monthly,* No. 291, pp. 13–22.

Coughlin, E. (1991). "Amid Challenges to Classic Remedies for Race Discrimination, Researchers Argue Merits of Mandatory School Desegregation." *The Chronicle of Higher Education* 38(7), A9, A11.

——— (1994). "Experts Add Their Voice to Welfare-Reform Debate." *The Chronicle of Higher Education* 40(48), A6–A7.

COWAN, A. (1992). "Milken to Pay $500 Million More in $1.3 Billion Drexel Settlement." *The New York Times,* February 18, p. A1, D10.

DE BEAUVOIR, S. (1949, 1961). *The Second Sex.* H. M. Parshley, translator and editor. New York: Bantam Books.

DELONE, R. H. (1979). *Small Futures: Children, Inequality, and the Limits of Liberal Reform.* New York: Harcourt Brace Jovanovich.

DE TOCQUEVILLE, A. (1835/1968). "Memoir on Pauperism." In *Tocqueville and Beaumont on Social Reform,* edited by S. Drescher, New York: Harper Torchbooks.

*Digest of Education Statistics 1997.* (1997). (Online; http://www.nces.ed.gov/pubs/digest97d97to92.html).

DUGGER, C. (1994). "Researchers Find a Diverse Face on the Poverty in New York City," *The New York Times,* August 30, pp. A1, B3.

EICHENWALD, K. (1994). "Brokerage Firm Admits Crimes in Energy Deals." *The New York Times,* June 28, pp. A1, D15.

*Evans v. Buchanan.* (1977). 416 F. Supp. 328.

FISCHER, C., ET AL. (1996). *Inequality by Design: Cracking the Bell Curve Myth.* Princeton, NJ: Princeton University Press.

FLIEGEL, S. (1993). *Miracle in East Harlem.* New York: Time Books.

FODERARO, L. W. (1988). "In Yonkers. A Measured Integration of Schools." *The New York Times,* September 25, pp. 1, 42.

"Forty Years and Still Struggling." (1994). *The New York Times,* May 18, p. A22.

*Freeman v. Pitts* (1992). Case No. 89-1290.

FRIEDAN, B. (1963). *The Feminine Mystique.* New York: W.W. Norton.

FRIEDMAN, M. (1994). "Once Again: Why Socialism Won't Work," *The New York Times,* August 13, p. 21.

FRIEDMAN, M., AND FRIEDMAN, R. (1980). *Free to Choose.* New York: Harcourt Brace Jovanovich.

*Fullilove v. Klutznik.* (1980). 448 U.S. 448.

GALBRAITH, J. (1998). *Created Unequal: The Crisis in American Pay.* New York: The Free Press.

GALLUP, A. M. (1986). "The 18th Annual Gallup Poll of the Public's Attitudes Toward the Public Schools." *The Gallup Report* 252, 11–26.

GILDER, G. (1981). *Wealth and Poverty.* New York: Bantam.

GLASSER, I. (1978). "Prisoners of Benevolence: Power vs. Liberty in the Welfare State." In *Doing Good: The Limits of Benevolence,* edited by W. Gaylin et al. New York: Pantheon.

GOERTZ, M., ET AL. (1982). *Plain Talk About School Finance.* Washington, DC: National Institute of Education.

GRANT FOUNDATION COMMISSION ON WORK, FAMILY AND CITIZENSHIP. (1988). *The Forgotten Half: Pathways to Success for America's Youth and Young Families.* Final Report. Washington, DC: Grant Commission.

*Green v. County School Board of New Kent County.* (1968). 391 U.S. 430.

GREENHOUSE, L. (1995). "Justices, 5 to 4, Cast Doubts on U.S. Programs that Give Preferences Based on Race." *The New York Times,* June 13, pp. A1, D25.

GROSS, R., AND ESTY, J. (1994). "The Spirit of Concord." *Education Week* 14(5), 36, 44.

HACKER, A. (1992). *Two Nations: Black and White, Separate, Hostile, Unequal.* New York: C. Scribner.

HARRINGTON, M. (1973). *Socialism.* New York: Bantam.

HASS, N., AND NAYYAR, S. (1994). "Barbarians Break the Bank." *Newsweek,* May 2, p. 55.

HENDRIE, C. (1997). "Judge Decides State Funds for Desegregation to End in K.C." *Education Week* 16(27), 1, 30.

HERRNSTEIN, R., AND MURRAY, C. (1994). *The Bell Curve.* New York: Free Press.

HINDS, M. (1994). "Schools Ordered to Desegregate in Philadelphia." *The New York Times,* February 5, p. 6.

HUFF, D. (1992). "Upside-Down Welfare." *Public Welfare* 50(1), 36–47.

"In Job-Bias Test, Colleges Get Passing Grade." (1975). *U.S. News and World Report,* August 18, pp. 73–74.

IVINS, M. (1997). "The Danger in Outrageous Fortunes." *The Newark Star-Ledger,* October 20, p. 13.

JASCHIK, S. (1992). "High-Court Ruling Transforms Battles Over Desegregation at Colleges in 19 States." *The Chronicle of Higher Education* 38(44), A16–A18.

———— (1995). "'No' on Black Scholarships." *The Chronicle of Higher Education* 41(38), A25, A29.

JENCKS, C., ET AL. (1970). *Education Vouchers.* Cambridge, MA: Center for the Study of Public Policy.

JORDAN, K. F., AND MCKEOWN, M. P. (1980). "Equity in Financing Public Elementary and Secondary Schools." In *School Finance Policies and Practices,* edited by J. W. Guthrie. Cambridge, MA: Ballinger.

KEMPER, V. (1993). "Rebuilding the Schoolhouse." *Common Cause Magazine* 19(1), 24–28.

KENISTON, K., AND THE CARNEGIE COUNCIL ON CHILDREN. (1977). *All Our Children: The American Family Under Pressure.* New York: Harcourt Brace Jovanovich.

*Keyes v. School District No. 1, Denver, Colorado.* (1973). 413 U.S. 189.

KIRP, D. (1992). "What School Choice Really Means." *The Atlantic Monthly,* November, pp. 119–132.

KLUGER, R. (1976). *Simple Justice.* New York: Knopf.

KRISTOL, I. (1978). *Two Cheers for Capitalism.* New York: Basic Books.

KUTTNER, R. (1991). "Notes From the Underground: Changing Theories About the 'Underclass.'" *Dissent,* Spring, pp. 212–217.

LEDERMAN, D. (1997). "Suit Challenges Affirmative Action in Admissions at U. of Michigan." *The Chronicle of Higher Education* 44(9), A27–28.

LEMANN, N. (1991). *The Promised Land: The Great Black Migration and How It Changed America.* New York: Knopf.

LEVINE, D. U., AND HAVIGHURST, R. J. (1989). *Society and Education.* Boston: Allyn & Bacon.

LEWIN, T. (1998). "Public Schools Confronting Issue of Racial Preferences." *The New York Times,* January 29, pp. 1, 42.

LIEBERMAN, M. (1994). "The School Choice Fiasco." *The Public Interest,* No. 114, pp. 17–34.

MANZO, K. (1998). "Curtain Falls on Desegregation Era in Nashville." *Education Week* 18(6), 3.

*Martin v. Wilks.* (1989). 490 U.S. 755.

McCloud, L. (1980). *The Effect of Racial Conflict in School Desegregation on the Academic Achievement and the Attitudes of Black Pupils in the Englewood Public Schools.* Doctoral dissertation, Rutgers University.

MEAD, L. M. (1988). "The New Welfare Debate." *Commentary* 85, 44–52.

MEIER, D. (1991). "Choice Can *Save* Public Education." *The Nation,* March 4, pp. 253, 266–271.

*Milliken v. Bradley.* (1974). 418 U.S. 717.

MILLS, N. (1994). "Introduction: To Look Like America." In *Debating Affirmative Action,* edited by N. Mills. New York: Dell.

MISCHEL, L. (1997). "Capital's Gain." *The American Prospect,* 33, 71–73.

*Missouri v. Jenkins.* (1995). Case No. 93-1823.

MORAN, B. (1987). *Inside a Gifted/Talented Magnet: An Analysis of the Enrollment and Curricular Patterns by Race and Gender in the Hillside School in*

*Montclair, New Jersey.* Doctoral dissertation, Rutgers University.

MURRAY, C. (1991). *Losing Ground: American Social Policy, 1950–1980.* New York: Basic Books.

——— (1994a). "Does Welfare Bring More Babies?" *The Public Interest,* No. 15, pp. 17–31.

——— (1994b). "What to do About Welfare," *Commentary* 98(6), 26–34.

OLSON, L. (1991). "Proposals for Private School Choice Reviving at All Levels of Government." *Education Week* 10(22), 1–10, 11.

ORFIELD, G. (1993). *The Growth of Segregation in American Schools: Changing Patterns of Separation and Poverty Since 1968.* Cambridge, MA: Report of the Harvard Project on school Desegregation to the National School Boards Association.

PATERSON, J. T. (1986). *America's Struggle Against Poverty: 1900–1985.* Cambridge, MA: Harvard University Press.

PEAR, R. (1998a). "Government Lags in Steps to Widen Health Coverage." *The New York Times,* August 9, pp. 1, 22.

——— (1998b). "H.M.O.'s Cut Off Medicare, Leaving Many in Quandary." *The New York Times,* October 19, p. A10.

"Philadelphia Loses Round in Court Ruling." (1996). *The New York Times,* September 12, p. A15.

PHILLIPS, K. (1990). *The Politics of Rich and Poor: Wealth and the American Electorate in the Reagan Aftermath.* New York: Random House.

PITSCH, M. (1991). "School-Choice Plan Could Endanger Entire Bush Proposal, Senators Warn." *Education Week* 10(39), 31.

PRINCE, H. (1997). "Michigan's School Finance Reform: Initial Pupil-Equity Results." *Journal of Education Finance* 22(4), 394–409.

*Putting Learning First.* (1994). Washington, DC: Committee for Economic Development.

RABINOVITZ, J. (1997). "Connecticut Welfare Cutoff Falls on Hundreds of Families." *The New York Times,* November 3, pp. B1, B5.

"Racial Quotas in the Workplace." (1991). *The Gallup Poll Monthly,* No. 309, June, p. 35.

REED, D. (1996). "Court-Ordered School Finance Equalization: Judicial Activism and Democratic Opposition." *Developments in School Finance, 1996.* (Online: http://www.nces.ed.gov/pubs97/97535.html).

*Regents of the University of California v. Bakke.* (1978). 438 U.S. 265.

*Richmonds v. A. J. Crosson Co.* (1989). 448 U.S. 469.

*Robinson v. Cahill.* (1972). Docket L-18704, Sup. Ct. of N.J., Hudson County.

*Robinson v. Cahill.* (1973). 62 N.J. 473, 303 A.2d 273.

ROSSOW, L., AND PARKINSON, J. (1994). "Introduction and Comment." *School Law Reporter* 36(10), 1–2.

SACK, J. (1998). "In Vermont's Funding Shakeup, A Bitter Pill for 'Gold Towns.'" *Education Week* 18(9), 1, 23.

SAFIRE, W. (1995). "The Newt Deal." *The New York Times,* January 5, p. A27.

ST. JOHN, N. (1975). *School Desegregation: Outcomes for Children.* New York: Wiley.

SAMUELSON, R. (1998). "A Tycoon for Our Times?" *Newsweek,* November 16, p. 65.

*San Antonio Independent School District v. Rodriguez.* (1973). 411 U.S. 1.

SCHORR, J. (1993). "California's Experiment on Your Schools." *The New York Times,* October 30, p. 21.

SCHUNDLER, B. (1994). *The Jersey City "Schoolchildren First" Education Act.* Jersey City, NJ: Save Our Schoolchildren.

*Serrano v. Priest.* (1971). 96 Cal. Rptr. 601, 437 P.2d 1241.

SHANKER, A. (1991). "Private Is Public." *The New York Times,* December 1, p. E7.

SIMON, W. E. (1978). *A Time for Truth.* New York: McGraw-Hill.

SLAVIN, R. (1997–1998). "Can Education Reduce Social Inequity?" *Educational Leadership* 55(4), 6–10.

SMITH, A. (1776/1976). *The Wealth of Nations.* Edited by Edwin Cannan. Chicago: University of Chicago Press.

SNIDER, W. (1988). "In Chicago, Implication of Reform Bill Please the Grassroots, Dismay Others." *Education Week* 8, 6.

SPRING, J. (1988). *Conflict of Interests: The Politics of American Education.* New York: Longman.

STEVENS, M. (1994). "State Orders DPS to OK Charter Plan." *The Denver Post,* July 19, pp. 1, 8.

*Swann v. Charlotte-Mecklenburg Board of Education.* (1971). 402 U.S. 1.

*Taxman v. Board of Education of Piscataway.* (1993). 832 F.Supp. 836 (D.N.J).

TAYLOR, W., AND PICHE, D. (1991). "Fiscal Equity and National goals." *Education Week* 10(26), 26.

*Thomas v. Stewart.* (1981). No. 8275 (Ga. Super., Polk County).

THUROW, L. C. (1980). *The Zero-Sum Society: Distribution and the Possibilities for Economic Change.* New York: Basic Books.

"The Tide Is Not Lifting Everyone" (1997). *The New York Times* (editorial), October 2, p. A18.

*Time for Results: The Governors 1991 Report on Education.* (1986). Washington, DC: National Governors' Association.

TURNER, R. (1994). "Round Two in Topeka." *Emerge,* May, p. 34.

*The Unfinished Agenda: A New Vision for Child Development and Education.* (1991). Washington, DC: Committee for Economic Development.

*United Steelworkers of America v. Weber.* (1979). 443 U.S. 193.

VERHOVEK, S. (1997). "Referendum in Houston Shows Complexity of Preferences Issue." *The New York Times.* November 6, pp. A1, A26.

VERSTEGEN, D. (1994). "The New Wave of School Finance Litigation." *Phi Delta Kappan* 76(3), 243–250.

"Views on Race: Progress Made, Needed." (1993). *The New York Times,* April 4, p. 16.

WALSH, M. (1998). "'Green Light' for School Vouchers?" *Education Week* 18(12), 1, 19.

WALSH, M. (1994). "Charter Ruling Sends Schools in Mich. Reeling." *Education Week* 14(13), 1, 16.

——— (1995). "Court Hears Arguments in K.C. Case." *Education Week* 14(17), 1, 19.

WEINRAUB, B. (1989). "Bush Wooing Educators, Urges Choice in Schools." *The New York Times,* January 11, p. B28.

WELLS, A., AND CRAIN, R. (1994). "Perpetuation Theory and the Long-Term Effects of School Desegregation." *Review of Educational Research* 64(4), 531–555.

WILKINSON, J. H. (1979). *From Brown to Bakke: The Supreme Court and School Integration, 1954–1978.* New York: Oxford University Press.

WILSON, W. J. (1987). *The Truly Disadvantaged: The Inner City, the Underclass, and Public Policy.* Chicago: University of Chicago Press.

# School Choice: For Family Choice or Against Vouchers

## POSITION 1: FAMILY CHOICE IN EDUCATION

As the twenty-first century unfolds, school choice will develop steam and become a dominant trend in education. Public support has grown to the point that almost half the states have started, or are considering, some form of choice program—many are turning to vouchers as one approach. To spur public voucher and choice programs, private enterprise has taken some leadership in providing grants for private school attendance, and this has produced some impressive results. Clearly, there is a high level of public interest in choosing the kind of education that best fits.

The School Choice Scholarships Foundation offered 1,300 vouchers to cover private school tuition to low-income children in New York City in 1997; 16,000 parents applied (Archer, 1997). This remarkably popular program is supported through private fund-raising, already over $7 million. Financier Theodore Forstman raised $170 million, and more than one million families applied for scholarships to private schools (Hartocollis, 1999). If public schools were successful, why would an enormous number of parents be discontent enough to seek private schooling? This shows the great public demand for, and public policy virtue of, school choice. A 1997 poll of residents of Washington, D.C. by The American Education Reform Foundation found that 61 percent of low-income residents would send their children to private schools if they could afford it. Family choice should not be limited by income; private vouchers offer the possibilities of choice.

The first private voucher program started in 1991 in Indianapolis, when an insurance company contributed $1.2 million to provide almost 750 vouchers. Rapid growth and unceasing demand for the vouchers has pushed other philanthropists, business leaders, and community organizations to start private voucher programs to help young people get a high-quality education. Over thirty private programs now exist in more than eighteen states, a doubling of private voucher programs in the past few years.

Private voucher programs are not intended to be permanent; instead, they offer an example of how well family choice programs work, how popular they are, and what they can do to improve education for many children. Relying on philanthropy for large numbers of children is not in the public interest, but neither is reliance on a massive and slow-moving bureaucracy that restricts parental decisions. Public policy can be improved by innovation in the private sector. Private voucher programs can help lead to a more rational publicly funded choice system, either through vouchers or through some other means to increase parental choice. The concept of choice is most important, not the particular form or model it comes in. Thus, the argument here is not limited to vouchers; vouchers are but one form of choice that allows families to decide which schooling best fits their family's needs. Florida, in 1999, was the first state to provide vouchers; other choice ideas will follow.

## The Idea of Choice

School and family choice hits a very responsive chord among American families, going well beyond the idea of vouchers. The idea of *family choice* captures the spirit of this position, and so it is the term we will use in this argument. The family choice idea merits consideration for three reasons: (1) public interest signifies the issue will not go away; (2) it gives many people, including officials at the highest levels of local, state, and national government, great hope for the future of American education; and (3) it is an idea of such intrinsic promise that it cries out for a fair test. Moreover, as Lynn Cheney, former chairperson of the National Endowment for the Humanities, has said: "Critics of choice are fond of saying that it is not a panacea, and they have a point; nevertheless, simply because of the forces it sets in motion, choice does have primacy among reforms. It is, as well, a change that seems long overdue" (Cheney, 1990, p. 24).

Family choice means that the family chooses the school its children will attend. The family can make this choice from among *all* of the *approved* schools within a reasonable commuting distance. Approved schools would be those that meet minimum standards, such as building safety and fiscal accountability; public, private, and parochial schools could all participate. This would include literally scores of schools in the more populous areas of the United States. But even if there were only five schools to choose from in a less populous area, that would be five times more choice than families have now.

To pay for the school of its choice, the family would receive a check (or voucher) from the government. The government would get the money for these checks from the taxes it collects. In other words, schools would still be supported by taxes, but a family would be able to get its hands on its share of the tax money and use that to buy the kind of education it *really* wants. All families would get the same amount of money per child, depending on the needs of the child. For example, checks (or vouchers) for children with handicaps would be for larger amounts than those for children without handicaps because it costs more to educate a child with disabilities. For all children in the same educational category, the amounts of the checks would be the same.

## The Benefits for Students

One of the recurring and most common complaints about American education is that it leaves students bored out of their skulls. You can judge for yourself how much this complaint echoes your own experience. The complaint has been around for a long time, but school officials have never had to do anything about it because neither children nor their parents have had other choices. Children had to go to school; they had to go to the school that some authority mandated; and they could end up in reform school if they did not attend the prescribed school. While youngsters may need to receive an education for their own and society's benefit, they at least should be able to go to a school they like.

The *literature* of professional education contains some truths that remain remarkably absent from the *practice* of education. One of these truths is that different children have different needs and interests. That's so obvious as to be a truism. Another truth (and another truism) is that students learn more when they are motivated than when they are longing desperately for the bell to ring. Family choice means that at long last these two fundamental truths of education may actually be *applied*.

As a matter of fact, the truths are being applied already, but for only a few students—those whose families can afford to send them to a school beyond the control of the local authorities. Family choice will give all of us a right that now exists only for the well-to-do. It is true that the poor can scrimp and save to send their children to parochial schools, but parochial schools for the poor are not markedly better, and from the student's point of view may be much worse, than the local public schools. Why should only the rich be allowed to have effective control over their children's education? Studies show that poorer American families also favor school choice ("School Choice Debate," 1997). Bret Schundler, mayor of Jersey City, fought to get a voucher program for the poor children of his constituency. As he put it:

> School choice has been a reality for the rich. They can move to suburban districts where the public schools are decent. Or if, like Bill Clinton, occupational requirements compel them to live in a city, they can send their children to high-quality private schools. The poor are largely denied that opportunity. They are compelled by law to attend government schools, even when some of these schools are dysfunctional. (Schundler, 1993, p. A27)

If a poor family can pick a school outside of its neighborhood, then minority families will be able to integrate their children into majority schools. As it stands now, American schools are notoriously and thoroughly segregated

(Orfield, 1993). It is easy to find a school populated overwhelmingly by minority students. It is just as easy to find an almost lily-white school. A tragedy of our times is that these schools can be found in such close proximity to each other: They are on opposite sides of an arbitrary and artificial line known as the school district boundary. Family choice on a nondiscriminatory basis offers real promise of getting past this disgraceful condition. It might mean that the student body of Phillips Academy, the elite boarding school in Andover, Massachusetts, will be as racially diverse as that of the Andover Public High School (Boaz, 1993). Nina Shokrai (1996) argues that private schools are more successful at recognizing and responding to parental interests for their children than are the public schools, and that low-income families do care about their children's education. She notes, in fact, that it is a destructive myth that low-income families don't care about the education of their children.

Racial and social integration of schools, to the extent it has been tried in the United States, has had a rocky history. In many cases, it seems to have done more harm than good, needlessly wasting time, energy, money, patience, and kids' lives. Such cases have all involved legally forced integration. With family choice, integration will come about naturally—that is, voluntarily. The kids in a given school may not have race or social class in common, but they will have common interests and needs. Those commonalities are more important to children than are the superficial characteristics of race and class that adults worry about.

Family choice is a way to honor children's good sense. The Hervey School in Medford, Massachusetts, offered such interesting programs that it attracted a multiracial student body (Bastian et al., 1985, p. 76). Some "choice" schools even organize around a theme of multiculturalism or integration. "Educational alternatives can be based on a newer conception of integration—multicultural education, which establishes cultural diversity as its founding principle" (Fantini, 1973, p. 229). It is paradoxical that today's racially segregated schools are pushing for multicultural education.

## The Rights of Parents

In the United States, parents have extensive and legally sanctioned control over their children. The theory that justifies this legal authority is that parents are the people most likely to understand the needs of their children and the people most concerned about their welfare. "In its unique opportunity to listen and to know and in its special personal concern for the child, the family is his most promising champion" (Coons and Sugarman, 1978, p. 53).

The rights of parents over their children are not unlimited, and should not be. Children have some needs that parents simply cannot meet and for which they have to rely on expert help. Medical care is one example. Education is another. Parents may lack pedagogical skills and have to turn to professional educators for assistance. However, professional educators have transitory relationships with children and never acquire the intimate knowledge and concern that parents have. Moreover, they do not have to live with the long-term consequences of having a miseducated and unhappy child. Therefore, parents should always be the senior partner in the educational team for their child. And they should certainly have the most to say about the primary educational decision: the school the child will attend.

Increasingly, they also have the right to choose the schools their children will not attend. The courts have affirmed that parents have the right to educate their children at home. Parents need only demonstrate their competence to deliver the basic education expected by the state. Home schooling is not widespread yet, but if parents could cash a voucher themselves instead of signing it over to a school, it would become financially feasible for more parents to do what they've always wanted—create family schools.

## Breaking the Educational Monopoly

Obviously, none of this would make any sense if the family could choose only from among schools that were all the same. That is why the idea doesn't make much sense in today's school market, where the vast preponderance of schools are interchangeable clones. "If we first implement choice, true choice among schools, we unleash the values of competition in the education marketplace" (*Time for Results,* 1986, p. 6). What family choice is intended to do, therefore, is to replace that amorphous mass of jelly that passes for education in America with some really solid alternatives. The public schools can afford to be arrogant and unconcerned because they have a monopoly on public funds for schools. They determine where you go and what you get for the vast majority of Americans who are not wealthy enough to send their children elsewhere.

Under family choice, the neighborhood school will no longer be forced on families until they have the money to buy their way out. "There's something galling about the idea that you're stuck in a particular school that's not working for you unless you are rich enough to buy yourself out of it" (Meier, 1991, p. 271). The captive clientele of today's schools will be set free. Family choice in education is a liberating act of the twenty-first century. And just as indentured servants of the eighteenth century who had worked off their period of servitude could either remain with their former owners or strike out on their own, families can stick with their neighborhood schools or go to some school that has deliberately fashioned itself to be attractive and interesting. Indeed, the neighborhood school will probably refashion itself in an effort to keep families from fleeing.

The possibilities for attractive and interesting schools are endless. For example, one of the public schools in the East Harlem section of New York City is a maritime academy, with the East River serving as a natural laboratory. The East Harlem schools also include a talented and gifted school, a performing arts school, a career academy, and a key (basic skills) school. The last four schools share space in what was once a large, impersonal, one-size-fits-all public school (Fliegel, 1993; Kirp, 1992). It is remarkable that these public schools in one of the worst sections of New York City have been made so attractive that they enroll 1,000 students from other parts of the city (Snider, 1990, p. 19)! Cleveland has an aviation high school whose curriculum includes flying lessons. Less dramatically, a school could be truly "user friendly" by using the experiences of the kids in the neighborhood as the building blocks of the curriculum (Raywid, Tesconi, and Warren, 1984, p. 24). The choice will be especially rich if families can select not only the public schools, but also the private and parochial schools in an area. This variety of schools already has some diversity to offer, but the choices will be multiplied many times as *all* schools scurry to attract parents with vouchers.

With declining patronage, a school will have decreasing income and will have to lay off staff. With few, if any, vouchers, a school will not have adequate resources to stay in operation and will have to shut down. These dismal prospects will cause schools to work harder than ever to attract customers and keep them satisfied. Up until now, a public school has not had to work hard at all because it has had a virtual monopoly on the education in its neighborhood. "Under a real competitive system of choice, what would a school board do if a school lost 40 percent of its students and 40 percent of its money? They'd give the principal a year to turn the damn place around or get out the door. There would finally be a reason why somebody had to care about these schools. It would work for the kids left behind even more than for the kids who move" (Clark, 1993, p. 53).

## Escaping Secular Humanism

In addition to the right to choose a good education for their children, parents have the right to protect their children from influences they feel are bad. One of the things that most worries parents is having their children come under "evil" influences. For example, some parents forbid their children to play with certain other children for fear their children will be led astray.

For many parents, especially among those who are devoutly religious, the public school itself is an evil influence because it is nonreligious. In its attempt to avoid indoctrinating children into any religion, the public school shuns all but the most neutral presentation of religion, treating religious faiths as purely historical phenomena. It presents all religions as equally valid and equally arbitrary manifestations of people's search for meaning. This obviously suggests to students that their family's religion is just one among equals and that it is certainly no more divinely inspired than any other, and maybe not at all.

Parents believe that the noncommittal approach of the public schools weakens their children's religious commitment. It turns children away from spiritual sources of certain truth to human sources that are uncertain and relative. Naturally, parents who find religion meaningful and whose beliefs guide their behaviors dread having their children drawn away from religion by the public schools. Some parents go so far as to say that because the public school's approach has consequences for their religion, it is, in fact, a form of religion itself. They call this form "secular humanism," a "religion" that elevates human beings to the highest moral realm. And that means that their children are in a school where a competing and hostile religion is subtly and insidiously taught.

Choice allows these parents to protect their children's spiritual lives as they see fit. It is a violation of religious freedom to require parents to send their children to an institution that undermines the parents' religious values.

The liberal reaction is that the diversity in a public school is worth maintaining even if it offends everyone in the school in some way. Indeed, offensiveness itself is presumed to have educative value. However, Nathan Glazer, a leading scholar of religious and ethnic conflict, articulates a much more realistic position:

> I am convinced the conflict of values in this country today, between the religious and the secular, the permissive and the traditional, those seeking experience and those seeking security and stability, between the culture of the coasts and the culture of the heartland, between the cosmopolitans of Los Angeles and New York and the staid inhabitants of smaller towns and cities (as well as most of the inhabitants of Los Angeles and New York), are so great that the vision of a truly common school, in which all are educated together, simply will not work . . . a decent opportunity for withdrawal to a more homogeneous and educationally effective environment is necessary and can be provided without destroying our democracy and/or our multiethnic society. (quoted by Lieberman, 1993, p. 38)

## The Benefits for Teachers

Family choice does not sit well with teacher unions because it appears to pose a threat to members' job security. Every family that pulls out of a school brings the teacher's job closer to extinction. If families are not allowed to pull out, the teacher can bask in the assurance of guaranteed employment—at least when birth rates are not falling. This negative attitude toward family choice paints teachers as wanting nothing more than to be civil service lifers. It is a demeaning portrait of teachers, and it ignores the positive aspects of family choice for them.

Despite the rhetoric of union leaders, the data show that public school teachers often select private schools for their own children. That is a devastating argument against the monopoly of the public schools and an argument in favor of parental rights to choose. Dennis Doyle (in "School Choice Debate," 1997), reported a compilation of U.S. Census data on the high percentages of public school teachers who chose to send their own children to private schools in many cities (table 2.1). What better testimony to the need to provide choice for all Americans than these data? If public school teachers recognize and take advantage of the values of private education for their own children, why should children of the less informed or less well-paid be denied the same opportunity?

**TABLE 2.1  Percent of City-Resident Public School Teachers Who Send Their Children to Private Schools**

| CITY | PERCENT |
| --- | --- |
| Baltimore | 32.9 |
| Boston | 49.6 |
| Cleveland | 46.5 |
| Grand Rapids | 50 |
| Los Angeles | 30.6 |
| New Orleans | 46.1 |
| Pittsburgh | 46.3 |

School choice offers more than personal and family advantages—it offers benefits for teachers. Family choice frees teachers to design schools as they wish. The deadening uniformity and ritualism of schools can be as enervating to teachers as to students. Most teachers would like to make school more exciting for themselves and their students, but they have no chance to do so because they are locked into a bureaucratic monolith. Teachers may want to do little more than a series of interest-arousing community explorations outside the standard organization of the school day. But they cannot do so because such an idea does not fit into the "system." David Kearns, former chairman and chief executive officer of the Xerox Corporation, as well as a U.S. Assistant Secretary of Education, says that America's public school system has to be broken up, just as business corporations had to be in recent years, and for the same reason: They have become bureaucratic dinosaurs that impede the productivity of their employees. Choice is the way to disassemble an outmoded system (Kearns and Doyle, 1988). If one of the most powerful corporations in the world, IBM, has been forced to do this, it is not too much to expect that public education will have to do the same.

All teachers can do now is struggle around the periphery of the dinosaur until they become exhausted, and then content themselves with going through the motions until retirement or get out of teaching altogether. Read the following description of the idealistic teacher who has become burned out and imagine what "choice" could mean for such a person.

> The classic example of Type II burnout is a young, well-educated, socially idealistic, politically involved young man or woman who comes to an impoverished inner-city or rural school brimming with ideas, enthusiasm, and confidence and who, after several months (or perhaps even years) of giving more and more—of depriving him or herself of sleep and/or a relaxing social life, of trying to find new, creative ways to motivate and teach children— senses that these efforts are not paying off, that he or she is ineffective and perhaps even mistrusted. (Farber, 1991, p. 91)

Family choice will give the bolder and more creative teachers an opportunity to break loose and start their own schools, perhaps on the basis of a shared enthusiasm for a particular approach to education or even on the basis of friendships among teachers, with the particular educational approach hashed out collegially and revised the same way (Raywid, 1987). If the school is small, the teachers will still be able to maintain their standard of living while saving a lot of the cost of administrative overhead. A sufficiently small school could be operated out of a home or store, so that both capital and custodial costs could be kept to a minimum.

Less adventurous teachers could redesign the schools they have been working in, perhaps dividing them into minischools. The school administrators who might be rendered superfluous by this action could take on more strictly educational duties, and they should welcome this prospect if they are truly committed to working with children.

Family choice, then, will have the effect of *empowering* teachers. Not only will they remain in direct contact with students, but there no longer will be a bureaucratic Maginot line between them and the parents or the school policies. Schooling will become a cooperative venture among three essential parties: students, teachers, and parents. This does not mean that all of the new schools will be better than any of the present schools. It means that students, teachers, and parents will be able to have the kind of school they feel comfortable in and have the most confidence in as well.

These prospects could solve the problem of a teacher shortage. People who would not deign to teach in the present system might be excited enough by the chance to be true educational professionals that they would switch careers. The Friedmans report that people have told them: "I have always wanted to teach [or run a school] but I couldn't stand the educational bureaucracy, red tape, and general ossification of the public schools" (1980, p. 169).

The charter schools movement is especially promising. The goal is to allow teachers and parents to take over the operation of their local public schools, relatively free of control by local boards of education or the state. By September 1997, 30 states had passed charter school laws and 24 states had charter schools in operation, with the total number of schools being 693 and the combined enrollment reaching 110,122 (Berman et al., 1998).

## Respecting Differences

Teaching children to respect differences among people is supposed to be a goal of today's public schools. However, the schools betray this goal in two major ways. First, they are segregated along racial and social-class lines. The message that this sends to students is that some people are more worthy of avoidance than respect. Second, the public schools are like giant food blenders that ground differences into mush. It's all right for teachers to talk about tolerance, but the kids don't get the chance to assert anything about themselves that could require toleration.

Religion, politics, esthetic sensibilities, and expressive styles are all carefully constrained in today's public school. No one is allowed to get too far out of line or to be too radical. Everyone walks on eggshells. Genuine self-expression is like a time bomb that must be defused. Eccentricity is a scandal, and in today's frantically vanilla schools it does not take much to be eccentric. The norms in poor urban schools may be different from those in affluent suburban schools, but they are just as limiting and oppressive. The frantically chocolate school leaves no more breathing room than the frantically vanilla.

Family choice means freedom for the misfits in today's schools—misfits not because of their own qualities, but because of the intellectual and social rigidity of the schools. These students are as likely to be supernormal as subnormal. Their only crime lies in falling outside a narrow field of tolerance. The only choice they have now is for an education that is either painful or inauthentic, and often both. If they display their true selves, they suffer rejection and ridicule from their peers and constant badgering by the school authorities. If they dissemble to get by, they feel false and dishonest, which can cause them to reject themselves. Family choice can widen the field of tolerance *across* schools, so that the misfits, some of whom are misfitted unto suicide, begin to belong. It may not increase the tolerance within a school—in fact, it could even reduce it—but at least children would know that society respected them enough to find comfortable places for all.

Choice, then, allows the creation of communities of interest and mutuality, as opposed to the current school communities of coercion. The genuine community nature of choice schools is their essential element, and that is what most guarantees the success they enjoy.

> What can choice be, then, if it finds support in so many different, ordinarily antagonistic quarters? The common element—for community organizers, for Catholics, for free marketers—is that in each case proponents of choice are arguing for the creation and support of communities. This may seem far-fetched with regard to the current choice movement—after all, the free market dissolves communities, it doesn't create them. But free choice in a free market environment for schooling does indeed permit the expression, creation, and maintenance of communities. And if choice is effective, as its advocates hope, in raising academic achievement, the primary reason will be because it re-creates community in schools in which the maintenance of community had become difficult or impossible. (Glazer, 1993, p. 650)

## Building in Safeguards

Family choice, of course, is vulnerable to abuse, with hucksterism the abuse that usually leaps to people's minds. Schools-for-profit are permitted—indeed, encouraged—by family choice. Some of the profiteers are going to be hucksters willing to use unscrupulous means to attract and bilk families. False advertising, misrepresentation, inflated claims, hidden charges, and bait-and-switch schemes are some of the practices that must be prevented. As with other businesses, the best way to circumvent these white-collar crimes is by developing a monitoring mechanism, then imposing swift and severe penalties on perpetrators. Dishonest educational practices are among the worst kinds of consumer fraud because the victims are children and the harm can be long-lasting. A well-staffed agency should be able to keep the abuses to a minimum and to catch quickly any that do occur.

Another potential abuse of the family choice system is discriminatory admissions practices. A school might want to make itself attractive to both families and teachers by excluding certain students, such as black students, low-achieving students, students with handicaps, or students from a minority religious group. It might be permissible to exclude students who perform poorly on a test that is related to the purpose of the school, or students who are so profoundly handicapped that the school is not equipped to educate them. Other schools will specialize in meeting the needs of these students. And academically elite schools, such as Boston's Latin School, should be allowed to continue their mission of serving those students who are academically talented without considering their nonacademic characteristics (Glenn, 1991). However, exclusion on the basis of race, religion, or other illegitimate criteria are abuses that the fair practices agency should be charged to prevent. A *Time*/CNN poll conducted in the spring of 1991 strongly indicated that the public wants more choice even if it means that some schools will be nearly all white and others nearly all black; 48 percent of those polled agreed to this, whereas 42 percent disagreed (Shapiro, 1991, p. 57). Equally noteworthy is a Gallup survey showing that 64 percent of those polled believe that parents should receive governmental financial support to send their children to religious schools (*The People's Poll on Schools and School Choice*, 1992). In sum, the public is prepared to endure racially and religiously segregated schools as long as people can freely choose these schools.

A third form of abuse would be the failure to provide the minimally adequate education expected for all children. A school may attract students because it is warm and friendly and fun to attend, but then not assist them in acquiring the academic skills needed for gainful employment and useful citizenship. Society has a right to establish minimum standards of achievement and to test students to ascertain that they are meeting these standards. Many states already have statewide standards and tests, so these states would simply maintain their tests under the family choice system.

A fourth problem is the cost of transportation. Students should be transported at public expense to any school in the region covered by the family choice system. Otherwise, a family's choices will be circumscribed by the cost of transportation. For poor families, this cost can be prohibitive, so they will have no real choice apart from the neighborhood school(s). It is not likely that suburban students would be attracted to an urban school if that school were nearly crammed to capacity with kids who are trapped in the neighborhood. Without a transportation allowance, the family choice system offers a lot less choice and may bring about very little racial and social integration. Obviously, if private schools are allowed to be part of a publicly funded choice system, they will have to play by these rules. They can't take government money and be free of government regulation. They will have to compete for students under the same constraints as those imposed on public schools. The line between private and public will largely be erased (Kemerer, 1992; Weinberg, 1992).

A fifth form of abuse has been alleged in Wisconsin. Milwaukee's Parental Choice Program is a publicly financed private school choice experiment, and its success (or failure) will greatly influence the future of choice. Thus, the research on this program is studied closely by advocates, opponents, and policymakers generally. Advocates claim that the researcher doing the official analysis is biased against choice and is rigging the research to discredit the Milwaukee program (Lindsay, 1994; McGroarty, 1994, 1996). This demonstrates the need to make the program data widely available for independent analysis by any interested researcher.

Once a choice system is under way, other dangers may appear, and other safeguards may have to be devised, but human ingenuity should be able to cope with these problems. It is possible to protect everyone's legitimate interest while expanding everyone's freedom, and the result will be education characterized by harmonious pluralism. "The ability to get the kind of education one wants for oneself or one's children serves both as a reward for those with a pedagogical interest and as a means of defusing fights between interests over who should have the ability to impose universal requirements on the system" (Kerchner, 1988, p. 390).

## POSITION 2: AGAINST VOUCHER PLANS

### Defining the Terms

Family and choice are powerful words in the American lexicon; they carry a lot of emotional baggage. Both the Democratic and Republican national parties invoke the word *family* as though it were a sacred mantra. And choice is something we instinctively associate with democracy as opposed to tyranny, which is characterized by the denial of choice. So when the words are combined into the term *family choice,* the unwitting listener or reader is disposed to agree with the proposal.

We could dispense with this nonsensical use of language by noting that no one, even in a democracy, has free and unfettered choice, and that *family* means very different things to different people. All choices are limited or restricted in some manner—choices about money, time, law, physics, other people's rights, energy, health, and mental capacity face a myriad of limits. We can't always do what we wish when we wish and how we wish. That doesn't mean that choice, even in limited form, is not a great and democratic idea that we support; it is just that the word *choice* used in a political or ideological battle can easily be misunderstood—with the implication that the opponents are evil tyrants bent on dictatorship. Choices are necessarily couched in personal and social contexts that need consideration before judgment.

*Family* is also a term that hides its complexity. Families can include two parents, one parent, two parents of the same sex, no parents, one person, five hundred people, nuclear families, extended families, humankind, teams and corporations, and nearly limitless other combinations. Families not only come in all sizes, shapes, and colors, they also come in a multitude of personalities, including destructive, caring, dysfunctional, loving, intrusive, manipulative, domineering, and long-suffering. Family choice, then, can be a very misleading term. In the pleasant form, we like family choice; we just don't trust what we think the other side means by it. We don't like vouchers or other mechanisms that can cripple or destroy the public school system and provide huge sums of taxpayer funds to support profit-making or religious enterprises.

It's a good debate tactic to give your side of the argument an appealing label. If the debate were just an intellectual exercise, no harm would be done by this, and one side would rack up a few points in the category of "best label." However, the issue under discussion here is one that has momentous implications for us all. The two parties to the debate are not nearly as important as the great party in-between: the American public. For the American public to judge the debate fairly and make a well-informed decision about the future direction of American education, it is imperative that it not be blinded by debaters' tricks. Therefore, we will not use the loaded term *family choice*, which plays into our opponents' hands, nor will we employ a loaded term of our own. Instead, we will use a more neutral term. The word *voucher* has developed value connotations, beyond those of accountants, but the use of this word will not cloud the debate, because it is widely accepted as a form of choice.

A voucher is simply a mechanism for choice; parents get a voucher (or check) from the government, which they use to pay for their child's education at the school they select. Charter schools are another form of choice. A group can organize a charter school, determine its focus and its standards for student admissions, competitively seek students, and obtain public funds for operations, and be exempt from many of the governmental controls that exist for other public schools. Charter schools differ from vouchers because vouchers go directly to parents to use for individual children, while charter schools obtain public funds for all the children in their school. There are, however, a number of common elements between vouchers and charter schools. They both divert public funds now used for existing public schools, and they both entail diminished requirements for public accountability. We will use the term *voucher* in this essay to represent the common elements of most school choice programs. While vouchers are but one form of choice, they are the logical end to which the other forms lead. For this reason, opponents of school choice suspect that the more limited forms of choice are stalking horses for vouchers.

## Preserving Diversity

A voucher system has many practical problems that we will address in later sections. The overriding problem, however, is philosophical. The American public school now functions as a crucible of democracy. This is especially true of the comprehensive high school, where students from a good-sized geographic area and with a wide range of interests and abilities are brought together. The public school is the most democratizing institution in America. It is the social institution most open to the most people for the longest time. Its primary purpose is to provide a sound education that can equalize opportunities for all children. No other institution—government, family, media, religion, or work—can equal the record of public education for expanding opportunities for the most people over the greatest period of time. Public schools, no matter their many faults, are the backbone of democratic American society.

Public schools are also responsive to the public will and to parental concerns as are no other social institutions. Governance and funding are under open public control through boards and elections. Schools are public buildings and, save for health and safety considerations, are open to public visit. Media scrutiny of public schools is intense. Parents, to the extent they are willing or able to participate, are active partners in school life.

Public schools also offer choice—not always a choice of school, but a choice of curricula and programs within the school. Students with different interests and abilities can take part in programs tailored to their needs. They also can easily switch from one program to another since all the programs are in a single school. Parents and students may choose and change. Thus, the individual has both choice and ease of choice, and also gains the benefit of a heterogeneous social environment. Students from different programs in the high school can mingle and engage in common activities; the *extra*curricular activities of the school are open to all regardless of their curriculum program. But even some of the academic courses mix students from different programs. For schools that have different programs but not ability grouping (or tracks) within the programs, the commingling is even greater.

The net result of this arrangement is that different kinds of people practice living together. The practice may, on occasion, be unsettling, even painful. However, it cannot be forestalled forever, and school is a semiprotected environment in which to gain the experience of democratic living and learn how to get along with others. In the comprehensive high school, "others" does not just mean others like oneself; it also means others with whom one does not have much in common. Students who develop the ability to interact smoothly with a variety of other people are likely to be successful and happy adults. They will know when to compromise and will understand what behaviors are offensive to what sorts of people. They will also understand the value of reciprocity in relationships. These abilities can only be developed in a setting with a variety of other people—that is, in the comprehensive high school.

A voucher system, by whatever euphemism and in whatever form, would replace the comprehensive high school crucible with a spice rack that physically isolates differences. It may be snug and comfortable for the students in each little container, but it is poor preparation for the real world. For American students, it is poor preparation for citizenship in a democracy. "The unifying function is not simply an ideal of the comprehensive high school model; it reflects an ideal central to our democratic republic. It is, in effect, an effort to act upon the motto of the United States, *E Pluribus Unum*—out of many, one" (Wraga, 1992, p. 42).

Learning how to socialize with people who share your interests and abilities is relatively easy, but hardly enough. There are other kinds of people in the world, and you cannot hide from them forever if you wish to have a rich and full life. A voucher system would cripple students socially and breed a divisive defensiveness among groups of people who have never gotten to know each other. At a time when states are trying to develop more truly multicultural curricula in recognition of the value of multiple perspectives in an interdependent world, it is ironic that some people are trying to make the school itself more unicultural.

## The Interests of Society

It is interesting to note how the voucher proposal is pitched to the self-interests of different groups. Parents are told that vouchers will give them latitude in deciding where their children go to school. Students are regaled with visions of candy store education where they will be able to go on shopping sprees. Teachers are led to believe that, finally, they will have total job control. Very little emphasis is placed on the *responsibilities* these groups will acquire—time-consuming, anxiety-provoking, selfishness-inducing responsibilities. Worse yet, no attention is paid to the interests of the whole, the common good. As a society, we have interests that transcend the self-interests of individuals and that cannot be left to individual whim. The more legitimate interests a society has, the less freedom each individual or group can be allowed. The public interest requires that we constrain the exercise of our selfish interests.

What are society's interests in education? First, all children need to acquire the communication skills and the knowledge of government necessary for full and active citizenship. When state authorities spell out these skills and knowledge areas in detail, a good part of the K–12 curriculum has been specified. This becomes more and more the case as democracy demands greater sophistication of its members.

Society's second major interest is in preparing young people for effective functioning in the world of work. This involves the development not only of marketable skills, but also of positive work habits and attitudes. This should eliminate from any "choice" equation schools whose principal attraction for students is low expectations. In addition to having high expectations of its schools, the state has an obligation to monitor the schools to ensure a satisfactory fulfillment of society's goals.

Society's third interest is negative. The state has a definite interest in keeping every school it pays for free of religious and ideological indoctrination.

Public schools—and all voucher schools would be publicly funded—cannot brainwash students into the agenda of any interest group. As the U.S. Supreme Court stated in a decision involving the teaching of Darwinian theory in Arkansas:

> Judicial interposition in the operation of the public school systems of the Nation raises problems requiring care and restraint. Our courts, however, have not failed to apply the First Amendment's mandate in our educational system where essential to safeguard the fundamental values of freedom of speech and inquiry and of belief. By and large, public education in our Nation is committed to the control of state and local authorities. Courts do not and cannot intervene in the resolution of conflicts which arise in the daily operation of school systems and which do not directly and sharply implicate basic constitutional values. On the other hand, "The vigilant protection of constitutional values is nowhere more vital than in the community of the American Schools."
> (*Epperson v. State of Arkansas*, 1969)

Preserving "freedom of speech and inquiry and of belief" means that many people will be ineligible for voucher money with which to impose their personal convictions on youngsters. Otherwise, we are going to see public subsidization of socially divisive and miseducative institutions such as white supremacist and black nationalist schools. Such cities as Detroit, Milwaukee, and New York have given serious thought to the establishment of public academies for black males (Chmelynski, 1990). Should such academies come into being, their curricula are likely to be Afrocentric to promote the self-esteem of the students. This goal may be laudable, but the instruction itself might amount to myth mongering.

## *Choosing When Ready*

A voucher system is both unnecessary and undesirable at the high school level, when students are more mature and can make informed decisions about programs, and schools are larger and allow more choices. A voucher system may seem justified at the elementary school level because students (and families) now have virtually no choice in these schools. Usually, a single neighborhood school provides a single curriculum for everyone. Moreover, that single curriculum has a stranglehold on elementary education across America. Voucher advocates imply that people indifferent to the needs of children developed this situation conspiratorially. The American elementary school system is a gulag archipelago, they suggest—nothing more than a national system of prisons for children.

This characterization is a gross slander of elementary school educators and an insult to the intelligence of the American people. The elementary schools of America are, in reality, the places where children's *common needs* are met. The schools are similar precisely because children's needs are similar. *All* children who are going to survive and thrive in our society need to learn the academic basics of reading, writing, and arithmetic. These are generative skills; they are tools for further learning. The fact that all schools teach these skills, along with the social studies and science future voters and workers need and the art and music that enrich life, simply reflects good sense. Computer literacy is now a part of this list because its importance has become obvious, and elementary schools are flexible and prudent enough to accommodate such a significant cultural adaptation. Do we really want to allow families to decide whether their children should have to learn basic skills that are of transparent benefit to them and to society?

Just how important and widely approved the elementary curriculm is can be seen in the state tests now under state development. Experts are designing tests in the core school subjects and grade-by-grade standards so that Americans will have a good gauge of how well their children are doing relative to those standards and to other children. State standards are being promulgated in more and more states. Because the tests are based largely on a common curriculum for all students across the nation, vouchers are not needed to mitigate mobility.

Because children's needs and the corresponding academic subjects are similar from school to school, and to some extent from grade to grade, children are able to transfer between schools without disrupting their academic progress. This portability has to be an important consideration for a people as mobile as Americans. It does not mean, however, that all children are expected to learn the basic academic skills in exactly the same way. Different schools have different teaching styles and materials, and this is true for students of different abilities within the same school. The styles and materials are best left to the judgment of trained professionals. Without denigrating the intelligence of parents and children, the indisputable fact is that they have not been trained to make the professional judgments of educators. Moreover, parents may wish to send their children to school outside the neighborhood just because it has become fashionable to do so, much as some college students wish to attend an out-of-state college. Even if the cost of transportation were only a dollar each way, that could amount to $400 a year per student, or millions of dollars for the transportation system. These funds would then be unavailable for the education system. Moreover, parents of even young children are apt to defer to their children's choices, and as the past president of the American Federation of Teachers predicted, "What most kids—and most adults—want is not to have to work very hard" (Shanker, 1993, p. E7). This certainly is not the best basis for choice.

Voucher advocates argue that the differences in styles and materials to be found in today's elementary schools aren't wide enough. Not even the differences that a school district creates when it makes each school a magnet site with its own unique theme are enough to satisfy many voucher advocates. They insist on a veritable multitude of choices, in the naive belief that children and parents are capable of wading through this wild abundance and making an intelligent selection. Elementary school children are too young to have this responsibility imposed on them, and most parents lack the time and expertise to make distinctions among a host of closely competing alternatives. The voucher proponents subscribe to the illogical notion that there can't be too many choices. But although choice can be a good thing, too many choices can be as paralyzing as taking too much cough medicine for a cold. If the public desires more choice, it should be brought about gradually and cautiously within an already proven system.

## *Inequality of Choice*

Should a voucher system succeed in bringing about a wide variety of schools, choosing will be difficult for even the most intelligent and assiduous parents. Ploughing through the promotional materials and independent assessments of many schools could entail an enormous amount of reading. Interpreting this material could require technical expertise the ordinary parent does not possess. Visiting schools that look good on paper to check out the reality is a task that many parents don't have time to carry out. Other parents lack the self-confidence to embark on such a bold venture (Winerip, 1998).

Obviously, not all parents are equal when it comes to choosing. The most educationally disadvantaged students are likely to have parents whose own poor educations did not equip them to make wise choices for their children. Every day, news disclosures shock us with revelations that many parents brutalize their children, and it may be unwise to trust some parents with their children's welfare in any way. Thus, the already educated and concerned parents will be able to take advantage of a choice system in ways that won't even occur to the ignorant or the indifferent.

Making the selection parameters equal will require considerable money for the production of reliable and cognitively accessible information packets, in more than one language, and will require a goodly number of qualified counselors. This money may have to be subtracted from the value of the vouchers, leaving less for the actual education of children. Mario Fantini's blithe suggestion that those who lack the ability to choose well can simply continue doing so by trial-and-error until they get it right (Fantini, 1973, pp. 74–75) ignores the huge educational and psychological cost for youngsters who wander from school to school, year after year.

The propagation of low social status across generations is something poor parents engage in unwittingly. In a voucher system, "parents will be able to send their children to schools that [may] reinforce in the most restrictive fashion the family's political, ideological, and religious views. That is, school will be treated as a strict extension of the home" (Levin, 1980, p. 251). The upshot will be that working-class parents will pick schools that stress discipline, basic skills, and learning to follow orders, while middle-class parents will select schools that foster independence and higher-order thinking skills. Working-class kids will learn how to be low-wage workers; middle-class kids will be readied for high-salaried professions. The working-class students will be limited by their parents' constrained conception of success.

Since minorities are represented disproportionately among the poor, social-class tracking by school will mean racially segregated schools. It is instructive to recall that the South used "schools of choice" to guarantee the continuation of a dual school system. Now that we know how fiercely northern communities have resisted desegregation, "it is fatuous to believe that the white community will permit a voucher system to operate so as to remove the barriers that they have laboriously erected to protect themselves and their children from what they consider to be the undesirable behavior patterns of the disadvantaged" (Ginzberg, 1972, p. 106). Whites will fight to make sure that "choice" is intradistrict only, leaving them safe to choose from among schools that will remain predictably white. New Jersey trumpets its "choice" initiatives, but with a few isolated exceptions, they are intradistrict plans, posing no threat to the suburbs of Newark or Trenton or Camden.

The same result is possible with interdistrict choice if schools are allowed to choose students after the students have indicated their choice of schools. Schools could establish admission criteria that would predetermine the composition of the student body, not just in terms of academic ability, but also socioeconomically and racially. An example of how this might work is the New York City school system, which has four tiers of high schools: academic schools, theme schools, vocational schools, and neighborhood schools. The top tier schools skim off the most able and manageable students, leaving the most needy, and therefore least desirable, students to the neighborhood schools (Bastian et al., 1985, p. 75). The choice for the disadvantaged is to stay put.

The segregative potential of "choice" plans is so great that some have recommended that vouchers be granted only to students who are failing in their present school. That would help ensure that vouchers have an overall positive effect on students (Elconin and Holahan, 1990). Moore and Davenport looked at the way choice operated in New York, Chicago, Philadelphia and Boston, and concluded:

> School choice has, by and large, become a new improved method of student sorting, in which schools pick and choose among students. In this sorting process, black and Hispanic students, low-income students, students with low achievement, students with absence and behavior problems, handicapped students, and limited-English-proficiency students have very limited opportunities to participate in popular-option high schools and programs. Rather, students at risk are proportionately concentrated in schools which . . . characteristically exhibit low levels of expectations for their students, deplorable levels of course failure and retention, and extremely low levels of graduation and basic skill achievement. (quoted in *Public Schools of Choice*, 1990, pp. 12–13)

Even in East Harlem's much-touted District 4, "creaming" (skimming the brightest and best from the top) occurs in subtle ways. Nonachieving students are encouraged to go elsewhere, while the junior high schools annually recruit the best sixth graders. Such practices explain why the highly esteemed Central Park East School in the district had so few children from welfare families

(Tashman, 1992). Robert Peterkin, director of the Urban Schools Programs at Harvard, has remarked on the "subtly selective" nature of the choice schools in Cambridge, Massachusetts, another district whose choice program has garnered a lot of favorable publicity (Peterkin, 1994). That kind of sorting is now taking place in Great Britain, where "choice" was made national policy in the late 1980s. British schools, desperately seeking to assure themselves of a student body, are screening out less desirable students, whether they are handicapped, troubled, or slow learners (Chira, 1992b). Their reasoning is that having undesirable students gives a school a poor reputation, and the only families willing to patronize such a school will be those with no other choice—perhaps because their children are also deemed undesirable.

## Keeping Teachers Sane

Teacher unions get a bum rap for being opposed to vouchers. The unions are accused of protecting the jobs of teachers above all else, the public be damned. If the voucher system is adopted, the public *will* be damned, just as surely as there will be a dramatic drop in the number of teachers.

No one wants to work in an insecure environment. Everyone seeks stability and predictability in employment. To ask teachers to subject themselves to precarious, insecure jobs for the rest of their working lives is to expect a sacrifice no other workers would willingly make. Each summer, teachers would have to wait for word that their schools had attracted enough students for them to return to work in September. Their anxiety would then end only briefly, since student transfers during the year (another choice in the radical voucher scheme) could put them back out on the street. It might be possible for a teacher in a low-drawing school to transfer to a high-drawing school, but this could require that he or she abandon a sincerely held teaching philosophy. The teacher's effectiveness would be seriously impaired by coerced insincerity. Certainly, job satisfaction would be diminished.

Over time, the constant tensions inherent in a voucher system are bound to have an insidious effect on even the most dedicated of teachers. They will know that their livelihoods are at stake in every interaction with their pupils. Dissatisfied pupils (and parents) will be able to pull out of school even if their dissatisfaction is unjustified. Many families will shop around for a good deal, not for a good education. Grade inflation, already at a scandalous level in American education, will render teacher judgments meaningless. Teachers will be in the untenable position of being the direct employees of the very people they are expected to evaluate. "Without an external incentive system that demands a certain kind of quality, success will be based on popularity rather than quality" (Shanker, 1994). *Caveat vendor* should not be the watchword of education.

This is not a call for the continuation of the tenure system for teachers. It is much more modest, and thus much less controversial. It is only a call for some continuity and independence in the professional lives of teachers so that they can do their jobs honestly. Vouchers will drive teachers into other careers, and the first teachers to go are likely to be those who value honesty the most.

## Controlling Temptation

This brings us to another consideration of honesty—or, rather, dishonesty. Voucher schools will be public schools insofar as they are funded publicly and open to the public. However, a salient feature of public schools is that they have historically been nonprofit institutions. Budgets are subject to public approval, including employee salaries, and no stockholders receive dividends or make capital gains. In short, the opportunities for public school officials to profit from their positions are severely limited, and in many cases could only occur through illegal or unethical conduct. Even then, the amount to be gained might be so small that very few would take the risk of detection and punishment.

The voucher system will put public education in the for-profit category. People who run the schools will be allowed to earn as much as they can wring from the public. The thickness of their wallets will no longer be limited to their salaries; public education will be transformed into just another capitalist venture. "Supply-side competition introduces strong incentives for providers to present superficial or inaccurate information on effectiveness, to package information to promote their product, and to protect as proprietary certain types of information that would be useful in making client choice" (Elmore, 1986, p. 34). If college recruiting brochures have only a coincidental relationship to the actual institution they supposedly portray, imagine all the misleading fluff that will go into the promotional materials of voucher schools.

We can glean some idea of this from California's open enrollment law, which allows parents to send their children to any public school within their school district. Schools are now running television commercials and placing newspaper advertisements to attract students (Newman, 1994). Even if the hype is restrained, the money and personnel time consumed in producing promotional materials could have been spent directly on education.

We need to make sure the American public does not have to bail out an array of corrupt voucher or charter schools as it has had to bail out corrupt savings and loan associations. A corrupt-practices control board for the voucher system will have its hands full. Its first order of business will be to figure out what constitutes a corrupt practice in this strange new form of business. No doubt it will encounter, among other abuses, those that have been so rife among proprietary schools: inflated claims of graduate placement; inflated projected earnings for graduates; elastic definitions of success, so that a person who becomes a file clerk in a public defender's office is credited with a career in law enforcement. The prohibited practices will likely be defined in general terms, so large gray areas are left where all kinds of shady practices can take place. The number of independent public schools will increase geometrically, and just conducting paper audits of each one could take up all the time of a well-staffed control board. On-site inspections would take place perhaps once every five years. The years between inspections would be duping and stealing time.

Voucher schools and charter schools will either conduct or commission studies of their own effectiveness. This is not a reassuring prospect, given the record to date. The public has been seeing a welter of conflicting research results. The Carnegie Foundation for the Advancement of Teaching captures page 1 of *The New York Times* with its report questioning the effectiveness of choice programs (Chira, 1992a). Prestigious researchers, such as Paul Peterson of the Harvard University government department (Lindsay, 1994), then challenge the data used by the prestigious Carnegie Foundation. District 4 in East Harlem had been nationally acclaimed for raising test scores and reducing dropout rates; but then Princeton University Press published a book demonstrating that both the test scores and the retention rates were misrepresented, if not deliberately rigged (Henig, 1994). This battle over choice programs does not give the public much basis on which to choose. Imagine what it would be like if voucher programs were enacted on a wide scale, with many jobs and much money at stake. The only group guaranteed to do well in such an environment would be the researchers-for-hire.

What makes these prospects all the more horrendous is that the families that are especially presumed to benefit from a voucher system—the poor—are most likely to be the victims of its abuses. They will be sold a bill of goods by sleazy operators who prey on their ignorance. The poor may even be sold a bill of ideological and racial goods so that they end up rallying to the defense of the people who stole their money and their children's futures.

If the profits to be made from voucher schools are large enough, members of the control board may find themselves looking the other way in order to get their piece of the action. In other words, all the travesties of corporate America will be visited upon public education. For centuries now, the young have been shielded from that danger by a public school system that has controlled corruption by controlling temptation. We must not throw teachers and students to the wolves of the profit system.

Fortunately, the danger may have passed. The defeat of voucher proposals in California, Colorado, and Oregon is one sign that the public has become skeptical. Nationwide, 54 percent of respondents to a Time/CNN poll oppose public vouchers for private and religious schools, with only 34 percent in support (Cohen, 1999, p. 38). And nonpublic schools are beginning to rethink the wisdom of participating in a government-run operation that will prohibit some of the things they are now doing and impose new demands on them (Corwin and Dianda, 1993; Trowbridge, 1993). Vouchers, which not long ago were touted as being in everyone's interest, are beginning to look as though they are in no one's interest (Walsh, 1999). The charter school movement, another malformed choice effort, will become less popular as their warts and blemishes begin to show in the early years of the twenty-first century.

## For Discussion

1. Contact two public schools and two private schools in your area. Ask for information about school programs, teachers, libraries, costs, class sizes, and extracurricular activities. Ask also about admission criteria, parent rights, school budgets, and how each school is governed. Ask about what

happens to students who have discipline problems. Ask for a brochure which highlights the school. Compare the responses to make a judgment about school choice. What are the advantages and disadvantages of each kind of school? What difference would it make for a student to attend one school rather than another?

2. How many of your friends or classmates went to public schools; how many to private schools? (Which did you attend?) What are the main reasons they give for those decisions? What do they perceive as the differences between public and private education, and how important do they believe those differences are? Do they recommend that all children attend the kind of school they attended?

3. Assume you had the opportunity to establish a new charter school in your community, based on your best ideas about how schools should operate and what they should emphasize. What would your school's mission be? What would your school's curriculum include? How would you select students? How would you advertise your school?

4. Choice can be built into a school system in many different ways. To illustrate:

**School Organization and Finance**

local district control, taxpayer community finance, central district administration

school-site control, taxpayer lump-sum budget to school, staff administration

contracting for services, taxpayer finance by contract and bids, district supervision

privatization and vouchers, taxpayer individual vouchers, self-administered/state supervision

**Admissions, Attendance, Staffing**

all residents can attend, attendance required for certain ages, teachers certified

special school for special interests, attendance required, teachers certified

lottery/test for admission, voluntary/can be expelled easily, teachers as suitable

charter mission determines admission, attendance, teacher requirements

These are different ways of organizing, financing, managing, and operating a choice system. The curricula may differ, according to state requirements and local options, along a wide spectrum. What would you add to these lists for making schools of choice? What would you limit? How should choice be exercised, and by whom?

5. The tables that follow show reasons that people in Europe and the United States give for choosing a school. Do these reasons make sense to you? Do they persuade you that school choice will be of educational benefit to children?

**TABLE 2.2  Reasons for Choosing a Swedish Compulsory School**
*(Entry ages 7, 10, 14)*

| Reason | Percentage of Parents |
|---|---|
| Friends/good peer atmosphere | 34 |
| Quiet/not violent/small classes | 21 |
| Good teachers/school leadership | 16 |
| Social factors/attention to pupils | 15 |
| Special pedagogical character (Waldorf, Montessori, etc.) | 12 |
| Geographical factors | 10 |
| Better equipment/facilities | 8 |
| Attention to pupils with problems | 7 |
| Special subject character (music, art, foreign language) | 5 |
| Good reputation | 5 |
| Possibility of parent influence | 4 |
| Special religious character | 2 |

**TABLE 2.3  Reasons for Choosing an English Secondary School**
*(Entry age: 11)*

| Reason | An Influential Reason (%) | One of the Three Most Important Reasons (%) |
|---|---|---|
| Child preferred school | 59.2 | 23.3 |
| Near to home/convenient for travel | 57.3 | 23.7 |
| Children's friends will be there | 56.1 | 14.5 |
| Standard of academic education | 55.7 | 21.0 |
| Facilities | 55.7 | 20.6 |
| School's reputation | 54.6 | 20.6 |
| Child will be happy there | 49.2 | 21.0 |
| School atmosphere | 44.7 | 5.0 |
| Policy on discipline | 42.0 | 11.5 |
| Standard of education in nonacademic areas | 40.8 | 6.5 |
| Examination results | 38.9 | 11.1 |
| What school teaches/ subject choices | 37.4 | 6.9 |

**TABLE 2.4  Reasons for Choosing a French Lycée**
*(Entry age: 15)*

| Reason | Most Important Reason (%) | One of Three Most Important Reasons (%) |
|---|---|---|
| Success at *baccalauréat* | 6.2 | 10.4 |
| Quality of teaching | 15.0 | 20.3 |
| Reputation | 13.7 | 25.1 |
| Discipline | 0.7 | 3.3 |
| Total of above 4 motives | 35.6 | 59.1 |
| Smaller classes | 2.0 | 4.3 |
| Subject option | 14.7 | 20.9 |
| Atmosphere | 1.0 | 6.9 |
| Continuity | 10.7 | 16.2 |
| Closeness | 27.0 | 51.7 |
| Sibling(s) | 2.6 | 10.1 |
| Child's preference | 6.5 | 12.4 |
| Total | 100.0 | 181.6 |

**TABLE 2.5  Reasons for Choosing a School, by United States Parents**

| Reason | Very or Fairly Important Reason (%) |
|---|---|
| Quality of teaching staff | 96 |
| Maintenance of school discipline | 96 |
| Curriculum/courses offered | 95 |
| Size of classes | 88 |
| Grades/test scores of students | 88 |
| Close proximity to home | 74 |
| Extracurricular activity | 68 |
| Athletic program | 53 |
| Racial or ethnic composition | 32 |

*Source: School: A Matter of Choice.* (1994). Paris, France: Organisation for Economic Co-operation and Development, pp. 26–27.

## References

ARCHER, J. (1997). "16,000 N.Y.C. Parents Apply for 1,300 Vouchers to Private Schools." *Education Week,* April 30.

BASTIAN, A., ET AL. (1985). *Choosing Equality: The Case for Democratic Schooling.* New York: New World Foundation.

BERMAN, P., ET AL. (1998). *A National Study of Charter Schools.* Washington, DC: U.S. Department of Education.

BOAZ, D. (1993). "Five Myths About School Choice." *Education Week* 12(18), 24, 36.

CHENEY, L. (1990). *Tyrannical Machines.* Washington, DC: National Endowment for the Humanities.

CHIRA, S. (1992a). "Research Questions Effectiveness of Most School-Choice Programs." *The New York Times,* October 26, pp. A1, B8.

—— (1992b). "Schools Vie in a Marketplace: More 'Choice' Can Mean Less." *The New York Times,* January 7, pp. 1, 12.

CHMELYNSKI, C. (1990). "Controversy Attends Schools with All-Black All-Male Classes." *The Executive Educator,* October, pp. 16–18.

CLARK, J. (1993). "Pro-Choice." *Mother Jones,* September, pp. 52–54.

COHEN, A. (1999). "A First Report Card on Vouchers." *Time,* April 26.

COONS, J. E., AND SUGARMAN, S. D. (1978). *Education by Choice: The Case for Family Control.* Berkeley, CA: University of California Press.

CORWIN, R., AND DIANDA, M. (1993). "What Can We Really Expect From Large-Scale Voucher Programs?" *Phi Delta Kappan* 75(1), 68–74.

ELAM, S., ROSE, L., AND GALLUP, A. (1994). "The 26th Annual Gallup Poll of the Public's Attitudes Toward the Public Schools." *Phi Delta Kappan* 76(1), 41–56.

ELCONIN, M., AND HOLOHAN, B. (1990). "Education Vouchers: A Win-Win Plan." *The New York Times,* May 9, p. A31.

ELMORE, R. F. (1986). *Choice in Public Education.* Madison, WI: Center for Policy Research in Education.

*Epperson v. State of Arkansas.* (1969). 393 U.S. 97.

FANTINI, M. D. (1973). *Public Schools of Choice.* New York: Simon & Schuster.

FARBER, B. (1991). *Crisis in Education: Stress and Burnout in the American Teacher.* San Francisco: Jossey-Bass.

FLIEGEL, S. (1993). *Miracle in East Harlem.* New York: Times Books.

FRIEDMAN, M., AND FRIEDMAN, R. (1980). *Free to Choose.* New York: Harcourt Brace Jovanovich.

GINZBERG, E. (1972). "The Economics of the Voucher System." *In Educational Vouchers: Concepts and Controversies,* edited by G. LaNoue. New York: Teachers College Press.

GLAZER, N. (1993). "American Public Education: The Relevance of Choice." *Phi Delta Kappan* 74(8), 647–650.

GLENN, C. (1991). "Controlled Choice in Massachusetts Public Schools." *The Public Interest* No. 103, 88–105.

GREENHOUSE, L. (1997). "Court Eases Curb on Providing Aid in Church Schools." *The New York Times,* June 24, p. A1, B9.

HARTOCOLLIS, A. (1999). "Private School Choice Plan Draws a Million Aid-Seekers." *New York Times* 148. April 21. pp A1, B4.

HENIG, J. (1994). *Rethinking School Choice: Limits of the Market Metaphor.* Princeton, NJ: Princeton University Press.

KEARNS, D. T., AND DOYLE, D. P. (1988). *Winning the Brain Race: A Bold Plan to Make Our Schools Competitive.* San Francisco: Institute for Contemporary Studies.

KELLY, M. (1996) "TRB from Washington." *The New Republic,* Dec 30, p. 29.

KEMERER, F. (1992). "The Publicization of the Private School." *Education Week* 11(16), 42, 56.

KERCHNER, C. T. (1988). "Bureaucratic Entrepreneurship: The Implications of Choice for School Administration." *Educational Administration Quarterly* 24(4), 381–392.

KIRP, D. (1992). "What School Choice Really Means." *The Atlantic Monthly,* November, pp. 119–132.

LEVIN, H. (1980). "Educational Vouchers and Social Policy." In *School Finance Policies and Practice: The 1980s, a Decade of Conflict,* edited by J. Guthrie. Cambridge, MA: Ballinger.

LIEBERMAN, M. (1993). *Public Education: An Autopsy.* Cambridge, MA: Harvard University Press.

LINDSAY, D. (1994). "Wis. Blocking Voucher Data, Researcher Says." *Education Week* 14(15), 14.

MCGROARTY, D. (1994). "School Choice Slandered." *The Public Interest* 117, 94–111.

———. (1996). *Breaking These Chains: The Battle for School Choice.* Rocklin, CA: Prima Publishing.

MEIER, D. (1991). "Choice Can Save Public Education." *The Nation*, March 4, pp. 253, 266–271.

NEWMAN, M. (1994). "California Schools Vying for New Students Under a State Plan for Open Enrollments." *The New York Times*, May 25, p. B9.

OLSON, L. (1995). "17-State Project Hammers Out Own Standards." *Education Week* 14(17), 1, 8.

ORFIELD, G. (1997a). "The Growth of Segregation in American Schools; Changing Patterns of Separation and Poverty Since 1968." *Equity and Excellence in Education* 27(1).

———(1997b). "Deepening Segregation in American Public Schools." Harvard Project on School Desegregation. April. Cambridge, MA: Report of the Harvard Project.

*The People's Poll on Schools and School Choice: A New Gallup Survey.* (1992). Princeton, NJ: Gallup Organization.

PETERKIN, R. (1994). "Strategies in Choice: The Cambridge and Milwaukee Experiences." Presentation to the Urban Superintendents' Issues Conference, Edison, NJ, November 14.

*Public Schools of Choice.* (1990). Alexandria, VA: Association for Supervision and Curriculum Development.

RAYWID, M. A. (1987). "The Dynamics of Success and Public Schools of Choice." *Equity and Choice* 4(1), 27–31.

———, Tesconi, C. A., and Warren, D. R. (1984). *Pride and Promise: Schools of Excellence for All the People.* Washington, DC: American Educational Studies Association.

"School Choice Debate." (1997). *Congressional Quarterly Researcher* 7(27) 625–648.

SCHUNDLER, B. (1993). "The Simple Logic of School Choice." *The New York Times*, October 28, p. A27.

SHANKER, A. (1994). "Charter Schools." *The New York Times*, June 26, p. E7.

——— (1993). "Students as Customers." *The New York Times*, August 8, p. E7.

SHAPIRO, W. (1991). "Tough Choice." *Time*, September 16, pp. 54–60.

SHOKRAI, N. (1996). "Free at Last: Black America Signs Up for School Choice." *Policy Review*, November/December.

SNIDER, W. (1990). "Convergence on Choice." *Teacher Magazine*, February, pp. 18–20.

TASHMAN, B. (1992). "Hobson's Choice: Free-Market Education Plan Voucher for Bush's Favorite Class." *Village Voice* 37(3), 9, 14.

*Time for Results: The Governors 1991 Report on Education.* (1986). Washington, DC: National Governors Association.

TIROZZI, G. (1997). "Vouchers: A Questionable Answer to an Unasked Question." *Education Week*, April 23, p. 43.

TROWBRIDGE, R. (1993). "Vouchers: Devil's Bargain for Private Schools." *The Wall Street Journal*, October 20, p. A20.

WALSH, M. (1999). "A Better Choice?" *Education Week on the Web.* Feb. www.edweek.org.

WEINBERG, H. (1992). "For School Choice: Let's Follow the F.A.A." *Education Week* 11(21), 40.

WINERIP, M. (1998). "Schools for Sale" *New York Times Magazine.* June 14, pp 42–9.

WRAGA, W. (1992). "School Choice and the Comprehensive Ideal." *Journal of Curriculum and Supervision* 8(1), 28–42.

# CHAPTER 3

# School Finance: Equity or Disparity

## POSITION 1: FOR EQUITY IN EDUCATION

### Gauging the Gap

The American system of free public education is touted as the great equalizer of opportunity. Education is offered to all children regardless of their parents' station in life. In virtually every state, the child and the parents have no choice but to take advantage of this educational opportunity, since school attendance is required by law up to a certain age, usually 16. Moreover, the guarantee of a public school education is good for several years beyond this required age. Because attending school is compulsory, and because the guarantee extends over so many years, the United States can justly pride itself on giving all its children an education, even those whose parents are residents only and not citizens.

This educational birthright for America's youth, however, is a prize that comes in many different dollar amounts, depending on various factors. For the child in an affluent suburb, it can be worth about $12,000 a year, the amount actually spent on his or her education in the local public school. For a child in a large city or a rural area, the prize may be worth only half that amount, or $6,000. The $6,000 difference multiplied over the twelve years of school adds up to $72,000 more education for the suburban child than for his or her urban or rural counterpart. Some actual in-state differences are even more glaring. In Alaska, it is $32,000 per pupil in one district to $6,000 per pupil in another district. In Montana, it's $25,000 to $2,000. In New York, $39,000 to $5,000. In Texas, $42,000 to $3,000 ("Savage Inequalities State by State," 1997). Such extreme spending differences within states are sometimes discounted as anomalous, but they are nonetheless real, and even lesser differences reveal real inequalities. All American children are guaranteed an educational opportunity, but there is no guarantee that the opportunity will be equal for all—and in reality, the opportunity is quite unequal. No wonder that

James Conant, a former president of Harvard University, was moved to write that "the contrast in money available to schools in a wealthy suburb and schools in a large city jolts one's notion of the meaning of equality of opportunity" (1961, pp. 2–3). What appalled Conant nearly forty years ago is appalling still.

The inequality is even more pronounced than these numbers indicate. The child in the plush suburb is likely to begin school with much greater educational advantages than the urban or rural child. The suburban child may have traveled abroad with his or her parents even before entering first grade, and foreign travel may be part of every summer vacation. The child may have been "prepped" for first grade by attendance at an expensive nursery school. "Young children of affluent parents, ages 3 to 5, are almost twice as likely to be attending preschool as are blue-collar youngsters" (Fuller and Holloway, 1998, p. 56). Books, including a variety of costly and up-to-date reference works, may abound in the child's home. The parents are likely to be proficient readers. Educational toys, including brain-developing manipulables, are probably plentiful. A personal computer is now a standard possession among children in suburbia, and the children are well-traveled on the information highway. Attending summer camps that feature specialized educational programs is an annual rite for many suburban kids. The very conversations that a suburban child has with his or her well-educated parents are intellectually enriching. "There is no mystery about it: the child who is familiar with books, ideas, conversation—the ways and means of the intellectual life—before he begins consciously to think has a marked advantage. He is at home in the House of Intellect just as the stableboy is at home among horses or the child of actors on the stage" (Barzun, 1959, p. 142). Add to all this the robust good health that proper nutrition and medical attention can assure.

Contrast this bountiful life with the austere life of the child from the inner city. The contrast starkly reveals an accumulation of privations for the inner-city child. This child has experienced no foreign travel, and perhaps not even intracity travel. Adolescents who have grown up in Brooklyn, for example, may have never been to Manhattan. The poor child sees no books other than comic books and a few superficial magazines left lying around at the local barber shop. A personal computer is as removed from possibility as a private spaceship. Perhaps the child might take a brief vacation at a charity summer camp, such as those sponsored by the Fresh Air Fund and the St. Vincent de Paul Society. Conversations with adults who use English badly put the child at a *disadvantage* in school. Actually, the child has few conversations with adults at all, and these are necessarily brusque because the only adult permanently in the home is a harried mother trying to hold her life together. Increasingly, neither a mother nor a father stays at home. Between 1970 and 1990, the proportion of American children without a mother or father at home rose from 6.7 percent to 9.7 percent (Gross, 1992). And that "home" may be a room in a welfare hotel (Kozol, 1988). Welfare reform his meant that welfare mothers have been forced to take "workfare" jobs, guaranteeing that they will be at home even less. The television set is the child's constant companion, purveying visions of distorted reality, false hopes, and the violent resolution of conflicts. The child's diet is junk food, or no food, and any medical attention is the perfunctory medical care one receives in a municipal hospital emergency room. Moreover, many serious injuries are never reported or treated because they are the result of child abuse, including sexual abuse. And some children suffer the injury for which there may be no cure: the brain damage inflicted on the fetuses of crack-addicted women. Many children born on crack are now of school age (Daley, 1991; Treaster, 1993). They join the ranks of children who suffer from fetal alcohol syndrome.

Outside the home, the ghetto child lives under the threat of becoming a victim or witness of a murder. Kotlowitz has recorded this situation in ghastly detail. The Chicago mother of the family he studied pays $80 a month for burial insurance on her five children, knowing the odds of collecting. This was the experience of one of her children:

> At the age of 10, Lafayette had his first encounter with death; he saw someone killed. . . . The first victim was a young Disciple nicknamed Baby Al, who was shot with a .357 Magnum, not far from [the building in which Lafayette lived]. Wounded, he ran into the high-rise, where, while trying to climb the stairs, he fell backward and lost consciousness. Lafayette came running out of his apartment to see what all the commotion was about. He watched as Baby Al bled to death. Two years later, his blood still stained the stairwell. . . . A couple of weeks later, as Lafayette and Pharaoh played on the jungle gym in midafternoon, shouting broke out. A young girl jumping rope crumpled to the ground. . . . They watched as paramedics attended to the girl, who luckily had been shot only in the leg. (1991, pp. 39–40)

No wonder that when Kotlowitz asked the mother if he could write about her children, she replied, "But you know, there are no children here. They've seen too much to be children" (p. x).

Consider this poem, scrawled on the side of a building in the South Bronx:

> I am the boy who lives in a slum surrounded by problems with no where to go
>
> I am the boy who has no hope, who solves his problems with a bag of smoke
>
> I am the boy who lives next door, whose father is a drunk and whose mother is a whore
>
> I am the boy who lives a rough life, who has to depend on a push-button knife
>
> I am the boy who must take the first swing
>
> I am the boy who must pull the trigger
>
> I am the boy who whitey calls nigger.
>
> (Vergara, 1991, p. 805)

Adolescent boys in Camden, New Jersey, spend a lot of time imagining their own, presumably imminent, funerals (Previte, 1994). And in Chicago, 11-

year-old Yummy Sandifer became famous as a gang shooter who was shot to death by his own gang (Gibbs, 1994).

Poor children require more than the rich when they get to school because they have so much less at home, and so much more trauma with which to cope. They come to school undereducated in the things that schools consider important, so they need *compensatory education* to bring them to the same starting line. What happens, instead, is that the disadvantage poor children bring to school is aggravated by the underfunding of their formal education, even as the advantage of the rich is augmented by generous funding. In short, the American system of education uses public money to favor the already favored. It is the great *disequalizer* of opportunity.

## Understanding the Cause

Before discussing specifics concerning the educational advantages that taxpayer money can buy in schools, we must explain why such glaring inequality exists between the schools of the rich and the poor. The answer, in two words, is *local control*. Because rich communities pay for their own schools and poor communities pay for theirs, there can be no equality. The rich can afford to pay more, so they have better schools. State governments try to smooth over the gaps by giving more state money to the poor schools. But except for Hawaii, where all public schools are funded by the state government, the gap between rich and poor schools is never closed completely. In many states, it is a yawning chasm.

You should be able to obtain from the education officials in your state a breakdown of how much each school district in the state, including the one you attended, spends per pupil. For example, in 1990, New York City spent an average of $6,644 per pupil. This was $22,814 less than the amount spent in Pocantico Hills, directly to the north in suburban Westchester County, and $39,330 less than the amount spent on Fire Island, off Long Island (Barbanel, 1992). Even if Pocantico Hills and Fire Island are dismissed as extreme examples, there was still a difference (in 1993) of $8,448 between New York City and Great Neck, Long Island (Winerip, 1993). In Texas and Illinois, the highest-spending districts spend almost seven times as much as the lowest-spending districts ("States' School Spending Disparities," 1992). If we look at the disparities from an interstate perspective, we see that Connecticut spent an average of $4,924 while Utah spent $1,782, even after adjusting for estimated cost-of-living differences (*Digest of Education Statistics*, 1997). "We must also take note of the fact that children from rich families stay in school longer than children from poor families. When we take this into account, we estimate that America spends about twice as much on the children of the rich as the children of the poor" (Jencks et al., 1972, p. 27). Acquiring the financing information for your own state may make you realize that you yourself have already been denied an equal educational opportunity as compared with other young people in your state. Of course, that same information could also reveal that the inequality was in your favor.

Local control explains the inequality in American education. It does not, however, explain the continuing American allegiance to that inequality. That explanation lies in the unequal power arrangements between rich and poor.

> We must recognize the ways in which powerful groups are able to arrange better opportunities for their children, despite the rhetoric of standard and therefore equal education. Families with the economic and political power to give their children an advantage are unlikely to relinquish that advantage willingly. Most people with influence over public education have at least some measure of such an advantage and are surrounded by associates who share it as well. They are likely to share a perspective that makes the maintenance of separate schools with superior human and material resources for the white middle class seem natural and necessary. Their vested interests are served by muting the recognition of differences in the opportunities offered by schools accessible to children of different races and social classes (Metz, 1988, p. 60)

The rich have reason to rig the system in their favor. "Significant changes toward a more equal educational system . . . would be associated with equally significant changes in the statistical relationship between education and the distribution of economic rewards . . . unequal schooling perpetuates a structure of economic inequality which originates outside the school system" (Bowles and Gintis, 1976, p. 248).

## *Specifying What the Gap Means*

Some people say that money cannot buy a good education. So let us see what it is that money can buy. You get some idea of this even before entering a school building. The building's exterior tells you whether the building is new, attractively designed, and in good repair, or old, fortresslike, and ramshackle. Many old city school buildings not only are ugly, but are in such disrepair as to be safety hazards. "Many schools have rundown physical facilities that are, in some cases, safety and health hazards. . . . If this sample of schools is any indication, the physical plants of many of the nation's urban schools need substantial rehabilitation and modernization" (*City High Schools*, 1984, p. 68). President Clinton acknowledged this in his 1998 State of the Union address. However, it costs so much to renovate old buildings or replace them with new buildings that urban districts make do year after year. In New Jersey, the cost of repairing and replacing buildings in the twenty-eight poorest districts has been placed at more than $2 billion (King, 1998). Nationwide, the cost has been estimated by the federal government to be $112 billion (Peterson, 1997) and while the President and Congress have begun to appropriate money for this purpose, the need could well outstrip the limited federal response.

Inside, a building may be bright with windows and fluorescent lights, cheery with decorative touches, and comfortable with carpeting and the latest in school furniture. Or it may be Gothic in style and gloomy. City (and rural) school buildings, because they are on average much older than suburban schools, are more likely to fall into the latter category. One elementary school in the late 1980s in the city of Camden, New Jersey, occupied a three-story building but had only one boys' and one girls' lavatory, both on the first floor. The building was so crowded that two of the classes had to be held in the cafeteria of another school (Lefelt, 1988, p. 32). The fact that situations like this are more likely to be corrected as a result of adverse publicity does not keep new problems from constantly cropping up, hidden or public.

More important than the buildings are the educational materials they house. Poor schools have small libraries with few recent additions to the book collection, only a few magazine subscriptions, and very little audiovisual equipment and software. The audiovisual equipment may be so old and unreliable that the teachers have given up on it in order to spare themselves awkward delays in trying to adjust or restart it. The libraries themselves serve mostly as study halls, but they often don't even have comfortable chairs. The libraries of suburban schools are much more richly endowed, and some are absolutely alluring in their architectural splendor and provision of creature comforts, not to mention the wide array of multimedia material available, including computer terminals with internet access.

The auditorium of a poor school may be little more than a cavern with chairs and a stage. For the rich school, it is a professional theater, with all the technical paraphernalia needed for live productions. These lavish productions not only instill school spirit among the students, but also inspire parental and community pride and support.

The suburban school is much more likely to have a swimming pool and a fully equipped gym, perhaps with a weight room, as well as a basketball court with spectator stands. The spacious grounds on which the school is located allow for regulation-size athletic fields, which are well-maintained by professional groundskeepers.

The vocational shops and the home economics rooms in a suburban school have all the latest gadgets, whereas their counterparts in the urban school contain equipment used by generations of students. New equipment is acquired in an incremental fashion, so that only a small portion of the equipment is ever really new. Poor vocational education prepares teenagers for jobs that no longer exist, or underprepares them for the new types of jobs available.

The labs of many urban schools would be laughable to someone seriously trying to teach science, with some test tubes, a few bunsen burners, a couple of microscopes, some old jars of chemicals, and a washbasin making up the entire inventory of supplies. Students do not have a variety of materials to learn from, and what they have is so limited that they have to wait their turn to share it. Suburban schools, in contrast, are likely to provide a state-of-the-art lab station for each student in the class.

Computers—the communication tool of our common tomorrow—are much more in evidence in rich classrooms than in poor ones. In some fortunate schools, each child is assigned his or her own computer, much as a textbook is assigned at the beginning of a course. Yet those are the schools whose students also have computers at home.

The textbooks used in English and social studies classes in some poor schools have been through thirty years of page turning, according to the president of the New York City teachers' union (Weiss, 1988, p. 60). Worse yet, not all the pages in these beat-up and out-of-date books are there to be turned. Supplementary reading consists of a desultory book collection approaching antiquity on a bookshelf in the back of the room. The pages of those fossils remain intact because no one ever turns them. Rich schools have spiffy new texts that catch your eye even if they don't hold your attention. A cornucopia of new paperback books lines the shelves for supplementary reading. Of course, the students in these schools have no trouble creating their own paperback libraries at home.

Jonathan Kozol visited city schools and observed the privations under which they function. East St. Louis Senior High School is just one example. Sewage backed into the school, including the school kitchen. The teachers ran out of chalk and paper. The football field did not have goalposts. The football uniforms were nine years old and were washed at a local laundromat. The science labs were not hooked up for water. The heating system and the building's insulation were so bad that it cost thousands of unnecessary dollars each year to maintain them (Kozol, 1991, pp. 23–32). If Kozol's book succeeded in ameliorating these atrocities, one can only wonder how long the unpublicized atrocities are allowed to continue.

The saddest commentary of all is that even the teachers in rich schools tend to be better than those in poor schools. They are better educated, having attended superior colleges and universities, and they acquire advanced degrees. They receive job offers from the rich schools, and such offers are eagerly sought, because these schools provide students who are relatively docile and pliable, and who, by and large, come prepared to learn regardless of the teacher's skills. Rich schools also have higher salary ranges than poor schools—so that good teachers become just another of the things they can afford to buy. When teacher salaries are computed by the number of students a teacher has, the poor school fares even worse because poor schools control costs by establishing large classes. Research shows that smaller classes enhance student achievement (HEROS, 1999). Higher salaries mean higher pension costs for teachers in rich schools. In New Jersey, where the state pays for all teacher pensions, the total amount in the affluent community of Millburn averaged out to $1,066 per pupil, whereas in the poor community of Camden it was only $522 (King, 1992). For poor schools, a sufficient supply of teachers requires an array of emergency certification schemes. This has rightly been characterized as using children as guinea pigs for grown-ups who are trying to become teachers on the quick.

## Equalizing Educational Opportunity

Those who say that money cannot buy a good education live in good neighborhoods with good schools that spend a lot of money. Some of these people do not deign to use even the good public schools in their neighborhoods; they send their children to private schools to buy what they say cannot be bought. If they are correct that money cannot buy a good education, it would seem that the poor have as much right to be disappointed by this fact as the rich (Coons, Clune, and Sugarman, 1971, p. 30). Some of the rich who patronize private schools are candid enough to admit the relation between money and quality education. The chairman of the board of trustees of the exclusive Peddie School said that "as one would expect, the more assets the better the education. . . . Funds are necessary to employ able teachers, to provide reasonable facilities and to provide a reasonable student-faculty ratio. If you achieve that, you can have a very fine education" (van Tassel, 1988, p. NJ3). The Peddie School should offer a fine education, indeed, since it recently received a $100 million donation from billionaire philanthropist Walter Annenberg.

Educational opportunity can be equalized in a simple and straightforward way by equalizing the money spent per pupil. It is necessary to do this within as well as between school districts because single districts often spend more on schools in their better neighborhoods. The parents in the better neighborhoods may be more demanding, so they succeed in getting for their children materials and programs, and even teachers, not available to schools in the poorer parts of town. Jonathan Kozol (1991) describes the heavy allocation of resources to the relatively affluent Riverdale section of the Bronx as compared with poorer schools elsewhere in the borough. The inequality extends from the number of computers to the quality of the teachers (pp. 84–85). In Los Angeles, parents in the poor neighborhoods won a court case, *Rodriguez v. Los Angeles Unified School District*, in which they alleged that the teachers assigned to their schools had less experience and were more likely to be unlicensed or to be substitutes than were the teachers in other Los Angeles neighborhoods. They also demonstrated the obvious overcrowding of their schools and the dilapidation of the facilities (Bradley, 1994). Such disparities can develop almost imperceptibly, so it is important for school districts to be on the watch for them.

This does not mean that districts cannot spend different amounts for students in different educational categories, for example, students with handicaps versus those without, or high school versus elementary school students. These differences result from real differences in the costs of educating different kinds of students. They are not the same as spending different amounts on students in the *same* educational category.

Equalizing educational opportunity *across* school districts is the state's responsibility. Under our constitutional system, education is a prerogative of state government, so states already have the authority to intervene in local school operations. What better justification for intervention could they have than to redress elemental fairness? The unfairness is so egregious that it forces the question of why states have allowed it to exist for so long. As already indicated, the answer is a political one: The people who profit from the unfairness are rich, and the rich have more political power than the poor. If the rich are going to continue exercising their power at the expense of the poor, then they should stop pretending that justice, fairness, and equality are characteristic of American education. If the children of the poor are going to be treated shabbily by the state simply because of the plight of their parents—a plight for which the children suffer enough as it is—then the state is as much an oppressor of its people as a Latin American oligarchy is.

It is desirable to equalize educational opportunity not just among schools and districts within a state, but also among the fifty states of the union. Different states spend widely differing amounts per pupil, even taking into account cost-of-living differences. So even if there were full equalization within states, the poor states would still be spending less than the wealthier ones. John Fischer, once president of Columbia University Teachers College, said: "If we really mean it when we say that every American child—rather than every Californian or every Arkansan—is entitled to equal educational opportunity, we must be prepared to use federal means to bring about such equality" (quoted by Herbers, 1972, p. E3). Only the federal government has the capacity to deal with inequality on this level, but the Constitution gives it no clear warrant to do so, and the political clout of the rich can be as intimidating to members of the U.S. Congress as it is to members of a state legislature. Perhaps the most we can expect from our national leaders is that they restrain their rhetoric about the greatness of the American educational system. We have as much reason to be ashamed of that system as we have to be proud of it.

Something the government could do immediately would be to increase the funding for Chapter I, the major federal program for poor students. It has at least retargeted the money so that it goes to districts with the highest concentration of poor students. The money was not doing much good when it was spread around almost half of the elementary schools in the country; some schools counted poor children as making up as little as 10 percent of the student body (Rotberg, 1994). The funding for Head Start should also be increased now that the accumulated evidence shows that the gains students make are longer-lasting than previously believed and that any fade-out is likely to be a result of poor subsequent schooling (Barnett, 1993; Viadero, 1994). Unfortunately, tax-cut fever and middle-class paranoia, make these changes an uphill struggle; a booming economy mitigates this.

Something the Clinton administration and the Republican Congress began to do in the late 1990s was to budget money for more teachers so that class sizes could be reduced. The state of Tennessee did the most thorough and best controlled study of the effects of class size reduction to date. Its study involved more than ten thousand students from seventy-five schools and went on for ten years. When class size was reduced from 22 to 25 down to 13 to 17, test scores increased an average of ten points (HEROS, 1999). Harold Wenglinksy (1997) explains that in a smaller class, the teacher is able to exercise more control and better reduce problem behaviors among students that detract from learning time. Class size reduction, then, is an area in which government at the state and local levels could wisely invest dollars.

## The Benefit to Society

John Donne's insightful statement that "No man is an island, entire of itself" is truer in today's interdependent world than it was when he wrote it. Its application to American education at the end of the twentieth century has been captured by Lester Thurow: "I am willing to pay for, indeed insist upon, the education of my neighbor's children, not because I am generous but because I cannot afford to live with them uneducated" (Thurow, 1985, p. 187).

As Thurow correctly understands, educating the children of the poor is in the interest of us all. It saves corporations the costs of searching extensively only to find minimally qualified employees or of educating those who come unqualified. It gives people legitimate opportunities so that they desist from taking illegal ones, with the corresponding costs in human and property loss.

Educating the poor necessarily entails some additional costs to compensate for the disadvantages they bring to school. For example, urban communities have unusually high percentages of students whose native language is not English, and these students are from literally scores of different language groups. A debate is underway about how best to help such students become proficient in English, but, it is generally agreed, it requires extra resources regardless of the approach. Urban districts also have security costs just to keep the schools safe. These districts must pay guards, and supply them with walkie-talkies that cost about $1,000 each. Suburban schools are spared these costs.

Philanthropists and corporate leaders acknowledge the need and the cost of successfully educating the poor and minorities. The Ford Foundation, after completing a national study of city high schools, came up with a list of twenty "lessons" it had learned. At least twelve of these lessons involve more money, and four of them specifically mention the need for more funds (*City High Schools*, 1984, pp. 66–68). The Carnegie Foundation for the Advancement of Teaching has issued a more recent report on urban schools, which concludes with a call for a national urban schools program. All eight of the points in this program are high-cost (Carnegie Foundation, 1988, pp. 37–38). The Institute for Educational Leadership examined teachers' working conditions in thirty-one schools in five large cities. The conclusion was that "urban teachers . . . labor under conditions that would not be tolerated in other professional settings. This is true of teaching in general, but the compounding of problems in urban schools creates extremely difficult and demoralizing environments for those who have chosen to teach" (Corcoran, Walker, and White, 1988, p. xiii). This study, too, emphasizes the lack of resources available to urban teachers. Imagine the outrage if the following applied to suburban teachers: "Urban teachers often do not have even the basic resources needed for teaching. There are serious shortages of everything from toilet paper to textbooks; teachers have limited access to modern office technologies, including copiers, let alone computers" (Corcoran, Walker, and White, 1988, p. xiii). The Committee for Economic Development, composed of chief executive officers of various

American corporations, in true businesslike fashion presented a list of "cost-effective programs" and "investment strategies" for helping the educationally disadvantaged. All of these recommendations cost more money than is now being spent (*Children in Need*, 1987). Wehlage et al. (1989) describe fourteen dropout prevention programs that have had marked success in keeping at-risk youngsters in school. A common feature of these programs is the intensive personal attention the students get, which requires additional professional personnel. Lucas, Henze, and Donato (1990) report on successful programs for Latino students, all somewhat costly. The New Jersey Supreme Court, after reviewing the evidence on what seems to work, ordered pre-school programs for children in the state's poorest school districts. It also ordered "whole school reform" models, such as Success for All, for the K–12 schools in these districts. The projected cost is in the hundreds of millions of dollars (*Abbott v. Burke*, 1998).

To be blunt, urban schools need more money. Moreover, they need more money per pupil than suburban schools do just to afford an equal chance at an effective education. Currently, they are struggling to make do with less money. This condition is not in our interest as an interdependent society, and the socially deleterious consequences should be obvious to all. The money spent on schools in poor neighborhoods can be an especially good social investment since formal education has a greater impact on poor students than it does on their better-off peers, as the largest study of education ever undertaken demonstrated over thirty years ago (Coleman et al., 1966). But perhaps the best reason for doing something now is to make us a more honest society. Investing in educating our poorest children will reduce not only the opportunity gap between rich and poor, but also the gap between our lofty rhetoric and the grim reality (Bell, 1976, p. 263).

Can we afford it? To answer this question, it is instructive to compare our effort with that of fourteen other industrialized nations. We rank *eleventh* in terms of the percentage of gross domestic product devoted to public spending on elementary and secondary schools. Our average expenditure of $3,398 per pupil puts us in sixth place in actual dollars spent (Nelson, 1991, p. 2). The Quality Education for Minorities Project of the Massachusetts Institute of Technology has come up with twenty-five programs the federal government could fund. Some of these programs are already in place, but with inadequate funding. Full funding of all the programs would cost $27.31 billion (*Education That Works*, 1990). Even the national media have jumped into the school reform business, with *Education Week* making twelve recommendations (Olson and Hendrie, 1998), and *Time* magazine offering four "lessons" (Wulf, 1997). Federal officials should bear all of this counsel in mind when they try to decide what to do with the surplus revenue that flows into the government during economic boom times. Should a tax cut for the middle class or a shoring up of the social security system take priority over giving the next generation of tax-payers an adequate education?

# POSITION 2: FOR FREEDOM IN SCHOOL FINANCING

## Gauging the Gain

There is, to be sure, a strong undercurrent of capitalism in American education. But instead of fretting over this fact and becoming defensive about it, people should assess the benefits it brings.

In education, as in the free enterprise system generally, inequality is both inevitable and desirable. The prospect of getting to the top or falling to the bottom motivates us as individuals to do our best. That is just basic human nature. When all of us are working hard to get to the top or to avoid falling to the bottom, the whole ship of state is buoyed up. The United States grows stronger, and we enrich ourselves materially, to the benefit of the poor and the rich.

Government-guaranteed equality denies people this basic drive. What's the point of striving if you can't advance beyond the level of the person who does nothing? Even communist countries, most notably those that made up the former Soviet bloc, have come to appreciate the motivating force of capitalist inequality. Inequality not only is a great goad to human effort, but it is a just way to distribute the blessings of liberty. You get what you earn; or, as the Bible says, you reap what you sow. To earn something is to *deserve* it. Capitalist inequality is intended to ensure that everyone is rewarded appropriately in the fair competition of the free marketplace. We are all aware that the system does not work perfectly, but what Winston Churchill (1947) said about democracy as a political system is also true of capitalism as an economic system: "No one pretends that democracy is perfect or all-wise. Indeed, it has been said that democracy is the worst form of government except all those other forms that have been tried from time to time." And despite its imperfections, the free enterprise system has created a wealth of opportunities for upward mobility. Millions of successful people have come from humble beginnings, so that the top ranks of government, the arts, the professions, business, and the military are filled with people whose origins were no more auspicious than those of Bill Clinton, Oprah Winfrey, Jonas Salk, Famous Amos, Colin Powell, Ross Perot, Bill Gates, or Jesse Ventura.

Education is a right of all Americans, and it is guaranteed to all Americans because it is essential to our progress as a nation and our fulfillment as individuals. However, the guarantee is only for a minimally adequate education. A general consensus exists that public education should be free through high school, but no agreement exists on what a student should learn by graduation. The higher the expectation, the more it will cost taxpayers to bring every student to that level. Frankly, it does not seem that the level need be very high to satisfy the needs of society.

> Our definition of a basic education is considerably . . . restricted. It consists of those things necessary for minimal effective functioning in a democracy. This includes the ability to read, write, and do basic arithmetic, and knowledge of

our democratic government. These goals are relatively clear-cut, and accomplishment is more easily measured than in other curricula. Most people would agree that they form the core of education, while few would agree on other curricular objectives. It should be possible to complete this basic education by the end of the eighth grade. (Garms, Guthrie, and Pierce, 1978, pp. 241–242)

We need not guarantee that everyone will graduate from high school, let alone go to medical school or law school. Education beyond the minimum guarantee is something that students should earn, just as we earn any other valued commodity. Moreover, society creates social dynamite by educating people beyond its capacity to absorb them into careers congruent with their educations. It is fashionable now to talk about the education needed for the cybernetic society of the twenty-first century. The implication is that everyone will be on the information superhighway, but no one will be part of a minimally skilled janitorial crew. Not only will there be many low-skill jobs in the information systems world, but this world will be but a small part of the overall job market, where low-skill jobs predominate. People who are overeducated for the jobs they hold are discontented workers, which makes them ripe for revolutionary appeals. Hayek (1944) found that this was part of Hitler's success: "The resentment of the lower middle class, from which fascism and National Socialism recruited so large a proportion of their supporters, was intensified by the fact that their education and training had in many instances made them aspire to directing positions and that they regarded themselves as entitled to be members of the directing class" (p. 117). The three occupations with the greatest projected *percentage* growth between 1992 and 2005 are home health aides, human services workers, and personal and home care aides. The occupation projected to have the greatest *numerical* growth is retail sales clerk. None of these four occupations requires more than a two-year college education, if that (Krugman, 1994).

The commodities children value are sometimes earned directly by the children. A child can use the money from a paper route to buy a bicycle. Another child can study and earn a scholarship to a private school. But usually parents earn the commodities for their children. They buy the bike and they pay the private school tuition. The most common way in which parents buy their children an education beyond the state's minimum guarantee is to buy a home in a community that has good schools.

Good schools are one of the most cherished blessings of liberty, and parents struggle very hard to earn a good education for their children by living near good schools. One of the great (if not the greatest) motivators for parents is being able to provide a good education for their children. One parent has written movingly of his decision to relocate his family to a small town so that his children would have good schools. He realized that in abandoning the city he violated some of his own convictions, but he concluded that *"no one is willing to sacrifice their children on the altar of their social principles"* (original author's emphasis; Nocero, 1989, p. 30). Real estate agents are well aware of this fact, which is why they reveal (or conceal) the quality of local schools as a selling point to prospective home buyers. To deny parents the right to influence the quality of their children's education in this way is worse than denying them a basic right as citizens in a free society; it is to deny them a *natural* right as parents. And it is to deny society the benefit of the parents' highly motivated labor.

## Equalizing How?

Egalitarians espouse noble sentiments that we all endorse to some extent. However, they avoid discussing those troublesome specifics that gravely weaken their case. When they exhort us to equalize per-pupil spending throughout an entire state, they fail to tell us in which direction and how far to do so. These are hardly minor details! Suppose the following is the situation in your state:

| | |
|---|---|
| Highest-spending districts | $10,000 per pupil |
| Average-spending districts | $7,000 per pupil |
| Lowest-spending districts | $4,000 per pupil |

Should the state allocate money to equalize everyone up to the top level of $10,000 per pupil? That's going to cost the state and its taxpayers, including poor folks who pay taxes, a lot of money. It may be more than taxpayers are willing to provide, and they'll make their reluctance known at the ballot box in good democratic fashion. Former Governors Florio of New Jersey, Weicker of Connecticut, and Cuomo of New York can tell you all about taxpayer revolts. Indeed, the ascendancy of the Republican Party in the 1990s was all about limited taxes (and government). Moreover, equalization will mean that the family already living in the $10,000 district has to pay additional taxes for the benefit of someone else's children. This family is already paying stiff taxes to guarantee its own children a good education, and those children will not benefit from the additional taxes paid. In fact, their education will become relatively devalued.

Perhaps the state should equalize everyone *down* to the level of the $4,000 districts. That would require putting a ceiling on how much the affluent districts could spend on their children and forbidding them to spend more. The poor districts would not get any more money; they would just have the spiteful satisfaction of knowing that everyone else was as bad off as they are. (Many conservative commentators have remarked on the symptoms of envy and greed among egalitarians; see, for example, Hayek, 1944, p. 139, and Kristol, 1978, p. 220.) The $10,000, and even the $7,000, districts would have to make major adjustments. Their budgets would be slashed by 60 percent and 42 percent, respectively. These are enormous reductions, and even if they were phased in gradually, the ultimate result would be a huge decline in the quality of education. People will not sit still and let something that disastrous happen to their children. If they cannot stop it from becoming law, they will surely find ways to get around the law. They would probably arrange all kinds of "voluntary" contributions to their schools to make up for the loss in official revenues. We would see bake sales galore. In fact, that sort of thing is already happening in Manhattan's better neighborhoods, where parents of public school children use their own money to hire teachers' assistants and buy supplies and equip the playgrounds (Chira, 1992; Freeman and Pollitt, 1991). School Chancellor Crew tried to draw the line on this when the Parent-Teacher Association at one of the schools began paying the salary of a fourth grade teacher, but his disapproval only meant that the PTA money would go for some other purpose, freeing up the school's money for the teacher's salary (Harrison, 1997; Jayson, 1997). Other communities are establishing educational foundations. These will allow the public schools to engage in private fund-raising on a grand scale, and the grandest communities will obviously be the ones to do so on the grandest scale. Public equality will once again, inexorably, be nullified by private inequality (Steinberg, 1997).

The middle ground is a compromise that avoids all of either approach while including a bit of both. The affluent districts could be equalized down to the $7,000 level, while the poor districts are equalized up to it. However, the affluent districts might not be much more willing to suffer a 30 percent reduction in their budgets than a 60 percent reduction, even though 30 percent is twice as easy to make up in bake sales. To avoid the problem of affronting the affluent, they could simply be left alone at their $10,000 level. However, egalitarians would no doubt declare this to be a cop-out, and people in the average districts would feel that the poor had been thrown into the same pot with them while the rich escaped the soup altogether.

There is another hitch to all this. The poor tend to be in large urban districts with lots of students. If they were fewer in number, the cost of equalization would be more bearable. The actual cost when one multiplies the per-pupil increase by the number of eligible pupils is outrageously high.

At any rate, it is not up to people who value educational liberty to work out a politically viable means of vitiating that liberty. It is up to the egalitarians. Even if they can come up with a scheme that citizens will support, it will prove to be a failure in the long run because it will contradict human nature and the values that have made the United States great. The U.S. Supreme Court upheld those values when it refused to strike down the Texas system of local school financing and found that system to be "rational" (*San Antonio Independent School District v. Rodriguez*, 1973). Unfortunately, people were not content to leave well enough alone after the Supreme Court ruled. Another case was brought, this time in the Texas state court system. It resulted in a victory for the egalitarians, and a court order that school financing be equalized in Texas. That led to a years-long battle over exactly how this was to be done, ending in a crazy "Robin Hood" scheme that left both the rich and the poor unhappy (Celis, 1994).

## Pouring Money Down Ratholes

All but one of the schemes discussed in the Position 1 essay have something in common: They would inject a large infusion of cash into poor school districts, in addition to the huge amounts of financial aid already extended to those districts over the past thirty years. Unfortunately, the recipient districts have a dismal record for spending money unwisely, and even illegally. The poor performance of their students is due as much to mismanaged money as it is to insufficient money. For example, some of the money is never spent on the targeted pupils. "Entitlement funds have frequently been treated as discretionary monies, and have been diverted from their original purposes" (Bastian et al., 1985, p. 30). Urban districts have taken state compensatory education money intended for remedial programs and used it to pay regular classroom teachers to continue what they had been doing all along. The districts justified this diversion by pointing to the money they were saving their taxpayers. The result was that suburban districts, with few remedial pupils, were spending roughly $150 on additional services for each of their neediest children, whereas one urban district was spending only $7 on each of its many needy youngsters (Carlson and Rubin, 1979).

Even when the districts spend the money on the targeted population, coordination is inadequate. How do we ensure that the expenditure an assistant superintendent approves results in a teaching tool that the teachers actually understand and use? Fancy instructional hardware gathers dust in the storerooms of poor school districts. Moreover, many of these districts simply have too many assistant superintendents and other administrators, all busying themselves with projects that never percolate down to the classroom. After the late Richard Green became chancellor of the New York City schools, he announced that he intended to clean out the board of education headquarters and send people out to the schools, where they might finally be able to do some good for the children. The fact that his successors, Joe Fernandez, Ramon Cortines, and Rudy Crew, have tried to do the same means there is still bloat. Cortines found that the personnel in central headquarters had been badly undercounted. The previous count had 3,468 people working in the central office; Cortines's count put the number at 7,078 (Barbanel, 1994a). The bloat was largely responsible for the fact that of the $7,000 per pupil spent in the New York City schools, only $3,500 reached each pupil for instruction (Barbanel, 1993).

Besides allowing people to spin their wheels for no apparent educational purpose, poor school districts, and urban districts in particular, are pestholes of corruption. The poor citizens who live in these districts lack the expertise to detect the corruption and the political skills to attack it. They are at the mercy of slick operators with education certificates who exploit them and their children, and who themselves are likely to live in suburbs where their own children are getting a decent education. These parasites who prey on the poor have a lot of taxpayer money to spend, and they keep much of it for themselves in the form of kickbacks. They do business with the companies they can extort the most money from, whether it benefits the students or not. They manage to give their friends and relatives no-show jobs on the district payroll, and then they take a share of the unearned paycheck. They treat themselves to lavish perks, such as expensive dinners when they're in town and luxurious travel accommodations when they're out of town (ostensibly on school business), and they're out of town a lot.

New York City witnessed the spectacle of an elementary school principal being arrested on the street near his school for making a drug purchase. He turned out to have a record of absenteeism from his job. A detailed report on the front page of the *New York Times* began: "Members of a community school board in Brooklyn formed an interlocking power base to secure jobs and promotions for relatives and friends and advance a major private development project, according to school employees, parents and personnel records" (Lewis and Blumenthal, 1989, p. 1). Lest anyone think this is how minorities behave, we must note that all the board members were white. In a report on the business practices of the Jersey City school district, a nationally known accounting firm listed a host of irregularities in the awarding of contracts, maintenance of payrolls, and the operation of the personnel office (Peat Marwick Main & Co., 1988). These irregularities were one of the major reasons why the state of New Jersey took over operation of the Jersey City schools. In Newark, a member of the board of education admitted that he offered to secure school principalships for pay, one of the reasons why the Newark schools, too, were taken over by the state. In a school district in the Bronx, central office administrators, including the superintendent himself, "rarely bothered to visit the schools they were charged with improving," and three board members pleaded guilty to various criminal charges (Berger, 1991, pp. B1–B4). The principal of a Queens public school for handicapped youngsters pleaded guilty to stealing more than $20,000 by faking bills for goods he never ordered and skimming money from fund-raisers (Berger, 1992a). In the Bronx, teachers who hoped to be appointed to principalships were expected "to work in the election campaigns of members of their school board, calling voters and chauffering election workers" (Berger, 1992b). In Brooklyn, a principal was charged with stealing nearly $10,000 in school funds and with coercing teachers to join a political club (Fried, 1994, 1995). In the poorest districts of the Bronx and upper Manhattan, school board members ran up huge travel expenses to such places as Las Vegas, Honolulu, and the Virgin Islands (McKinley, 1994). Retired New York City teachers have been allowed to collect their pensions while being retained as "consultants" making $200 a day (Barbanel, 1994b). One consultant was paid $4,000 to make a recommendation as to whether another consultant should be hired (Dillon, 1994). Since all these examples come from a limited geographic area, one shudders to think of the scope of the problem nationwide.

Until honest and effective people take control of poor school districts, it would be foolish for the taxpayers of a state to send care packages in the form of extra revenue to crooks and incompetents. As Henry Levin (1976) put it after studying the impact of expenditure increases on school effectiveness: "Spending increases will have a much greater effect on the economic status and employment of educational professionals than they will on the educational proficiencies of children" (p. 194). The spending did continue to increase after Levin wrote this. During the 1980s, state and local education revenues increased 39.1 percent (after removing price increase effects) and went up 27.8 percent on a per-pupil basis (Alexander, 1997). The rate of increase declined in the 1990s, as schools tried to become more efficient, but the increase by no means disappeared (*Digest of Education Statistics*, 1997). William Bennett, a former U.S. Secretary of Education, noted that between 1960 and 1993, spending on elementary and secondary schools increased more than 200 percent and average SAT scores dropped 73 points (1994, p. 82). Bennett can add to his argument against mindless education spending by citing the dismal showing of U.S. students on the Third International Test of Mathematics and Science in 1996.

## Throwing Dollars in the Dark

We know how we do not want to spend school money: on waste and corruption. But we are not sure how we do want to spend it. Educational research and past experience do not tell us clearly what works.

> Research currently available in this arena is deficient in both focus and rigor, findings often are nonconfirmatory or contradictory. For example, teaching experience and advanced degrees are major determinants of teachers' salaries, but these variables are not clearly related to improvements in school outputs. . . . Education has not been able to provide cost/benefit data as readily as have some other public services . . . (McCarthy and Deignan, 1982, p. 102)

Even programs that appear to work in one locale defy successful transplantation to other sites, as Eric Hanushek (1997) laments. Hanushek's work is often cited by those who would reduce school spending, but, to be fair, we must note that others challenge his statistical methods (Hedges, Laine, and Greenwald, 1994; Greenwald, Hedges and Laine, 1996). In the further interest of fairness, we also must note that Hanushek (1994) claims that his critics themselves use dubious methods. Policymakers with authority to legislate on school finance have an obligation to study both sides of the debate, not just cite the data that bear out their own positions. If they do, they may be forced into the agnostic approach that other researchers adopt when they review the evidence. As James Guthrie puts it:

> Everybody's arguing for more school decision making, and the school finance people and the economists say they don't know how to advise them on the appropriate spending of resources. What the field needs is to better understand how money is spent inside a school, what are we buying, and what is it we ought to buy, and what leads to more learning. (quoted by Colvin, 1989, p. 13)

The so-called effective schools research that yielded a list of nostrums has itself come under attack for the narrow assumptions it was based on—for example, that a successful school is one whose students score well on standardized tests in math and reading. Whole books are now devoted to critiques of the effective schools research (Knapp and Shields, 1990). Some research results are presented in such turgid detail that they defy comprehension. One research report entitled "Early Schooling of Children at Risk" (Reynolds, 1991) would be of obvious interest to urban school officials, but they might abandon the effort to fathom it about halfway through. Researchers tend to write for other researchers, not for the people who are in a position to implement the research recommendations. As Ralph Tyler (1988) has said: "Researchers are accustomed to looking to the university for guidance and rewards. Practitioners are accustomed to looking to school and community leaders for guidance and rewards. It is therefore difficult to get them together and establish a tradition of working together" (p. 177).

Some of the things that seem to work at first in poor schools peter out after a while. It is as though what really works is novelty. But even then, some novelties do not work as well as others, or at all. Some of the steps that seem to work either are beyond the school's control or cannot be bought. Good families and stable neighborhoods seem to work, and this makes intuitive sense; but these conditions are largely the responsibility of individuals, other government agencies, and private charities. Parental participation in school seems to work, but suburban schools are able to get this without paying for it. Principals who take an interest in the quality of classroom instruction seem to be more effective, but this does not cost more money, only a reordering of the principal's priorities. Aligning the curriculum with the tests that assess student achievement should not cost much money, and this step is so commonsensical that it should have been done long ago. Keeping students on task and not distracting them with administrative interruptions is another method that does not cost money and is patently desirable.

Given all this uncertainty about the programs that cost money and the much greater certainty about the programs that don't, spending more money on poor schools is like throwing dollars in the dark and hoping they will land where they can do some good. The uncertainty is not restricted to poor schools; rich schools spend money on many things that have no demonstrated effect on the schools' goals. An Olympic-size swimming pool is certainly nice to have, but it is hardly essential. Luxuriantly carpeted and paneled offices create an elegant ambiance, but their relationship to staff or student productivity is elusive. The same is true for beautifully manicured grounds surrounding the school building. The difference is that rich schools spend (or waste) their own money; poor schools are asking for money from people who don't use these schools and don't live anywhere near them. Poor schools cannot expect anyone to invest in them before they establish a record for getting results with their own money.

It is not at all impossible that poor school districts already have enough money to do the job. They may have only half as much per pupil as a rich district, and their students may have a lot of educational handicaps, but by emphasizing a few really important goals they could concentrate their staffs' energy on the essentials. If the vast majority of the students are deficient in the basic skills of reading, writing, and arithmetic, the poor districts should focus their time and money on those areas. Full-fledged art and music programs may be luxuries that poor districts cannot afford and that detract from students' real needs. Robert Slavin and his colleagues at Johns Hopkins University have been operating an intensive pre-K-to-6 reading program in 750 schools and achieving well-documented success. They are using the same federal Chapter 1 funds that the other schools get. The difference is that they spend the money in a concentrated, systematic way, with a focus on what young children need most to learn (Fashola and Slavin, 1998). Given the dialectic of educational research, even the success Slavin claims has come under attack for dubious methodology and analysis (Veznesky, 1999; Pogrow, 1998; Jones, Gottfredson, and Gottfredson, 1997).

Dedicated urban educators can get results without waiting for more largesse from the state or federal treasury. Jaime Escalante, a math teacher in California, got such startling results that his story was made into the movie *Stand and Deliver*. Joe Clark, a New Jersey high school principal, was lionized in a *Time* magazine cover story and in the movie *Lean on Me*. And surely every state has its Jim Caulfield, a district superintendent whose schools spend less, have proportionately fewer administrators and teachers, and still get higher student test scores than similar districts (O'Neill, 1994). Whatever one thinks of these individuals' tactics, the fact is that they had latitude for action without needing more money, and they acted.

The simple fact that a rich district spends twice as much money per pupil as a poor district could mean that the rich district is wasting half its money on frills its students don't need. However, it could also mean that the students are so educationally advanced that they require expensive programs and materials in order to continue their intellectual development. When a school has a sizable number of students who are able to handle expensive laboratory equipment and learn from doing so, buying that equipment is a legitimate educational expense. But to buy that equipment for students who are incapable of comprehending it is to pay for a foolish equality. Educationally backward students don't need sophisticated equipment, and they are not likely to have much respect for equipment that they find frustratingly difficult. The propensity of students from poor communities to engage in destructive behavior often leaves schools with expensive, unused, and *damaged* equipment. Equal education for rich and poor students does not mean the same education; it means equally appropriate education. Rich students tend to do better in school than do poor students, so it is a good social investment to spend more on them. These students *earn* the additional expenditure by dint of their hard work and better-developed ability.

### Making Students Responsible

Society gives students a free start in life but not a guaranteed finish. Students are the adults of the future, and they must learn responsibility in school in order to assume their adult roles. They must learn and act on the conviction that they are the major determiners of their fates.

A society that insists on excusing student transgressions does a tremendous disservice to young people. It gives them the notion that others are always to blame for their behavior. In the case of poor students, it is often society itself that is supposedly at fault. These children are pitied to the point of being denied all free will. That attitude, however charitably grounded, is insulting and damaging to poor children. It has the effect of maintaining them in poverty and dependency. The lesson these children must learn is that society simply cannot afford to give everyone an unending free ride. After going a certain distance, the riders must make some payment. The ability and willingness to make such payments are traits of responsible, self-sufficient individuals. Students in poor schools may not be able to make cash payments toward their education, but they can certainly make payments of effort. If they do, they will find their own children attending suburban schools, just as so many earlier generations of the poor worked their way out of poverty.

This may already be happening, if minority student performance on standardized tests is an indicator. The scores are increasing on a variety of tests. For example, increasing numbers of minority students are taking the Scholastic Aptitude Test, one of the most consequential, and they are doing better all the time. Between 1979 and 1989, black students' scores rose by 49 points. Mexican-Americans' scores by 31 points, and Puerto Ricans' scores by 33 points. Anglo students' scores rose by only 10 points. Thus, minorities were catching up during a period when they were supposedly increasingly discriminated against economically (*Education That Works*, 1990, Table 2).

## For Discussion

1. Find out the current per-pupil expenditure for your home school district, and then compare the figures with other members of your class. Or get official expenditure numbers from the state education department (in some states, this is called the department of public instruction) and then compare several school districts within your state. How tolerable are the spending disparities across school districts?

2. The Committee for Economic Development lists the following as major reasons why children do poorly in school. Try to devise cost-free or inexpensive means of dealing with these conditions. Is it really necessary to spend more money on schools where these conditions are endemic?

   Children may come to school poorly prepared for classroom learning or not yet ready developmentally for formal education.

   Their parents may be indifferent to their educational needs.

   They may be children of teenagers who are ill-equipped for parenting.

   They may have undiagnosed learning disabilities, emotional problems, or physical handicaps.

   They may have language problems or come from non-English-speaking homes.

   They may experience ethnic or racial prejudice.

   They may have access only to schools of substandard quality.

   *Source: Children in Need: Investment Strategies for the Educationally Disadvantaged.*
   (1987). New York: Committee for Economic Development, p. 8.

3. It is often said that the one who pays the piper picks the tune. States that start giving more money to poor school districts will try to exercise more control over these districts to make sure the money is spent well. Make a list of the areas over which states should be exercising direct, prescriptive,

uniform control. Then make a list of the areas that should be left to the judgment of local officials, no matter how much money the state is contributing. Items on your lists might include hiring and evaluating personnel, the determination of curriculum content and teaching materials, assessment of student achievement, the requirements for a high school diploma, the length of the school year, and the safety standards for buildings. Do your lists indicate that you prefer a centralized statewide school system or a localized system?

4. Michael Kirst points out that reducing class size, though it seems good for children, entails so much expense that it may make the result simply too costly. Imagine a school of a certain total pupil enrollment and average class size, then reduce the class size by 20 percent. Do a rough calculation of all the expenses you incur.

*Source:* Kirst, M. (1997). "Smaller Classes Aren't a Cure-All." *The New York Times,* August 18, p. A19.

## References

*Abbott v. Burke.* (1998). New Jersey Supreme Court Syllabus. *Raymond Abbott et al. v. Fred G. Burke et al.* [online]. (Available at http://www-camlaw.rutgers.edu/decisions/supreme/a155-97)

ALEXANDER, N. (1997). "The Growth of Education Revenues from 1982–83 to 1991–92: What Accounts for Differences Among States?" *Journal of Education Finance* 22(4), 435–463.

BAKER, K. (1991). "Yes, Throw Money at Schools." *Phi Delta Kappan* 72(8), 628–631.

BARBANEL, J. (1992). "Long Island District Illustrates Paradoxes of School Financing." *The New York Times,* February 12, p. A23.

BARBANEL, J. (1993). "School Financing Not Less for the Poor, Study Says." *The New York Times,* October 5, p. B3.

——— (1994a). "Cortines Says Board Payroll Was Misstated." *The New York Times,* February 11, pp. B1, B3.

——— (1994b). "Some Retired Teachers Evade Income Restrictions." *The New York Times,* March 15, p. B3.

BARNETT, S. (1993). "Does Head Start Fade Out?" *Education Week* 12(34), 40.

BASTIAN, A., ET AL. (1985). *Choosing Equality: The Case for Democratic Schooling.* New York: New World Foundation.

BARZUN, J. (1959). *The House of Intellect.* New York: Harper & Row.

BELL, D. (1976). *The Cultural Contradictions of Capitalism.* New York: Basic Books.

BENNETT, W. (1994). *The Index of Leading Cultural Indicators.* New York: Simon & Schuster.

BERGER, J. (1991). "Report Sharply Rebukes School District in the Bronx." *The New York Times,* April 23, pp. B1, B4.

——— (1992a). "Principal Admits Misusing School Funds." *The New York Times,* February 21, p. B3.

——— (1992b). "Trade-Off in the Schools: Principals Pay Political Dues to Get Jobs." *The New York Times,* February 7, pp. B1.

BOWLES, S., AND GINTIS, H. (1976). *Schooling in Capitalist America: Educational Reform and the Contradictions of Economic Life.* New York: Basic Books.

BRADLEY, A. (1994). "Equation for Equality." *Education Week* 14(2), 28–32.

CARLSON, K., AND RUBIN, L. (1979). *Analysis of the Development and Implementation of Local and Statewide Standards in Basic Skills in the State of New Jersey: A Final Report.* Washington, DC: National Institute of Education.

CARNEGIE FOUNDATION FOR THE ADVANCEMENT OF TEACHING. (1988). *An Imperiled Generation: Saving Urban Schools.* Princeton, NJ: Princeton University Press.

CELIS, W. (1994). "A Long-Running Saga Over Texas Schools." *The New York Times Education Life,* April 10, pp. 30–31.

*Children in Need: Investment Strategies for the Educationally Disadvantaged.* (1987). New York: Research and Policy Committee of the Committee for Economic Development.

CHIRA, S. (1992). "Quality Time for Quality Schools." *The New York Times,* March 30, pp. B1, B4.

CHURCHILL, W. (1947). Address to House of Commons, November 11, 1947.

*City High Schools: A Recognition of Progress.* (1984). New York: Ford Foundation.

COLEMAN, J. S., ET AL. (1966). *Equality of Educational Opportunity.* Washington, DC: Government Printing Office.

COLVIN, R. (1989). "School Finance Equity Concerns in an Age of Reforms." *Educational Researcher* 18(1), 11–15.

CONANT, J. B. (1961). *Slums and Suburbs.* New York: McGraw-Hill.

COONS, J. E., CLUNE, W. H., III, AND SUGARMAN, S. D. (1971). *Private Wealth and Public Education.* Cambridge, MA: Harvard University Press.

CORCORAN, T. B., WALKER, L. J., AND WHITE, J. L. (1988). *Working in Urban Schools.* Washington, DC: Institute for Educational Leadership.

DALEY, S. (1991). "Born on Crack and Coping with Kindergarten." *The New York Times,* February 7, pp. 1, D24.

*Digest of Education Statistics, 1997.* (1997). (Online; available at http://www.nces.ed.gov/pubs/digest97/d970002.html).

DILLON, S. (1994). "School Board Said to Misuse Consultants." *The New York Times,* August 10, pp. B1–B2.

*Education That Works: An Action Plan for the Education of Minorities.* (1990). Report of the Quality Education for Minorities Project. Cambridge, MA: Massachusetts Institute of Technology.

FASHOLA, O., AND SLAVIN, R. (1998). "Schoolwide Reform Models: What Works?" *Phi Delta Kappan* 79(5), 370–378.

FREEMAN, J., AND POLLITT, K. (1991). "Islands of Quality, Sea of Decay." *The New York Times,* March 16, p. 23.

FRIED, J. (1994). "Principal Charged With Stealing Funds." *The New York Times,* May 19, p. B3.

FRIED, J. (1995). "More Corruption Charges Against Former Principal." *The New York Times,* March 1, p. B3.

FULLER, B., AND HOLLOWAY, S. (1998). "Child-Care Combat." *Education Week,* 17(22), 56, 37.

GARMS, W. I., GUTHRIE, J. W., AND PIERCE, L. C. (1978). *School Finance: The Economics and Politics of Public Education.* Englewood Cliffs, NJ: Prentice-Hall.

GIBBS, N. (1994). "Murder in Miniature." *Time,* September 9, pp. 54–59.

GREENWALD, R., HEDGES, L., AND LAINE, R. (1996). "The Effect of School Resources on School Achievement." *Review of Education Research* 66, 361–396.

GROSS, J. (1992). "Collapse of Inner-City Families Creates America's New Orphans." *The New York Times,* March 29, pp. 1, 20.

HANUSHEK, E. (1997). "Applying Performance Incentives to Schools for Disadvantaged Populations." *Education and Urban Society* 29(3), 296–315.

HANUSHEK, E. (1994). "More Money Might Matter Somewhere: A Response to Hedges, Laine, and Greenwald." *Educational Researcher* 23(4), 5–8.

HARRISON, D. (1997). "The Real Class Divide." *The New York Times,* September 24, p. A27.

HAYEK, F. A. (1944). *The Road to Serfdom.* Chicago: University of Chicago Press.

HEDGES, L., LAINE, R., AND GREENWALD, R. (1994). "Does Money Matter? A Meta-Analysis of Studies of the Effects of Differential School Inputs on Student Outcomes." *Educational Researcher* 23(3), 5–13.

HERBERS, J. (1972). "School Financing: A New Way to Foot the Bill." *The New York Times,* March 12, p. E3.

HEROS (1999). (Online Available at http://www.totalink.net/~heros>).

JAYSON, K. (1997). "Our Unfair Share." *The New York Times,* September 26, p. A27.

JENCKS, C., ET AL. (1972). *Inequality: A Reassessment of the Effect of Family and Schooling in America.* New York: Basic Books.

JONES, E., GOTTFREDSON, G., AND GOTTFREDSON, D. (1997). "Success for Some: An Evaluation of the Success For all Program." *Evaluation Review* 21(6), 643–670.

KARP, S., ET AL., EDS. (1997). "Savage Inequalities State by State." In *Funding for Justice.* Milwaukee: Rethinking Schools Publications.

KING, P. (1998). Report of Special Master to the New Jersey Supreme Court. Trenton, NJ.

KING, W. (1992). "Florio's Educational Panel Offers Many Changes, at a Hefty Price." *The New York Times,* January 9, p. B7.

KNAPP, M., AND SHIELDS, P., EDS. (1990). *Better Schooling for the Children of Poverty: Alternatives to Conventional Wisdom—Volume II: Commissioned Papers and Literature Review.* Menlo Park, CA: SRI International.

KOTLOWITZ, A. (1991). *There Are No Children Here.* New York: Doubleday.

KOZOL, J. (1988). *Rachel and Her Children: Homeless Families in America.* New York: Crown.

—————— (1991). *Savage Inequalities: Children in America's Schools.* New York: Crown.

KRISTOL, I. (1978). *Two Cheers for Capitalism.* New York: Basic Books.

KRUGMAN, P. (1994). "Technology's Revenge." *The Wilson Quarterly* 18(4), 56–64.

LEFELT, S. (1988). Abbott v. Burke. *Initial Decision.* Trenton, NJ: State New Jersey Office of Administrative Law.

LEVIN, H. M. (1976). "Effects of Expenditure Increases on Educational Resource Allocation and Effectiveness." In *The Limits of Educational Reform,* edited by M. Carnoy and H. M. Levin. New York: David McKay.

LEWIS, N. A., AND BLUMENTHAL, R. (1989). "Power Base vs. Schools in Brooklyn District." *The New York Times,* February 10, p. B4.

LUCAS, T., HENZE, R., AND DONATO, R. (1990). "Promoting the Success of Latino Language-Minority Students: An Exploratory Study of Six High Schools." In *Strategies for Success: What's Working in Education Today.* Cambridge, MA: Harvard Educational Review.

MADDEN, N., ET AL. (1993). "Success for All: Longitudinal Effects of a Restructuring Program for Inner-City Elementary Schools. *American Educational Research Journal* 30(1), 123–148.

McCARTHY, M. M., AND DEIGNAN, P. T. (1982). *What Legally Constitutes an Adequate Public Education?* Bloomington, IN: Phi Delta Kappa.

McKINLEY, J. (1994). "School Districts Assailed on Travel Expenses." *The New York Times,* February 11, p. B3.

METZ, M. H. (1988). "In Education, Magnets Attract Controversy." *Issues '88,* special edition of *NEA Today.*

NELSON, F. (1991). *International Comparison of Public Spending on Education.* Research Report of the American Federation of Teachers. Washington, DC: American Federation of Teachers.

NOCERO, J. (1989). "The Case Against Joe Nocero." *The Washington Monthly,* February, pp. 22–31.

OLSON, L. AND HENDRIE, C. (1998). "Pathways to Progress." *Education Week,* January 8, pp. 32–50.

O'NEILL, T. (1994). "Where Schools Work." *New Jersey Reporter* 23(6), 30–34.

PEAT MARWICK MAIN & CO. (1988). *Executive Summary of Jersey City Schools Investigation.* Trenton, NJ: New Jersey Department of Education.

PETERSON, B. (1997). "School Facilities at Crisis Level." *Funding For Justice.* Milwaukee: Rethinking Schools Publications.

POGROW, S. (1998). "What Is an Exemplary Program, and Why Should Anyone Care?" *Educational Researcher* 27(7), 22–29.

PREVITE, M. (1994). "What Will They Say at My Funeral?" *The New York Times,* August 7, p. E17.

REYNOLDS, A. (1991). "Early Schooling of Children at Risk." *American Educational Research Journal* 28(2), 392–422.

ROTBERG, I. (1994). "Separate and Unequal." *Education Week* 13(24), 44.

*San Antonio Independent School District v. Rodriguez,* (1973), 411 U.S. 1.

SEXTON, P. C. (1961). *Education and Income: Inequalities in Our Public Schools.* New York: Viking.

"States' School Spending Disparities." (1992). *Education Week* 11(39), 28.

STEINBERG, J. (1997). "Fair or Not, Rules Are Bent to Bankroll Public Schools." *The New York Times,* September 24, p. 1, B3.

SULLIVAN, J. (1989). "School Official Admits Guilt in Bribery Case." *The New York Times,* January 24, p. B3.

SURO, R. (1991). "Equality Plan on School Financing Is Upsetting Rich and Poor in Texas." *The New York Times,* October 9, p. A-10

THUROW, L. C. (1985). *The Zero-Sum Solution.* New York: Simon & Schuster.

TREASTER, J. (1993). "For Children of Cocaine, Fresh Reasons for Hope." *The New York Times,* February 16, pp. A1, B4.

TYLER, R. (1988). "Utilization of Research by Practitioners in Education." In *Contributing to Educational Change: Perspectives Research and Practice,* edited by P. Jackson. Berkeley, CA: McCutchan.

VAN TASSEL, P. (1988). "Keeping the Peddie School's Aims Alive." *The New York Times,* December 11, p. NJ3.

VEZNESKY, R. (1999). "An Alternative Perspective on Success for All." In K. Wong, editor, *Advances in Educational Policy* (Vol. 4). Greenwich, CT: JAI Press.

VERGARA, C. (1991). "New York's New Ghettos." *The Nation* 252(23), 804–810.

VIADERO, D. (1994). "'Fade-Out' in Head Start Gains Linked to Later Schooling." *Education Week* 13(30), 9.

WEHLAGE, G., ET AL. (1989). *Reducing the Risk: Schools as Communities of Support.* London: Falmer Press.

WEISS, P. (1988). "The Education of Chancellor Green." *The New York Times Magazine,* December 4, pp. 42–44, 60–62, 81, 92–94, 109.

WENGLINSKY, H. (1997). *When Money Matters.* Princeton, NJ: Educational Testing Service.

WINERIP, M. (1993). "America Can Save Its City Schools." *The New York Times Education Life,* September 7, pp. 16–18.

WULF, S. (1997). "Teach Our Children Well: It Can Be Done." *Time,* October 27, pp. 59–69.

# CHAPTER 4

# School Integration: Compulsory or Voluntary

## POSITION 1: FOR LEGAL INTEGRATION

### Where Are We Now?

Nearly fifty years after the Brown decision, can we say our schools are integrated? By 1997, the percentage of white American adults over age 25 who held a bachelor's degree was about 25 percent, but the percentage of African American adults over age 25 who held a bachelors degree was about half that, 13 percent. Similarly, black women made up 12 percent of the work force in the past five years, but only 6.6 percent of the people in managerial positions. And the number of federal, state, local, and administrative law judges in the United States is about 60,000; but the number of black judges is 1,680, a mere 2.8 percent of the total ("Vital Signs," 1998).

These indicators do not show the kind of social progress we might have desired by this time, given the high hopes for integration. But things are clearly better than before we embarked on the just course of integration. For example, black students now succeed in completing college at a rate four times higher than in 1960. Black students now enter college at a rate over seven times the rate in 1960. By 1970, six times as many blacks held white-collar positions (36 percent) than was true in 1940 (6 percent; Masci, 1998). From the time of slavery, when blacks were legally prohibited from enjoying the basic rights of citizens and were denied schooling, they have suffered untold miseries, and society has lost the benefit of their contributions. Centuries of segregation are not overturned quickly. Integration, long and difficult though the process may be, is obviously better for all.

### The Residue of Segregation

The major and most often quoted reason for outlawing racial segregation in American schools, as defined by the U.S. Supreme Court in 1954, is that segregation does psychological damage to black students. The damage may be so severe that it can never be repaired, said the Court. In the Court's exact words: "To separate them [blacks] from others of similar age and qualifications solely because of their race generates a feeling of inferiority as to their status in the community that may affect their hearts and minds in a way unlikely ever to be undone" (*Brown v. Board of Education of Topeka*, 1954). The Court, however, could only look at "legal" segregation, that is, segregation imposed by law. The Court ruled that this type of segregation was, in fact, illegal: It violated the highest law in the land, the U.S. Constitution.

The Supreme Court ruling against legal segregation has caused profound changes in society. The civil rights movement gained tremendous momentum from the ruling; schools throughout the nation were desegregated; blacks secured opportunities for better education, employment, and housing. Some blacks even received preferential treatment over whites in securing these benefits. Black progress during the past half-century was perhaps symbolized most dramatically by the presidential campaigns of Jesse Jackson, Douglas Wilder, and Allan Keyes, and the much-hoped-for presidential bid of Colin Powell.

And yet, after all the tumult and all the genuine progress of the past five decades, where does the United States stand today? It is still a racially segregated society. Several American cities now have majority black populations, including Atlanta, Baltimore, Birmingham, Detroit, Memphis, Newark, New Orleans, and Savannah, as well as Washington, D.C. (*Statistical Abstract of the United States*, 1994, pp. 44–46). In many areas of the country, the segregation in schools is more extensive than it was twenty years ago. In 1972–1973, the percentage of blacks and Latinos attending predominantly minority schools was 64 percent and 57 percent, respectively. By 1991–1992, these percentages had increased to 66 percent and 73 percent. Ironically, the most segregated states in the union are now those in the north and the west: Illinois, Michigan, New York, New Jersey, and California. Segregation of black students is worse now than it was before the Supreme Court's first busing decision in 1971. And Latino students are far more likely than black students to attend segregated schools (Orfield, 1993). Moreover, "both African American and Latino students are much more likely than white students to find themselves in schools of concentrated poverty. Segregation by race is strongly related to segregation by poverty" (Orfield, 1993, p. 1). The segregation is so extreme in the urban areas of the north that social scientists have new names for people trapped in the ghettos: "the underclass" and "the truly disadvantaged." The underclass and the truly disadvantaged are worse than poor; they are without hope. They can see no legitimate way to escape their poverty, or to find a way of escape for their children. Many take the illegitimate route of crime in an attempt to escape their plight, leading only to prison or death.

The plight of these people passes from generation to generation because they are isolated in the ghetto without opportunities and without positive role models. When the races were totally segregated, successful blacks lived in the ghetto and could serve as guides and role models for black children. Now they are able to escape to residences in the suburbs, leaving the black children who are still in the central cities with nothing but models of defeat. William Julius Wilson, in examining the cities of New York, Chicago, Los Angeles, Philadelphia, and Detroit, found the following.

> Although the total population in these five largest cities decreased by 9 percent between 1970 and 1980, the poverty population increased by 22 percent. Furthermore, the population living in poverty areas grew by 40 percent overall, by 69 percent in high-poverty areas (i.e., areas with a poverty rate of at least 30 percent), and by a staggering 161 percent in extreme poverty areas (i.e., areas with a poverty rate of at least 40 percent). It should be emphasized that these incredible changes took place within just a ten-year period . . . the significant increase in the poverty concentration in these overwhelmingly black communities is related to the large out-migration of nonpoor blacks. (Wilson, 1987, pp. 46, 50)

The result of this massive and sudden dislocation is that the people left behind

> experience a social isolation that excludes them from the job network system that permeates other neighborhoods and that is so important in learning about or being recommended for jobs . . . in such neighborhoods the chances are overwhelming that children will seldom interact on a sustained basis with people who are employed or with families that have a steady breadwinner . . . the relationship between schooling and postschool employment takes on a different meaning. . . . In such neighborhoods, therefore, teachers become frustrated and do not teach and children do not learn. (Wilson, 1987, p. 57)

The schools of the underclass are a national disgrace. They catch the contagion of hopelessness from the ghettos and add to the despair and hostility the students bring from the streets. Black students make up 16 percent of the total school enrollment nationwide, whereas white students make up 70 percent. However, black students account for a much greater proportion than 16 percent of students with special needs and problems, and for only 8 percent of gifted and talented students. Thus, black students are not well served by the schools they attend. Most of them attend segregated schools.

The acuteness of urban school problems led the National Governors Association to recommend that states take over urban school districts locked in a cycle of failure (*Time for Results,* 1986). The state of New Jersey has already taken over the Jersey City, Paterson, and Newark school systems, on the grounds that the schools of these cities have demonstrated repeatedly that they are unable to provide an adequate education. The state has replaced the boards of education and the chief school administrators of these cities with its own appointees. In the Chelsea school district in Massachusetts, the local authorities asked Boston University to assume management of the schools because they felt powerless to overcome the impact of poverty. The Hartford, Connecticut, board of education signed a contract to let a private firm, Educational Alternatives, Inc., run the public school system, having repeatedly failed to improve the beleaguered schools. The private corporation was not successful, either.

Obviously, the plight of the American underclass has reached crisis proportions. The newsmagazines feature cover stories on it; the *New York Times* carries periodic front-page reports; and the television networks run prime-time specials. This means that the problem has risen to the top of the national political agenda. As we formulate answers, we need to first heed the U.S. Supreme Court's words from nearly fifty years ago.

## Focusing on Effects, Not Intentions

It was almost five decades ago that the Supreme Court spoke of the possibly permanent damage racial segregation does to youngsters. The Court's remedy at that time was to outlaw various forms of legal segregation. If the segregation was not imposed by some law, and it just happened to come about as a result of private choices that individuals made, then it passed Constitutional muster. But that did not mean that the psychological harm caused by this second kind of segregation was any less potent.

Moreover, it can be impossible to tell whether the segregation is due to official action or just to a series of innocent choices. For example, the United States population is now largely divided into cities and suburbs. Blacks tend to be clustered in the cities and whites in the suburbs. When the suburbs were being established by state incorporation laws after World War II, lawmakers may have *intended* to create racially segregated communities. They must certainly have known that racial segregation would result from their action. Indeed, the federal courts, including the Supreme Court, found that this was the case in several metropolitan areas in the north (for example, *Keyes v. Denver School District No. 1*, 1973; *Evans v. Buchanan*, 1976). If segregation was *deliberately* instituted in other metropolitan areas of the north—and this seems probable, given the prejudices of the period when the suburbs were developing—none of those responsible would admit it today. Thus, all we can know with certainty is the *effect* that the state incorporation laws had: white suburbs and black cities, white schools and black schools. "Requiring proof of intentional segregation before calling for any remedy is . . . not the most sensible [policy]. The injury that children suffer from racial separation has nothing to do with its cause" (Kirp, 1982, p. 285).

The answer to America's apartheid, then, is to integrate our country. The constitutionality of the segregation we now have may be debatable, but the harm it is doing is not (Shipler, 1997). There are some obvious strategies that we can (and must) use to bring about an integrated society.

## Integrating the Schools

The first and cheapest strategy is to redraw school district boundaries. One of the reasons why the south has had more success with school desegregation than the north has had is that southern school districts are countywide. The districts cover areas large enough to include a good mix of students from both races, although busing may be necessary to move children from their respective neighborhoods to a common school. When a state has large, racially mixed school districts, it is much harder to flee to a lily-white district. And the desire to flee also abates, since the integration is spread out enough to allay white panic.

The north has many racially segregated and economically inefficient little school districts that could be consolidated profitably into large, integrated districts. Getting students of different races to the same school may require some busing, but not as much as opponents claim. Black (and Hispanic) students who live on the periphery of the city may already live closer to the nearest suburban school than they do to the city school they now attend. The reverse is true for some suburban students whose homes are near the city line.

Interdistrict integration is the only kind of integration feasible now, since city schools have become predominantly black and suburban schools almost exclusively white. "Desegregation in a society where whites have run to the suburbs to establish a 'white noose' around decaying, predominantly minority central cities requires metropolitan desegregation" (Mahard and Crain, 1983, p. 124). Evidence also suggests that integration in a limited area engenders more resistance than large-scale integration (Hochschild, 1984, pp. 54–70, 147). This may be due to the fact that large-scale integration has effects that are popular with whites as well as blacks. "A range of desirable goals for an effective school desegregation program—such as furthering genuine integration, cost and transportational efficiency, equity, and parental choice—can all be more effectively advanced within a metropolitan context" (Pettigrew, 1981, p. 163).

Even if better racial proportions existed within the cities, it is fairer to integrate over a larger geographic area. When the schools of the working-class Irish and blacks in Boston were integrated under court order, noted Harvard psychiatrist Robert Coles had the following reaction:

> The busing is a scandal. I do not think that busing should be imposed like this on working-class people exclusively. It should cross these lines and people in the suburbs should share it. . . . [Working-class whites and blacks] are both competing for a very limited piece of the pie, the limits of which are being set by the larger limits of class which allow them damn little, if anything. (quoted in Lukas, 1985, p. 506)

Metropolitan desegregation of schools does not guarantee classroom integration, however. Even well-intentioned communities with magnet schools designed to promote integration find that, over time, the classrooms of these integrated schools segregate (McLarin, 1994). This raises delicate questions regarding ability grouping and maintaining the support of high-status parents, usually the wealthier and whiter parents in town. The federal government's Magnet Schools Assistance Program requires such schools to demonstrate how they have increased interaction among students of different racial and social backgrounds (Schmidt, 1994); the government itself should be monitoring the situation to make sure that a good amount of the interaction is taking place *within* classrooms. Racial hatred runs deep (Peebles, 1997), and forceful government pressure is needed.

## The Benefits for Students

People typically want to know what educational rewards will result from such large-scale reorganization and the added time and cost of busing. Those who ask this question usually think of educational benefits in terms of such quantifiable measures as math, reading, and SAT scores. They seem unaware that children can learn through associating with children from other backgrounds. This kind of knowledge can contribute to their success in later life, and it is absolutely indispensable for nullifying the poison of the racial past and present in this country. Such an attitudinal change may not be as easy to measure as gains in academic achievement, but it is no less important for the future of the United States.

We know that schools can be integrated successfully. Children, black and white, need not sacrifice academic achievement to reap the benefits of a multiracial, multicultural environment (Schiff, 1999). "White children almost never experience declines in performance on standardized achievement tests as a result of desegregation. Minorities benefit academically from desegregation much more often than they experience negative effects" (Hawley, 1981, p. 151).

This is especially true if minority students receive the "wise" schooling Claude Steele writes about. Schooling of this kind overcomes the double fear that minority students have—fear of failing and fear of being devalued. It allows them to relax and achieve as they are encouraged to undertake successively more difficult tasks (Steele, 1992).

We must also realize that the *process* of creating an integrated school can be a valuable learning experience. Integration has to happen not just in the school, but also in its classrooms. Classroom integration permits cooperative learning tasks, with black and white students working together toward common goals. This usually has a positive effect on the racial attitudes of both groups (Conard, 1988; Schofield and Sagar, 1983, pp. 78–85). Adults are somewhat sheepishly aware that young people are more adaptable in such situations. But what we must understand most keenly is how necessary it is to prepare the next generation to handle the vicissitudes of a multiracial world better than we have. It is a world in which Anglo-Americans are becoming a progressively smaller proportion of the population, both worldwide and in the United States.

A large, integrated school district can offer several other advantages. Because it is large, it can purchase school supplies and equipment in quantity at discount prices. It can offer special programs, such as four years of Russian or Chinese, because it has enough students to make these programs economical. And a large district does not have to be a bureaucratic nightmare. Indeed, it should require fewer administrators than several small districts serving the same overall number of pupils, and the savings in administrator salaries can go directly toward instruction. A large district can be broken down into fairly independent units, with each school having considerable self-governance. It can even include schools-within-schools to give students a greater sense of belonging, as in the Central Park East Schools in New York City (Bensman, 1987). Thus, a large district makes racial (and cultural) integration possible; it makes a richer education program possible; and it does not preclude decentralized control.

## Integrating the Neighborhoods

School integration can accomplish only so much. Its benefits end each day when the students return to their segregated neighborhoods. And not only do the black and Hispanic students return to segregated neighborhoods, but they are likely to return to poor neighborhoods as well. Many of these neighborhoods are crime- and drug-ridden, which discourages the students who live there from doing well in school. They find it difficult to concentrate on homework assignments because of the turmoil around them. Neighborhood hoodlums tell them it is not cool to be a good student, or to attend school at all. They constantly face the threat of physical harm because of the rampant violence in a neighborhood marked by desolation and hopelessness. And very often, and tragically, these conditions have seeped into the home as well.

The abolition of ghettos is the only way to fully liberate the youngsters living in them so that they can lead successful and lawful lives. But abolishing ghettos requires that the people now trapped in them have the means to live elsewhere. They will need housing allowances, since their meager incomes do not permit them to buy or rent decent housing now (Dreier and Moberg, 1996). They also will require *available* housing outside the area. Fortress suburbia must open up to make room. The fair housing law makes this goal explicit. It stipulates that all federal agencies "shall administer their programs and activities relating to housing and urban development in a manner affirmatively to further the purposes of this title [housing integration]" (quoted in Orfield, 1978, p. 436).

Suburban communities have erected barricades against the poor; these barricades are called "zoning laws." One zoning law says that no house can be built on a lot smaller than two acres in size. The cost of such a lot alone would drive the price of the house beyond the reach of poor people. Another zoning law says that no house can be occupied by anyone but the immediate nuclear family. This requires that families abandon their grandparents to live elsewhere, and it assumes that the grandparents or other relatives can afford separate housing. Another zoning law says that no house can be smaller than so many thousand square feet; but the larger the house, the greater the cost. Still another law forbids apartment housing and mobile homes, often the only kind of housing the poor can afford.

Residents defend these laws with the argument that they keep the community "nice." "Nice" means rich and mostly white. It is as though being poor means you are not entitled to live in a nice neighborhood—even if you are a full-time worker performing a vital job, but at a poverty wage.

These artificial barriers can be broken down, as the state of New Jersey has shown. The New Jersey Supreme Court ordered the state's suburban communities to change their zoning laws to permit the construction of housing for people with low and moderate incomes. Builders have agreed to put up low- and moderate-income housing, even though they will not make much profit from it, because this allows them to also build expensive and profitable housing. Unfortunately, even low-income housing is too expensive for many families, which is why housing allowances are needed. In the absence of housing allowances, court rulings may not effect much change. The ultimate ineffectiveness of the New Jersey court ruling was reflected in remarks made by the chief justice of the state Supreme Court:

New Jersey today, like much of this country, is a collection of islands, not happy with each other at all, potentially hostile, a black and Hispanic population overwhelmingly and disastrously poor, a white population trying to make ends meet, not having it easy at all. Our separateness is frightening: The public school enrollment of our biggest cities is more than 90 percent minority. (Wilentz, 1991, p. 7)

Neighborhood integration on a national level, as urged a quarter century ago, requires government intervention in the housing market, with much more government control over what the housing industry is allowed to do, and more incentives to get the industry to do the right things (Downs, 1973; U.S. Commission on Civil Rights, 1974). Hartford, Connecticut, has considered forcing the issue by razing some of its low-income housing projects, thereby pressuring the state to order the construction of low-income housing in some of the surrounding suburbs. This would distribute the poverty population more evenly throughout the metropolitan area (Johnson, 1991).

It is ironic that rich folks want to keep poor folks out, and yet rich folks themselves are now invading the neighborhoods of the poor. The well-to-do are engaging in a process called "gentrification," purchasing city dwellings in poor neighborhoods, evicting the poor or hiring thugs to terrorize them, refurbishing the dwellings, and then selling or renting them to other rich folks. The reason rich people want to live in cities like New York is to be close to where they work and to the cultural events the region offers. Alas, the poor pushed out to make room for the rich cannot afford to move to the suburbs. Many of them end up in welfare hotels or in abandoned buildings without heat or running water. Others take to living on the streets as part of the growing population of homeless people.

Those who maintain that the races will not reconcile during our lifetimes and that neighborhood integration is a dream should look to the city of Shaker Heights, Ohio, where the dream has been a reality for more than thirty years. That reality exists because of the city's determination. For example, the city provides low-cost loans to black or white families who move into neighborhoods dominated by the other race. The elementary schools offer race sensitivity training. The city even makes attempts to make sure that block parties are integrated. Shaker Heights is an affluent community that decided it could integrate without losing that affluence. And it was sophisticated enough to realize that integrating in a racist nation requires a continuing effort (Wilkerson, 1991a).

In a similar vein, the town of Matteson, Illinois, forty miles south of Chicago, launched a $37,000 advertising campaign to attract affluent white families and stabilize the town's racial balance ("Illinois Town, Fearing Racial Imbalance, to Advertise for Whites," 1995).

Unless the suburbs, too, are integrated, the pattern in Boston will remain the national pattern:

So desegregation does not get pushed very far—instead, we get a little, but not too much. Virtually no scholar looking at Boston and lacking any personal interest in defense of the desegregation process there has failed to see that the lower classes did the desegregating, the middle classes did the fleeing, either immediately or after a short trial (some stayed because their children traveled on insulated or relatively "safe" tracks to the sixth grade and then escaped into the six-year Latin schools), while the affluent were exempt from the start. (Formisano, 1991, p. 232)

## Making the Only Choice

It might seem too costly to integrate the schools and communities of the United States. The busing costs for school integration might be low enough for the tax-payers to take on this burden, but the cost of housing allowances for residential integration could demand too much sacrifice. Given the federal budget deficit, housing allowances could also be what former President Reagan referred to as "budget busters." Taxpayers might well resent using their hard-earned income to subsidize the housing of people they consider unworthy. Politicians have successfully exploited resentment toward the poor by promising to "roll back all those government handouts."

To a large extent, in fact, that is what happened with the "Welfare Reform" of 1996. The middle and upper classes staged a political backlash against the poor. It became popular to think that the problems of poverty could be dealt with *cheaply;* in some circles, increased misery was even considered the most effective way to snap the poor out of their poverty. In addition, the genetic argument arose. Some said that the poor were poor because they were "natu-rally" dumb and shiftless. They were born that way, just as if they had been born with an incurable disease. Nature *meant* them to be poor, and they were too brutish even to resent it much.

This kind of thinking has resurfaced in the writings of people like Herrnstein and Murray (1994) and Levin (1998), but it is an indulgence the United States no longer can afford. It is selfish thinking; but, ironically, the best answer is selfish thinking *that is more realistic.* It is unrealistic to think that the problems of the poor do not affect the rest of us.

We may not want to incur the costs of school reorganization and busing, but those costs can still be smaller than the property and insurance losses due to urban crime, and the productivity losses due to high jobless rates. We may not want to bear the costs of integrated housing, but such housing can still be cheaper than building prisons for criminals whose breeding ground is the ghetto. We may wish we could forego the initial tensions, suspicions, and hostil-ity of intergroup association, but these feelings are still easier to cope with than the riots and physical assaults—or even just the constant threat of them—that result from group alienation. We may want our children to acquire a competi-tive edge in the occupational marketplace against the children of the poor, but with the United States workforce declining numerically, with the structure of future work so difficult to predict, and with a growing elderly population requiring support, it might well be in our mutual interest to fully develop *everyone's* talents. We might wish to treat our minority citizens as though they were citizens of a developing country, but we can hardly expect to be spared Los Angeles-type rioting if we do.

## Is the Problem Solved After Almost Fifty Years?

We can choose to ignore the problems of segregation in our society and hope that they will vanish in time. We can do as we've done for so long: treat the problems with Band-Aids and lip service. Or we can determine that the problems must be eliminated. The last choice is the one most clearly in our self-interest, and in the interest of our consciences. Moreover, public opinion is swaying in this direction. In 1971, 43 percent of the public thought that integration improved education for black children, and 23 percent thought it also helped white children. In 1988, 55 percent thought that it helped blacks and 35 percent believed that white students benefit, too, an increase of 12 percent in each category. Additionally, in 1973, 30 percent of the public thought that we should do more to integrate the schools; in 1988, this figure was 37 percent (Gallup and Elam, 1988, p. 39). And this was at the end of the Reagan era, after a long federal retreat from integration as a goal. In 1993, a majority of both blacks and whites said in a *New York Times*/CBS poll that they favored full integration (Jones, 1994). Obviously, some will define the term more restrictively than others, but the general sentiment that integration is good reveals the angels to whom the appeal for full integration should be addressed.

In 1994, the *New York Times Magazine* carried an article entitled "We're All Racist Now" (Bissinger, 1994). The title quote is from a white woman who sent her daughters to the newly integrated school in her community and who worked to make that school a success. Her discouragement at the behavior of the black students and the indifference of their parents is what prompted her remark. You may think that her experience and reaction would better support Position 2 of this chapter. But her experiences are the cautionary note this side of the debate must end on.

As a society, we must address some ominous signs. Integration works, and it is consistent with the American ideals of a diverse society of equal people. But integration, after so many years of slavery and then segregation, requires more than laws and press statements. The general will to make integration a reality forms as we correct the long-term systems that oppress or restrict opportunities for minorities. Affirmative action is but one example of a way to correct previous discrimination, but it provides some good examples of the problem. When the board of trustees of the University of California system, over the protests of faculty and administration, voted to end affirmative action in admissions, the admission of African American students at the Berkeley campus law school dropped 81 percent. African American admissions to the undergraduate programs at Berkeley made up 7.6 percent of the total in 1997, before the board's action, and they dropped to 2 percent in 1998. Much of this decline occurred because qualified African Americans did not feel comfortable at such an institution and applied elsewhere. Proposition 209 in California outlawed affirmative action; if it were a nationwide policy, it would further increase segregation. The struggle to end slavery was long and difficult, as was the struggle for civil rights a hundred years later—and the last struggle, for a fully integrated society, will be a long one as well. We have no choice but to get on with it, patiently and persistently, and to leave a legacy for which future generations will be profoundly grateful.

## POSITION 2: AGAINST LEGAL INTEGRATION

### Keeping Government Off Our Backs

Let's not mince words: "Legal" integration is simply a euphemism for *forced* integration. Integration forced on us by law is as objectionable as segregation forced on us by law. Legal integration is as contrary to the freedoms the U.S. Constitution guarantees us as legal segregation was. Integration must stand on its own, with public support. Thinking whites and blacks recognize the falsity and hypocrisy of forced integration, just as they recognized it in forced segregation.

States like Colorado, Ohio, and others are moving toward policies like Proposition 209, which passed in California and eliminates racial preferences by any government agency (Masci, 1998). This referendum approach to cutting back govenment interference is a legitimate reaction to overkill by rabid integrationists. They had instituted race-based quotas to legally force integration in schools and workplaces, but it backfired. Neither apartheid nor "togetherheid" will ensure lasting peace between the races; people's decisions and behaviors determine whether living together or apart works best.

One can be an integrationist without being rabidly so. The rabid integrationist is willing to invoke all the forces of government to bring about a goal the Constitution does *not* guarantee. Our slave-owning Founding Fathers did not even envision a racially integrated society, let alone guarantee it (Higginbotham, 1978). However desirable a racially integrated society may be, it is not the government's role to force such a society on free individuals, black and white. If an integrated society is to emerge in the United States, it must happen through the *uncoerced* interactions of individuals. What kind of integration occurs under the pressure of courts and police? Look how busing has transformed local schools into warring camps and merely reinstituted segregation.

Federal Judge John Parker, "a moderate jurist who had issued several racially progressive rulings" (Wilkinson, 1979, p. 81), interpreted the *Brown* decision in the only reasonable way:

> A state may not deny to any person on account of race the right to attend any school that it maintains . . . but if the schools which it maintains are open to children of all races, no violation of the Constitution is involved even though the children of different races voluntarily attend different schools, as they attend different churches. Nothing in the Constitution or in the [*Brown*] decision of the Supreme Court takes away from the people the freedom to choose the schools they attend. The Constitution, in other words, does not require integration. It does not forbid such discrimination as occurs as the result of voluntary action. It merely forbids the use of governmental power to enforce segregation. (*Briggs v. Elliott*, 1955)

Exactly forty years later, Supreme Court Justice Clarence Thomas, in his concurring opinion in the *Missouri v. Jenkins* case (1995), echoed Judge Parker's opinion.

The freedoms the Constitution guarantees us are largely freedoms *from* government. The Founders had fought a war to rid themselves of the restraints of a repressive British government. They wanted a government that would be restrained from interfering in the affairs of its citizens. As Thomas Jefferson said, "That government governs best which governs least."

Tyranny can creep up on us in small steps, and so government must not take any steps that are not absolutely essential for the common good. Even when the proposed government action appears benevolent, we must raise the question as to whether the result of that action is worth the loss of individual freedom that will inevitably occur.

For example, in 1974, members of the U.S. Congress became dismayed at the number of deaths resulting from automobile accidents. They then passed a law requiring all newly manufactured cars to contain an alarm system that would continue sounding until a car's occupants had fastened their seat belts. People who hated to buckle up might find that the sound drove them crazy as they traveled, but "better nuts than dead" was Congress's reasoning. Others reasoned differently: However benign its intention, Congress was protecting a large number of people *against their will* and had thereby abrogated too much basic human freedom. Congress soon rescinded the law, at the urging of both liberals and conservatives. (The increasing cost of automobile insurance may have caused people to be more forbearing toward state laws requiring the use of seat belts.)

The next time you are tempted to support government interference in the private lives of your fellow citizens for their own good—perhaps, for example, in the form of a government ban on all tobacco smoking—pause to consider some of the many actions the government could compel you to do in support of your best interests. Do you like whipped cream, high-quality beefsteak, watching TV into the wee hours and suffering sleep deprivation? The government could control most of your waking hours in the sincere belief that it was protecting your health and safety and making you a better person. But each time the government gets to control you at all, it acquires an argument for controlling you further. People who are behaving well *under duress* have hardly been ennobled.

## The Affront to Blacks

One assumption compulsory integrationists make is so offensive that it demands discussion in a section by itself. This is the belief that blacks long for the chance to live and work among whites. This assumption brings integrationists close to being racists. Behind it is the further assumption that blacks *should* want to live and work with whites. However, the integrationists do not generally make the reverse assumption—that whites should want to live and work with blacks. Thus, the compulsory integrationist position is insulting and condescending to blacks because it presumes to know and represent their real feelings. The last Gallup poll to sample opinions about busing to integrate schools showed that fully 31 percent of blacks opposed it (Gallup and Elam, 1988). Since 78 percent of whites also opposed busing, it may be that both races want good schools for their children, period. They do not necessarily crave the chance to mingle with each other.

By 1988, the Gallup organization no longer asked about busing, but just whether enough was being done to integrate the schools. Fifty-four percent of the respondents thought it was ("Special Report on Education," 1988). By 1989, Gallup had switched to asking what could be done to improve inner-city schools. The 1994 Gallup poll contained no questions on integration or urban schools, reflecting the prevalence of other educational concerns among the public (Elam, Rose, and Gallup, 1994).

It is true that black organizations, particularly the National Association for the Advancement of Colored People (NAACP), have initiated much of the school desegregation litigation. However, it is overreaching to infer from this that blacks want integration per se. As Ogbu points out:

> Blacks and Mexican Americans who supported desegregation did so primarily because they believed that desegregation would enable their children to receive the same kind of education as white children. The underlying black assumption . . . is that chances are greater that their children will receive equal or quality education if they attend the same classes with white children. Many parents said that in a desegregated school, classroom minority and white children would be exposed to the same curriculum materials and other resources and would most likely be treated alike by teachers and other school personnel . . . *the perspective on the desegregation situation given by these parents is not the same as that held by social scientists* [emphasis added]. (1986, p. 40)

Thus, what blacks want is not necessarily integration, but equal educational opportunity. This is what Kenneth Clark, the black psychologist whose evidence was so influential in the Supreme Court's *Brown* decision, meant when he argued for equal schools regardless of integration (Clark, 1965). It is what the advocates of Afrocentric schools mean when they demand equality of resources while recognizing that Afrocentrism itself is a powerful antidote to the paucity of resources:

> The biggest problem with Afrocentrism, at least as it's practiced at the grade school level, is that it has distracted attention from far more pressing issues like overcrowding, crumbling facilities, the violence in and around schools, lagging technology, the dearth of even the most basic supplies. . . . In these circumstances, tinkering with the curriculum can help when it lifts spirits, motivates teachers, parents, and children, and inspires a commitment to excellence. (Mosle, 1993, p. 82)

This is not a call for integration, but for educational opportunity and excellence. It echoes the pride Vern Smith feels when he recalls the segregated school he attended in Mississippi: "By the conventional wisdom of the day, we were the lowest of the low: black kids in a segregated school in the poorest, most violent of the Southern states. But we never saw ourselves as powerless victims; [our] teachers drummed into us that it was possible to overcome, but it took preparation. Knowledge was power, so we strove to empower ourselves." The success rate for the graduates of that segregated school is remarkable (Smith, 1994, p. 53).

The pride that blacks take in their own schools and the success they enjoy through these schools is now becoming evident at the collegiate level. In the push for integration, the federal courts are threatening the existence of historically black colleges in the southern states. The survival of these colleges has become a major goal among blacks, who see in them a nurturing environment absent from integrated institutions (Constantine, 1994; Smothers, 1994; Ware, 1994; Sowell, 1999).

John Ogbu notes that blacks are often disappointed by desegregated schools. They find that the schools become segregated inside, with the black children shunted disproportionately into special classes for problem students (Ogbu, 1986, p. 41). After all the agony Bostonians endured to integrate their schools so that children would have better educational opportunities, what was the result? "Far and away the gravest failures in the Boston story concern the continuation of generally poor instruction. The number of students denied promotions is still significant, and it reveals a sorry state of affairs. Academic achievement has been improved in a few schools but such is not the case in most" (Dentler and Scott, 1981, p. 233).

Integration is palatable to many whites only when their children constitute a large majority of the students in an integrated school. When white representation drops below 75 percent of the student body, the "tipping point" is reached, and whites start pulling out. Therefore, the usual integration pattern is to send black youngsters from segregated schools where they are a majority to integrated schools where they are a distinct minority. Metropolitan integration is intended to keep blacks in this minority status so that whites will not become unduly alarmed. The predictable result for black children—for any children—when they are put into a strange and hostile environment is that their self-esteem drops. "Many researchers have found that black children tend to indicate a higher degree of self-esteem than white children, but that desegregation often has a discouraging effect . . . desegregation tends to threaten the self-esteem of minority children" (St. John, 1981, p. 91). Another researcher reports:

> The desegregated experience, then, is one of enhanced awareness of the broader society's negative attitudes towards one's race. . . . In segregated settings, the self-esteem of black children from separated or never-married families is just as high as that of children from intact families; but in the desegregated setting, it is substantially lower. In addition, in desegregated settings, black children are more likely to be poorer than those around them than in the segregated settings. In several important respects, social comparisons tend to be more unfavorable in desegregated than in segregated settings. (Rosenberg, 1986, pp. 186–187)

What black parent should be expected to subject his or her child to the psychological torment attendant on integrated education? Some might find this a reasonable price for their children to pay in exchange for improved academic performance. Unfortunately, the evidence for the effect of integration on black academic achievement is not at all clear. The data are "mixed and ambiguous" (Granovetter, 1986, p. 99). "The very best studies available demonstrate no significant and consistent effects of desegregation on black achievement" (Armor, 1984, p. 58). Is this indeterminate result worth the price paid in lower self-esteem?

An illuminating study on this issue is that of Meier, Stewart, and England (1989). They looked at what they call "second-generation discrimination," that is, discrimination that occurs in desegregated schools. They examined schools in 174 districts, of at least 15,000 students each. They found that black students were *overrepresented* in classes for the educable mentally impaired and the trainable mentally impaired; among students receiving corporal punishment, suspensions, and expulsions; and among dropouts. Black students were *underrepresented* only among students in gifted classes and among those graduating. The more desegregated the school, the higher the level of resegregation within. A school with a high percentage of black teachers and relatively affluent black families is much less likely to experience this internal segregation. Should black parents in the 21st century be expected to relegate their children to in-school conditions that may well be as damaging as the between-school conditions that existed prior to 1954?

Now that they are familiar with the alleged benefits of school integration, blacks themselves have lost enthusiasm for it. In Louisville, Kentucky, the local chapter of the NAACP did not oppose a proposal to eliminate school busing and return to racially segregated neighborhood schools, though in previous years it had been an ardent advocate of busing (Marriott, 1991). The NAACP continues to face a sizable and strong internal challenge to their long-held support for integration; at their 1997 meeting, the anti-integration movement had become a very vocal and increasingly large minority of NAACP members (Hentoff, 1997).

Ward Connerly is an African American member of the board of trustees for the University of California. He is the leader of the successful effort to dismantle that university's quota-based affirmative action program for admissions. He believes quota policies actually damage black and other minority students because the standards for college admission or jobs are lowered for these students in order to meet an arbitrary quota. Connerly argues that some of the minority students or employees fully meet all criteria, but their qualifications are diminished by the perception that all minorities were admitted on a quota basis. Those who do not meet the full criteria, says Connerly, get the mistaken idea that they do not have to compete directly with their white counterparts, and they drop out in large numbers when they encounter that competition. Further, race quotas hide the educational deficiencies of schools in ghetto areas; it is those schools that need to change, not the college admission departments or employers. Race quotas force an artificial integration that dissolves into bitter resegregation.

## Giving Government Manageable Tasks

Nothing breeds disrespect for government so much as its failures. We have become used to hearing such expressions as a "government mess" and a "real government foul-up." The messes and foul-ups often occur because the government arrogantly decides to take on a task beyond its capability. Even if it does so reluctantly in response to public pressure, the result may be the same. The job may be so complicated that no human agency can do it well, ensuring failure.

Sometimes the government invites predictable disasters, which then make it such an object of ridicule that people start breaking the law in contempt for the government's bungling. A good example of this is the widespread practice of cheating on taxes. Many people rationalize that it's all right to cheat because even officials of the Internal Revenue Service concede that the tax collection system is unnecessarily confusing and unfair. At other times, the law so tramples on a cherished right that breaking the law becomes an honorable pastime. Prohibition violated people's assumed right to drink alcohol, and they defied it with zest. Exceeding the 55 m.p.h. speed limit on highways is another example. In instances such as these, the government is reduced to ignoring or repealing its laws or facing public defiance that would make enforcement a nightmare.

The right of association is a cherished American right from the Bill of Rights. The government has already curtailed this right by prohibiting people who engage in most forms of commerce from discriminating. This government action is designed to prevent a harm: the denial of fair opportunity to minorities. For the government to go the next step and insist that people integrate (associate) with groups they dislike is to provoke wholesale defiance of the law. "Most groups (racial and ethnic) prefer to live among their own kind. While this may look and have the same effects as prejudice, it really is different. For one thing, it may affect blacks in the same way as whites. For another, the housing decision is not one based on prejudice against a specific group" (Glazer, 1981, p. 138). Henry Louis Gates has captured how rich and emotionally fulfilling life can be for blacks in a segregated community in his memoir of growing up in such a community in West Virginia (Gates, 1994). As a black woman who grew up in Alabama puts it: "We had our own doctors, our own soda shops. We didn't have the psychic pressure of feeling uncomfortable, of feeling less than. We didn't have or need a Jesse Jackson on the national level saying 'I am somebody,' because it came from our teachers, our churches, the man who ran the movie theater" (Nellie Hester-Bailey, quoted by Jones, 1994, p. 40). And integration may actually harm black businesses (Rymer, 1998). Moreover, people, both black and white, who live in the suburbs consider their residence a reward for achievement. They will not tolerate government intrusion into that hard-earned sanctuary. If a person's home is his or her castle, the neighborhood around it is the moat. And to maintain the dollar value of the castle, it is necessary to maintain the quality of the moat.

The task of enforcing compulsory integration would be monumental even if it were tolerated. Many, many more government officials would have to be hired to carry out this task alone. They would have to keep track of racial proportions community by community to ensure that each area achieved the "correct" balance. They would, of course, first have to decide what the correct balance should be for each community and school. As the proportions became imbalanced, they would need to make continual adjustments to restore the right racial mix. School attendance patterns would be redrawn regularly—perhaps every year—to make the numbers satisfy some bureaucrat. Housing allowances for families and construction permits for builders would be subject to constant government manipulation. Altogether, it would be a tremendous task of social engineering—one that government already has proved unable to handle, and one that would cause endless exasperation for everyone concerned. It might succeed in uniting blacks and whites, but only in their disgust with the government. A good example of how the best-laid plans of government can go awry in large-scale social planning appears in Daniel Patrick Moynihan's aptly titled book *Maximum Feasible Misunderstanding* (1969). He details some of the consequences of the War on Poverty program that *no one* intended.

The U.S. Supreme Court raised a series of questions that suggested how difficult the task of metropolitan school integration would be when it rejected the attempt to integrate the Detroit metropolitan region:

> Entirely apart from the logistical and other serious problems attending large-scale transportation of students, the consolidation would give rise to an array of other problems in financing and operating this new school system. Some of the more obvious questions would be: What would be the status of authority of the present popularly elected school boards? Would the children of Detroit be within the jurisdiction and operating control of a school board elected by parents and residents of other districts? What board or boards would levy taxes for school operations in these 54 districts constituting the consolidated metropolitan area? What provision could be made for assuring substantial equality in tax levies among the 54 districts, if this were deemed requisite? What provisions would be made for financing? Would the validity of long-term bonds be jeopardized unless approved by all of the component districts as well as the State? What body would determine that portion of the curricula now left to the discretion of local school boards? Who would establish attendance zones, purchase school equipment, locate and construct new schools, and indeed attend to all the myriad day-to-day decisions that are necessary to school operations affecting potentially more than three-quarters of a million pupils? (*Bradley v. Milliken*, 1974)

These questions suggest the tumult that will ensue if any government body attempts metropolitan desegregation, a step that has no Constitutional imperative and is likely to thwart any educational rationale.

It is important to bear in mind that the compulsory integrationists do not limit their benevolence to blacks. They are more altruistic than that. They also seek to integrate into the American mainstream Hispanics and the poor in general. The grander the goals of the integrationists, the greater the government action needed to achieve them. So all the difficulties we have been discussing are going to become even worse. Moreover, the huge expansion of the public, or government, sector of society called for by the integrationists' ambitious agenda will necessarily reduce the size of the private, or productive, sector. In other words, the *revenue-producing* sector of society will be reduced and the *revenue-consuming* sector will grow. This obviously will have negative consequences for the health of the U.S. economy, but just how negative will depend on how zealously the compulsory integrationists pursue their dreams.

The Kansas City, Missouri, schools are a case in point. The federal judge presiding over that district did not *compel* metropolitan integration, but he was hell-bent on fostering it. He succeeded in forcing the people of Missouri to pay a sharply higher tax so that the schools in Kansas City could be made more attractive, with the hope that these schools would then lure suburban white students. More than $1.3 billion was spent on this effort, with no significant effect either on integration or on the performance of the black students (Celis, 1995). Surely Missouri has pressing economic needs that would have been much better served by leaving this money in the taxpayers' hands. The judge's gamble, like all overweening government schemes, is but one example of the danger of know-it-all government. The judge's most recent ruling that the Kansas City schools would remain under his desegregation order until the students' test scores had improved was a horrible conflation of racial neutrality with academic performance. Fortunately, the parties agreed to try to work their way out of this quagmire through negotiations (Schmidt, 1995), and the Supreme Court has curtailed the district judge's control of the Kansas City schools (*Missouri v. Jenkins*, 1995).

We can get some sense of the risk by looking at the state of the former Soviet economy. The Soviets had a centrally planned society with a massive government bureaucracy, and their budget deficit grew to be as high as 20 percent of their national income (Shelton, 1989). Our deficit has been kept below 6 percent, which explains why former communists are trying to become capitalists. We should not be adopting practices they are rejecting after long and bitter experience, when disentangling from these practices is a nightmarish ordeal.

## Challenging Other Integrationist Assumptions

All the aggravation and pervasive government control of our lives might be worth bearing if the results could be predicted, with some certainty, to be beneficial. However, we cannot know beforehand whether the results will be beneficial at all, let alone how beneficial. The compulsory integrationists act as though their *assumptions* about the benefits are already proven facts. In making these assumptions, the integrationists may be guilty of nothing more than excessive optimism about human nature. But even so, to base social policy on their Pollyanna attitudes is to take a dangerous gamble.

A corollary to the assumption that all blacks want to be integrated with whites is the assumption that different groups will grow to respect each other if they are forced to live and work in close contact. The danger is that they might, in fact, grow to dislike each other so much that instead of having a productive relationship, they will develop bitter enmity. It is true that some cases of forced integration have turned out reasonably well. Unfortunately, these cases are more than offset by cases in which physical violence was a recurring event, and even now, years later, mutual antagonism and tension exists between the groups. A series of studies on the interactions between blacks and whites in integrated schools in both the south and the north reached the following conclusions:

> The racial cleavage reported time and again in these studies suggests that while the student populations may have been desegregated, they were not integrated . . . For most participants, school desegregation spelled trouble, and to keep it at arm's length was thought to be success enough. . . . Violence was thought to be just below the surface of daily behavior . . . the racial attribute of being 'white' carried high status, while that of being a member of a racial minority carried low status. Given that so many members of the minority groups were also economically poor meant that status characteristics were reinforced with class characteristics. (Rist, 1979, pp. 8–10)

What worked in the more positive cases may be unique to the contexts they unfolded in, and since we cannot be sure what *those* were, we cannot know how to apply the lessons from these cases to other situations. But we do know there were a lot of unhappy cases. One sad situation developed at a senior prom a few years ago at Brother Rice High School, an integrated Catholic school in Chicago. The black students, who constituted only about 12 percent of the senior class, felt so excluded from the prom planning that they held their own, separate prom (Wilkerson, 1991b). There is just too much at stake for us to rely on government by guess and wishful thinking in the matter of integration. As a California newspaper said in opposition to the forced integration of the Berkeley schools: "The board of education is destroying a city to test a theory" (quoted in Kirp, 1982, p. 161).

A second assumption of the compulsory integrationists is that the downtrodden will respond to kindness with gratitude. "Just give 'em a chance and they'll come around," is the thinking. However, it's possible that the downtrodden will perceive kindness as a weakness to exploit. During the high-tide years of the War on Poverty in the late 1960s and early 1970s, the poor and minorities spent a good deal of time not reforming their lives, but ripping off the system that was trying to help them (Lemann, 1988–1989). If the abuses are not as great today, it's because the benefits have been cut back, so there are fewer opportunities for abuse. The integrationists may have naive notions about human nature, or, at least, notions that cannot be generalized to *every* human being. At any rate, it is possible that some people's personalities have been so damaged, either by genetic predisposition or life experience or both, that kindness is a medicine that will no longer work. The bleeding-heart integrationists refuse to acknowledge that such a grim situation is even possible.

## Sparing the Innocent

It is indisputable that the United States has a horrible history of racism. In recent decades, however, we have made remarkable progress in removing its overt manifestations. This progress has affected attitudes as well, so that racism no longer constantly lurks in the American mind as it once did. The laws that forbade racist behavior among the older generations of Americans have gradually caused many people of those generations to purge themselves of racist attitudes, which they now look back on with shame. The younger generations, with a few well-publicized exceptions are generally far freer of racist behavior, and they have learned from schools and the media that racist attitudes are discreditable.

And yet it is the younger generations from whom the compulsory integrationists expect the greatest sacrifice in their bold experiment. Young married couples and their children are being asked to redeem the United States from its legacy of racism. School integration will involve them directly; all the trauma will be visited upon them as though they personally must make restitution for the crimes of others. Worse, it will be visited on them by people who have arranged to avoid it for themselves, as Nathan Glazer has noted:

> The leading advocates of transportation for integration—journalists, political figures, and judges—send their children to private schools which escape the consequences of these legal decisions. This does raise a moral question. The judges who impose such decisions, the lawyers who argue . . . for them would not themselves send their children to the schools to which, by their actions, others poorer and less mobile than they are must send their children. Those not subject to a certain condition are insisting that others submit themselves to it, which offends the basic rule of morality in both the Jewish and Christian traditions. (quoted in Wilkinson, 1979, p. 210)

If we could be sure that the school integration experiments would go smoothly, it would be reasonable to subject innocent children to the inconveniences for the long-term good of society. The resistance is not to an integrated society per se, or even to using children in bringing about that goal. The resistance, the absolute refusal, stems from fear of gratuitous harm to the innocent of both races.

This harm can take several forms, as past integration experiments have shown. First, children are forced into close and constant association with other children who have violent tendencies. For whites to connect violence with black youngsters is not irrational when the number of firearm homicides among blacks aged 19 or younger is greater than that for their white peers, even though there are far fewer adolescent blacks than adolescent whites (*The State of America's Children*, 1994, p. ix). How the violent children get that way is beside the point; they threaten and sometimes inflict physical harm on children who have done nothing to provoke it. And the possibilities of physical harm do not stop short of killing. The innocent child may not even be an intended victim but just someone who was in the path of a stray bullet. Second, some children may use the threat of physical harm to extort money from frightened peers. Some schoolchildren have gone without lunch because other students were extorting their lunch money, and they were too terrified to tell even their parents. Third, the availability of drugs in or near the school is likely to increase, as are the pressures to engage in drug abuse. This risk is made all the more intolerable as newer drugs are formulated for easy manufacture, some of which irreparably damage the body. Fourth, the school's academic mission will become more diffuse as it must accommodate students of different abilities. As the school's focus blurs, energy and resources will be spread more thinly than when they were more narrowly concentrated. Everyone will lose. Fifth, a less homogeneous (less segregated, if you will) school community will cause a loss of school spirit. Neither students nor parents will be able to identify with the school as they did when it more fully reflected their own values and aspirations.

The list of the harms that can and do result from school integration experiments indicates that blacks as well as whites run the risk of a worse educational experience. For blacks who are transported from a predominantly black school near their homes to an overwhelmingly white school miles away, the sense of being an unwelcome outsider can be most dispiriting. Just as innocent white children ought not to be victimized by the integrationists' grand schemes, innocent black children should not lose their most valuable possession—their sense of self-worth. Putting that in jeopardy is a serious matter, and it should not be done given the weaknesses of our present state of social policy forecasting.

Finally, the fundamental difference between the compulsory integrationists and those who oppose them is not the goal they want to achieve. We all wish for an integrated society. The difference lies in each group's sense of the possible, and in the opposing group's conviction that good intentions are not enough. It would be wonderful to have a better society but, given the fragility of human relationships, it would be quite easy to create one that's worse.

It is fitting that some final word be given to William Bradford Reynolds, the U.S. assistant attorney general for civil rights during the Reagan administration. Reynolds fought hard, in the face of much slander, to restore morality and common sense to American education:

> We have learned something from this unfortunate social experiment, which has led needlessly to the sacrificing of quality education on the altar of racial balance. It is a lesson that should not soon be forgotten, with respect to school desegregation or civil rights generally. We must always be aware of the danger to an individual's civil rights that lurks in group-oriented policies grounded on racial preferences, racial balancing, and proportionality. If we ever succumb to this threat, the great civil rights movement will have tragically, and unnecessarily, exhausted all credibility. Once the noble ideal of equal opportunity is compromised, it is not easily retrieved, and all Americans suffer. (1986, p. 13)

## All in Due Course

Integration is taking place in the United States because of the natural goodwill of the American people. "From 1980 to 1990, the black population in the suburbs grew by 34.4 percent, the Hispanic population by 69.3 percent, and the Asian population by 125.9 percent. By contrast, the white population in the suburbs increased by 9.2 percent" (DeWitt, 1994, p. 1). Moreover, "the percentage of all black families earning incomes of $50,000 or more (as adjusted to 1992) dollars rose from 10.2 percent in 1970 to 16 percent in 1992. . . . The percentage of blacks in professional or managerial jobs rose from 10 percent to 16.8 percent in the same period. And the percentage of blacks 25 to 29 years old who had completed at least four years of college more than doubled, from 6 percent in 1970 to 12.7 percent in 1989" (Jones, 1994, p. 40). The percentage of blacks 18 to 24 years old enrolled in college compares favorably with the percentage of whites of this age (Bennett, 1995, p. 9). School completion rates are almost identical (Rothstein, 1998).

Current generations are well-motivated in matters of race; we can be trusted to do the right thing. Big Brother schemes that attempt to accelerate progress beyond its natural flow create eddies and currents that only make the progress more difficult and may even reverse its course.

The great black leader and educator, W. E. B. DuBois, said it best sixty years ago:

> To sum up this: Theoretically the Negro needs neither segregated schools nor mixed schools. What he needs is Education. What he must remember is that there is no magic, either in mixed schools or in segregated schools. A mixed school with poor and unsympathetic teachers, with hostile public opinion, and no teaching of truth concerning black folk, is bad. A segregated school with ignorant placeholders, inadequate equipment, poor salaries, and wretched housing, is equally bad. Other things being equal, the mixed school is the broader, more natural basis for the education of all youth. It gives wider contacts; it inspires greater self-confidence; and suppresses the inferiority complex. But other things seldom are equal, and in that case, Sympathy, Knowledge, and the Truth, outweigh all that the mixed school can offer. (1935, p. 335)

## For Discussion

1. In 1972–1973:

   64 percent of black children, and

   57 percent of Latino children
   > attended schools that were predominantly minority segregated

   by 1994–1995:

   67 percent of black children, and

   74 percent of Latino children
   > attended schools that were predominantly minority segregated

   *Source:* Orfield, G., Bachmeier, M., James, D., and Eitle, T. (1997). *Deepening Segregation in American Public Schools.* Cambridge, MA: Harvard University School of Education.

   What does this say about desegregation and integration? What are the plausible reasons for this increasing segregation? What are the most suitable responses to this shift?

2. When given several choices and asked for the three most effective strategies for improving schools, over one thouand adults in a recent survey in the Detroit area responded as is shown in Table 4.1.

   What accounts for the consistencies and inconsistencies between the views of whites and blacks in this survey? Why would both groups rate integration so low compared with the other items? What would you hypothesize would have been the responses in 1960? What do you think they might be in 2020?

3. If, as William Julius Wilson contends, black children in the inner city are isolated from good role models as well as from good job contacts, how can we

**TABLE 4.1 Survey Responses on School Improvement in the Detroit Area**

| Improvement | Percentage | |
|---|---|---|
| | Whites | Blacks |
| More or better teachers | 67% | 54% |
| More or better teaching materials | 45 | 49 |
| More programs for stronger students | 18 | 10 |
| More programs for weaker students | 49 | 55 |
| More programs to help parents cope | 22 | 29 |
| More security in schools | 17 | 39 |
| Better buildings | 6 | 12 |
| More discipline for students | 62 | 48 |
| **School Integration** | **6** | **4** |

Source: Welch, S., et al. (1997). "Race or Place: Emerging Perspectives on Urban Education." *Political Science and Politics* 30(3), 456.

break this isolation? What effects do you think this isolation has on black children and on white children? How would policies supporting integration or segregation influence these effects? How do local practices that shift communities toward or away from integration influence these effects?

4. Racial integration or segregation can be measured in a variety of ways. Since going to college is one noted pathway to economic and social success, measuring the number of black college students can provide one small indicator of the course of integration in society. Large state universities offer comprehensive academic programs that attract a variety of students, and state financial support keeps tuition costs lower. Table 4.2 shows the trends in black student enrollment at some of these state universities.

What might account for the increase or decline in the porportion of black students at these universities? Check a library for the U.S. Department of Education statistics for college enrollment of minority students in your state for the past several years. What do they show in regard to integration?

5. Different regions of the United States differ in the percentage of black students who attend schools that are at least 90 percent minority. The most segregated schools are *not* in the south, where some of the most devastating legal and social segregation occurred prior to the *Brown* decision. In fact, western and southern states have about the same proportion of the most segregated schools in the United States. Figure 4.1 shows the proportions.

What are some possible reasons for the disparity by region? What are the schools like, in terms of integration, in your hometown? in your college town? If integration fails, where does that leave the American society? What impacts can you expect in education, jobs, neighborhoods, social structure, and general lifestyle?

**TABLE 4.2  Black Students as a Percentage of All Students**

|  | 1980 | 1993 |
| --- | --- | --- |
| University of Illinois | 3.9% | 6.0% |
| University of California, Berkeley | 3.6 | 5.4 |
| University of Michigan | 5.3 | 7.8 |
| University of Oklahoma | 3.9 | 6.4 |
| Ohio State University | 5.1 | 6.6 |
| University of Georgia | 4.5 | 5.8 |
| University of Virginia | 7.2 | 8.9 |
| University of Missouri | 3.7 | 4.0 |
| University of Connecticut | 3.6 | 3.6 |
| University of Arkansas | 5.7 | 5.0 |
| Rutgers University | 10.2 | 7.3 |
| Indiana University | 5.6 | 4.0 |

*Source:* Slater, R. B. (1996). "The Progress of Blacks at the Flagship State Universities." *Journal of Blacks in Higher Education* 11, p. 72. Compiled by the Journal using statistics from the U.S. Department of Education. Enrollment data are for the years shown only.

FIGURE 4.1

**Percentage of Black Students Attending Highly Segregated Schools, 1991–1992**

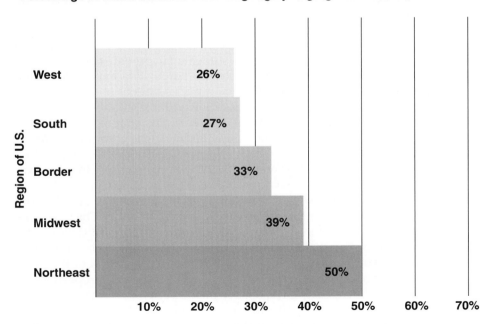

**Source:  Jost, K. (1996). "Rethinking School Integration."** *Congressional Quarterly Researcher* **6(39), p. 916.**

# References

ARMOR, D. (1984). *The Evidence on Desegregation and Black Achievement.* Washington, DC: National Institute of Education.

BENNETT, C. (1995). *The Black Population in the United States: March 1994 and 1993.* Current Population Reports P20–480. Washington, DC: Bureau of the Census.

BENSMAN, D. (1987). *Quality Education in the Inner City: The Story of the Central Park East Schools.* New York: Central Park East Schools.

BISSINGER, H. (1994). "We're All Racist Now." *The New York Times Magazine,* May 29, pp. 27–33, 43, 53–56.

*Bradley v. Milliken.* (1974). 418 U.S. 717.

*Briggs v. Elliott.* (1955). 132 F. Supp. 776.

*Brown v. Board of Education of Topeka.* (1954). 347 U.S. 483.

CELIS, W. (1995). "Kansas City's Widely Debated Desegregation Experiment Reaches the Supreme Court." *The New York Times,* January 11, p. B7.

CLARK, K. (1965). *Dark Ghetto: Dilemmas of Social Power.* New York: Harper & Row.

CONARD, B. D. (1988). "Cooperative Learning and Prejudice Reduction." *Social Education* 52(4), 283–286.

CONSTANTINE, J. (1994). "The 'Added Value' of Historically Black Colleges." *Academe* 80(3), 12–17.

DENTLER, R. A., AND SCOTT, M. B. (1981). *Schools on Trial: An Inside Account of the Boston Desegregation Case.* Cambridge, MA: Abt Books.

DEWITT, K. (1994). "Wave of Suburban Growth Is Being Fed by Minorities." *The New York Times,* August 15, pp. A1, B6.

DOWNS, A. (1973) *Opening Up the Suburbs: An Urban Strategy for America.* New Haven, CT: Yale University Press.

DREIER, P. AND MOBERG, D. (1996). "Moving From the Hood." *The American Prospect.* No. 24, pp. 75–9.

DUBOIS, W. E. B. (1935). "Does the Negro Need Separate Schools?" *Journal of Negro Education,* July, pp. 328–335.

ELAM, S., ROSE, L., AND GALLUP, A. (1994). "The 26th Annual Phi Delta Kappan Gallup Poll of the Public's Attitudes Toward the Public Schools." *Phi Delta Kappan* 76(1), 41–56.

*Evans v. Buchanan.* (1976). 416 F. Supp. 328.

FORMISANO, R. (1991). *Boston Against Busing: Race, Class, and Ethnicity in the 1960s and 1970s.* Chapel Hill, NC: University of North Carolina Press.

GALLUP, A., AND ELAM, S. (1988). "The 20th Annual Gallup Poll of the Public's Attitudes Toward the Public Schools." *Phi Delta Kappan* 70(1), 33–46.

GATES, H. (1994). *Colored People.* New York: Knopf.

GLAZER, N. (1981). "Race and the Suburbs." In *Race and Schooling in the City,* edited by A. Yarmolinsky, L. Liebman, and C. S. Schelling. Cambridge, MA: Harvard University Press.

GRANOVETTER, M. (1986). "The Micro-Structure of School Desegregation." In *School Desegregation Research: New Directions in Situational Analysis,* edited by J. Prager, D. Longshore, and M. Seeman. New York: Plenum.

HAWLEY, W. D. (1981). "Increasing the Effectiveness of School Desegregation: Lessons from the Research." In *Race and Schooling in the City,* edited by A. Yarmolinsky, L. Liebman, and C. S. Schelling. Cambridge, MA: Harvard University Press.

HENTOFF, N. (1997) "The Undercutting of Thurgood Marshall—by the NAACP." *The Washington Post,* July 12.

HERRNSTEIN, C., AND MURRAY, C. (1994). *The Bell Curve.* New York: Free Press.

HIGGINBOTHAM, A. (1978). *In the Matter of Color, Race and the American Legal Process: The Colonial Period.* New York: Oxford University Press.

HOCHSCHILD, J. L. (1984). *The New American Dilemma: Liberal Democracy and School Desegregation.* New Haven, CT: Yale University Press.

————. (1997) "Is School Desegregation Still a Viable Policy Option?" *Political Science and Politics* 30(3), 458–465.

"Illinois Town, Fearing Racial Imbalance, to Advertise for Whites." (1995). *The New York Times,* April 30, p. 36.

JOHNSON, K. (1991). "Take Our Poor, Angry Hartford Tells Suburbs." *The New York Times,* February 12, pp. 1, B5.

JONES, C. (1994). "Years on Integration Road: New Views of an Old Goal." *The New York Times,* April 10, pp. 1, 40.

*Keyes v. Denver School District No. 1.* (1973). 413 U.S. 189.

KIRP, D. L. (1982). *Just Schools: The Idea of Racial Equality in American Education.* Berkeley, CA: University of California Press.

LEMANN, N. (1988–1989). "The Unfinished War." *The Atlantic Monthly* 263(1): 37–56; January 1989, pp. 53–68.

LEVIN, M. (1998). *Why Race Matters.* Westport, CT: Praeger.

LUKAS, J. A. (1985). *Common Ground: A Turbulent Decade in the Lives of Three American Families.* New York: Knopf.

MAHARD, R. E., AND CRAIN, R. L. (1983). "Research on Minority Achievement in Desegregated Schools." In *The Consequences of School Desegregation,* edited by C. H. Rossell and W. D. Hawley. Philadelphia: Temple University Press.

MARRIOTT, M. (1991). "Louisville Debates Plan to End Forced Grade School Busing." *The New York Times,* December 11, p. B13.

MASCI, D. (1998). "The Black Middle Class." *Congressional Quarterly Researcher* 8(3), January 23.

McLARIN, K. (1994). "Specter of Segregation Returns." *The New York Times,* August 11, pp. B1, B9.

MEIER, K., STEWART, J., AND ENGLAND, R. (1989). *Race, Class and Education: The Politics of Second-Generation Discrimination.* Madison: University of Wisconsin Press.

*Missouri v. Jenkins.* (1995). Case No. 93–1823.

MOSLE, S. (1993). "Separatist But Equal?" *The American Prospect,* No. 15, 73–82.

MOYNIHAN, D. (1969). *Maximum Feasible Misunderstanding: Community Action in the War on Poverty.* New York: Free Press.

OGBU, J. U. (1986). "Structural Constraints in School Desegregation." In *School Desegregation Research: New Directions in Situational Analysis,* edited by J. Prager, D. Longshore, and M. Seeman. New York: Plenum.

ORFIELD, G. (1978). *Why Must We Bus? Segregated Schools and National Policy.* Washington, DC: Brookings Institution.

————. (1993). *The Growth of Segregation in American Schools: Changing Patterns of Separation and Poverty Since 1968.* Cambridge, MA: Report of the Harvard Project on School Desegregation to the National School Boards Association.

————, ET AL. (1997). *Deepening Segregation in American Public Schools.* Cambridge, MA: Harvard University School of Education.

PEEBLES, R. (1997). "Inherently Unequal?" *Education Week* 16(20), 64.

PETTIGREW, T. F. (1981). "The Case for Metropolitan Approaches to Public-School Desegregation." In *Race and Schooling in the City,* edited by A. Yarmolinsky, L. Liebman, and C. S. Schelling. Cambridge, MA: Harvard University Press.

REYNOLDS, W. B. (1986). "Education Alternatives to Transportation Failures: The Desegregation Response to a Resegregation Dilemma." *Metropolitan Education* 1, 3–14.

RIST, R. C. (1979). "Introduction." In *Desegregated Schools: Appraisals of an American Experiment,* edited by R. C. Rist. New York: Academic Press.

ROSENBERG, R. (1986). "Self-Esteem Research: A Phenomenological Corrective." In *School Desegregation Research: New Directions in Situational Analysis,* edited by J. Prager, D. Longshore, and M. Seeman. New York: Plenum.

ROTHSTEIN, R. (1998). "Richard Rothstein Replies," *Dissent,* Winter, pp. 45–97.

RYMER, R. (1998). "Integration's Casualties," *New York Times Magazine,* Nov. 1, pp. 48–56.

SCHIFF, J. (1999). "Organizational Context for Student Achievement." Paper Presented at American Educational Research Association, Quebec, April.

SCHMIDT, P. (1995). "Accord Set in Desegregation Case in K.C." *Education Week* 14(23), 1, 4.

———. (1994). "New Magnet-School Law Emphasizes Desegregation." *Education Week* 14(13), 20.

SCHOFIELD, J. W., AND SAGAR, H. A. (1983). "Desegregation, School Practices, and Student Race Relations." In *The Consequences of School Desegregation,* edited by C. H. Rossell and W. D. Hawley. Philadelphia: Temple University Press.

SHELTON, B. (1989). *The Coming Soviet Crash: Gorbachev's Desperate Search for Credit in the Western Financial Market.* New York: Free Press.

SHIPLER, D. (1997). *A Country of Strangers.* New York: Knopf.

SMITH, V. (1994). "We Wanted to Be the Best." *Newsweek,* July 18, p. 53.

SMOTHERS, R. (1994). "Mississippi's University System Going on Trial." *The New York Times,* May 9, p. A10.

SOWELL, T. (1999). "Failure 'Pays' in Education." *Lansing* [MI] *State Journal.* Apr. 4.

"Special Report on Education." (1988). *The Gallup Report* No. 276, pp. 41–53.

*The State of America's Children.* (1994). Washington, DC: Children's Defense Fund.

*Statistical Abstract of the United States.* (1994). (114th edition). Washington, DC: U.S. Bureau of the Census.

STEELE, C. (1992). "Race and the Schooling of Black Americans." *The Atlantic Monthly,* April, pp. 68–78.

ST. JOHN, N. H. (1981). "The Effects of School Desegregation on Children: A New Look at the Research Evidence." In *Race and Schooling in the City,* edited by A. Yarmolinsky, L. Liebman, and C. S. Schelling. Cambridge, MA: Harvard University Press.

*Time for Results: The Governors 1991 Report on Education.* (1986). Washington, DC: National Governors Association.

U.S. Commission on Civil Rights. (1974). *Equal Opportunity in Suburbia.* Washington, DC: Government Printing Office.

"Vital Signs." (1998). *Journal of Blacks in Higher Education.* 20, 83.

WARE, L. (1994). "Will There be a 'Different World' After *Fordice?*" *Academe* 80(3), 7–11.

WELCH, S., ET AL. (1997). "Race or Place: Emerging Public Perspectives on Urban Education." *Political Science and Politics* 30(3), 454–458.

WILENTZ, D. (1991). Commencement Address to Rutgers University School of Law, Newark, June 2.

WILKERSON, I. (1991a). "One City's 30-Year Crusade for Integration." *The New York Times,* December 30, pp. 1, 11.

———. (1991b). "Separate Proms Reveal an Unspanned Racial Divide." *The New York Times,* May 5, pp. 1, 36.

WILKINSON, J. H. (1979). *From Brown to Bakke: The Supreme Court and School Integration, 1954–1978.* New York: Oxford University Press.

WILSON, W. J. (1987). *The Truly Disadvantaged: The Inner City, the Underclass, and Public Policy.* Chicago: University of Chicago Press.

# CHAPTER 5

# Gender: Easing Discrimination or Making Legitimate Distinctions

## POSITION 1: EASING DISCRIMINATION

Rosalind Miles (1989) starts her historical work with the comment, "The story of the human race begins with the female. . . . Yet for generations of historians, archaeologists, anthropologists, and biologists, the sole star of the dawn story has been man" (p. 3). Males dominated the writing of these histories, as they dominated the traditional positions of power in society, letters, religion, the law, academia, and the professions—with one exception: women held most positions as teachers of elementary children. Even in education, administrators and college teachers were usually males. Females, often unwed because married women were expected to stay at home, were considered best suited for nurturing young children, but not suited to management, leadership, or scholarship.

In the Western tradition, men were supposed to be strong, protective, and dominant; women, sweet, nurturing, and submissive. In early times men worked as hunters and warriors, while women were berry pickers and child tenders. According to tradition and to the male-drafted literature that supported it, hunting and warmaking were admirable tasks, involving skill, strength, and courage; berry picking and child care were considered necessary but lesser activities. One role was for leaders, heroes, and those who govern; the other for homemakers, nurturers, and those being governed. The current study of history in schools conveys some of the same belief, with extensive coverage of wars and politics, inhabited overwhelmingly by males, and virtually no coverage of domestic life.

In economic terms, the separation of the sexes meant that men were understood to be the primary breadwinners while women were the primary homemakers. This division of labor follows from a long belief that gender differences necessarily control destiny, position, status, and power. Of course, it also provided a rationale for discrimination that subjected women to subservient positions and inferior status.

## Segregating by Gender

The concept of clearly bifurcated sex roles was enthusiastically developed by male scholars, who suggested that it conferred some survival value in epochs such as the Ice Age. Their premise was that hunting large beasts with crude weapons required physical strength, not to mention testosterone-driven aggression. Babies required mother's milk and care. It was a fairly neat symbiotic arrangement for the survival of the species, and it fit an emerging patriarchial pattern for social and family structure. Reconsideration of the evidence beyond the male-written archaeologies and histories has suggested that the neat segregation into dominant and submissive roles resulted not from the natural or genetic characteristics of each gender, but from practical considerations.

Margaret Ehrenberg (1989), for instance, finds there was not much division of labor between the sexes in earliest times, but that hunting larger animals with newly developed tools required mobility and free hands, not easy to come by when one is pregnant or looking after young children. People of this period lived only about twenty years, so the social needs for protecting the young and providing sustenance were strong. Separation by sex may well have developed to ensure the survival of the community, not to fulfill some innate gender differences. Ehrenberg also reports anthropological evidence that gender equality occurred much more in nomadic, foraging societies, in which private property and ownership were not prevalent and economic or political dominance and submission roles were not strong. Women and men of foraging societies shared in food gathering, even with gender separation of particular tasks, but each had equal status. Ehrenberg concludes that "although the social status of women has long been inferior to that of men, it must be remembered that the foraging societies of the palaeolithic and mesolithic spanned an immense period. . . . Throughout human history, the great majority of women who have ever lived had far more status than recently, and probably had equality with men" (p. 173). Thus, separation by gender does not have to result in a status difference. Gender equity and gender neutrality have existed in many societies. But status differences appear to have developed in a later period, when the agrarian and industrial revolutions created conditions conducive to the merger of property and power. In these later societies, political and economic dominance mattered a great deal.

Social customs, laws, and family pressures developed to maintain the separation of roles, power, and expectations between the sexes. Psychological histories are replete with traumas suffered by people at odds with the traditional roles and expectations for their genders. Deviants from the norms were punished by legal restriction, ostracism, and estrangement; even stoning, lynching, branding, and torture were meted out to those who strayed from the social norms of sex roles, showing the force of gender-separated traditions. Some of the basic concepts of property, viewing women as chattel and giving women no rights to own property or to govern, derived from this gender separation.

Education, one of the major means to individual improvement, also derived as a gender-separated institution. Girls were unable to attend beyond grammar school, and thus they were excluded from advanced learning, the professions, or careers. This double-bind pattern, in which women cannot access an advanced education and are then considered lower status because they don't have that education, is well-documented by Kathleen Hall Jamieson (1995). As Belenky, Clinchy, Goldberger, and Tarule (1986) point out, "Most of the institutions of higher education in this country were designed by men, and most continue to be run by men. In recent years, feminist teachers and scholars have begun to question the structure, the curriculum, and the pedagogical practices of these institutions" (p. 190).

Even the origins of evil, usually defined by men, have disproportionately been ascribed to women to help explain a theology where God is good, but evil exists. Noddings (1989), in making this point, notes that "women's bodies have been suspected of harboring evil and menstrual taboos were established in congruence with this belief" (p. 10). Gender discrimination has influenced philosophy, theology, politics, economics, sociology, and education. Certainly, a wide variety of historical power differences between men and women were based on this separation. It is in the interests of those with power to preserve it.

The weight of historic gender discrimination and its denial of equality to one-half of the world's population can easily produce nihilism, negativism, pessimism, or radicalism. It is easy to draw the conclusion that nothing will change, little can be done, no improvement is likely to occur, or that gender equality will come only with upheaval and revolution. Certainly, looking back through the long periods of oppression, denigration, and exclusion based on gender could cause melancholy or despair. Many feminists have decried this history of repression, and some have promoted radical change. Others promote more gradual alteration in the relations between the sexes, with equality as a longer-term goal. From the pens and actions of such independent women as Aphra Ben, the first Englishwoman to become a professional writer in the late seventeenth century, Mary Wollstonecraft, Elizabeth Cady Stanton, Susan B. Anthony, Lucy Stone, Emma Goldman, Virginia Woolf, Mary Ritter Beard, and Simone de Beauvoir came the inspiration for much of the current feminist determination to seek gender equity (Spender, 1983). Modern feminism traces back to the work of Betty Friedan in the 1960s, continuing through the writings, scholarship, and political efforts of such feminists as Naomi Weisstein, Kate Millett, Germaine Greer, Barbara Ehrenreich, Deirdre English, Andrea Dworkin, Gloria Steinem, Ti-Grace Atkinson, Susan Brownmiller, Lois Weis, Jane Roland Martin, and Nel Noddings.

The work of these early pioneers and their later colleagues produced significant modifications in the ways we think about women in society and in the roles we expect women to play. It is true that many serious gaps still exist, and women continue to struggle to achieve gender equity, but the outlines of a brighter future are becoming more distinct. The struggle, however, requires constant vigilance in the face of countervailing efforts to deride feminism and the women's movement ("Equal Time," 1999).

## *Redefining Sex Roles: Increasing Gender Neutrality*

Dichotomized survival roles for men and women are less imperative as civilization develop, but economic and political status remains separated by gender.

Agrarian economies required different field and house work, but both genders were capable. The industrial society has a variety of "light industry" jobs that do not require much physical strength. Even in the traditionally heavy industries robotization has lightened the load for both men and women. Today's high tech, service, and information industries are more cerebral than physical. Sitting for long stretches is often the most arduous physical exertion, and carpal tunnel syndrome is the most common industrial injury. Neither of these is gender-related. Moreover, the service sector of the economy—the human interaction part—rewards social skills. People with empathetic natures possess these skills disproportionately, regardless of gender.

Now we have increasing numbers of examples of gender-neutral or shared responsibilities for nearly all work and home activities. We still see remnants, many very strong, of earlier gender role differentation. Many males still insist on their version of human history and the status differences that conveys. And many people still cling to established habits that relegate certain activities to males and certain others to females. Of course, individual deviation from those older norms is still subject to some abuse: name calling, derision, and isolation; and various forms of overt and hidden discrimination still permeate much of society. But the evolution of our notions of civil rights, equality, and justice, along with increased economic productivity, offers a significant expansion of gender neutrality in work, play, and home.

Civilization has thus brought us closer to a gender-neutral economy and society. You will be hard pressed to think of an occupation that is necessarily for men or women only. Obviously, some disparities exist in the current actual proportions of each gender in some occupations, but that is the result of the long tradition of gender separation, continuing male control of access to certain jobs, and individual choices women and men make. You have probably seen female police officers and firefighters, hard hat construction workers, and race drivers, as well as male nurses, secretaries, and hairdressers. Among the higher-income, higher-visibility, and higher-status positions, previously held almost entirely by men, women are making headway. It is not a time for complacency, but there is evidence of improvement.

There is a continuing income gap between men and women in upper-level corporate and academic life, but that gap is decreasing. The gender gap in income has been stubbornly persistent; women now earn about 74 cents for each dollar earned by men, but that gap has declined by about 5 cents in the past twenty years ("Gender Gap," 1998). On the minus side, women make up by far the largest proportion of those living in poverty and of those raising children in a single-parent family. This remains a worrisome situation for society, the women involved, and the children. It is a pattern that emerges from the historic disparate status between the genders, and it demands the attention of government and other agencies devoted to democratic life. It is for this kind of issue that we need more women in positions of power to adequately represent the interests of this female underclass.

Women are increasingly holding more important positions in American life. Sherry Lansing headed Twentieth Century Fox movie and television production;

Tina Brown has been in charge of *Vanity Fair* and *The New Yorker*; Kathryn Graham was the boss at *The Washington Post*; Madeleine Albright has been Secretary of State and Ambassador to the United Nations. Women are ambassadors to many nations; they are Supreme Court justices, members of Congress, cabinet members, state governors, corporate executives, lawyers, doctors, engineers, architects, professional athletes, and financial entrepreneurs. The notable exception to date is the presidency, but that is only a matter of time. Eleanor Smeal (1984) shows how important the women's vote has become, and how the political gender gap can influence elections.

## *Altering Motherhood*

The growing representation of women at all levels of the workforce is a sure sign of women's liberation from many constraints of the past. Women are free to participate in the economic realm, at least up to that level referred to as the "glass ceiling," which separates women from the highest echelons of corporate America. Even so, the International Labour Office data for 1994–1995 show that the United States has more women in administrative and managerial jobs than any country except Australia ("Women in Management," 1998). But have women in the corporate world been freed from their previous roles as mothers and homemakers so they are not required to be superwomen who have to do it all? The answer is mixed but promising.

Just as technology has helped to make the workplace more gender-neutral, it has made homemaking less labor intensive. Appliances abound in the modern home, so cooking is almost instantaneous (at least, in the microwave), laundry goes through wash and dry cycles while humans are off doing other things, disposable diapers reduce laundering, hair dryers reduce grooming time, vacuum cleaners make cleaning faster and more thorough, dishwashers offer more leisure time and more sterility than hand dishwashing. These appliances are regularly improved for efficiency, and new household technologies are constantly coming on the market.

There is some dispute among feminists about whether or not the new household technologies are always improvements, since the evidence is that many technological advances for homes actually complicate housework and make it less efficient (Bose and Bereano, 1983). Many innovations in home technology are devoted more to profit making for industry than to efficiency or effectiveness. And technology has not redistributed household chores away from the mother and to other family members, and thus has not reduced demands on women. But technology has provided some relief in some areas of housecare, and it holds the potential for a major redistribution of housekeeping roles. As more women take on high-level positions, we might expect a demand for product improvements more attuned to gender equality in the home.

In today's economy, mothers are often expected, or desire, to work outside the home to maintain a decent family living standard and/or to further a career. Of course, they should not be expected to do this with no decrease in their domestic responsibilities. The outside work benefits the family economically; it is in the family's interest; it is a fulfillment, not an abdication, of the mothering role. For many families, mothering itself has been outsourced to the emergent childcare industry, with day care centers and nursery schools springing up all over. Professional childcare is becoming a condition of employment for parents so that the demands on their time and energy are more reasonable. The government now provides tax incentives for childcare while parents work, a recognition of this shift in social and economic customs.

Mothering may seem to be female-specific. Pregnancy, childbirth, and nursing certainly are; but increasingly, fathers, too, can fill a nurturing role. They need not even be biological fathers: adoptive fathers and stepfathers qualify. Gay and lesbian couples can adopt and become parents. In some cases, gay and lesbian parents are already biological parents, having been in heterosexual relationships before coming to terms with their homosexuality. Human cloning, should it come to pass, will allow asexual reproduction, revising the concept of mothering again. In sum, "mothering" may no longer be gender-specific but more of a gender-neutral concept of nurturing a child. Good parents can be found in a variety of relationships, and their roles have been made more flexible by household technology and a decline in traditional gender barriers.

## *Curricular Liberation*

School is preparation for the adult world. The curriculum should reflect changes in sex roles and altered attitudes about those changes. Alas, in most cases, schools serve to retard progress in these areas, rather than to advance it. Many schools, often with parental complicity, continue to refer girls more often to homemaking and boys to woodshop, girls to the humanities and boys to the sciences, girls to cheerleading and boys to sports teams, girls and boys to traditional, gender-separate occupational choices and preparations. A raft of studies have shown the curricular discrimination against female students. The 1992 report of the American Association of University Women (AAUW, 1992) and Sadker and Sadker (1994, 1995) provide good overviews of these studies.

Although gender discrimination has often been most damaging to females, males are also subject to discrimination in schools. Many troubling indicators of discrimination crop up because of gender separation in school operation:

- In early school years, girls excel beyond boys in speaking, reading, and counting, but they end up behind, especially in math and science scores on standardized tests.
- Girls receive only 36 percent of the National Merit Scholarships each year because of PSAT test results.
- Girls are more invisible in schools, receiving less praise, fewer teacher interactions with complex and abstract questioning, and less participatory instruction than boys.
- Girls exhibit lower self-esteem than boys in secondary and higher education.
- Girls in urban areas who drop out of school are far less likely to return than are boys.

- Girls, despite federal laws, receive far less than half of the athletic budget of colleges.
- Boys with learning, reading, or mental disabilities are more likely to be identified than are girls with similar problems.
- Boys are more subject to reprimands and disciplinary action than girls.
- Boys are estimated to be nine times more likely to be hyperactive than are girls.

*Source:* Adapted from Sadker, M., and Sadker, D. *Teachers, Schools, and Society.* (1997). 4th ed. New York: McGraw-Hill.

The AAUW issued a new report in 1998, showing that girls are falling well behind boys in computer literacy. Girls are more heavily enrolled in clerical and data entry computer courses, while boys are more heavily represented in advanced computer courses (AAUW, 1998). Since the gap between boys and girls in math and science course registration has been narrowing, there is no reason why the gap should be widening in computer courses. The studies of gender differences in academic performance reveal the subtle, and not so subtle, ways that teachers, counselors, and school administrators send messages of female inaptitude to students. Teachers don't call on girls as often as boys and are less likely to ask girls follow-up questions (Sadker and Sadker, 1995). They compliment girls for being quiet and orderly, not jumping into class interactions or engaging in arguments. The message this conveys is that girls' opinions do not count as much as those of boys.

Matthews et al. (1997) trained a class of fifth grade students to spot this gender discrimination for themselves. When students are sensitized to the subtle forms discrimination can take, they are alert to it and quick to challenge it. Every teacher who is nondefensive and eager to have a more gender-equitable classroom can easily familiarize the students with things to watch for. The students can speak up in a friendly spirit and send a powerful message about fairness. Obviously this applies to grades K–12, and it is especially pertinent in subjects in which girls have traditionally been shunted aside (math and science). Teachers can even make these subjects more female-friendly, apart from distributing interactions with individual students more equally. The content can be altered to better engage the interests of girls. Successful women scientists and mathematicians, and there are many, can address classes and serve as role models. A critical review of the research on gender discrimination in schools can be found in Mael (1998). He concludes that single-sex classes and schools for girls can be advantageous. It may be desirable to set up single-sex laboratories in co-ed schools so the girls can do their work without falling into the shadow of the boys (Rop, 1998).

The new enlightenment about gender equality has led to an awareness and abatement of discriminatory curricular practices. However, in some cases it may actually, if inadvertently, exacerbate the discrimination. A history textbook with special (and often sporadic) sections on the accomplishments of a few famous women gives the impression that women in general have not done much of significance. The few women who get special mention prove the point by their exceptionality, and the mention itself seems to be sop to political correctness, not a sincere attempt to make women as integral to the history textbook as they were to history itself. Too many history texts remain "great man" histories, and nearly all retain a primary focus on politics and war, areas in which women have historically been significantly underrepresented.

## Guidance and Gender

Guidance counselors participate in gender discrimination by steering girls into courses that prepare them for traditional female careers. The counselor may be well-intentioned—he or she may want to keep girls from pursuing careers they are supposedly "unsuited" for intellectually, physically, or temperamentally. That view is premised on the invalid assumption that all girls possess similar intellectual, physical, and temperamental profiles that differ distinctly from those of boys.

Another assumption that guidance counselors often make is that test scores are valid indicators of ability. For example, the vaunted gender difference on the SAT math exam is assumed to reveal a basic difference between males and females in math ability. But alternative explanations also merit consideration. Test scores are affected by variability; scores for males are more variable (boys produce more very high and very low scores) than scores for females. This variability affects the mean score for each gender. When it is accounted for statistically, the mean difference between boys' and girls' scores disappears on the PSAT or SAT verbal tests and exhibits only a small difference on the math tests (Feingold, 1992). Unfortunately, this adjustment is not commonly made. The raw mean scores are therefore the scores professional educators and the public take as truth.

## Extracurricular Opportunities

Federal law (Title IX) has made equal funding of boys' and girls' sports a must. This has helped school-sponsored girls' sports programs to blossom. One long-term effect of this has been the professionalization of women's sports. Women's basketball teams now have their own professional leagues and draw good crowds as well as television coverage. Women boxers often appear in preliminary bouts on the same card as male championship fights. Advanced athletic competition, as well as professional sports, requires the development of a core of athletes from the early years. Discrimination against young women and girls in sports diminishes the opportunities, and the talent supply, for advanced and professional athletics.

Of course, gross inequality in athletic opportunities for women also severely limits large numbers of women who will not enjoy participatory sports experiences as part of a well-rounded life. Health and leisure activities should not be the exclusive province of male-dominated athletic programs. Repercussions from this discrimination ripple throughout the society.

It is not that girls did not want to participate in sports before the advent of Title IX; it is that they were denied the equal opportunity and support. Title IX passed as part of the Education Amendments of 1972. National Collegiate Athletic Association data show that, one year earlier, in 1971, only about a quarter of a million girls participated in high school sports. By 1996, almost 2.5 million girls participated, an eight-fold increase in twenty-five years. Soccer, for example, attracted 11,000 female participants in 1977 and almost 210,000 in 1996. At the college level, where fewer women have participated historically, the numbers soared during the same period from about 30,000 to almost 120,000 women in a variety of recognized sports activities (Worsnop, 1997).

These developments were obviously assisted by the increased public acceptance of athletic activity as natural and beneficial for girls. However, equalizing the spending on boys' and girls' sports has not been easy because boys' sports tend to be the bigger revenue producers. It requires careful monitoring to ensure that girls are not shortchanged. If their teams are underfunded, the inducement to participate is diminished. The lack of participation then supports the claim that girls do not really care about sports, except as spectators at the boys' games. This situation is another example of a double bind for women.

Title IX has not abolished sex discrimination in sports. It only codifies the concept of equity in financial support and permits adjudication as a remedy. An increasing number of gender-equity lawsuits are being filed under Title IX. The *Cohen v. Brown* case, in which eleven members of the women's gymnastics and volleyball teams sued Brown University for sex discrimination when their teams lost university funding, captured national interest (Worsnop, 1997). Brown University lost in decisions at the District and Appeals court levels; and despite the fact that Brown had the backing of sixty other universities, the U.S. Supreme Court let the Appeals court decision stand in April 1998.

Amy Cohen, whose name appears on the case, is now an elementary school teacher in Baltimore, and one can imagine that her school makes a serious attempt to equalize opportunities for girls and boys (Milloy, 1998). Many more challenges will arise as parents of girls begin to question the allocation of resources for sports programs at local schools and community-sponsored youth activities. As Marcia Saneholtz, Washington State University Senior Associate Athletic Director, says: "More attention needs to be focused on gender-equity issues at the grass-roots level [junior high school and community-sponsored sports]. We're not going to be any more equitable at the collegiate level than we are at those lower levels, which is where our student-athletes come from" (Worsnop, 1997, p. 339).

Support for girls' teams can be more than financial. Teachers and staff are often in the stands at the boys' football and basketball games, and may even find time to discuss the games in class. Female athletes would no doubt respond to this kind of interest as much as the male athletes do. In time, girls may play on the traditionally boys' teams, and the reverse. If the eligibility requirement is athletic prowess, any person who has it should be allowed to play, regardless of gender. Another example of support is hiring female coaches for women's and girls' teams. In many cases, as equity provisions of Title IX provide for more funds and higher public visibility for women's sports at the college level, women coaches are actually replaced by men who have had more opportunities for intercollegiate experience. This will likely self-correct, however, as more women coaches get exposure and experience.

Class offices are another area in which girls can and should be encouraged to vie with boys. The class president does not *have* to be male. Students who always fill supporting roles cannot gain the full range of organizational and leadership skills. School officials should discourage a we-they contest of boys versus girls for elective offices. The elections should be issue-oriented, just as we wish for elections in the world outside the school. However, if the only way to get girls to go for the top offices is to make gender itself a campaign issue, then that may be a necessary stage in the evolution of political equality for girls. The political nature and power of the women's rights movement may need to become more apparent, and girls may need to be encouraged to become active in that movement.

## *Worldwide Discrimination Against Women*

Discrimination against women has been widely documented over a long period of time. The women's movement of the nineteenth century was a battle against certain aspects of the Old Order, a patriarchial system in which "authority over the family is vested in the elder males, or male. He, the father, makes the decisions that control the family's work, purchases, marriages. Under the rule of the father, women have no complex choices to make, no questions as to their nature or destiny: the rule is simply obedience" (Ehrenreich and English, 1978, pp. 6, 7).

The United States has a sordid history of gender discrimination, with many remnants still in evidence. But the U.S. appears to be trying to address and correct this through legislation, education, and more enlightened public opinion. That, sadly, is not the case for the vast majority of women around the world. Women actually do about two-thirds of the work in the world, but they receive only a tiny fraction, about 10 percent, of the world's income. They are prohibited from holding property in some places, holding only about 1 percent of the land in the world. In many parts of the globe, they are unable to vote and unable to make decisions about their lives, health, mates, dress, labor, finances, or education. Largely because of worldwide gender discrimination, women account for two-thirds of all illiterates in the world, and they head 85 percent of all single-parent families (Clark, 1997).

Following World War II, the United Nations recognized disparities in the treatment of women; the 1948 Universal Declaration of Human Rights called upon all nations to gauge the status of women. Women's status was an issue then, and it remains an issue of international human rights. Thirty years later, in 1979, the United Nations established a Convention on the Elimination of All Forms of Discrimination Against Women. Over 162 nations have ratified that convention, a minimal effort to redress gender discrimination across the globe. Unfortunately for our oft-trumpeted espousal of human rights, the United States has signed but not yet ratified this important international convention. In truth, we have ratified only three of the eight U.N. human rights treaties, but one of those was the International Convention on the Elimination of All Forms of Racial Discrimination. It is not clear why the United States would not have also ratified the convention on gender discrimination in the twenty years since the U.N. adopted it. The fact that U.S. women now face less discrimination than women in many other societies is scant reason for complacency about the remnants of discrimination here or for a lack of concern about the plight of women in far more discriminatory societies.

## Summary

Eliminating gender discrimination is a worthy goal for the nation and the world. More than a goal, it is a necessity in a civilized nation that purports to be democratic or in a world that aims to provide equity in human rights. Further, discrimination restricts not only the individuals and groups that it is used against, it limits the contributions these people could otherwise make to the culture, economy, and life of the society. Discrimination against women is discrimination against one-half of the human race, a tragic loss to humankind and an extremely short-sighted policy. Speeches, marches, banners, demonstrations, and media blitzes may help raise public recognition of this problem, but long-term solutions require thoughtful legislation, enforcement, sanctions against those who continue discrimination, and a strong educational program to lead younger generations to improve. Schools are central to this work, but schools also have a history of gender discrimination. One of the most productive steps we could take to extinguish gender discrimination is to eliminate it from all aspects of schooling and to institute a progressive approach to education for a gender-neutral future.

The easing of gender discrimination is clear in recent U.S. history, but we still have a ways to go to do justice to our ideals of equity.

## POSITION 2: MAKING LEGITIMATE DISTINCTIONS

### No More P.C. Pressure

In recent years, the initials *PC* have become a powerful symbol. "Politically correct" has become a phrase that signifies no distinction, no difference, no individuality, and no accuracy—just a set of words that demands a standard of conformity. The mavens of politically correct speech dictate that we should never ruffle anyone by disagreeing or by discussing real issues that separate people. These advocates claim to know better than the rest of us where the truth lies and what ideologies deserve favored treatment. Indeed, they can get quite testy when their pontifical certitude is called into question. Fortunately, their intemperate self-righteousness has become a subject of satire. And their Pollyannalike facade has proven to be hypocritical. Elitism and social control are the handmaidens of the PC movement.

The PC brigades have been especially outspoken on the topic of gender. Feminists dominate this aspect of discourse, ignoring the desires of many women and the obvious fact that members of the male gender can have legitimate and pertinent views of gender questions. Not all females wish to be militant feminists or grasping careerists, and not all males are evil and malevolent manipulators. Under the aegis of the feminists in PC garb, it is not considered fashionable or sophisticated to point out the important differences between the sexes, even though many people of both sexes appreciate these differences and want to maintain the traditional gender roles as a personal choice and as a service to families and to society. Many women and men prefer separate roles as homemakers and breadwinners; they do not appreciate being told that they are out of synch with modern thinking or with a monolithic sisterhood of women. They do not like to have their right to choose a traditional and more comfortable role threatened by pressure from the PC crowd.

For a while, the "politically correct" folks actually succeeded in making women fearful of admitting that they preferred the traditional homemaker role and were not flaming feminists. Not surprisingly, a backlash against this PC intimidation has arisen, with more and more women feeling free to gravitate to the role that seems most natural to them. This is a refreshing movement, consistent with a free society. Karen Lehrman (1995) notes that the term *liberated woman* has become an epithet: "Stripped of its original promise of strength, independence, and adventure, the phrase had been media-sentenced to represent the worst stereotype of the women's movement: a saggy-breasted, hairy-legged, man-hating militant who spends her days denouncing capitalism and Western culture and her nights doing God knows what with other women" (p. 7).

If many women are still compelled to work outside the home to make family ends meet, that may partially be the result of the feminist movement hectoring women into the workforce to demonstrate their independence from men. This leaves many women in a difficult position; they feel they can't assume the more traditional women's role in the home without sacrificing the economic well-being of their family or disservicing their gender. It has the additional negative effect of significantly increasing the supply of workers, thereby lowering the wages for both sexes. It now takes two wage earners to maintain many households, whereas in the prefeminist days, one was sufficient. Feminism has taken its toll on women as well as men. We could argue that the stridency of feminism contains seeds as bitter for women as sexism did.

Many women do not want to work outside the home. They consider, rightly, that homemaking is legitimate, difficult, and intelligent work, deserving more respect than it gets from the women's movement. They believe that children should have a mother at home. They want to provide a nurturing, caring home for their families. They want the media and movies to return to positive portrayals of women as homemakers. Not all women desire to be like Thelma and Louise or the CEO of General Motors. Many women want to be at the center of the home, conveying family values and keeping the hearth. This is a powerful, not powerless, position. They resent being considered pawns of "patriarchial oppressors," or being considered stupid or dupes. Feminists, rather than taking the side of these women and supporting their courage and integrity and their freedom to choose, turned against them and made them feel alienated and unworthy. It is not, as some feminists allege, evil patriarchy that denigrates these women, it is the feminists themselves.

## *Feminism and Femininity*

The Independent Womens Forum (IWF) in Washington D.C. is a group of professional, business, working, and stay-at-home women who speak out for the right of women to make their own decisions. One might think that the feminist movement would have the same goal, but the IWF is devoted to deconstructing feminism. IWF is one of the groups involved in the backlash against the feminist ideology, believing that women are threatened by it and that women's rights are trampled under its conformist views. The feminist movement started as a way to improve the status of women in society, but it has been turned into another special interest group committed to self-protection; feminism became elitist, negative, anti-male, and unconcerned with ordinary women living ordinary lives (Clark, 1997). *Newsweek* wondered in print whatever happened to the women's movement and its ideals ("Sisterhood was Powerful," 1994).

*Feminism* should be a neutral term that merely incorporates the idea of feminine characteristics or womanly traits. *Masculinity,* of course, describes characteristics peculiar to men. Both terms include positive and negative aspects, but they are separable traits. Ironically, the feminist movement is dominated by women who want to pursue a political agenda based on the view that no differences exist between the sexes or that the differences don't matter. Feminism has lost its feminine core, the essence that attracted broad support. It is ironic that *feminism* is linguistically based on the term *feminine,* describing separable traits of women. Even as some feminists argue for a unisex society without gender separation, the feminist movement has become a battlefield of competing ideologies that subverts the women's movement. It has separated the women in the movement into fiefdoms.

There are Feminists for Free Expression, Feminists for Life, and Christian Feminists. Feminism has split into other factions, sometimes identified as "difference feminists," who stress the miscommunication between women and men; "equity feminists," who pursue equality with men in all matters; "gender feminists," who attack males for their power and control; "victim feminists," who lay the blame for all significant women's problems on sexism; and "power feminists," who take self-responsibility very seriously (Clark, 1997). One of the perversities of the feminist movement is its attack on homemaking, nurturing, caring, family, and traditional women's roles. Their lack of concern for family values and personal character in sexual relations is shown by their silence in the face of highly publicized allegations of President Clinton's gross sexism and sexual harassment. This is beyond irony, bordering on hypocrisy.

Karen Lehrman (1995) identifies four basic problems with the current course of ideas coming from feminists:

1. Gender feminists undermine the first purpose for feminism—liberating women from oppression. They have substituted an "inflexible set of political opinions, professional goals, and androgynous behaviors and attire" (p. 10).
2. The expectations of some feminists are actually in opposition to the interests and desires of many women.

3. Many feminist goals (for example, restricting sexual harassment and sexist speech) are unachievable or inconsistent with governmental control. Even if attainable, they portend censorship and a lack of due process.
4. Much of the backlash against feminists is "legitimate resistance by both women and men to the extremes of establishment feminism" (p. 10), and not an orchestrated male response. Some of the feminist rhetoric is "anti-male, anti-sex, anti-family, anti-beauty, anti-religion, or anti-nature" (p. 10).

A 1998 Time/CNN poll shows the extent to which feminism is passe for today's women. Only 48 percent of the female respondents thought feminism was relevant for women, and only 28 percent thought it relevant for them personally. Between 1989 and 1998, the percentage of women who looked unfavorably on feminism rose from 29 to 43 (Bellafante, 1998). Clearly, feminism is fading because most women find themselves living in a fundamentally gender-fair society. Susan Faludi (1991) recognized the backlash against feminism among women but attributed it to conservatives' political manipulation, an explanation that does not explain the widespread disatisfaction with feminism or give credit to thoughtful women who are not mere pawns in another liberal-conservative political struggle. Christina Hoff Sommers (1994), professor of philosophy at Clark University, presents a strong argument that feminist leaders are elitistic and out of touch with most women in the society, and that they have misused information to overstate how victimized women are by sexism. Elizabeth Fox-Genovese (1996), a historian at Emory University, makes a similar case that the feminists have lost touch with common women and their concerns.

## Vive la Difference

Among the factors ignored by the more strident members of the feminist movement is that there really are two genders, with significant physical, mental, and emotional differences. The feminist tendency to trivialize the differences between men and women and treat the sexes as essentially identical does violence to reality as well as to what people know intuitively. There are major differences in the electrochemical structuring of men's and women's brains, and these have consequences for psychological functioning. Men and women are "wired" differently and react to the world differently as a result. Feminists suggest that these felt differences are merely cultural artifacts that we can easily overcome once we recognize how superficial they are. That suggestion causes people to engage in the struggle to overcome traits that, in truth, are deep-seated and enduring.

In a practical sense, it does not matter whether gender differences are primarily caused by genetics or culture—the resulting behaviors and attitudes still exist. Over time, genetic and culturally imposed distinctions become inseparable because of their interaction, fueling what is referred to as "genetic evolution" (Kiernan, 1998). They develop into ingrained differences in the individual and in society. Thus, gender differences cannot be brushed aside by the claim that they are only "cultural," either through a simple effort of the will, or through the pressure of ideology and a political agenda. These differences, and their social importance, have formed over evolutionary time and have therefore become "natural."

More than a quarter century ago, Steven Goldberg (1973) tried to find a culture, either historical or contemporary, in which male dominance was not the norm. To be sure, in some societies, women and men performed roles usually associated with the opposite sex. But even in these societies, males occupied the *high-status* roles, the most prized roles. Goldberg attributed the universalism of male dominance to the testosterone-driven aggression in males. Anthropologist Lionel Tiger (1995) has also long argued that the relation between gender and aggression is as biologically based as it is socially produced. "The single glistening fact is that sex is about reproduction and genetics as well as social roles, attitudes, and cultural assumptions" (p. 82). No amount of feminist rhetoric can offset this. Only fiction can create Amazon societies.

Neuroscientists at Yale, led by a woman, have been mapping the brain differences between men and women. Using Positron Emission Technology (PET) scans and Magnetic Resonance Imaging (MRI), they have produced graphic pictures of functioning male and female brains. The pictures show that men and women do not use the same parts of the brain to solve the same task. Women employ both spheres, while men employ only one side (Shaykin et al., 1995). Gazzaniga (1992) reported a confirmatory finding, showing that male stroke victims who suffer damage to one side of the brain are less likely to recover than females, who are able to enlist the help of the undamaged side. Still other research shows that women's brains do not lose cells as rapidly as men's as they pass into middle age and beyond (Cowell et al., 1994; Shaykin et al., 1995). Obviously, most of these gender differences are favorable to women. The point is that there *are* gender differences in mental functioning, and these logically lead to different capabilities and propensities. It is also logical to assume that more gender differences will be uncovered as neuroscientific research proceeds.

These cerebral differences may well explain the traditionally superior performance of one or the other sex in a given academic subject. A University of Chicago comprehensive review of these differences found that boys clearly outperform girls on math tests, while girls do markedly better than boys on verbal tests, including reading tests (Hedges and Nowell, 1995). The Educational Testing Service came to the same conclusion, using the results of 74 nationally used tests for twelfth graders (Lawton, 1997). To persistently ignore these differences as fleeting cultural phenomena is to distort reality and create unfair expectations.

## The Religious Prescription and Proscription

Proper gender roles are derived from a variety of authorities: psychologists, philosophers, political theorists, ideologues, and so on. For many people, the single definitive authority is the literature of their religion. All the fundamentalist religious groups, be they Christian, Muslim, or Jewish, find the proper roles for men and women spelled out commandingly in the ancient testaments of their faith. And for all these groups, the role prescribed for women is to be submissive to men. Under these articles of faith, women are to continue in the paths their foremothers took when the holy words were scripted.

Not all religions are fundamentalist, holding firmly to a prescribed set of rules about the conduct and roles of men and women. In some religions, women hold key roles in the ministry and in leadership, even though they are still considered different from men. These women hold positions different from the men's, but they are not considered inferior—merely different. These traditions are of great moment for the religions. They are matters of theology, doctrine, or long-term practice. A radical feminist movement intent on the destruction of gender differences in all aspects of human life has no right to destroy these deeply held beliefs. Some religious hierarchies have tried to change the gender role situation without reliance on radical feminist rhetoric. Hoover (1999), for example, argues that women deserve ordination in the Catholic religion based on her interpretation of theological traditions, not because of some feminist tract or position on gender neutrality. Each religious denomination must examine these issues in light of the best interests of its people and its understanding of its basic views; this is not a proper place for feminist propaganda.

Even groups such as the Promise Keepers, Christian men who project an image of modernity, have been criticized for their paternalistic attitudes toward their wives. Needless to say, the wives in fundamentalist religions readily acquiesce to their subservient (but protected) status. They are as steadfast in the faith as the men. The gender role differentiation usually does not preclude careers for women, but it does make personal fulfillment dependent on much more than (or entirely other than) a career. Being a homemaker and mother can provide personal fulfillment, despite feminist rhetoric.

## The Role of the Public School

Schooling has become one of the most visible sites for feminist attack. Nearly every aspect of school, from gyms to classroom activities, has been subjected to feminist critique. Critics almost always find the school wanting and advocate draconian measures as correctives. Altering standardized tests, equalizing expenditures for athletics, mandating quotas for admissions, forcing teachers to change class discussion techniques, imposing new unisex curricula, and demanding changes in teaching materials are some of those measures. This can destroy basic elements of public schooling, including teacher freedom, individual rights, and integrity in testing, school admissions, and scholarship.

If feminist correctives are to be incorporated into the curriculum, as sound ones should be, then it is important to make sure that the "correctives" are not just fresh errors. If feminists assert that premenstrual syndrome is purely the product of a male-oppressive culture and has no biological basis (Delaney, Lupton, and Toth, 1975), school personnel should certainly scrutinize such a counterexperiential claim. When Naomi Wolf (1992) alleges that 150,000 American women die each year in a holocaust of anorexia, school officials should seek corroborative evidence and hold action until the evidence is clear. If as august a body as the American Association of University Women announces that girls' self-esteem plummets at puberty, school people should know that boys mature later than girls and may retain immature notions of grandeur longer (Sommers, 1994). The methodology of the widely reported AAUW self-esteem study has, in fact, been faulted for a variety of defects (Schmidt, 1994).

In their aptly titled book, *Professing Feminism: Cautionary Tales from the Strange World of Women's Studies* (1995), Daphne Patai and Noretta Koertge listed the distortions found in college women's studies programs. Among these is TOTAL REJ, rejecting anything masculine as tainted. This is a form of misandry, or hatred of men, and it is no more defensible than misogyny. Another distortion is GENDERAGENDA, which reduces every issue to a question of gender only, no matter how complex the issue is in reality. BIODENIAL is another distortion, whereby any negative female traits are attributed to social construction rather than biology. (Negative male traits, on the other hand, are the nature of the beast!) These distortions can creep into the precollege curriculum if misguided people think it is necessary to "spin" the facts in order to capture students' attention or to proselytize for the feminist cause.

We cannot redress historical injustice to women by spreading contemporary lies, no matter how well-meaning we are. Schools have a responsibility to present the most accurate depictions science allows. Similarly, the most solid and responsible history, literature, economics, sociology, psychology, anthropology, and other academic studies should be the benchmark for inclusion in the curriculum, not an unfounded and unsupported set of claims and generalizations.

Disparities in test scores between boys and girls have a basis in reality. Whatever the reasons, the long-term evidence shows that girls tend to perform better in language and humanities, boys in math and science. In the early grades, girls do better in math, but they trail off over time in school. Girls tend to select advanced math and science courses less often than boys. Girls get better grades in general, and boys get into trouble more. The much-touted research that was supposed to show that girls are shortchanged in school has apparently "disappeared," and other studies show no pattern of consistent teacher favoring of boys or girls (Kleinfeld, 1999). Academic test scores differ by gender, but girls are not "silenced" in school.

If schools ignore the clear and undeniable data and pretend there are no gender differences, it can only lead to error in counseling students into courses and programs and in classrooms. If the differences are entirely attributable to lower self-confidence in girls, how is ignoring or papering over the test score differences going to correct the problem? If girls of a certain age generally have less self-confidence, that could signal a real difference between the sexes or simply another manifestation of the prejudices of society. But how does it help young girls or boys, or reduce those prejudices, if we try to act as though differences in test scores, interests, self-confidence, or other characteristics do not exist? If the feminists, through shrillness and stridency, have not yet boosted girls' math test scores or self-confidence, how can we expect favored treatment in schools to make that change? To some boys, it already appears that girls are favored in school.

Perhaps the answer is single-sex courses, programs, or schools. This may allow for the fuller maturation of both sexes separately, and the elimination of competition between the sexes for grades, scores, school offices, and favorable treatment in school. That separation was common in the early years of education in America; some high schools actually still have signs for separate entrances for boys and girls. But doesn't the provision of separate courses and schools support the contention that some gender differences do matter? The American Association of University Women (AAUW) determined that single-sex schools may raise math scores for girls, give them more confidence in competition, and encourage them to take risks, but the AAUW also fears that such schools will reinforce sexual stereotypes. The President of the New York City National Organization for Women (NOW) argues that separate but equal does not work. There is, in the feminist ideology, a persistent belief that "boy" and "girl" are merely social constructed categories. NOW and the AAUW "can't bring themselves to accept that there are differences between the sexes." ("Feminists Will Be Feminists," 1998, p. 17).

Schools would be well-advised to stop thinking of girls as the only victims of gender discrimination. Boys suffer, too, from biased educational practices. More than thirty years ago, Patricia Cayo Sexton (1969) reported on the feminization of the American elementary school, with its predominantly female authority figures and feminine norms. More recently, William Pollack (1998) of the Harvard Medical School noted the greater difficulty that boys have learning to read and write, and the fact that boys are greatly overrepresented in special education classes and among those diagnosed with attention deficit disorder. Pollack shares Sexton's view that boys' temperaments and energy levels tend to be at odds with the school's agenda. Even a mainstream publication, *Parents* magazine, recognizes that gender differences exist and matter. A recent article by a noted psychologist expressed one of the differences: "Even tomboy girls think that boys are too wild" (Kutner, 1998). How does gender neutrality square with the real world children and adults know? Feminists could increase their credibility by paying some attention to this side of the story.

## Stretching the Athletic Dollar into Political Activism

Title IX of a 1972 act providing federal funds for education outlaws sex discrimination in any education programs which receive federal funds. While the elimination of discrimination is a valuable goal, the means used to measure discrimination and to mitigate it are sometimes well beyond reason. They often involve increasing governmental intervention in the lives of individuals, result in a destructive polarization between people of goodwill, and impose even worse conditions to remedy the problem. Using Title IX to deal with gender inequity in schools provides us with striking examples of each of these problems.

Although Title IX was intended to address discrimination based on sex in all education programs receiving any federal support, it has had its most obvious impact on athletics in high school and college. The Education Department's Office of Civil Rights determined that the measure of compliance with Title IX for sports programs includes an acceptable answer to at least one of the following:

1. Are the men's and women's sports participation opportunities substantially proportional to male and female enrollments?
2. Is there a history and continuing practice of program expansion for the underrepresented gender?
3. Has the program fully and effectively accommodated the interests and abilities of members of the underrepresented gender?

Item one appears to be an example of government intervention into the affairs of schools and colleges and the individual decisions of students; it suggests a quota system based on enrollment, considering nothing about the nature of the institution, its students, or its sports program. All criteria insert a divisive hatchet into sports programs, offering opportunists a chance to undercut viable programs by challenging whether such programs are available to the opposite gender. This pits women's sports against men's in destructive ways. Further, these criteria can easily lead to the abolition or severe restriction of successful men's sports merely to meet a hypothetical quota for what may be unsuccessful women's sports—a worse condition than existed before Title IX.

The case of *Cohen v. Brown University* illustrates this problem. As is true at most universities, men at Brown are far more interested in participating in intercollegiate athletics than women are, so a quota system based on university enrollment by gender is an unrealistic approach to allocating the athletic budget. Should we force women to participate in intercollegiate sports in the same proportions as men? Or should we force men out because a smaller proportion of women want to participate? This is a crazy way to address equity.

Some sports are very expensive; some make enough money to support others; students are interested in watching some sports more than others. These points do not translate well into equal budgets. Interestingly, Brown had a history of expanding opportunities for women's sports well before Title IX became the law of the land. This early progressive effort, unfortunately, makes the Brown University record of providing improved sports opportunities for women appear weaker because the efforts predated Title IX and would show, therefore, less proportional improvement since Title IX. The measure for improvement, dating from Title IX, is, thus, unrealistic and unrelated to a school's actual history. Brown University was penalized for trying to expand women's sports before the government, under feminist pressure, told it to.

*Reason* magazine (Olson, 1998) reports that the California State University (CSU) system provides another example of the problems created under Title IX by its assumption that men and women have equal needs and interests in athletics. CSU agreed to settle a court case by using quotas related to male and female enrollments at the many CSU campuses. According to Olson, as a result:

- By 1997, massive cuts were made to men's athletics.
- CSU Northridge dropped baseball, a program that had ranked in the top 20 nationally.

- CSU Bakersfield drastically cut its premier program in men's wrestling.
- CSU San Francisco, Fullerton, Hayward, Chico, and Long Beach dropped men's football.
- Various campuses have eliminated about 200 men's teams with about 17,000 players.

CSU Bakersfield, for example, enrolls many women ages 40 to 50 who have no interest in sports participation. Since women make up 64 percent of the student population, men's sports suffer.

The next targets, of course, are the high schools and then the junior highs. By equalizing sports programs through quotas, we lose sight of the differences between boys and girls, and of the value of treating those differences as legitimate and important to the well-being of both genders.

## Summary

Gender is an important variable in humans because of the differences between males and females, not because of their commonalities. If those differences are covered up, it creates pressures and tensions far beyond those experienced when differences are appreciated. Society is enhanced by differing gender characteristics, interests, talents, and perceptions. Forcing those underground in some charade of gender neutrality is not only unnatural, it is destructive. The feminist movement has shifted from its proper concern with relieving discrimination against women to increasing discrimination against certain women and against many men.

Feminism has lost its feminine quality—an intuitive, insightful, congenial quality that can bring peace and pleasantness to fractious surroundings. Feminism has created a deep chasm in the women's movement, slowed and weakened its progress, and caused misery for women who feel pressured to bear the superwoman image at work and at home. Schools, under some feminist influences, have retreated from knowledge and truth to political correctness and a veneer of gender neutrality. We need to extol and enjoy the differences between genders, not hide and repress them.

## For Discussion

1. Recently, the U.S. Department of Education caused the scoring system for the Preliminary Scholastic Aptitude Test (PSAT) to be altered so that girls would get higher scores and be eligible in greater numbers for National Merit Scholarships. The verbal score, usually the higher one for female test-takers, is doubled (Murray, 1998). What evidence shows that girls were unfairly disadvantaged before this adjustment? Why should any or all tests on which girls tend to score lower than boys be adjusted to eliminate the gender difference? How does this change address the idea of equity?

2. In 1998, the Horatio Alger Association announced the results of its annual survey of youth aged 14 to 18 in the United States (Horatio Alger Association,

1998). The researchers claim the results are nationally representative, and they show the following gender breakdown on some of the items. How do you think authors and organizations which contend that girls are victimized in school would interpret the numbers? What factors do you think account for these gender differences in opinions about schooling?

|  | *Percent of Responses* | |
| --- | --- | --- |
|  | Female | Male |
| School courses are preparing me for the future. | 73% | 65% |
| It is important to teachers that I do my best. | 72 | 63 |
| I try to take the most challenging courses. | 60 | 45 |
| The amount of work I do is important to later success. | 73 | 59 |
| It is personally important to do my best in school. | 81 | 65 |
| Hard work leads to more opportunities. | 75 | 67 |
| I have opportunities for open discussion in classes. | 33 | 18 |
| I received mostly A's on my last report card. | 49 | 31 |
| Homework is a higher priority than other activities. | 49 | 31 |

*Source:* Adapted from Horatio Alger Association. (1998). *Annual Survey of youth 14–18 in the United States.* Online: http://www.horatioalger.com/pubmat/state98.htm. Numbers rounded.

3. Following are some data from a 1995 survey conducted by Louis Harris for the Feminist Majority Foundation, based on interviews with 1,364 adults. What accounts for the differences in the level of support for the "women's movement," the "feminist movement," and other movements? How would you define and describe the various movements? What would you predict if this survey were to be conducted in another ten or twenty years?

|  | *Percent* | |
| --- | --- | --- |
|  | In Support | Against |
| Women's Movement | 69% | 19% |
| Feminist Movement | 51 | 34 |
| Pro-Choice Movement | 58 | 30 |
| Pro-Life Movement | 57 | 30 |
| Civil Rights Movement | 78 | 14 |

*Source:* Adapted from "Women's Equality Poll 1995," conducted by Louis Harris for the Feminist Majority Foundation. In Clark, C. S. (1997). "Feminism's Future." *Congressional Quarterly Researcher* 7(8), 173.

4. If you believe that gender differences are primarily due to genetics, what are the social policy implications of that position? What are the educational implications?

   If you believe that gender differences are primarily due to cultural influences, what are the social policy implications of that position? What are the educational implications?

Design a hypothetical school consistent with your ideas on the primary causes of gender differences. Would the building be different from those you know now? What curricula would you adopt, and how would you organize extracurricular activities? How would you organize the teaching staff, class times, and teaching materials used?

## References

AMERICAN ASSOCIATION OF UNIVERSITY WOMEN. (1998). *Gender Gaps: Where Schools Still Fail Our Children.* Washington, DC: AAUW.

——— (1992). *How Schools Shortchange Girls.* Washington, DC: AAUW.

APPLEYARD, B. (1998). *Brave New Worlds.* New York: Viking.

BELENKY, M. F., CLINCHY, B. MC., GOLDBERGER, N. R., AND TARULE, J. M. (1986). *Women's Ways of Knowing.* New York: Basic Books

BELLAFANTE, G. (1998). "Feminism: It's All About Me!" *Time,* June 29, pp. 54–62.

BIRD, C. (1995). *Lives of Our Own: Secrets of Salty Old Women.* Boston: Houghton Mifflin.

BOSE, C. E. AND BEREANO, P. L. (1983). "Household Technologies: Burden or Blessing." In *The Technological Woman,* edited by J. Zimmerman. New York: Praeger.

CLARK, C. S. (1997). "Feminism's Future." *Congressional Quarterly Researcher* 7 (8) 69–92.

COWELL, P., ET AL. (1994). "Sex Differences in Aging of the Human Frontal and Temporal Lobes." *The Journal of Neuroscience* 14(8), 4748–4755.

DELANEY, J., LUPTON, M., AND TOTH, E. (1975). *The Curse: A Cultural History of Menstruation.* New York: Knopf.

EHRENBERG, M. (1989). *Women in Prehistory.* Norman: University of Oklahoma Press.

EHRENREICH, B., AND ENGLISH, D. (1978). *For Her Own Good: 150 Years of the Experts' Advice to Women.* Garden City, NY:Anchor Press/Doubleday.

"Equal Time." (1999). *Ms* 9(2), 1.

FALUDI, S. (1991). *Backlash: The Undeclared War Against American Women.* New York: Crown.

FEINGOLD, A. (1992). "Sex Differences in Variability in Intellectual Abilities: A New Look at an Old Controversy." *Review of Educational Research* 62(1), 61–84.

"Feminists Will Be Feminists." (1998). *National Review* 50(6), 17–18.

FOX-GENOVESE, E. (1996). *"Feminism Is Not the Story of My Life": How Today's Feminist Elite Has Lost Touch with the Real Concerns of Women.* New York: Doubleday.

FRIEDAN, B. (1997). *Beyond Gender: The New Politics of Work and Family.* Edited by B. O'Farrell. Washington, DC: Woodrow Wilson Center Press.

GAZZANIGA, M. (1992). *Nature's Mind: The Biological Roots of Thinking, Emotions, Sexuality, Language, and Intelligence.* New York: Basic Books.

"Gender Gap Adds to Income Inequality." (1998). *Congressional Quarterly Researcher* 8 (15), 346.

GOLDBERG, S. (1973). *The Inevitability of Patriarchy.* New York: William Morrow.

HEDGES, L., AND NOWELL, A. (1995). "Sex Differences in Central Tendency, Variability, and Numbers of High-Scoring Individuals," *Science* 269, 4045.

HOOVER, R. (1999). "Consider Tradition: A Case for Ordaining Women." *Commonweal* 126(2), 17–20.

HORATIO ALGER ASSOCIATION. (1998). *Annual Survey of Youth 14–18 in the United States.* Online: *http://www.horatioalger.com/pubmat/state98.htm.*

JAMIESON, K. H. (1995). *Beyond the Double Bind: Women and Leadership.* Oxford: Oxford University Press.

KIERNAN, V. (1998). "Are Human Behavior and Culture Products of Our Biology?" *The Chronicle of Higher Education* 45(4), A18, A22.

KLEINFELD, J. (1999). "Gender and Myth," *Current* 11, May, 3–10.

KUTNER, L. (1998). "Why Children Split into Same-Sex Groups." *Parents* 73(4), 112–114.

LAWTON, M. (1997). "ETS Disputes Charge of Gender Bias." *Education Week* 16(33), 1,21.

LEHRMAN, K. (1997). *The Lipstick Proviso: Women, Sex and Power in the Real World.* New York: Doubleday.

LEVAY, S. (1993). *The Sexual Brain.* Cambridge, MA: MIT Press.

MAEL, F. (1998). "Single-Sex and Coeducational Schooling: Relationships to Socioemotional and Academic Development." *Review of Educational Research* 68(2), 101–129.

MATTHEWS, C. ET AL. (1997). "Challenging Gender Bias in Fifth Grade." *Educational Leadership* 55(4), 54–57.

MILES, R. (1989). *The Women's History of the World.* Topsfield, MA: Salem House.

MILLOY, M. (1998). "Amy Cohen". *Ms.* 8(4) 52–4.

MURRAY, D. (1998). "The War Against Testing." *Commentary* 106(3), 34–37.

NODDINGS, N. (1989). *Women and Evil.* Berkeley: University of California Press.

OLSON, W. (1998). "Title IX From Outer Space." *Reason* 29 (9), 50–51.

PATAI, D., AND KOERTGE, N. (1995). *Professing Feminism: Cautionary Tales from the Strange World of Women's Studies.* New York: Basic Books.

POLLACK, W. (1998). *Real Boys.* New York: Random House.

POLLITT, K. (1994). *Reasonable Creatures: Essays on Women and Feminism.* New York: Alfred Knopf.

ROP, C. (1998). "Breaking the Gender Barrier in the Physical Sciences." *Educational Leadership* 55(4), 58–60.

SADKER, D. AND SADKER, M. (1994). *Failing at Fairness: How America's Schools Cheat Girls.* New York: Macmillan.

SADKER, M., AND SADKER, D. (1995). *Failing at Fairness: How Our Schools Cheat Girls.* New York: Touchstone Press.

———— (1997). *Teachers, Schools, and Society.* 4th ed., New York, McGraw-Hill.

SCHMIDT, P. (1994) "Idea of 'Gender Gap' in Schools Under Attack." *Education Week* 15(4) 1, 16.

SEXTON, P. (1969). *The Feminized Male: Classrooms, White Collars, and the Decline of Manliness.* New York: Random House.

SHAYKIN, A., ET AL., (1995). "Normative Neuropyschological Test Performance Effects of Age, Education, Gender, and Ethnicity." *Applied Neuropsychology* 2, 79–88.

"Sisterhood was Powerful." (1994). *Newsweek,* June 20, p. 68.

SMEAL, E. (1984). *Why and How Women Will Elect the Next President.* New York: Harper and Row.

SOMMERS, C. (1994). *Who Stole Feminism?* New York: Simon & Schuster.

SPENDER, D., editor. (1983). *Feminist Theorists.* New York: Pantheon Books.

TIGER, L. (1995). Review of Campbell. *Men, Women, and Aggression in Society* 32(3) 79–83.

WHEELER, D. (1998). "Neuroscientists Take Stock of Brain-Imaging Studies." *The Chronicle of Higher Education* 45(3), A20–21.

WOLF, N. (1992). *The Beauty Myth: How Images of Beauty Are Used Against Women.* New York: Doubleday.

"Women in Management: It's Still Lonely at the Top." (1998). *World of Work: The Magazine of the International Labour Office,* No. 23, February, pp. 6–9.

WORSNOP, R. I. (1997). Gender Equity in Sports." *Congressional Quarterly Researcher* 7(15)337–360.

# CHAPTER 6

# Affirmative Action: Progressive or Restrictive

## POSITION 1: FOR AFFIRMATIVE ACTION

### Different Views of the Same Situation

A 1997 Gallup Poll survey of 3,076 randomly selected black and white Americans asked how blacks are treated in their communities.

Black respondents in the following proportions answered that:

| | |
|---|---|
| They were treated as well as whites: | 49% |
| They were not treated very well: | 38% |
| They were treated badly: | 7% |

White respondents answered that:

| | |
|---|---|
| Blacks were treated as well as whites: | 76% |
| Blacks were not treated very well: | 15% |
| Blacks were treated badly: | 2% |

Thirty years earlier, Gallup Poll data on the same issue showed even more disparity between the views of blacks and whites. Only 26 percent of the blacks surveyed in 1968 thought they were treated as well as whites in their communities, but 73 percent of the whites thought so—not far from the 1997 proportion of whites. By 1980, the proportion of blacks who responded that they were treated as well as whites had risen to 40 percent, against 68 percent of whites (Masci, 1998). Part of this increasing sense of equity on the part of blacks is attributable to affirmative action programs designed to equalize opportunities for minorities and women in education and work. The need for affirmative action progams is not likely to be as clear to whites because the vast majority of them think equity already exists, and, of course, they have thought so for over thirty years.

In the 1997 Gallup survey, when asked how they felt about affirmative action programs, 53 percent of the black respondents wanted to increase them; while less than half as many whites, 22 percent, wanted an increase in affirmative action. An equal proportion—29 percent—of both black and white respondents wanted affirmative action retained as it is. But the highest proportion of white respondents, 37 percent, and the smallest proportion of blacks, 12 percent, wanted to decrease affirmative action (Masci, 1998). Clearly there are disparities in black and white perceptions on how well blacks are doing and whether affirmative action is working.

## Affirmative Action for all Minorities and Women

Affirmative action is not limited to equalizing opportunities for black Americans; it offers opportunities to Native Americans, Hispanic Americans, Asian Americans, women, and others who have suffered discrimination in education or in work. Diversity in education and the workplace have increased, partly thanks to affirmative action programs. Schools and businesses look more realistically like the broad rainbow of people in U.S. society.

Schools are more multicultural than ever, reflecting a diverse and vibrant society. The artistic, intellectual, and athletic talents of a much larger spectrum of people are developed and enhanced through this diversity in education, offering more back to society as well. From 1972 to 1995, the percentage of law degrees awarded to women increased from about 6 percent to almost 50 percent. Affirmative action helped to make that possible. Thomas (1990), one of the founders of the diversity movement, credits affirmative action as essential in correcting the imbalance in the workforce. Diversity has been good for schools and businesses, significantly increasing the social and economic contributions of previously underrepresented groups. Increased productivity, more responsiveness to the consumer base around the world, and greater understanding of cultural differences and similarities are examples of improvements diversity has wrought in business.

## A Policy Seeking Its Own Demise

Affirmative action is a peculiar social policy. It developed as a means to counter centuries of discriminatory policies and practices, and to remedy the disadvantages that discrimination placed upon members of minority groups. Legal challenges to discrimination evolved in legislation and in court decisions and provided a technical avenue to redress grievances. But society still needed to correct an ingrained policy that depended upon prejudice and fostered segregation. That prejudice, even when legal supports for discrimination were destroyed and new policies were put in place, still wafted through schools and businesses. We can abolish discrimination by law, but it is not easy to abolish it in day-to-day life. Even if we could succeed in eliminating all current prejudices, the harm done to minority families over the decades of discriminatory practice could not be undone in one year or five.

Affirmative action arose as one idea to jump-start the correction to this generations-old problem. The idea was to give preferential treatment to members of minority groups who demonstrate they have equal qualifications for entry into school programs or jobs. That premise—that members of groups who have suffered because of discrimination deserve an extra, affirmative boost—is a ringing tribute to American concepts of civil rights and democracy.

One of the peculiarities of affirmative action is that it is a policy that, if successful, should lead to its own destruction. When affirmative action succeeds in leveling the playing field for minorities and women, so that they are no longer underrepresented in admission to colleges, to specialized training, and to professions, we will no longer need affirmative action.

## The Persistence of Prejudice

Many people question how long we must "put up with" affirmative action. Opponents of affirmative action answer this question with a rhetorical question of their own: Hasn't affirmative action lost whatever usefulness it may have once had?

Both questions miss the primary point. We should start not with a question about affirmative action, but about the phenomena that gave rise to it (Bond and Reed, 1991). The real question, then, is: Do racial, ethnic, and sexual prejudices still exist in America, and do these prejudices keep people from exercising equal opportunity?

Not only do the prejudices still exist, but they have resurfaced in recent years in more overt forms. The prejudices have acquired a patina of acceptability by being published in "respectable" journals such as *Commentary* and *The Public Interest*. The prejudices have also been the subject of a lot of mush-mouthing among intellectual and government "leaders." These high-falutin' variations of prejudice mostly blame the victims for their situation. Anyone who thinks we are discussing only racial prejudice here should read Susan Faludi's *Backlash* (1991) for its extended description of the forces undermining feminism, or David and Myra Sadker's *Failing at Fairness: How America's Schools Cheat Girls* (1994) for its host of examples showing how girls still suffer under sexism.

Politicians have seen the value of appealing to bigots; the notorious Willie Horton commercial of the 1988 Bush presidential campaign provides the most obvious example. The Bush administration long delayed enactment of the 1991 Civil Rights Act on the grounds that it would result in racial quotas, even though the bill expressly prohibited such quotas. The administration did not capitulate until Bush saw the need to distance himself from the demagoguery of David Duke, a Louisiana politician with a long history of race baiting, who was only saying what the White House had been saying.

Although the Clinton administration's position on affirmative action and performance were an improvement, Clinton himself showed a willingness to back off when resistance began to coalesce. He abandoned his nominee for assistant attorney general for civil rights, Lani Guinier, after the *Wall Street Journal* dubbed her a "quota queen." All she had suggested was that people *consider* some voting changes to ensure that minorities were not completely powerless in our democracy. For example, suggested Guinier, if a town had six openings on the town board, instead of having to vote for one candidate for each opening, a voter could cast all six of his or her ballots for a single candidate. This "cumulative" voting would increase the chance that the town's minority citizens would win at least one of the six slots and not be left unrepresented on the town board (Guinier, 1994, 1998).

It is strange indeed that affirmative action is challenged at a time when prejudice is becoming much more palpable. Although the challenge often comes from sources that seem well-intentioned, it also often comes from a source with a lengthy record of hostility toward minorities. The 1994 elections turned control of the Congress over to the Republicans for the first time in many years. Among the Republicans elected or reelected were many whose positions were contrary to the interests of minorities. Advocating for the abolishment of affirmative action is but one of these positions (Holmes, 1995a). The attacks on programs and policies of benefit to minorities, including affirmative action, are a manifestation of the prejudice—or, at the very least, the insensitivity—that makes affirmative action necessary.

Expressions of racial, ethnic, and gender-based prejudice are demonstrably on the increase, as the popularity of hate-filled radio talk shows so readily attests. Thus, the case for abandoning affirmative action has to be based on the idea that prejudice is unrelated to educational and employment opportunity. In fairness, the case is not as brazenly illogical as it sounds. The argument is that the laws now in place prevent prejudice from controlling school admissions or hiring and promotion decisions. However, anyone who has ever had to make such a decision knows the effort involved in keeping personal prejudices out of the picture, even when race, ethnicity, and gender are not at issue. We can never know the success of the effort for certain.

It is ridiculous to expect judges to understand the thought processes of an admissions officer or an employer better than that individual does him or herself. The most a judge can determine is whether the negative decision is completely at odds with the rejected candidate's qualifications (and those of the accepted candidate). Admissions officers and employers no longer are likely to make such patently indefensible decisions. For that, we can thank the antidiscrimination laws. Alas, below that threshold there is plenty of room for the subtle and indiscernible exercise of prejudice. Without affirmative action to promote some positive results, minorities and women would be left at the mercy of the antidiscrimination laws, which, at best, can guard them only against the grossest displays of prejudice.

Moreover, an antidiscrimination law can provide justice for a person who has been victimized by prejudice only if that person invokes the law. The cost of doing so can be huge, greater even than the value of the unfairly denied opportunity. There are time costs, which translate into lost-work (or wage) costs. There are the direct costs of legal assistance, especially now that the general slash in government services has sharply reduced the availability of free legal aid for the poor. There are emotional costs, which mount as the case drags on month after month, year after year. Recent rulings by the conservative majority on the U.S. Supreme Court have made it more difficult to bring a case and to win a case once brought (*Patterson v. McLean Credit Union,* 1989; *Wards Cove Packing Co., Inc. v. Atonio,* 1989).

It takes a determined and persevering nature to embark on such a journey. All those who lack the heart, and all those who start but then stop, forsake press coverage as well as justice. We know only about the stalwart few who persist and ultimately prevail. The publicity their victories attract makes the law seem more efficacious than it is. Affirmative action gives the unheralded losers another small chance at justice.

Cornel West, professor of Afro-American Studies and the Philosophy of Religion at Harvard University, captures well the prophylactic nature of affirmative action:

> Progressives should view affirmative action as neither a major solution to poverty nor a sufficient means to equality. We should see it as primarily playing a negative role—namely, to ensure that discriminatory practices against women and people of color are abated. Given the history of this country, it is a virtual certainty that without affirmative action, racial and sexual discrimination would return with a vengeance. Even if affirmative action fails significantly to reduce black poverty or contributes to the persistence of racist perceptions in the workplace, without affirmative action, black access to America's prosperity would be even more difficult to obtain and racism in the workplace would persist anyway. (West, 1994, p. 95)

## The Value of Inclusiveness

For a long time, colleges and private schools, especially those whose reputations allowed them to be very selective in admissions, tried to select a geographically diverse student body. This diversity, the schools believed, would yield a variety of perspectives, which would enrich the education of all the students. Diversity had educational value. The student who could provide it was considered to have an extra qualification for admission.

Geographic diversity is only one kind of *cultural* diversity. With the mass media homogenization of America, the white, male, middle-class student from Oregon may not differ significantly from his Pennsylvania peer. The two will probably share a lot of cultural referents and values. Educationally enriching differences are more likely to be found between blacks and whites, Latinos and Anglos, males and females. *Affirmative action,* then, is simply a catchall term for any attempt to give students the benefits of diversity. It is certainly as defensible to apply affirmative action to racial, ethnic, and gender differences as to geographic differences. There would be a strange inconsistency if geographic origin were the only desirable kind of difference, as indeed it was when U.S. education was officially racist and sexist.

Chang-Lin Tien is an Asian American who serves as the Chancellor of the University of California at Berkeley. He has no trouble thinking of ways in which a diverse student body enriches the education of all students:

> The medical student who plans to set up practice in East Los Angeles needs to learn how to interpret the way her patients perceive and describe symptoms,

patients whose families come from Mexico, Guatemala, El Salvador, Korea, China, Taiwan, and Japan.

The journalism student who aspires to one of California's major dailies—such as the *Los Angeles Times, San Jose Mercury News,* the *San Francisco Chronicle,* or others—must be versed in interviewing and reporting on all constituencies. The story about flooding in a Central Valley farm town will be based on accounts from Mexican field hands. The story about new directions in Silicon Valley will require interviews with engineers born in Taiwan and India.

The business administration major who hopes to climb the corporate ladder will head a workforce predominated by women and ethnic minorities. The education student will one day teach classes populated by youngsters of different ethnic and language backgrounds. The law student whose sights are set on political office must become familiar with the needs of a multicultural electorate in order to win votes. (1994, pp. 239–240)

Cultural diversity is at least as desirable in K–12 schools as it is in higher education. It can prevent children from forming prejudices at an age when students are especially suggestible. A mixed student body is the focus of the chapter on integration; affirmative action serves to integrate a school's *staff.* Ghetto students are already likely to have white teachers, so the benefits of affirmative action go to students in suburban schools who would not otherwise have a black or Hispanic teacher. Students in both kinds of schools who might otherwise think that only men can be school principals or superintendents, benefit when women are hired for these positions (Shakeshaft, 1998).

A New Jersey case highlights this idea. A high school had to dismiss one of the teachers in its business department because of declining pupil enrollment. The two most junior teachers both had the same length of service. One of the teachers was black in an otherwise all-white department. The school decided to keep her on in the interest of diversity. As the school superintendent explained, "Piscataway High is 52 percent minority. We think that students need to have both role models for them in the school. We also feel we have to have faculty members who represent the cultural differences in the school when we make judgments, policy and decisions about student programming and services" (Philip Geiger, as quoted by Gladwell, 1994, p. 33). The Bush administration argued in court against this action; the Clinton administration decided to support the action because it recognizes that cultural diversity is a legitimate *educational* interest (Rosen, 1994), then urged the Supreme court not to review the case (Elgasser and Peres, 1997).

Inclusiveness also has value in the workplace. Indeed, it can have a direct dollar value—a positive effect on the major focus of the workplace: profits. A company that excludes or that denies advancement to people solely on the basis of their skin color or sex can hardly maintain good public relations with the groups these people come from. The company may even run the risk of a boycott from those potential customers. By threatening such a boycott, Jesse Jackson was able to persuade several major corporations that their personnel mix should better reflect their mix of customers. It is, therefore, in a company's bottom-line interest to hire a diverse workforce. Awareness of this business reality is one of the reasons why the National Association of Manufacturers has given affirmative action a ringing endorsement (Urofsky, 1991, pp. 36–37). "Market penetration" is not the noblest of motives, but it serves a good cause if it broadens employment opportunities. If a company's marketing staff, sales-people, and advertising personnel include a representative mix of the American population, the company can easily gear its product image to a variety of sub-groups. Its own employees can tell it what the subgroups are likely to respond to.

Who now thinks it strange or off-putting that Jane Pauley should be one of NBC's senior news broadcasters, or Cokie Roberts one of ABC's? Both women are convinced their careers would never have taken off if affirmative action laws had not placed pressure on the networks (Reeves, 1995).

What does *employment* opportunity have to do with education, the focus of this book? Actually, the two are powerfully linked. The prospect of qualifying for a good job is a great inducement for students to gain an education. Students who foresee no occupational dividends can be expected to drop out. If students believe their sex or skin color vitiates the value of education, they will not see much point to spending time in school, other than for the social life it affords.

The employment-education link is of interest to society, as well as to the individual. Society seeks to get as much productivity out of individuals as pos-sible. The bigger the boost an individual can give to the national economy, the better. The key employment consideration should be the ability to do the job. To subvert this consideration with petty prejudice is as injurious to the society as it is to the individual. For a long time in U.S. history, ending only in the latter half of the twentieth century (and then far from completely), whole classes of people who had done well in school were kept from making the most of their educa-tion. We will never know how much more advanced and secure the national economy would be today if our system had not suppressed so much talent.

## The Long History of Preferential Treatment

Affirmative action was first made federal law in 1961 by an executive order of President Kennedy. Whatever preferential treatment women and minorities have received as a result can only have occurred since that year. The 174 years of U.S. history prior to 1961 were the era of preferential treatment for white men of European (and Christian) ancestry. In terms of numbers of years alone, white European men have received about six times as much preferential treatment as the groups that are now benefiting from it. The preferential treatment that accrues to minority groups or women does so with a good deal of fanfare. The preferen-tial treatment that still redounds to white men receives no attention at all.

One of the most obvious and ongoing forms of this historical preference is that of the Ivy League "legacies." Legacies are students who are given prefer-ence in admission to the Ivy League colleges because they are the children of alumni. "For more than forty years, an astounding one-fifth of Harvard's stu-dents have received admissions preference because their parents attended the school. . . . Offspring of [Yale alumni] are two-and-a-half times more likely to be accepted than their unconnected peers. Dartmouth this year admitted 57 percent of its legacy applicants, compared to 27 percent of nonlegacies. At the University of Pennsylvania, 66 percent of legacies were admitted last year" (Larew, 1994, p. 248). And the practice is not limited to the Ivy League; fully 25 percent of Notre Dame students are legacies (Lamar, 1991; Leslie, Wingert, and Chideya, 1991). The legacies contribute affluence and Anglocentricity to the student body, so one has to look to affirmative action for other ingredients.

Though whites fear massive displacement in colleges by minorities under affirmative action programs, affirmative action has not produced a huge increase in the number of black students in colleges. In 1990, black students constituted about 9 percent of the collegiate student body in the United States; in 1996, they made up only about 10 percent of that student population ("Vital Signs," 1998, p. 83.) More women, Asians, Hispanics, Native Americans, and others now attend and graduate from colleges, but white enrollments have declined less than 5 percent in the past ten years. And that decline cannot be attributed to affirmative action; the proportion of whites of that age group has decreased by the same amount. Further, the percentage of whites who have attended college for at least four years grew from 8 percent in 1960 to 24 percent in 1995; the percentage of blacks grew from 3 percent to 13 percent in the same period.

One of the specious arguments put forth against affirmative action college admission programs is that they are responsible for high dropout rates for black students. This argument, based on the mistaken presumption, or prejudice, that the black students admitted are of inferior quality, simply does not fit the facts. A study conducted in 1997 by the *Journal of Blacks in Higher Education* (Cross, 1998) assessed the black and white graduation rates at the most prestigious colleges and universities (Table 6.1).

Cross also determined that schools which have no affirmative action program, the historically black colleges and universities, have high dropout rates, obviously for reasons other than affirmative action. The reasons for

**TABLE 6.1. 1997 White and Black Graduation Rates at Selected Colleges and Universities**

|  | White Graduation Rate | Black Graduation Rate |
| --- | --- | --- |
| Amherst | 97% | 95% |
| Bryn Mawr | 84% | 80% |
| Claremont McKenna | 88% | 86% |
| Harvard | 97% | 95% |
| Haverford | 92% | 91% |
| Princeton | 95% | 92% |
| Yale | 96% | 88% |

*Source:* Survey by the JBHE research department and 1997 NCAA Division 1 Graduation Rates Report. In Cross, T. "Why Affirmative Action Is Not Responsible for High Black Dropout Rates." *Journal of Blacks in Higher Education* 20, 91–99.

high withdrawal rates at these and many other colleges are complicated; they include general social conditions, a long history of discrimination, continuing disparity in socioeconomic status between blacks and whites, much higher unemployment rates for black youth compared to white, and significantly smaller endowments and student support money in colleges other than the most prestigious. These factors have nothing to do with affirmative action; indeed, affirmative action may offer some mitigation from them for blacks, women, and other minority students.

Along with other types of preferential treatment, children of the favored have been guaranteed job slots in such industries as the printing and construction trades and in municipal services such as police and fire departments. These father-son job bequests have long enjoyed the blessings of the labor unions. This preferential treatment was a form of discrimination since employment, like college admission, is a zero-sum game. Antidiscrimination laws were used to break down these barriers in several notable cases. However, affirmative action programs were also valuable tools since they could get results much more quickly than a years-long court case based on an antidiscrimination law. President Nixon used an affirmative action decree, known as the Philadelphia plan, to set numerical goals and enforcement procedures for the desegregation of the construction trades (Urofsky, 1991, p. 18).

Try to imagine how civil harmony would be disrupted if police and fire departments had not been integrated to reflect the communities they serve. Would ghetto communities want to be "protected" by people they have come to perceive as an invading force, a colonial power? If the Los Angeles police officers who repeatedly clubbed Rodney King in 1991 had been of his race, their behavior would have been no more excusable; but the community reaction to their acquittal would likely have been nonviolent rather than sparking days of violent rioting and looting. The integration of the municipal services was brought about, in large measure, by affirmative action plans. And schooling was one of the affected municipal services. No longer were minority families required by law to entrust the education of their children to people from outside the community who were unfamiliar with and even hostile to its ways—so hostile, in fact, that they could not use the community's traditions as building blocks in the education of its children. All the outsiders did was instill in the children a sense of shame for their roots, and rage eventually erupted from the shame.

## The Myth of Potential

A widely held belief exists that it is possible to measure a person's potential for success and to calibrate this potential with a high degree of precision. There are all kinds of "ability tests" that are supposed to do just that. The readers of this book no doubt have acquired a good deal of personal experience with such tests. The Scholastic Aptitude Test (SAT), the American College Test (ACT), and the Graduate Record Exam (GRE) are ability tests, or tests of potential. So are all those screening tests that business, government, and the military use to decide who gets in the door and which slot he or she can best fill.

If one believes in the validity of these tests, that they really tell us what they claim to tell us, then it would be both stupid and cruel not to rely on them in making decisions about a person's fate. It would be stupid because talent would sometimes go unused, and tasks would sometimes be carried out by incompetents. It would be cruel because both the talented and the incompetent would suffer frustration and despair. By overriding the results of ability tests, affirmative action earns the reputation of being both stupid and cruel.

But is it? It is only if one shares two common assumptions about ability tests. The first is that these tests measure something innate that the environment cannot affect. For a long time, the Educational Testing Service (ETS) made that claim for the SAT, saying that coaching could not change one's predestined score because that score reflected innate ability; or, at least it reflected knowledge obtained over a long period that could not be quickly acquired. In recent years, the ETS has conceded that coaching can raise the score considerably; it now even sells its own SAT coaching products (Crouse and Trusheim, 1989; "SAT Coaching," 1991; "Ten Myths About the SAT," 1989). The ability to raise one's score, of course, had long been obvious to parents who paid a great deal of money to have their children coached. The SAT, like all so-called ability tests, is really an *achievement* test. Achievement is a product of native endowment plus experience, and coaching is just one experience that affects the score. Another factor is school experience; if women and minorities tend to score lower than white males on the SAT, one should look to differential school experience for an explanation.

The second assumption one has to make to conclude that affirmative action is wrongheaded is that an ability or achievement test allows us to target a person into the place where he or she can perform best. The U.S. Supreme Court, in *Griggs v. Duke Power Company* (1971), struck a heavy blow against this assumption. The Duke Power Company had used a general intelligence (IQ) test to determine whom to hire and where to put them to work. Blacks, on average, scored lower than whites because they had received poorer educations, so they were either rejected or consigned to the lower-paying jobs. The Court recognized the experiential component of an IQ score. More importantly, the Court found the test was not job-related. A general intelligence test does not predict how well someone will perform a particular job, any more than SAT scores are good predictors of how well people, especially women, will do in college (Wainer and Steinberg, 1992). What tests like this do is make screening decisions easy, not wise.

When assumptions about test validity are successfully challenged, affirmative action ceases to seem stupid and cruel. What is stupid is giving people tests on which they are doomed to do poorly because of past discrimination and not taking the discrimination into account when interpreting the test scores. What is cruel is denying people an opportunity to overcome the effects of past discrimination and instead using those effects to justify further discrimination. Affirmative action is intended to break what otherwise would be an unending cycle of discrimination.

One way to avoid the unfair use of screening tests, other than to prohibit their use altogether, is to conduct differential "norming" of the results. For example, SAT scores should be adjusted to improve their predictive validity for women.

The tests could compare (norm) women with each other and not lump them together with the men. For a while, such norming was actually done for racial and ethnic groups. An employer was allowed to hire the top-ranked black even if the black's score was lower than that of the top-ranked white; society recognized that the black had overcome obstacles to get to that point and would probably do well on the job. The Civil Rights Act of 1991 banned further norming of this type, but Robyn Dawes (1993) is right in her conclusion about race norming:

> Yes, racial norming does involve unfairness to some majority applicants, but there is no way to treat everyone fairly at once. Is it fair to penalize a minority applicant from a poor background who had few opportunities to develop a relevant aptitude by interpreting test scores in a color-blind manner? Is it fair to penalize the majority applicant who scores higher for lacking a poor background by race-norming our test results? As President Kennedy once said, "Life is not fair." Reality prohibits fairness. What we can do is minimize unfairness. Racial norming of tests, which adversely affects only those majority group applicants with the lowest scores, is a coherent way of minimizing unfairness. The problem with racial norming is that it is also explicit, and therefore open to objections and alternative proposals that are not coherent. I argue, however, that social policy should be coherent. (p. 34)

## Much Ado About Little

Affirmative action has recently become a blackjack for beating up women and minorities. That might be sufferable if the size of the blackjack were proportional to the actual impact affirmative action has had.

A good way to get a firsthand sense of this impact is to ask a working parent, "How has affirmative action affected your place of employment?" (If you have work experience of your own, ask yourself this question.) You may have to push the parent (politely) for some actual evidence, since affirmative action is the subject of countless unfounded and horrific rumors.

The truth is that the government simply does not have, nor does it want to have, enough monitors to check on the thousands and thousands of businesses and educational institutions that fall under affirmative action requirements. Enforcement was either lukewarm or nonexistent even during the Carter presidency (Stasz, 1981). During the Reagan and Bush presidencies, the executive branch of the federal government was ideologically opposed to affirmative action, hardly an attitude conducive to strict enforcement. Indeed, the U.S. attorney general's office was openly engaged on the side of interests that opposed the civil rights laws. An ideological shift occurred with the advent of the Clinton presidency. Clinton's assistant attorney general for civil rights, Deval Patrick, was actively supportive of affirmative action, to the point of reversing hostile decisions his predecessor had made ("Affirmative Action Without Fear," 1994).

This is not to suggest that no minorities or women benefited from affirmative action in the 1980s or 1990s. They did, but it is impossible to know how much of this benefit was *undeserved*. And that, after all, is the crucial question.

Ask your working parent, or yourself, "Are your female and minority cowork-ers incompetent at their jobs? How is their competence judged?" If they are as competent as the other workers, they were entitled to the jobs all along. If it took some pressure from the government to get them preferential treatment so that they could obtain long-delayed *equal* treatment, that is not *their* fault and they should not be beaten with a blackjack for it. "When reverse discrimination does *not* lead to visible differences in performance, the clear implication is that the selection criteria on which blacks ranked lower than whites were inappro-priate to begin with and should be abandoned" (Jencks, 1992, p. 63).

Something we can know for sure at this time is the economic and educational status of minorities relative to that of whites. The data show that black progress ceased, and in some cases reversed, during the 1980s (Jaynes and Williams, 1989). In 1969, black men earned $694 for every $1,000 white men earned. By 1989, the figure for black men had increased by only $22, to $716 (Hacker, 1992b, p. 101). Similarly, from 1970 to 1990, the percentage of black physicians increased from 2.2 percent to only 3.0 percent; of lawyers, from 1.3 to 3.2 percent; and of professors, from 3.5 to 4.5 percent (Hacker, 1992a, p. 24). In answer to the question "So what, why should blacks get special treatment?" one can quote Jim Sleeper:

> Blacks who demand preferments on the basis of past oppressions have more right behind them than do other interest groups, whose justifications are far more specious. Therefore, it is hypocritical for us to hold blacks, even those who trade irresponsibly on their status as special creditors, to standards of social reci-procity we certainly don't apply to savings-and-loan sharpies who come to us for bailouts and civil servants who demand pension increases. (1990, p. 309)

Data also show that women's progress has halted as well. Women bump up against the "glass ceiling," that level in the hierarchy of business that they can-not climb above. For example, women hold 43.5 percent of the low-level jobs in state and local government, but only 31.3 percent of the high-level jobs. They hold only 6 percent of the top jobs in the largest American corporations ("Few Women Found in Top Public Jobs," 1992). These numbers were compiled by the Federal Glass Ceiling Commission, which has since found that white men are now circling the wagons to remain the controlling group in corporations. They do this through mentoring and shared life-styles (Kilborn, 1995a, 1995b).

These objective data indicate that affirmative action was never a forceful federal program. That is why the outcries against it seem especially churlish. Nevertheless, those outcries reach the ears of poll takers and, thus, of politi-cians. The politicians are also aware of the popularity that conservatives such as David Duke, Jesse Helms, and George Pataki have garnered by opposing affirmative action, even though most politicians repudiate the more extreme statements of these men. A good gauge of the gutlessness of politicians con-cerning the affirmative action issue is found in the statements of the Democratic contenders in the 1992, 1996, and 2000 presidential races. And this does not augur well for Democratic platforms in the future.

All this reveals what everyone knows: large elements of racism and sexism spur the opposition to affirmative action, and politicians are prepared to pander to those elements. This may make affirmative action a losing cause, but it also makes its necessity clear.

## Acceptable Costs

The most painful aspect of affirmative action is the unavoidable hurt it causes innocent people. If someone with a higher score on the Medical College Admissions Test is passed over for admission to medical school in favor of a person with a lower score, the rejected applicant is bound to feel disappointment, if not bitterness. The applicant may realize that both test scores are within the range deemed acceptable by the medical school, that the lower scorer was handicapped by an impoverished education, and that the lower scorer will use his or her medical training to serve a poor community in dire need of doctors. And yet the rejected applicant is also aware that he or she was in no way responsible for the conditions that justify the affirmative action acceptance. Bearing no personal responsibility for the wrongs of the past, the rejected applicant cannot help but wonder why he or she must bear the burden of rectifying those wrongs. Nevertheless, the zero-sum nature of medical school enrollments demands that some individual do penance for society's sin. The old victims are replaced with new ones.

The policymakers who create affirmative action requirements are not personally inconvenienced by them. Their hopes are not shattered, and they may even be able to assuage their consciences at no personal cost. They pass the costs on to someone else, usually someone much younger than they and much less implicated in the evil being redressed. The opponents of affirmative action often say that the policy substitutes one wrong for another, and that two wrongs don't make a right. Alas, social order among all species is a series of trade-offs in which the interests of some are sacrificed to the interests of the whole. It is in the United States' self-interest to progress beyond the injustices of the past, and there is no way to do this without providing compensatory justice to the victim groups. Their plight is real; it is without redeeming purpose; it is a disgrace that demeans us all. Those relatively few persons whose aspirations are thwarted by affirmative action should at least have the satisfaction of knowing they are taking part in a historic struggle toward establishing a victimless society.

We should all be able to take satisfaction in the successes of that struggle. Read the words of Stephen Carter (1991), an unapologetic beneficiary of affirmative action:

> I got into law school because I am black. As many black professionals think they must, I have long suppressed this truth, insisting instead that I got where I am the same way everybody else did. Today I am a professor at the Yale Law School. I like to think that I am a good one, but I am hardly the most objective judge. What I am fairly sure of, and can now say without trepidation, is that were my skin not the color that it is, I would not have had the chance to try. (p. 11)

What Carter graciously avoids adding is that for *centuries* the color of his skin would have been enough to keep him *out* of law school.

Finally, we may all admire the reaction of Paul Spickard, a white man with degrees in Asian history from Harvard and Berkeley, after he was twice turned down for college teaching jobs because the colleges wanted a person from a minority:

> My family came over on the *Mayflower* and made money in the slave trade. Doctors, lawyers, judges, and comfortable businesspeople go back several generations in my clan. . . . I am standing on the shoulders of my ancestors and their discriminatory behavior.
>
> Contrast my experience with that of a Chicano friend, whose immigrant father had a fourth-grade education and ran a grocery store. Without affirmative action and the social commitment it symbolizes, my friend might not have gone to Amherst, nor to Stanford Law School. . . . Our society would be poorer for the loss of his skills. . . . Affirmative action may not always be fair. But I'm willing to take second best if overall fairness is achieved. After all, for biblical Christians, fairness—often translated in our Bibles as "justice" or "righteousness"—is a fundamental principle by which God calls us to live. And affirmative action is an appropriate program aimed at achieving the godly goal of putting others' welfare before our own. (Spickard, quoted in Urofsky, 1991, pp. 28–29)

## Meanwhile . . .

We do continue to make progress. There is action, and it is affirmative.

Texas Southern University has created the Black Male Initiative, a program that intervenes in the lives of high school students to get them on the college-bound track and keep them at Texas Southern until they graduate. The fact that almost three thousand students attended the recruitment meetings in 1994 is evidence of the program's value (Zook, 1994).

The Compact for Faculty Diversity is a thirty-six-state consortium working to get two hundred minority students a year into doctoral programs. These students will be among the college faculty members of the future, serving as role models and mentors to the minority students of that era (Mercer, 1994).

Affirmative action programs at America's elite colleges have paid handsome dividends to society (Bok and Bowen, 1998).

Do these programs amount to preferential treatment? Yes. Is it a preferential treatment that will benefit all of us? Absolutely.

## POSITION 2: AGAINST AFFIRMATIVE ACTION

### From Goals to Quotas

In its earliest incarnation, affirmative action was only a reach-out program. Federal contractors were expected to reach out to minorities and women to make sure that these groups knew about available jobs and had a chance to apply. The reach-out effort added to employer costs and raised a question: Why couldn't these job hunters learn about job openings the way everybody else always has? Even so, the initial version of affirmative action was fairly benign.

Then the ominous mutations began. The employer's good faith efforts at reaching out, which were easy to document, were not enough if they did not lead to actual hires of women and minority group members. The employer was expected to establish hiring goals and timetables for reaching the goals. Employers knew that they would be suspected of bad faith if they reached out and set goals and timetables, but the composition of their workforce did not change. The goals inexorably mutated into quotas as employers felt more and more pressure to meet them and became more and more determined to do so.

U.S. Representative Edith Green of Oregon testified to her colleagues in Congress about how irrational the pressure on employers could be. Federal officials told a Portland company that it would receive no federal contracts until it had 15 percent minority employees in every single job category. It was impossible for the company to meet this demand unless it was willing to give jobs to highly unqualified people just for the sake of show (Maguire, 1980, p. 34).

Large companies such as Coca-Cola faced more than government pressure. Jesse Jackson's Operation PUSH (People United to Save Humanity) threatened to boycott these companies' products if their hiring demands were not met. Pressure also came from comparisons. One company would contrast the composition of its workforce with that of other companies in the same industry. Colleges and universities developed tables and graphs to show how well they were scoring in the affirmative action contest as compared with their competitors. To score well meant relieving a lot of pressure from Big Brother. It also meant a public relations victory.

The victories proved somewhat Pyrrhic when the public learned the price at which they were achieved. At the Georgetown University Law Center, a student who was hired to file student records began to notice some anomalies. He then did an analysis of a random sample of the records. He found:

> The average white student accepted by GULC had a score of 43 on the Law School Aptitude Test (LSAT) out of a possible 48 on the scale then in use; his average black counterpart had a score of 36. The average white student accepted by the school had maintained an undergraduate grade-point average (GPA) of 3.7; for the average black, the figure was 3.2. (Maguire, 1992, p. 50)

Numbers like these impelled a white student to bring a suit against the University of Texas Law School. The case of *Hopwood v. Texas* was decided in favor of the student. No college in the region can have minority quotas.

The sundry pressures that transform official goals into unofficial quotas will continue to exist under the Civil Rights Act of 1991. The law itself may contain language prohibiting quotas, but it has other language that will make employers anxious to meet their "goals" (Holmes, 1991). The distinction between a goal and a quota vanishes in these circumstances. A goal treated as a quota is, for all intents and purposes, a quota by whatever euphemism it is called. The *Hopwood* case has put an end to this charade in Texas, Louisiana, and Mississippi.

## Fabricating Ability

Employers and colleges are caught on the horns of a dilemma in pursuing their affirmative action interests. On the one hand, they cannot blatantly fill openings with unqualified people. Nor can they justify giving an opening to an affirmative action applicant whose qualifications are well below the standards for other applicants. They need *relatively qualified* affirmative action applicants.

These constraints put employers, colleges, the government, and affirmative action applicants in collusion to pad applicants' abilities. The most common way to do this is to interpret low ability in the most positive light. An applicant's low score on a screening test may be explained away by saying that the score is remarkable given the inferior education the applicant was subjected to in a racist (or sexist) society. The fact that the applicant scored even this well is a sign of perseverance against obstacles, a trait that surely means the person will perform well on the job.

The practice known as race norming institutionalizes this kind of score interpretation. The General Aptitude Test Battery (GATB) is a screening test whose use is encouraged by the U.S. Department of Labor. This battery was originally accepted as a reasonably valid way to predict how someone would do at a particular job. It was a job-related test. The problem was that minorities scored lower on the test than others did. Thus, if an employer were to be guided by the scores alone, minorities would be hired at much lower rates than other people, and at rates much lower than their percentage of the population.

Therefore, labor officials decided that two adjustments had to be made. First, the raw scores were converted into percentile scores. This is a common practice and is not objectionable on the face of it. But in this case, the percentile scores were computed *by category*. The percentile score for African American test takers was figured only against the scores of other African Americans who had taken the GATB. The percentile score for Hispanics was calculated against the scores of other Hispanics. All the other test takers were lumped into a third category called "other." The result of this race norming was that an African American could have a much lower raw score than a white (an "other") but be in the same percentile. A low test score could put someone at the 70th percentile among African Americans; a high score could put someone at the 70th percentile among "others" (Blits and Gottfredson, 1990a, 1990b). The employer would be free to hire the lower-scoring applicant, and would in fact be under government pressure to do so.

The 1991 Civil Rights Act prohibits the further use of race norming (Clymer, 1991). However, one cannot be sure that a new scheme for inflating low scores will not soon emerge. Besides, now that employers cannot use the GATB to satisfy their affirmative action interests, they may well turn to more congenial screening devices.

One such device is to discount the value of test scores in light of "other considerations." A low-scoring student can be accepted if it is presumed the student will benefit his or her classmates simply by being a member of an approved minority. Or it might be anticipated that the minority student will use his or her education to serve or advance the interests of the minority group. The most common way of justifying the acceptance of a lesser applicant is to say that he or she is entitled to preference in compensation for past sufferings.

None of these justifications is an empirical proposition. They are all faith statements, and empirical data can easily shatter the faith. Consider the last statement about compensation. As Lino Graglia (1993), the Cross Professor of Law at the University of Texas, notes:

> Persons who have been unfairly disadvantaged should undoubtedly be made whole to the extent feasible, but race is neither an accurate nor an appropriate proxy for such disadvantage. It is inaccurate because not all and not only blacks have suffered from disadvantage. Indeed, racially preferential admissions to institutions of higher education ordinarily help not those most in need of help, but middle-class and upper-middle-class blacks. (pp. 29–30)

Thus, a large amount of wishful thinking goes into these rationales, and their nebulousness allows almost anything to happen in the name of affirmative action. Tests and test scores, for all their problems, do provide a comprehensibility that permits us to discuss them meaningfully.

## The Problem of the Protected Category

Affirmative action is inherently corrupted by the terms it must deal in. Unlike the antidiscrimination laws, which provide remedies for *individuals* who have been discriminated against and can prove it in court, affirmative action refers to whole *categories* of people, all of whose members are presumed to have been discriminated against and none of whom has to prove anything. This immediately raises the sticky problem of deciding what these lucky categories are. For the federal government, the protected categories have been blacks, the Spanish-surnamed, Asians, Native Americans, and women. Governments at other levels have been free to decide what categories to include in affirmative action programs. If a large number of Italians live in a town, town officials can decide that the historical discrimination against Italians in the United States warrants preferential treatment for Italian Americans. This happened when the City University of New York added Italians to its preferred hiring list (Hacker, 1990, p. 7). Such self-serving mischief is called affirmative action. More and more we hear about others who would like to put themselves on board the affirmative action bandwagon; for example, the overweight, the elderly, the short. Northeastern University announced its intention to give hiring preference to gays, lesbians, the disabled, and veterans (Cage, 1994), so it is likely only a matter of time before other institutions will succumb to pressure to do the same. If there is no end, everyone will eventually belong to an affirmative action category and we will be back to square one.

Thinking only in terms of the five federal categories does not make matters much more palatable. Consider, for a moment, the Spanish-surname category. An Anglo woman who took the last name of her Hispanic husband would qualify for special treatment. So might a person of mixed parentage, both of whose parents were well-to-do. So, for that matter, would Linda Chavez (1991, 1994), the most vociferous Spanish-American opponent of affirmative action. Chavez's counterpart in the Asian community is Dinesh D'Souza (1991). The group mistakenly thought to have the largest number of people benefiting from affirmative action—African Americans—includes such prominent opponents as Thomas Sowell (1990). Sowell has studied the disastrous consequences of affirmative action programs in countries around the world, and he sees much more harm than good flowing from these programs. Other black scholars, such as Glenn Loury (1989; 1997) and William Julius Wilson (1987, 1991), are not ready to abandon affirmative action at this time, but have serious reservations about its efficacy and make a case for race-neutral programs to help the poor of all races. It is bizarre for supporters of affirmative action to insinuate that its opponents are bigots when so many of those opponents are among the putative beneficiaries.

What the opponents all share is an uneasiness about the sweeping nature of the categories. *Every* African American and *every* Spanish-surnamed person and *every* Asian American and *every* Native American and *every* woman are treated as victims entitled to special government treatment. This broad labeling is but another kind of stereotyping that ignores individual differences. It allows the wealthy Ivy League graduates in these groups to be accorded preferential treatment on the assumption that they have been victims of oppression. By this all-encompassing definition, the wife of the chief executive officer of the Cable News Network—Jane Fonda—is as much a victim of oppression as a woman in Appalachia raising a family of six on her own. Indeed, it is a melancholy fact of affirmative action that the people who have best been able to take advantage of it are those who are already relatively advantaged. Affirmative action actually widens the gap between these people and the less advantaged members of their group.

The five federal categories are problematic for who they exclude as much as for who they include. Homosexuals, for example, are not included. They have to depend solely on antidiscrimination laws to get fair treatment, and cannot get preferential treatment. And yet it is obvious that homosexuals have historically been much more maligned as a group than women. Given the voters' rejection of state initiatives designed to safeguard homosexuals against discrimination, it can be argued that gays and lesbians continue to be at greater risk of discrimination than heterosexuals in any affirmative action category. Neither do the poor constitute a protected category, even though they are the neediest group in terms of sheer survival. Poverty is considered to be a less compelling case for government intervention than is membership in one of the five official categories. Poverty is not an immutable—that is, unchangeable—characteristic, but race, ethnicity, and gender are. Therefore, the government assumes that the poor person is free to change his or her status with a little effort. In a recession economy, even a lot of effort may not be enough to do the trick, especially if the poor person has to wait to see what, if any, jobs are left after the affirmative action placements have been made. An employer, when forced to choose between hiring an unemployed white man with several young children or an already employed African American woman with no dependents, is on notice that giving the job to the white man could cause trouble with the government. On the other hand, giving the job to the African American woman will improve his hiring profile, if the government should come looking.

In fact, hiring the African American woman is a double bonus since the employer will have satisfied two of the categories in a single stroke. For that reason, a needy African American *male* applicant is not going to be as attractive to an employer as a Spanish-surnamed female applicant with an independent source of income. It is almost amusing to think about the ideal affirmative action hire in the near future—perhaps a Puerto Rican lesbian of African ancestry.

The important point is that the opponents of affirmative action are champions of the poor. It is their concern for the needy that causes them to oppose a program that so often bypasses the poor and benefits those who already have a step up. The opponents of affirmative action are the supporters of a means-tested program targeted to the truly disadvantaged, regardless of race, gender, ethnicity, sexual orientation, age, body shape, or veteran status. Paul Starr, a liberal, notes the static affirmative action creates in the antipoverty campaign:

> With the positive effects of racial preferences have come many unhappy ones—sustaining racism, stigmatizing much minority achievement as "merely" the result of affirmative action, creating a sense of grievance among whites who then feel entitled to discriminate, and blocking the formation of biracial political alliances necessary to make progress against poverty. (Starr, 1992, p. 14)

## Perpetuating Prejudice

Affirmative action is marked by many ironies, several of which we just discussed. The most tragic is that it exacerbates the very condition it was designed to help transcend. Racism is still pervasive in America, and affirmative action provides much of the fuel. Those who rightly resent the unfairness of affirmative action go beyond attacking the program to attacking the groups the program covers. This is a terrible mistake, but one that was predicted when the program was set up. As government pressure to force results increased, the prediction became increasingly true. Affirmative action became an albatross around the necks of the people it was supposed to help, the vast majority of whom received no benefit at all. Those who did benefit from affirmative action did so at the cost of increased hostility from all those who have not. Affirmative action is now an attack weapon against minorities in the hands of Rush Limbaugh and Jesse Helms. Mainstream politicians use it more sneakily, but to the same end. Affirmative action has thus caused a backlash against minorities. The way this backlash evolved and the Republican party's responsibility for instigating and capitalizing on it are the subjects of a book by Thomas and Mary Edsall (1991). The 1994 election gave their book a genuinely prophetic quality.

The prejudice affirmative action engenders can directly affect the beneficiaries themselves. They may feel great about being hired for a particular job or admitted to a certain school, but they immediately confront the animosity of their coworkers or of other students. Often they also have to contend with condescension from supervisors or faculty. Whereas the government treats them as victims entitled to special treatment, their coworkers and fellow students often *react* to them as political extortionists undeserving of the concessions they have gained. Those women and minority group members who earned their jobs or college placements without special consideration cannot wear sandwich boards advertising this fact; they themselves may not even be sure whether affirmative action played a role in their success. Thus, they are stigmatized as the *woman* forklift operator or the *black* Ph.D. candidate, with everyone understanding the implication about their right to be where they are.

Because of the unwelcoming work environment, the minority employee may either remain aloof or quit; either behavior reinforces the prejudice that precipitated it. The psychodynamics of these situations are explored in fascinating detail by Shelby Steele (1991). And two young blacks who were admitted to the exclusive St. Paul's and Phillips Exeter Academy prep schools became the subjects of gripping books about the trauma they experienced (Anson, 1987; Cary, 1991).

On college campuses, this affirmative action backlash results in segregation. The college may have succeeded in assembling a mixed student body, but minority and majority students don't mix with each other outside the classroom. When minority students choose "minority majors," such as African American or Puerto Rican studies, even the in-class mixing between groups is kept to a minimum. Minority clubs and minority fraternities or sororities further institutionalize the separation. Reality nullifies the diversity rationale for affirmative action.

The worst cases are those of the employer or college administrator who maintains a "good" hiring or admissions record by using the "revolving door" policy (Jacobs, 1989). A high-risk student or worker is admitted, which puts an end to special assistance. Without assistance, the high-risk student or worker fails, and a new one then takes his or her place. Studies show that colleges have lowered their admission standards to admit minority students who were likely to fail out without remedial help, and yet the help was not forthcoming (Hacker, 1989). Moreover, coworkers and fellow students receive little preparation, and there are no spelled-out sanctions against bigoted behavior toward the newly admitted minority. The speech codes that some universities developed to protect minorities against verbal assault have been overturned by the courts as undue infringements on a bigot's First Amendment rights. The minorities are therefore left to swim or sink in a sea of taunts. After a drowning, another hapless newcomer is admitted to the company or college. That person will count toward an affirmative action target until he or she goes under, and someone else is brought in. The company, college, or school district has invested virtually nothing in ensuring the success of the individual; it has cynically exploited an individual to win a numbers game it plays with the government. And every time an affirmative action prospect fails, the failure is attributed to others in the same category, tarring them all.

Jay Walker's case is emblematic of the syndrome. Walker was one of three black lawyers in a two-hundred-member law firm. He was never told he was an affirmative action hire, but he was always made to feel like one:

You always want to believe you were hired because you were the best. You work seven days a week, you wear Brooks Brothers suits, you play golf. But everything around you is telling you were brought in for one reason: because you were a quota. No matter how hard I worked or how brilliant I was, it wasn't getting me anywhere. It's a hell of a stigma to overcome. There are only twenty-four hours in a day.

When Walker left the firm, another black took his place. "It's a revolving door," Walker concluded (Walker, quoted by Wilkerson, 1991, p. 28).

Women, too, must contend with the stigma of affirmative action. From 1960 to 1990, the proportion of women among students earning doctorates increased from 11 to 36 percent (Stimpson, 1992). In 1994–5, almost 18,000 women earned doctorates (The Nation, 1998). For these women to realize that the value of their doctoral degrees has been cast in doubt by affirmative action policies that benefited very few of them is a terrible cruelty. In business, the proportion of senior vice presidencies held by women increased from 14 percent in 1982 to 23 percent in 1992, and women now occupy more than 40 percent of all managerial positions (Ingraham, 1995). As these presumed beneficiaries of affirmative action become increasingly aware of the extent to which they, too, have actually been victims of it, it will pass into history as a sincere but misguided attempt to bring justice.

## The Emerging Dismantlement

The affirmative action edifice is being dismantled, and with little protest. The federal government laid the cornerstones, and those will probably be the last to go—although the walls are already tumbling at the state and local levels.

During the 1990s, New York City Mayor Rudolph Giuliani discontinued the practice of steering city contracts to female- and minority-owned businesses. "This administration believes in hiring the best person or best company irrespective of race, color, creed, or sexual orientation. All such decisions are based solely on merits" (Giuliani, as quoted by Hicks, 1994, p. B1).

In California, the voters decided in 1996 to abolish the state's affrmative action program. Even prior to that, the University of California board of regents was asked to discontinue the university system's affirmative action policy. A black member of the board made the request; he wanted to do away with ethnic outreach and replace it with economic outreach to the poor. The university predicted that the Caucasian proportion of the freshman class at Berkeley would climb from 30 to perhaps 37 percent, while the African American proportion would drop from 6 to 2 percent. Also predicted were a significant increase for Asian Americans and a significant drop for Hispanics (Lubman, 1995). The African-American proportion dropped in 1998, but is returning to previous levels.

Nationally, the Republican contenders for the Presidency in 1996 lined up in opposition to affirmative action, and President Clinton announced a review of all 160 federal programs to determine which have outlived their usefulness. In the 21st century, affirmative action will be gone as a quota system.

The Supreme Court looks even more skeptically at affirmative action. In *Adarand Constructors v. Pena*, the Court decided that all affirmative action programs are suspect and must be strictly scrutinized to see if they really serve a "compelling government interest" (Greenhouse, 1995). The Court also let stand a lower court ruling in *Podberesky v. University of Maryland* that race-based scholarships awarded by public universities are unconstitutional (Holmes, 1995b).

Affirmative action was always a delicate balance between need and merit. Basing it on categories such as race and gender confused both sides of the issue. If such programs are to be continued, they should be recast in terms that more clearly capture the original purpose. *Need* and *disadvantage* must be defined in ways most Americans can agree with and can endorse; preferential action must be based on legitimate individual need and a proven ability to overcome personally encountered obstacles. Quotas do not do that. Affirmative action outlived its early concerns. It is time to put it to rest.

## For Discussion

1. The United States counts among its citizens people from many nations and ethnic groups, as well as two sexes. Affirmative action programs are designed to increase opportunities for members of minority groups or genders who are underrepresented in education or work—partly because of past discrimination or unfair practices. Table 6.2 records the proportions of different populations in the United States in recent and projected years. Given these data, what could you say about the current affirmative action policies in school and work, and what would you predict about them over the next fifty years? Examine census statistics for data about educational attainment and employment for each of these groups, and discuss how affirmative action is or could be negative or positive for them.

**TABLE 6.2. Population Proportions, Past and Projected, for Minority Groups in the United States**

|  | 1980 | 2000 | 2050 |
|---|---|---|---|
| Whites | 86% | 82.1% | 74.8% |
| Blacks | 11.8 | 12.9 | 15.4 |
| Asian/Pacific Islanders | 1.6 | 4.1 | 8.7 |
| AmerIndians, Eskimos, Aleuts | 0.6 | 0.9 | 1.1 |
| *Hispanics |  |  |  |
| Males (all groups) | 48.6 | 48.9 | 49.1 |
| Females (all groups) | 51.4 | 51.1 | 50.9 |

*Hispanic Origin can be of any race. The proportion of HIspanic Origin people in the United States for the same years is or is projected to be: 1980 = 6.9%; 2000 = 11.4%; 2050 = 24.4%.
*Source: Statistical Abstract of the United States.* (1997) U.S. Department of Commerce, Bureau of the Census. Washington, DC: U.S. government Printing Office.

2. It is often said that women, blacks, or Hispanics are "underrepresented" at one college or another.
   a. What are the percentages of these groups in the student body of your college? (The dean of students should be able to tell you.)
   b. What are the percentages among the faculty? (The director of personnel or the affirmative action director should know.)
   c. Are the percentages of blacks, Hispanics, and women "high enough?" How is "high enough" determined?
3. Andrew Hacker claims that if affirmative action is applied only on the basis of economic need, minority students will have less chance of getting into college than they have now. He thinks that is because minority students in economic need have lower SAT scores than their poor white counterparts (Hacker, 1991). Can you find evidence of SAT differences among these groups? Under this logic, would Asians, who get higher SAT scores than whites, receive less affirmative action? How would Hacker's idea affect women, Hispanics, Native Americans, or other groups? What do you make of Hacker's logic?
4. Table 6.3 shows the high school completion rates for white, black, and Hispanic students in the United States from 1989 to 1995. What would account for these differences? If affirmative action policies were applied at the high school level, what would the affects likely be? What would you expect to be the relationship between language and school completion? How will new efforts to eliminate or decrease bilingual education influence these rates? What are the possible interrelations among various policies of affirmative action, desegregation, English-only instruction, and national standards?

**TABLE 6.3. Black, Hispanic, and White High School Completion Rates, 1989–1995**

|          | 1989  | 1991  | 1993  | 1995  |
|----------|-------|-------|-------|-------|
| White    | 89.3% | 89.8% | 91.2% | 92.5% |
| Black    | 82.3  | 81.8  | 82.7  | 86.8  |
| Hispanic | 61    | 56.7  | 60.9  | 57.2  |

*Source: Congressional Quarterly Researcher.* (1998). 8(35) 823. From *Latino Education: Status and Prospects,* National Council of La Raza, July 1998; National Center for Education Statistics, June 1996; *Educational Attainment in the United States,* Census Bureau, March 1995.

## References

"Affirmative Action Without Fear." (1994). *The New York Times,* September 19, p. A16.

ANSON, R. (1987). *Best Intentions: The Education and Killing of Edmund Perry.* New York: Random House.

BLITS, J., AND GOTTFREDSON, L. (1990a). "Employment Testing and Job Performance." *The Public Interest* No. 98, 18–25.

———— (1990b). "Equality or Lasting Inequality?" *Society* 27(3), 4–11.

BOK, D. AND BOWEN, W. (1998). *The Shape of the River*. Princeton: Princeton University Press.

BOND, J., AND REED, A. (1991). "Equality: Why We Can't Wait." *The Nation* 253(20), 733–737.

CAGE, M. (1994). "Diversity or Quotas?" *The Chronicle of Higher Education* 40(40), A13–A14.

CARTER, S. (1991). *Reflections of an Affirmative Action Baby*. New York: Basic Books.

CARY, L. (1991). *Black Ice*. New York: Knopf.

CHAVEZ, L. (1994). "Just Say Latino." In *Debating Affirmative Action*, edited by Nicolaus Mills. New York: Dell.

———— (1991). *Out of the Barrio: Toward a New Politics of Hispanic Assimilation*. New York: Basic Books.

CLYMER, A. (1991). "Senate Passes Civil Rights Bill, 95–5, Ending a Bitter Debate Over Job Bias. *The New York Times*, October 31, p. A20.

CROSS, T. (1998). "Why Affirmative Action Is Not Responsible for High Black Dropout Rates." *Journal of Blacks in Higher Education* 20, 91–99.

CROUSE, J., AND TRUSHEIM, D. (1989). *The Case Against the SAT*. Chicago: University of Chicago Press.

DAWES, R. (1993). "Racial Norming: A Debate." *Academe* 79(3), 31–34.

D'SOUZA, D. (1991). *Illiberal Education: The Politics of Race and Sex on Campus*. New York: Free Press.

EDSALL, T., AND EDSALL, M. (1991). *Chain Reaction: The Impact of Race, Rights, and Taxes on American Politics*. New York: Norton.

ELGASSER, G., AND PERES, J. (1997). "Supreme Court Asked to Ignore Appeal in Affirmative Action Case." *Chicago Tribune*, June 6, p. 4.

FALUDI, S. (1991). *Backlash: The Undeclared War Against American Women*. New York: Crown.

"Few Women Found in Top Public Jobs." (1992). *The New York Times*, January 3, p. A12.

GLADWELL, M. (1994). "How Far Can an Affirmative Action Plan Go?" *The Washington Post National Weekly* 11(49), 33.

GRAGLIA, L. (1993). "Affirmative Discrimination." *National Review* 45(13), 29.

GREENHOUSE, L. (1995). "Justices, 5 to 4, Cast Doubts on U.S. Programs that Give Preferences Based on Race." *The New York Times*, June 13, pp. A1, D25.

*Griggs v. Duke Power Company*. (1971). 401 U.S. 424.

GUINIER, L. (1994). *The Tyranny of the Majority*. New York: Free Press.

————. (1998). *Lift Every Voice*. New York: Simon and Schuster.

HACKER, A. (1990). "Affirmative Action: A Negative Opinion." *The New York Review of Books*, July 1, p. 7.

———— (1989). "Affirmative Action: The New Look." *The New York Review of Books*, October 12, pp. 63–68.

———— (1991). "Playing the Racial Card. *The New York Review of Books*, October 24, pp. 14–18.

———— (1992a). "The Myths of Racial Division." *The New Republic*, March 23, pp. 21–25.

———— (1992b). *Two Nations: Black and White, Separate, Hostile, Unequal*. New York: Scribner's.

HICKS, J. (1994). "Giuliani Is Halting or Scaling Back Affirmative Action Efforts." *The New York Times*, August 23, pp. B1, B3.

HOLMES, S. (1995a). "Backlash Against Affirmative Action Troubles Advocates." *The New York Times*, February 7, p. B9.

———— (1995b). "Minority Scholarship Plans Are Dealt Setback by Court." *The New York Times*, June 23, p. B9.

———— (1991). "Lawyers Expect Ambiguities in New Rights Law to Bring Years of Lawsuits."*The New York Times*, December 27, p. A20.

*Hopwood v. State of Texas.* (1994). 861 F. Supp. 551.

INGRAHAM, L. (1995). "Enter, Women." *The New York Times*, April 19, p. A23.

JACOBS, J. (1989). *Revolving Doors: Sex Segregation and Women's Careers.* Stanford, CA: Stanford University Press.

JAYNES, G., AND WILLIAMS, R., EDITORS. (1989). *A Common Destiny: Blacks and American Society.* Washington, DC: National Academy Press.

JENCKS, C. (1992). *Rethinking Social Policy.* Cambridge, MA: Harvard University Press.

KILBORN, P. (1995a). "White Males and Management." *The New York Times*, March 17, p. A14.

———— (1995b), "Women and Minorities Still Face Glass Ceiling." *The New York Times*, March 16, p. A22.

KLEIN, J. (1995). "The End of Affirmative Action." *Newsweek*, February 13, pp. 36–37.

LAMAR, J. (1991). "Whose Legacy Is It, Anyway?" *The New York Times*, October 9, p. A–25.

LAREW, J. (1994). "Who's the Real Affirmative Action Profiteer?" In *Debating Affirmative Action*, edited by Nicolaus Mills. New York: Dell.

LESLIE, C., WINGERT, P., AND CHIDEYA, F. (1991). "A Rich Legacy of Preference." *Newsweek*, June 24. 59.

LOURY, G. (1989). "Why Should We Care About Group Inequality?" In *The Question of Discrimination: Racial Inequality in the U.S. Labor Market*, edited by S. Shulman and W.Darity, Jr. Middletown, CT: Wesleyan.

————. (1997). "How to Mend Affirmative Action." *The Public Interest.* No. 127, pp. 33–43.

LUBMAN, S. (1995). "Campuses Mull Admissions Without Affirmative Action." *The Wall Street Journal*, May 16, pp. B1, B10.

MAGUIRE, D. (1980). *A New American Justice: Ending the White Male Monopolies.* New York: Doubleday.

MAGUIRE, T. (1992). "My Bout with Affirmative Action." *Commentary* 93(4), 50–52.

MASCI, D. (1998). "The Black Middle Class." *Congressional Quarterly Researcher* 8(3), 49–72.

MERCER, J. (1994). "Ambitious Program Aims to Produce Minority Ph.D.'s." *The Chronicle of Higher Education* 40(35), A36.

"The Nation." (1998). *Chronicle of Higher Education.* 45(1), 26.

*Patterson v. McLean Credit Union.* (1989). 491 U.S. 164.

REEVES, R. (1995). "Affirmative Action Does America Good." *The Newark Star-Ledger*, May 10, p. 18.

ROSEN, J. (1994). "Is Affirmative Action Doomed?" *The New Republic* 211(16), 25–36.

SADKER, D., AND SADKER, M. (1994). *Failing at Fairness: How America's Schools Cheat Girls.* New York: Macmillan.

"SAT Coaching: Reality vs. Cover-up." (1991). *FairTest Examiner* 5(4), 1–2.

SHAKESHAFT, C. (1998). "Wild Patience and Bad Fit." *Educational Researcher.* 27(9), 10–12.

SLEEPER, J. (1990). *The Closest of Strangers: Liberalism and the Politics of Race in New York.* New York: Norton.

SOWELL, T. (1990). *Preferential Policies: An International Perspective.* New York: Morrow.

STARR, P. (1992). "Civil Reconstruction: What to Do Without Affirmative Action." *The American Prospect* No. 8, 7–14.

STASZ, C. (1981). *The American Nightmare: Why Inequality Persists.* New York: Schocken Books.

STEELE, S. (1991). *The Content of Our Character: A New Vision of Race in America.* New York: St. Martin's Press.

STIMPSON, C. (1992). "It Is Time to Rethink Affirmative Action." *The Chronicle of Higher Education* 38(19), A4.

"Ten Myths About the SAT." (1989). *FairTest Examiner* 3(4), 8–9.

THOMAS, R. R. (1990). "From Affirmative Action to Affirming Diversity." *Harvard Business Review.* March/April.

TIEN, C. (1994). "Diversity and Excellence in Higher Education." In *Debating Affirmative Action,* edited by Nicolaus Mills. New York: Dell.

UROFSKY, M. (1991). *A Conflict of Rights: The Supreme Court and Affirmative Action.* New York: Scribner's.

"Vital Signs." (1997). *Journal of Blacks in Higher Education* 20, p. 83.

WAINER, H., AND STEINBERG, L. (1992). "Sex Differences in Performance on the Mathematics Section of the Scholastic Aptitude Test: A Bidirectional Validity Study." *Harvard Educational Review* 62(3), 323–336.

*Wards Cove Packing Co., Inc. v. Atonio.* (1989). 109 S. Ct. 2115.

WEST, C. (1994). *Race Matters.* New York: Vintage.

WILKERSON, I. (1991). "Remedy for Racism of Past Has New Kind of Shackles." *The New York Times,* September 15, pp. 1, 28.

WILSON, W. (1987). *The Truly Disadvantaged: The Inner City, the Underclass, and Public Policy.* Chicago: University of Chicago Press.

———— (1991). "Racism and Race-Conscious Remedies." *The American Prospect* No. 5, 93–96.

ZOOK, J. (1994). "Recruiting Black Males." *The Chronicle of Higher Education* 41(13), A34.

## PART TWO

# What Should Be Taught?

## INTRODUCTION

Part II concerns the idea of knowledge. It should not be surprising to find that a book about schooling spends considerable space on knowledge, but what makes it an issue? Communicating knowledge, most people agree, is the core purpose of schools. The issues arise because of major disagreements over how to define knowledge, whose knowledge should prevail in the schools, how to package that knowledge, and how to organize and teach that knowledge. These disputes are often at the center of various school wars, since the control of knowledge is the control of society. Significant arguments arise over such issues as:

- What knowledge is most valuable?
- What knowledge should we teach, and in what sequence?

- Which knowledge should be required study, which should be elective, and which should be censored out of school?
- Who gets to decide what knowledge we will teach?
- Who should get access to which kinds of knowledge?

Not only are these theoretical concerns linked to the school curriculum, they are also practical concerns basic to teaching and learning. Should schools emphasize the classics of Western literature, computer technology, basic skills, moral behavior, employable job skills, test taking, citizenship, the arts, science, language, recreational activities, or some combination of these or other topics? Should the schools aim to produce broadly educated people, specialists in academic subjects, social critics, book learners, industrial workers,

**193**

college material, athletes, consumers, patriots, or something else? Should all students be required to take courses each year in English, social studies, math, science, and the arts? Who should be selected for admission to programs in law, medicine, auto mechanics, flower arranging, or accounting? Who should decide?

Obviously, the most valuable knowledge should be taught in school, but that begs the question of who decides what is worth knowing. The struggle to control what is accepted as valued knowledge is inevitably a struggle for power. To control people's minds is to control their expectations, their behavior, and their allegiance. Deciding which students get access to which knowledge has a powerful impact on social policy and politics, with results that can lead in opposite directions: more social egalitarianism or more elitism, more social-class separation or more social integration. Such decisions can enable or restrict individual achievements and enhance or detract from democracy. Thus, these decisions have enormous implications for individuals and for society.

In ancient times, when magic and witchcraft were socially credible, sorcerers enjoyed great power and status. Their pronouncements were often translated into laws and policies. Only a select few had the opportunity to learn their secret rites. Later, when knowledge of witchcraft came to be viewed as evil knowledge, sorcerers were burned; in modern societies where scientific knowledge is prized, "sorcerers" are considered interesting eccentrics. This demonstrates how societies change the definition of valuable knowledge. The postmodern society suggests new definitions and a new

school curriculum for the twenty-first century (Stanley, 1992; Greene, 1994).

Knowledge incorporates the concept of literacy. In an age of witchery, a literate person is one who shares the language and values of the sorcerer's form of knowledge. In an age of technology, a literate person may be defined as one who shares the language and values of technological knowledge. Thus, the term *literate* may be thought of as a verbal badge given to those who possess knowledge considered socially valuable. Schools provide literacy credentials in the form of diplomas, degrees, and various types of professional certificates.

The school curriculum of each society reflects the definitions of knowledge prevalent in that society and in that time. The content of the school curriculum is shaped by what a society's leading groups consider valuable knowledge. These definitions often conflict—the arts versus the sciences, the practical versus the theoretical, how to promote social cohesion versus individual independence. Typically, the traditional school subjects coexist in the curriculum until a new topic arises that challenges that emphasis. When test scores revealed a deficiency among U.S. students in the basic skills of reading, writing, and arithmetic, many elementary schools decreased the curriculum time spent on science, social studies, and the arts and shifted it to reading and arithmetic. When computer education became socially valuable, the schools made space to fit it into a crowded school curriculum.

The specific mix of courses and the emphasis within the curriculum depend on the prevailing visions of the "good" individual and the "good" society. In every age, people hold disparate views on what kinds of individuals and society are most desirable.

Some want to assist individuals to be free, independent, and critical; others advocate behavior modification to control deviation and ensure social conformity. Some want to mandate that each person acquire specific, standard information; others recommend unlimited variety and creativity. Some demand that schools instill prescribed moral values and beliefs; others demand release from moralisms and prescriptions. Some desire respect for authority; others prefer challenges to authority. Some would use schooling to supply society's needs for workers, managers, engineers, and doctors; others would promote broad schooling with no vocational orientation. Driving each of these competing views are concepts of the "good" individual and the "good" society.

## PRACTICAL, THEORETICAL, AND MORAL SCHOOLING

The literature of all societies is filled with disputes over how school should develop the good individual and the good society. Aristotle considered the state the fulfillment of our social drives and saw education as a state activity designed to provide social unity. He said that "education is therefore *the* means of making it [the society] a community and giving it unity . . . Education should be conducted by the state" (Aristotle, 1962, pp. 51, 333). In his introduction to and discussion of Chapter 2, Book 8, of *The Politics*, Aristotle discussed the controversy over whether schools should teach practical knowledge, moral character, or esoteric ideas:

The absence of any clear view about the proper subjects of instruction: the conflicting claims of utility, moral discipline, and the advancement of knowledge. . . . At present, opinion is divided about the subjects of education. All do not take the same view about what should be learned by the young, either with a view to plain goodness or with a view to the best life possible; nor is opinion clear whether education should be directed mainly to the understanding, or mainly to moral character. (pp. 333–334)

Contemporary curriculum debate continues to focus on the relative emphasis schools should give to practical, theoretical, and moral schooling. What type of knowledge will best fulfill the needs of individuals and society to (1) develop the skills for doing practical work; (2) pursue advanced, theoretical knowledge in such areas as mathematics, literature, logic, and the arts; and (3) provide a set of moral guidelines and ethical values for judging right from wrong?

No one has resolved the disputes over the kinds of knowledge schools should convey. Contemporary comprehensive public schools offer some useful applied educational programs, such as reading, writing, music, wood shop, home economics, computer operation, physical education, and vocational training. They also offer the study of theoretical concepts in English, math, social studies, the arts, and science. And schools provide various forms of moral education; students study selected literary and historical materials that convey ideas of the good person and the good society, and they learn from school rules and teachers to be respectful, patriotic, loyal, and honest.

The exact mix of these forms of education varies as different reforms become popular and as local communities make changes.

The school reform literature of the 1980s and the reactions of the 1990s were marked by arguments over whether to emphasize practical, theoretical, or moral knowledge in the schools. The National Commission on Excellence in Education, the lightning rod of the reform movement, proposed a high school graduation requirement of four years of English, three years of mathematics, three years of science, and a semester of computer science (National Commission on Excellence in Education, 1983). It is significant that the Commission ignored vocational education, a prominent feature of the school reforms of the 1930s and 1940s, in this report. Physical education, an emphasis in major school reforms between 1910 and 1920, was also dismissed. The arts received only passing reference in the National Commission report, but the proposed emphasis on computer science was actually in support of a practical course, not unlike the business education proposals of the 1920s and 1930s. The entire report was framed as a way to restore America's competitive edge in international business and national defense. These are practical purposes, and suggest that the required core of courses should tend toward knowledge useful in business. Economic utility, as Goodlad (1999) notes, continues to be the "drumbeat" of school reform.

Boyer's *High School*, an influential 1980s reform book from the Carnegie Foundation for the Advancement of Teaching, describes four essential functions of a high school. A high school should help students:

1. Develop critical thinking and effective communication skills.
2. Learn about themselves, the human heritage, and the interdependent world.
3. Prepare for work and further education.
4. Fulfill social and civic obligations. (Boyer, 1983)

These functions incorporate practical, moral, and higher or theoretical knowledge. Boyer's curriculum proposal includes required courses in writing, speech, literature, the arts, foreign language, U.S. and world history, civics, science, technology, and health, as well as a seminar on work and a senior-level independent applied project. The idea was to cover as many bases as possible to help students cope with an "interdependent, interconnected, complex world." Boyer included each of the practical, moral, and esoteric topics that Aristotle had posed as disputable in education.

In the 1990s, public opinion shifted to the idea that the school reforms of the 1980s were essentially mechanistic and "top-down." The presumption in the 1980s was that the president, governors, legislators, and national commissions could tell the schools what and how to teach in order to correct educational ills. Their prescriptions—for increased course requirements, longer school days and school years, more homework, more testing, and force-feeding knowledge to students in factorylike schools—have not proved their curative abilities.

Edward B. Fiske (1991), former education editor for the *New York Times*, argues:

> The time for tinkering with the current system of public educa-

tion is over. After a decade of trying to make the system work better by such means as more testing, higher salaries, and tighter curriculums, we must now face up to the fact that anything short of fundamental structural change is futile. We are trying to use a nineteenth-century institution to prepare young people for life in the twenty-first century. (p. 14)

Fiske argues against highly centralized school authority, standardization, and bureaucracy. He presents a case for students who can think for themselves; for decentralized and shared school decision making, with teachers taking responsibility for making the most important school decisions; for cooperative learning; and for moving beyond multiple-choice standardized testing to measure student knowledge. These views suggest a significantly different approach to knowledge than the prescriptions for particular courses, test score improvements, and imposed requirements that the 1980s school reform movement advocated. In the Fiske proposal, knowledge is much more holistic and integrating, and valued knowledge is defined by those closest to the classroom.

In the beginning years of the twenty-first century, external forces still largely determine the formal curriculum in American schools. Since Colonial times, the curriculum has evolved from a narrow interest in teaching religious ideals to multiple, and often conflicting, interests in providing broad knowledge, skills, and values relevant to nearly every aspect of social life. In U.S. schools, the medieval curriculum of "seven liberal arts"—rhetoric, grammar, logic, arithmetic, astronomy, geometry, and music—has given way to a list of subjects too long to enumerate. And the formal curriculum is certainly not all that students are expected to learn in school.

## THE HIDDEN CURRICULUM

In addition to the formal school curriculum, which is composed of the various courses prescribed for or offered to students, there is also a hidden curriculum consisting of unexpressed and usually unexamined ideas, values, and behaviors conveyed more informally to students. These are the subtle, often unintended, things students (and teachers) learn as they go about their lives in school. They represent underlying ideologies, root ideas about human values and social relations.

Two brief examples illustrate the hidden curriculum at its simplest level. Teachers tell students to be independent and to express their own ideas, but they often chastise or punish the student who exhibits independence and expresses ideas the teacher doesn't like. What does the student learn? In history courses, students hear that justice and equality are basic American rights, yet they see that compliant and well-dressed students earn favored treatment. What do they learn? The hidden curriculum is a vast, relatively uncharted domain that is often much more effective than the formal curriculum in shaping student learning.

At a deeper level, the discrepancies between what a teacher says and what that teacher does may raise a more significant concern about competing ideologies. Often, the hidden curriculum is in conflict with the stated purposes of the visible curriculum. The stated curriculum values diversity; the hidden curriculum expects conformity. The stated curriculum advocates critical thinking; the hidden curriculum supports docility. The visible curriculum emphasizes equal opportunity; the hidden curriculum separates students according to social-class background, gender, race, or other factors.

Critical literature examines the hidden curriculum and its ideological bases (see, for example, Anyon, 1979, 1980; Apple, 1990; Cherryholmes, 1978, 1988; Giroux, 1988; Giroux and Purpel, 1983; Popkewitz, 1987; Stanley, 1992; Young, 1970). From this critical view, the "great debates" about schooling that are extensively covered in the media and the mainstream educational literature are actually narrowly constructed differences between liberals and conservatives. At bottom, they do not raise ideological concerns about the control of knowledge and its social consequences; they tinker with the stated curriculum but leave the powerful hidden curriculum intact. That is the reason superficial school reforms do very little to change schooling, and neither mainstream liberals nor conservatives really want much change.

At the surface level, where much school reform debate occurs, a discussion about whether to spend more school time on computers, math, and English and less on the arts and social studies is a trivial matter; it hides more fundamental disputes about whose interests are served and whose are maligned. Shallow arguments about whether the curriculum should stress the basics, provide vocational courses, allow electives, or emphasize American values should lead to deeper, more critical examinations of who controls the school curriculum and the consequences of that control. In mainstream discourse, those basic issues (surrounding class, gender, race, and age controls) are hidden.

## *CURRICULUM CONTROL*

Control of knowledge, and of the school curriculum, is a product of both prevailing social goals and prevailing social structures. During most of the United States' formative years, religion was the basis for the school curriculum. Although differences existed among the colonies, most people expected that all young children would be taught religious precepts at home or at dame or writing schools. The purpose was to thwart the efforts of "that ould deluder, Satan," who sought to keep human beings from knowledge of the scriptures. After learning to read and write, however, most girls were not permitted further education. They returned home to learn the art of homemaking, while boys from more affluent homes continued their schooling at Latin grammar schools. African Americans and Native Americans were virtually excluded from the schools.

Historically, the struggle for the control of knowledge has paralleled social-class differences (Spring, 1998). The assumption was that workers needed practical knowledge, the privileged class needed higher knowledge, and both needed moral knowledge, but with great disparity in the kinds of moral knowledge they required. Craft apprenticeships to acquire practical knowledge were for the masses. Formal schooling to learn critical thinking and to study philosophy, science, and the arts was for the aristocratic class. In terms of moral instruction, the masses were to gain the moral character to obey, to respect authority, to work hard and be frugal, and to suffer with little complaint. Members of the privileged class were supposed to gain the moral character to rule wisely, justly, and with understanding.

One of the central purposes of schooling is to prepare the future leaders of society. But when the powerful class controls education and decides what is to be taught, the essential curricular question is: What should members of the ruling class know? In more democratic societies, which make an effort to educate the masses, the curricular questions revolve around what *all* members of the society need to know.

Even in democratic societies, however, the additional curricular needs of those identified as potential leaders receive special attention. We can see this in the higher academic tracks and honors programs that characterize many modern high schools. The correlation between social expectations, social-class structure, and what schools teach deserves ongoing examination. Marrou (1956/1982), for example, notes that in ancient Arabia the "upper class is composed of an aristocracy of warriors, and education is therefore of a military kind . . . training character and building up physical vigour rather than developing the intelligence." He found similar conditions in ancient Asian, Indian, and Western educational systems (pp. xiv, xv).

R. H. Tawney (1964), observing that "educational policy is always social policy," criticized the elite "public boarding-school" tradition of the wealthy in England, and advocated improvements in the developing system of free schools for the working classes. Tawney saw how the very nature of the elite system was a part of the hidden curriculum, teaching the sons of the wealthy "not in words or of set purpose, but by the mere facts of their environment, that they are members . . . of a privileged group, whose function it will be, on however humble a scale, to direct and command, and to which leadership, influence, and the other prizes of life properly belong" (1964, p. 83).

Social class is not the only major factor lying behind curricular decisions. Race, gender, national origin, and religion are other conditions that influence decisions about which people receive what knowledge in a society. The concept of privilege, and the education that privilege brings, has been linked to racism and sexism in American and other national histories. Educational discrimination against racial minorities, women, Jews, Catholics, Native Americans, Eskimos, and others is a sorry tradition in a democratic society.

About half a century ago, psychologist Kenneth Clark, whose studies were a significant factor in the Supreme Court decision that found segregated schools unconstitutional (*Brown v. Board of Education*, 1954), put the case clearly:

> The public schools in America's urban ghettos also reflect the oppressive damage of racial exclusion. . . . Segregation and inferior education reinforce each other. . . . Children themselves are not fooled by the various euphemisms educators use to disguise educational snobbery.

From the earliest grades a child knows when he has been assigned to a level that is considered less than adequate. . . . "The clash of cultures in the classroom" is essentially a class war, a socioeconomic and racial warfare being waged on the battleground of our schools, with middle-class and middle-class-aspiring teachers provided with a powerful arsenal of half-truths, prejudices, and rationalizations, arrayed against the hopelessly outclassed working-class youngsters. (Clark, 1965, pp. 111–117)

Similar condemnations of educational discrimination based on religion, nationality, and gender are common in the critical literature (Hofstadter, 1944; Clark, 1965; Katz, 1971; Feldman, 1974; Spring, 1976; Apple, 1979, 1990; Sadker and Sadker, 1982; Walker and Barton, 1983; Grimshaw, 1986; Lather, 1991; Weiler, 1991; Giroux, 1991; Spring, 1998). As Rosemary Deem (1983) comments: "Women have had to struggle hard against dominant patriarchal power relations, which try to confine women to the private sphere of the home and family, away from the public sphere of production and political power" (p. 107). Weiler (1991) essentially agrees in a critique of the western system of knowledge, arguing that feminist pedagogy is rooted in a critical, oppositional, and activist vision of social change. Schooling that provides different types of knowledge and skills to students who differ only in race, gender, class, religion, or nationality contributes to continued inequality of treatment and to stereotypes.

The chapters of Part II examine some of the current curriculum disputes that have emerged as part of the reform movement in education. These disputes clearly relate to the question of what knowledge is most valuable in our society, a question that, in turn, relates to our differing visions of what constitutes the good individual and the good society.

## SOCIAL EXPECTATIONS: BASIC EDUCATION VERSUS CRITICAL THINKING

Chapter 7 poses a question about what schools should teach: should they concentrate on subject knowledge of historic and socially approved value, or on material that encourages critical thinking and student interest? It raises the issue of external versus internal determination of the curriculum. If individual students are expected to develop independent and critical judgment so they can participate actively in improving the democratic society, we should expect schooling that leads to that goal, and we can expect educated individuals to have an impact on the society. If society values a structure in which only a few people have power and most people are expected to be docile and to conform to social norms, we should expect schooling that leads to that end, and the resulting society.

Those two hypothetical statements seem to suggest the choice is simple; it is not. There are complex and changing relationships between the kinds of individuals we desire, the society we want to develop, and the schooling we provide. These relationships often send conflicting signals to schools, and the conflicts become enshrined in the school curriculum. Society wants students to become self-sufficient individuals—but not too self-sufficient too early, so students have little latitude in deciding what to study until they reach college. We desire a society that is democratic and inspires voluntary loyalty, but we do not trust open inquiry, so we require courses that stress nationalistic patriotism.

"Individual-making" encourages self-development and fulfillment, and "society-making" instills social values and socially valuable knowledge and behaviors. Arguments over what we expect students to learn in school relate to the twin goals of individual-making and society-making, because critics differ in their views of the kinds of individuals and society we should have. This reflects the potential power of the school in influencing succeeding generations.

Some people enjoy mathematics. For others, reading history or literature is a great joy. Some like to dissect white rats in biology class, to saw wood in the shop, or to exercise in the gym. Others are completely baffled or utterly bored by textbooks and teachers. Different strokes, as they say, for different folks. But aren't there some things that *everyone* should know, whether they enjoy it or not? Is there a set of skills that all should master? Should we require that anyone who graduates from high school be literate? Who should decide the criteria for literacy? What does it take to be educated in this beginning decade of the twenty-first century?

## READING: PHONICS OR WHOLE LANGUAGE?

Quite often in public disputes one finds that the controversy is on the surface, and secretly the

parties mostly agree. . . . The dispute over reading instruction is just the opposite: . . . everybody now claims allegiance to a "balanced approach" incorporating whole language and phonics, but the truth is that the two sides have one of the purest and angriest disagreements I've ever encountered. We're in the midst of a huge war. . . . (Lemann, 1997, p.129)

Chapter 8 provides two perspectives on this long-standing war of words.

Reading is generally acknowledged to be fundamental to student success. Few people question reading's place at the center of the elementary curriculum, but no one agrees on how schools should introduce reading to students. This is not new. Reading has always been surrounded by controversy, and the history of reading instruction is a record of bitter disagreements, both political and academic. One way to gain some perspective on the current debate is to briefly consider some earlier disputes.

For most of history, reading has been taught privately and has been the instructional concern of wealthy families educating their own children. When continental philosophers such as Voltaire and Rousseau wrote about selecting the most appropriate books for young children, they pictured a private tutor working one-on-one with a young boy. Thomas Jefferson and Benjamin Franklin broadened the audience for reading instruction and changed its focus. They supported universal literacy—the ability of every citizen to read books and write letters—in support of democracy and freedom. This was not only a break with the European tradition, it was also a departure from an American colonial practice that had linked reading to religious ends.

The Puritans of colonial New England believed that reading knowledge was essential for personal salvation. No priest or pastor formed an intermediary between man and his maker. Every individual church member needed to read the scriptures in order to know truth and avoid evil. In 1647, the Puritans ordered every town of fifty households to hire a teacher to instruct children in reading and writing. Reading would help students fend off the "old deluder, Satan" and unmask the tricks he used to keep men from the knowledge of the Scriptures. Reprints of the *New-England Primer,* an early reader first used in 1680, highlight the political and religious goals of reading instruction. In the first few pages of the *Primer,* students were asked to memorize a four-line verse that began, "I will fear God, and honor the King," and ended, "I will submit to my elders."

Reading instruction methods appear to have been limited to a great deal of private memorization, followed by public recital of memorized material and repeated drill (Shannon, 1989, p. 4). Biblical rhymes and moral admonitions helped students learn the alphabet. Students would begin: *A—In Adams's Fall, We Sinned All;* and later, *F—The Idle Fool is Whipt at School.* After committing the alphabet to memory, students memorized whole words of increasing complexity, beginning with single-syllable words—God, great, and good—and then more complex words—Be-witch-ing, God-li-ness, Glo-ri-fy-ing, Hu-mi-li-ty, Ad-mi-ra-ti-on, and For-ni-ca-ti-on (Ford, 1962).

Literacy evolved slowly and unevenly, its definition constantly changing. The current debate between whole language advocates and phonics supporters, for example, traces back to nineteenth-century disagreements between the followers of Horace Mann and of Noah Webster. Webster, the lexicographer whose name is associated today with dictionaries, believed in phonics. In the preface to his *Blue-Backed Speller,* first published in 1783, he explained that students must begin reading by learning what he called the sounds of English and their correspondence to the letters of the alphabet. Webster wrote,

> Language is the expression of ideas by articulate sounds. . . . Letters are the marks of sounds. . . . A vowel is a simple articulate sound formed without the help of another letter. . . . A consonant is a letter which has no sound, or an imperfect one, without the help of a vowel. . . . (Webster, quoted in Flesch, 1955, p.45)

Horace Mann, the Massachusetts legislator and educational reformer, believed in the look-and-say method, a reading technique that asked children to recognize and read whole words instead of memorizing the sounds associated with letters. Critics argued that the look-and-say method ignored the basic sound-letter relationships of English and asked students to learn to read as if they were learning a nonphonetic system of Chinese characters or Egyptian hieroglyphics. Phonics and look-and-say advocates battled one another for nearly a century. In his 1955 book, *Why Johnny Can't Read,* Flesch blamed the look-and-say method for the reading crisis of his day. According to Flesch, young students were asked to memorize words through a series of repetitive drills and lifeless texts. To teach the word *sat*, for example, by the look-and-say method, teachers would ask students to read the following story:

> "Quack, quack," said the duck. He wanted something. He did not want to get out. He did not want to go to the farm. He did not want to eat. He sat and sat and sat. (Flesch, 1955, p.6)

Flesch did not want to visit this sort of reading experience on anyone. He wrote that children were being exposed to a "series of horrible, stupid, pointless, tasteless little readers, the stuff and guff about Dick and Jane or Alice and Jerry visiting the farm and having birthday parties" (Flesch, 1955, pp.6–7). His remedy was to abandon look-and-say and return to the time-tested phonics approach:

> When a schoolboy in ancient Rome learned to read, he didn't learn that the written word *mensa* meant a table, that is, a certain piece of furniture with a flat top and legs. Instead, he began by learning that the letter *m* stands for the sound you make when you put your lips together, that *e* means the sound that comes out when you open your mouth about halfway, that *n* is like *m* but with the lips open and the teeth together, that *s* has a hissing sound, and that *a* means the sound made by opening your mouth wide. Therefore, when he saw the word *mensa* for the first time, he could read it right off and learn, with a feeling of happy discovery, that this collection of letters meant table. (Flesch, 1955, p.4)

Whole language teachers, who Flesch believes are the direct descendants of the look-and-say methodologists, blame today's reading crisis on mind-numbing phonics drills and the misguided focus of basal readers. Basals are skill-based textbook reading materials used in nearly 90 percent of elementary classrooms. They are integrated systems for teaching reading by grade level. Phonics kits include skills materials for students to master, graded series of books for the students to read, teachers' manuals telling teachers what to do and how to teach, workbooks and handouts for students to complete, and sets of tests to assess reading skills.

Ken Goodman, one of the leaders in the field of whole language, has led the attack on phonics-based basals. He writes, "Let's not beat around the bush. Basal readers, workbooks, skills sequences, and practice materials that fragment the process [of reading] are unacceptable to whole language teachers. Their presentation of language phenomena is unscientific, and they steal teachers' and learners' time away from productive reading and writing" (Goodman, 1986, p.29).

Whole language teachers argue that children learn to read by really reading, not by developing skills about reading, studying the sounds of the letters, or doing phonics exercises. Whole language teachers point out that their approach to reading does not center on specific materials or classroom activities. Whole language focuses on whole texts from the very beginning of reading instruction, and the texts and stories can vary as the children do. "Just as activities do not define whole language, neither do texts. Using song lyrics for the purpose of enjoying or learning the song is congruent with whole language premises. Using the same lyrics to teach rhyming words or spelling patterns is not" (Edelsky, Altwerger, and Flores, 1991, p.8).

The International Reading Organization (http://www.reading.org), an umbrella group for those interested in the practice and research of reading instruction, has long maintained that no one approach to reading is best for all students. In 1997, the IRO issued a position statement asserting three basic principles concerning phonics and reading instruction:

1. The teaching of phonics is an important aspect of beginning reading instruction. . . .
2. Classroom teachers in the primary grades value and teach phonics as part of their reading program. . . .
3. Phonics instruction, to be effective in promoting independence in reading, must be embedded in the context of a total reading/language arts program. (Braunger, and Lewis, 1997, pp. 38–39).

Calls for a balanced approach to teaching reading, which would unite whole language and phonics, have failed to mollify critics or bring the two sides together. Phonics folks argue that a balanced approach does not go far enough to emphasize the significance of phonics in learning to read. Whole language teachers argue that a balanced approach brings "too much attention to phonics and detracts from [reading as] the construction of meaning" (Braunger and Lewis, 1997, p.39). As you read chapter 8, try to keep several questions in mind:

1. Which group—the phonics side or the whole language side—has the more convincing arguments and research evidence?

2. Which views fit better with your view of how children learn and how instruction should be organized?
4. Are the two sides ultimately compatible, or are their differences irreconcilable?
5. Which approach would you prefer for the students in your class or for your own children?
6. Are disagreements between phonics and whole language teachers political or academic?

## MULTICULTURAL STUDIES OR WESTERN CLASSICS?

Chapter 9 includes two views of another curriculum question: whether to stress diversity or unity in schools. In the twenty-first century, an increasing proportion of the nation's population will be able to claim membership in an ethnic minority. That sets the stage for another battle over knowledge in schools.

Among the reasons offered for multicultural education are:

1. The increasingly global nature of political affairs, increasing global democracy, and the world leadership role of the United States.
2. The need to understand peoples of varying backgrounds and values, to avoid stereotypes, and to address a shocking U.S. tradition of racism and prejudice.
3. To correct Americans' appalling ignorance of other cultures' high-quality contributions to literature, science, history, and the arts.

Those who advocate multicultural education want much more than mere token additions of ethnic history and culture to textbooks, International Day celebrations once a year, and learning about quaint customs, habits, and holidays in world history classes. Most want multiculturalism to permeate school and classroom activities, significantly altering the misconceptions and stereotypes many children have of other people in other places. Some advocates call for an era beyond multiculturalism, a large-scale educational reform that empowers people to make society more equitable and more respectful of cultural differences (Cheng, 1998).

One of the concerns of those who advocate multicultural studies is that the traditional Western heritage taught in schools focuses almost entirely on the works of white men. The domination of this Western tradition perpetuates the discrimination against the works of women and minorities. Knowledge is obviously not limited to a select group of white men in certain locations.

In opposition to those who support multicultural education are those who argue for national unity. They say that emphasizing diversity decreases unity and enhances factionalism. Multicultural education, they argue, reinforces each subgroup's myths without any unifying core for all. Separationist education, stressing the differences among groups, easily leads to factions and conflicts. In contrast, the canon of Western civilization, at the root of American education, provided generations of immigrants with knowledge that strengthens national unity. The Western tradition in literature, history, politics, and ethics undergirds democratic life in this country and encompasses the universal ideas common to all humans. We are a

Western society, and that heritage is what each new generation must learn. If we diminish or ignore that heritage, our society suffers. Americans must know about our country's Founders, political traditions, historic social values, and Western literature.

This critical issue in education is among the most volatile. It is a regular feature on newspaper pages and in popular newsmagazines and has been the subject of disputes on college campuses, in discussions about changing state and local school curricula, and in national politics.

## CURRICULUM CONTROL: NATIONAL MANDATE OR LOCAL OPTION?

The essays in chapter 10 focus on the value of a national or a local school curriculum. The formal curriculum is one of the most visible parts of a school, indicating the relative value the school puts on various forms of knowledge. Actually, individual schools do not make a separate determination of the relative values of parts of the curriculum; a number of factors influence what most schools teach and contribute to a relatively standard curriculum in U.S. schools.

The various states mandate certain courses that state legislatures believe are necessary for all students, such as English and American history. Many states also encourage or require other courses, such as drug and alcohol education, providing special funding or applying political pressure to add these courses to the curriculum. Accrediting agencies in each region examine schools periodically, and they review the curriculum to see if it conforms to their standards. A school that does not have a standard curriculum or its equivalent is threatened with loss of accreditation. Publishers, aiming at a national market, produce teaching materials that fit a national curriculum. A school that deviates from that pattern will have trouble finding textbooks. And school district curriculum coordinators and department heads attend national conferences and read journals that stress standard curricular structures. Thus, a broad outline exists for a general national curriculum based on common practices, even though the specific curricula in each state could differ.

Many political permutations affect the question of a national versus a local curriculum, but we can agree on a basic social interest in this aspect of the struggle over control of knowledge: the concern for and definition of literacy. Schools are the major means for young people to gain access to socially approved knowledge, and literacy, defined in differing ways, has become the goal of schooling. This goal, however, is far from simple because the definition of *literacy* changes. Should we prescribe a national curriculum for all students, or should local communities be able to define the nature of literacy and the schooling students need to develop it?

## TRADITION VERSUS LIBERATION

A central issue in the struggle for the control of knowledge is whether traditional knowledge provides enduring wisdom or promotes social oppression. Chapter 11 illustrates two views on what schools should teach—traditional values or liberating knowledge.

Religious literacy and values dominated the school curriculum in early America. In the earliest secondary schools, boys of the wealthy class learned Latin, Greek, catechism, and the Bible to prepare them to go to college, where many would prepare for the ministry. Religious beliefs continue to influence schooling, primarily in parochial schools, but they also form the basis for many of the values taught in public education today.

Prior to the American Revolution, religion was waning as the primary social glue. National political interests emerged. The schools changed to meet changes in frontier life, city development, and more secular and sectional economic interests. After the Revolution, and into the nineteenth century, nationalism replaced religion as an educational force. Literacy became important not for religious salvation, but for patriotism, the preservation of liberty, and participation in democracy.

The political-nationalistic tradition remains strong in U.S. schools, with a call for renewed emphasis each time social values seem threatened. During the period of overt racism in the United States, and as a reaction to the legal abolition of slavery, some regions used literacy tests to restrict voting rights. Since slaves had been prohibited, by law in some states, from receiving an education, these tests were intended to keep former slaves and the poor from voting. Their proponents also used them to limit the participation of immigrants. David Tyack (1967) quotes an imperial wizard of the Ku

Klux Klan as saying, "Ominous statistics proclaim the persistent development of a parasitic mass within our domain. . . . We have taken unto ourselves a Trojan horse crowded with ignorance, illiteracy, and envy" (p. 233).

The "red scare" of the 1920s, McCarthyism in the 1950s, and anticommunist political rhetoric in the 1980s were also periods when people perceived social threats; the effect was to strengthen a nationalist viewpoint in history, government, literature, and economics curricula. International competition in technology and trade threatens Americans today and translates into an increased curricular emphasis on mathematics, science, technological subjects such as computers, and foreign languages.

In opposition to the traditional use of literacy as a tool of the dominant class to separate and control the masses is the idea of literacy as a tool for liberation, Paulo Freire's revolutionary concept (Freire and Berthoff, 1987). Freire, born in one of the most impoverished areas of Brazil, came to know the plight of the poor. He vowed to dedicate his life to the struggle against misery and suffering, and his work led him to define the "culture of silence" he saw among the disadvantaged.

Freire realized the power of knowledge and recognized that the dominant class used education to keep the culture of silence among the victims. He developed a program to teach adults to read in order to liberate them from their silence. As a professor of education in Brazil, he experimented with this program to erase illiteracy, and his ideas became widely used in private literacy campaigns there. Freire was considered a threat to the government and was jailed after a military coup in 1964. Forced to leave his native country, he went to Chile to work with UNESCO, came to the United States, and then joined the World Council of Churches in Geneva as head of its educational division.

Freire's program involves the development of critical consciousness, using communication to expose oppression. Teacher and student are "co-intentional," sharing equally in dialogues on social reality and developing a critical understanding that can liberate them from the culture of silence.

Henry Giroux, citing Freire, argues that we need a redefinition of literacy in order to focus on its critical dimensions. Mass culture via television and other electronic media is under the control of dominant economic interests, and it offers only immediate images and unthoughtful information. This creates a "technocratic" illiteracy that is a threat to self-perception, to critical thought, and to democracy. Giroux (1988) states:

> Instead of formulating literacy in terms of the mastery of techniques, we must broaden its meaning to include the ability to read critically, both inside and outside one's experiences, and with conceptual power. This means that literacy would enable people to decode critically their personal and social worlds and thereby further their ability to challenge the myths and beliefs that structure their perceptions and experiences. (p. 84)

Should schooling emphasize traditional values or liberation? What are the other options?

## *BUSINESS INFLUENCE ON EDUCATION*

Chapter 12 examines the issue of whether or not business and industry should dominate the struggle for control of ideas expressed in schools. The movement toward common schools in the United States has included seeking support from business and labor leaders. Preparation for employment is now considered one of the basic purposes of schools. Vocational education evolved in response to a dual problem—satisfying the needs of business and alleviating the dropout rate. Many parents want schools to give their children the skills that will make them employable. Many families pressure their children to study subjects that will pay off in economic terms. The question becomes, What will help get the student into the right law school or medical school to ensure future economic success?

Even the way schools are organized and operate reflects the influence of business. Members of school boards are often elected because they promise to bring "businesslike efficiency" to the schools. Businesspeople often participate in blue-ribbon boards and committees that are asked to review school operations. School administrators are required by state licensing laws and university degree requirements to study management material taken from the business school literature and translated into school management practices. Textbooks on school administration advocate business management techniques.

Businesses provide considerable financial and other types of support for schools. School districts are pleased to include "ratables," taxable businesses that pay for schools but produce no students. Businesses also give large sums of money to local schools for various programs and teaching materials and for the sponsorship of school events.

One major social factor influencing the school curriculum is the traditional American interest in practical innovations within the ethos of capitalism. Benjamin Franklin serves as the prototype of the American captivated by invention and utility. Andrew Carnegie, John D. Rockefeller, Jay Gould, J. Paul Getty, and Donald Trump, among others, illustrate the American belief in entrepreneurship and the values of free enterprise. The idea of rugged individualism that permeated our early national literature glorified the individual who could survive by wits and invention and a determination to succeed at any cost.

The idealization of capitalism in U.S. society creates a need for adequately prepared engineers, technicians, assembly-line workers, maintenance and secretarial personnel, salespeople, and managers, as well as eager and knowledgeable consumers of new products. The schools are under pressure to prepare people with skills and attitudes that enhance capitalism, just as they earlier were expected to prepare people for religious and nationalistic loyalty. Schools are also expected to train people in the skills necessary for employment, and to promote the attitudes that will help them succeed in the workplace; television and videotape equipment is widely available in most schools; and personal computers are provided free or at very low cost to stimulate mass computer education and entice eager consumers.

The Industrial Revolution assisted the demise of the classical curriculum and the rise of applied subjects. Latin, Greek, ancient history, philosophy, and many of the arts are no longer considered useful knowledge, whereas vocational subjects, commercial courses, the physical and biological sciences, and economics are. Schools emphasize computer literacy for all students, courses in reading and writing for employment purposes, "free enterprise" course requirements in some states, and the development of entrepreneurial programs and management science in colleges.

Industrialization creates social problems that also influence the school curriculum. Urbanization and suburbanization follow employment opportunities and social-class patterns, and this creates social and individual difficulties that schools are often expected to ameliorate. Violence, crime, alcohol and drug abuse, broken families, suicide, unemployment, prejudice, dislocation, and financial chaos are among the many examples of social issues schools are expected to address.

The stress associated with contemporary life in a capitalistic society is the subject of books, lectures, and the new industry called human resource development. The school curriculum has changed since 1900 to provide courses in sociology, psychology, urban problems, financial planning, family studies, drug education, sex education, and death and dying.

At the college and university level, businesses provide major funding for many research and teaching projects. Grants from businesses to education total many millions of dollars per year. Businesspeople are often the strongest advocates of schools, offering speakers, part-time employment for students, educational material, and myriad other subsidies.

Although these business relationships may seem positive, they pose both obvious and subtle threats to education. The influence business exerts on what schools teach is enormous. The visible and hidden curricula are subject to business manipulation. And business is not without blemish itself; it is scarcely an ideal model for social values and ethics. Should corporate interests dominate the definitions of knowledge and literacy? Chapter 12 presents two of the many divergent views on what the relationship between business and the schools should be.

## STANDARDIZED TESTING AND WHAT IS TAUGHT

Standardized testing has become the most commonly used device to determine student achievement and proficiency, the measure of how well schools teach. Chapter 13 considers the role and impact of standardized testing as a critical educational issue.

U.S. students take as many as 300 million standardized tests each year, most of them in public schools. A typical high school graduate has been subjected to six batteries of standardized achievement tests in twelve years of schooling (Mehrens and Lehmann, 1987, p. 2). Test taking is one of society's more widely shared experiences; it is unusual to find anyone who has not taken at least one such exam.

Proponents of standardized tests argue that machine-scored multiple-choice tests are the best available measures of academic merit and educational quality. Well-designed and well-used tests, they note, can provide schools with the objective information needed to make curricular decisions. Test programs can inform educators about the effectiveness of their teaching methods, comparing the test takers with students of earlier years or other schools. Standardized testing can also help hold schools accountable, forcing them to demonstrate that the money they spend on education is used prudently.

Opponents maintain that standardized tests are crude, imprecise measures that reward superficiality, ignore creativity, and penalize test takers who read too much into the questions. Instead of informing the public, they argue, tests confuse people with results shrouded in mathematical terms. Rather than offer accountability, testing mistakenly applies the simple-minded methods of cost accounting to the complexities of the teaching-learning process. To meet the demands for a large-scale testing program, testing and measurement experts have had to design instruments for a machine-scored multiple-choice format. Critics claim that few concepts of significance can be reduced to discrete bits and measured by a series of short-answer, timed questions.

Standardized tests are one of the more controversial applications of social science to education. Despite the extent to which they have permeated every level of school experience, they are a relatively recent development. Civil service examinations were first administered centuries ago in China, but it was not until the nineteenth century that standardized exams became a common part of social and economic life. Nineteenth-century Britain, in the throes of an expanding domestic economy and of becoming an international empire, found it could not satisfy the demand for large numbers of middle-class managers through the traditional patronage appointments. There simply were not enough privileged males—the sons of civil servants, members of Parliament, or others of wealth and connections—to fill all the vacancies worldwide. Competitive exams were introduced to open the civil service to a broader range of male applicants.

The United States also used testing to democratize the selection of government workers. Political abuse, through patronage, was rampant in the late nineteenth century. Civil Service reform began with the Pendleton Act of 1883, which established competitive exams for prospective government employees.

Standardized tests were introduced in Boston's public schools in 1845 to measure student knowledge and determine who was eligible for secondary education (Travers, 1983). In many ways, performance on standardized tests still controls access to education and power in society (Eggleston, 1984).

Chapter 13 presents two competing perspectives on standardized testing and assessment. One position argues against testing, maintaining that tests measure little of value and that testing is biased, stifles student creativity, and perpetuates social injustice (Broadfoot, 1984; Crouse and Trusheim, 1988; Owen, 1985). The opposing position argues that formal and objective evaluations can measure worthwhile educational achievements and can be used to hold schools accountable (Mehrens and Lehman, 1987).

# References

ANYON, J. (1979). "Ideology and U.S. History Textbooks." *Harvard Educational Review 7*, 49–60.

———. (1980). "Social Class and the Hidden Curriculum of Work." *Journal of Education 162*, 67–92.

APPLE, M. (1979, 1990). *Ideology and Curriculum.* 2d ed. New York: Routledge.

———. (1982). *Education and Power.* London: Routledge & Kegan Paul.

ARISTOTLE. (1962). *The Politics of Aristotle,* translated by E. Barker. Oxford: Oxford University Press.

BERNSTEIN, B. (1977). *Class, Codes, and Control.* Vol. 3. London: Routledge & Kegan Paul.

BOURDIEU, P., AND PASSERON, J. (1977). *Reproduction in Education, Society, and Culture.* London: Sage.

BOWLES, S., AND GINTIS, H. (1976). *Schooling in Capitalist America.* New York: Basic Books.

BOYER, E. L. (1983). *High School.* New York: Harper & Row.

BRAUNGER, J., AND LEWIS, J. P. (1997). *Building a Knowledge Base in Reading.* Newark, DE: International Reading Association.

BROADFOOT, P., EDITOR. (1984). *Selection, Certification and Control: Social Issues in Educational Assessment.* London: Falmer Press.

*Brown v. Board of Education of Topeka, Shawnee County, Kansas, et al.* (1954). 74 Sup. Ct. 686.

BUTTS, R. F. (1955). *A Cultural History of Western Education.* New York: McGraw-Hill.

CARNOY, M. (1975). *Schooling in a Corporate Society: The Political Economy of Education in the Democratic State.* 2nd ed. New York: McKay.

———. and Levin, H. (1985). *Schooling and Work in America.* Stanford, CA: Stanford University Press.

Cheng, L. (1998). "Beyond Multiculturalism." Chapter in Pang, V., and Cheng, L. *Struggling to Be Heard.*

Albany, NY: State University of New York Press.

Cherryholmes, C. (1978). "Curriculum Design as a Political Act." *Curriculum Inquiry 10*, 115–141.

———. (1988). *Power and Criticism: Poststructural Investigations in Education.* New York: Teachers College Press.

Clark, K. (1965). *Dark Ghetto.* New York: Harper & Row.

CROUSE, J., AND TRUSHEIM, D. (1988). *The Case Against the SAT.* Chicago: University of Chicago Press.

DEEM, R. (1983). "Gender, Patriarchy and Class in the Popular Education of Women." In *Gender, Class and Education,* edited by S. Walker and L. Barton. London: Falmer Press.

EDELSKY, C., ALTWERGER, B., AND FLORES, B. (1991). *Whole Language, What's the Difference?* Portsmouth, NH: Heinemann.

EGGLESTON, J. (1984). "School Examinations—Some Sociological Issues." In *Selection, Certification and Control,* edited by P. Broadfoot. London: Falmer Press.

FELDMAN, S. (1974). *The Rights of Women.* Rochelle Park, NJ: Hayden.

FISKE, E. B. (1991). *Smart School, Smart Kids.* New York: Simon & Schuster.

FLESCH, R. (1955). *Why Johnny Can't Read—And What You Can Do About It.* New York: Harper & Row.

FORD, P. C., EDITOR. (1962). *The New-England Primer: A History of Its Origin and Development.* New York: Teachers College.

FREIRE, P. (1970). *Pedagogy of the Oppressed,* translated by M. B. Ramos. New York: Herder and Herder.

———. and Berthoff, D. (1987). *Literacy: Reading and the World.* South Hadley, MA: Bergin & Garvey.

GIROUX, H. (1981). *Ideology, Culture, and the Process of Schooling.* Philadelphia: Temple University Press.

———. (1988). *The Teacher as Intellectual.* South Hadley, MA: Bergin & Garvey.

————, editor. (1991). *Postmodernism, Feminism and Cultural Politics.* Albany: SUNY Press.

————. and Purpel, D. (1983). *The Hidden Curriculum and Moral Education.* Berkeley, CA: McCutchan.

GOODLAD, J. (1999). "Flow, Eros, and Ethos in Educational Renewal." *Phi Delta Kappan* 80(8), 571–58.

GOODMAN K. (1986). *What's Whole in Whole Language?* Portsmouth, NH: Heinemann.

GREENE, M. (1994). "Postmodernism and the Crisis of Representation." *English Education,* 26, 206–219.

GRIMSHAW, J. (1986). *Philosophy and Feminist Thinking.* Minneapolis: University of Minnesota Press.

HANSON, F. A. (1993). *Testing, Testing: Social Consequences of the Examined Life.* Berkeley: University of California Press.

HOFSTADTER, R. (1944). *Social Darwinism in American Thought.* Philadelphia: University of Pennsylvania Press.

KATZ, M. B. (1971). *Class, Bureaucracy, and Schools.* New York: Praeger.

LANGER, J., EDITOR. (1987). *Language, Literacy and Culture: Issues of Society and Schooling.* Norwood, NJ: Ablex.

LATHER, P. (1991). *Getting Smart: Feminist Research and Pedagogy Within the Postmodern.* New York: Routledge.

LEMANN, N. (1997). "The Reading Wars." *The Atlantic Monthly,* November, 1997, pp. 128–134.

MARROU, H. (1956/1982). *A History of Education in Antiquity,* translated by G. Lamb. Madison: University of Wisconsin Press.

MEHRENS, W. A., AND LEHMANN, I. J. (1987). *Using Standardized Tests in Education.* 4th ed. New York: Longman.

NATIONAL COMMISSION ON EXCELLENCE IN EDUCATION. (1983). *A Nation at Risk.* Washington, DC: U.S. Department of Education.

NELSON, J., CARLSON, K., AND LINTON, T. (1972). *Radical Ideas and the Schools.* New York: Holt, Rinehart and Winston.

OAKES, J. (1985). *Keeping Track: How the Schools Structure Inequality.* New Haven, CT: Yale University Press.

OWEN, D. (1985). *None of the Above.* Boston: Houghton Mifflin.

POPKEWITZ, T. (1977). "The Latent Values of the Discipline-Centered Curriculum." *Theory and Research in Social Education* 13, 189–206.

————. (1987). *The Formation of School Subjects.* New York: Falmer Press.

SADKER, P., AND SADKER, D. M. (1982). *Sex Equity Handbook for Schools.* New York: Longman.

SHANNON, P. (1989). *Broken Promises: Reading Instruction in Twentieth-Century America.* Granby, MA: Bergin and Garvey.

SPRING, J. (1976). *The Sorting Machine.* New York: McKay.

SPRING, J. (1998). *American Education.* 8th ed. New York: McGraw-Hill.

STANLEY, W. (1992). *Education for Utopia: Social Reconstructionism and Critical Pedagogy in the Postmodern Era.* Albany: SUNY Press.

TAWNEY, R. H. (1964). *The Radical Tradition.* London: Allen & Unwin.

TRAVERS, R. M. W. (1983). *How Research Has Changed America.* Kalamazoo, MI: Mythos.

TYACK, D. (1967). *Turning Points in American Educational History.* Waltham, MA: Blaisdell.

WALKER, S., AND BARTON, L. (1983). *Gender Class and Education.* London: Falmer Press.

WEILER, K. (1991). "Freire and a Feminist Pedagogy of Difference." *Harvard Educational Review* 61, 449–474.

YOUNG, M. F. D., EDITOR. (1970). *Knowledge and Control.* London: Collier-Macmillan.

*CHAPTER 7*

# Basic Education: Traditional Disciplines or Critical Thinking

## POSITION 1: TEACH THE BASIC DISCIPLINES

Schools continue to fail at the one thing society charges them to do—provide students with a basic education. Declining test scores and the painfully obvious evidence of basically illiterate citizens demonstrate the serious deficiencies in U.S. schooling. As a recent report of the Center for Educational Reform notes, "Intellectually and morally, America's educational system is failing far too many people" (1998). Despite the enormous amount of money we pour into our schools, our students do not compare favorably with students in Japan, Germany, or most modern industrialized nations. We spend more than most nations do on our schools, ranking fourth among OECD nations (Hoff, 1998), but we have less to show for it. Academically, the United States ranks with developing countries.

We are a third-rate nation producing generations of graduates who can't read, write, compute, or respond intelligently to questions about history, geography, economics, or literature. Our 17-year-olds are incompetent in the humanities (Ravitch and Finn, 1987); in science and math, they are even worse, and they also perform poorly when tested on general information about society and contemporary affairs. (*National Review,* 1990; *USA Today,* 1990; *Fortune,* 1990; Samuelson, 1991; Perry, 1993; Peltzman, 1994; Finn, 1995; Center for Educational Reform, 1998, McNamara, 1998).

Baker and Smith (1997) performed a comprehensive analysis of multiple studies of math and science achievements, comparing U.S. schools with schools in other nations over a recent three-year period. They note that "U.S. performance ranks in the middle of each study and never among the best-performing countries." (p. 16). The Third International Mathematics and Science Scores (TIMSS) rated the performance of U.S. students as "among the worst in the world" (McNamara, 1998). These depressing data on academic achievement show the enormous lack in our educational system. Even in an area that the United States used to excel in, high school graduation rates, we are now declining behind other nations ("U.S. Drops in Education Rankings," 1998). Although high school graduation rates in the United States hide the weak program of studies that many U.S. students take, we have still fallen behind other nations whose students take much stronger academic programs (Hoff, 1998).

The basic purpose of schools is to teach fundamental knowledge and skills to the young, including the body of important information and values that stems from our cultural heritage. Fundamental skills, such as mature reading, writing, and computation, are necessary to survive and be productive in contemporary society. Our cultural heritage has evolved over time and has also served society well. It incorporates history, literature, and the elements of national character that make the United States what it is. Yet, even in these basic tasks of schools, we see failure.

## School Failure in the Basics

Despite two decades of increased funding and attention, the "rising tide of mediocrity" in American schools has not been stemmed. In 1983, a national panel provided a devastating analysis of educational performance (National Commission on Excellence in Education, 1983) that identified thirty-seven different study findings, including the following:

- Average academic achievement test scores are lower than in 1957, when *Sputnik* was launched.
- SAT test scores were in continual decline from 1963 to 1980.
- Test scores in science steadily declined from 1969 to 1977.
- Remedial math courses in college increased by almost 75 percent.
- In comparison with students in other industrialized nations on nineteen academic achievement tests, U.S. students never scored first or second, and they scored last seven times.
- Textbooks have been written at lower reading levels ("dumbing down") to accommodate declining reading abilities.
- About half the new teachers of math, science, and English are not qualified to teach these subjects.
- Average school grades rise, however, as real student achievement falls.

Since the publication of the National Commission's *A Nation at Risk*, school funding and teacher salaries have increased, national goals have been set, and some states have set new requirements to improve the schools. Still, there has been no actual move to return the basics to their rightful place in the curriculum (*Time*, 1989; Shaw, 1993; Perry, 1993).

Fifteen long years later, a conference sponsored by the Heritage Foundation, the Center for Educational Reform, Empower America, and the Thomas G. Fordham Foundation produced *A Nation Still at Risk: An Educational Manifesto* (Center for Educational Reform, 1998), following up the startling report of the 1983 National Commission. They found no improvement. This 1998 Manifesto reported that many educators and commentators responded to the persistence of mediocre performance in schools by engaging in "denial, self-delusion, and blame-shifting" (1998, p.1). Such notable intellectuals as William Bennett, Chester Finn, E. D. Hirsch, and Diane Ravitch, part of this distinguished and concerned group, offered suggestions to deal with the continuing educational problem:

1. Set and maintain high standards, national competitive assessments, and strict accountability.
2. Provide plural avenues to schooling, competing with public schools and offering choice to parents (for example, charter schools, school choice, vouchers).
3. Require rigorous subject field tests for teachers.
4. Reinstitute order and discipline in schools.
5. Institute merit pay for teachers and administrators.
6. End the monopoly of colleges of education over teacher education.
7. Limit the excesses of such school efforts as bilingual education and multi-cultural education.
8. Teach the essential academic skills and knowledge.

This is a good set of practical strategies to return schools to their primary purpose, to institute and monitor significant improvements in the quality of schooling, and to provide competition and choice to keep schools effective. We do not have sufficient space to examine all of these suggestions. Our focus, instead, will be on one of the key elements—improving school performance by increasing the emphasis on the essential academic skills and knowledge. That could signal a significant return to basic education, and a move away from social welfare or personality manipulation in the schools.

Shaw (1993) points out that despite the failure of schools, Americans have become educated through the media and interactions with their families and peers. Industrial growth has continued even though we have seen a steady decline in reading scores since 1930. Consider what might have happened if the schools were doing their job. There is a superficial idea that schools have improved, but it is similar to the sham of grade inflation that engulfed schools; magically, grade-point averages increased while real student achievement declined. Evidence of a real return to basic education and solid improvement in student knowledge simply is not there. The much-heralded and temporary fads hide the underlying erosion of school quality. Schools move like sludge, and the 1990s showed no better overall student performance in academic subjects.

Schools just do not have enough time or resources to deal with every possible topic. We need to decide which areas are important, and then focus our schools' energies on doing them well. That means we have to decide what to jettison and what to improve as we consider what has happened in our schools.

## The Dumping-Ground School

It is clear that schools have taken on far too many tasks, have failed in the most significant ones, and have been forced into the position of replacing parents, church, and society.

Instead of teaching the necessary academic skills and knowledge, today's schools serve as places to learn a set of ideological ideas and engage in utopian, liberal pet projects. These include such preposterous and intellectually squishy topics as:

Saving the environment and establishing world peace

Gaining parenting skills

Learning self-respect

Adjusting to society

Getting a job

Having safe sex

Driving a car

Appreciating the arts, often with gay and lesbian overtones

Adopting secular morality and values

Abolishing racism, sexism, and evil; embracing the "multicultural"

Ironically, the schools' attempts to fulfill these more frivolous tasks have also been unsuccessful. Further, the frivolous take energy away from the basic purpose of education. Some people may desire to have the schools take over all responsibilities for children, but they don't recognize the threat this represents to our free society. Government-operated or -supervised schools have a severely limited capacity to know what's best. Financing those behemoth operations strains the tax budget without improving solid learning. Samuelson (1998), noting that the United States spends over half a trillion dollars each year on its schools, found that waste and test failure are typical outcomes.

Unfortunately, the school curriculum has become a dumping ground for every special interest group's pet idea for solving a human problem. If we have a problem with crime, we think we can solve it by teaching about crime in schools. When the topics of teen-age sex and pregnancy show up on the front pages of newspapers, a new course is proposed for schools. A war occurs somewhere in the world, and we find calls for "peace education" in schools. We presume to stop the threat of nuclear war by teaching a class on peace. A student commits suicide, and an elaborate effort begins to develop antisuicide classes and courses in "improving one's self-concept." The AIDS epidemic leads to special courses and instructions on using condoms; meanwhile, the epidemic of actual school failure is ignored. Some students fail tests, and the schools respond not by giving the student additional work on the subject area, but by taking up curricular time with courses on study habits and how to take tests.

If one could find evidence that these frill courses actually eliminated crime, teen-age pregnancy, war, suicide, academic failure, and AIDS, there might be some grounds for including them in the curriculum. But the simpleminded idea that the schools should use their valuable time to address each social problem, or that they could actually deal effectively with social problems, has put the real curriculum in danger. While students are starved for quality academic work, schools crowd their time with frills and foolishness. Some of these topics are important social issues, but the school is ill-equipped to address them.

There are several reasons we need to get the schools out of the social welfare business and back into teaching students the basics. First, schools have limited time and have other, more significant, purposes. Second, these topics are heavily laden with values, and our children should not be subjected to a teacher's interpretation of "proper" values. And third, it is folly to believe that students who have difficulty reading and calculating, or who lack basic knowledge and experience, can adequately deal with such topics as crime and nuclear war.

Then there are the courses that have no important social value but which pander to fads and fun while taking up students' time and absorbing their interest. Schools should not devote time to such absurd classes as Being Me, Making Conversation, Informed Shopping, Hairstyling, or All About Cars. Underwater Basket Weaving may be a satirical course title to illustrate the silliness of some schoolwork, but a heavy layer of nonacademic school time exists in virtually every school. Spending curricular time on driver's education, school safety, baton twirling, school newspaper production, marching band, sports, home maintenance, and the like drains valuable time and energy from the study of literature, history, geography, math, and science.

## Schools Fail Even in the Nonessentials

Even if we agreed that schools were appropriate places in which to study society's problems or help students with low self-esteem, have those problems been solved by tackling them in the schools? If anything, we have even more social problems. The school has not been successful in teaching fundamentals, nor has it been successful in the misguided effort to correct all of society's ills or to produce happy and confident students.

In examining the list of excessive tasks taken on by schools, we find only one that they have performed moderately well—though at great cost. Driver's education may help young drivers slightly in driving more safely and gaining lower insurance premiums, but that has been accomplished by sacrificing valuable school time, using expensive teachers in very inefficient settings with a small number of students, eliminating a skill area parents could teach to their children, and saddling school budgets with unnecessary costs for automobiles, insurance, equipment, and teaching time.

This is not a diatribe against teaching students how to drive, but is an example of limited and costly success in a mistaken area of the school curriculum. School is not the best place to use time and money to teach students how to drive.

Consider other items on the list. Is school the best, or even a good, place for children to learn parenting, self-respect, drug avoidance, safe sex, and morality? Daily newspaper stories show that parenting, self-respect, and morality have declined in American society, even as the schools have sought to teach these subjects. It is also clear that drug usage has not abated after years of school efforts to teach its dangers, and students' unsafe sex practices seem to be at epidemic levels. Beyond this, the backbone of American society, the family, has eroded because schools, not families, have taken the responsibility for these educational areas.

It is no coincidence that family life has declined in the twentieth century as schools have begun to take over many family responsibilities. Contemporary family life, in the homes where parents still live together, appears to consist of providing a place to sleep and eat, to watch television, and to wave goodbye as parents go to work or the child goes to school. How can children gain respect for their parents and other relatives when they abdicate basic family responsibilities to a government institution? The historic and appropriate tasks of families include providing security and nurturing. The nurturing purpose is essentially educative, as families providing guidance and values for the young. And those families that take nurturing seriously run the risk of running into a different set of values in school. Obviously, this is a particular problem for religious families.

## Adjustment and Conformity

Among other items on the list of extraneous school responsibilities are teaching students to adjust to society, get along with others, obtain a job, and appreciate the arts. This list smacks of Big Brother. One of America's claims to world leadership rests in our diversity and individuality. Who is to decide what adjustment, behaviors, and arts we should honor? Do we want monolithic schooling that requires each student to adjust to whatever the school determines is good for society?

Life adjustment education, brought in by the "progressives" just after World War II, assumed that educators knew what society needed and could determine how students would adjust. This was a form of social engineering that failed. The emphasis was on vocational courses designed to prepare people for work, not to provide intellectual or cultural enrichment. It was based on the false premise that over half of America's students could not benefit from traditional learning and were destined to a working-class existence. This movement opposed academic study and substituted such trivial activities as learning to dance, playing party games, selecting good movies, and relieving tensions. This period of silly curricula passed, thankfully, but remnants still remain in the schools.

A school curriculum built on current fads and the latest social issues is one that has no lasting value and cannot hope to prepare young people for productive lives. Similarly, a curriculum designed simply to make students feel better about themselves does not develop maturity; rather, it is likely to exaggerate personal problems and dependency on others. Meanwhile, these kinds of curricula rob students of time and energy that should be devoted to real education. Students should be learning many important subjects and skills that are consistent with the basic purposes of education. We need to identify the essential skills needed for learning and the time-tested knowledge that all educated citizens should acquire. This is the basic rationale for compulsory schooling; otherwise, why require all children to attend school?

In a well-reasoned book published almost half a century ago, historian Arthur Bestor (1953) called attention to this educational issue:

> The disciplined mind is what education at every level should strive to produce. . . . The idea that the school must undertake to meet every need that some other agency is failing to meet, regardless of the suitability of the classroom to the task, is a preposterous delusion that in the end can wreck the educational system without in any way contributing to the salvation of society. . . . The school promises too much on the one hand, and too little on the other, when it begins to think so loosely about its functions. (pp. 59, 75–76)

Bestor further proposed identification of the fundamentals needed in schools: "Educational reform must begin with the courageous assertion that all the various subjects and disciplines in the curriculum are *not* [original author's emphasis] of equal value. Some disciplines are fundamental. . . ." It is those fundamental studies in science, math, language, and history that should return to primacy in the schools. Bestor directed his attack toward the progressive educationists who claimed not to "teach history," but to "teach children." He correctly pointed out the inanity of this claim. Clearly, the idea of teaching children is vapid; children must be taught *something*. Bestor argued strongly for intellectual content. He supports public education, but not education about nothing, or about everything but with no intellectual focus.

Thirty years later, Gilbert Sewall, education editor of *Newsweek*, visited about thirty schools in eight states and reviewed many of the contemporary writings about schools. In summarizing his findings, Sewall wrote of the contemporary American schools:

> For youngsters of all backgrounds and capabilities, academic outcomes are low and, at least until very recently, have been shrinking. Why? To begin with, few pupils at the secondary level are required to take courses in the basic subjects—language, math, history, science—in order to qualify for a high school diploma. . . . Even more disturbing, curricular revisions have steadily diluted course content. New syllabuses in basic subjects have appeared, purged of tedious or difficult units. Vacuous electives have proliferated, allowing some students to sidestep challenging courses altogether. . . . Endless courses in family life, personal adjustment, consumer skills, and business have crowded out more rigorous subjects, notably in science and foreign language. (Sewall, 1983, pp. 6, 7)

Sewall concludes his book with strong support for teaching fundamental disciplines and basic subjects, with high expectations and clear standards for student performance. He argues that the schools have taken on "new and distracting duties to care for every unfortunate and antisocial child, increasingly acting as flunkies and surrogates for self-absorbed, overburdened, or negligent parents" (p. 177). The schools should return to their primary purpose, allow other social institutions to conduct their proper social welfare functions, and recognize that the best route to vocational education is solid preparation in fundamental knowledge.

The distressing list of curricular failures in areas of fundamental knowledge indicates that the nation is at risk. We must move to correct the accumulated problems of education by refocusing on the basics.

## Stress the Basics and Necessary Skills

No solid argument contradicts the wisdom of teaching the traditional skills of reading, writing, and arithmetic. Disputes arise as to how we should teach these skills, for how long, and how to measure their mastery, but even hard-core "happy children" advocates agree that children need to be able to communicate in language and numbers.

This agreement would seem sufficient to guarantee a strong emphasis on these skills in schools. And yet, large numbers of students are not acquiring these skills, and will suffer as they try to make their way in society. The society will suffer as well, since these otherwise productive workers will not have the capability to survive in the workplace (Szabo, 1992). Many other students manage to pick up some fundamental skills, but not enough to be competitive. These young people are destined to take marginal positions in society and to be the recipients of social welfare programs.

One of the reasons the schools fail in this basic curriculum is that they spend insufficient time to ensure that children master these skills. Too many distractions interfere at school, including the dumping-ground problems. A second reason for the failure is that schools teach these skills in isolation from the disciplines of knowledge students will confront as they move through school. Instead of reading literature or history, children learn to read from texts especially designed to avoid ideas and to present only insipid stories using "a limited vocabulary." A third reason for failure, tied to the second, is that schools do not expect enough of many students, and the children become bored and shut out education. Students in earlier periods could read complicated material that stretched their minds. Today's texts, "dumbed down" to meet a minimal standard, are demeaning to students and stultify their development.

## Beyond the Fundamental Skills

Not only do we need to reemphasize the fundamental skills in elementary schools, but we also need to insist upon rigorous evaluation of those skills before we allow students to continue in school. The purpose for requiring that students obtain skills in the early years is to permit full use of those skills in further study of important knowledge. Thus, we do a disservice to students who have not mastered the skills, as well as to those who have, if we merely pass them on to higher grades.

The knowledge we have acquired over a long period, and with great effort, is collected in the major disciplines schools have traditionally taught. All new generations must learn this intellectual and cultural heritage in order to preserve and extend the culture. The development of disciplines has helped us to establish categories of knowledge and methods of study that make access to the cultural heritage easier and more systematic. Learning is difficult work, and it should be, but the study of the basic disciplines provides a logical avenue to reach understanding.

The basic disciplines represent differing ways humans have organized wisdom, and together they offer the means to intellectual power. Among these basic disciplines are:

Math, because we live in a world where quantity and numerical relationships are important.

Language, because accumulated knowledge is communicated in various languages.

Sciences, because they provide an understanding of our environment and its workings.

History, because an understanding of current life requires us to study the past.

Of course, one can study other disciplines as well in the process of becoming an educated person, but the basic four deserve particular attention in the schools. These are the *liberal arts* disciplines, meant to *liberate* people from ignorance. Although the liberal arts have changed over time, they still represent the storehouse of knowledge an educated person should have. Modern society needs citizens who are grounded in math, language, science, and history in order to take on the responsibilities and challenges of democratic governance.

A thorough understanding of mathematical and scientific principles is necessary for life in a technological world. A thorough understanding of the humanities, represented by literature and history, is necessary if we are to comprehend the human condition and to communicate effectively. This combination is the essence of education. To proceed with schooling that fails to educate our children in these areas is to short-circuit the educative process and to condemn our children to ignorance.

## Summary

Basic school studies take time and concentration. One cannot master fundamental skills and the principles of our cultural heritage on a part-time basis, while devoting considerable time to learning how to "get along with others," or "improve self-respect," or even "learning how to learn." The focus on current fads and personal problems trivializes our heritage, consumes precious school time, and compromises our children's and our society's future. Furthermore, it is clear that schools have not solved social problems and, as a result of spending time trying to, are not very successful in teaching the basics.

The most valuable education for individual students and for society is to build basic skills and emphasize the liberal arts disciplines.

## POSITION 2: TEACH FOR CRITICAL THINKING

Political turmoil surrounding school reform over the past twenty years has obscured the most important purpose of schooling. In the clamor to improve test scores that require students to recall bits of information, we have ignored the need to develop students' abilities to engage in critical inquiry. Backward-looking, rigid disciplinarians should not be allowed to put intellectual blinders on the critical work of the schools in order to push their school and social agenda. Traditionalists would like us to move back to drill and memorization in a few selected school subjects in order to raise test scores. They want to restrict new generations to old ideas, filtered through their narrow vision of education. They want to limit controversy and thinking, control teachers, and make schools dull and deadly places where test scores rule. But controversy, as Nel Noddings (1999) properly comments, is necessary to democratic education.

A democratic nation cannot long survive simply on math and reading skills, or on a body of memorized standard information. The world requires thinking people to critically examine issues and policies, and this means actively engaging students in inquiry. Of course, it is impossible to fully engage in inquiry without developing good reading, writing, and calculation skills. So it is absurd to argue that basic skills and knowledge are not important areas of learning in progressive schools. But it is also absurd to argue that basic education should be limited to traditional fields of knowledge, studied only in a certain way. That narrow and academically invalid perspective seriously compromises a good education. The effort to return U.S. schools to memorization, recitation, and skill drill is misguided and intellectually restrictive.

Further, it is a myth that teaching for more than test scores and traditional information diminishes our students' knowledge. On a wide variety of measures, including but going beyond test scores, U.S. students stack up very well. For political and ideological purposes, conservatives manufactured a fictitious crisis in American education in the 1980s (Berliner and Biddle, 1995). Misinterpretations of test quality, student scores, and differing contexts in different nations and times have misled the public. Researcher Gerald Bracey's annual reports on the condition of public education and his many articles clearly show no massive failure in the schools (Bracey, 1998, 1999). Lemann (1998) notes in an article about American schools in *Atlantic Monthly*, "The rhetoric of failure is simply wrong. . . . Public education is by far the largest and most important function performed by government in this country. In no way is it in systemic crisis" (pp. 92–93). Ideologues and much of the media have maligned public schools. The mistreatment helps people get elected, sells newspapers, and furthers the right-wing agenda to gut public education and control social values.

Certainly individual school districts, schools, and classrooms may be unsatisfactory and in great need of correction and improvement, but there is no large scale decline across our schools. If a problem exists in education now, it is that traditionalist school reforms, stimulated by the fictional crisis, have stifled teacher creativity and chilled efforts to improve schools in their most important functions.

The primary purpose of schooling is to stimulate critical thinking so that young people can improve themselves and the society. How can we hope to accomplish this lofty ideal if we continue to burden students with learning material irrelevant to their lives and to future society and rob them of the opportunity to raise questions about what they are learning and about society?

Much of the past decade's school reform craze has focused on learning sterile trivia in order to pass tests designed by and for an earlier generation of students. We are so driven by silly concepts of competition in test scores that we limit the time left for creativity, innovation, and reflection on matters of importance to the child and to our society. Critical thinking has been abandoned by the one social institution that should most defend it. In an educational absurdity, students must seek opportunities to develop critical thinking by looking outside the school (Caywood, 1994).

A backward-looking curriculum and lack of mental stimulation combine to rob contemporary students of their right to a liberating education. School has become an onerous period of separation from reality. What students learn does not prepare them for understanding or reflecting on life. As Howard Gardner (1991a) expresses it: "Specifically, school knowledge seems strictly bound to school settings" (p. 119). Gardner's studies show that school knowledge may show up in students' scores on school-related tests, but that school knowledge has limited relation to improved knowledge of the real world (Gardner, 1991b). The movement to mandate national standards of basic education is restrictive, counterproductive, and, ultimately, a national folly (Ohanian, 1999).

## Basic Education Is Not Critical Thinking

*Basic education* has become a code term to describe a sterile and conformist school environment that feeds externally defined skills and lists of information to children. It depends heavily on indoctrination and regurgitation; there is, presumably, one right way to learn and one set of right "facts" to obtain. Robert Ennis (1991) defines critical thinking, however, as "reasonably reflective thinking that is focused on deciding what to believe or do" (p. 6). It depends on the engagement of the thinker in the process.

You can't just tell someone to think critically in the same way that teachers in traditional schools try to explain history or science. Critical thinking requires active involvement in the reflective act and goes well beyond the mechanical recitation of information imparted by a teacher or textbook. This means that student interest must be stimulated to activate participation. Students, then, have a serious stake in critical thinking, and schools cannot ignore student interests and motivations. Critical thinking cannot operate in top-down schooling, which has no regard for the learner or for real learning situations.

The artificiality of traditional basic education in schools is obvious. These schools are disconnected from society, from the lives of children, from families, and from reality. Bells signal when one is supposed to start learning. Children are drilled to memorize terms that hold no meaning for them. Tidiness and punctuality substitute for thought. Platitudes abound about a life that is not recognizable in the children's experience. Students are required to learn categories of information that do not relate to their lives, and they are tested on trivial details. The public then falsely presumes that the students' scores represent what they know about the world, and we pretend that this is preparation for life. School takes children who are living a real life and gives them artificiality, claiming that this is education.

Students thus begin to dread school, hating the regimen of rules, boredom, inert ideas, and stuffiness. We all start with immense curiosity about the world, and most of us are eager to start school. That curiosity is quickly stifled and that eagerness is dulled as we progress through schools that deny us the chance to engage in critical thinking. Isn't that an incredibly ironic situation? The institution intended to stimulate learning about the world is, instead, the institution that presents the most obstacles to that learning.

The academically successful student in such schools is usually not the most curious or creative, but the one best able to follow the teacher's directions and to remember what the books say when it's time for a test. The schools reward conformity and obedience, not diversity and independence. Schooling becomes training, not education. Students become passive receptacles for adult ideas, and student learning is defined by adult-constructed measures. The student is a bystander in schooling. Sizer's (1984) study of high school students showed they were compliant and docile and lacked initiative. He attributed this to the heavy emphasis on getting right answers and to too little emphasis on being inquisitive. Goodlad (1983), after examining data from observations in over a thousand classrooms, documented the high degree of passivity among students and the lack of time or concern afforded student interests and opinions.

Students need, and deserve, to participate actively in the learning process, and they require materials that stretch their imaginations, their pre-existing conceptions, and their intellectual capacities (Duckworth, 1987; Bamberger, 1991; Begley, 1993; Tice, 1994). These are basic elements in developing critical thinking. School reform at the end of the twentieth century has glossed over these elements in favor of old-fashioned basic skill drills. We continue to suffer from this backward stance.

Students were the most hidden part of the school reform movement of the 1980s; in fact, they were essentially invisible. The most ignored curriculum concern was critical thinking. Virtually every report, government statement, and proposed legislation focused on basic skills, the school organization, or school officials. The concern was to make some organizational or operational change in the structure of the institution. No interest was shown in the students or in their lives in school, and the idea of developing critical judgment as a primary school goal was lost in the pages of data on test scores. More tests, higher standards set by adults outside the school, longer school days and years, more homework, more stress on teachers and administrators, and less enjoyment in learning were the major educational achievements of the 1980s.

In a particularly clear-eyed review of the 1980s reform movement, English teacher Susan Ohanian (1985) summarized this point:

We must be ever wary of wasting some youngster's life just because of a dubious notion that a rigorous, regimented curriculum will help restore to the U.S. a better balance of trade. . . . At best, the recommendations of the commissions and task forces on school reform are hallucinatory; at worst, they are soul-destroying. Let us teachers not succumb to the temptation of asking what we can do for General Motors; let us continue to ask only what we can do for the children. (p. 321)

## Wrong First Question

The essential concern in education should not be what we teach, but what students learn. For too long, we have posed the wrong question in considering the school curriculum. Certainly we need to consider what is, or should be, taught, but that is a secondary issue. The primary focus should be on what is, or should be, learned. We can't properly address what we want to teach in schools without first determining the nature of learning and of the learners. Curriculum artificiality is borne on the presumption that we can ignore the needs and interests of children and their long-term development in favor of a set of pronouncements on what subjects they must learn.

The false claim behind the idea that schools should be reformed to teach basic reading, writing, and arithmetic skills is that schools are not now teaching these skills. Communication and mathematics are necessary parts of an education, but they are too limited to be the only goal of schooling. These skills are important, but they are important because of their value to individual children in making sense of their experience and in the critical thinking necessary for social improvement. They are not important simply because previous generations had to learn them. The view that everyone has to learn the same information in the same way leads to a stultifying but easily measured standardization. Information is essential, but why must everyone know the same things? The pronouncement that only the knowledge certain adults have deemed important is important to children may be satisfying for those adults. However, it is not adult satisfaction but human experience that determines what knowledge is of value.

The idea that schools should be devoted to discipline and to producing high test scores pleases those who would restrict freedom and control others. Discipline and high test standards are nothing more than means to restrict and to ensure social conformity. Schools should make individual creativity, human development, and rational social purposes their goals, not externally imposed discipline and academic standards. This is not a new school problem, but it has recurred in the current age of educational repression.

Over half a century ago, John Dewey's remarkably cogent book, *Experience and Education*, differentiated between traditional and progressive education. Dewey divided the two on the basis of a long-term schism that "is marked by opposition between the idea that education is development from within and that it is formation from without. . . ." (Dewey, 1938, p. 17) He notes that traditional education consists of information and skills that "have been worked out in the past," that its standards and rules of conduct are prescribed by adults, and that the school operates as though it were separate from the lives of children and the rest of society. The school imposes the subject matter and rules of conduct on the children, and the attitude of pupils must "be one of docility, receptivity, and obedience" (p. 18). The school molds or forms the child.

Progressive education, Dewey says, arose out of discontent with this traditional approach:

> To imposition from above is opposed expression and cultivation of individuality; to external discipline is opposed free activity; to learning from texts and teachers, learning through experience; to acquisition of isolated skills and techniques by drill, is opposed acquisition of them as a means of attaining ends which make direct vital appeal; to preparation for a more or less remote future is opposed making the most of opportunities of present life; to static aims and materials is opposed acquaintance with a changing world. (p. 20)

Unfortunately, the schools have never taken progressive education—developing the learner from within—seriously. Cosmetic changes have made schools appear more humane, but they have not shed their basic, misplaced authoritarian efforts to impose selected information and morals on children. Traditional education seeks to pour information into students, discouraging critical thinking and creativity. Schools continue to teach as though education were not part of life itself, but preparation for some later event. They ignore individual children in favor of standardization of curriculum and test scores.

The premise for education must be the child's development, not the adult's wish to mold the child's knowledge, values, and behavior. When we focus on subjects that "must" be taught, we are inclined to forget about the students and thinking. We are more likely to produce lists of concepts imposed on us that we now wish to impose on students. We introduce the teacher as an authority, rather than as a wise guide. And we structure schools to systematically destroy the creative interests of children by forcing them all to learn the same material.

A focus on what is to be learned permits consideration of the learner. Of course, it is possible to avoid that consideration by assuming that students will learn whatever they are taught, but that only increases the artificiality of the school. What students really learn is what has meaning for them, no matter what is taught and what is on the examination. It is this focus on the learner that makes what is learned the primary question.

## Natural and Unnatural Learning

A substantial battle has raged in the long history of educational thought between those who think that people learn naturally from within and those who believe that external force must be brought to bear to assure learning. This battle is illustrated currently by the difference of opinion between those who want students to be free to pursue their natural inclinations to learn and those who want to impose a set of conditions and ideas on the minds and actions of students. This battle is also illustrated by a quote from Nat Hentoff (1977):

One afternoon as we were walking down the street, Paul Goodman turned to me and said, "Do you realize that if the ability to walk depended on kids being taught walking as a subject in school, a large number of citizens would be ambulatory only if they crawled." (p. 53)

The first position, in support of freedom, does not mean letting students do whatever they please. Among the false criticisms of progressive education and of John Dewey's work is the claim that the child determines everything. That is either a misreading or a calculated attempt to discredit the position. Dewey insisted that the most mature person in the classroom, the teacher, must ultimately take responsibility for what is taught, but that the teacher's decision must be predicated on the needs and interests of the child. It is the child, or learner, who determines what is learned. Thus, the child-centered, or learner-centered, curriculum is designed with the child's development first in mind. The teacher must, in this curriculum, remain sensitive to the learner. License to do whatever one pleases, whether teacher or learner, is inconsistent with this view. Freedom encourages innovation and stimulates critical thinking.

The learner-centered curriculum stands in opposition to the subject- or discipline-centered curriculum, which begins by considering how the discipline is organized. The traditional discipline-centered curriculum represents the imposition of information, categories, and ideas without concern for the learner. It is thus an unnatural and external structuring of what is learned. The learner-centered curriculum rests on the conviction that students want to learn. What destroys that natural curiosity is the authoritarian nature of traditional approaches to schooling.

## Defects in the Traditional Structure of Schooling

The discipline-centered school has several defects. It imposes an externally determined body of information on children, it ignores natural learning interests and stifles curiosity and creativity, and it requires schools to be authoritarian. This last point, on the authoritarianism of schools, deserves further discussion. If one starts with the premise that children are curious, imaginative, and eager to learn, what happens to make schools impose so many restrictions on students? The main reason is that schools have traditionally been expected to homogenize individual children into an adult view of what society should be.

The structure of traditional schooling is consistent with the old-fashioned view that schools should be cheerless places where the young are trained to become adults by learning what adults think they should know and behaving in ways adults think they should behave. Schools are expected to impart to the younger generation skills and information based on past ideas; they are expected to train students to behave according to a set of rules and standards; and they are to do it all as efficiently as possible in order to save time and tax money.

From this viewpoint, schools are organized to distill the adult world for children, to impose a set of ideas and morals on them, and to require them to undergo processing as though they were in a food-packing or auto-assembly plant. As a result, schools classify students by grade and test scores to make teaching more efficient, set up severe time schedules, and rely on teacher or textbook presentation of standard information, required courses, and excessive testing to ensure that all students are trained the same way.

As a result, traditional schools are static institutions that stress conformity and adult concepts that have limited meaning in the lives of students. Yet students are dynamic, growing, and concerned about their own individuality. It is remarkable that the resilience of youth permits them to survive in such a stifling environment. Good teachers recognize the paradox between traditional schooling and the needs of youth, and they try to find ways to match static material with a changing society. They also ameliorate the demand for conformity by trying to recognize the individual differences among their students, and they attempt to enlarge the students' horizons by building on their experiences. But the efforts of good teachers are undermined by the traditional structure of schooling, by standardized tests, and by pressure from vocal advocates of the past.

In traditional schools, we reward those who do as we tell them whether it involves thinking or not. The main purpose of much schooling is for students to get the "right answers," not to encourage them to engage in critical thinking. The thinking student might challenge the way the school operates, the uninteresting material, the stress on conformity, and why certain answers are "right." Schools are not usually prepared to respond to such challenges, and teachers and administrators often resort to fear, ridicule, repression, and isolation to squelch them. Students learn quickly that it does not pay to raise serious questions, and they withdraw into the safer haven of going along with the system.

Schools present artificial barriers to learning, and they stimulate fear and repression. The typical student responds to school in one of the following ways:

- Drop out or fail
- Slip through without meaningful engagement
- Please the teacher and succeed
- Resist school rules and suffer penalties
- Wait for something more interesting

None of these responses represents the best form of intellectual development. Do we think our schools are excellent when large numbers of students drop out, fail, or set aside their curiosity?

## Student and Teacher Experiences

The primary way that people learn, as opposed to being taught, is through experience. Learning is an active, not a static process. When we are involved in some physical activity, such as organizing a group project, building a model village, playing a game, or measuring a room, we are learning. We make errors, seek advice, modify actions, and gain understanding in a real situation. Most teachers will admit, for example, that they learned the most about a subject when they had to teach it, not when they were sitting in a college class. We learn more about cars by trying to fix them than by hearing how to fix them.

Not all experiential learning involves physical activity or actual situations. Such vicarious experiences as reading a book or listening to a speaker can provide pertinent learning. And, of course, it is impossible, and would not even be desirable, for students to physically experience all learning situations. Active engagement, mental *or* physical, is what produces learning.

Curiosity, interest, or the need to resolve a problem makes reading or listening a learning situation in which active engagement can take place. Simply being told that something is important, or that something must be learned for a test, does not necessarily stimulate active engagement. Perfunctory reading of a book or listening to a teacher may appear to be learning, but the student with an active mind may be off on a different tangent. The teacher teaches and assigns readings; the student appears to be listening and reading, but what does he or she learn? The student learns to cope with dry and uninteresting material in a school filled with boring routines. That is not the experience good teachers desire, and many are themselves tired of the dullness and boredom. Certainly, it is not the experience students desire. But too many traditional schools operate this way.

It is clear that not all experiences are equally beneficial as learning situations; some are actually detrimental. We may like the taste of excessively fatty and salty foods, but that can lead to poor nutritional habits. Smoking cigarettes may lead to health problems. It may take only one experience of jumping out of a window to stop learning entirely. It is not simply experience that matters, but the quality and developmental nature of that experience. The teacher's role, then, becomes one of seeking and providing experiences for students that stimulate their interest and enrich their learning. Success, of course, depends on the wisdom and knowledge of the teacher and on the teacher's sensitivity to the students. As previously noted, a learner-centered curriculum encourages the teacher to guide and challenge rather than to act as an authority and keeper of the truth.

## The Subjects Learned

The learner-centered curriculum might appear to have no content, to be so loose and free that nothing intellectual is accomplished. Actually, the opposite is true. In the tightly organized and past-oriented traditional curriculum, the meticulously structured content largely has no meaning in the lives of students, and memorizing material for a test is scarcely intellectual. A properly developed learner-centered curriculum, however, requires the intellectual involvement of students in examining topics those students can comprehend and utilize. What is lacking in the learner-centered curriculum are what Alfred North Whitehead so eloquently derided in his 1929 classic, *The Aims of Education,* as 'inert ideas'—that is to say, ideas that are merely received into the mind without being utilised, or tested, or thrown into fresh combinations" (Whitehead, 1929, p. 13). He goes on to note that education is "overladen with inert ideas." And he states that "education with inert ideas is not only useless: it is, above all things, harmful. . . ."

The traditional school is filled with inert ideas, bits and pieces of information that fit no pattern and have no vitality for most students. Consider the standard school day: students go from English class, with a mixed lesson on spelling, vocabulary, and story reading; to history, where they hear about America's victory in some past war; to science, where they watch the teacher mix chemicals; to math, where they put answers on the chalkboard; to art, where they draw; and to gym, where they do calisthenics and study the rules of a game. Every period of inert ideas is followed by another period of different, apparently unrelated, inert ideas. Each teacher acts as though his or her ideas are very important, and will soon appear on a test, and the student goes through the expected motions. Schools are like giant jigsaw puzzles, except that the box cover with the picture of the completed puzzle is missing.

The material taught—which is different from the material learned—is a series of disconnected and lifeless bits of information that have little meaning for students. The student learns that English is separate from history, which is separate from economics and science and math and the arts and physical education. And the student learns that school is separate from life, and certainly from social and individual problems. How can a student understand and try to resolve a personal or a social problem using traditional school subjects? Are shyness, feelings of failure, apprehension, death in the family, and acne the kinds of problems traditional subjects can address? Does the student see problems of poverty, alcoholism, war, and human rights as resolvable by using the bits and pieces learned in math or science or history or English as taught in the schools? Is it reasonable or desirable for students to suffer through school and to look forward to life outside of school? That inverts what school should be, and what knowledge should provide.

Subjects taught in the traditional manner are not intellectual; they do not stimulate thinking and the consideration of diverse ideas. Intellectual vitality arises from life, not from the unrelated segments of knowledge we throw at students. We need to abolish this disconnectedness and restore the vitality of learning. That does not mean we would ignore or destroy the information gained from scholarly study of a subject; it means that we need to help students understand the connections that make knowledge valuable and learn how to utilize that knowledge in solving problems.

## Knowledge and Problems

We need to focus on what areas of knowledge are important for students to use in dealing with human problems. Thus, we must start with those problems and determine what knowledge exists that can help us understand and address them. That is certainly different from the old-fashioned approach, which starts with categories or subjects and presumes that the students need to learn them regardless of their value to the learner. Real human problems cannot be treated simply as literature or history or chemistry problems. Under the traditional curriculum, teachers resort to contrived "problems" in each of the subjects in an attempt to motivate student interest. Standard math story problems are notoriously unreal; U.S. history usually presents problems that the student sees as already resolved and unrelated to current life. Why not start with a problem the students can easily identify, and then find knowledge—regardless of the subject field it comes from—that we can utilize in solving that problem? This method recognizes knowledge as interrelated and useful, not as compartmentalized and ornamental.

The adult and traditional manner of organizing knowledge into apparently discrete categories, such as English and American literature, physics, political science, drawing, biology, algebra, European and U.S. history, botany, geometry, economics, psychology, chemistry, and drama, may work well for those who devote their careers to advanced study in one of these areas. (Interestingly, some of the most advanced thinkers in each of these fields recognize the connections among subjects and seek to find theories that draw fields together rather than separate them.) These distinct categories may not be as useful for students in elementary and secondary schools, where the need is greater to see that knowledge is seamless and valuable in examining life's problems.

The identification of problems to study should be a mutual process, with students and teacher jointly engaged. Some pervasive human problems revolve around such values as justice, equality, freedom, democracy, and human rights. And a myriad of individual problems are related to these broader human challenges. To solve them may require knowledge from such fields as math, science, history, economics, psychology, literature, the arts, and politics. It may also require skills in reading, writing, calculating, organizing, categorizing, and critical thinking. As students mature, they develop interests in different problems, different types of knowledge, and different levels of skills. An active problems approach to learning, based on student interests and freedom to choose, leads to the development of critical thinking.

## Summary

Traditional schooling continues to emphasize rote memory, achieving high scores on tests over relatively trivial material, and amassing information taught for its own sake. This type of schooling fails to connect to students and their lives, and it suppresses critical thinking because that type of thinking disrupts the teacher's authoritarian role. Schooling should, instead, open ideas that stimulate students to examine their own experiences and to engage in the critical examination of social problems. This goal requires a new focus on students and on critical thinking.

Students come with a variety of personalities, backgrounds, and interests. We need a curriculum that recognizes this individuality as an opportunity and sees the students as a dynamic resource. The static, traditional curriculum pushes them into molds and stamps them with a list of subjects studied. The learner-centered critical thinking curriculum develops the student's inner curiosity and energy and his or her ability to utilize knowledge in addressing human problems.

## *For Discussion:*

1. Construct and defend several hypothetical school curricula that you believe would ensure each of the following goals.
   a. Graduates would be able to operate successfully in society.
   b. Individual students' rights and interests would be given credible expression.
   c. Critical thinking would be a high priority for all students.
   d. Basic education would be at the core of the curriculum.
2. You have had experiences as student in several different levels of schooling. Which of the following potential school topics would you identify as a frill? Which are, to you, fundamentals? On what basis do you make the distinction?

   Athletics

   Group play

   Penmanship

   Landscaping

   American history

   Writing letters

   Games and rules

   Reviewing movies, newspapers, and television

   Literary classics

   Balancing a checkbook

   Advanced science and math

   Japanese, Russian, Chinese, and Spanish languages

   Astrology

   Myths and legends

   Latin and Greek

   Social living

   Economic theory

   Parts of speech

   Clothing design

   What would you add that is clearly a frill? What could you add that is obviously a fundamental?
3. If the roles of adults and children were reversed to allow children to determine what adults should know for a basic education, what would the curriculum be like?

S

# References

BAKER, D. P., AND SMITH, T. (1997). Trend 1: The condition of Academic Achievement in the Nation. *Teachers College Record* 99 (1), 14–17.

BAMBERGER, J. (1991). *The Mind Behind the Musical Ear.* Cambridge, MA: Harvard University Press.

BEGLEY, S. (1993). "Doin' What Doesn't Come Naturally." *Newsweek 122, 84.*

BERLINER, D. AND BIDDLE, B. J. (1995). *The Manufactured Crisis: Myths, Fraud, and Attack on America's Public Schools.* Reading, MA: Addison-Wesley.

BESTOR, A. *(1953). Educational Wastelands.* Urbana: University of Illinois Press.

BRACEY, G. (1998). "The Eighth Bracey Report." *Phi Delta Kappan.* Oct.

———. (1999). "The Demise of the Asian Math Gene." *Phi Delta Kappan.* 80(8), 619–620.

CAYWOOD, C. *(1994).* "Critical Thinking: A Critical Need." *School Library Journal* 40, 46.

Center for Educational Reform. (1998). *A Nation Still at Risk: An Education Manifesto.* Washington, DC: Center for Educational Reform.

DEWEY, J. (1938). *Experience and Education.* New York: Macmillan.

DUCKWORTH, E. (1987). *The Having of Wonderful Ideas and Other Essays.* New York: Teachers College Press.

ELIAS, M., AND KRESS, J. (1994). "Social Decision Making and Life Skills Development." *Journal of School Health* 64 (2), 62–66.

ENNIS, R. *(1991).* "Critical Thinking: A Streamlined Conception." *Teaching Philosophy* 14, 5–24.

FINN, C. (1995). "The School." *Commentary* 99, 6–10.

*Fortune.* (1990). Special Issue: "Saving Our Schools." Spring, p. 121.

GARDNER, H. (1991a). "The Tensions Between Education and Development." *Journal of Moral Education* 20, 113–125.

——— (1991b). *The Unschooled Mind.* New York: Basic Books.

GOODLAD, J. (1983). *A Place Called School.* New York: McGraw-Hill.

HENTOFF, N. (1977). *Does Anybody Give a Damn?* New York: Knopf.

HOFF, D. J. (1998). "U.S. Graduation Rates Starting to Fall Behind." *Education Week on the Web,* Nov. 25.

LEMANN, N. (1998). "Ready, Read!" *Atlantic Monthly* 282(5), 92–104.

MCNAMARA, J. B. (1998). "The Morality of Mediocrity." *Vital Speeches of the Day* 64(16) 497–501.

NATIONAL ASSESSMENT OF EDUCATIONAL PROGRESS. (1994). *NAEP 1992 Trends in Academic Progress.* National Center for Educational Statistics. Washington, DC: US Department of Education.

NATIONAL COMMISSION ON EXCELLENCE IN EDUCATION. (1983). *A Nation at Risk.* Washington, DC: U.S. Department of Education.

*National Review.* (1990). "Knowing So Much About So Little (Poor Performance of American Schools)." 42, 14–15.

"A Nation Still at Risk: An Educational Manifesto." (1998) *Policy Review* 90, 23–29,

NODDINGS, N. (1999). "Renewing Democracy in Schools." *Phi Delta Kappan.* 80(8), 579–83.

OHANIAN, S. (1985). "Huffing and Puffing and Blowing the Schools Excellent." *Phi Delta Kappan* 66, 316–321.

——— (1999). *One Size Fits Few: The Folly of Educational Standards.* Westport, CT: Heineman.

PELTZMAN, S. (1994). *USA Today.* 122, 22–25.

PERRY, N. J. (1993). "School Reform: Big Pain, Little Gain." *Fortune* 128, 130–135.

"Political Factors in Public School Decline." (1994). *The American Enterprise* 4, 44–49.

RAVITCH, D., AND FINN, C. (1987). *What Do Our 17-Year-Olds Know?* New York: Harper & Row.

RICHBURG, R. (1994). "Jump-Start Thinking." *The Social Studies* 85(2), 33–35.

ROSENBERG, A. (1994). "Futurescape." *Instructor* 103(6), 44–45, 84.

SAMUELSON, R. J. (1991). "The School Reform Fraud." *Newsweek* 117, 44.

——— (1998) "The Wastage in Education." *Newsweek* 132, 49.

SEWALL, G. T. (1983). *Necessary Lessons: Decline and Renewal in American Schools.* New York: Free Press.

SHAW, P. (1993). "The Competitiveness Illusion: Does our Country Need to Be Literate in Order to Be Competitive? If Not, Why Read?" *National Review* 45, 41–45.

SIZER, T. (1984). *Horace's Compromise: The Dilemma of the American High School.* Boston: Houghton Mifflin.

SZABO, J. C. (1992). "Boosting Workers' Basic Skills." *Nation's Business* 80, 38–41.

TICE, T. N. (1994). "Critical Plus Open." *Education Digest* 59, 42–44.

*Time.* (1989). "Mixed Review: Some Progress, More Needed." 133, 68.

"U.S. Drops in Education Rankings." (1998) *San Diego Union Tribune* 7(328), 1, 17.

*USA Today.* (1990). "Skills Lacking for Tomorrow's Jobs." 119, 11+.

WHITEHEAD, A. N. (1929). *The Aims of Education.* New York: Macmillan.

# CHAPTER 8

# Reading: Phonics or Whole Language

## POSITION 1: THE PHONICS ARGUMENT

When Alexis Muskie talks about her daughter's experience learning to read, she begins to cry. Muskie, whose father-in-law was the late Senator and Secretary of State Edmund Muskie, lives in Peterborough, New Hampshire. Before her daughter, Olivia, entered first grade, it became apparent that she would need some extra help, and so she received phonics tutoring in addition to her classroom instruction. But the school district had adopted the "whole language" approach to teaching reading. "There was a conflict between the special-ed teacher and the whole language teacher," Muskie says. "The whole language teacher was saying I can't send her to that program." The tutoring ended, but Olivia's reading didn't improve, and in second grade she became scared and frustrated. "She was literally pulling her hair out," Muskie remembers, her voice cracking. A year later, Muskie found a reading clinic that used a phonics method. "It took them six days," Muskie says, "and Olivia could read." (Collins, 1997, p. 1)

Across the centuries, methods to help the beginning reader attend to the sequence of letters and their correspondence to speech patterns have been a core element of most approaches to literacy instruction in alphabetic languages . . . We use the term *phonics* to refer to such methods. In order to understand written text, the reader must be able to derive meaning from the strings of printed symbols on the page. (Adams and Bruck, 1995, p. 7)

We all learn to use oral language through a natural process. We imitate the sounds we hear in our environment, connect those sounds to things and people, and eventually utter them in patterns others can understand. We learn informal oral communication skills without any direct instruction. You are unlikely to hear people arguing about "the best way to teach young children to speak" or discussing the "speaking crisis in our schools," and you may never run across a book entitled *Why Johnny Can't Speak!* Learning to read, on the other hand, is not an automatically acquired, natural process. The relationship between sounds and letters is an arrangement by convention; there is nothing natural about the letters assigned to sounds of the English language. Left to themselves, children will not automatically learn to associate sounds and letters, a fundamental prerequisite for successful reading. The weight of research evidence indicates that children will not learn to read without direct instruction (Grossen, 1998). Children need to be explicitly taught how to break the code of letters we use to represent the sounds of our language.

Reading instruction is a matter of serious concern. Nothing better predicts the future academic success of children than their ability to read. Unfortunately, as many as one in five children have reading difficulties, and those children are likely to be headed for a life of academic struggle and a world of diminished promise. Children who are behind in reading at an early age, in kindergarten and first grade, fall further behind every year they are in school. In a review of research conducted by the National Institute of Child Health and Human Development, one researcher found that nearly three-fourths of the children diagnosed as "reading disabled" in the third grade remained disabled in the ninth grade (Grossen, 1998, p. 6).

What makes this all the more unfortunate is that we know how to teach young children to read. Recent research evidence is overwhelming: To become good readers, children need to be taught the "alphabetic principle": that is, words are made up of letters, and letters correspond to speech in consistent and specific ways. In experimental treatments comparing direct instruction in letter-sound correspondence (phonics) and less direct methods (whole language), the children receiving direct instruction "improved in word reading at a faster rate and had higher word-recognition skills" than the other children (Foorman et al., 1998, p. 37).

Why do children need to know the sounds of letters? The answer is disarmingly straightforward: Words and syllables are composed of short sound units called phonemes. Research indicates that deficits in phonemic awareness—the ability to understand how to break words into component sounds—is at the heart of most reading problems (Grossen, 1998, p. 6). For children to be successful readers, teachers need to begin reading instruction with direct, explicit lessons in the relationships between sounds and letters. As one researcher points out, children who are not taught to link sounds and letters are in academic trouble: "You have to understand what happened to kids who don't learn sound awareness . . . They just don't make it. They don't make it in school and they don't make it in life. It is extremely important and it is not something you can 'pick up'" (Gursky, 1998, p. 12)

Reading is a technical field, but don't be thrown by terms such as *letter-sound relationships, phonemic awareness,* and *phonics.* These terms are nothing more than the ways reading scholars describe how oral language relates to written language. Consider the following example of several phonemic awareness tasks for young children. On the left side are the technical terms for the reading subskills a phonics teacher would help children master. On the right side are the classroom questions a teacher would ask to help students develop those skills.

| | |
|---|---|
| 1. Phonome deletion: | What word would be left if the /k/ sound were taken away from *cat?* |
| 2. Word-to-word matching: | Do *pen* and *pipe* begin with the same sound? |
| 3. Blending: | What word would we have if we put these sounds together: /s/, /a/, /t/? |
| 4. Sound isolation: | What is the first sound in *rose?* |
| 5. Phoneme segmentation: | What sounds do you hear in the word *hot?* |
| 6. Phoneme counting: | How many sounds do you hear in the word *cake?* |
| 7. Deleting phonemes: | What sound do you hear in *meat* that is missing in *eat?* |
| 8. Odd word out: | What word starts with a different sound: *bag, nine, beach, bike?* |
| 9. Sound-to-word matching: | Is there a /k/ in *bike?* (Grossen, 1998, p. 10) |

## *The Romance of Whole Language*

Are you familiar with *Emile,* by Jean-Jacques Rousseau? One section reads,

> Everything is good as it leaves the hands of the Author of things; everything degenerates in the hands of man. He forces one soil to nourish the products of another, one tree to bear the fruit of another. He mixes and confuses the climates, the elements, the seasons. He mutilates his dog, his horse, his slave. [Man] turns everything upside down; he disfigures everything; he loves deformity, monsters. He wants nothing as nature made it, not even man; for him, man must be trained like a school horse; man must be fashioned in keeping with his fancy like a tree in his garden. (Rousseau, 1979, p. 37)

What does this have to do with reading? Rousseau (1712–1778) might seem an unlikely participant in a discussion of today's "reading wars," but his insistence on the natural goodness of man and children's natural inclination to take the right educational path provide some background to the current dilemma. Rousseau's pedagogic focus on the wishes of the child and his insistence that children learn best when allowed to do exactly what they want provides the ideologic basis for present-day progressive education and whole language reading instruction. Progressives assume that children naturally want to learn, to study, to improve. Any imposition on a child's natural bent is considered a corruption of nature and an impediment to progress.

Emile, Rousseau's hypothetical pupil, was led by a tutor to discover scientific and moral truths by using his inherent creativity and curiosity. Emile learned by observing nature, by cultivating a garden and discovering nature's rules about competition and survival, and by experiencing the world around him. He learned useful trades and the principles of good character formation. Emile, guided by his tutor, had a natural education. The basic purpose of Rousseau's world was to facilitate the happiness of humankind. Happiness was part of God's plan, and it could be seen everywhere in nature. The obstacles to achieving happiness were put into the minds of children by misguided educators who insisted on teaching inert facts and other useless information. True learning was the road to happiness, and it could only be discovered individually. False learning was standardized and taught by drill and repetition. Rousseau would never have had Emile memorize multiplication tables, the parts of speech, or the sounds of the letters.

Whole language thinking is a direct descendant of Rousseau's philosophy, by way of John Dewey and A. S. Neill. Whole language methods do not require a private tutor for every child, but teachers are asked to draw on the natural curiosity of each individual child in the classroom. Whole language advocates reject drill and phonics worksheets as corrupting and unnatural, in the same way that Rousseau rejected the conformity of school and the rules of civilized society. Whole language may be attractive at first glance, and it would be very appealing classroom methodology if it were effective in teaching children to read, but it is not. In fact, the appeal of whole language does not extend beyond its rhetoric, and in practice it nearly visited disaster on the children from one state that adopted it.

## Whole Language Problems in California

> Why are California's schoolchildren reading so poorly? The whole language method. (Grossen, 1995, p. 43)

California's experience offers an interesting case study of the failure of whole language instruction as a practical method for teaching reading. During the 1980s, William Honig, the Superintendent of Public Instruction in California, was responsible for the education of the state's 5 million school children. Honig was not an expert on reading, but he was taken by what he heard about whole language. He was impressed by whole language advocates' arguments that children would benefit from spending more time reading "real books" and less time performing repetitive classroom drills. The skill-and-drill approach to reading made an easy target. The image of classrooms filled with joyful children reading "real literature" was appealing, and the siren call of a literature-based whole language approach to reading was hard to resist. Whole language advocates are optimistic about schooling; they convey a genuine love of children and literature; and they argue that whole language instruction will bring young children the joy of reading. To Honig and others, whole language seemed both innocent and promising.

By 1987, California bought into whole language hook, line, and sinker. A committee that Honig appointed recommended that the state abandon phonics and adopt the recently designed English-Language Arts Framework, a curriculum approach based largely on the principles of whole language (Lemann, 1997). Teachers were told to discard their old phonics methods and texts and embrace the new literature-based classroom methods. Schools cast aside phonics and research on reading as the state adopted untested whole language approaches.

As phonics educators had warned, the approach did not go well. The failures of whole language methods were not immediately apparent to outsiders.

It was not until the state published nationally normed test results that Californians learned about the problem and were shocked into action. The reading portion of the National Assessment of Education Progress exam (a test described in chapter 13) placed California children in a tie for last place in the nation. Whole language reading instruction was not working; children's reading skills were declining. As one member of the California State Board of Education later put it, "Unfortunately for California children, the unsubstantiated claims and enthusiastic visions of whole language ideologues proved to be disastrous when applied to real children" (Palmaffy, 1997, p. 3). California's experience provides a clear message: When reading teachers ignore phonics instruction, reading scores plummet. William Honig would later turn away from whole language and acknowledge that phonics teaching was a prerequisite for developing successful readers. Before they can become proficient readers, children need to learn phonics.

In 1995, California enacted legislation that required the State Board of Education to exercise greater oversight over reading instruction and include "systematic, explicit phonics" (Grossen, 1995, p. 43). California later strengthened the language of this legislation to ensure that reading instruction in grades K through 6 conformed to the rules of phonics, and that teachers provided direct instruction in letter-sound correspondences, letter by letter, word by word. During a typical phonics lesson under the new regulations, teachers would ask children to produce the sounds of letters that appear both singly and combined in words. Phonics was back. Faith in reading research was restored.

## Research on Reading

For over thirty years, at a cost of more than $200 million, the National Institute of Child Health and Human Development (NICHD) has conducted research that supports the essential link between learning to read effectively and the use of phonics. The NICHD program was formed in 1965 to study children who were experiencing reading difficulties. In 1985, its mission was expanded to examine ways to improve the quality of reading research. NICHD division head Reid Lyon, described as a "nightmare figure for the whole language movement" because of his insistence on research evidence, led as many as one hundred researchers in several fields, including medicine, psychology, and education (Lemann, 1997, p. 132). Working in fourteen different centers, Lyon and his colleagues designed longitudinal studies to uncover the factors that were causing 20 to 40 percent of the population to exhibit persistent reading problems.

The findings were interesting: Children's reading difficulties appear to occur independent of IQ or other academic abilities such as listening comprehension or mathematics. Children's difficulties in reading relate to an inability to decode the sound/letter relationship; disabled readers typically have trouble "sounding out" single words. For example, when asked to say *cat* without the /t/ sound, good readers have no problem, while disabled readers have difficulty. This indicates their trouble with a skill called "phonological awareness" (Grossen, 1998, p. 5).

Based on these studies, Lyon has become an opponent of whole language methods and an enthusiastic supporter of the teaching of phonics (Lemann, 1997). Lyon's findings are by no means new or unique. For the past fifteen years, researchers have documented the success of phonics instruction over any competing approach. In 1985, the U.S. Department of Education released a report, "Becoming a Nation of Readers," which concluded that "the issue is no longer . . . whether children should be taught phonics . . . [but] how it should be done" (Palmaffy, 1997, p. 3). More recently, in a study of 285 first and second graders, the greatest reading gains were found among children receiving direct instruction on the correspondence between letters of the alphabet and the sounds they make. These children learned to recognize words at a faster rate and with a higher degree of accuracy than children receiving instruction of other sorts, including whole language techniques (Foorman et al., 1998).

## Why Are People Opposed to Phonics?

> Good people do believe in alchemy at various points in our history. (California's State Superintendent of Public Instruction, quoted in Lemann, 1997, p. 133)

You may well ask, If the weight of research evidence in support of phonics is so overwhelming, why are the voices in opposition so insistent? The answer may be quite simple: For a long time, reading teachers have known that children must learn that written letters correspond to the sounds in spoken words, but phonics-based teaching methods have been less than stimulating. Consider the following example:

> It is October 1921, and forty first graders are seated at rows of desks. The teacher stands at the front of the class and points with a long wooden pointer to a wall chart that contains columns of letters and letter combinations. As she points to a column of short vowel and consonant *b* combinations, the class responds with the sound of each combination: /ab/, /eb/, /ib/, /ob/, /ub/. She goes to the next column and the class responds, /bab/, /beb/, /bib/, /bob/, /bub/. Then the teacher asks, 'What's the rule?" The children respond in unison, "In a one-syllable word, in which there is a single vowel followed by a consonant . . ." So it went day after day, "with letter-sound relationships and pronunciation rules done to death." (Diederich, 1973, quoted in Beck and Juel, 1995, p. 24)

Phonics theory was tarnished by the dreariness of early phonics instruction. Phonics became a synonym for "skill and drill" and "heartless drudgery." None of us wants to teach or be taught with these kinds of methods. We know today that children do not learn to read by memorizing abstract rules about the sounds of letters. Children need lots of practice with interesting materials to help them learn the patterns of written language. Today's phonics instruction and the basal programs that use phonics convey the principles of phonics through compelling teaching approaches. Instead of memorizing strings of abstract rules, children are introduced to meaningful reading, and they practice with real books and real words that teach sound/letter relationships.

During preservice and inservice teacher education, students take two or three courses in teaching reading. Such classes teach in far greater detail than we can outline here the various approaches to teaching reading and how to organize the classroom for reading instruction. In the following section, we describe some of the characteristics of a phonics-based basal approach to teaching beginning reading, and we outline some of its assumptions and describe the array of materials available to teachers. If you have not already explored these materials on your own, your courses on reading methods will introduce you to them. We think you will be surprised by their richness and pleased by the explicit link between the research evidence about how children learn to read and the reading materials teachers can now use to teach young learners. No matter who the publisher is, today's phonics materials are unlike the basals you may have used as a student.

## Today's Phonics Basals

What are the practical differences between a phonics approach and a whole language approach to reading instruction?

You may be surprised to find there are more similarities than differences between the teaching applications of the two camps. As you explore some of today's reading basals, you will learn that most new phonics-based basals incorporate many of the best literature teaching ideas formerly associated with whole language. The publisher of "Open Court" states that the series uses a "blended variety of approaches to reading instruction and that . . . whole language and phonics need not be mutually exclusive."[1] The new balanced approach to basals offers a very rich resource for teachers in kindergarten through sixth-grade classrooms who want to give their students a sound introduction to phonics and an exposure to authentic classic and contemporary literature. If you are planning to teach at the elementary level, or if you just want to know how elementary teachers teach children to read, explore one of these kits. These examples of the newer basals, taken from "Open Court," are typical of the materials you will find for children in the first grade:

- *Real literature in a phonics base:* Children are reminded that literacy is a powerful tool gained through learning the written code. Children's literature experience begins with Big Books (oversize story books) and extends to both contemporary and classic fiction and nonfiction. Literature selections include such familiar works as "Hey, Diddle, Diddle" and "The House That Jack Built," as well as poetry by William Blake (1757–1827) and selections from some of today's award-winning children's authors.

    The literature cuts across subject lines and affords children an integrated curriculum. The Big Book *Animals* introduces students to biology,

---

[1] The "Open Court" basal series is published by the Open Court Publishing Company, Chicago and Peru, Illinois, a division of SRA McGraw-Hill.

and *Captain Bill Pinckney's Journey* introduces social studies concepts through the tale of a solo sail around the world. In addition, children learn natural reader-response to literature by watching the teacher and their classmates respond as they read authentic texts.

- *Research-based phonics instruction:* As one of the basal authors notes, "In order for children to learn to read, they have got to break the code. And by teaching them about how the sound structure of their language works, you're only making it much easier for them to break the code" (Hirshberg, 1995, p. 17F). This basal series offers direct instruction in phonics through a variety of research-validated techniques. For example, sound/spelling cards introduce students to the sounds and spellings of English phonemes. Students are taught to be active learners and to construct meaning from multiple sources. They are encouraged to use "inventive spelling" and to explore the relationships between sounds and words and the application of phonics knowledge to writing.

- *Teacher support:* Even the most able and best-prepared new teacher needs help in weaving together the complex activities of a beginning reading program. Phonemic awareness cards, phonics cards, sound spelling cards, learning framework cards, activity sheets, Big Books, individual sound/spelling cards, letters cards, alphabet flash cards, take-home phonics books, and the like can form a dizzying array of materials. Teacher's guides offer practical advice about how to structure and pace a lesson, how to individualize instruction, and how to integrate the various aspects of the basal program. In addition, a series of fifteen letters to parents (written in English and Spanish) solidify the home/school connection by informing parents what's going on in the classroom and how they can help their child learn to read.

Phonics instruction is based on sound, research-based teaching strategies, and we believe that the new basal series are nothing short of a bonanza for the new teacher. The new basals are an effective component of phonics instruction that incorporate the best of other reading approaches (invented spelling, constructed knowledge, authentic literature, reader-response) while eliminating the dull routine formerly associated with phonics. Using phonics to teach reading is not new; however, today's basals help to make it an exciting approach to beginning reading. Check this approach out thoroughly.

## POSITION 2: THE WHOLE LANGUAGE ARGUMENT

When Carol Avery talks about her goddaughter's experience learning to read, she . . . begins to cry. Avery, from Millersville, Pennsylvania, recently served as president of the National Council of Teachers of English. Like most members of that organization, she is a committed, sincere believer in whole language. "Mary knew how to read when she got to the first grade," Avery says. "I asked her what she read in school, and she said, `We don't read stories; we do papers.'" By "papers" Mary meant phonics worksheets. "She had a terrible time that year," Avery continues, now holding back tears. "She cried every night.

She had to stand in the corner with her nose against the wall for having too many mistakes on her worksheets. That's the sort of experience I fear too many children will have with what's happening with phonics now." (Collins, 1997, pp. 1–2)

There is a significant gap between how reading is learned and how it is taught and assessed in the vast majority of classrooms today. This gap is perpetuated by the basal reading series that dominate reading instruction in roughly 90 percent of the elementary classrooms in the United States. Such textbooks series are often viewed as complete systems for teaching reading, for they include not only a graded series of books for the students to read but teacher's manuals telling teachers what and how to teach, workbooks and dittos for the students to complete, sets of tests to assess reading skills, and often various supplementary aids. (Weaver, 1990, p. 58)

Whole language is a perspective on reading and education that assumes, among other things, that learning to read and write is not very different from learning to talk. The roots of whole language reading instruction can be traced to the work of Ken and Yetta Goodman in the 1970s, but whole language did not become widely known in the United States until the late 1980s. The whole language approach to reading is harder to define than the phonics approach. It is not a program or a package of materials for the classroom. It is easier to think of whole language as a perspective on the ways children learn and teaching methods that spring from that perspective (Watson, 1989).

Whole language theorists and researchers argue that children learn to read by interacting with the world of print in natural exchanges. One instructional key to whole language is to encourage students to do real reading and real writing and not waste effort on repetitive exercises and isolated drills commonly found in basal programs. Whole language teachers use genuine texts—children's literature, song lyrics, poetry, and story books—not artificially written material designed for instructional purposes. However, the real difference between phonics and whole language is not necessarily in the material, but in the ways teachers use the materials. Whole language teachers and phonics teachers may read the same poem with their students. The whole language teacher is likely to have selected the poem so that children can learn from it and enjoy its message. Phonics teachers are likely to use it to isolate its rhyming patterns, letter sounds, or some other feature (Edelsky, Altwerger, and Flores, 1991, p. 8). In whole language classrooms, teachers expect children to do real reading, real writing, and real learning. Students and teachers pursue whole texts at the very beginning of reading instruction. Whole language teachers do not try to break texts into fragments. They do not use "readiness activities" to prepare children for reading someplace down the road. They begin with texts, not skills. They do not rely on basals.

"Let's not beat around the bush," writes Ken Goodman, "basal readers, workbooks, skills sequences, and practice materials that fragment the process are unacceptable to whole language teachers" (Goodman, 1986, p. 29). Reading is not a mechanical process acquired in isolated steps. Whole language teachers do not ignore phonics, but they do not center their instruction on the sounds of language. Whole language teachers teach phonics in the context of real reading and understanding whole texts. Whole language teachers view phonics as one way to understand printed text, but certainly not the only way.

## Definition of Reading: Constructed Meanings

> Reading is not a matter of "getting the meaning" from text, as if that meaning were *in* the text waiting to be decoded by the reader. Rather, reading is a matter of readers using the cues print provides and the knowledge they bring with them . . . to construct a unique interpretation. (Edelsky, Altwerger, and Flores, 1991, pp. 19–20)

The real difference between the whole language approach and the phonics approach to reading lies in separate and competing perspectives and differing definitions of what it means to read. If someone were to ask you, "Can you read English?" How would you interpret the question, and how would you answer? Would you understand the question to refer to your ability to *pronounce* English words? In that case, you might respond that you could also "read" a host of foreign languages including Spanish, French, Portuguese, Romansch, and Latin. Most of us can sound out words in those languages although we may not know what they mean, and we ordinarily do not confuse the languages we can *read* with those we can merely *pronounce.*

Do you believe reading means decoding the words to find out what the author meant when she wrote them? Do you believe that meaning is embedded in the word and to "read English" is to engage in a code-breaking process of unlocking the author's meaning? Many people accept this definition, and if you are among them, you may be comfortable with the phonics arguments about reading. The conception of reading as decoding or unlocking the meaning embedded in text and a phonics approach to reading instruction go hand in glove.

On the other hand, if you believe that reading is a complex process in which a person brings meaning to the text, you are likely to be more comfortable in the whole language camp (Braunger and Lewis, 1997, p. 7). This view of reading as a way to construct meaning is one of the unifying threads among whole language advocates. The text has a certain inherent meaning for whole language teachers, but understanding text depends mainly on what the individual reader brings to it. Not every child will interpret the written material in the same way. Teachers emphasize "individual understanding" of text over the "author's intent." Whole language classrooms encourage multiple interpretations of printed material.

Whole language is based on research principles derived from several fields, including linguistics and cognitive psychology. Whole language teachers are a diverse, creative group, and not all whole language classrooms look the same, nor should you expect them to. If you spend time with a whole language teacher, you are likely to see a wide range of classroom activities designed to encourage reading and writing, but not every teacher uses the same set of classroom strategies. You are likely to find, however, that whole language teachers do share a number of perspectives and principles about literacy:

- Learning to read is a natural, social process, much like learning to speak. Children encounter reading and speaking as ways of communicating meaning. Children will learn to read when teachers and other literate adults find ways to engage them in written language (Edelsky, Altwerger, and Flores, 1991; Freeman and Freeman, 1998).

- Reading instruction should involve students in choosing books of interest to them. Students should often read silently, since most reading is silent in "real life" (Goodman, 1998).
- The materials children read in classrooms should connect to their lives.
- Phonics teaches children unreal relationships between the sounds of oral language and the letters of written language. It is silly to teach that "when two vowels go walking, the first does the talking." That only holds in limited cases, and the reader must know the exceptions to make sense of the rule (Goodman, 1986, p. 37). Whole language teachers teach phonics, but only in the context of the books they are reading. They teach skills as students need them.
- Readers use their prior experiences to make sense out of texts (Goodman, 1986, p. 38).
- Whole language focuses on children, and whole language teachers plan with children what they will read and write.
- Some classroom practices support reading instruction; others do not. The International Reading Association lists practices that hinder reading development: "Emphasizing only phonics, drilling on isolated letters or sounds . . . focusing on skills rather than interpretation and comprehension, constant use of workbooks and worksheets, fixed ability grouping, blind adherence to a basal program" (Braunger and Lewis, 1997, p. 65).
- Classroom teachers, not textbook publishers, should exercise the greatest authority over reading instruction. Whole language harnesses the creativity of the teacher to cast and recast activities to help children learn written language.
- Basal readers, workbooks, and skill sheets are not needed to teach reading. Children are better served when classrooms are filled with books children want to read—real literature, such as poetry, fiction, and nonfiction, some books specially designed for schools, such as beginning dictionaries, and some real world texts, such as phone books (Goodman, 1986, p. 33).
- Reading is not a decoding of text. It is a construction of meaning from text that requires readers to be active and build their own understandings (Braunger and Lewis, 1997, p. 29).
- Reading knowledge is not something teachers build in students brick-by-brick. Teachers create academic scaffolding that supports individual students in constructing their own meanings from text.

## What Are Whole Language Methods?

Whole language is not a single method, a series of methods, a package, or even a program. As noted earlier, it may be more helpful to think of whole language as a perspective on language and learning. Although whole language has no core methods, some classroom approaches fit better than others with a whole language perspective. In your reading classes, you will learn about methods commonly associated with whole language, such as self-selected reading, literature studies, theme cycles, interactive journal writing, Big Books, predictable texts, and creating literature-rich environments (Edelsky, Altwerger, and Flores, 1991, p. 42). We do not go into great detail on those methods here. Our goal is to provide an overview and an introduction that will assist in your own exploration of whole language teaching.

As Ken Goodman notes, the organization of the whole language classroom may not be obvious to the casual observer (1986, p. 31). It is beliefs rather than specific methods that distinguish different kinds of reading teachers. A whole language teacher and a skills teacher may both use phonic activities and decoding strategies. The difference between the teachers will be the role they assign to these activities and whether such activities are the focus of instruction. A whole language teacher, for example, would not teach phonics in isolation apart from the text or as a prerequisite skill for reading and writing.

Other visible differences may also appear subtle at first glance. A skills-oriented phonics teacher may try to correct every error a child makes in oral reading. Phonics teachers expect readers to strive for accuracy as they decode the printed text and convert it into oral language. Because whole language teachers are more interested in having the reader derive meaning from the text, they are less concerned about whether the child reads every word correctly. Whole language teachers consider teacher-corrected errors in reading (referred to as "miscues") a distraction from the central task of making sense of the text. Goodman emphasizes student *self*-correction. "When *they* [the students] realize something has gone wrong, *they* will take the opportunity to locate the problem and fix it. There's no good reason to call their attention to miscues that don't disrupt the process of making sense" (1996, p. 115).

## What Really Happened to the Reading Ability of California's Children?

In the mid 1990s, critics of whole language tried to blame whole language teaching for California's problems in reading achievement. California had introduced a new English-Language Arts Framework that shifted the focus of literacy instruction from a skills-based to a literature-based approach to reading, writing, and language arts. Scores on the National Assessment of Educational Progress (NAEP) indicated that the reading levels of California's fourth graders were very low. In 1992, California's students ranked fifth from the bottom nationally. On the next NAEP exam, an analysis of reading scores found California students tied for last place among students from the fifty states, and ahead only of students from Guam (Lemann, 1997). California's own statewide test, the California Learning Assessment System, also indicated student problems in reading (McQuillan, 1998).

Something had to be done. William Honig, the Superintendent of Public Instruction who had endorsed the literature-based reading, an approach associated with whole language, was no longer in office. Both economic conditions and California electoral politics had changed. Less money was available for public schools. A new Superintendent was in office, and a conservative had replaced a liberal governor. NAEP reading scores were low, and state officials blamed the literature-based approach to teaching reading. Critics quickly condemned whole language instruction as a mistake that caused the decline in reading scores. Whole language provided a scapegoat, and phonics promised a cheap remedy. Unfortunately neither action was academically responsible or warranted.

If you have taken a course in logic, you have probably learned about errors of reasoning, sometimes referred to as "logical fallacies." Among these errors is one referred to as the *post hoc, ergo propter hoc* fallacy ("after this, therefore because of this"). You are guilty of committing this error in logic if your reasoning holds that because event A precedes event B, then event A must be the cause of event B. For example, if A, a rooster crowing in the morning, is followed by B, a sunrise, would you conclude that A caused B? When California politicians and school leaders blamed declining scores on whole language instruction, they were committing this logical fallacy. When the legislature of California enacted legislation mandating phonics instruction in 1995, they were sacrificing sound logic to political expediency.

California's experience reveals little about the effectiveness of whole language. First of all, it is not clear that California's reading test scores actually declined. California's children were not doing well, to be sure, but to attribute a decline in test scores to a curriculum change, test data must be collected over time—both before and after the implementation of the new curriculum. No such test data existed for California children taking the NAEP exam. The NAEP data do not provide evidence of a decline, only scores that were low and that continued to be low. On the California state test, reading scores were stable despite the introduction of the whole language curriculum in 1987. Students were performing at about the same level in 1985, before the adoption of the Framework, as they were in 1990, after the introduction of the new curriculum (McQuillan, 1998, p. 13). The scores were not good, but they were not declining.

In the rush to indict whole language, critics ignored two interesting findings from the NAEP assessment: (1) In 1992, as part of the assessment, fourth-grade teachers were asked to indicate their methodological approach to teaching reading and to identify the term that best described their approach: whole language, literature-based, or phonics. The average scores for children of teachers using each approach were then compared; children in classrooms with a heavy emphasis on phonics did the worst (McQuillan, 1998, p. 14). (2) A major feature of whole language is silent reading of student-selected books. NAEP results indicate that students who read silently in school and students who choose their own books to read had higher test scores on average than students who did not participate in these features of instruction (Goodman, 1998, p. 6).

Despite the heated rhetoric and political maneuvering, no real evidence indicates that California's reading scores have declined over the past ten years, and even less indicates that whole language teaching methods are to blame in any reading problems. However, phonics advocates castigated whole language while ignoring many factors that affect student performance. For example,

California, once a leader in public education, had experienced dramatic changes in its classrooms. In the 1970s, under spending-limit initiatives proposed by then-Governor Ronald Reagan, the state spent less money on public education. In 1965, California was fifth in the nation in per capita spending on public education; by the time of the 1992 NAEP exam, its rank had slipped to thirty-seventh (Lemann, 1997, p. 134). The new Language Arts Framework was introduced as California was experiencing further budget cuts.

As a result of an economic downturn in the 1980s and early 1990s, California's schools were not as well funded as they had been, and many teachers found themselves teaching between thirty-two and thirty-six students in cramped classrooms where it was not uncommon to hear three or four different native languages. To make matters worse, Californians had fewer library books per child than national standards called for, and California ranked dead last in the number of librarians per pupil (Freppon and Dahl, 1998).

It's hard enough to switch to a literature-based reading approach in large classes, without adequate books or library facilities, but to make matters worse, California's teachers were asked to change the emphasis of their reading instruction without being given adequate support to help them make the transition. Fewer than 2 percent of the teachers were introduced to whole language principles and techniques during in-service workshops (Murphy, 1998, p. 165). As one teacher educator admitted:

> Many beginning teachers were not well-prepared to teach reading. In California, the teaching credential is earned in fifth-year programs after earning a bachelor's degree. This results in one (or possibly two) literacy courses in that fifth year . . . It's simply not possible to teach everything beginning teachers need to know about reading in a single course. (Freppon and Dahl, 1998, p. 246)

Did the reading scores of California's schoolchildren really decline? If they did, what was the cause? Unfortunately, no one can answer the first question with certainty because no longitudinal data exist. Clearly, California's children were not doing well on standardized tests, but no one can say for sure whether spending cuts, class size, lack of support for teachers, or the implementation of a literature-based reading instruction and a deemphasis on phonics was to blame.

## The Politics of Reading

> The "reading wars," as they have been dubbed in the press, are not wars between teachers who believe in phonics or in whole language. The war is political and ideological, a product of the new capitalism . . . The battle is for power, for control, and of course for profits. (Taylor, 1998, p. 259)

> "God Believes in the Beauty of Phonics" . . . The primary push for intensive, systematic phonics comes originally—especially—from the religious right . . . and more generally from the far right, which currently wields considerable influence and power in our national and state governments. (Weaver and Brinkley, 1998, pp. 128–129)

Whole language teaching came to public attention through media accounts of the NAEP assessment data and the California's Reading-Language Arts Framework. Newspapers and magazines reported a new "school crisis." Children were at-risk; whole language teachers were villains; parents were understandably alarmed.

Whole language teachers and teacher educators were taken unawares. Certainly they knew that not everything was right with reading in the schools. They agreed that students should read more, with greater understanding, and derive more pleasure from reading. Whole language teachers were stunned, however, that the media had declared a "reading crisis." Teachers who kept up with research knew that U.S. children were reading as well as their parents had a generation ago (see Berliner and Biddle, 1995). A review of the NAEP testing from 1971 to 1996 showed some fluctuations in performance, but it failed to indicate a national decline in reading scores (McQuillan, 1998).

Whole language teachers were further surprised to learn from media accounts that they were at "war" with phonics advocates. Although whole language teachers begin reading instruction with real literature, not by teaching the sounds the letters make, they are not opposed to phonics teaching or phonics teachers. Most whole language educators found themselves comfortable with a National Council of Teachers of English resolution that called for all students to learn a range of reading strategies, including phonics, but that phonics be considered only one part of the socially constructed intellectual process we call reading (Taylor, 1998). Does that sound like the rhetoric of a war?

Whole language educators have come to realize that the reading crisis was largely a media invention, and if whole language was at war, it was not necessarily at war with other reading camps. Whole language teachers might instead be in a battle with commercial publishers on one front and the far right on another. Given their support for children's choice in literature and individualized reading assignments, whole language teachers are likely to favor increases in library budgets and filling libraries floor-to-ceiling with trade books. They may not support schools spending money on commercially prepared (and expensive) basals. Reading represents a large, lucrative market. Publishers invest heavily in instructional reading materials for schools, and they expect significant returns. If schools adopted whole language more widely, children would be reading more, but they would be using commercially prepared basals less.

Other whole language adversaries represent the extremes of the political and religious right. Whole language instruction emphasizes a child's individual interpretation of literature. Readers are encouraged to bring their own meanings to texts and develop their own constructions of what is important in the books they read. This approach may raise the ire of those who believe that texts have definite, embedded meanings that learners are to unlock. For some, the interpretative nature of whole language is a threat to the authority, control, and tradition of text materials. For others, whole language represents an attack on the notion of "absolute truth" and "literal interpretation of text" (Weaver and Brinkley, 1998, pp. 129, 132). As one whole language educator notes:

One reason that fundamentalist Christian parents value reading so highly and favor an emphasis on phonics and spelling is that they believe these skills will lead to a more careful reading of the Bible. Studying biblical texts closely, attending to precision in language, and carefully weighing the meaning of each word are especially valued, since fundamentalists depend on their accurately reading and interpreting Bible messages as a way to keep them focused on God's will for their lives. (Brinkley, 1998, p. 59)

Phonics is associated with order and structure and a less interpretative, more direct "transmission model" of education, a notion that what is taught is learned just as the textbook authors and curriculum planners intended (Weaver and Brinkley, 1998). Some whole language critics believe that phonics will afford them greater control over what children learn and think because it limits the range of children's interpretations. Many on the far right see phonics as a way to control the messages of the school curriculum (Taylor, 1998, p. 319).

The so-called "reading wars" are a reminder to educators that we cannot separate the processes of teaching and learning from politics and economics. The contest over teaching reading and writing to young children is much more than a set of academic differences between phonics teachers and whole language teachers. The battle over reading is really about controlling the school curriculum, and ultimately about controlling information and determining what counts as knowledge. Whole language teachers need to do a better job of explaining the value of real reading and literature-based instruction to parents and the media. Literacy teachers are among society's least combative people, but others have besieged them. Whole language teachers did not initiate the conflict, but they will continue to fight back and defend their approaches to teaching reading and writing because these approaches are best for children.

## For Discussion

1. As you have read, phonics advocates argue that successful readers need to understand the sound-letter relationships in words. Guessing a word from context does not always equal word recognition. In the following text, taken from Jack London, the blanks indicate parts a child was unable to decode (Grossen, 1998, p. 14). It is possible to predict the missing words from context, as whole language teachers advocate?

He had never seen dogs fight as the w_____ish c_____f_____t, his first_____ex t_____t him an unf_____able l_____n. It is true, it was a vi_____ ex_____, else he would not have lived to pr_____it by it. Curly was v_____. They were camped near the log store, where she, in her friend_____ way, made ad_____ to a husky dog the size of a full-_____ wolf, th_____ not so large as _____he. _____ere was no w_____ing, only a leap in like a flash, a met___clip of teeth, a leap out equal_____swift, and Curly's face was ripped open from eye to jaw.

2. In 1998, the California State Department of Education prohibited schools from spending funds for any teacher development program that uses reading methodologies emphasizing contextual clues in place of decoding, or that encourages inventive spelling in writing instruction. Whole language teachers argue that the state and federal government should not be involved in defining what is and what is not good reading instruction (Taylor, 1998). Whole language advocates further contend that decisions about the most appropriate reading programs are academic decisions that should be left to classroom teachers and reading educators. Do you agree? Should classroom teachers have the right to choose the methods of reading instruction? What about parents? Should they have the right to select the methods of instruction for their children? Who should select the books children read in elementary schools?

3. William Honig, the former Superintendent of Instruction for California, among others involved in the debate about reading instruction, now advocates a "balanced approach" to reading instruction. Honig recommends one hour a day of direct instruction on teaching letter/sound correspondence (phonics) and an additional hour a day for shared reading, reading children's literature, and writing instruction (a literature-based strategy characteristic of whole language teachers. (Freppon and Dahl, 1998, p. 242). A survey of elementary teachers indicates that the majority prefer such a "balanced approach" to reading instruction (Baumann et al., 1998). Do you think a balanced approach is desirable? Do you think this approach would resolve the "reading wars"? Interview teachers in public schools and colleges of education to learn their opinions.

## *References*

ADAMS, M. J., AND BRUCK, M. (1995). "Resolving the 'Great Debate.'" *American Educator,* (Summer), pp. 7–20.

BAUMANN, J. F., HOFFMAN, J. V., MOON, J., AND DUFFY-HESTER, A. M. (1998). "Where Are the Teachers' Voices in the Phonics/Whole Language Debate? Results from a Survey of U.S. Elementary Teachers." *The Reading Teacher 51,* May 1998, pp. 636–651.

BECK, I. L., AND JUEL, C. (1995). "The Role of Decoding in Learning to Read." *American Educator,* Summer 1995, 8, 21–25, pp. 39–42.

BERLINER, D., AND BIDDLE, B. (1995). *The Manufactured Crisis: Myths, Fraud, and the Attack on America's Public Schools.* Reading, MA: Addison-Wesley.

BRAUNGER, J., AND LEWIS, J. P. (1997). *Building a Knowledge Base in Reading.* Newark, DE: International Reading Association.

BRINKLEY, E. H. (1998). "What's Religion Got to Do with Attacks on Whole Language?" In Goodman, K. (1998). *In Defense of Good Teaching: What Teachers Need to Know About the "Reading Wars."* York, ME: Stenhouse.

COLLINS, J. (1997). "How Johnny Should Read: A War Is On Between Supporters of Phonics and Those Who Believe in the Whole-Language Method of Learning to Read. Caught in the Middle—The Nation's Schoolchildren." *Time,* October 7, pp. 1–7 (http://web.lexis-nexis.com)

EDELSKY, C., ALTWERGER, B., AND FLORES, B. (1991). *Whole Language, What's the Difference.* Portsmouth, NH: Heinemann.

FOORMAN, B. R., FLETCHER, J. M., FRANCIS, D. J., AND SCHATSCHNEIDER, C. (1998). "The Role of Instruction in Learning to Read: Preventing Reading Failure in At-Risk Children." *Journal of Educational Psychology 90,* pp. 37–55.

FREEMAN, D., AND FREEMAN, Y. S. (1998). "California Reading: The Pendulum Swings." In Goodman, K. (1998). *In Defense of Good Teaching: What Teachers Need to Know About the "Reading Wars."* York, ME: Stenhouse.

FREPPON, P. A., AND DAHL, K. L. (1998). "Balanced Instruction: Insights and Considerations." *Reading Research Quarterly 33,* June 1998, pp. 240–251.

GOODMAN, K. (1986). *What's Whole In Whole Language.* Portsmouth, NH: Heinemann.

———— (1996). *On Reading, A Common-Sense Look at the Nature of Language and the Science of Reading.* Portsmouth, NH: Heinemann.

———— EDITOR. (1998). *In Defense of Good Teaching: What Teachers Need to Know About the "Reading Wars."* York, ME: Stenhouse.

———— (1998). "Who's Afraid of Whole Language? Politics, Paradigms, Pedagogy, and the Press." In Goodman, K. (1998). *In Defense of Good Teaching: What Teachers Need to Know About the "Reading Wars."* York, ME: Stenhouse.

GROSSEN, B. (1995). "Preventing Reading Failure." *Effective School Practices,* Fall, pp. 43–44.

———— (1998). "30 Years of Research: What We Know About How Children Learn to Read." *The Center for the Study of the Future of Teaching & Learning,* November 11, 1998. (http://www.cftl.org/30years/30years.html)

GURSKY, D. (1998). "What Works for Reading." *American Teacher,* March, 1998, pp. 12–13.

Hirshberg, J. (1995). *Framework for Effective Teaching: Grade 1—Thinking and Learning About Print, Teacher's Guide, Part A.* Chicago: Open Court.

HONIG, W. (1996). *Teaching Our Children to Read: The Role of Skills in a Comprehensive Reading Program.* Thousand Oaks, CA: Corwin.

LEMANN, N. (1997). "The Reading Wars." *The Atlantic Monthly,* November, pp. 128–134.

McQUILLAN, J. (1998). *The Literacy Crisis: False Claims, Real Solutions.* Portsmouth, NH: Heinemann.

MURPHY, S. (1998). "The Sky is Falling: Whole Language Meets Henny Penny." In Goodman, K. (1998). *In Defense of Good Teaching: What Teachers Need to Know About the "Reading Wars."* York, ME: Stenhouse.

PALMAFFY, T. (1997). "See Dick Flunk." *The Journal of American Citizenship Policy Review,* November/December. pp. 1–12. (http://web.lexis-nexis.com)

ROUSSEAU, J-J. (1979). *Emile, or On Education,* introduced and translated by A. Bloom. New York: Basic Books.

TAYLOR, D. (1998). *Beginning to Read and the Spin Doctors of Science: The Political Campaign to Change America's Mind About How Children Learn to Read.* Urbana, IL: National Council of Teachers of English.

WATSON, D. (1989). "Defining and Describing Whole Language." *The Elementary School Journal 90,* 208–221.

WEAVER, C. (1990). *Understanding Whole Language, From Principle to Practice.* Portsmouth, NH: Heinemann.

———— AND BRINKLEY, E. H. (1998). "Phonics, Whole Language, and the Religious and Political Right." In Goodman, K. (1998). *In Defense of Good Teaching: What Teachers Need to Know About the "Reading Wars."* York, ME: Stenhouse.

# CHAPTER 9

# Multicultural Education: Representative or Divisive

## POSITION 1: FOR A MULTICULTURAL PERSPECTIVE

When I am asked to talk about the opening of the American mind, or the decentering of the humanities, or the new multiculturalism . . . I have to say my reaction is pretty much Mahatma Gandhi's when they asked him what he thought about Western civilization. He said he thought it would be a very good idea. (Gates, 1992, p. 105)

After Negro students have mastered the fundamentals of English, the principles of composition, and the leading facts in the development of literature, they should not spend all of their advanced time on Shakespeare, Chaucer, and Anglo-Saxon. They should direct their attention also to the folklore of the African, to the philosophy in his proverbs, to the development of the Negro in the use of modern language, and to the works of Negro writers. The leading facts of the history of the world should be studied by all, but of what advantage is it to the Negro student in history to devote all of his time to courses bearing on such despots as Alexander the Great, Caesar, and Napoleon, or to the record of those nations whose outstanding achievement has been rapine, plunder, and murder for world power? (Carter G. Woodson, 1933, quoted in Gordon, 1995)

Multicultural education is subject to a variety of competing definitions. For some scholars in the field, it is a political process designed to free students and schools from society's oppressive influence over school curricula (Chavez and O'Donnell, 1998). For others, it is a philosophic method for critiquing society that goes well beyond education and that offers political and moral correctives (Giroux, 1997; Sleeter, 1996; Willett, 1998). Glazer (1997) argues that "we are all multiculturalists," because whether you may favor or oppose it, multiculturalism is here, necessary, and unavoidable. All groups—ethnic, religious, racial—belong in our study of American culture because of their unique contributions and perspectives. Glazer argues that some groups have been denied appropriate recognition. "Multiculturalism," Glazer writes, "is the price America is paying for its inability or unwillingness to incorporate into its society African Americans, in the same way and to the same degree it has incorporated so many groups" (p. 147).

Although you may like some other definition of multiculturalism, in this section, we draw upon Professor James Banks for ours. He writes:

> Multicultural education is a field of study and an emerging discipline whose major aim is to create equal educational opportunities for students from diverse racial, ethnic, social-class, and cultural groups. One of its important goals is to help all students acquire the knowledge, attitudes, and skills needed to interact, negotiate, and communicate with people from diverse groups in order to create a civic and moral community that works for the common good. (1995, p. xi)

## The Best That Is Thought and Known?

We all see the world from slightly different perspectives. We bring separate understandings to events based not only on our academic experiences but on the interpretive lenses through which we view the world. Women, minorities, and new immigrants, for example, may see the world from a different view than men, majority group members, and long-established American families. They have developed separate frames of reference and different perspectives because of their differing experiences. Multiculturalism may be considered a struggle to incorporate a wider range of perspectives into the way we make meanings in school (Gordon, 1995; Takaki, 1993).

Multiculturalists argue that the views of groups previously marginalized or excluded because of gender, class, race, or sexual orientation must be given representation in the school curriculum. Public schools should be places where students hear the stories of many different groups. The curriculum should present the perspectives of women as well as men, the poor as well as the rich, and it should celebrate the heroism not only of conquering generals but of those who are victorious in the struggles of everyday life. In a multiculturally reconfigured curriculum, the voices of all Americans would find legitimacy and academic consideration (Apple, 1979, 1982). Multiculturalism is not about pitting one group against others or claiming that any one perspective is more valid or more valued. In the past, schools have done a disservice to their students by assuming a narrow view or discounting the nature of knowledge as including multiple truths and multiple perspectives. Multiculturalists encourage schools to approach knowledge as a reflection of society, and a multicultural society will inevitably have competing views of truth.

Unfortunately, not many schools offer a multicultural curriculum. Most use a standardized presentation of the dominant culture. Instead of being tailored to reflect the varied needs and aspirations of the children in the classroom, the curriculum is, by design, an idealized, uncritical account of what the most powerful members of society believe children should know. Harking back to Matthew Arnold, traditional curriculum writers envision schools as beacons of a single, unified, high culture, passing on the best that is thought and known in the world. Writing in the late nineteenth century, Arnold, a literary critic, poet, and educator, fretted about what he saw as the "vulgar" tastes of the economically powerful but culturally unformed middle classes of England. He believed—as do many of those who now control the curricula of public schools—that appropriate tastes, judgments, and habits could and should be dictated from above. Members of the English upper class of Arnold's day, although losing their economic dominance, considered themselves culturally superior, possessing the most appropriate tastes, habits, and virtues. The upper class therefore defined the behaviors, knowledge, and virtues the schools were to prize and pass on to the next generation. Arnold believed the middle classes would be better off if they would follow the lead of their social betters. Reflecting traditional values rather than actual merit, one body of literature came to dominate. One set of writers, poets, artists, and musicians was acclaimed superior to others. One body of knowledge prevailed in the schools, and other forms were ignored. Politically powerful minorities imposed their views on the less powerful.

## Different Voices

Curriculum change is always a slow-moving process characterized by widespread disagreement. Be careful—the argument between multiculturalists and traditionalists is not a simple academic debate about textbooks or approved reading lists: The struggle over the curriculum is a political battle over the control of knowledge. Sort through the rhetoric carefully. Look for the political implications embedded in education arguments. In the end, you should ask one question: Would children benefit more from a multicultural or a traditional school curriculum?

If you were to believe the critics of multiculturalism, you might conclude that multiculturalists are bent on destroying not only the schools but the whole of Western civilization. E. D. Hirsch (1987, 1996), for example, tried to convince his readers that the nation would disintegrate unless schools required all students to study a common curriculum. Allan Bloom (1987) warned that multiculturalism poses the threat of cultural relativism, a disease, he says, that regards all values as equally valid, and that would likely cause the decline of the West. Another critic of multiculturalism, Diane Ravitch, argues that multiculturalism would lead to the death of education and the fragmentation of American society. She asks us to examine the elementary school curriculum of what she believes was a better time, the first decade of the twentieth century, when children were exposed to a common culture and high expectations:

> Most children read (or listened to) the Greek and Roman myths and folklore from the "oriental nations." . . . The third grade in the public schools of Philadelphia studied "heroes of legend and history," including "Joseph; Moses; David; Ulysses; Alexander; Roland; Alfred the Great; Richard the Lion Hearted; Robert Bruce; William Tell; Joan of Arc; Peter the Great; Florence Nightingale." (Ravitch, 1987, p. 8)

This represents a rich literature, to be sure, but, like the canon championed by Hirsch and Bloom, it is skewed toward a white, Western, male orientation. No people of other races were represented in classroom readings during the "good old days," and for women to find their way into the curriculum, they either had to be burned at the stake or to pioneer as nurses! Henry Louis Gates, Jr. refers to this as the antebellum aesthetic position, "when men were men, and men were white . . . when women and persons of color were voiceless, faceless servants and laborers, pouring tea and filling brandy snifters in the boardrooms in the old boys' clubs" (Gates, 1992, p. 17).

## Multicultural Perspectives

What do the multiculturalists want? Are they a threat to schools and the social cohesion of the country? Are they trying to impose political correctness on all Americans? Take a look at some of the multiculturalist arguments for curriculum change in the schools and decide for yourselves.

As we stated earlier, multiculturalists are a diverse group that includes feminists, Afrocentrists, social critics, and many people who defy labels but who simply want to transmit the variety of American culture more faithfully to their children. The charge that multiculturalists want to purge the school curriculum of Western culture is simply false. Multiculturalism does not require us to eliminate the contributions of white males from the curriculum and substitute the experiences of women, gays, African Americans, and other exploited and disadvantaged persons (Sobol, 1993). Multiculturalists ask only for a fair share of curricular attention, an honest representation of the poor as well as the powerful, and the reasonable treatment of minority as well as majority cultures. The United States is a multicultural country, and our ethnic and religious mix is becoming increasingly diverse, owing to recent immigration laws and the influx of people from non-European countries. Whatever the outcome of the current struggle over cultural representation in the curriculum, the world our students know is already multicultural (Gates, 1992, p. xvi). The curriculum must reflect this society, or it becomes irrelevant to the students' lives.

We might think of the multiculturalist reaction against the traditional curriculum as a "victims' revolution," a repudiation of the top-down approach to literature, art, music, and history. It is a demand for change coming from those who have been discounted and otherwise harmed by traditional approaches to schooling. Multiculturalists ask us to tell the cultural tale in a way that weaves the experiences of the disadvantaged and the marginalized into the tapestry of the United States' rise to prominence. Multiculturalism is a call for fairness and a better representation of the contributions of all Americans. Multiculturalists do not discount the role the school curriculum plays in developing a cohesive, national identity. At the same time, however, schools must guarantee that *all* students can preserve their ethnic, cultural, and economic identities (Banks, 1994).

Schools are obligated to teach multiple perspectives in the name of academic fairness and historical accuracy. Few events of significance can be clearly understood from only one perspective, and viewing them from diverse and competing viewpoints leads to a fuller and more complete representation of truth. For example, school textbooks typically emphasize the role the white abolitionists of the nineteenth century played and discuss how white people struggled to achieve integration in the twentieth century. This is, of course, appropriate; many whites have played vital and significant roles in the struggle for social justice. But these same textbooks typically minimize the stories of African American resistance to slavery, as well as their efforts to achieve integration and equality (Asante, 1987, 1991). These omissions alienate young African American students and present an inaccurate picture to their white peers. The story of slavery must be told from many sides, including the perspective of African Americans as agents in their own history and not simply as people who were colonized, enslaved, and freed by others (Asante, 1995). A multiculturally educated person would be able to see the slave trade from the view of the white slave trader as well as from the perspective of the enslaved people. The point is not to replace one group's story with another, but to tell the whole story more fully. To include women, the poor, and minorities is not to eliminate the lessons of culture or history; it is simply a way to make them richer and more complete.

## Monoculturalism and Minority Alienation

Curriculum change may come from the top down or from the bottom up, but it never comes easily. By the mid 1980s, the majority of the students at the University of California at Berkeley were people of color. The faculty was 90 percent white, and the school lacked a multicultural requirement for graduation. One Berkeley professor recalls the alienation the students felt: "The students, without having to speak, said to us as the faculty, 'Read our faces. We don't see ourselves on the faculty. We don't read about ourselves in the books you're requiring us to read, and we don't hear our voices in the lectures'" (*Harvard Educational Review*, 1997, pp. 170–171).

The goal of multiculturalists is to bend education around the lives of students so all students can experience a real chance at school success. Anyone familiar with schools knows that the most effective way to teach is to make the curriculum relevant to students. A curriculum has more meaning when students find characters like themselves in the books they read, and instruction has a better chance of engaging students when the subject matter speaks to their experiences. Exclusion of particular groups of students and their history from the literature alienates the student and diminishes academic achievement. Everyone benefits from multicultural education. Children of immigrants from northern and western Europe hear tales that resonate with their experiences. They also learn about the experiences of others and how they view their lives. Children of new immigrants from Asia and Latin America need to know about the lands they left, their new home, and their varied new neighbors. They need to examine the cultural baggage they have brought with them so they can better understand how it fits into the cultures that shape America. These children need to know that a pluralistic society welcomes cultural differences, and that they do not have to distance themselves from their families and cultural traditions and homogenize to be considered "good Americans." Schools in a democratic society have no choice but to be multicultural. Children who find themselves and their culture underrepresented in the school curriculum cannot help but feel lost and resentful. Without a multicultural emphasis, minority children feel like outsiders. As Asante (1991) writes:

> The little African American child who sits in a classroom and is taught to accept as heroes and heroines individuals who defamed African people is being actively decentered, dislocated, and made into a nonperson, one whose aim in life might be to one day shed that "badge of inferiority": his or her Blackness. (p. 171)

## A Bold Step Toward a Multicultural Curriculum

Multicultural education reform has spread to many states (Banks and Banks, 1995) and nations (Patel, 1994). The experience of New York State is an interesting example because of the state's ethnic complexity and its combination of urban, suburban, and rural school districts. In the late 1980s, the New York State Commissioner of Education invited scholars and curriculum writers to review the appropriateness of the state's K–12 social studies curriculum and recommend any needed changes.[1] Task Force members were asked to examine the curriculum and address questions about its fairness and balance. Did this curriculum speak to the varied needs of female as well as male students, of African Americans and Asian Americans as well as European Americans, of the disadvantaged as well as the advantaged? On the basis of the reviewers' recommendations, New York developed a new curriculum that promises a fresh focus on the treatment of all students in the state.

The report, *A Curriculum of Inclusion, 1989,* recognized that New York's curriculum was not fairly representing minorities. Although the nation had opened its doors to millions of new immigrants, their ways of life, their foods, their religions, and their histories were not found in the curriculum. Instead, the new immigrants were socialized along an "Anglo-American model" (New York State, 1991). Despite some demographic projection that white, Anglo-Saxon Protestants will be a minority in this country by the middle of the next century, New York was still asking new immigrants to exchange their families' habits and rituals for an homogenized American culture. The unstated curricular message asked new immigrants to abandon the cultures of their forebears and learn to prize the literature, history, traditions, and holidays of the Anglo-American Founding Fathers.

This is a familiar model of cultural assimilation. Proponents of state-funded education in the nineteenth century encouraged schools to teach immigrants the social behaviors and patriotic rituals designed to encourage "Americanization." Such assimilation worked reasonably well for white Europeans who came to this country in the nineteenth century, but it did not work for other immigrants. Now, in the face of new immigration patterns, it seems to be an untenable ideal. A significant demographic difference distinguishes today's immigrants from

---

[1]For a detailed and sympathetic examination of multicultural curriculum reform in New York and California, see Cornbleth, C., and Wauch, D. (1995). *The Great Speckled Bird: Multicultural Politics and Educational Policymaking.* New York: St. Martin's Press.

those of the past. In the nineteenth century, most of the nation's voluntary immigrants came from Europe, and socialization toward an Anglo-American model of behavior may not have been terribly discontinuous with their heritage. Now, the majority of immigrants are from Asia and South America. People newly arrived from Korea and Colombia are less likely to find resonance in the Anglo-American cultural ideal than those who came to the United States from Ireland, Germany, and Italy.

In 1990, New York State impaneled a second committee to offer curriculum recommendations. This committee's report acknowledges the importance of socialization and nation building for an increasingly diverse population, but it also fosters respect for cultural diversity. No longer should immigrants—old or new—be encouraged to abandon their cultural pasts in order to be considered Americans. When the report's recommendations are fully implemented, schools will be asked to reflect the cultural diversity of the nation by helping students develop a multicultural perspective. As defined in the report:

> A multicultural perspective, then, means that all of the applicable viewpoints of the historical and social protagonists should be explored, paying special attention to the ways in which race, ethnicity, gender, and class generate different ways of understanding, experiencing, and evaluating the events of the world. Because interpretations vary as experiences differ, a multicultural perspective must necessarily be a multiple perspective that takes into account the variety of ways in which any topic can be comprehended. (New York State, 1991, p. 17)

## Social Construction of Reality

The New York curriculum report recognizes that reality is socially constructed. Social reality—those taken-for-granted beliefs about life, such as who we are and how we should behave—is shaped by the books we read, the ways in which we argue and discuss ideas, and the cultural perspectives of our schools and families. The subject matter we teach in schools should be considered provisional, as is all knowledge. "Knowledge," as the New York report reminds us, "is the product of human beings located in specific times and places; consequently, much of our subject matter must be understood as tentative" (New York State, 1991, p. 29).

In a pluralistic society, students must learn that there are many and varied sets of socially constructed realities. We believe what we do, in part, because of who we are and how we are raised. Knowledge about the social world is not objective, but is a human product that differs for different groups of people, based on their cultural differences and unique histories. Schools should encourage students to develop a broad understanding, considering competing viewpoints. Students should learn to appreciate the different social realities stemming from human differences in language, gender, socioeconomic class, religion, sexual orientation, age, and physical challenges. One of the guiding principles in the New York plan is that teaching "should *draw and build on the experience and knowledge that students bring to the classroom.*" The authors of the New York report argue that "such pedagogy not only validates a student's sense of worth, but also fosters developmentally appropriate and meaningful learning" (New York State, 1991, p. 29).

The New York State plan seeks to remedy the single perspective schools formerly presented. The older New York curriculum, like those in most schools, was Eurocentric and unidirectional; that is, it tended to reflect what Europeans thought and believed and did to others. The designers of the newer New York curriculum have attempted to promise children that the material they study will represent America's story fairly. Students will consider social and historical phenomena from many perspectives. This is a goal other states should consider. It promises to change the ways in which we define education.

The new social studies curriculum is a long way from implementation, and its effects will not be evident for some time. In 1995, New York issued a document entitled *A Preliminary Draft Framework for the Social Studies*. While some have attacked it as a retreat from the boldness of earlier drafts, it still contains the language and spirit of multicultural education. Its authors remain steadfast in their belief that multiculturalism and multiple perspectives will allow students to "develop greater tolerance and empathy for people holding varying viewpoints" (Ward, 1995, quoted in Grant, 1997, p. 104).

The multiculturalist argument is not that Eurocentric views are wrong or evil or that children of Asian or African descent should not learn about the European cultural legacy. Multiculturalism asks that we subscribe to one simple educational truth: tolerance cannot come without respect, and respect cannot come without knowledge (Gates, 1992, p. xv). Multiculturalism begins by recognizing the cultural diversity of the United States, and it asks that the school curriculum explore that diversity. To be well-educated in a multicultural sense means to learn about the histories, literature, and contributions of the varied people who have fashioned the complex tapestry of American life. All students should sample broadly from all of the cultures and all of the ideas that have contributed to the making of the United States.

## POSITION 2: FOR THE COMMON CULTURE

Until lately, the West has regarded it as self-evident that the road to education lay through great books. No man was educated unless he was acquainted with the masterpieces of his tradition. There never was very much doubt in anybody's mind about which the masterpieces were. They were the books that had endured and that the common voice of mankind called the finest creations, in writing, of the Western mind.

In the course of history, from epoch to epoch, new books have been written that have won their place in the list. Books once thought entitled to belong to it have been superseded; and this process of change will continue as long as man can think and write. It is the task of every generation to reassess the tradition in which it lives, to discard what it cannot use, and to bring into context with the distant and intermediate past the most recent contribution to the Great Conversation. (Hutchins, 1952, p. xi)

Conceptually and programmatically, multicultural education is in virtual dis-array. The case has yet to be made that it can deliver on its promises, and that it is not a means of perpetual differences-accentuation, despite the "good inten-tions" of its advocates. (Webster, 1997, p. 58)

## Schools and the Cultural Heritage

For the past one hundred and fifty years, public schools have had three broad objectives: to educate individual citizens for democratic participation; to encour-age individual achievement through academic competition; and to promote, encourage, and teach the values and traditions of the American cultural heritage. The United States has been enriched by every ethnic and racial group to land on these shores, and the immigrants, in turn, have been well served by the nation and the nation's schools. The public schools have their share of detractors, to be sure, but the multiculturalists' attack on the schools' curriculum seems mis-guided. A fair assessment would find it difficult to fault the success schools have had in passing the common culture of the United States to new generations of Americans—immigrants and native-born citizens alike. No mean accomplish-ment, the transmission of the cultural heritage requires an appreciation for the complex aspects of U.S. history, literature, and political traditions (Ravitch, 1990; Schlesinger, 1992). American culture is, after all, a hybrid—a mix of European, Asian, and African cultures—and it is the job of the schools to transmit this cul-tural legacy faithfully in all its complexity. The school's role in cultural transmis-sion has been one of brilliant success for well over a century.

The nineteenth-century proponents of public education recognized that the United States was a dynamic nation, with succeeding waves of immigrants changing and invigorating the cultures. The new arrivals came from every cor-ner of the world, and they brought energy, talent, and cultural variation never before gathered in one nation. When they arrived in the United States, they spoke different languages, they were of many races, and they practiced many religions. What they shared was an eagerness to succeed economically and politically, and to learn how to become "American," to fit into a unique, unprecedented cultural amalgam.

The common schools of the nineteenth century, influenced by the Western ideas of philosophic rationalism and humanism, were an expression of opti-mism concerning human progress and democratic potential. Advocates of mass public education saw the schools as a vehicle of social progress, and they shared a common belief in education, "an education, moreover, which was nei-ther a privilege of a fortunate few nor a crumb tossed to the poor and lowly, but one which was to be a right of every child in the land" (Meyer, 1957, p. 143). The common schools succeeded beyond anyone's expectations. The chil-dren of the poor as well as the rich received a public education; the children of immigrants read the same texts and learned the same lore as the children of native-born Americans. The mix of immigrants now coming to the United States is far richer and more diverse than the founders of the common schools could ever have envisioned. The need for the schools to transmit the common culture has never been greater; the preservation of democratic tradition has never been more difficult.

The United States has always been a haven for those seeking political freedom and political expression. In the nineteenth century, million of immigrants came to this country, in large measure to enjoy the fruits and accept the burdens of participating in a democratic society. This is still true today, but unlike the immigrants of the former times, today's new arrivals typically have had little or no direct experience with democratic traditions. For example, in the 1840s, after the collapse of the Frankfurt diet, immigrants from Germany flocked to America seeking the democratic political expression they had been denied in their homeland. Today's immigrants may want democracy, but when they come from autocratic regimes in Asia and South America, they have had no experience with the responsibilities of democratic living. They are less prepared for assuming a role in a democratic society than any previous generation of immigrants. It is clearly up to the schools to induct the children of the new immigrants into the complexities of U.S. democratic culture.

Although the schools should expose children to the common culture, they need not pretend to a cultural homogeneity or deny the ethnic experiences of individual students. Schools are obligated to represent the range of cultural voices—male and female, African American, Asian American, and European American—but these voices must be trained not for solo performances but to be part of a chorus. Schools must encourage individual identification with one central cultural tradition, or the United States might fall prey to the same ethnic tensions that are undermining the sovereignty of Lebanon and the nations of Eastern Europe and Africa. Students should learn about the common Western ideals that have shaped the United States and that bind us together as a nation: democracy, capitalism, and monotheism.

## Particularism

> What happens when people of different ethnic origins, speaking different languages and professing different religions, settle in the same geographical locality and live under the same political sovereignty? Unless a common purpose binds them together, tribal hostilities will drive them apart. Ethnic and racial conflict, it seems evident, will now replace the conflict of ideologies as the explosive issues of our times. (Schlesinger, 1992, p. 10)

The United States stands to benefit—economically, politically, and socially—from the infusion of talent brought by the new immigrants, as it has in the past. Assimilated new immigrants pose no threat to U.S. growth or nationhood. Instead, the United States faces a threat from those who deny that the schools should teach a common American tradition or that a common culture even exists! Diane Ravitch calls these people particularists; they argue that teaching a common culture is a disservice to ethnic and racial minorities. "Particularism," writes Ravitch, "is a bad idea whose time has come" (Ravitch, 1990, p. 346).

Particularists demand that the public schools give up trying to teach the commonalities of cultural heritage in favor of teaching a curriculum that centers on the specific ethnic mix represented in a given school or community. Students in predominantly white schools would have one focus, children in predominantly African American schools another, and so on. It is not at all clear where the particularists would stop in the Balkanization of the curriculum. Would a school with a predominantly Asian population have an Asian-focused curriculum, or would they further divide the curriculum into separate strands of Korean, Chinese, Vietnamese, Filipino, and Cambodian culture (Fox-Genovese, 1991)?

The extreme arguments of the particularists do not lend support to the unifying and democratic ends that the founders of the common schools envisioned. Asante, for example, advocates an Afrocentrist curriculum that would teach young African American children about their African cultural roots at the expense of teaching them about Western traditions. He denounces those African Americans who prefer Bach and Beethoven to Ellington and Coltrane. An African American person, he believes, should center on his or her cultural experience; any other preference is an aberration. Asante argues that majority as well as minority students are disadvantaged by the "monoculturally diseased curriculum." He writes that few Americans of any color "have heard the names of Cheikh Anta Diop, Anna Julia Cooper, C. L. R. James, or J. A. Rogers," historians who contributed to an understanding of the African world (Asante, 1991, p. 175). He is probably right, but for better or worse, the most enduring mainstream white historians—for example, Spengler, Gibbon, Macaulay, Carlyle, and Trevelyan—are not likely to enjoy greater recognition.

The cultural focus of the curriculum is a serious matter, and although petty and irrational arguments exist on all sides, the real issue is the role the schools must play in transmitting the common cultural heritage. Schools must teach children that regardless of race, gender, or ethnicity, one can achieve great feats. This is the record of the past and the promise of the future. The public school curriculum should allow all children to believe that they are part of a society that welcomes their participation and encourages their achievements. As Ravitch (1990) writes, "In their curriculum, their hiring practices, and their general philosophy, the public schools must not discriminate against or give preference to any racial or ethnic group. . . . They should not be expected to teach children to view the world through an ethnocentric perspective that rejects or ignores the common culture" (p. 352).

Schools cannot fulfill their central mission to transmit the common culture if they cater to particularist demands for teaching the perspective of every minority group. Ravitch argues that in the past, generation upon generation of minorities—Jews, Catholics, Greeks, Poles, and Japanese—have used private lessons, after school or on weekends, to instill ethnic pride and ethnic continuity in their children. These may be valuable goals, but they have never been the public schools' province, nor should they be. The public schools must develop a common culture, "a definition of citizenship and culture that is both expansive and *inclusive*," one that speaks to our commonalities and not our differences (Ravitch, 1990, p. 352). The public school curriculum must not succumb to particularists' demands to prize our differences rather than celebrate our common good.

## Anticanonical Assaults

Among the greatest absurdities the particularists have produced is their attack on the canon, denouncing it as racist, sexist, Eurocentric, logocentric, and politically incorrect. Before we put these distortions to rest, a few words about the nature of the canon. The term *canon* (from the Greek word *kanon*, meaning a measuring rod), which originally referred to the books of the Hebrew and Christian Bibles, meant Holy Scripture as officially recognized by the ecclesiastic authority. Today, it has taken on secular and political meanings. The canon represents, first of all, the major monuments to Western civilization, great ideas embodied in books that form the foundation of our democratic traditions. The "great books" of the Western tradition (for example, the writings of Plato, Aristotle, Machiavelli, and Marx, to name but a few) have shaped our political thinking, whether we trace our origins to Europe, Africa, or Asia; Homer, Sophocles, George Eliot, and Virginia Woolf inform our sense of literature whether we are male or female. Every major university offers courses in the Western canon, and as the late Alan Bloom noted, generations of students have enjoyed these works. He wrote, "wherever the Great Books make up a central part of the curriculum, the students are excited and satisfied, feel they are doing something that is independent and fulfilling, getting something from the university they cannot get elsewhere. . . . Their gratitude at learning of Achilles or the categorical imperative is boundless" (Bloom, 1987, p. 344).

The particularists' attack on the canon is new and somewhat surprising. The value of the canon has long been taken for granted as the cornerstone of quality education. As Searle writes, educated circles accepted, almost to the point of cliche, that

> there is a certain Western intellectual tradition that goes from, say, Socrates to Wittgenstein in philosophy, and from Homer to James Joyce in literature, and it is essential to the liberal education of young men and women in the United States that they receive some exposure to at least some of the great works in this intellectual tradition; they should, in Matthew Arnold's overquoted words, know the best that is thought and known in the world. (Searle, 1990, p. 34)

In the past, support for the canon was an article of faith, not belabored or examined at length. People considered these works and the ideas they contained to be of enduring worth, part of a timeless literary judgment—as Samuel Johnson spoke of it—and quite apart from the hurly-burly of politics. Canonical authors were acknowledged representatives of the triumphant march of Western civilization, "an unbroken crescendo from Plato to NATO" (Perry and Williams, 1991, p. 55). No longer. Particularists and multiculturalists attack the canon at every turn. Searle writes that the cant of the anticanonicals runs something like this:

Western civilization is in large part a history of oppression. Internally, Western civilization oppressed women, various slave and serf populations, and ethnic and cultural minorities, generally. In foreign affairs, the history of Western civilization is one of imperialism and colonialism. The so-called canon of Western civilization consists of the official publications of the system of oppression, and it is no accident that the authors in the "canon" are almost exclusively Western white males. . . . [The canon] has to be abolished in favor of something that is "multicultural" and "nonhierarchical." (Searle, 1990, p. 35)

The particularists and multiculturalists are trying to do to the public school curriculum what they tried unsuccessfully to accomplish at universities: to politicize the curriculum. In the name of justice and equity, they encouraged universities to broaden the curriculum and include non-Western as well as Western authors. Of course, curriculum is a zero sum game; that is, if a school adds something, it must also take something else out.

The case of Stanford University is instructive. In the late 1980s, Stanford University proposed adding authors from developing countries and both women's and minority perspectives into the curriculum of the Western Culture course. These changes would come at considerable cost. Plato's *Republic* and Machiavelli's *Prince* would be replaced by works such as *I, Rigoberta Menchu*, the story of the political coming-of-age of a Guatemalan peasant woman, and Franz Fanon's *Wretched of the Earth*, a book that encouraged violent and revolutionary acts among citizens of third world countries (D'Souza, 1991). Although campus radicals demonstrated in support of the proposal, chanting, "Hey, hey, ho, ho, Western Culture's got to go," cooler heads won the day. The required course in Western Culture retained its reading list but added some optional assignments that provided a non-Western focus.

Stanford's approach to curriculum reform underestimated the power great literature has to capture the imaginations of minority students and the ability minority students have to appreciate Western classics. Sachs and Thiel, Stanford students during the time of the "great curriculum wars," argue that Stanford multiculturalists rejected the universalism of Western culture and the power of ideas. They write:

There exist truths that transcend the accidents of one's birth, and these objective truths are in principle available to everyone—whether young or old, rich or poor, male or female, white or black; individual (and humanity as a whole) are not trapped within a closed cultural space that predetermines what they may know. (1995, p. 3)

## Misguided Curriculum Reform

Stanford successfully resisted the social engineering of the multiculturalists, as have most universities; the public schools have been less successful. New York State has plunged headlong into the maelstrom of multiculturalism in reaction to a report critical of the state's social studies curriculum. The New York proposal is filled with problems. Consider a few: One of the guiding principles of the report is that "[t]he subject matter content should be *treated as socially constructed* and therefore tentative—as is all knowledge." The document goes on to assert: "Knowledge is the product of human beings located in specific times and places; consequently, much of our subject matter must be understood as tentative."

This is distressing. As Searle writes, "If you think that there is no reality that words could possibly correspond to, then obviously it will be a waste of time to engage in an 'objective and disinterested search for truth' because there is no such thing as truth" (1990, p. 40). What is it that we are passing on to succeeding generations if not the fruits of our culture's pursuit of truth? Why should parents be required to send their children to school, and why should taxpayers be expected to fund such tentative and subjective ends?

The New York State curriculum proposal ("One Nation, Many Peoples: A Declaration of Cultural Independence," New York State, 1991) has been criticized for its intellectual dishonesty and its potential for divisiveness. Albert Shanker, the late president of the American Federation of Teachers, argued that "multiculturalism" is an appealing idea but is likely to degenerate into stereotyping about minority views when applied in the classroom:

> For a teacher presenting a historical event to elementary school children, using multiple perspectives probably means that the teacher turns to each child and asks the point of view about the event. To the African American child this would mean, "What is the African American point of view?" To a Jewish child, "What is the Jewish point of view?" And to the Irish child, "What is the Irish point of view?" (Shanker, 1991, p. E7)

Shanker pointed out that multiculturalism is, in practice, a racist approach: it assumes that every single African American child shares the same perspective, as do all members of any religious and/or ethnic group. The rhetoric of cultural relevance and a curriculum centered around the child's sociocultural experience is, on the surface, attractive. However, it treats culture as a heritable or biological characteristic. This is a cruel distortion. Culture is learned, much as language is learned. Ravitch reminds us that the adoption of multiculturalist assumptions limits our ideas of human freedom and potential and "implies a dubious, dangerous form of cultural predestination" (Ravitch, 1990, p. 346).

Multiculturalism also represents a distraction from the rest of the curriculum, which ultimately works to the disadvantage of poor and minority children. Consider this: Educators generally acknowledge that middle-class children come to school with a greater store of knowledge about the world around them than children of the poor do. Poor children are less likely to have taken family vacations, traveled to distant places, or had highly literate adults read to them. Unless schools can make up the deficit and help poor children develop the ability to read and write and to interpret the world around them, the cognitive gap between rich and poor will widen. As Hirsch (1996) notes,

> Students from middle and upper classes, coming from educated homes, learn more in school and become more competent than educationally less advantaged students because the intellectual capital derived from their homes enables them

to derive a great deal more from . . . schooling than can students [with] little home-provided knowledge. (p. 212)

All students need exposure to the common culture to succeed. Poor and minority children need more school help to overcome the deficits they face when they begin school. A multicultural education unintentionally robs children of the intellectual capital they need to do well in school.

## Political Correctness

The New York State curriculum report enshrines the shrillest voices of the political correctness choir, forcing adherence to the political attitudes and social mores of the liberal left. Political correctness is not entirely bad; it has made us more sensitive about the language we use. We can credit it with making people realize how inappropriate it is to refer to mature women as "girls" and black men as "boys." However, there seems to be no stopping the tidal wave of "correctspeak" and politically correct behavior. You no doubt have heard some wag report that it is no longer acceptable to call people "short"; instead they are "vertically challenged humans." The deceased may be labeled "permanently horizontal"! We could take this lightly if it were not such a serious matter. Political correctness, which has become the multiculturalists' enforcement arm, has narrowed the range of acceptable public discourse—the things we can speak about openly—and has enlarged the American lexicon with neologisms. It protects people from a range of tyrannies never before imagined. For example, Smith College in Northampton, Massachusetts, calls students' attention to several types of "oppression," including "ableism," "heteroism," and "lookism." Consider these definitions:

Ableism: Oppression of the differently abled by the temporarily able.

Heteroism: Oppression of those of sexual orientation other than heterosexual, such as gays lesbians and bisexuals; this can take place by not acknowledging their existence.

Lookism: The belief that appearance is an indicator of a person's value; the construction of a standard of beauty/attractiveness; and oppression through stereotypes and generalization of both those who do not fit that standard and those who do. (Schlesinger, 1998, pp. 120–121)

One shudders to think what would happen if ableism and lookism were ever to be ruled violations of the Constitution. Would medical schools be forced to accept applicants no matter what their ability? Would Miss America contests be decided by lottery?

Consider another example of an adventure into the misguided world of political correctness. A New Jersey high school decided not to announce the names of graduates in alphabetical order at senior commencement because to do so would group together the school's large number of Asian-Indian students. It seems that during past commencement ceremonies, members of the audience would snicker at the large number of graduates with the last name

Patel. "As each got up, some people would yell 'Patel number one,' 'Patel number two,' and so on," reported one school administrator. The school superintendent said, "We were teaching students about sensitivity to race and ethnic background. [We] were grouping the students by last names. It was a type of segregation. It didn't make sense" (Jaffe, 1994, p. 14).

The whole business does not make sense. Why did the school need a special new policy? What happens in schools where the most common surnames are Smith, Jones, and Johnson? Do administrators there consider calling names randomly at commencement? Or does political correctness force a new, self-conscious, and unnatural attention to these matters?

The state of New York, for all its good intentions, appears to have fallen victim to the extremes of political correctness. In its most recent curriculum revision, it struck references to "slaves," using "enslaved persons" instead so as to "call forth the essential humanity of those enslaved, helping students to understand from the beginning the true meaning of slavery (in contrast to the sentimental pictures of contented slaves, still found in some texts)" (New York State Social Studies Review and Development Committee, 1991, p. 43). The state has scrutinized textbooks for potentially offensive language. References to the "Far East," a Western term, are to be replaced by "East Asia," which the state of New York assumes is less offensive to the people who live there. In a similar vein, the "Middle East" will be known as "Southwest Asia and North Africa," and the "New World" will become the "Western Hemisphere." (Calling the West the "New World" is considered potentially offensive to Native Americans.)

In a dissenting opinion appended to the New York State report, historian Arthur Schlesinger argued that the defining experience for Americans has not been ethnicity or the sanctification of old cultures, "but the creation of a *new* national culture and a *new* national identity." It is foolish, he argues, to look backward in empty celebration of what we once were. Instead, the schools need to look forward and blend the disparate experiences of immigrants into one American culture (New York State Social Studies Review and Development Committee, 1991, p. 89). Schools should continue to serve the nation by passing on to children the elements of the common culture that defines the United States and binds its people together. This is not to say that the schools should be asked to portray the culture as unchangeable or force students to accept it without question. The culture of a nation changes as a reflection of its citizens; U.S. culture will continue to change. School curricula will of necessity expand and sample more broadly from the various influences that have shaped our culture. However, to turn the schools away from the Western ideals of democracy, justice, freedom, equality, and opportunity is to renounce the greatest legacy one generation ever bequeathed to the next. No matter who sits in American classrooms—African Americans, Asian Americans, Latin Americans, or European Americans—and no matter what their religion or creed, those students and their nation have been shaped by the democratic and intellectual traditions of the Western world, and they had better learn those traditions or risk losing them.

## For Discussion

1. According to John Searle (1990), a well-educated person should be characterized by the following abilities:
   a. The person should know enough of his or her cultural traditions to know how they evolved.
   b. The person should know enough of the natural sciences that he or she is not a stranger in that world.
   c. The person should know enough of how society works to understand the trade cycle, interest, unemployment, and other elements of the political and economic world.
   d. The person should know at least one language well enough to read the best literature that culture offers in the original language.
   e. The person needs to know enough philosophy to be able to use the tools of logical analysis.
   f. The person must be able to write and speak clearly and with candor and rigor.

   Do you agree or disagree with his listing? Who should decide these matters—the individual? the school? the parents? the state? the federal government?

2. One body of research suggests that students respond to learning situations in different ways, based in part on their social backgrounds and cultural experiences. In a review of the literature of learning styles and culturally diverse students, Irvine and York (1995) summarize findings about the learning styles of African American students, Hispanic students, and Indian (Native American) students, as follows:

   African American students tend to
   1. respond to things in terms of the whole instead of isolated parts.
   2. prefer inferential reasoning as opposed to deductive or inductive reasoning.
   3. approximate space and numbers rather than adhere to exactness or accuracy.
   4. focus on people rather than things.
   5. be more proficient in nonverbal than verbal communication.
   6. prefer learning characterized by variation and freedom of movement.
   7. prefer kinesthetic/active instructional activates.
   8. prefer evening rather than morning learning.
   9. choose social over nonsocial cues.
   10. proceed from a top-down processing approach rather than a bottom-up approach.
   11. prefer vervistic learning experiences.

   Hispanic students tend to
   1. prefer group learning situations.
   2. be sensitive to the opinions of others.
   3. remember faces and social words.
   4. be extrinsically motivated.

5. learn by doing.
6. prefer concrete representations to abstractions.
7. prefer people to ideas.

Indian (Native American) students tend to
1. prefer visual, spatial, and perceptual information rather than verbal information.
2. learn privately rather than in public.
3. use mental images rather than word associations to remember and understand words and concepts.
4. watch and then do rather than employ trial and error.
5. have well-formed spatial ability.
6. learn best from nonverbal rather than verbal mechanisms.
7. learn experientially and in natural settings.
8. have a generalist orientation, interested in people and things.
9. value conciseness in speech, slightly varied intonation, and limited vocal range.
10. favor holistic presentations and visual representations. (pp. 490–491)

What implications do these characteristics have for teachers in diverse classrooms? Can a teacher apply the characteristics for a group to individual group members? Should minority students always receive instruction in their preferred learning style?

3. What arguments support a "multicultural education" course as a college/university graduation requirement? If a school has such a graduation requirement, what courses at your institution would you recommend to satisfy that requirement? Would you count courses on feminism? What about modern language courses or courses in ancient Greek? Would you allow a Mexican American student, for example, to satisfy the requirement by taking a course in Hispanic Studies?

4. Population demographers predict that by the year 2020, one of every three people in the United States will be a member of a group now labeled a "minority." By the middle of the next century, if current trends continue, white Anglo-Saxon Protestants may be a new minority.

Assuming these projections are correct, do they offer support for the multicultural argument that schools should teach many cultural perspectives and histories? Or do the projections support the argument of those calling for a renewed emphasis on teaching the common culture? Is there a middle ground—a position that could satisfy both sides?

## References

APPLE, M. W. (1979). *Ideology and Curriculum.* Boston: Routledge and Kegan Paul.
———— (1982). *Education and Power.* Boston: Routledge and Kegan Paul.
ASANTE, M. K. (1987). *The Afrocentric Idea.* Philadelphia: Temple University Press.

———— (1991). "The Afrocentric Idea in Education." *Journal of Negro Education 60* (2), 170–180.

———— (1995). *African American History: A Journey of Liberation.* Maywood, NJ: The Peoples Publishing Group.

BANKS, J. A.

———— (1994). "Transforming the Mainstream Curriculum." *Educational Leadership 51* (8), 4–8.

———— AND BANKS, C. A. MCGEE, EDITORS. (1995). *Handbooks of Research on Multicultural Education.* New York: Macmillan.

BLOOM, A. (1987). *The Closing of the American Mind.* New York: Simon & Schuster.

CHAVEZ, R. C., AND O'DONNELL, J., EDITORS. (1998). *Speaking the Unpleasant: The Politics of (non) Engagement in the Multicultural Education Terrain.* Albany: State University of New York Press.

D'SOUZA, D. (1991). "Illiberal Education." *The Atlantic Monthly,* March 1991, pp. 51–79.

FOX-GENOVESE, E. (1991). "The Self-Interest of Multiculturalism." *Tikkun 6* (4), 47–49.

GATES, H. L., JR. (1992). *Loose Canons: Notes on the Cultural Wars.* New York: Oxford University.

GIROUX, H. A. (1997). "Rewriting the Discourse of Racial Identity: Towards a Pedagogy and Politics of Whiteness." *Harvard Educational Review 67* (2), 169–187.

GLAZER, N. (1997). *We Are All Multiculturalists Now.* Cambridge, MA: Harvard University Press.

GORDON, B. M. (1995). *Knowledge Construction, Competing Critical Theories, and Education.* In *Handbook of Research on Multicultural Education,* edited by J. A. Banks and C. A. McGee Banks. New York: Macmillan.

GRANT, S. G. (1997). "Reading the New York State Social Studies Framework—Is Appeasing the Right Missing the Point?" *Social Education 61,* (2), 102–106.

HARVARD EDUCATIONAL REVIEW. (1997). "Ethnicity and Education Forum: What Difference Does Difference Make?" *Harvard Educational Review 67* (2), 169–187.

HIRSCH, E. D., JR. (1987). *Cultural Literacy: What Every American Needs to Know.* Boston: Houghton Mifflin.

———— (1996). *The Schools We Need, and Why We Don't Have Them.* New York: Doubleday.

Hutchins, R. M. (1952). *The Great Conversation: The Substance of a Liberal Education.* Chicago: Encyclopedia Britannica.

IRVINE, J. J., AND YORK, D. E. (1995). *Learning Styles and Culturally Diverse Students.* In *Handbook of Research on Multicultural Education,* edited by J. A. Banks and C. A. McGee Banks. New York: Macmillan.

JAFFE, J. (1994). "Flunking Bigotry," *The Newark Star Ledger,* June 22, p. 14.

MEYER, A. E. (1957). *An Educational History of the American People.* New York: McGraw-Hill.

NEW YORK STATE SOCIAL STUDIES SYLLABUS REVIEW AND DEVELOPMENT COMMITTEE. (1991). *One Nation, Many People: A Declaration of Cultural Independence.* Albany: The State Education Department, State University of New York.

PATEL, K. (1994). *Multicultural Education in All-White Areas: A Case Study of Two ESG Projects.* Aldershot, England: Avebury.

PERRY, R., AND WILLIAMS, P. (1991). "Freedom of Hate Speech." *Tikkun,* July/August, pp. 55–57.

RAVITCH, D. (1987). "Tot Sociology, Grade School History." *Current,* December, pp. 4–10.

———— (1990). "Multiculturalism, E Pluribus Plures." *American Scholar,* Summer, pp. 337–354.

SACHS, D. O., AND THIEL, P. A. (1995). *The Diversity Myth: "Multiculturalism" and the Politics of Intolerance at Stanford.* Oakland, CA: The Independent Institute.

SCHLESINGER, A. M. (1992/1998). *The Disuniting of America*. New York: W.W. Norton.

SEARLE, J. (1990). "The Storm Over the University." *The New York Review of Books*, December 6, pp. 34–41.

SHANKER, A. (1991). "Multiple Perspectives." *The New York Times*, October 27, 1991, p. E7.

SLEETER, C. E. (1996). *Multicultural Education as Social Activism*. Albany: State University of New York Press.

SOBOL, T. (1993). "Revising the New York State Social Studies Curriculum." *Teachers College Record*, Winter, pp. 258–272.

TAKAKI, R. (1993). *A Different Mirror: A History of Multicultural America*. Boston: Little, Brown.

WEBSTER, Y. O. (1997). *Against the Multicultural Agenda: A Critical Thinking Alternative*. Westport, CT: Praeger.

WILLETT, C., EDITOR. (1998). *Theorizing Multiculturalism: A Guide to the Current Debate*. Malden, MA: Blackwell.

# CHAPTER 10

# Curriculum Control: National or Local

## POSITION 1: FOR A NATIONAL CURRICULUM

### A Modest Proposal

Nothing radical is being proposed here. The idea of a national curriculum, with national standards to demonstrate that students have mastered that curriculum, is not a suggestion that we overhaul U.S. schools completely. We offer no list of school defects or problems here, no demand for large-scale school reform. Indeed, this is the most modest of proposals because it will result in so little change.

A national de facto curriculum already exists for American schools. In his book *Horace's Compromise* (1984), Theodore Sizer includes a chapter entitled "What High School Is." His book would not have sold so well if the readers wondered which high school he was talking about. Of course, it was *their* high school, and the high schools they were familiar with because the American high school is a constant in so many respects. This is especially true for the curriculum, as you and your fellow college students can quickly establish by compiling and comparing lists of the high school courses you took. Individual student and school variations are minor compared to the common concepts and subjects schools offer across the nation.

Imagine that you were kidnapped and blindfolded and then parachuted out of an airplane somewhere over the United States. Wherever you landed, the institution that would seem the least strange would likely be the local public school. In your mind's eye you can see the flag in front, the paintings of U.S. Presidents, the school offices, the classrooms, and the various common facilities like the library and laboratories. The students at this school might speak in accents you find a bit strange, like those in Boston, the deep South, or Southern California. They might wear comparatively odd-looking clothes—the latest student fashions in this location—and listen to different music. But the basic ideas they would be learning in class would be much the same as what you were learning when you were in high school at home.

An unofficial national curriculum exists for many reasons. Employers in companies in all states expect their employees to have a basic set of skills and knowledge that they learn in school. Admission to most colleges requires a common set of courses and exams based on a common curriculum, and high schools must provide these courses or the colleges will not admit their students. Students, teachers, and school administrators know what schools are teaching through the Internet, journals, conferences, friends, and family. Thousands of teachers attend national teachers conventions and read the same professional journals. Administrators are an even more tightly woven group. Parents also convey an expectation for a national curriculum. They read magazine and newspaper accounts about education, and they recall what they learned when they were in school. Also, the majority of people change residence at some point in time, and they expect the new school to offer certain classes and experiences to their children.

Of course, we also have nationally used textbooks. "Given that most teachers rely on textbook content for course content, and given that the large majority of textbooks are nationally distributed, how local could curricula be in practice? Sure, some states require unique course content. Requirements for social studies courses on a state's history or constitution provide an example. But, that's a pittance" (Phelps, 1993).

The national college entrance exams, national teacher conferences, and national communication and transportation systems are part of a national culture. The present proposal would simply make more systematized and deliberate that which is now somewhat random and coincidental. The reason we need to make it more systematic is to plug the knowledge gaps so many students now suffer from. In other words, we need to *guarantee* that all students will be taught the crucial components of our cultural heritage.

## *Providing Accountability*

A national curriculum and national standards will give the public some assurance that students are learning *something*. Naturally, this means we will have to institute national tests to measure how well students are mastering the national curriculum. Students are not now judged by how many nationally significant ideas or subjects they have learned, but by how many things they have learned that the teachers in their particular schools think are important. Not all teachers make sound judgments about what is genuinely important. Some emphasize trivial ideas of personal interest, and some don't even expect their students to learn much about *those* areas. Teachers are professionals, but they are as fallible as members of any other profession. The American public is entitled to hold teachers to some uniform standards. "Once you have a curriculum on which everyone agrees, you have an answer to the question of how to train teachers: They have to be able to teach the common curriculum. You also have an answer to the question about the level of understanding and skill student assessments should call for because you can base assessments on the common curriculum" (Shanker, 1991).

Some schools may offer trivial subjects—notorious Mickey Mouse courses like basket weaving. Other schools may appear to offer a straightforward academic curriculum, but the course content is watered down. Some offer adequate content but do not expect students to master much of it. A U.S. Department of Education study found that students in high-poverty schools earn A's and B's for mastering no more content than students who get C's and D's in suburban schools (Shanker, 1994). Students graduate from the poor schools with impressive transcripts but little knowledge.

The public is entitled to more accountability. The only way to get it is to have a national curriculum and standards for all schools. The public agrees, as a recent Gallup poll indicates: A whopping 73 percent of those polled think it is very or quite important to require students to pass national tests based on a national curriculum in order to earn grade promotion and to graduate (Elam, Rose, and Gallup, 1994).

Poor performance on the tests should disqualify a student for federal college aid (Samuelson, 1991). The tests could even replace the Scholastic Aptitude Test (SAT) and the American College Test (ACT) as college admission tests (Finn, 1991). The SAT and ACT are not subject-specific and so are less valid measures of a student's academic ability than national subject-matter tests would be. The test results of students who choose not to go on to college could provide prospective employers with useful information as they make hiring decisions (Kean, 1991).

## Promoting Economic Competitiveness

In a world where a nation's economic competitiveness depends on how well educated its people are, we simply cannot afford to be slack any longer. It is important that we be economically competitive so that all our citizens can maintain a decent standard of living.

To be competitive, we need people with high levels of technical expertise, but these people must also be educated broadly enough to understand how to use their skills and how to work within a society. Mortimer Adler, the renowned philosopher and founder of the Great Books program, puts it in the following terms:

> There is no question that our technologically advanced industrial society needs specialists of all sorts. There is no question that the advancement of knowledge in all fields of science and scholarship, and in all the learned professions, needs intense specialization. But for the sake of preserving and enhancing our cultural traditions, as well as for the health of science and scholarship, we need specialists who are also generalists—generally cultivated human beings, not just good plumbers. We need truly educated human beings who can perform their special tasks better precisely because they have general cultivation as well as intensely specialized training. (Adler, 1988, p. 43)

Although Adler thinks we can accomplish this through a prescribed set of required courses, E. D. Hirsch correctly recognizes that required courses do not guarantee that teachers will focus on specific content. Thus, we need to specify content so that children across the United States will learn common things.

Hirsch believes that content is preliminary to problem solving. "Yes, problem-solving skills are necessary. But they depend on a wealth of relevant knowledge. Meanwhile, street-smart children in the Bronx and elsewhere demonstrate outside school that they already possess higher-order thinking skills . . . what these students lack is not critical thinking but academic knowledge" (Hirsch, 1993). Hirsch and his colleagues made a major contribution defining and providing this knowledge with *The Dictionary of Cultural Literacy* (Hirsch, Kett, and Trefil, 1988). Hirsch (1991) also developed a recommended curriculum for the elementary grades.

## *Easing Geographic Mobility*

A national curriculum is especially important in a geographically mobile society like the United States. It may be personally satisfying to learn about the history of your own town, West Overshoe, or your own ethnic group, Transylvanians; and there will still be time to do so. But young people have to be prepared to function in the larger world. Before they die, they are likely to live in several towns and in more than one state. They need a broad perspective that they can share with the people they will encounter along their way. This broad perspective, this common frame of reference, will vastly facilitate social and business communication. It will hold us together as a people, serving as the cultural cement of our society. It will reduce the culture shock and the period of adjustment we all face in moving from one locale to another. Indeed, national geography standards will assure that we know how to get from one place to another and have a sense beforehand of the new location's topography, climate, and natural resources (The Geography Education Standards Project, 1994).

Without a common culture, the United States may become dangerously pluralistic. When groups have so little in common that they become strange to one another, the strangeness can breed suspicion, then hostility, and finally a descending spiral of violence. We do not have to look to the Middle East or Eastern Europe for examples of this phenomenon; we need look no farther than the Howard Beaches and Crown Heights and Los Angeles Centrals of America, or wherever else the next ethnic explosion occurs.

A national curriculum will ease geographic mobility for students. As the former president of the American Federation of Teachers argues: "National curriculums mean that kids moving from one school district to another do not have to waste time by repeating the material they already know or struggle to catch up on stuff they've missed" (Shanker, 1992). The American Federation of Teachers is now calling for the United States to adopt a common academic curriculum and a national exam for high school students ("Largest Teachers' Union . . . ," 1995).

## *Building National Cohesion*

No nation can survive if its people lack a sense of nationhood. Studying the history of the nation helps provide this sense of unity. The stirring examples of our nation's leaders, the enormous obstacles overcome in times of national peril, the daily struggles of ordinary people, the evolution of social institutions—knowledge of all these awakens us to our common heritage and our shared destiny. "Indeed, we put our sense of nationhood at risk by failing to familiarize our young people with the story of how the society in which we live came to be. Knowledge of the ideas that have molded us and the ideals that have mattered to us function as a kind of civic glue" (Cheney, 1987, p. 7). President Reagan spoke to this concern in his farewell address when he commented that patriotism, which he defined as an informed love of country, is promoted when students learn of the United States' great triumphs. For the dean of Yale College, the common culture is the "system of laws and beliefs that shaped the establishment of the country, a system developed within the context of Western civilization. It should be obvious, then, that all Americans need to learn about that civilization to understand our country's origins and share in its heritage, purposes, and character" (Kagan, 1991).

Another way to bring a people together in national unity is through their literary past. The great works of prose and poetry—the canon of American literature—unite us through our shared delight. These literary treasures give us rich insights into ourselves, making it impossible to ignore the humanity we have in common with our fellow citizens. "Something of value is lost when there is no coherent literature curriculum. . . . Such a curriculum, beginning in the early grades, helps young people understand how the culture came to be what it is, how it was shaped, which writers defined it and thereby changed the way we see ourselves" (Ravitch and Finn, 1987, p. 10).

This "cultural" curriculum can be honest about America's past by acknowledging the shameful episodes and giving credit to groups whose contributions were formerly ignored. The national standards for United States history attempt to do just that, drawing numerous examples from minority cultures, heroes, and travails. Imagine elementary school students reading the diaries of Harriet Tubman, *Tales from the Gold Mountain* by Paul Yee, and *The Cat Who Escaped from Steerage* by Evelyn Meyerson, vicariously experiencing the lives of slaves and of Chinese and Jewish immigrants (Crabtree and Nash, 1994, pp. 126, 146). At the same time, such a curriculum can avoid multiculturalism's America bashing and ethnic breast thumping. It can be a curriculum that unites us through mutual understanding and shared appreciation (Schlesinger, 1992).

## Improving Reading Ability

One of the reasons why so many adults cannot, and will not, read even the local newspaper is that it contains too many terms they don't recognize. Many don't have the time or patience to look up these terms in dictionaries, encyclopedias, or atlases. In other cases, the reader lacks the background knowledge to understand the real meaning of the term:

> The recently rediscovered insight that literacy is more than a skill is based upon knowledge that all of us unconsciously have about language. We know instinctively that to understand what somebody is saying, we must understand more than the surface meaning of words; we have to understand the

context as well. The need for background information applies all the more to reading and writing. To grasp the words on a page we have to know a lot of information that isn't set down on the page. (Hirsch, 1987, p. 3)

If students are thoroughly educated in the general culture of their country, they will be able to draw on this knowledge as needed. A passing newspaper reference to the First Amendment or the Korean War, for example, will not create confusion. Such references will not cause the daily newspaper to take on the esoteric quality of a technical journal. Rather, readers who know their country's history will readily grasp the references and put them into context. Without this information, readers will become discouraged from reading, compounding their lack of understanding. Schools, then, must give children the basic information they need to undergird their lifelong intellectual development.

## Enlightening the Electorate

If Americans are not able to *stay* informed because they have never been informed, there is not much hope for democracy. People become apathetic about public affairs when they don't have the background to understand the issues. Even worse, they vote without knowing the issues well enough even to realize what is in their own interest. Politicians can manipulate uninformed people with slick slogans. Lies become as credible as truths. More and more ruthless demagogues will take power, until eventually a despot inveigles the ignorant masses into letting him or her take control. "True enfranchisement depends upon knowledge, knowledge upon literacy, and literacy upon cultural literacy. To be truly literate, citizens must be able to grasp the meaning of any piece of writing addressed to the general reader" (Hirsch, 1987, p. 12).

Recent presidential campaigns may have underscored this point for you. With as many as seven candidates involved in a single debate during the primaries, each trying to score points with high-sounding rhetoric and claims to special expertise, the viewer needed a lot of background knowledge to avoid being completely flummoxed. Persons lacking this knowledge probably gave up trying to understand what the election was all about and voted without logical reason or did not bother to vote at all.

Issues the electorate is expected to make judgments on are becoming more complex. The numerous technical details are difficult to comprehend, and the consequences of action are less predictable than they were when the world was simpler. A cursory review of national health care and welfare reform proposals, or global strategy, is all it should take to drive this point home. Thus, it is imperative that voters be able to fathom the issues in some depth if democratic decision making is not to become as random as a lottery drawing.

R. Freeman Butts (1995) has expressed these concerns in the following way:

> It will not be easy, but a gigantic effort must be launched to counteract the superficial political opinions of citizens now molded by TV attack ads, by radio squawk-talk, and by organized floods of faxes—what *New York Times* reporter Michael Wines has called the "electronic din" of a "500-channel

democracy." The public is so easily influenced by negative campaigning because they know less than they need to about what government is and should do. The only long-term hope of revivifying a cynical electorate is serious and sustained study and learning of basic principles of constitutional democracy like those invoked by Jefferson. (p. 48)

Butts was a senior consultant and advisor to the National Civic Standards Project. Those standards now exist; schools across the United States should adopt them to assure the vitality of democracy in the twenty-first century (*National Standards for Civics and Government,* 1994).

## Uplifting the Poor

Americans are better off when all citizens are well-informed. Those who will reap the greatest benefits, however, are those who are now the least informed. The poor, especially the poor minorities who are so ignorant of mainstream culture, will learn the vocabulary needed to converse on equal terms with the higher social classes. Communication will no longer block their upward mobility; outsider feelings will diminish; and a major reason for resentment and ridicule will be removed. Cultural literacy will give *power* to the poor so they will be able to compete in the job market and in the political arena on a more equal footing. The black Harvard historian and sociologist Orlando Patterson expressed this view:

> The people who run society at the macrolevel must be literate in this culture. For this reason, it is dangerous to overemphasize the problems of basic literacy or the relevancy of literacy to specific tasks, and more constructive to emphasize that blacks will be condemned in perpetuity to oversimplified, low-level tasks and will never gain their rightful place in controlling the levers of power unless they also acquire literacy in this wider cultural sense. (Patterson, quoted in Hirsch, 1987, pp. 10–11)

Minority cultures certainly add richness to the United States; there is no secret plot to drown these cultures in the mainstream. In fact, the intention is to make minorities truly bicultural. By learning about the common culture, they will be able to retain their original cultures but will no longer be *trapped* in them. Furthermore, they will no longer be patronized as the larger culture celebrates meretricious aspects of their particular cultures; if the Zulus had no Tolstoy, we will not need to attempt to inflate a minor writer to that status. Better that minorities be given the tools they need to cross into the dominant culture as they choose. If an evil plot is underfoot, it is the work of those who pretend to value minorities by keeping them "pure" (and poor) in their lack of literacy and knowledge of the mainstream culture. They are creating separate ghettos for minority children's minds.

## Not a Task for the Weak

Drafting national standards and developing tests in a variety of subject areas is not an easy job. We could spend enormous time just getting input from a broadly representative array of constituencies. Sifting and assembling the input into a coherent document is another time-consuming task. And it is certain that those who had no input or were not consulted will second-guess the final product.

Criticism of the national standards (and tests) will be keenest in the subject areas that are the most subjective—the social sciences and the humanities. The United States history standards, and, to a lesser extent, the world history standards, have provoked a firestorm of criticism. The U.S. Senate denounced the United States history standards by a vote of 99 to 1 (Johnston and Diegmueller, 1995). The standards were discredited because they were illustrated with teaching activities that emphasized minorities and their oppression.

Had the suggested teaching activities been more traditional, they would have been criticized for that reason. Striking a universally popular balance is probably not possible. However, the authors of the standards responded to the criticisms by seeking further input and displaying a willingness to compromise.

This demonstrates that the creation of national standards is itself both a democratic and an educational process. And since it is the supporting activities and not the standards themselves that have come under attack, it appears we have reached a consensus on the latter:

> The standards represent an impressive breakthrough in linking the subject matter of history with new understanding of how children can and do learn at different stages of their development . . . these standards make available to elementary- and high-school students—our future citizens—the analytical tools and skills they need to come to their own understanding of history, skills that will enable them to differentiate between historical facts and historical interpretations and to consider historical events and characters from multiple perspectives. The standards offer nothing less than an escape from the rote learning of factual matter that has bedeviled the introductory study of history in this country for more than a century. (Jones, 1995, B1)

In short, the process of creating national standards in history has worked. If it can work in an area as subjective as history, it can work in any discipline. And it has worked in the best American tradition: "The new standards are sprawling, messy, both too little and too much, just like the process that produced them. Focus groups do not create elegant, coherent curriculums, but they do keep the democratic juices flowing" (Gluck, 1994).

## Escaping Indoctrination

A national curriculum will surely mean a loss of local control, and this alarms many people. However, the national curriculum not only will get children beyond the parochial and often trivial knowledge they are taught at the local level, but it also will give them a broader *value* perspective. Instead of being indoctrinated in the values of the fundamentalist Christian or Jewish or liberal or conservative community where they happen to live, they will be exposed to the positions of all these groups. If the *National Standards for United States*

*History* (Crabtree and Nash, 1994) were adopted nationally, we would have some guarantee that students in Podunk were learning more about the minority cultures of the United States. This exposure would challenge provincial values and perspectives and might cause students to rethink and modify some of their views. This possibility is what alarms some community members. They worry that outside influences will corrupt their children.

These fears are understandable, but the reaction—the desire to impose an ostrichlike education, with everyone's head stuck in the sand—is not. That kind of education is designed to keep children ignorant; it is not an education at all. It tells young people that the only way we can get them to believe what we tell them is to keep them from hearing anything else. Truth, however, arises from the competition with other "truths," not from silence. Besides, with all the mass communications systems in the United States, it is futile to try to keep kids in a soundproof darkroom. Fiber optics and satellite dishes are giving us so many television channels that "channel surfing" is the newest labor-intensive activity. Who will block the screen and drown the sound when something heretical appears? Computers put kids on the information highway—which is often strewn with litter—but who will stand astride it waving warning flags? Any attempt to do so would be counterproductive. Every new sight or sound that breaks through will have a special allure for youngsters because they will recognize it as something they're *not supposed to* see or hear.

The national curriculum, therefore, will help save children from the narrow-mindedness of their communities. The elders in a community might still refuse to let their children learn certain topics in school, but this enforced ignorance will be reflected in the youngsters' national test scores. The adults will soon realize that their attempts to preserve an unknowing innocence are made at the expense of the youngsters' educational and occupational mobility. That realization should at least cause them to reconsider the values they took for granted for so long.

## POSITION 2: FOR LOCAL DETERMINATION

### Maintaining Local Interest

Local public schools are a local investment, a local pride, a local interest, a local contribution to society. They are the main root of America's grass roots. "Community" does not mean a national government or a national bureaucracy imposing its will and conformist standards on all. Community is instead a group of local people who come together because of residence, work, communication, or interest. Community represents our shared concerns and goals, often in a particular locale. We like and want community schools because they are responsive to us. Do we feel any kinship to the national IRS office in town? Or are we drawn as a community to the national FBI or post office nearby? We may like the people who work there, and they may be part of our comunity, but the agency itself does not make a community. Local schools will lose even more of their community character, and their focus as a community resource, if a national curriculum and standards are imposed.

## Local Decisions to Provide Similar Schooling

Granted, there already is a haphazard national curriculum. It would be a disaster to solidify this further through national mandates and testing. Nothing is more certain to depress local interest in schools than to take away local control over what the schools are doing. In recent years, local control has been severely eroded by all kinds of state requirements and monitoring. The state requires specific courses; students take state achievement tests in these courses, as well as in basic skill areas such as math and reading; and state legislatures keep adding to the requirements rather than subtracting. "If the school day weren't so overcrowded already by the pressure of the factologists, maybe there would be more time for teachers to teach and students to learn" (Ohanian, 1987, p. 21).

"It seems as though every journal or newspaper education section either reports on or calls for new standards. The calls and reports are always written by professors of education, politicians, federal or state education department officials, or people with a special interest in a discipline like mathematics or biology. Can you imagine a group of teachers indignantly rising up to demand more standards? Sounds like material for a stand-up comic to me" (Schwarz, 1994, p. 44). It is worth noting that Schwarz is the codirector of the highly acclaimed Central Park East Secondary School in Harlem.

To carry the logic of the accountability schemes to the national level is to repudiate the wisdom of the Founders. Education is a power reserved to the states, according to the U.S. Constitution. Even within states, local school districts still maintain some limited amount of curricular control. This is a wise policy for several reasons. First of all, the *informal* national curriculum that we already have ensures that no local district will get too far out of line. Second, the recent spate of state incursions into the curriculum created fairly rigid prescriptions that local districts must follow. What local districts need, then, is not more direction from above, but continued discretion over those few areas of the curriculum that they can still tailor to their particular needs. Harold Howe II, a former U.S. Commissioner of Education, recommends that national standards "be as vague as possible" so that teachers will continue to "have the freedom that will motivate them to take on the burdens of becoming true professionals" (Howe, 1995, p. 376).

It is not enough to let local people control what remains after the central government flexes its muscles. The educational program the local people desire must receive as much respect as the central government's plan does. Otherwise, the message sent is that the local education program is merely a frill, and teachers should concentrate their time and energy on satisfying the national and state bureaucrats. This message effectively repudiates the legitimacy of determining curricula locally.

The message will come across loud and clear if the national tests have "high stakes," meaning that a lot is riding on them in terms of students' careers and schools' reputations. There is not much point in having the tests if these consequences do not follow. That is why the National Coalition of Advocates for Students opposes national tests ("Steps Toward Improving Student Assessment," 1992). Furthermore, writes Cuban (1993)

> when tests are wired to an official curriculum and scores carry heavy consequences for individual students, teachers, and schools, the official district curriculum will narrow to what is on these high-stakes tests. Even this freezing and narrowing of the curriculum pales next to compelling evidence of test-score pollution that has occurred in schools responding to high-stakes state tests. "Test-score" pollution means that standardized-test scores rise because students practice with questions similar to ones that will be on the test. (p. 25)

National standards and tests will narrow the curriculum; as other countries already have experienced this phenomenon (Celis, 1993). High stakes standards cause school officials to cheat (Carlson, 1996).

Greater control of curricula at the national level may be part of the conservatives' agenda for U.S. schools, but it contradicts another part: parental choice. If all the schools are bent on teaching one version of cultural literacy, there won't be much for parents to choose (Henig, 1988).

## Preventing Mediocrity or Lowering to a Common Denominator

A national curriculum and tests necessarily mean a national set of standards. How obliged local school people will feel to focus on those standards will depend, of course, on what the payoffs are. If the chances increase, of getting their graduates into good colleges, with financial aid, local officials will take the national standards very seriously. The national curriculum will become the local curriculum, and teachers will spend a lot of time preparing students for the national tests. This will narrow what students learn to a curriculum a single level of government has ordained. And since the national standards will likely be determined by national committee consensus, they will be *compromise* standards.

For some schools, the national standards may be higher than their present requirements, so their students will be challenged to reach new criteria. We do not equate standards with quality, so the new standards may not provide any better education, even for these students. Alas, for many schools, the compromise standards lower the bar. The expectations for these students will drop. As Lorie Shepard has said about the new math standards of the National Assessment of Educational Progress: "If all fifty states have to agree to them, I can bet you you'll get a lower set of standards than if you let ambitious states go off on their own. . . . You'll get lowest-common-denominator standards, not world-class standards" (Shepard, quoted in Rothman, 1991b).

A pressure to weaken the standards arises from the standards mania itself. Every subject area wants to get in on the act; that means national standards and tests in English, social studies, mathematics, science, and foreign languages. And since each of these subjects breaks down into component subjects, the efflorescence will be boggling. Social studies alone already includes a set of U.S. history standards, a set of world history standards, a set of civics and government standards, a set of geography standards, standards for economics, and an umbrella set of social studies standards that tries to include all the subfields. The U.S. history standards total 271 pages! Soon, every other social studies subject will have weighed in with its standards, since failing to set national standards means risking dislodgement from the curriculum. This is a political, not an educational, battle.

The chairman of the social studies department in Gloucester, Massachusetts, has reacted to this wild abundance: "I have a major concern about being held accountable for all this. I'm already trying to fit ten pounds into a five-pound bag. If all these documents come out this way, somebody's going to have to take a sabbatical to read it all" (Richard Aieta, quoted in Viadero, 1994, p. 25).

Thus, every subject area will come under pressure to be less piggish with its standards to leave room in the pen for the standards of every other subject. The new, pared-down standards will be couched in such all-embracing terms that they will mean nothing. Paul Schwarz gives a doozy of an example: "Students will value the principles and ideals of a democratic system based on the premises of human dignity, liberty, justice, and equality" (Schwarz, 1994, p. 44). Sweeping generalities like this cause one to actually yearn for the mediocre.

## Deciding What Is Important

If students lack the cultural literacy that people like Hirsch, Finn, and Ravitch think is important, it may be that students have yet to be convinced of its importance. The only other possibility is that schools are not teaching it to the students, which means that teachers are not themselves persuaded of its importance. But this does not mean that students learn nothing in school, or that teachers teach nothing. All it means is that students and teachers are not learning or teaching what someone else has declared important.

Let's take an example from Hirsch's book. One of the terms Hirsch thinks should be in the vocabulary of a literate person is *Occam's razor*. This is a wonderful term tracing back to the fourteenth century. As you probably know, it describes a philosophical rule that the assumptions that underlie an explanation should not be multiplied unnecessarily. If you hear an explanation for a stock market crash that requires you to first accept the truth of ten prior assumptions, and if a simpler alternative explanation requires only five such assumptions, the alternative is more likely to be true because it entails fewer assumptions that must also be true. Students would certainly not be *harmed* by learning the term *Occam's razor*. But what about another philosophical term of even more ancient vintage: *Anselm's ontological argument.* This is an argument for the existence of God. It posits that an attribute of perfection is existence; since God, by definition, is perfect, God must exist. This term is not on Hirsch's list.

Obviously, Hirsch thinks the first term is important, and the second is not. That's his right—but in exercising it, he has engaged in an arbitrary judgment. And he has tried to impose his personal preference on other people. Thus, the issue is not whether schools should make students culturally literate; of course they should. The issue is *what constitutes cultural literacy.* For Hirsch, one of the crucial items is Occam's razor. For someone of a more theological bent, it is Anselm's argument. (For a teenager, it might be Jim Carrey or Adam Sandler.)

Hirsch has a biased view of American culture, as do we all. "One could waste many happy hours looking things up in Hirsch's tome in an effort to characterize the American culture he imagines. He includes William Faulkner but not Zora Neale Hurston, the Beatles but not the Rolling Stones, Bob Hope but not Lenny Bruce, Chappaquiddick but not SDS, the Monroe Doctrine but not the Truman Doctrine, Solidarity but not the Wobblies" (Margaronis, 1989, p. 14). Hirsch's vision of American culture has a marked conservative bias. If Hirsch attempts to overcome this criticism, he may fulfill the prophecy of Neil Postman (1992): "We may be sure that Hirsch will continue to expand his list until he reaches a point where a one-sentence directive will be all he needs to publish: 'See the *Encyclopedia Americana* and *Webster's Third International'*" (p. 176).

After witnessing the seemingly interminable debate among math educators concerning national standards, Lauren Resnick noted that other disciplines are even more contentious than math. "It's going to be very difficult in this country to deal with the concept of a canon, to say which knowledge and pieces of the culture are going to be considered the nation's culture" (Resnick, quoted in Rothman, 1991a, p. 25). Thus, the effort at creating a national curriculum may be a fool's errand foredoomed to failure (Ohanian, 1999).

## Avoiding the Merely Ornamental

You might wonder why terms such as *Occam's razor* and *Anselm's ontological argument* are worth learning about at all. It might suddenly have occurred to you that you rarely come upon these terms in your schoolwork or general reading. Even rarer are the occasions when you yourself might employ the terms.

But wait a moment. Now that your memory of these terms has been refreshed, you might find yourself deliberately dropping them in a term paper (no pun intended) or a class discussion. Wouldn't that impress the professor and intimidate your classmates? It should, but only if the point you were trying to make when you slipped in the terms was itself impressive and intimidating. Otherwise, all you have done is momentarily dazzle people with a sheen of culture. This would make you a *dilettante,,* another term that, interestingly, does not appear on Hirsch's list. The "literacy" of a dilettante, or dabbler, is only ornamental. It dazzles people in order to distract them from shallowness.

No matter how high you pile the baubles, bangles, and beads of this ornamentation—even if you adorn yourself with *all* the terms in Hirsch's dictionary (Hirsch, Kett, and Trefil, 1988)—in the long run, others will judge you on the power and logic of your thinking. You may be culturally literate in Hirsch's terms, but you will be a functional illiterate in the real world unless you can think well. Good thinking consists of locating relevant data and synthesizing them into meaningful wholes in order to solve problems. Terms alone do not enable you to think; they only enable you to sound like a deep thinker until people get wise to your superficiality. Knowing Hirsch's terms is no better than knowing the answers in Trivial Pursuit or Jeopardy.

The argument thus far may have seemed congenial because you think of yourself as liberal and Hirsch is being derided for his conservatism. But liberals make lists, too. A good example is the *National Standards for United States History* (Crabtree and Nash, 1994). This tome was so skewed to the left that it had nineteen references to McCarthy and McCarthyism, but no mention of Soviet aggression in Eastern Europe (Ravitch, 1994), and it cited Harriet Tubman far more often than George Washington (Winkler, 1995). In time, we may have not just one set of national standards per subject area, but a set for each ideological persuasion within each area. Perhaps we should also produce multiple versions of Trivial Pursuit and Jeopardy for the dilettantes in each ideological camp.

## Shunning Elitism and Imperialism

It is likely that the average assembly line worker in a Detroit auto factory would have trouble understanding Hirsch, who is a professor of English at the University of Virginia, or the authors of the national history standards, who are professors at UCLA. The autoworker would lack familiarity with the terms and ideas the professors toss around. One solution to this communication problem would be to drill the autoworker on the professors' language. This, in fact, is the kind of solution the professors and others are offering. They are saying that other people should learn to understand *them*. If the rest of us become fluent in the cultures of academe, human communication will be enhanced.

No doubt it will. But communication would also be enhanced if academics learned the culture of the autoworker, or even the culture of the colleague whom they so cavalierly dismiss. The idea that "My culture is better than yours, so you should learn mine, but I don't have to bother with yours" is an example of cultural imperialism. The autoworker would probably use a pithier term: snobbery. To say that my culture is more important than yours because my group is more powerful than yours is to talk power politics. It is saying that you have to please me because I am one of the people in charge of the world. That's not education; that's domination. Education is about learning to understand *each other*.

Granting for the sake of argument that it is desirable for the poor to learn the culture of the better-off, we would still argue that the $400 million it will cost to design and administer national tests would be better spent on upgrading the education of the poor rather than once again demonstrating their inadequacy (Schwebel, 1994). This is why such groups as the National Education Association, the National Association for the Advancement of Colored People, the National Parent-Teacher Association, and the American Association of School Administrators have urged that we forego national testing at this time (Neill, 1991). The Clinton administration has tried to defuse this opposition by proposing we also set opportunity-to-learn standards to ensure that poor kids have a fair chance to perform well on the national tests (Massell and Kirst, 1994). Working out these standards, which are sure to entail large costs and increased federal involvement in education, may be a politically impossible task.

If national tests are not to be elitist and imperialistic, does this mean we have to learn all the terms of the academics' culture and all the terms of the autoworker's culture and all the terms of every other culture, including that of blacks, Hispanics, women, and gays? That is obviously impossible. The most we can reasonably expect is that the national standards and tests deal respectfully with many major cultural groups. What the major groups are will depend, to some extent, on the particular community. For example, a Texas coastal community with a large influx of Vietnamese refugees should include the culture of these people in the curriculum. In order to do this, the Texas town needs some control over the curriculum of its own schools. That is why a national curriculum with a lot of spelled-out details would be unwisely restrictive. "Students should have thorough exposure to the core of basic skills, but they should also have a curriculum which is relevant to their social environment . . . and which recognizes cultural diversity as a resource, not a deficit, in learning" (Bastian et al., 1985, p. 47). A national curriculum without a lot of detail but just lofty rhetoric is not worth the paper it takes to publish it.

One group whose culture should always be prominent in the curriculum but seldom is, is youth. The youth culture of the United States (and the local community variation on it) is a most appropriate subject of study in school. The fact that this culture is constantly changing does not mean that its current manifestations are frivolous. On the contrary, young people—who are, after all, the clients of schools—respond eagerly to these manifestations. Schools should let their clients know that their culture is an important matter, and not something to be ignored until it is outgrown. Schools should cease suggesting to students that people become important only after they leave school.

## Having a Common Culture

The concern that local control will produce too much diversity and keep children from learning a common culture necessary for communication and career success is unwarranted. In the United States, the common culture is learned not only in school, but also through family, peers, mass media, and the Internet. There are only a handful of major television networks, including the cable stations. Syndicated radio talk shows like Rush Limbaugh's are national town halls. The number of newspapers in the United States has been dwindling for a long time now, and we even have a national paper, *USA Today*. Few newsmagazines have survived, and Hollywood makes fewer movies than in the past. This all encourages a centralization and homogenization of culture—fostering a mass culture, even if it is not the high culture that appeals to Hirsch and others.

The mass culture is the primary basis upon which people relate to each other. Most understand its terms. Of course, most of us also need to know certain subcultures in depth in order to get by in the world; these subcultures belong to our jobs, religions, ethnic groups, and so on, and we learn about them by living in them. It is the height of arrogance to insist that one's subculture be made the common culture; as Margaronis explains:

> What standardized cultures are meant to do is distinguish their owners from the barbarians . . . by classifying the knowledge "we" have and "they" don't . . . it marks the difference between those for whom cultural literacy comes

"naturally"—i.e., those who absorb the information and its context from home and social circles—and those who must acquire it, who feel the rift between their lived experience and what is considered important at school. (Margaronis, 1989, p. 14)

## *Avoiding Big Brother*

In his classic novel *1984*, George Orwell warns against a society in which the few exercise total control over the many. The few who have total control (totalitarians) are referred to as Big Brother. If all the schools in the United States are going to teach a single notion of cultural literacy, then the United States will need a Big Brother to spell out the details of that notion. Who should it be? Hirsch? You? Us? A committee of really, really smart people? A committee of people from every important cultural group? Members of Congress? We saw how they handled the impeachment trial of President Clinton, and we heard about how our President comported himself to bring the trial upon him. Are these the people you want to decide on a national curriculum?

Before we can answer this question, we need to think about another: Who decides who gets to decide? If someone or some group is going to be America's cultural czar, then the people who get to pick the czar must be selected very carefully.

As you can see, this process is very complicated and fraught with risk. The risks and effort might be worth it if we really needed national standards and tests, but we don't. The Republican-controlled 104th Congress had threatened to put an end to the effort to establish a national curriculum and standards by refusing further funding, but that failed on the shoals of partisan politics. If we want to cut unnecessary costs and keep the national government off our backs as much as possible, the national standards movement is a good place to begin. Left-leaning U.S. history standards have given the Republicans an added incentive for scuttling the movement (Diegmueller, 1995). To those on the left, however, the same U.S. history standards appear to be right-wing, a nationalistic and patriotic papering over of America's problems. In fact, a draft set of the U.S. history standards drew attack from some on the right for not featuring more American heroes and Americanistic stories. In order to retain funding and the power to determine standards, historians modified the draft standards to placate the right-wing critics. Is this a way to establish the validity of knowledge—by changing what is supposed to be necessary knowledge in order to gain the approval of one side of the political spectrum? This unfortunate set of developments illustrates one of the main problems in the national curriculum/standards movement—the power of politics to control and limit the search for knowledge (Ohanian, 1999). It can happen at the local level, but there are a lot of locals, so they can't impose their views on other locals. People can then choose the community with the standards they desire.

## *Teaching for Critical Literacy*

Instead of giving students a false sense of culture by urging them to memorize big words, we should be making them *critically* literate. Brazilian educator

Paolo Freire (Freire and Macedo, 1987) and his North American colleagues, including Stanley Aronowitz and Henry Giroux (1985), expressed this notion. Being critically literate means being able to understand and cope with the real world. Students learn how to think intelligently about their own lives and to analyze their own culture. But, in turn, they also have to analyze the larger culture for its impact on their lives. This is functional literacy of the highest sort. It not only enables people to survive in their culture, but it empowers them to change the culture's negative aspects.

If young people were to analyze American culture critically, they would surely find that the kind of cultural literacy academics are advocating bears faint resemblance to the kind of literacy that pays off with good jobs and high salaries in our society. They would quickly realize, if they don't already, that their elders are much better at preaching than practicing:

> We honor ambition, we reward greed, we celebrate materialism, we worship acquisitiveness, we commercialize art, we cherish success and then we bark at the young about the gentle arts of the spirit. . . . Kids just don't care much for hypocrisy, and if they are [culturally] illiterate, their illiteracy is merely ours, imbibed by them with scholarly ardor. They are learning well the lesson we are teaching—namely, that there is nothing in all the classics in their school libraries that will be of the slightest benefit to them in making their way to the top of our competitive society. (Barber, 1987)

A good way to tackle *critical* literacy would be to involve students in the debate over *cultural* literacy. In the process, they would have to decide what is important to learn and defend their decisions. As Gerald Graff argues: "The best way to deal with the conflicts over education . . . is to *teach them*—teach the conflicts themselves" (quoted in Greene, 1989).

The standards movement may be well on the way to self-destruction because of its driven quality. So many groups have been beguiled that we now have national standards for arts, civics, economics, English, foreign languages, geography, health, history, mathematics, physical education, science, and social studies. This, plus the fact that all the states are weighing in with their own versions ("Struggling for Standards," 1995), means such a wild efflorescence of standards that people will soon get lost and head for a clearing.

## For Discussion

1. In 1859, John Stuart Mill, the English philosopher, issued the following warning in his classic work *On Liberty:*

   > All that has been said of the importance of individuality of character, and diversity in opinions and modes of conduct, involves, as of the same unspeakable importance, diversity of education. A general State education is a mere contrivance for molding people to be exactly like one another; and as the mold in which it casts them is that which pleases the predominant power in the government . . . in proportion as it is efficient and successful, it establishes a despotism over the mind. . . .

   How would you relate this quote to the cultural literacy movement?

2. It has often been said that schools are supposed to optimize each child's educational experience by individualizing instruction according to the child's background and abilities. How is this compatible with the goal of uniform cultural literacy for all?

3. At the end of his book *Cultural Literacy: What Every American Needs to Know*, E. D. Hirsch, Jr., has a sixty-four-page appendix of terms that every American should know. Following are several of these terms. How many do you know? What do you make of your relative "knowledge" or "ignorance"?

| | | |
|---|---|---|
| Potato famine, Irish | *Pride and Prejudice* | Prokofiev, Sergei |
| pragmatism | prima donna | proletariat |
| precipitate (chemistry) | primate | Prometheus |
| premier (prime minister) | primrose path | Promised Land |
| pre-Raphaelite | probation | pro rata |
| Presley, Elvis | Procrustes' bed | prose |
| Pretoria | Prohibition | |

4. Following are books recommended by teachers and principals honored as educators of the year in 1988. Does this list fit the 21st century? Should this be a nationally required reading list? Would you modify the list in any way? Why?

**Preschool**

Dr. Seuss series, Dr. Seuss

*Mother Goose Stories*

*The Little Engine That Could*, Watty Piper

*Where the Wild Things Are*, Maurice Sendak

*Make Way for Ducklings*, Robert McCloskey

**Primary School (K–3)**

*The Velveteen Rabbit*, Margery Williams

*Alexander and the Terrible, Horrible, No Good, Very Bad Day*, Judith Viorst

*Ira Sleeps Over*, Bernard Waber

*The Tale of Peter Rabbit*, Beatrix Potter

*Winnie-the-Pooh*, A. A. Milne

*Charlotte's Web*, E. B. White

*Where the Wild Things Are*, Maurice Sendak

**Elementary School (4–6)**

*Charlotte's Web*, E. B. White

*Tales of a Fourth Grade Nothing*, Judy Blume

*Where the Red Fern Grows*, Wilson Rawls

The Laura Ingalls Wilder series, Laura Ingalls Wilder

*Little Women*, Louisa May Alcott

**Junior High School (7–9)**

*Where the Red Fern Grows,* Wilson Rawls

*Anne Frank: The Diary of a Young Girl,* Anne Frank

*The Red Badge of Courage,* Stephen Crane

*The Call of the Wild,* Jack London

*Huckleberry Finn,* Mark Twain

*Treasure Island,* Robert Louis Stevenson

*The Outsiders,* S. E. Hinton

**High School (10–12)**

*The Grapes of Wrath,* John Steinbeck

*To Kill a Mockingbird,* Harper Lee

*Huckleberry Finn,* Mark Twain

*The Scarlet Letter,* Nathaniel Hawthorne

*A Tale of Two Cities,* Charles Dickens

*Macbeth,* William Shakespeare

*The Catcher in the Rye,* J. D. Salinger

*Source: Education Week,* October 19, 1988, p. 30.

5. Lynn Cheney, former chair of the National Endowment for the Humanities, funded the development of national standards for U.S. history. However, the final draft, developed by some well-known historians, left her unhappy. Cheney thought the standards were skewed to the left, overrepresenting some topics and underrepresenting others. Table 10.1 illustrates her concerns. Do you share them? What would you propose as necessary historical knowledge for all Americans? The historians modified the standards in response to Cheney and other critics. Discuss your view of how standards should be decided and modified.

**TABLE 10.1 Citations on Famous People and Events in the Draft U.S. History National Standards**

| | |
|---|---|
| Paul Revere, Thomas Edison, the Wright Brothers | 0 |
| Seneca Falls | 9 |
| Harriet Tubman | 6 |
| Ulysses S. Grant | 1 |
| Robert E. Lee | 0 |
| Lincoln's Gettysburg Address | 1 |
| American Federation of Labor | 8 |
| Senator Joseph McCarthy | 19 |
| Ku Klux Klan | 17 |

# References

ADLER, M. (1988). "The Paideia Proposal: Rediscovering the Essence of Education." In *Innovations in Education: Reformers and Their Critics,* edited by J. M. Rich. Boston: Allyn & Bacon.

ARONOWITZ, S., AND GIROUX, H. A. (1985). *Education Under Siege: The Conservative, Liberal and Radical Debate Over Schooling.* South Hadley, MA: Bergin & Garvey.

BARBER, B. (1987). "What Do 47-Year-Olds Know?" *The New York Times,* December 26, p. 23.

BASTIAN, A., ET AL. (1985). *Choosing Equality: The Case for Democratic Schooling.* New York: New World Foundation.

BUTTS, R. (1995). "Antidote for Antipolitics: A New 'Text of Civic Instruction.'" *Education Week* 14(17), 38, 48.

CARLSON, K. (1996). "No School for Scandals." *New York Times,* September 1, p. NJ13.

CELIS, W. (1993). "The Fight Over National Standards." *The New York Times Education Life,* August 1, pp. 14–16.

CHENEY, L. (1987). *American Memory: A Report on the Humanities in the Nation's Public Schools.* Washington, DC: National Endowment for the Humanities.

CRABTREE, C., AND NASH, G. (1994). *National Standards for United States History.* Los Angeles: National Center for History in the Schools.

CUBAN, L. (1993). "A National Curriculum and Tests." *Education Week* 12(39), 25, 27.

DIEGMUELLER, K. (1995). "Backlash Puts Standards Work in Harm's Way." *Education Week* 14(16), 1, 12–13.

ELAM, S., ROSE, L., AND GALLUP, A. (1994). "The 26th Annual Phi Delta Kappa Gallup Poll of the Public's Attitudes Toward the Public Schools." *Phi Delta Kappan* 76(1), 41–56.

FINN, C. (1991). "Education Reform vs. Civil Rights Agendas." *The New York Times,* May 18, p. 23.

FREIRE, P., AND MACEDO, D. (1987). *Literacy: Reading the Word and the World.* South Hadley, MA: Bergin & Garvey.

THE GEOGRAPHY EDUCATION STANDARDS PROJECT. (1994). *Geography for Life.* Washington, DC: National Geographic Research and Exploration.

GLUCK, C. (1994). "History According to Whom?" *The New York Times,* November 19, p. 23.

GREENE, E. (1989). "'Teach the Conflicts, Teach the Conflicts,' Preaches This Humanist." *The Chronicle of Higher Education* 35(22), A3.

HENIG, J. R. (1988). "Which Way, Mr. Bennett?" *The Washington Post National Weekly Edition,* September 12–18, p. 27.

HIRSCH, E.D. (1987). *Cultural Literacy: What Every American Needs to Know.* Boston: Houghton Mifflin.

——— (1993). "Teach Knowledge, Not 'Mental Skills.'" *The New York Times,* September 4, p. 19.

——— KETT, J. F., AND TREFIL, J. (1988). *The Dictionary of Cultural Literacy: What Every American Needs to Know.* Boston: Houghton Mifflin.

——— (1991). *What Your 1st Grader Needs to Know* and *What Your 2nd Grader Needs to Know.* New York: Doubleday.

HOWE, H. (1995). "Uncle Sam Is in the Classroom!" *Phi Delta Kappan* 76(5), 374–377.

JOHNSTON, R., AND DIEGMUELLER, K. (1995). "Senate Approves Resolution Denouncing History Standards." *Education Week* 14(18), 14.

JONES, A. (1995). "Our Stake in the History Standards." *The Chronicle of Higher Education* 41(17), B1–B3.

KAGAN, D. (1991). "Western Values Are Central." *The New York Times,* May 4, p. 23.

KEAN, T. (1991). "Do We Need a National Achievement Exam? Yes." *Education Week* 10(31), 28, 36.

"Largest Teachers' Union Calls for National High School Exam." (1995). *The New York Times,* July 6, p. A15.

MARGARONIS, M. (1989). "Waiting for the Barbarians: The Ruling Class Defends the Citadel." *Village Voice Literary Supplement,* January/February, pp. 12–17.

MASSEL, D., AND KIRST, M. (1994). "Determining National Content Standards: An Introduction." *Education and Urban Society* 26(2), 107–117.

*National Standards for Civics and Government.* (1994). Calabasas, CA: Center for Civic Education.

NEILL, M. (1991). "Do We Need a National Achievement Exam? No." *Education Week* 10(31), 28, 36.

OHANIAN, S. (1987). "Finding a 'Loony List' While Searching for Literacy." *Education Week* 6(5), 21–22.

———. (1999). *One Size Fits Few.* Portmouth, NH: Heinemann.

PHELPS, R. (1993). "The Weak and Strong Arguments Against National Testing." *Education Week* 12(34), 30.

POSTMAN, N. (1992). *Technopoly: The Surrender of Culture to Technology.* New York: Knopf.

RAVITCH, D. (1994). "Standards in U.S. History: An Assessment." *Education Week* 14(14), 40, 48.

——— AND FINN, C. (1987). *What Do Our 17-Year-Olds Know? A Report on the First National Assessment of History and Literature.* New York: Harper & Row.

ROTHMAN, R. (1991a). "On the Road to National Standards, Math Educators Debate Assessments." *Education Week* 10 (32), 1, 25.

——— (1991b). "Researchers Say Emphasis on Testing Too Narrow, Could Set Back Reforms." *Education Week* 10(38), 25.

SAMUELSON, R. (1991). "Why School Reform Fails." *Newsweek,* May 27, p. 62.

SCHLESINGER, A. (1992). *The Disuniting of America: Reflections on a Multicultural Society.* New York: Norton.

SCHWARZ, P. (1994). "Needed: School-Set Standards." *Education Week* 14(12), 34, 44.

SCHWEBEL, M. (1994). "Educational Pie in the Sky." *The Nation,* May 2, pp. 591–592.

SHANKER, A. (1994). "All 'A's' Are Not Equal." *The New York Times,* September 11, p. E7.

——— (1991). "Developing a Common Curriculum." *The New York Times,* February 24, p. E7.

——— (1992). "National Standards and Exams." *The New York Times,* March 1, p. E7.

SIZER, T. (1992). "A Test of Democracy." *The New York Times,* January 30, p. A21.

——— (1984). *Horace's Compromise.* Boston: Houghton Mifflin.

"Steps Toward Improving Student Assessment." (1992). *New Voices* 2(1), 3.

"Struggling for Standards." (1995). *Education Week Special Report,* April 12.

VIADERO, D. (1994). "Standards in Collision." *Education Week* 13(17), 25–27.

WINKLER, K. (1995). "Who Owns History?" *The Chronicle of Higher Education* 41(19), A10–A11, A18.

# CHAPTER 11

# Values and Character: Traditional or Liberational

## POSITION 1: TEACH TRADITIONAL VALUES

American public schools commonly operate without an ethical compass. Relativism keeps such schools and their students adrift in a sea of personal and social temptations. Relativism in schools reflects the ideas that (1) all values are relative, with none superior; (2) there is no enduring set of ethical standards; and (3) personal character is a matter of individual choice and particular situations. Sommers (1998), in a perceptive analysis of the moral and educational chaos that faces young people, summarizes her position: "The last few decades of the twentieth century have seen a steady erosion of knowledge and a steady increase in moral relativism" (p. 33). She recalls the other school problems linked to the fact that Johnny can't read, write, or count, and continues, "it is also true that Johnny is having difficulty distinguishing right from wrong. . . . Along with illiteracy and innumeracy, we must add deep moral confusion to the list of educational problems" (p. 31).

Far too many public schools lack a central core of fundamental morals and give students no ethical basis for guidance through life. Instead, secular domination of education mistakenly keeps religious values at bay, while self-absorption becomes a primary focus for students. Is it any wonder that society is crumbling, violence is increasing, families are in disarray, and civility has disappeared?

Education that emphasizes selfishness, personal freedom, and permissiveness is a major contributor to the significant decline in social and family values (Sowell, 1992). An increase in crime and abuse is a natural outcome of schooling that preaches self-indulgence. Charles Colson (1994) argues that the secularization of American society is responsible for the increase in violent crime. Where can one gain a deep respect for other people, property, and social traditions if the schools assume the relativist stance that these things do not matter? The liberal view of education—that traditional values don't matter and that students should decide basic value questions for themselves without guidance from educators, religious leaders, or parents—has an eroding effect on the cornerstones of American society. It does not take a rocket scientist to recognize that the common values that undergird the civility, manners, and courtesies once dominant in the United States have given way to the self-indulgent values of greed, destruction, and fear of others. This erosion has been the companion of the permissive attitudes fostered in schools since progressive education concepts enveloped the school in the 1930s (Bennett, 1994).

It is no wonder that family values have declined in the face of an educational philosophy based on individualism and libertine lifestyles (Anderson, 1994; Roberts, 1994). Evidence of moral disaster surrounds us: extraordinarily high divorce rates, child and spouse abuse, lack of ethics in business and government, drug and alcohol addiction, out-of-control teen-age pregnancy rates, excessive reliance on child care outside the home, acceptance of immorality on television and in the arts, cheating scandals and explosive violence in the schools (Colson, 1994). We even have a recent U.S. President who admitted to moral corruption in his private life and deception in his public life, even as important public figures claimed that his behavior did not matter. This is a snapshot of life when we do not provide a strong education in traditional values.

Schools have lost their moral focus and, thus, their ability to educate youth in the most important of areas—morality. Without a moral focus, other learnings are shallow. Bryce Christensen (1991), director of the Rockford Institute Center on the Family in America, argues persuasively that schools have become ideological centers for crusades against family and traditional values. He buttresses his points with numerous quotations, including an apt insight from sociologist Kingsley Davis: "One of the main functions of [the school system] . . . appears to be to alienate offspring from their parents" (p. 6).

Christensen raises important questions about teachers who presume to supersede parents in implanting moral values in children. Further, he cites the work of Paul Vitz and Michael Levin, who document an aggressive feminist bias in school texts and teachings—a feminist bias in opposition to traditional American family values. Traditional parenthood and family life are virtually censored from school materials, while the same materials convey romantic images of adventurous single women. Similarly, reports Christensen, traditionalist parents have good reason to worry about amoral messages in literature that denounces religion and espouses adultery or other antifamily values.

Radical feminism is not the only culprit in the theft of morality from the schools. Similar attacks on American family values have appeared under the banners of "diversity," "multiculturalism," and "sexual orientation." These banners share the root idea of moral relativism, the idea that all views are equally valid in the classroom—from mercy killing to abortion to gay and lesbian advocacy. As it destroys traditional values, moral relativism substitutes immorality as a guide to life. While claiming that no values are more important than any others, advocates propose a set of special interests that they claim deserve special treatment in classrooms and textbooks: mercy killings, abortions, and homosexuality are examples of perfectly acceptable conduct, while praying in school is not. This is hypocrisy.

## *Traditional Values Can Be Restored to Schools*

Although it is possible to differentiate among the topics of values, ethics, morals, and character, school programs under the labels "values education," "ethics education," "moral education," and "character education" often use the same principles, purposes, and general practices. Often they are so similar as to be interchangeable, and we will treat them as such. At the core of the best of these programs is an effort to restore traditional values to the schools and to students: and these good programs work.

There is a tight relationship between good families and good schools in a society based on common values. The increasing disillusionment many Americans feel concerning the drift of the nation and the decline of schools causes them to want to stem the downward trend. The good news is that efforts to bring schools and society back to their moral base can yield positive results. A decade ago, a coalition of groups supporting family values and school morality were successful in elections in San Diego County in California, putting strong citizens in about two-thirds of the open seats on school boards and city councils. Pat Robertson's Christian Coalition described San Diego as a model of what we can do in local communities to reestablish morality in schools and society. Local agendas now include maintaining traditional values in the school curriculum; stemming the tide of antifamily education, such as providing birth control classes; and fighting to bring religion back as basic to schooling (Rabkin, 1995). A continuing series of elections which replace liberal politicians with more conservative ones reflect the general discontent with the direction the United States took during the Progressive Period.

Among the agenda items in the new movement for family values is the restoration of religion to U.S. schools. The Freedom Alliance works to restore America's first principles: traditional morality, close and strong families, free enterprise, solid schools, and vigorous national defense. Other indicators of success include the increasing number and quality of educational materials available for teachers and parents. The Character Education Institute provides teaching materials aimed at instilling universal values in students: honor, honesty, truthfulness, kindness, generosity, helpfulness, courage, convictions, justice, respect, freedom, and equality (Character Education Institute, 1998). The Bureau of Essential Ethics Education in California maintains a Character Education Center on the Internet. The Education Index listed the Center as one of the best education-related sites on the Internet, and *USA Today* featured it as a "Hot Site" in 1998. The Bureau advocates core ethical values, and it has created a system to help children understand these values by relating them to parts of the body:

1. Positive mental attitude (mind)
2. Respect (eyes and ears)
3. Integrity (mouth)
4. Compassion (heart)
5. Cooperation (hands)
6. Perseverance (stomach or guts)
7. Initiative (feet)

The Bureau's research studies followed children over a twenty-year period, the most comprehensive ethics education study ever done in the United States. The studies found extraordinarily high levels of success in students' ability to identify and write knowledgeably about these ethical values after participating in the Bureau's educational programs.

Stimulated by a concern about character education in schools, a variety of private foundation and government grants have emerged to assist in the movement for improved character education. Some grants from the U.S. Office of Eucation have enabled the establishment and development of model centers and special programs for character education in a number of states, including North Carolina, California, Iowa, New Mexico, Utah, Connecticut, Maryland, Washington, Missouri, Kentucky, New Jersey, and South Carolina. These efforts indicate large-scale interest in recharging the schools with moral, ethical, and character education. The centers sponsor such activities as programs devoted to creating safe and orderly school environments, encouraging students to take responsibility for their conduct and for others, preventing violence, and reinforcing efforts to curb drug abuse and weapons in school. Character education is developing quickly into one of the most important new projects in the schools; it offers the opportunity to correct generations of deficient schooling.

## Schools Are Rooted in Moral Values

Schools in America were founded to provide a moral foundation, and they were effective. Colonial schools had as their core a firm commitment to morality, ethics, and traditional values. Basic to these values was a firm belief in religion, even though the denominations differed among the various colonies.

The first school laws, passed in Massachusetts in 1642 and 1647, mandated that communities provide schooling for young people and that those schools preserve religious and social values. The *New England Primer,* the colonial schoolbook used to teach the alphabet and reading, incorporated moral virtues in its teaching of basic skills. All school books followed this pattern for many generations. Early Americans clearly recognized the link between a good society and solid religious, family, and school values. Religion continues to be a firm foundation for teaching traditional values, and it should not be kept out of public school classrooms (Schiltz, 1998).

Religion affords a good moral base for young people, but it isn't the only source of traditional values. Ethical personal behavior also derives from deep-rooted family and social values. The good society depends on citizens who have developed keen concern for others, awareness of personal responsibility, and habits of moderation (McFarlane, 1994). Etzioni (1998) argues that values education has broad and deep support among the American public, and he proposes that "we just teach the values that most American agree upon" (p. 448). Sommers (1998) presents a clear case for classical moral education for students, the "core of noncontroversial ethical issues that were settled long ago. . . . We need to bring back the great books and the great ideas" (pp. 33,34).

The basic ethical traditions that undergird strong and positive character traits are necessary in a civil society, but many people in our modern, selfish, and individualistic world have forsaken them. Not all families or social groups exhibit values conducive to the good society because they themselves are in deep moral decay. That is why schooling to preserve and protect traditional values is so essential. Schools, unfortunately, have fallen prey to the same selfish and corrupting ideas that have destroyed some families and some segments of society.

## Secular Humanism and the Loss of Values

Schools no longer lead in the reaffirmation of traditional family and religious values, but instead have become leaders in spreading secular humanism and its selfish pursuits. Secular humanism, with its relativistic and narcissistic values, has corrupted much of public life. It has permeated the public schools; it has fostered permissiveness and kept students from developing a personal core of values. This is certainly one reason why family life has fallen apart and why religious involvement has declined. Most young people of the post-World War II generation were indoctrinated with secular humanism in school, even though they may not have recognized its pernicious influence. Thus, it is easy to understand how family and religious life would suffer as that generation became parents. Now at least two generations have gone through the program, and American society is reaping the social discontent that secular humanism can produce.

Secular humanism holds that the state is more important than religion, and that humans can create and change their values without reference to a greater being. This means that any current fad can become the ethical code for the society. If enough people want to do something, they simply do it, no matter how much it may damage society or moral law. If what they want to do is illegal, they flout the law and put pressure on public officials to ignore higher values. In some instances, they alter the law to erode basic values further. Legalized gambling and easy abortions are examples of this practice.

Secular humanism, and the relativistic values it promotes, caters to the basest of human desires. Because it provides no guidelines for behavior or thought, it represents permissiveness at its most extreme. Secular humanism is now the dominant view in the public schools.

Jerry Falwell (1980) described the destruction of American education:

> Until about thirty years ago, the public schools in America were providing . . . support for our boys and girls. Christian education and the precepts of the Bible still permeated the curriculum of the public schools. . . . Our public schools are now permeated with humanism. . . . children are taught that there are no absolute rights or wrongs and that the traditional home is only one alternative. (pp. 205, 210)

Senator Strom Thurmond, a strong Constitutionalist, wrote a ringing criticism of Supreme Court decisions that "assault the Constitution." Among the decisions he criticizes as leaving the country open to communism, collectivism, and immorality are the Court's actions to prohibit prayer and Bible reading in public schools. He asserts:

> They [parents] ought to have a right to insist that their children are educated in the traditions and values of their own culture. Above all, they have a right to see that their children are not indoctrinated in a secular, Godless point of view which contradicts the values that are taught at home. (Thurmond, 1968, p. 28)

## How Schools Destroy Values

In many schools, children are taught that the values they learn in the home or at church are a matter of choice. Through teachings such as "values clarification," children are led to believe that right and wrong are purely matters of individual opinion. There is no moral guideline for conduct or thought. In values clarification, the teacher may ask a child to publicly identify situations when his or her father or mother was wrong and to present his or her own view of what the parent should have done. Teachers ask children personal questions about their family lives and private thoughts. And they present lists of antisocial behaviors and ask the children to rank them according to their own opinions of whether the behaviors are "good" or "bad." The teacher does not present correct responses or try to explain why a particular view is right. There are no criteria children can use to weigh right and wrong. Instead, the teacher encourages each child to determine his or her own set of values.

In class discussions on values, children who present their personal opinions with conviction can influence other children, and the teacher is not to intercede for fear of impeding the "clarification" of values. It is possible for an entire class to agree that tying cans to a cat's tail, euthanizing people who are old or ill, or remaining seated during the salute to the flag may be acceptable behavior. Children also learn to report on their parents and to ridicule those who support traditional values concerning discretion and privacy.

Dr. Elmer Towns, in a hard-hitting book, documents the failures of public education and the resulting threat to U.S. society. In a chapter entitled "The Smell of Deterioration," he writes:

> What has "had it" in public schools? Bible reading and prayers are not legal; they have "had it." The Puritan/Protestant ethic as a style of life has been edged out by the new morality; it has "had it." Dedication to academic pursuits is no longer prized by the majority of educators; it has "had it." Correct behavior, according to respected society norms, is no longer enforced; it has "had it." . . . the question that screams for an answer is, "Has our nation 'had it'?" (Towns, 1974, p. 23)

It is ridiculous to assert that young children can exert self-restraint and make critical judgments without proper training. The government requires school attendance but neglects and undercuts the moral basis required for a proper education in values.

## Confusing Values in the Current Curriculum

The school curriculum and textbooks schools now use present a wide array of relativistic values that only confuse children. Secular humanism is not defined as a school subject, and schools offer no courses in it. Instead, it filters into nearly all courses and often goes unrecognized, even by teachers. Because there is no specific curriculum that stresses traditional morals and values, it is easy for teachers and courses to present differing views, and to lead students to believe there are no eternal or universal values, only personal ones. If the courses and the teachers do not attest to a common core of morality, students are left morally rudderless. This spawns confusion or self-indulgence at best, and scorn for morality at worst.

The teaching materials children learn from are often either vapid, without any connection to moral thought and behavior, or confusing, because they display multiple values of supposedly equal weight. Current reading materials in school include nonsensical stories with no moral conclusions, trash that directs attention to the values of the worst elements of society, and adult stories well beyond the moral development of children. In civics and history, the focus is on political power, not virtue. Children are taught how to manipulate others and how interest groups get their way. History texts are bland and noncommittal concerning basic values and treat religion with disdain. Sex education instruction tends toward the belief that students will engage in promiscuity and sexual freedom, not exercise abstinence and responsibility (Whitehead, 1994). Science ignores religious views and substitutes the "value-free: ideas; any scientific experiment is okay. And the arts include the study of depraved artists and music, rather than uplifting and positive arts. Instead of protecting and encouraging innocence, schools savage and debase it (Rafferty, 1968).

The results of this permissive and selfish education are apparent. We are subject to increasing abuse in contemporary life. We have seen a startling increase in child abuse, so prevalent we now have twenty-four-hour telephone hotlines to report it. Spousal abuse is another item featured almost daily in the newspapers. Animal abuse is so common it no longer makes news. And sex and drug abuse have become epidemic.

Other abuses abound in the current world. We abuse our ideals, our respect, our heroes, our national honor, and our religious base. Political and business leaders abuse the public trust through cheating and corruption. Young people no longer understand why we fought wars to protect our liberties. Some children refuse to recite the Pledge of Allegiance or to sing the "Star-Spangled Banner." Graffiti covers many of our national monuments and our statues of heroes. Children no longer honor their parents or respect their elders.

What is the reason for this decline in our values? There are many reasons, but the foremost is that the schools have foresaken the responsibility to teach solid values. Instead, they have substituted highly relativistic opinions that undermine parental and religious authority. Children are taught that all values are equal, so whatever they value is fine. We can't hold children responsible for this rejection of common morality because their natural tendency is to be selfish.

Parents must teach children to share and to respect traditional social values. Historically, we have relied on the school to reinforce and extend the basic ethical code families, churches, and other religious institutions teach. In those unfortunate circumstances when parents are unable, or refuse, to teach children right from wrong, the school has usually supplied this important function. Those who now run the schools have forgotten their history, and people who forget will repeat the mistakes of the past.

With the current high divorce rates and parents' lack of attention to their children's moral development, the schools should be expected to play an even more significant role in conveying American values to children. In times of family and social stress, the schools should exert expanded influence to ensure the continuation of our heritage. Active membership in religion is beginning to increase as people recognize the insidious moral vacuum created during the most recent period of permissiveness. But many of our young parents grew up during the 1960s and 1970s, when there was a sharp decline in religious participation and a significant increase in immorality. Without the value base that strong religious and national traditions provide, the United States will be in trouble. Schools must assume an increased responsibility for training students in the traditional values our society needs.

## What Should Be Taught: Traditional Values as the Focus

Clearly, schools need to rediscover their proper role and function in a moral society. The United States was founded on Judeo-Christian ideals. We have survived, and thrived, because of these ideals. They form the basis of our concepts of justice and democracy. Schools were established to transmit those values to the young in order to preserve the values and the society.

Early American schooling was deliberately intended to instill a belief in God and support for traditional values. Schools had a clarity of purpose and a solid direction. Children did not receive mixed messages about morality and behavior, and they did not get the impression that they could make up and change their values on a whim.

The curriculum should include a prominent focus on traditional values at all levels. In elementary school, reading material should emphasize ideals (Anderson, 1994). Stories of great heroes, personal integrity, resoluteness, loyalty, and productivity should dominate. The main emphasis should be on the positive aspects of U.S. history and literature, showing how individuals working together toward a suitable goal can succeed. Teachers should stress and expect ethical behavior, respect, and consideration. Classes should study various religions with the purpose of understanding their common values and how those values apply to life. Providing time in school for children to reflect on their personal religious beliefs would be appropriate.

Signs and symbols in school should reinforce American values. Pictures, displays, and assemblies on morality offer students a chance to see how important those values are to society and the school. Inviting speakers into classes, showing films, and taking students to see significant monuments to American values are techniques that can help. Teachers can emphasize good values by providing direct instruction on moral precepts and rewarding students for good citizenship.

At the secondary level, the emphasis on traditional values should continue with more sophisticated materials and concepts. There is no need for a special course on sex education if family values are covered in other courses. A student honor roll, citing acts of outstanding school citizenship, might be as prominently displayed as the athletic trophies that now typically dominate glass cabinets near the principal's office. Libraries are good places to set up special displays of books that feature the kinds of thoughts and behaviors we seek to encourage.

Literature classes should teach U.S. and foreign literature that portrays the rewards of moral behavior and the negative consequences of immorality. Schools might sponsor essay contests on subjects that convey a concern for morality. American history classes should express the ideals for which we stand and our extraordinary historical achievements. Science courses should feature stories of hard work and perseverance in making scientific discoveries, as well as stories of how basic values and religious views have guided many scientists in their work.

The arts are a rich place to show values through the study of paintings, compositions, sculptures, and other art forms that express the positive aspects of human life under a set of everlasting ideals. Not only can religious music and art be a part of the curriculum, but there are thousands of examples of non-religious art that idealize such values as the golden rule and personal virtue. The vocational subjects afford numerous ways to present good attitudes toward work, family, responsibility, loyalty, decency, and respect. Sports are an especially important place in which to reaffirm these same values; numerous professional and college teams pray together before matches, and many players are leading figures in setting high standards of moral conduct.

## Teachers for American Values

The kinds of teachers we need are those who demonstrate a strong personal commitment to traditional values and whose behaviors and lives exhibit that commitment. These teachers are the key to improved values education. Changes in curriculum or teaching materials will have no impact if the teachers who work directly with the young do not meet strong moral standards. Obviously, determining a teacher's moral beliefs goes beyond examining his or her college transcripts, since the subjects a person studies bear little relation to his or her moral conduct.

To preserve and protect American values in schools, states have a right to require high moral standards from those who obtain state licenses to teach in the public schools. Colleges that prepare teachers should examine potential students' records and deny entry to those with criminal or morally objectionable backgrounds (for example, a history of cheating or dishonesty). Applicants for teaching credentials should be expected to submit references that speak to their moral character. Since we ask this of lawyers who take state bar exams, why shouldn't we expect it of people going into teaching? As a part of the application procedure for teaching positions, schools should require applicants to prepare essays discussing their values. Clearly, the period of student teaching and the first few years of full-time teaching provide ample opportunity to screen young teachers to ensure that they uphold moral standards. If these criteria are clearly and publicly stated, they have fair warning. Teachers found wanting may need to find employment in some other occupation. They should not be retained in positions where they can influence the ideals of young people.

With a strengthened corps of teachers in the schools, we can rebuild American values. These teachers will demand better curricula, better teaching materials, and better student behavior. There will be an infectious quality about this renewed commitment to ethical behavior that will influence parents, government, and the media. The schools have a rich opportunity.

## Summary

It is possible to restore basic American values to the schools and to our young people. But a potential opportunity is not enough. It is crucial that we move quickly to reinvigorate our school leaders with the resolve to do it. We are facing a crisis of values in society, and the crisis is reflected in our schools. Our society is extremely vulnerable. The school must reassume its original responsibility for moral teachings.

From the *New England Primer* through McGuffy's *Readers,* the content studied in school was consistent with America's traditional values. We can learn much from the moral stories these old works present. Children learned it was wrong to misbehave at home, in the community, and at school. They learned the consequences of affronting the common morality by reading about what happened to those who did. They gained respect for proper authority in families, churches, society, and school. We need to reject the permissiveness and valuelessness of the current schools and return to emphasizing moral precepts and proper behavior. It will require considerable effort to rethink the curriculum and redirect teaching. The crisis in education has the same origin as the crisis in society: a decline in basic values. Correction in the schools is the main avenue to correction in society.

## POSITION 2: FOR LIBERATION

The primary purpose of education is liberation. Liberation from ignorance is the basis beneath freedoms from slavery, from dictatorship, and from domination. The freedom to know underlies the freedom to participate fully in a democracy, to enjoy justice and equality, and to live a healthy and satisfying life. The freedom to think and the freedom to act are based on the freedom to know. Any society that intends to be free and democratic must recognize an elemental equation: liberation = education. Schools that restrict and contort the minds of the young oppose that principle, and democratic civilization is the victim. The principles of liberation and education operate whether students are learning basic skills and knowledge, or values, ethical conduct, morality, and character development.

School is not a neutral activity. The very idea of schooling expresses a set of values. Social and individual decisions to provide and to participate in education are based on a set of values. The daily activity of education is value-laden. Everything schools do and decide not to do reflects a set of values. No school is value-free; neither are teachers or students. We educate and we are educated for some purpose we consider good. We teach what we think is a valuable set of ideas. How else could we construct education? It would be absurd to have schools without goals, teaching without purpose, curriculum without objectives. Schools, then, are heavily involved in a series of value-based decisions related to the kind of person and the kind of society we want to produce. *The Humanist* magazine, in 1998, reprinted a 1947 article by Thayer (1947/1998) that persuasively argued that effective character education (1) grows out of active relationships, and (2) is positive, not negative. Thayer's premise grew from educational philosopher W. H. Kilpatrick's observation that children learn what they live and live what they learn. This expresses the idea that children's values and ethics are influenced by their real environments, not by the dogma of hypocritical pronouncements, moralisms, or memorized do-nots. Schools provide values education through a variety of forms, whether they intend to or not.

## School Decisions About Values Education

The issue is not whether schools should be engaged in values education, since all are by their very nature. Rather, the issue is what kinds of values should be central to schoolwork. Teachers, textbooks, and schools in general all teach some set of values to young people. Schools can be organized and can operate in ways that develop conformity, obedience to external authorities, and passive and docile behavior. Schools can also work to develop thoughtful critics of society's problems, students who are willing to challenge social norms and pursue the continued improvement of humankind into the future (Kidder, 1994; Haydon, 1995). There are many variations on these purposes of either socializing students to conform to social values or liberating them to engage in social improvement.

Unfortunately for those who believe the schools have more significant social purposes, much of the activity in contemporary schools is devoted to producing docile and passive students who will be unlikely to challenge the status quo. Current materials for teaching values and character in schools are also intended to protect the status quo, to make students vessels for conformist behavior, and to offer a noncritical perspective on religious views. Kohn (1998), for example, provides ample evidence that "conventional character education rests upon behaviorism, conservatism, and religious dogma" (p. 455). Even more unfortunately for students and society, the schools are often successful in this purpose. School life focuses far too much on conformity, placing extreme pressure on all students to think, behave, and view life in the same way. The "standard model" approach to values leads to a stultifying school life based on rigid moral pronouncements and outdated slogans. This not only is hypocritical, since many adult citizens and educators do not adhere to the moralistic standards prescribed, but it destroys the creativity and energy of our young people.

John Stuart Mill (1859/1956) defines the commonplace conformist education of his time:

> A general State education is a mere contrivance for moulding people to be exactly like one another; and as the mould in which it casts them is that which pleases the predominant power in the government—whether this be a monarch, a priesthood, an aristocracy, or the majority of the existing generation—in proportion as it is efficient and successful, it establishes a despotism over the mind, leading by natural tendency to one over the body. (p. 129)

Mill's comments are still appropriate today. It is a sad commentary that many schools aim to produce obedient citizens to assure social control, not critical thinking.

In traditional schools, students are force-fed moralisms and value precepts that are inconsistent with what students see for themselves in society. Poorly paid teachers preach honesty while wealthy financiers, bankers, and politicians loot the public. Well-heeled or well-connected people who commit so-called white-collar crimes are seldom punished, although a few may be sent to luxurious detainment centers for brief stays. However, people from lower-social-class backgrounds who commit similar crimes often receive long and debilitating sentences in the worst prisons, where they learn more criminal behavior. This obvious disparity in our concept of justice is evident to students. Similar examples of disparity in equality and justice abound in our national life. Students are well aware of these inequities. A moralistic slogan does not hide the defect.

This is not an essay in favor of abandoning the civilizing characteristics of human society, including decency, respect, responsibility, courage, and magnanimity. Indeed, it is the opposite—a plea in favor of values that give students the power to develop and enhance civilization without hypocrisy. We cannot impose traditional, externalized values on schoolchildren without allowing criticism of those values. Students learn to conform in school in order to avoid problems, and, as a result, they learn to ignore social injustice and inequality. Instead of questioning and acting to improve society, students are expected to sponge up moralisms and be quiet. Philosopher Maxine Greene (1990) stated that moral choice and ethical action should be the products of careful and critical thought. That occurs when the community provides freedom and encouragement for individual students and teachers to engage such thinking.

## Liberation Education

Liberation education is obviously not a prescribed set of teacher techniques, a specific lesson plan, or a textbook series for schools to adopt. There is no mechanistic or teacher-proof approach that will produce liberation. Devious and robotlike educational theories, such as behavioral objectives and mastery learning, are not part of liberation education. Indeed, liberation is in direct opposition to the conformist mentality that produced such ideas. Liberation is the emancipation of students and teachers from the blinders of class-dominated ignorance, conformity, and thought control (Shor, 1987; Clark, 1990;

Ahlquist, 1991). It is dynamic, viewing students and teachers as active participants in opposing oppression and improving democracy (Giroux, 1991).

Liberation education is complex, because the social forces it addresses are complex. The central purpose is to liberate the individual and society from oppression and to broadly distribute liberating power. That, of course, requires a set of values, including justice and equality, to serve as ideals in opposition to oppression. It further requires a critical understanding of the many cultural cross-currents in contemporary society and the mechanisms of manipulation that hide ideological purposes. Liberation education uncovers the myths and injustices evident in the dominant culture. It also embraces the expectation that the powerless can, through education, develop power. This requires us to recognize that the forms of knowledge and schooling are not neutral, but are utilized by the dominant culture to secure its power.

Schools must become sites where we examine the conflicts of humankind in increasing depth in order to understand the ideological and cultural bases on which societies operate. The purpose is not merely to recognize those conflicts or ideologies, but to engage in actions that constrain oppression and expand personal power. This profound and revolutionary educational concept goes to the heart of what education should be. Schools themselves need to undergo this liberation, and we should take actions to make them more truly democratic. Other social institutions also merit examination and action. It is obvious that *liberation education,* a redundant term, is controversial in contemporary society. Liberated people threaten the traditional docility and passivity that schools now impose.

## *Mainstream Mystification*

There is too little in popular educational literature that speaks to liberation, opposition to oppressive forces, and the improvement of democracy. Most mainstream educational writing raises no questions about the context the school sits within; the writers seem to accept the conservative purposes of schools and merely urge us to "fine-tune" them a bit. Standard educational writing does not examine our schooling system to the depth of its roots, ideologies, and complexities. Instead, teachers and teachers-in-training read articles on implementing teaching techniques and making slight modifications in curriculum. There is nothing critical in these pieces, and there is no liberation of the mind from the strictures of a narrow culture. The dominant concern is to make the school more efficient, more mechanical, more factorylike, more conformist.

Mainstream educational literature rests on a mainstream of thought in American society. This thought is bound by a narrow band between standard conservative and liberal ideas. It is not considered good form to read materials, pose ideas, or raise criticisms from outside this band. Those who do are labeled radical or "un-American" and are viewed with suspicion. Outside ideas and criticisms have no public credibility. Mainstream thinkers disdain the effort to improve the way democracy works by subjecting it to critical evaluation, and neither conservatives nor liberals are pleased to see schools critically examine American democracy.

Conservatives and liberals do seem to agree that U.S. schools should support democracy. Numerous platitudes about schools preparing citizens for democracy, or about the school as a minidemocracy, fill the mainstream literature. This literature can be classified as mystification because it uses high-sounding phrases to cover its ideology, a continuation of the status quo and the power of the already dominant class. It is not active democracy, with its liberation values, that this literature commends. The real purpose of this line of thought is to keep the masses content as uncritical workers who believe themselves to be free but are actually bound and powerless. The function of mainstream writing, in other words, is to mystify readers with a rhetoric of freedom while maintaining the domination of the powerful.

Current educational terms, such as *excellence, standards, humanistic,* and *progressive,* fill mainstream periodicals. Although the terms may be useful in discussing education, they often serve as camouflage. Conservatives use the terms *excellence* and *standards* to mask the interests of the dominant classes in justifying their advantages and the interests of business in the production of skilled but docile workers. Liberals use the terms *humanistic* and *progressive* to hide a soft and comfortable individualism that ignores the basic problems and conflicts in society. Together, the terms combine the business ideology that dominates schools and society and the narcissism that prevents groups from recognizing the defects in that ideology. That is mystification—an effort to mystify the public and hide the real school agenda.

That agenda is to maintain what Joel Spring (1976) calls a "sorting machine," sorting the different social classes into various categories of citizenship. Raymond Callahan (1962) documents this agenda as a business orientation in schools, designed to prepare the masses to do efficient work and the elite to manage. Jean Anyon (1980) exposes the actual curriculum of docility and obedience taught to the lower classes. Henry Giroux (1988) describes the hidden curriculum that imposes dominant class values, attitudes, and norms on all students. And Aronowitz and Giroux (1991) identify the need for a strong schooling in criticism to buttress students against the crippling effects of the traditional values society imposes.

The mass media amplify the conservative and liberal arguments about schooling, but, in fact, little separates them. The schools can and do, by making slight modifications every few years, accommodate each side for a while. The pendulum swings in a narrow arc from the center, but schools remain pretty much the same, with only cosmetic changes. When conservatives are in power, people express more concern about competition, grading, passing tests, and knowing specific bits of information. Liberals try to make students feel happy, to allow more freedom in the curriculum, and to offer more student activities.

With regard to democracy and schooling, the differences between the conservative and liberal views lie in how narrowly democracy is defined and at what age students are to begin practicing democracy. The conservative rhetoric calls for a narrower definition and for the development of good habits and values among students before they can participate. That usually means that school is the place to learn the narrow definition and to learn the precepts of democracy without yet practicing it. Liberals call for a somewhat broader definition and for the establishment of schools as places where students can actually practice a form of democracy.

Neither the conservative nor the liberal mainstream view raises questions about the basic nature of democracy or the means we use to achieve it. Neither view is critical of existing class domination over knowledge and schools. Neither sees democracy as problematic, deserving continuing critical examination in order to improve it. Both views assume there is a basic consensus on what democracy is, and that the schools are an agency for achieving it. As a result, conservative and liberal views about schooling in a democracy differ very little. The two groups express only shallow differences over what subjects schools should emphasize and how much freedom students should have. Those may sound like important differences, but debates over such matters as how tough grading practices should be or whether students need extra time for reading drill do not address the serious and significant issues of democratic life. Ideologically, conservatives and liberals share basic beliefs.

## *Reactionary Indoctrination and Cultural Reproduction*

Only the reactionary fringe on the far right appears to desire schools and a society that are basically undemocratic in purpose and operation. At least the far-right wing is honest and direct, if wrong in their approach. These reactionary groups, including religious fundamentalists, are clear that a hierarchical social order must be imposed on children in schools. There is nothing democratic in that premise. Right-wingers are open advocates of indoctrination and censorship. If you know the *truth*, why would you present other ideas? Dissent, of course, should be stifled because it confuses children of all ages, and deviation cannot be tolerated. It is refreshing to see such clarity and determination in the face of the general uncertainty of the modern world, but this view has potentially disastrous consequences for any democracy and its schools.

Interestingly, both conservatives and liberals expect indoctrination, but they are loath to tell anyone because it sounds undemocratic. Instead, since they control the schools and the society, they can impose their dominant views by more subtle means. Through state laws, this coalition controls the school curriculum, textbook selection, school operation, and teacher licensing. State agencies—for example, a state department of education—monitor schools and prescribe limits. The news media, which are also dominated by mainstream conservative and liberal forces, persuade the public that the democracy and the schools are working relatively well. We see very little thoughtful criticism of either in the media; the news mainly reports minor disagreements on tactics and personalities. Ideological disputes are not confronted because no real disputes arise between the standard conservative and liberal views.

So schools are expected to indoctrinate students into the mainstream culture, and the mainstream has the power to require conformity. "Cultural reproduction" means that each generation passes on to the next the dominant cultural ideology that was imposed on it. In the United States, this cultural reproduction takes two forms: (1) a set of positive beliefs that the United States is a chosen country, with justice and equality for all and the best of economic systems; and (2) a set of negative beliefs that any views that raise troubling questions about American values are automatically anti-American. This two-fold reproduction ensures that teachers and students will not engage in serious critical thinking, but will merely accept the dominant ideologies. Thus, the very nature of democracy, and the means for improving it, are perceived as naturally existing and beyond the school's scope of inquiry.

In school, students read mainstream literature, hear mainstream views from teachers and peers, see mainstream films, listen to mainstream speakers, and engage in mainstream extracurricular activities. The school library carries only mainstream periodicals and books. It is virtually impossible to find an examination of highly divergent ideas. When students are not in school, they read the mainstream press, watch mainstream TV, and live in families of people who were educated in the same manner. Teachers prepare in colleges where they study mainstream views of their subjects and of the profession of teaching. It is no wonder that schools are prime locations for cultural reproduction; they contain no other sources of ideas. To have mainstream ideas broadly represented in schools is certainly not improper, but to suppress the critical examination of those ideas, and to limit students to such a narrow band of ideas, is not liberating.

Students are often surprised to stumble on a radical journal or book that legitimately challenges basic assumptions about capitalism and U.S. politics and their impact on justice and equality. Those students are rightfully concerned about an education that did not permit them to consider opposing values and ideologies. Unfortunately, the vast majority of students never come across radical materials, or they automatically and unthoughtfully reject any divergent views because the schools have effectively sealed their minds.

## Mainstream Control of Knowledge

Not only do schools sort and label students and limit the range of views that undergo examination, but they also provide class-biased knowledge to differing groups of students. Michael F. D. Young (1971), a British sociologist, has argued that "those in positions of power will attempt to define what is taken as knowledge, [and] how accessible to different groups knowledge is. . . ."

Essentially, those in power in schools guard the knowledge they consider high-status and use it to retain power and to differentiate themselves from the masses. High-status knowledge is thus determined by those who already have power. Although some auto mechanics, for example, must use complex skills and knowledge, it is not considered high-status knowledge. Law and medicine, which also utilize complex skills and knowledge, are considered high-status. Access to these professions is restricted.

As Michael Apple (1990) notes, a relationship exists between economic structure and high-status knowledge. A capitalist, industrial, technological society values the knowledge that most contributes to its continuing development.

Math, science, and computer study have demonstrably more financial support than do the arts and humanities. A master's degree in business administration, especially if it is from a "prestigious" institution, is more valuable than a degree in humanities. Technical subjects, such as math and the sciences, are more easily broken into discrete bits of information, and are more easily testable than are the arts and humanities. This leads to easy stratification of students, often along social class lines. The idea of school achievement is to compete well in the "hard" technical subjects where differentiation is easiest to measure. Upper-class students, however, are not in the competition, since they are protected and usually do not attend public schools. The upper middle class provides advantages for its children; the working-class child struggles to overcome disadvantage.

The separation of subjects in the discipline-centered curriculum serves to legitimize the high status of hard subjects and the academic preparatory sequence. Few critically examine the organization of knowledge or understand it as class-based or problematic. Instead, schools present information in segments and spurts, testing on detail and ranking students on how well they accept the school's definitions. We pretend that knowledge is neutral, that the numerous subject categories and titles are merely logical structures to assist understanding. This separates school learning from social problems, reinforces the existing authority's domination over what is important to know, and maintains students as dependent and uncritical thinkers.

## What Should Be Taught

Liberation education requires us to blend curriculum content with pedagogy. We cannot separate what students study from how they study it. The basis of this approach to schooling is to engage students in critical study of the society and its institutions with the dual purpose of liberating themselves from simple cultural reproduction and liberating the society from oppressive manipulation of the masses. Critical study involves both method and content. It expects an open examination and critique of diverse ideas and sees the human condition as problematic. That places all human activity within the scope of potential curriculum content and makes all activity subject to critical scrutiny through a dynamic form of dialectic reasoning.

Obviously, students cannot examine all things at all times. Thus, the selection of topics for study depends on several factors, including what students have previously studied, and the depth of those investigations; which contemporary social issues are significant; the interests and maturity level of the students; and the knowledge of the teacher. There is no neatly structured sequence of information that all students must pass through and then forget. Knowledge is active and dynamic; it is complex and intertwined. Students should come to understand that, and to examine the nature of knowledge itself. That can lead to liberation.

Among the topics of early and continuing study should be ideologies. Students need to learn how to strip away layers of propaganda and rationalization to examine root causes. Ideology, in its most literal sense, is the study of ideas. Those ideas may be phrased in a language intended for mystification, or designed to persuade people. Critical study looks below the surface expression to find the roots of ideas.

Ideology can also mean basic, undergirding values and beliefs. Racism and sexism are not considered acceptable public views in the United States, and yet they often lie behind high-sounding pronouncements and policies. We can rationalize using test scores from culturally biased tests to segregate students for favored treatment in neutral-sounding nonracist and nonsexist terms, but the basic causes and the consequences may well be racist or sexist. Imperialism is not considered proper in current international relations, but powerful nations do attempt to control others through physical or political-economic means while labeling their actions defensive or even "freedom fighting." Ideological study can help students situate events in historic, economic, and political settings that are deeper and richer than the surface explanations.

## The Dynamic Dialectic

Liberation education requires teachers and students to engage in a dynamic form of dialectic reasoning to uncover ideological roots. A dialectic requires students to analyze ideas by considering opposing sides, delving deeper into the basis of each to attempt a more reasoned understanding of the issue. There are at least two forms of dialectic reasoning. One, proposed by Plato, structures and limits the discourse to lead students to one fixed idea of truth. For example, Socrates knew the truth and led students to it by asking them questions, then subjecting their answers to further questions until the students came to accept Socrates' view. This is an authoritarian and false form of dialectic.

A dynamic dialectic opens topics to examination. It does not impose a set of absolutes with a known truth, but operates more like a spiral, digging deep into rationales. It examines the topic in its total social context, not in segments as in the discipline-centered curriculum. And it requires a vision of liberation that allows students to dig beneath the surface of the topic to uncover its basic relationships to the structure of society and to dominant interests. The purpose of the dialectic is to encourage students to transcend their traditional non-active, sterile roles and to accept active roles as knowledgeable participants in the improvement of civilization. In theory, the dialectic is never-ending, since civilization is in continual need of improvement. In practice in the schools, the dialectic is limited by time, energy, interest, and the topics under study.

Liberation education expects that schools will explore highly divergent ideas. But this in itself is insufficient. These divergent ideas must be examined in a setting where they can be fully developed and are perceived as legitimate, rather than strange or quaint. Adequate time and resources must be available, and censorship and authoritarianism kept at bay.

To ensure a truly liberated society, one cannot expect less of schools than education for liberation. An emancipatory climate in schools will regenerate students and teachers to fully use their intellects and creativity. Those are fitting and proper goals for schools, unachievable under the restricted mainstream forms of schooling our society now practices. This is values education.

## *For Discussion*

1. You have been asked to appoint ten members to a statewide advisory council. The council's charge is to identify how the schools should approach values education.

    a. What kinds of people would you select, and how many of each? Why?

    b. What educational background should be required?

    c. What occupations should be represented, and in what proportions?

    d. What groups or agencies should be represented, and in what proportions?

    e. What age, gender, or ethnic categories should be represented, and in what proportions?

    f. What other characteristics would you look for?

    g. What kinds of people would you want to exclude? Why?

2. An advisory council appointed in New Jersey compiled the following list of values to be taught in New Jersey schools:

    Civic responsibility, based on:

    acknowledgment of authority

    global awareness

    justice, fairness

    patriotism

    property rights

    Respect for the natural environment, based on:

    care and conservation of all living inhabitants

    care and conservation of land, air, water

    conduct based on interdependence of environment

    Respect for others, based on:

    compassion and service

    courtesy and cooperation

    honesty

    loyalty

    moderation

    recognition and understanding of various religions

    regard for human life

    tolerance

    Respect for self, based on:

    accountability

    courage

    diligence, commitment, reliability

frugality, thrift

knowledge, learning

moral courage

self-esteem, pride

What do you think of this list? What would you change? Do you think the schools can and should convey these values to students? Are there inconsistencies or conflicts among the values? How should these be addressed? Whose interests are served by the values in this list? Are the values more consistent with traditional views or with liberation education?

3. Paulo Freire, an advocate of liberation education, claims that traditional teaching is fundamentally "narrative," leaving the subject matter "lifeless and petrified." Freire writes:

> The teacher talks about reality as if it were motionless, static, compartmentalized, and predictable. Or else he expounds on a topic completely alien to the existential experience of the students. His task is to "fill" the students with the contents of his narration—contents which are detached from reality. . . . The more completely he fills the receptacles, the better a teacher he is. The more meekly the receptacles permit themselves to be filled, the better students they are. (1970, pp. 57, 58)

Does this description fit your experience in schools? Criticize Freire's view of this "banking" form of education. Has he properly characterized what happens in schools? Should it happen? What are the social costs of changing to liberation education? What are the costs of not changing?

4. Many people agree that we should teach values in school, but they disagree about which values and who makes that choice. Some propose everlasting universal values; others propose utilitarian short-term values; some propose general and vague social values; and still others propose values based on individual or immediate circumstances. What is a reasonable way to determine what kind of values education we should be teaching in U.S. schools? What possible social consequences can you foresee for the various forms of values education?

## References

AHLQUIST, R. (1991). "Critical Pedagogy for Social Studies Teachers." *Social Studies Review* 29, 53–57.

ANDERSON, D. (1994). "The Great Tradition." *National Review* 46, 56–58.

ANYON, J. (1980). "Social Class and the Hidden Curriculum of Work." *Journal of Education* 162, 67–92.

APPLE, M. (1990). *Ideology and Curriculum.* 2nd edition. London: Routledge & Kegan Paul.

ARONOWITZ, S., AND GIROUX, H. A. (1991). *Postmodern Education: Culture, Politics, and Social Criticism.* Minneapolis: University of Minnesota Press.

BENNETT, W. J. (1994). "America at Risk." *USA Today* 123, 14–16.

CALLAHAN, R. (1962). *Education and the Cult of Efficiency.* Chicago: University of Chicago Press.

CHARACTER EDUCATION INSTITUTE. (1998). Online available at http://www.charactered-ucation.com.

CHRISTENSEN, B. (1991). "Pro: The Schools Should Presume that Parents have the Primary Authority to Determine the Cultural Traditions to Be Transmitted to Pupils." Debates in Education. *Curriculum Review* 31, 6–10.

CLARK, M. A. (1990). "Some Cautionary Observations on Liberation Education." *Language Arts* 67, 388–398.

COLSON, C. (1994). "Begging for Tyranny." *Christianity Today* 38, 80–81.

ETZIONI, A. (1998). "How Not to Discuss Character Education." *Phi Delta Kappan* 79, 446–448.

FALWELL, J. (1980). *Listen, America!* Garden City, NJ: Doubleday.

FREIRE, P. (1970). Pedagogy of the Oppressed. New York: Herder and Herder.

GIROUX, H. (1988). *Teachers as Intellectuals.* Granby, MA: Bergin & Garvey.

——— (1990). "Curriculum Theory, Textual Authority, and the Role of Teachers as Public Intellectuals." *Journal of Curriculum and Supervision* 4, 361–383.

——— (1991). "Curriculum Planning, Public Schooling, and Democratic Struggle." *NASSP Bulletin* 75, 12–25.

GREENE, M. (1990). "The Passion of the Possible." *Journal of Moral Education* 19, 67–76.

——— (1991). "Con: The Schools Should Presume that Parents Have the Primary Authority to Determine the Cultural Traditions to Be Transmitted to Pupils." Debates in Education. *Curriculum Review* 31, 6–10.

HAYDON, G. (1995). "Thick or Thin: The Cognitive Content of Moral Education." *Journal of Moral Education* 24, 53–64.

KIDDER, R. (1994). "Universal Human Values." *The Futurist* 28, 8–14.

KOHN, A. (1998). "Adventures in Ethics Behavioral Control." *Phi Delta Kappan* 79, 455–460.

MILL, J. S. (1859/1956). *On Liberty,* edited by C. V. Shields. Indianapolis: Bobbs-Merrill.

LATHER, P. (1991). *Getting Smart: Feminist Research and Pedagogy Within the Postmodern.* New York: Routledge.

MCFARLANE, A. (1994). "Radical Educational Values." *America* 171, 10–13.

RABKIN, J. (1995). "Let Us Pray." *The American Spectator* 28, 46–47.

RAFFERTY, M. (1968). *Max Rafferty on Education.* New York: Devon-Adair.

READ, L. (1968). *Accent on the Right.* Irvington-on-Hudson, NY: Foundation for Economic Education.

ROBERTS, S. V. (1994). "America's New Crusade." *U.S. News and World Report* 117, 26–29.

SCHILTZ, P. (1998). "Don't Leave Religion Out of the Classroom." *U. S. Catholic,* 63,22–23.

SHOR, I. (1987). *Pedagogy for Liberation.* South Hadley, MA: Bergin & Garvey.

——— (1989). "Developing Student Autonomy in the Classroom." *Equity and Excellence* 24, 35–37.

SOMMERS, C. H. (1998). "Are We Living in a Moral Stone Age?" *Current,* 403, 31–34.

SOWELL, T. (1992). "A Dirty War." *Forbes* 150, 63.

SPRING, J. (1976). *The Sorting Machine: National Educational Policy Since 1945.* New York: McKay.

THAYER, V. T. (1947/1998). "The School as a Character-Building Agency." *The Humanist* 58, 42–43.

THURMOND, S. (1968). *The Faith We Have Not Kept.* San Diego, CA: Viewpoint Books.

TOWNS, E. T. (1974). *Have the Public Schools "Had It"?* New York: Nelson.

WEILER, K. (1991). "Freire and a Feminist Pedagogy of Difference." *Harvard Educational Review* 61, 449–474.

WHITEHEAD, B. D. (1994). "The Failure of Sex Education." *The Atlantic Monthly* 274, 55–80.

YOUNG, M. F. D. (1971). *Knowledge and Control.* London: Collier-Macmillan.

# CHAPTER 12

# Business Influence: Positive or Negative

## POSITION 1: FOR INCREASED BUSINESS INFLUENCE

Good schools are simply good business. Businesspeople, from the small shop-keeper to the executive of a major corporation, recognize that there may be no more important work in American society than the improvement of schools. America's vitality and the health of our economy depend on schools. The president of the National Education Association, in announcing a new form of responsible unionism, stated: "Despite the political rhetoric, public schools and business are natural allies" (Chase, 1998).

Consistent with these beliefs, business leaders are in the forefront of efforts to reform schools (Ramsey, 1993). Goals 2000, the national strategy to improve schools, identifies the business community as essential to such improvements—business will "jump-start" the design of the new U.S. schools, will use new national tests to aid in hiring, and will provide resources to lead the changes (*America 2000*, 1991, p. 23). Business stands ready to take on this task (Szabo, 1990; Miller, 1991). In fact, business leaders spearheaded the 1992 establishment of the Education Excellence Partnership, a coalition including the Business Roundtable, the U.S. Department of Education, the American Federation of Teachers, the National Education Association, the National Governors Conference, and the U.S. Chamber of Commerce.

A recent demonstration of the strength of the business community's interest in schools is the production of *A Common Agenda for Improving American Education* (1997), a joint statement by the chairs of the Business Roundtable Education Task Force, the U. S. Chamber of Commerce, and the National Alliance of Business. The agenda stems from the concern that "the graduates of America's schools are not prepared to meet the challenge posed by global economic competition. . . . business continues to have trouble finding qualified workers" (p. 1). This somber concern stimulates U.S. business leaders to help improve education. Steps they advocate in the agenda include:

1. Help educators and policymakers establish tough academic standards to be applied to every student.
2. Assess the performance of students and school systems against the standards.
3. Use information from the assessments to improve schools and hold them accountable, providing rewards for success and consequences for failure.

The agenda also encourages business leaders to be more active in school reform, to consider the commitment of various states to high academic standards in making business location decisions, and to offer philanthropy to support school improvement initiatives. Businesses can make a significant positive impact on American education. Organizations of business leaders have already started the process.

The Business Roundtable includes the CEOs of 200 of the most prominent U.S. corporations, companies that employ about 34 million people. After major national reports on the quality of American education, the Business Roundtable made a ten-year commitment to reform the public education system. By 1996, almost all of the member businesses had formed school partnerships for educational improvement. These corporate-supported school activities focused on such diverse areas as academic instructional improvement, career awareness, civic and character education, drug prevention, dropout prevention, and programs for the disadvantaged. Corporations help schools in these key areas because they recognize the value of helping students reach their full potential. This is not a new role for business leadership in U.S. schools; business–education relations have a long and positive history. The perception of crisis in the U.S. education system has stimulated increased interest.

## Why Should Business Be Concerned?

Serious problems confront the United States because schools fail to provide students with solid skills and workplace values. Many who seek employment have inadequate skills or attitudes. Schools have not sufficiently prepared them for work. The magazine *Nation's Business* (Bates, 1998) reports a significant increase in the number of CEOs who have reported over the past several years that they were lowering corporate earnings estimates because of a shortage of skilled workers. In 1992, only 27 percent reported this type of negative economic impact caused by the poor skills of workers; by 1995, almost half reported the problem, and by 1998, almost 70 percent of the CEOs indicated that company earnings would be lower because of workers' educational defects. About half of the CEOs surveyed said they were unsatisfied with the quality of job applicants. William Brock, former U.S. Secretary of Labor, stated, "Public education today is totally inadequate to the task. Our schools are not designed for the workplace" (Bates, 1998).

As the surveys indicate, significant numbers of those already employed are illiterate or lack good work habits. Because of this, in addition to directly supporting schools, U.S. business spends billions of dollars annually on remedial education for employees. The United States is losing its competitive advantage because the workforce is undereducated. This crisis is particularly hurtful in a time of rapid technological change, especially when workers' skills are improving in other nations. A dramatic shift has already occurred in the production of electronics, automobiles, furniture, and other consumer goods: High-quality products are now manufactured in Japan, Taiwan, Korea, and other places.

We need people who are competent in basic skills, who can understand technical manuals and operations, and who can work with management in a cooperative effort to strengthen the nation's economy. In far too many schools, students have trouble following simple written forms and directions, understanding low-level technical information, and maintaining interest in their work. As *Newsweek* education editor Gilbert Sewall (1984) describes it:

> For at least 23 million Americans, the instructions in a laundromat are mystifying; reading a repair manual or filling out a job application accurately is impossible. Bluntly stated, these citizens do not have the survival skills to compete in a highly specialized service economy that values, above all, mental agility and reliability. Consequently, they have little or no stake in the future of democratic capitalism. These functional illiterates are condemned to live on the fringe of the polity as menial laborers, as welfare recipients, as outlaws, as the emotionally tortured and spiritually broken. Doomed to insecure, insolvent, and possibly violent futures, they are what society considers failed people. (pp. 3–4)

## *Preparing Non-College-Bound Students for Employment*

In addition to our general need to improve instruction in basic skills and workplace attitudes for all young people, we also need to better prepare non-college-bound students for employment. A considerable part of the current school reform movement has been directed at improving the academic quality of schools for those who plan to go to college. The majority of students, however, take jobs immediately after graduating from high school or drop out before graduation and try to find employment.

The Commission on Work, Family, and Citizenship, sponsored by the W. T. Grant Foundation, produced a report on the issue of work and non-college-bound youth. One of their criticisms of schooling for students not planning to go to college is that "a larger percentage of them are finding it harder than ever to swim against the economic tide" (*The Forgotten Half*, 1988, p. 410). The commission agrees "with those who say that America needs to 'work smarter' and raise productivity in order to be competitive with other nations" (p. 412).

The commission recommends a number of ways to bridge the gap from school to work, including intensive training in basic skills, a monitored work experience of apprenticeships and preemployment training, improved vocational education, incentives from businesses and mentors to do well in school, and better career counseling.

An important recommendation of the commission is to foster stronger alliances between employers and schools. Business leaders can come into the schools to teach, to talk with students, and to help teachers and guidance counselors develop programs to improve student skills and attitudes. In addition, students can visit places of employment. The alliances can establish work–study arrangements for students, produce teaching materials, and provide financial support for improving school technology and career guidance. Many businesses participate in "Adopt-a-School" programs that enrich the school's ability to prepare students for employment. Other businesses invite teachers to visit, provide summer employment and other opportunities for teachers to learn about their operations, and prepare free teaching materials. Business has a strong interest in improving education (Gilbert, 1993; Crain, 1994). Industries cannot survive without a well-prepared workforce, and they recognize this.

The Boston Compact, for example, established a partnership between Boston's schools and the Boston Private Industry Council. Businesses promised students jobs if the schools were able to raise test scores and decrease dropout rates. This alliance has provided jobs for over a thousand graduates, and reading and math scores have improved (Fiske, 1988, p. B8).

Mann (1987) examined school–business partnerships and concluded that "partnerships between businesses and the schools have made positive contributions to the public schools . . . [they] have offered concrete assistance to the schools in a number of ways" (p. 228). These contributions included cash, services, sympathy, and assistance in political and economic coalitions. Mann notes several problems with school–business alliances as well, but cites a large number of examples where businesses have been particularly helpful in improving local schools.

## Education and the Changing Nature of Employment in the United States

Prominent changes in the nature of employment in American society have had major implications for schools. Historically, the shift was from agricultural to manufacturing jobs; now the shift is from manufacturing to service. In the short space of the last fifty years, the proportion of farmers and farm workers has declined from almost 20 percent of the workforce to only 3 percent; manufacturing jobs have declined from about 32 percent to 27 percent of total employment, whereas service jobs have increased from about 53 percent to 69 percent. The service sector has grown primarily in social and producer services (for example, health and medical technology), rather than in personal services (for example, hairdressing or domestic work) or distributive services (sales and delivery). The most prominent change has been in the kinds of jobs available. White-collar jobs rose from about 45 percent of the labor force in 1940 to over 70 percent by the mid-1980s. Blue-collar jobs declined from about 42 percent to about 27 percent over the same period.

In educational terms, this means students need more and better schooling. Many agricultural jobs no longer demand just sheer physical labor, but involve technical work that requires strong academic skills. White-collar jobs typically require increased education. In a report on economic trends in the United States, a group of Oxford scholars commented: "Indeed, it is well-documented that over recent decades a person's job and level of income have become influenced more and more by his or her level of education and formal qualifications" (Oxford Analytica, 1986, p. 68). Blau and Duncan (1967), in a classic study of the relationship between education and jobs, reported a high correlation between job status and education. Social class and occupational experience were also considered influential in employment status, but education had the greatest effect. More recently, a U.S. Census Bureau report demonstrated that high school graduates earn only about 50 percent of the average income college graduates earn (*Educational Attainment in the United States: March 1998*).

In earlier times in U.S. history, basic literacy could be recommended purely for its inherent values; it had no special relation to people's work requirements. In a period when most citizens lived rural, agricultural lives, reading, writing, and calculating were nice to know, but not necessary for securing employment. Even in those times, however, obvious links existed between education and employment. A study conducted in 1867 by the Commonwealth of Pennsylvania, for example, showed that income related directly to literacy: Those who could not read earned an average of $36 per month; those who could read, but were otherwise poorly educated, earned an average of $52 a month; and those who were well-educated earned an average of $90 a month (Soltow and Stevens, 1981). Other studies have corroborated this point. But literacy for business purposes does not mean just proficiency in reading and writing. As Soltow and Stevens, in examining the history of literacy in the United States, note, "To be literate, as we have seen, did not simply mean to be competent at a specific level of reading mastery. It meant, perhaps more importantly for the employer, exposure to a set of values compatible with a disciplined workforce" (pp. 127–128). There is clear evidence schools should give more importance not just to reading but to basic skills and workplace values.

For all students, college-bound or not, we need to improve our instruction in the knowledge and attitudes that contribute to our society. Permissive education has led to indolence, narcissism, and a rebellious attitude against all forms of authority. The mistaken notion that we can do as we wish has caused our society to suffer. Schools need to redirect their energies toward developing students' pride in workmanship, increasing productivity, and fostering good citizenship in a nation where competition and free enterprise offer the most opportunities for all.

## Democracy, Capitalism, and the Business of Education

The strength of U.S. society lies in the fortuitous combination of democracy and capitalism. We not only offer freedom and opportunity in politics (the democratic concept), but also in economics. The freedom to engage in enterprise without obstructive governmental interference provides opportunities and incentives for everyone. Free enterprise is a basic condition for releasing the entrepreneurial spirit in humans, and entrepreneurs built and developed this great nation. People of merit and ideas of merit rise to the top. In order for the meritorious to stay at the top, the free marketplace requires continual improvement. This nation has moved from being a minor colony to a world power because of this spirit of freedom and ingenuity. Many other nations have tried to emulate American entrepreneurship.

The complete breakdown of most communist countries at the end of the 1980s illustrates the flawed nature of socialism. The death of communism will find the early twenty-first century a world of competing capitalist nations. This new scenario requires even more U.S. commitment to an education-business partnership. Schooling that will maintain our leadership in international business competition is a top priority. Schools have not demonstrated their ability to produce qualified students in the quantities required for international leadership. Business must enter into new and more intertwined partnerships with schools to ensure that the United States keeps its competitive edge in global markets.

## Business Approaches to School Operation

Not only do schools fail to give students basic skills and good workplace attitudes, but a corollary problem arises in the way schools operate. Schools are inefficient. Their organization and operation have not changed during the twentieth century, while industry has made remarkable progress in becoming more efficient and more productive. If U.S. industry had been as stultified as the schools, it would have failed long ago. In fact, those businesses that have not improved their efficiency and productivity *have* failed; private enterprise cannot survive stagnation. Yet we have protected our schools from this necessary competition, and they now lack the motivation to improve. Schools are sheltered; they consume significant amounts of tax money but face little accountability. They have not been required to make the improvements that any contemporary business would need to make simply to remain competitive.

Improved technology and increased productivity could limit the need for costly employees. School budgets represent one of the biggest expenses in most communities, and staff salaries constitute about 80 percent of that expense. Savings in payroll could be used to upgrade technology and improve student skills, or to reduce taxes. The ratio of students to teachers has been stable, about 25 to 1, in comprehensive school districts for years. In many suburban schools, the ratio is less than 20 students to each teacher. Yet there is no evidence that fewer students per class means a better education. And much of what a teacher does in a classroom could be accomplished more efficiently with larger groups of students by using video or computer equipment.

It is important for a teacher to guide instruction, but it is very expensive to have each teacher work with a small number of students. If innovative technologies came into play, the teacher could present material to larger groups, and individual students could work on computers under the general guidance of the teacher or a teacher's aide. This would mean schools would be organized very differently, but that is what we need. Businesses are constantly reorganizing to achieve better productivity because competition demands it. Schools should not be exempt from similar requirements.

The proportion of school administrative overhead in the budget has increased significantly, while the total student population has declined and then increased slightly. Schools also employ large numbers of workers to provide services that could be carried out more economically by contract with private industry. Such employees are usually on some form of civil service and keep their jobs regardless of reorganization. Teachers have tenure and lifetime security, and union contracts limit their workdays and work years. Schools suffer a wide variety of inefficiencies.

## Using Business Principles

School buildings are often large, inefficiently utilized, and costly to build and maintain. In districts where student enrollment has declined, expensive school buildings have been sold, destroyed, or renovated at great public financial loss. Some school buildings are used less than half of the year and then for only one-third of the day. The practice of issuing bonds has passed the debt for building these behemoths on to future generations.

Many small schools, with separate buildings and school staffs, could be reorganized into less costly regional districts if we applied business concepts. Individual school districts purchase millions of dollars' worth of books, equipment, and teaching materials at high cost, when a coordinated effort could decrease such expense considerably. Small, expensive schools operate out of pride, not economy.

Meanwhile, businesses have shown that they can train large numbers of employees by using video and computer systems, lectures, programmed materials, self-study, and other devices that do not consume the high levels of precious human resources that schools use. Furthermore, this training occurs in facilities used extensively for the whole of each year. The educational activities of these businesses are actually a response to the failings of the schools; business has shown that it can train people more effectively and more economically.

If schools could prove that expensive buildings and personnel increase productivity, there would be no problem. In fact, however, student test scores have been declining, students do not have work values that enhance their employment, and student social behavior is a public disgrace in many locations.

This is not a time for schools to continue the failures of the past—it is a time to change schools, and business-proven techniques can effect the changes. The structure of business based on a competitive marketplace has withstood the most severe tests of war, depression, and dislocation. We need to introduce contemporary business management—management concerned with improved efficiency and productivity—into education.

It is a social and educational necessity that we reorder our schools to give students solid skills and good, positive workplace values. It is an economic necessity that we reorganize school operations to more closely approximate good business practices.

All in all, business has much to offer education, much more than just the money schools need to continue their work (Feulner, 1991; Mandel, 1995; Oravitz, 1999). Financial support alone would do little to confront the crisis in education. To develop basic skills, to improve workplace attitudes and values, to increase the productivity of U.S. business, to enhance our competitive stance in international markets, and to make schools more efficient are goals business and the schools share. For the good of our young people and for our future as a nation, we need to encourage them to form an alliance to reach these goals.

## POSITION 2: LIMIT THE INFLUENCE OF BUSINESS

The business community should mind its own business first. If businesses could demonstrate a clear tradition of quality, ethics, and efficiency in their operation, then they might be in a position to claim that schools should follow that example. Schools have many problems, but they will not be remedied by thoughtlessly adopting business practices or following the dictates of the corporate world.

The unfortunate traditions of shoddy products, shady operations, inefficiency, and shaky ethics have long haunted U.S. business enterprises. Obviously, not all businesses share these traditions, but too many concentrate on making a profit with little regard for workers, ethics, the environment, or justice. Businesses are notorious for granting excessive salaries to CEOs and elaborate expense accounts to executives even as they cut workers' benefits and pay. Businesses are notorious polluters. The frequent recall of defective goods, fines levied for consumer deception or fraud, and constant consumer complaints about business practices should cast a chill over the idea of holding up business as a model for schools.

Further, society should have strong doubts about the wisdom of allowing business leaders to influence how students are educated. Corporate self-interest clouds the altruistic rhetoric about supporting good schools for all children. Corporations would like the taxpaying public to pay for the kinds of education they want their employees to have, and they would like schools to convey a positive view of business, no matter what its defects. Businesses can serve their own interests if their ideas control the schools. But schools exist for society's benefit; society is not served by having business interests dominate the schools (Marina, 1994). Business seeks profit, not enlightenment. Even profit in schooling is a business target (Buchen, 1999).

"America 2000" and "Goals 2000" are two names for the same strategy two presidents, Bush and Clinton, have offered. This strategy calls upon the business community to jump-start education reform by financing teams to design new schools, using new national tests to hire personnel, and trying to "catalyze needed changes in local schools, communities, and state policies" (*America 2000*, 1991). This rhetoric emphasizes business's intrusion into the schools. Such ideas raise a menacing cloud over education and reflect an ignorance of the social and human injuries business has inflicted in the past.

### A Corporate Model for Schools

Imagine allowing U.S. corporations to design the new models for schools of the twenty-first century. What values would they express? Certainly, humane values, protection of the environment, caring and mutual support, skeptical consumerism, health and safety, and positive images of labor unions would not be in the curriculum. Businesses would probably severely curtail the freedom to study diverse views of U.S. society, economics, politics, and history. Would an examination of the robber barons, the savings-and-loan fiasco, excessive cost overruns government contracts have allowed business, industrial pollution, unjustifiably high salaries for corporate executives, corruption of corporate officials, and related information about business operations be part of the curriculum in these corporate-sponsored schools?

Many business executives advocate using national test scores as the main criterion in hiring workers. This is little more than a simplistic and bean-counting method for pressuring schools into using and reporting the tests, demeaning the more important evaluation approaches that better express the complexities of human knowledge. Executives whose lives are determined by "the bottom line" are likely to seize on a single test score as the essence of each worker's talents and abilities. Test scores would become even more oppressive in covering up the multifaceted personalities of students and employees. Business would also insist on significantly influencing the construction of the tests themselves. As Carnegie and other notorious industrialists showed us, whoever controls all elements of an industry also controls prices and profits. The same can happen with industry-controlled schooling. Those who control test design and usage can manipulate employment levels, wages and benefits, labor contracts, and profits. They would also come to control the school curriculum through the tests.

Finally, consider asking business to "catalyze" educational reform. This request assumes that business knows what needs reform. Most of the negative statements corporate leaders make about schools refer to lacks in basic skills and workers' values. Students certainly need basic skills, but who should decide which skills? Must they be employment-related? And the idea of educating students to develop workers' values imposes a misguided and improper burden on schools. Human values and ethical conduct are proper goals of education, but employer values often contradict human and ethical values. Schools are not the place to insist on "worker" values.

## *The Notorious Contributions of Business to Civilization*

The record of U.S. business in its own domain has not been exemplary. While there are many fine and humane businesspeople, there are also many whose interests are inconsistent with social improvement. There is a stark and dark side of American business—our history is replete with evidence of it. A partial list includes sweatshops, child labor, virtual slavery of migrant workers, unhealthy and unsafe workplaces, pollution, linkages with corrupt politicians, secret coalitions to set falsely high prices, anticonsumer tactics, deceptive advertising, dissolution of pension funds, bankruptcy laws that permit executives to retain major assets while middle-class stockholders lose their life savings, taxpayer subsidies to cover up inept corporate management, and corporate lawyers and corporation-influenced laws that absolve corporations from accountability or responsibility for their wrongdoing. Are these the ideas and values we want to emulate in schooling?

Unfortunately, students in U.S. schools have been shortchanged, and American society has been deluded, by the imposition of business views on education for the past century (Apple, 1984, 1990; Callahan, 1962). It is deceptive to train the masses to conform to business interests while providing the elite with increased privileges. This is the most insidious educational trick in the new reform movement. Millions of students are relegated to nonthinking, menial work as preparation for poor jobs, and the schools are expected to make them think they are happy and well-educated.

Historian Christopher Lasch (1984) says there is

> a new system of industrial recruitment, centered on the school. The modern system of public education, remodeled in accordance with the same principles of scientific management first perfected in industry, has replaced apprenticeship as the principal agency of training people for work. The transmission of skills is increasingly incidental to this training. The school habituates children to bureaucratic discipline and to the demands of group living, grades and sorts them by means of standardized tests, and selects some for professional and managerial careers while consigning the rest to manual labor. . . . A willingness to cooperate with the proper authorities offers the best evidence of "adjustment" and the best hope of personal success, while a refusal to cooperate signifies the presence of "emotional problems" requiring more sustained therapeutic attention. (pp. 48–49)

American schools have been dominated by the values of business and industry since the beginning of the twentieth century, and schools have lost their primary purpose: enlightenment for the improvement of social justice. Rather than being liberating, schools are now indoctrinating institutions. They provide docile and hard-working employees business can rely on to gain a profit. Further, these future employees are taught an ideology that supports business regardless of ethical considerations and conditions them to unquestioningly accept the authority of a managerial elite.

## School Reform and Business Interests

Reform movements in education in the United States have often victimized the underclasses on the pretext of making them "fit for work and for citizenship." Schools tell students to be obedient, punctual, frugal, neat, respectful, patriotic, and content with their lot in life. A duality, a dialectic, exists between what is good for business and what is good for society. The work ethic, drawing from Puritan views, is of great value to industrialists who desire uncomplaining and diligent workers. This ethic has become the school ethic. Employment has become the curriculum of the schools, enabling business to sustain a receptive workforce. The carrot of democratic citizenship, however, is mythological, since the economic facts of life are that the elite remain in power while the masses do the work. Education for democratic participation, in the pursuit of justice and equality, is still in the rhetoric of school literature, but is not acted on in the schools.

This disparity in the schools' purposes—preparing students to participate as workers versus preparing them to participate as equal citizens in striving for justice in society—is overlooked in much of the reform literature. As historian Barbara Finkelstein (1984) notes:

> Nineteenth-century reformers looked to public schools to instill restraint in increasingly large numbers of immigrants and native children, while at the same time preparing them for learning and labor in an industrializing society. . . . They saw no contradiction in the work of schools as economic sorting machines and enabling political institutions. . . . Contemporary calls for reform reflect a retreat from historic visions of public education as an instrument of political democ-racy, a vehicle of social mobility, a center for the reconstruction of community life. . . . Rather, the educational visions of contemporary reformers evoke historic specters of public schools as crucibles in which to forge uniform Americans and disciplined industrial laborers. (pp. 276–277)

Finkelstein also discusses how corporate leaders are expanding their influ-ence on public education in order to assure a competent and compliant work-force. She illustrates this with examples from a business–education alliance at George Washington Carver High School in Atlanta, where business conducts the daily activities of the school by providing work-study in semiskilled jobs in local businesses, making moral pronouncements to promote industrial disci-pline in students, and establishing public rituals, such as "Free Enterprise Day" and "passports to job opportunity." This, and other business intrusions into schools, leads to "an effective transfer of control over education policy from public school authorities to industrial councils. . . . For the first time in the history of school reform, a deeply materialistic consciousness seems to be over-whelming all other concerns." (Finkelstein, 1984, p. 280)

## Is Business a Good Model for Schools?

The 1990s have shown the truth of Finkelstein's insight. We have become very good at teaching students to be avaricious, greedy, selfish, and conniving. Academic students are especially eager to get good grades in order to get into the right colleges and get high-paying jobs. They seem uninterested in intellec-tual development unless it pays off in employment and salaries. They seem uncaring about the homeless, the starving, and others who are disadvantaged, as well as the rest of the world. They are excessively competitive with each other and press for competitive advantage over other groups. Ethical consider-ations, including the pursuit of justice, do not seem to pose an obstruction to their efforts. Cheating, buying term papers, using parental influence, taking drugs to temporarily enhance performance, paying someone to take a college admission test, and falsifying a résumé may be part of the process. Those who aspire to be yuppies understand that winning is important in order to secure high pay; how one wins is not important.

Interestingly, this pattern of beliefs is drawn from big business. Wall Street companies have engaged in securities fraud, insider scandals, and various scams. Banks and insurance companies appear to have taken advantage of deregulation and loose public control to plunge the country's banking and insurance systems into serious trouble. Calavita and Pontell (1991), after reviewing government documents from congressional hearings on the savings and loan and insurance industries, described many top management actions as "collective embezzlement." Major corporations, including Chrysler and Lockheed, conducted business in a most unbusinesslike manner, leading to virtual bankruptcy. Taxpayers then bailed them out, turning the principles of "free enterprise" upside down.

Big business "sweetheart" contracts negotiated with current and former government officers have fattened profits and increased taxpayer costs exorbitantly. The Pentagon's extravagant contracts for military supplies are the obvious example, but many other federal, state, and local government contracts also overpay for work and supplies. The widely publicized Pentagon padding scandals are not the only example of questionable alliances between big business and government. Sematech, formed in 1986, presumably to regain America's competitive edge in semiconductors, was a consortium of fourteen major semiconductor corporations funded by the federal government. Taxpayers contribute about $100 million per year to this operation. In 1980, the United States had 75 percent of the worldwide semiconductor market; by 1991, we had only 45 percent. Sematech has neither made any technical breakthroughs nor regained our competitive edge.

The big business of professional athletics, until the public became outraged, condoned and supported drug use by athletes to improve their performance. Fraud, misrepresentation, cheating, using or peddling improper influence, falsifying or hiding records, and abusing drugs for business purposes appear to be acceptable ethical standards for many in business. This curriculum is one many students have picked up.

The unethical operations of business are manifold, and we hear about them often enough to suggest that business is not the place to look for educational views on ethics. Even if one grants that the unethical is not the standard but the exception in business, there remains a serious concern about the business view of social justice and responsibility. Industrial waste pollutes the land, water, and air, but industry does not accept the responsibility to clean it up. Strong protests by the corporate world have been effective in slowing and stopping the public regulation of worker health and safety, consumer protection, and improvement in public utilities and services. As Michael Apple (1990) describes it, "Economic and cultural power is being increasingly centralized in massive corporate bodies that are less than responsive to social needs other than profit" (p. 12).

## Educational and Social Consequences of a Corporate Takeover

The corporate takeover of schooling affects everyone, but the greedy and already advantaged stand to benefit the most. Those who are not going to college, and who are less likely to share the American business dream of success, are subjected to second-class treatment in schools and in careers. The industrial curriculum is designed to give them skills, not the ability to think, and is intended to make them believers, not thinkers. Industrial education increases the gap between these groups and is meant to produce workers willing to be manipulated.

Business leaders criticize the schools because new employees do not possess basic skills and do not have proper work attitudes. The basic skills business wants do not include critical judgment or the persuasive skills that could be useful in reconstituting the moribund union movement or in challenging management dictates. Rather, the basic skills business wants students to learn are fundamental reading and computation skills that make one more efficient in carrying out management's policies. A job candidate who demonstrates the ability to read radical left-wing literature and to raise questions about worker safety, environmental hazards, and excessive salaries and disparate benefits provided to owners and executives is not likely to be hired. A candidate who can calculate the differences in value between the worker's effort and the pay received, or between labor and management perks in health care and leisure provisions, is not likely to be hired. It is the moral curriculum rather than the academic that is of most interest to business. Managers want workers who believe that what is good for business is good for the nation, and who agree that management knows what is good for business.

Several states now require a high school course in "free enterprise," instead of a solid course in economics. Obviously, this course is not neutral; it is an advocacy course intended to indoctrinate youth to the idea that corporate practices, under the label of free enterprise, are good for the nation. In English class, students fill out job application forms and answer "help wanted" ads. Math is preparing students to work in stores and make change. History classes incorporate myths about the virtues of American business leaders, the appropriate power of corporations, and the threat of governmental interference in business. And, as Harty's (1980) study of business-produced teaching materials showed, students are given biased material that supports corporate views of environmental, social, and governmental actions. Harty (1989) more recently updated her analysis of corporate attempts to sell their wares and values by manipulating school materials, and found the practice continuing. Throughout the schools, students are treated as junior workers required to be punctual, to have good "work habits," to show deference to management, and to refrain from critical thought. This hidden curriculum of business has been very successful.

Business has been a major influence on education for a long time, yet it still complains about the product of an institution and a curriculum dominated by its ethos. Raymond Callahan (1962) conducted a historical study of what most influenced the development of contemporary public education in its formative period in the early twentieth century:

> At the turn of the century, America had reason to be proud of the educational progress it had made. The dream of equality of educational opportunity had been partly realized . . . the basic institutional framework for a noble conception of education had been created. . . . The story of the next quarter-century of American education—a story of opportunity lost and of the acceptance by educational administrators of an inappropriate philosophy—must be seen . . .

the most powerful force was industrialism . . . the business ideology was spread continuously into the bloodstream of American life. . . . It was, therefore, quite natural for Americans, when they thought of reforming the schools, to apply business methods to achieve their ends. (pp. 1, 5)

Callahan considered this business influence tragic for education and society because it substituted efficiency for effectiveness: We got cost control at the sacrifice of high-quality schooling for all. The business dominance stuck, and in the first decade of the twenty-first century, schools are still controlled by a corporate value system. This explains the factory mentality of schools. It explains why teachers are so poorly paid and badly treated—they are considered laborers. It explains why students are treated as objects in a manufacturing process on school assembly lines. It explains the conformity and standardization, the excessive testing, and the organization and financing of schools. It also explains the lack of concern for social justice and ethics, issues the schools were making progress on until business gained influence.

Upton Sinclair, an author whose devastating criticism of the meat packing industry for ignoring public health and worker safety (*The Jungle*, 1906, 1938) helped spur federal legislation to regulate food products, also published two books that showed the detrimental effects of business influence on education. *The Goose Step* (1922) detailed how major industrialists determined educational policies and controlled appointments and promotions to professorships in the most important universities in the United States. Leaders of big business dominate the boards that govern most colleges and universities—a point Thorstein Veblen (1918) made long ago. Veblen found that business practices and values detracted from the primary purpose of academic institutions: to liberate students. Sinclair also spent two years studying the public schools and found heavy-handed control over school policies and practices by business leaders across the United States. In *The Goslings* (1924), he stated, "The purpose of this book is to show you how the 'invisible government' of Big Business which controls the rest of America has taken over the charge of your children" (p. ix).

There is considerable evidence that nothing has improved in the seventy-five years since Sinclair wrote about schools and business. Schools teach what business wants them to teach. They should teach what society needs and justice requires them to teach. We need to return to the civilizing purposes of schooling—justice and ethics—and to wrench control of the schools away from those who see the school as just another agency to support the interests of big business. Certainly, the role of business in society should be studied, but not whitewashed, as it is now.

## Summary

Large segments of U.S. business have a grasping and greedy history, whereas education serves essentially civilizing purposes. Among the schools' most positive goals is to enable students to improve the society by increasing justice and expanding social ethics to incorporate a stronger concern for others. This ensures the future of American democracy and poses a significant challenge to schools to strive continually for social development. And that requires knowledge, critical thinking, cooperative endeavor, and a set of values based on justice.

Critical examination of business values and practices, in terms of social justice and human ethics, are of great import. We need to invert the current situation, in which business controls schools, to one in which education influences business values and practices, encouraging responsibility and enlightenment. This would put education in its proper role, monitoring the improvement of society by examining various social institutions, including business. It would certainly improve education, and it might improve business.

## For Discussion

1. The Business Roundtable developed a survey question for their Internet web site that featured a question about schools: Which of the following statements most closely matches your own view?
   a. Schools need a complete top-to-bottom overhaul.
   b. The present system just needs minor tuning.
   c. We should try new things like home-schooling and vouchers.
   d. We should just leave the public schools alone.
   The default answer set on the site was a.
   Responses (as of 1999) were: a = 31%; b = 9%; c = 10%; d = 50%

   What is your response? What explains the responses the Business Roundtable obtained? Can you construct a similar survey question about business reform in the United States? What results would you anticipate?
2. What would you change in the current k–12 school curriculum to produce graduates more satisfactory as
   a. employees in U.S. business enterprises?
   b. consumers of goods, services, and advertising?
   c. fellow members of society?
3. If school leaders were asked to reform U.S. business, what advice would you expect them to give? How would business take that advice?
4. The following graph, figure 12.1, shows the relationship between educational attainment and average annual income.
   Obviously, the graph documents that income goes up as education level increases.
   a. What other factors, beside education, could account for this increase in income?
   b. These are general data. How do they account for some relatively low-paying fields that usually require a graduate degree—for example, librarians, teachers, and social workers?
   c. How do such data inform the debate over business involvement in schools?

FIGURE 12.1

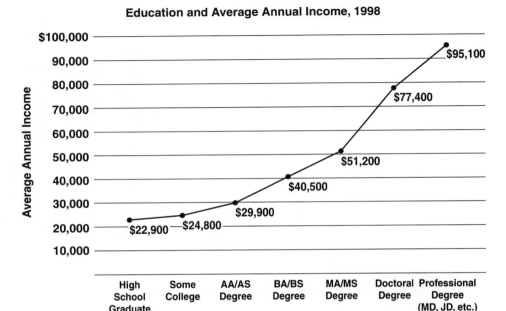

### Education and Average Annual Income, 1998

Average Annual Income vs. Educational Attainment

- High School Graduate: $22,900
- Some College: $24,800
- AA/AS Degree: $29,900
- BA/BS Degree: $40,500
- MA/MS Degree: $51,200
- Doctoral Degree: $77,400
- Professional Degree (MD, JD, etc.): $95,100

*Source:* U.S. Census Bureau. Current Population Survey, March 1998.

5. Identify a list of skills needed to succeed in today's economy. Are these taught in the schools you know? Should they be taught in school or at work? How should they be taught? Who should teach them?

## References

*America 2000.* (1991). Washington, DC: U.S. Department of Education.

APPLE, M. (1984). *Education and Power.* New York: Routledge & Kegan Paul.

——— (1990). *Ideology and Curriculum.* New York: Routledge, Chapman & Hall.

——— (1991). "The New Technology: Is It Part of the Solution or Part of the Problem in Education?" *Computers in the Schools* 8, 59–80.

BATES, S. (1998). "Building Better Workers." *Nation's Business* 86, 49.

BLAU, P., AND DUNCAN O. D. (1967). *The American Occupational Structure.* New York: Wiley.

BUCHEN, I. (1999). "Business Sees Profit in Education." *The Futurist* 33(5), 38–44.

CALAVITA, K., AND PONTELL, H. (1991). "Other People's Money Revisited: Collective Embezzlement in the Savings and Loan and Insurance Industries." *Social Problems* 38, 94–112.

CALLAHAN, R. (1962). *Education and the Cult of Efficiency.* Chicago: University of Chicago Press.

CHASE, R. (1998). "Changing the Way the Schools Do Business." *Vital Speeches of the Day* 64, 444–446.

*A Common Agenda for Improving American Education.* (1997). Washington, DC: Business Roundtable, July 2.

CRAIN, F. (1994). "Saving our Schools: Our Highest Priority." *Advertising Age* 65, 28.

*Educational Attainment in the United States: March 1998.* (1998). U.S. Bureau of the Census. Washington, DC: Government Printing Office.

FEULNER, E. J. (1991). "What Business Leaders Can Teach the Educators." *Chief Executive,* September, pp. 16–17.

FINKELSTEIN, B. (1984). "Education and the Retreat from Democracy in the United States, 1979–1980." *Teachers College Record* 86, 276–282.

FISKE, E. (1988). "Lessons." *The New York Times,* December 21, p. B8.

*The Forgotten Half: Non-College-Bound Youth in America* (Interim Report). (1988). Washington, DC: W. T. Grant Foundation.

GILBERT, T. (1993). "Corporate Influence by 2010." *Education Digest* 59, 25–27.

HARTY, S. (1980). *Hucksters in the Classroom.* Washington, DC: Center for Responsive Legislation.

——— (1989). "U.S. Corporations: Still Pitching After All These Years." *Educational Leadership* 47, 77–79.

LASCH, C. (1984). *The Minimal Self.* New York: Norton.

MANDEL, M., ET AL. (1995). "Will Schools Ever Get Better?" *Business Week,* Apr. 17, pp. 64–68.

MANN, D. (1987). "Business Involvement and Public School Improvement, Part 2." *Phi Delta Kappan* 69, 228–232.

MARINA, A. (1994). "Can the Private Sector Save Public Schools?" *NEA Today* 12, 10–12.

MILLER, W. H. (1991). "Bush Bucks It to Business: The President's Education-Reform Plan Relies on Business to Attain Goals." *Industry Week* 240, 70–72.

ORAVITZ, J. V. (1999). "Why Can't Schools be Operated the Way Businesses Are?" *Education Digest* 64(6) Feb., 15–17.

OXFORD ANALYTICA. (1986). *America in Perspective: Major Trends in the United States Through the 1990s.* Boston: Houghton Mifflin.

RAMSEY, N. (1993). "What Companies Are Doing." *Fortune* 128, 142–150.

"Saving Our Schools." (1990). *Fortune.* Special Issue, Spring, p. 121.

SEWALL, G. T. (1984). *Necessary Lessons: Decline and Renewal in American Schools.* New York: Free Press.

SINCLAIR, U. (1906, 1938). *The Jungle.* London: Cobham House.

——— (1922). *The Goose Step.* Pasadena, CA: Sinclair.

——— (1924). *The Goslings.* Pasadena, CA: Sinclair.

SOLTOW, L., AND STEVENS, E. (1981). *The Rise of Literacy and the Common School in the United States: A Socioeconomic Analysis to 1870.* Chicago: University of Chicago Press.

SZABO, J. C. (1990). "Grass-Roots Education Reform." *Nation's Business* 78, 65–67.

VEBLEN, T. (1918). *The Higher Learning in America.* New York: Heubsch.

# CHAPTER 13

# Standardized Testing: Restrict or Expand

## POSITION 1: FOR RESTRICTING TESTING

> A young Ojibwa student . . . was tested by several professionals and classified as having certain learning and behavioral problems. In part, this classification was based upon his staring into space, completing tasks very slowly, and giving "non-reality-based" responses to questions. As it turned out, the boy had a special relationship with his traditional Ojibwa grandfather, who encouraged his dreaming . . . In Ojibwa thought and language, *ga-na-wa-bun-daw-ming*, which means seeing without feeling (objectivity), carries less value than *mu-zhi-tum-ing*, which means feelings that you do not see (subjectivity). (McShane, 1989, cited in Madaus, 1994, p. 80)

### Vexing Tests

In a witty attack on standardized testing, Banesh Hoffmann (1962) recounted a debate played out on the pages of the London *Times*. A letter to the newspaper's editor asked for help in solving a multiple-choice problem from a battery of school tests the letter writer's son had taken. At first glance, the question seemed to be straightforward and not surprising to anyone who has taken school tests. It asked, "Which is the odd one out among cricket, football, billiards, and hockey?"

The letter writer believed the answer must be billiards because it is the only one of the four games played indoors. He admitted to being less than sure of his answer, and he reported there was no agreement among his acquaintances. One of his neighbors argued that the correct choice was cricket, because in all of the other games the object was to put a ball in a net. The writer's son had selected hockey because it was the only one that was a "girl's game." The letter writer asked readers of the *Times* for help.

Ensuing letters and arguments succeeded only in muddying the waters, since the logic supporting one choice was no more compelling than the logic supporting any other. For example, billiards could be considered the odd one out because it is the only one of the four games listed that is not ordinarily a team game. It is the only one in which the color of the ball matters. It is the only one in which more than one ball is in play, and it is the only one played on a green cloth rather than a grass field. Unfortunately, equally convincing briefs could be submitted in behalf of the other choices.

Hoffmann fumed about the inherent bias in the question. He assumed that the test was designed to measure reasoning ability and not sports knowledge, but he argued that the test taker might be disadvantaged by too little experience with athletics; for example, not all students with good reasoning skills may know how cricket is played. Test takers who know too much about sports might also be disadvantaged; they might choose hockey as the odd one out because it is really two different games that share the same name: in England and in several other countries, hockey is a game typically played on grass by players who receive no salary; elsewhere it is a game played on ice, often by professional athletes.

The language of this test item may also trip up students, preventing it from measuring reasoning ability. For example, many working-class students may not be familiar with either cricket or billiards. This item favors the language and culture of the middle and upper-middle classes, and low scores may reflect measures of social standing more than achievement or ability (Neill and Medina, 1989). Americans could also be disadvantaged by the language of the test item, which asks test takers to select the "odd one out." The same question in the United States would probably be, "Which of the following does not belong?"

Test questions of this sort seem silly. There is no readily apparent "right" answer, and test takers have no opportunity to demonstrate the thought processes that led them to their decisions. As Hoffmann noted, "What sense is there in giving tests in which the candidate just picks answers, and is not allowed to give the reasons for his choice?" (Hoffmann, 1962, p. 20). Multiple-choice questions are an unnatural problem-solving format incongruous with solving problems in real life. Rarely are life's dilemmas delineated by four answers, one of which is guaranteed to be correct. Good problem solvers in the real world are seldom locked away, deprived of books, computers, and human contact; they are seldom told to respond to a set of timed, multiple-choice questions that have no practical meaning.

If multiple-choice questions, such as the one that vexed *Times* readers, were nothing more than a parlor game, a form of Trivial Pursuit played for amusement, we would have little objection to them. However, as everyone knows, standardized testing has serious consequences, and for public school students, the stakes are particularly high. Standardized test results help determine placement in reading groups, admission to the college-track programs in public high schools, entrance into elite colleges, scholarship awards, admission into medical and law schools, and licensing to practice a profession or trade.

## If Testing Is the Answer, What Was the Question?

In the early twentieth century, defining "native intelligence" and attempting to measure it through standardized examinations instigated one of the most controversial legacies of the testing movement (Gould, 1981). Sir Francis Galton in

England and Alfred Binet in France attempted to measure mental capacities through standardized tests (Cremin, 1961). Binet developed his test at the request of the French government, to identify those children who were "mentally subnormal" and not able to function adequately in regular classrooms. Louis Terman translated Binet's tests into English for American students, and he and his colleagues adjusted the tests to comport with their own sense of how intelligence was distributed. For example, Terman believed that men are more intelligent than women and that rural people are less intelligent than urban dwellers. Therefore, when girls outscored boys, Terman changed the test items that girls scored unusually well on. He made no changes on items where urban children outscored rural children (Garcia and Pearson, 1994).

Terman argued that intelligence tests make schools more efficient. He claimed that the tests could be used to sort children into differentiated curricula designed to prepare them for their appropriate lot in life:

> Preliminary investigations indicate that an IQ below 70 rarely permits anything better than unskilled labor; the range of 70–80 is preeminently that of semiskilled labor; from 80–100 that of skilled or ordinary clerical labor; from 100–110 or 115 that of semiprofessional pursuits; and that above all of these are grades of intelligence which permit one to enter the professions or other large fields of business. (Terman, 1922, in Wolf et al., 1991)

Psychologists working for the United States government during World War I introduced the first wide-scale use of intelligence tests. The army was interested in classifying all new recruits, giving special attention to two groups: those of exceptional ability and those unfit for military service. Binet and Terman had used individual IQ tests that were not well-suited to large-scale testing; under the direction of American psychologists, the army developed the first mass testing program in history (Gumbert and Spring, 1974, pp. 87–112).

The army used the tests to answer questions about the placement of soldiers: Who would best fit where? How could the army best use the varied talents and abilities recruits brought with them? After the war, colleges and universities bought the surplus exams. The language of the army tests required only slight modification for use in the schools. The original instructions given to soldiers read:

> Attention! The purpose of this examination is to see how well you can remember, think and carry out what you are told to do in the army . . . Now in the army a man often has to listen to commands and carry them out exactly. I am going to give you these commands to see how well you carry them out . . .

In schools, these instruction were changed to read:

> Part of being a good student is your ability to follow directions . . . When I call "Attention," stop instantly what you are doing and hold your pencil up—so. Don't put your pencil down on the paper until I say "Go." . . . Listen carefully to what I say. Do just as you are told to do. As soon as you are through, pencils up. Remember, wait for the word "Go." (Gumbert and Spring, 1974, p. 94)

For many years, schools used IQ tests to track children based on their test performance. Intelligence was viewed as the "raw material" required for schooling, and students judged to have less intelligence received less education. This reliance on IQ tests produced the unintended result of limiting students' educational access (Darling-Hammond, 1994). Students performing at the lowest levels on IQ tests received an education designed to prepare them to be tractable, unskilled laborers. Only the highest-achieving students would be introduced to the most complex skills. Intellect was viewed as a biological trait much like height or eye color: It was (and in some quarters, still is) thought to be inherited, measurable, and fixed (Herrnstein and Murray, 1994). IQ tests allowed schools to sort students into appropriate curricula and thus into their later place in society (Callahan, 1962; Wolf et al., 1991). Too frequently, these tests excluded students from the best opportunities the school offered. More often than not, the best education and the most promising futures were reserved for those who performed well on standardized tests.

## IQ Tests Biased Against Poor

In the United States, Americans of European descent score more than 15 points higher on average than African Americans do on standardized tests. There are also significant gaps between the standardized test scores of European Americans, Mexican Americans, and native Americans. Some advocates of standardized testing believe that most of the differences in IQ scores are attributable to genetic endowment (Jensen, 1969; Herrnstein and Murray, 1994). However, many in the academic community doubt that intelligence is a single biological trait that paper-and-pencil tests can measure, and they criticize IQ tests for their bias as well as their failure to tap the test taker's full range of abilities (Gardner, 1983; Gould, 1981; Graves, 1996). Anthropologists and educational sociologists, for example, argue that IQ is more reflective of the child's socioeconomic status than his or her native ability (Ogbu, 1978). They point out that when children are grouped according to family background and academic experiences, the differences in achievement scores tend to disappear (Garcia and Pearson, 1994). Some researchers claim that there is bias in the tests themselves. They argue that the tests "reflect the language, culture, or learning style of middle-to-upper-class whites. Thus scores on these tests are as much measures of race or ethnicity and income as they are measures of achievement, ability, or skill" (Neill and Medina, 1989, p. 691). Gardner (1983) argues that children have seven forms of "intelligence," and that schools typically emphasize only two of the multiple forms. (See Discussion Question 2.)

Teachers of poor and minority children report that they spend more time teaching to the test and are more likely to rely on data from standardized tests than do teachers of students from moderate- and high-income families (Garcia and Pearson, 1994). Poor and minority children spend more time on workbook exercises and busy-work assignments. They are less likely than middle-class students to have access to classes where they can discuss what they know, read real books, write, or solve problems in mathematics, science, or other school subjects (Darling-Hammond, 1994). Students from poor families and children of minorities have been awarded an education of less substance because of their poor performance on standardized tests. As Madaus (1994) points out:

> Clearly, the unintended negative outcomes brought about by the widespread policy use of IQ tests disproportionately disadvantaged minority populations. Despite Binet's original purpose to identify children in need of instructional assistance, the IQ test in this country led to blacks and Hispanics being disproportionately placed in dead-end classes for the "educable mentally retarded." (p. 86)

## Misleading the Public

> Validation was once a priestly mystery, a ritual performed behind the scenes, with the professional elite as witness and judge. Today it is a public spectacle combining the attraction of chess and mud wrestling. (Cronbach, 1988, p. 3)

Until the last few years, despite question about the validity of individual test items on standardized tests (Crouse and Trusheim, 1988; Hoffmann, 1962; Nairn, 1980; Owen, 1985), test takers were never able to see a list of the "right" answers after they had taken the exams. The Educational Testing Service (ETS)[1] of Princeton, New Jersey, and other test developers published only a few sample questions, claiming that full disclosure would compromise the tests. To make the tests reliable,[2] they argued, many items had to be repeated from year to year, and the answers therefore must be held back from public scrutiny. The ETS admitted it was possible to construct new equivalent exams every year; however, it would be an expensive process, and test takers would ultimately bear the costs.

Recognizing the power standardized exams have on the lives of individual test takers, and failing to be persuaded by ETS's arguments, New York and California enacted legislation that allowed test takers to see the answers after they had taken the exams. These truth-in-testing laws revealed ambiguity in test items. In some instances, more than one answer was correct. The ETS and other test makers took the issue to court, and in 1990 a federal district court judge in New York set aside the requirements of the test disclosure law on the grounds that it interfered with copyright laws. The truth-in-testing laws have

---

[1] The Educational Testing Service (ETS) of Princeton, New Jersey, is the world's largest testing company. Formed in 1947 to develop and administer college entrance exams for returning World War II veterans, the company now administers 9 million exams annually and reports earnings of $411 million. ETS also sells materials and services that help students prepare for the tests the company develops. ETS advertisements proclaim, "We prepare the tests—Let us prepare you." (Nordheimer and Franz, 1997).

[2] Reliability in testing can be thought of as a synonym for stability, consistency, or dependability. Kerlinger's simile might be useful in understanding this concept. He writes:

> A test is like a gun in its purpose. When we measure human attributes and abilities and achievements, we want to measure "true" amounts of attributes that individuals possess. This is like hitting a target with a gun. With a test we want to hit the attribute. If a gun consistently hits a target—the shots cluster close together at or near the center of the target . . . we say it is reliable. Similarly with psychological and sociological measures. If they hit the target, they are reliable. (Kerlinger, 1979, p. 133)

cast doubt on the ability of tests to measure what they claim to measure, and have opened the issue of validity[3] to public examination.

There is good reason for public suspicion. Some people have intentionally used the results of standardized tests to mislead the public. Take the case of the "magic mean," uncovered by a physician in West Virginia. According to newspaper accounts, he learned that the students in his state were performing above the national average on standardized tests. This intrigued him, considering that West Virginia had one of the highest rates of illiteracy in the nation. Further checking revealed that no state using the test was reported to be below the mean. The tests compared student achievement with outdated and very low national norms. Therefore, the test results made even the worst test taker (and the school systems that bought the tests) appear to be above average. As one testing critic notes, "standardized, nationally normed achievement tests give children, parents, school systems, legislatures, and the press inflated and misleading reports on achievement levels" (Cannell, 1987, p. 3).

Indeed, by the late 1990s, it was hard to find any school districts or states that scored below the mean on nationally normed standardized tests. These data have contributed to what has been termed the Lake Wobegon Effect, after the mythical Minnesota town created by Garrison Keillor in which "the women are strong, the men are good looking, and all the children are above average" (Fiske, 1988; Mehrens and Kaminski, 1989; Phillips, 1990). Testing designs of this type are not uncommon, and we need to exercise caution before making inferences about quality of education based on the data from standardized testing (Judson, 1996; Linn, 1993). For the past fifty years, psychometricians and companies that market tests have convinced the public that short-answer tests are objective, scientific measures deserving of public confidence and faith, when in fact these tests suffer from vagueness, ambiguity, imprecision, and bias. There is nothing scientific or objective about these items; highly subjective human beings write, test, compile, and interpret each item (Owen, 1985). Standardized testing programs may serve better as public relations devices than as indicators of student ability or learning.

## *Bias*

The SAT and the ACT claim to be:
a) measures of academic achievement by students.
b) predictors of whether students will graduate from college.
c) reliable predictors of college performance, race notwithstanding.
d) measures of academic rigor of local school systems.
e) none of the above.
(Chenoweth, 1997, p. 20)

---

[3]Validity refers to the ability of a test to measure what the test maker wants to measure. Kerlinger uses the following example:

Suppose a group of teachers of social studies writes a test to measure students' understanding of certain social concepts: justice, equality, and cooperation, for instance. The teachers want to know whether their students understand and can apply the ideas. But they write a test of only factual items about contemporary institutions. The test is then not valid for the purpose they had in mind. (Kerlinger, 1979, p. 138)

The results of standardized testing programs are further marred by their bias against women and minorities. Consider the Scholastic Assessment Exam (SAT), a test college-bound high school students commonly take. The ETS has encouraged colleges and universities to consider the SAT exam a scientific predictor of students' success in college. Consequently, SAT scores are often part of the data colleges use in making admission decisions. According to ETS, students with higher SAT scores should earn higher grades during their first year in college. In fact, the SAT, similar to the ACT exam, measures how well a student is likely to do during the first year of college, and it does so accurately only about half the time. For African American and Latino students, the test scores *overpredict* their first-year grades. When these students earn 1200 SAT scores, for example, they do not do as well during their first year in college as white students with identical test scores (Chenoweth, 1997).

For women, the SAT *underpredicts* their first-year grades. In one study, the gap between average male and female scores on the test is 61 points. Female test takers scored 50 points lower on the Math Section and 11 points lower on the Verbal Section of the exam. If the SAT accurately predicted grade point average, males would have higher first-year grade point averages than female students. But this is not the case. Despite lower scores on the SAT, women earned higher grades than men (Rosser, 1987). The SAT does not predict what it is supposed to predict: success in college. The scores students get on SAT exams have less meaning than ETS has promised. Rosser concluded that because of sex bias on the SAT exam, women have less chance of receiving financial aid, being accepted to college, and being invited to join programs for the gifted. Because of an invalid exam, women are likely to earn less money and lose out on appointments to positions of leadership. In 1989, a federal district court ruled that New York State's Regents Scholarship, based on a student's performance on the SAT exam, discriminated against women. Women had previously won only 43 percent of the scholarships. After the decision, which required the State of New York to consider high school grades as well as standardized test scores, women won 51 percent of the awards (Arenson, 1996).

## Tests Drive School Curriculum

Standardized tests are terribly flawed, but despite their problems they continue to exert great influence on schools. Every teacher knows that testing drives the curriculum: What is tested is taught. No teacher wants his or her students to perform poorly on standardized achievement tests, and no school administrator wants his or her school to rank below others in the state or district. Everyone in education knows that, too often, the newspapers report the results of statewide testing in much the same way they report basketball standings. "We're Number One" or "County Schools Lowest in State" are not uncommon headlines in many local newspapers. To avoid such invidious comparisons, schools gear instruction to the test. Over time, material not tested tends not to be taught. Teachers and administrators fall victim to test makers' promises and the public's misplaced faith in testing. In truth, there is no compelling reason to subject students to large-scale multiple-choice exams.

National testing has become a national obsession. Encouraged by then-Governor Bill Clinton and then-President George Bush, the education community began to develop "New World Standards" in each of the "five core subjects" in the early 1990s (U.S. Department of Education, 1991, p. 11). In response, test makers began falling over themselves in a mad scramble to rush testing plans to market and have touted a national system of assessment as a means to chart the progress of schools on their march to the new higher standards (Jennings, 1998; Linn, 1993). However, Monty Neill of FairTest, among others, argues that all the proposals to bring about school reform through a renewed emphasis on assessment are based on premises that an examination of recent history does not support:

> During the 1980s, U.S. schoolchildren became probably the most overtested students in the world—but the desired educational improvement did not occur. FairTest research indicates that our schools now give more than 200 million standardized exams each year. The typical student must take several dozen before graduating. Adding more testing will no more improve education than taking the temperature of a patient more often will reduce his fever. (Neill, 1991, p. 36)

There is an antidote to standardized testing that does not sacrifice accountability. In every community, teachers, parents, and administrators should select appropriate content based on the students' interests, experiences, goals, and needs. Teachers should teach that content with all the skill at their command, and evaluate the extent of student learning with a wide variety of instruments. Students should be encouraged to demonstrate their ability to think through written exercises, verbal expression, and informal papers, and they should be given ample opportunity to demonstrate the reasons for their choices. The assessment of student learning requires that educators develop a broader, richer array of measures. We should not try to reduce student achievement to a single numerical score. Multiple-choice tests cannot tell the story of academic success. Assessment programs should be designed to improve student learning, not to measure one student against another or to measure a student's progress against some arbitrary standard (Neill, 1997).

Assessment programs should focus on the individual student. A student's record of school achievement should include a rich portfolio of papers, essays, videos, poems, photographs, drawings, and tape-recorded answers, not a series of test scores.

## POSITION TWO: FOR EXPANDING TESTING

In the American context [standardized, objective] tests are necessary to achieve excellence and fairness. They function as achievement incentives for students and teachers, as ways of monitoring students' progress in order to remedy their deficiencies, and as essential helps in the administrative monitoring of classrooms, schools, and districts. Without effective monitoring, neither good teaching nor educational administration is possible. Finally, and above all, objective tests are needed for academic fairness and social equity—the chief reasons that Americans, to their credit, have been pioneers in developing objective tests. (Hirsch, 1996, p. 117)

Why standards and tests? . . . The simple answer is that the focus on what is taught and learned is the proper one if student achievement is to be raised. Many elements are important in determining whether a student learns, but the school must first be clear about what is to be learned—and American education has not always been structured in such a way that there is a clear academic goal. (Jennings, 1998, pp. 183–184)

Public education has been "rediscovered" and carefully examined as an issue of social concern. Researchers, critics, and government officials have raised questions about the quality of teaching, student learning, and school leadership. Public education has been rescued from years of neglect, dusted off, and reassessed. After a long period of inattention, it is not surprising when problems are discovered everywhere, from the head to the tail of the academic procession. The public schools, it has been generally concluded, are in need of reform. Academic standards have slipped and students are passing from grade to grade without mastering the content that would allow them to be successful in life. Many educators recognize that the nation's schools need high standards for student achievement and scrupulously fair assessments of student performance or we will lose our competitive place in the world.

Previous generations of education reformers concerned themselves with making education available to children of all classes and races, and to a large extent they were successful. By the 1990s, a higher percentage of students were completing high school than ever before, but questions arose over what a high school diploma signaled. Instead of focusing on availability, the current generation of reformers is now forced to consider the quality of school experiences. As Mortimer Adler (1982) argues, we cannot satisfy the legal mandates for education simply by guaranteeing all children access to education. In order to satisfy the educational responsibilities of a democratic society, public education must demonstrate that each student is acquiring requisite skills and knowledge. We can no longer measure educational outcomes only in quantity—years of schooling and the number of high school diplomas granted. Schools must guarantee that the education they offer has a demonstrably positive effect on students. Schools must show that students benefit from their years of attendance; that an increased investment in schooling shows up in a measurably greater ability to read, write, and do mathematics; and that moving up the academic ladder from grade to grade is based on merit rather than social promotion.

The issue of educational quality raises a broad range of questions:

How good is the education provided students in kindergarten through grade 12?

How do the students of today compare with former students?

How do students in School A or District A or State A compare with others?

How can prospective employers know that students who graduate from high school possess a minimum level of skills, knowledge, and ability?

How can taxpayers know that the dollars given over to public education are well spent?

If changes are made in public education, how can we determine whether the changes are having a positive effect on learning?

Answers to these questions must be based on high-quality data. Schools need quantifiable measures of student performance and teacher effectiveness if they hope to maintain public support. Policymakers must make intelligent decision based on objective information. Although no single means of data collection is sufficient, the data that well-designed standardized tests generate are crucial to an understanding of school outcomes. Good tests and good testing programs permit schools to gather information about curricula and students that are not available to them through other means. Without these data, schools cannot make appropriate decisions about the quality of the curriculum or the power of specific programs to enhance learning.

Standardized testing is part of the scientific base that supports the art of teaching. Scientific testing permits us to measure the teacher's art, complementing as well as assessing classroom practice. Formal testing programs were introduced into schools in the nineteenth century to counter charges of examiner bias and subjectivity. Today, standardized testing programs also provide the yardstick society uses to chart the progress and shortcomings of education, and their results allow schools to report the status of education to public officials and parents. Test and measurement experts are often at odds with others in education, and they have suffered abuse from critics who are skeptical about the power of testing and fearful of the testing agencies' power to influence public policy. The purpose here is not to answer the critics or submit a brief in support of the Educational Testing Service or the National Assessment of Educational Progress. Instead, we will argue that (1) standardized testing is an essential tool for examining the measurable dimensions of education; and (2) education has entered an era of accountability. School officials must demonstrate that the money taxpayers spend for education is paying dividends in quality.

## Testing for the Good of Schools and Students

Standardized testing is an essential element of rational curriculum work. The data that testing programs generate help curriculum planners determine whether the measured outcomes of a given set of instructional inputs match the intended goals. In other words, tests can help educators find out if a specific program is working the way it was designed to work. When taxpayers are asked to foot the bill for a new science program in the high school or a new math program in the elementary school, they should be informed of the likely effects of these programs. They should also have hard data by which to judge how well these programs have worked elsewhere. This is a simple matter of cost accounting and fiscal responsibility.

Effective change does not occur by chance. Educational decisions must be made about student progress, the rate of achievement of proximate goals, and the best choice among the competing paths to the next objective. Educational planners need to choose appropriate measures of student attainment. Impressionistic data are not sufficient; anecdotal evidence is not scientific. It is not enough that a program "seems to be working" or that the teachers "claim to like" this method or that approach. Schools need to have better answers to direct questions about the curriculum. At what grade level are students reading? What do diagnostic and prescriptive tests tell us about a child's performance in academic skill areas? How much of the required curricula have students mastered?

Standardized testing should not be viewed as a report card but as part of an assessment system that permits schools to make decisions about curriculum and instruction. Standardized achievement tests are objective measures of performance. They are not designed to provide apologies for ineffective programs, nor do they offer arbitrary norms of excellence. Standardized tests are designed to measure the extent to which the nation is meeting its goals and responsibilities to provide educational quality to all children.

## Shooting the Messenger

In 1991, Congress created the National Council on Educational Standards and Testing, and it charged the Council to offer advice on the desirability of national standards and national testing. Six months later, the Council recommended that Congress take action to adopt high national standards for all children and develop a system of assessment to measure the extent to which students were meeting those standards (Jennings, 1998; Linn, 1993). These recommendations still have not yet been fully implemented. Until the United States establishes national standards and a national assessment system, we will not be able to measure educational quality across state boundary lines. At the present time, the United States has no national curriculum, and although education is essentially an enterprise run by the individual states, Americans have a right to know how well their children's education compares to the education children in other states and regions are receiving.

Since 1969, the federal government has financed an assessment program known as the National Assessment of Educational Progress (NAEP).[4] Administered since 1983 by the Educational Testing Service of Princeton, New Jersey, the NAEP gathers data about the knowledge, skills, and attitudes of students across ten subject areas: art, career and occupational development, citizenship, literature, mathematics, music, reading, science, social studies, and writing. Students in four age groups (ages 9, 13, 17, and young adults) take the tests. Educational planners need to have the information that tests such as the NAEP instruments yield in order to reform schools.

---

[4]The most up-to-date assessment data from NAEP, "The Nation's Report Card," can be found on the worldwide web at http://nces.ed.gov.naep. The Educational Testing Service maintains a website at http://www.ets.org. You may also want to check the website of the National Center for Fair and Open Testing (FairTest) at http://www.fairtest.org. On its website, FairTest is described as "an advocacy organization working to end abuses, misuses, and flaws of standardized testing and ensure that evaluation of students and workers is fair, open, and educationally sound."

Unfortunately, much of the test data has been negative; schoolchildren appear to know less today than in previous periods in our history. Although these findings grab headlines and cause a great deal of collective hand wringing, they should be viewed as a step toward school reform rather than an end in themselves. The NAEP is designed to help us reconsider the quality of teaching and learning in public schools. Too often, the response to negative findings has been to blame the test makers instead of addressing the cause of poor scores. More energy has been expended attacking the validity of standardized testing than in examining the conditions the tests reveal.

In 1985, a project funded by the National Endowment for the Humanities and administered by the staff of the NAEP assessed students' knowledge of history and literature (Ravitch and Finn, 1987). The results were unequivocal: The eight thousand 17-year-olds who took this exam were, in the words of the authors, "ignorant of much of what they should know." The sample was stratified for sex, race, ethnicity, geography, and private school attendance, in order to reflect a national population. Among all test takers, only 20 percent could identify Joyce, Dostoyevsky, Ellison, Conrad, or Ibsen; fewer than 25 percent were able to identify Henry James or Hardy; only one in three knew that Chaucer is the author of *The Canterbury Tales;* 65 percent did not know what *1984* or *Lord of the Flies* is about. Three-quarters of the students did not know when Lincoln was president; one-third were unfamiliar with the *Brown* decision; 70 percent could not identify the Magna Carta.

Critics screamed that the test was not valid—that it did not measure knowledge of the history and literature students learn in school. This criticism cuts to the heart of testing (Wainer and Braun, 1987). The goal of psychometric testing is to provide policymakers with valid data on which to base decisions. Too often, criticisms of standardized tests come from people uninformed about the field of measurement. (Admittedly, this technical area seems to defy the understanding of the general public and many educators.)

The National Assessment of History and Literature (NAHL) was certainly a valid exam. It was written in cooperation with public school teachers, and most of the questions were drawn directly from the most important material covered in the textbooks and curriculum. Most of the questions were designed to cover fundamental material that students of this age might reasonably be expected to know. Citing a handful of the literature questions—such as biblical references—relating to content not typically taught in school, critics raged that the test put certain students at a disadvantage.

The detractors of the NAHL were apparently unmindful of the goal of the exam. The NAHL was not meant to grade students in the hope of failing many of them. It was designed to determine what students know so that educators could improve the curriculum and the nature of instruction. The test did not try to identify individual or typical 17-year-olds. Its results were to be used as one body of objective data for considering what students learn in schools. The NAHL was not intended to replace teacher tests or substitute the judgment of the test makers for the individual judgments of state legislators or curriculum workers.

Standardized test results cannot be ignored. One of the goals of the NAHL was to provide baseline data for future assessments in history and literature. Relatively little is known about these fields of instruction other than enrollment statistics. It is frankly shocking that critics have attacked the test so viciously.[5]

Although testing is far from a perfect science, at present there are no measures that can compete with standardized tests for gathering economical, valid, and reliable data about what children have learned in school. Unfortunately, the testing community has been charged with delivering an unpleasant message. For the past two decades, U.S. students have taken standardized exams that compare their performance in a variety of subject areas (for example, math, science, reading, and geography) to student performance around the world.

Consider what the 1994–1995 assessment of science and math (TIMSS) tells us about science and math education in the United States. TIMSS is a large-scale, complex study of both educational outputs (test scores) and the cultural and academic processes (the processes of schooling). About fifty countries were involved in one or more aspects of the study. Evaluators looked at 628 textbooks and 491 curriculum guides from around the world and analyzed data on teacher practices in the United States and other countries. The result is an interesting as well as distressing portrait of how American students are taught and how they measure up against others around the world. In math, U.S. students lag two years behind, and in science they are almost a year behind.

To be honest, findings that indicate U.S. students are behind in one subject or another are no longer surprising (Stedman, 1997). Other studies have shown that American students lag behind others in essential reading and writing skills, and they lack basic knowledge of history, geography, and civics. This time, TIMSS reviewers in the United States wanted to go beyond reporting the bad news to provide an explanation for the poor performance of U.S. students. The report of the U.S. team examining TIMSS entitled their report *A Splintered Vision* (Schmidt et al., 1996). It points to a problem that surrounds science and math instruction in U.S. schools. Williams Schmidt, lead author of the report, writes:

> There is no one at the helm of U.S. mathematics and science education. In truth, there is no helm. No single coherent vision of how to educate today's children dominates U.S. educational practice in either science or mathematics. There is no single, commonly accepted place to turn for such visions. The visions that shape U.S. mathematics and science education are splintered. This is seen in what is planned to be taught, what is in textbooks, and what teachers teach. (Schmidt et al., 1996, p. 1)

---

[5]The assessment community takes seriously the role testing plays in individual lives, and testing companies know they must be fair and open with the public. Consider, by way of example, what happened when problems were discovered with one Scholastic Assessment Test. Colin Rizzo, a student who had taken the SAT I: Reasoning Test in October 1996, believed that the testing company might not have interpreted one question the way he had. The math problem used the latter $a$ to represent a number, and test makers assumed it to be a positive number. Rizzo assumed $a$ could also be a negative number. After receiving an e-mail from Rizzo, the Educational Testing Service, which administers the exam, agreed with Rizzo and rescored 350,000 tests. While very rare, cases such as this are embarrassing to the company, and ETS behaved responsibly when it learned of the mistake (Tabor, 1997).

The message from the assessment community could not be more clear. American students are not to blame for poor performance on tests that compare them with others; it's the absence of a national curriculum and the lack of agreement about what and how to teach. As the TIMSS authors note, "There is no single, coherent, intellectual vision underlying our efforts in math and science (Schmidt et al., 1996, p. 121). If you find this an unpleasant message, don't blame the messenger.

## Limits to Authentic Assessment

Most of us are familiar with tests that indirectly measure what we know. For example, a test maker who wanted to determine a student's woodworking ability might devise a test composed of a series of multiple-choice items. The student might be asked:

Which of the following tools would you need to make a wooden bowl?
   a) a ball peen hammer
   b) a lathe chisel
   c) a screw driver
   d) a wrench

Other questions might probe the student's knowledge of various types of wood, appropriate procedures for using power tools, types of finishing materials, and safety procedures. These items taken together might indicate a student's knowledge of bowl making, but the student's score would tell the test maker very little about the student's actual ability to fashion a wooden bowl. A better measure of that ability would entail taking the student into a fully equipped woodworking shop to watch him or her set about making a bowl from a block of wood. This authentic measure of performance would allow the test taker to demonstrate actual ability in a real-life situation, and it would allow the test giver to ask why the student followed certain procedures or omitted others (Cizek, 1991).

Performance or authentic assessments evaluate a student's ability to complete real-life tasks. Used as part of the instructional process, it allows teachers to see if students have mastered one set of skills before they move on to teach others. The NAEP first used performance components on tests in 1990; in 1992, it experimented with having students establish writing portfolios to assess writing ability, and it is planning to further expand the use of performance items. Performance assessment is one of the more exciting new developments in evaluation design, and it promises to give educators at the local level answers to questions previously available only through high-inference measures or proxy measures of ability. Performance testing can tell teachers, parents, and students whether a student can write an essay, conduct a science experiment, or make a wooden bowl.

Test makers and psychometricians are eager to design assessment instruments that allow test takers to demonstrate what they know in authentic situations. Assessment programs are changing: In 1994, the verbal section of the SAT began to place greater emphasis on reading and reasoning; the mathematics section now places more emphasis on data interpretation and real-life mathematics, and students are asked to demonstrate how they arrived at correct answers. "Multiple-guess" will no longer be a valid synonym for multiple-choice on such assessments. The latest generation of performance-based tests is not being used to group students by ability or measure them against arbitrary criteria; authentic assessment is designed to inform teachers about their students' abilities so they can improve learning for all students (Darling-Hammond, 1994). Performance testing is not without its faults. The testing community is well aware of its strengths and weaknesses, and it urges other educators not to discard the successes of standardized testing programs too quickly (Linn, 1993).

Since 1988, Vermont has been developing statewide performance programs in mathematics and writing in order to generate data about student achievement. Careful reviews of the Vermont process suggest that such data may be very difficult, if not impossible, to obtain through performance evaluation alone. Scoring writing portfolios is particularly difficult. It is generally agreed that when evaluators want to determine the quality of student writing, a performance review of actual student writing collected over time has clear advantages over a multiple-choice exam that covers the rules of grammar and the mechanics of writing. However, unlike scoring standardized exams, the evaluation of writing samples is highly subjective. A single reviewer may not offer a reliable assessment of writing, and it is often difficult to find two reviewers who agree about the quality of written work. We thus cannot assume that portfolio assessments are less biased or more fair than standardized testing programs unless the assessment undergoes rigorous examination for bias and discrimination (Supovitz and Brennan, 1997).

The assessment of student learning always entails problems. Although policymakers would prefer assessments that are easy, accurate, and inexpensive, assessment designs must be complex to account for variations among students, teachers, and curricula (Koretz et al., 1994; Linn, 1993). Performance or authentic assessment has a great deal of promise, but it must be viewed with caution. It allows teachers to observe the effects of instruction directly; students demonstrate the extent to which they have mastered the subject. However, performance testing alone does not provide data about how well students are performing compared with those in other districts, states, or nations. It permits students to exhibit real-world mastery of skills, but it doesn't compare one student with others of the same age and educational level.

Performance assessment is not a substitute for high-quality standardized testing. It offers the education community the promise of a fuller picture, but taken alone, the results of performance testing offer a snapshot too grainy to shape policy. As yet, there are no substitutes for objective data, standardized tests, and other measures that allow test takers to know where students stand in comparison to others and that permit policymakers to gauge the progress of educational change.

## For Discussion

1. Monty Neill, co-chair of the National Forum on Assessment, a group critical of standardized testing, argues that the primary purpose of assessment is to enhance student learning and that teachers should employ a wide range of assessment techniques. "These include," he writes, "structured and spur-of-the-moment observations that are recorded and filed; formal and informal interviews; collections of work samples; use of extended projects, performances, and exhibitions; performance exams; and various forms of short-answer testing. In this context, teachers could use multiple-choice questions, but as the Forum recommends, they would have a very limited role" (Neill, 1997, p. 35).

   As a student, do you like to be evaluated in the manner just described? What are the advantages and disadvantages? As a prospective teacher, is this manner of assessment appealing or unappealing? How do you think parents, state legislators, college admissions and scholarship committees, and people interested in making national and international comparisons of pupil achievement would view Neill's proposals?

2. Howard Gardner (1983) argues that children have "multiple intelligences" that afford them differing patterns of strengths and weaknesses. His research identifies seven domains of intelligence:

   1. Linguistic Intelligence: the ability to use written and oral language well
   2. Logical-Mathematical Intelligence: the ability to identify patterns and relationships and use numbers effectively
   3. Spatial Intelligence: the ability to recognize and mentally manipulate forms and objects
   4. Musical Intelligence: the ability to understand, perform, or compose music as a means of expression
   5. Bodily-Kinesthetic Intelligence: the ability to use one's motor skills in sports or performing arts
   6. Intrapersonal Intelligence: the ability to understand one's inner feelings and ideas
   7. Interpersonal Intelligence: the ability to get along well with other people

   Which forms of intelligence are standardized multiple-choice tests most likely to tap? Assuming that Gardner's research is valid, should schools supplement standardized testing programs and design instruction around multiple forms of intelligence, or should we limit the forms of intelligence and ability that schools recognize and reward?

3. Students demand fairness in testing and grading, and they often argue that evaluations of their written work are subjective and that an essay one professor evaluates negatively might be awarded a better grade by another. In a controlled study of "writing ability," 53 different evaluators graded 300 student papers (15,900 evaluations overall). More than one-third of the papers (101) received every possible grade from A through D, and no paper received fewer than five different grades (Hirsch, 1996, pp. 183–184).

Hirsch argues that research findings such as those just described cast doubt on the validity and reliability of performance assessments to measure writing ability. To demonstrate your writing ability, do you prefer to write essays, constructed and evaluated by your teacher, or do you prefer to take commercially prepared, standardized multiple-choice exams scored by a neutral party? Could each form of assessment be reliable and valid? Does your preference for essay or short-answer evaluation extend to other subject areas? Should students have a choice between standardized multiple-choice exams and essay exams to assess their performance in classes?

## *References*

ADLER, M. J. (1982). *The Paideia Proposal: An Educational Manifesto.* New York: Macmillan.

ARENSON, K. W. (1996). "College Board Revises Test to Improve Chances for Girls." *New York Times,* October 2. (http://www.nytimes.com)

CALLAHAN, E. (1962). *Education and the Cult of Efficiency.* Chicago: University of Chicago Press.

CANNELL, J. J. (1987). *Nationally Normed Elementary Achievement Testing in America's Public Schools: How All 50 States Are Above the National Average.* 2nd ed. Daniels, WV: Friends for Education.

CHENOWETH, K. (1997). "A Measurement of What?" *Black Issues in Higher Education 14,* 18–22, 25.

CIZEK, G. J. (1991). "Innovation or Enervation? Performance Assessment in Perspective." *Phi Delta Kappan 72,* 695–699.

CREMIN, L. (1961). *The Transformation of the School: Progressivism in American Education, 1876–1957.* New York: Knopf.

CRONBACH, L. J. (1988). "Five Perspectives on Validity Argument." In *Test Validity,* edited by H. Wainer and H. I. Braun. Hillsdale, NJ: Lawrence Erlbaum.

CROUSE, J., AND TRUSHEIM, D. (1988). *The Case Against the SAT.* Chicago: University of Chicago Press.

DARLING-HAMMOND, L. (1994). "Performance-Based Assessment and Educational Equity." *Harvard Educational Review 64,* 5–30.

FISKE, E. B. (1988). "America's Test Mania." *New York Times, Education Life,* April 10, pp. 16–20.

GARCIA, G. E., AND PEARSON, P. D. (1994). "Assessment and Diversity." In *Review of Research in Education,* edited by L. Darling-Hammond. Washington, DC: American Educational Research Association.

GARDNER, H. (1983). *Frames of Mind: The Theory of Multiple Intelligences.* New York: Basic Books.

GOULD, S. J. (1981). *The Mismeasure of Man.* New York: Norton.

GRAVES, J. L., JR. (1996). "The Pseudoscience of Psychometry and *The Bell Curve.*" *Journal of Negro Education 64,* 277–294.

GUMBERT, E. B., AND SPRING, J. H. (1974). *The Superschool and The Superstate: American Education in the Twentieth Century, 1918–1970.* New York: John Wiley and Sons.

HERRNSTEIN, R. J., AND MURRAY, C. (1994). *The Bell Curve: Intelligence and Class Structure in American Life.* New York: Free Press.

HIRSCH, E. D., JR. (1996). *The Schools We Need and Why We Don't Have Them.* New York: Doubleday.

HOFFMANN, B. (1962). *The Tyranny of Testing.* New York: Crowell-Colliers.

JENNINGS, J. F. (1998). *Why National Standards and Tests? Politics and the Quest for Better Schools.* Thousand Oaks, CA: Sage.

JENSEN, A. R. (1969). "How Much Can We Boost IQ and Scholastic Achievement?" *Harvard Educational Review 39,* 1–123.

JUDSON, G. (1996). "What Makes the School Shine? Test Tampering, Officials Say." *New York Times,* May 1. (http://www.nytimes.com)

KERLINGER, F. N. (1979). *Behavioral Research.* New York: Holt, Rinehart and Winston.

KORETZ, D., STECHER, B., KLEIN, S., AND MCCAFFREY, D. (1994). "The Vermont Portfolio Assessment: Findings and Implications." *Educational Measurement: Issues and Practice 13,* 5–16.

LINN, R. L. (1993). "Educational Assessment: Expanded Expectation and Challenges." *Educational Evaluation and Policy Analysis 15,* 1–16.

MADAUS, G. F. (1994). "A Technological and Historical Consideration of Equity Issues Associated with Proposals to Change the Nation's Testing Policy." *Harvard Educational Review 64,* 76–95.

MEHRENS, W. A., AND KAMINSKI, J. (1989). "Methods for Improving Standardized Test Scores: Fruitful, Fruitless, or Fraudulent?" *Educational Measurement: Issues and Practice 8,* 14–22.

NAIRN, A., AND ASSOCIATES. (1980). *The Reign of ETS: The Corporation that Makes Up Minds.* Washington, DC: Nairn and Associates.

NEILL, D. M., AND MEDINA, N. J. (1989). "Standardized Testing: Harmful to Educational Health." *Phi Delta Kappan 70,* 688–697.

NEILL, D. M. (1991). "Do We Need a National Achievement Exam? No: It Would Damage, Not Improve Education." *Education Week* April 24, pp. 36, 28.

———. (1997). "Transforming Student Assessment." *Phi Delta Kappan 79,* 34–40, 58.

NORDHEIMER, J., AND FRANZ, D. (1997). "Testing Service, Expanding and Competing, Draws Fire from All Sides." *New York Times,* September 30, 1997. (http://www.nytimes.com)

OGBU, J. (1978). *Minority Education and Caste: The American System in Cross-Cultural Perspective.* New York: Academic.

OWEN, D. (1985). *None of the Above.* Boston: Houghton Mifflin.

PHILLIPS, G. W. (1990). "The Lake Wobegon Effect." *Educational Measurement: Issues and Practice 9,* 3, 14.

RAVITCH, D., AND FINN, C. E., JR. (1987). *What Do Our 17-Year-Olds Know?* New York: Harper and Row.

ROSSER, P. (1987). *Sex Bias in College Admissions Testing: Why Women Lose Out.* 2nd ed. Cambridge, MA: FairTest.

SCHMIDT, W., MCKNIGHT, C., AND RAIZEN, S., IN COLLABORATION WITH SIX OTHERS. (1996). *A Splintered Vision: An Investigation of U.S. Science and Mathematics Education.* Boston: Klumer Academic Publishers.

STEDMAN, L. C. (1997). "International Achievement Differences: An Assessment of a New Perspective." *Educational Researcher 26,* 4–15.

SUPOVITZ, J. A., AND BRENNAN, R. T. (1997). "Mirror, Mirror on the Wall, Which Is the Fairest Test of All? An Examination of Portfolio Assessment Relative to Standardized Tests." *Harvard Educational Review 67,* 472–502.

TABOR, M. B. W. (1997). "Student Discovery of Flaw Forces Rescoring of SAT." *New York Times,* February 7, 1997. (http://www.nytimes.com)

TERMAN, L. M. (1922). *Intelligence Tests and School Reorganization.* Yonkers-on-Hudson: World Book Company.

U.S. DEPARTMENT OF EDUCATION. (1987). *What's Happening in Teacher Testing: An Analysis of State Teacher Testing Practices.* Washington, DC: U.S. Government Printing Office.

————. (1991). *America 2000: An Education Strategy.* Washington, DC: U.S. Government Printing Office.

WAINER, H., AND BRAUN, H. I., EDITORS. (1987). *Test Validity.* Hillsdale, NJ: Erlbaum.

WOLF, J. B., BIXBY, J., GLENN, J., AND GARDNER, H. (1991). "To Use Their Minds Well: Investigating New Forms of Student Assessment." In *Review of Research in Education*, edited by G. Grant. Washington, DC: American Educational Research Association.

## PART THREE

# How Should Schools Be Organized and Operated?

The five chapters in Part III focus on how schools should be organized and managed. One central strand running through the chapters calls your attention to the role teachers should play in schools. It is an issue that goes back to ancient times. What should be the nature of teachers' work? How much decision-making authority should teachers have? Among the oldest traditions of education is the view that teachers are the obedient servants of the state. Plato, who is often cited as the first philosopher of education, paid scant attention to the needs of teachers. His concern was the creation of a just society governed by the most able citizens. Education to prepare students for their place in society was under the heavy-handed control of the state. Schooling was compulsory up to age 20. Plato proposed that censors scrutinize the curriculum to make certain it contained no reference to anything that did not serve public ends. Plato's writing urged teachers to slavishly follow the curriculum; any deviation could only be for the worse. He wrote:

> In short, then, those who keep watch over our commonwealth must take the greatest care not to overlook the least infraction of the rule against any innovation upon the established system of education either of the body or of the mind. When the poet says that men care most for 'the newest air that hovers on the singer's lips,' they will be afraid lest he be taken not merely to mean new songs, but to commending a new style of music. Such innovation is not to be commended, nor should the poet be so understood. The introduction of novel fashions in music is a thing to beware of as endangering the whole fabric of society. (Cornford, 1968, p. 115)

**351**

Few people today would deny teachers the right to innovate in the classroom. Unlike Plato, most people believe in the potential of progress and the value of change. However, many believe that control of the curriculum remains the rightful province of the state or community and not the teacher. To empower teachers with authority over the curriculum is to disempower taxpayers, their elected representatives (boards of education), and school administrators.

Consider yourselves, for a moment, not as teachers or prospective teachers, but as taxpayers with children in public schools. Would you be comfortable paying hefty tax bills while having little or no say in the education of your children? Would you be willing to leave decisions about curriculum, textbooks, teaching methodology, and evaluation to teachers who are not accountable to you? Or would you prefer to have these policy matters rest in the hands of school administrators and elected school boards who are responsible to you as a citizen and community resident? Clearly, a strong case can be made for community control of schools.

Some argue with equal conviction that school reform has failed in the past largely because reformers have ignored the role teachers play. For schools to become more satisfying and more thought-provoking for children, they must first become better places for teachers. Teachers must be allowed to assume their rightful place as professionals with genuine authority in the school; they should control matters of curriculum, instruction, and policy. Teachers should be able to assume a responsible role in shaping the purposes of schooling (Aronowitz and Giroux, 1985). As a prospective teacher, would you want to work for a school district that refused to listen to you about matters of curriculum and instruction?

Arguments about the organization and management of schools lie along a continuum of political thought. The left, or liberal, end of the continuum includes those who tend to be sympathetic toward the rights of workers and toward teacher empowerment. It also includes those with positive views of unions and union involvement in school policy matters, as well as those who champion academic freedom for public school teachers. The right, or conservative, end of the continuum includes those who are more comfortable with the traditional exercise of authority in the schools. They tend to oppose any attempt to weaken community control of schools by granting greater power to teachers. Those on the right tend to be less sympathetic toward unions, often viewing them as the protectors of incompetent teachers and as unwise meddlers in local school management. Conservatives typically share a less than charitable view toward academic freedom for public school teachers, regarding it as an overused shield for spreading ill-founded and even dangerous ideas in the classroom.

Of course, we need to be cautious about painting with too broad a brush. Unions tend to be on the left end of the spectrum—but former Presidents Reagan and Bush enjoyed great support among union members. Similarly, community control of schools is typically considered a plank in a conservative political platform, but those on the left were the main champions of the decentralization of New York City's school system in the 1960s. Our goal is not to label school critics, but to make you more aware of the competing perspectives. As you think about what teaching should be, look to the arguments of both left and right. Where do you find yourself along the spectrum of opinion on each issue?

## SCHOOL LEADERSHIP: TEACHER-DIRECTED OR ADMINISTRATOR-CONTROLLED?

Teaching has been described as a "careerless profession," a job which offers only limited opportunity for promotion or increases in authority and salary (Etzioni, 1969; Lortie, 1975). Upon graduation from college, most people pursue a series of work experiences and job-related career moves that bring them additional responsibilities and greater remuneration. A few teachers—mainly those who move from classroom teaching through the principalship to central office administration—follow a similar ascent. However, teachers typically do not have access to a promotion path that includes a series of increasingly rewarding positions, and teachers are not allowed to participate in the reform and growth of education.

One teacher reported, somewhat tongue in cheek, that she had been "too busy too notice" that her husband, a hospital pharmacist, was participating in the development of his profession to a far greater extent than she was in hers. She slowly came to realize that her husband's work had allowed him to grow, while her role as a classroom teacher denied her similar professional development. She noted that the knowledge base of her husband's field had expanded, and

the techniques of pharmacy had grown and changed. More important, practitioners in the field had developed the advances and eagerly shared them with colleagues across the country. She wrote:

> Meanwhile, in my school district, classroom lessons looked the way they had in the fifties. Behind closed doors for the most part, teachers lectured, quizzed, and tested. Students "did" their workbooks and end-of-chapter questions, just as they had when I was in school myself. . . I want a database, too. I want up-to-date bibliographies on issues that directly affect the students I teach. I need . . . access . . . to colleagues who are testing solutions to the same problems I encounter. (Swart, 1990, pp. 315–316)

Schools, unlike most other large workplaces, are characterized by a flat organizational structure. Most employees occupy a single, undifferentiated job category: classroom teacher. Schools typically do not offer enough routes out of the classroom (for example, guidance counselor, building principal, curriculum coordinator, department chair) to permit the career mobility common to other fields (Sikes, Measor, and Woods, 1985). The majority of teachers begin their work in the classroom and end their careers as classroom teachers, without taking on additional responsibilities or gaining direct influence in running the school. Some sociologists have argued that because of its structure, teaching is an occupation that has better met the work needs of women than men (Lortie, 1975). Women, the argument goes, can begin teaching, drop out to raise a family, and return to the classroom when their children no longer need them at home without missing a beat.[1]

In the past, teaching and teachers' work were largely ignored as issues of public concern. If the public was satisfied with the quality of schools and the performance of teachers, its satisfaction was expressed inaudibly. When schools appeared to be functioning well, communities rarely considered the problems of a teaching career. As long as student learning appeared to be high and student discipline was relatively unproblematic, few people outside of education concerned themselves with teachers' salary structures, the role teachers should play in schools, or the difficulty of attracting and retaining talented faculty.

By the 1980s, evidence suggested a variety of problems with public schooling. Educational expenditures had never been higher, but scores on standardized achievement tests were hitting all-time lows. Restive teachers demanded higher salaries, while the popular press delighted in printing stories of increases in school violence, crime, and the numbers of poorly educated students. Studies criticized everything from student learning to teacher preparation (Archibold, 1998; Boyer, 1983; Goodlad, 1984; Goodlad, 1990; National Commission, 1983; Sizer, 1984). The schools were said to be in crisis and the nation was declared at risk because of the poor quality of teaching and learning. Teachers

were held up to public scrutiny, and their work was weighed, measured, and assessed. Everywhere, researchers found dull, lifeless teaching; an absence of academic focus; bored, unchallenged students; and teachers mired in routine and paperwork. Implicit in this new focus was the idea that teachers were not doing, or were not able to do, the job expected of them.

School problems were recognized by those on both sides of the desk. Neither immune to public criticism nor insensitive to school problems, teachers became increasingly dissatisfied with their work. A poll conducted by the National Education Association indicated that if they could start over, only 25 percent of the female and 16 percent of the male teachers would again choose teaching as a career (*Status of the American Public School Teacher*, 1982). The Carnegie Forum (1986), among others, suggested that a major cause of teacher dissatisfaction was the structure of schools, and it predicted a diminished pool of high-quality teachers in the future unless schools reorganized to make teaching more attractive.

Many have suggested that there is something very wrong with the ways schools organize teachers' work and career paths. In the late 1980s and early 1990s, nearly everyone advocating "restructuring" for school reform sought ways to include teachers in making decisions about curriculum and teaching. The arguments supporting teacher inclusion in decision making fall into three general areas: (1) Improved student performance: If teachers have greater decision-making authority, they will use their special knowledge about teaching to develop innovative approaches that enhance student learning. (2) Increased teacher

[1]Critics of this analysis note that it fails to account for the fact that women have multiple commitments, including career and family. Teaching may permit women to meet multiple obligations, but that does not mean that teaching satisfies their career needs any better than it does men's (Feiman-Nemser and Floden, 1986; Valentine, 1995).

professionalism: Teachers will have enhanced status if they are recognized as part of the decision-making team. They will have a greater sense of responsibility for school problems, and they will share a deeper commitment to work for school improvement. (3) Better role models for students: Shared decision making presents teachers as active, empowered workers. It provides students with role models for workplace democracy (Weiss, 1993, pp. 69–70).

Chapter 14 presents two positions on restructuring the work and role of teachers. Position 1 calls for teachers to exert influence well beyond the walls of their classrooms in order to improve their job satisfaction and performance. This position recommends restructuring schools to grant teachers decision-making authority in organizing the curriculum, running the schools, and charting the reform agenda. Position 2 argues that teacher empowerment would be to the detriment of students and communities. It argues that schools should consider teacher input, but professional administrators must make the decisions that best serve children, their parents, and the needs of the community.

## ACADEMIC FREEDOM: TEACHER RIGHTS OR RESPONSIBILITY

If you view teachers as the leaders in schools, then you are likely to believe that their right to teach should be protected. If, instead, you see teachers as practitioners who have no responsibility other than to serve the needs of children, then you may be less willing to grant them the same freedoms enjoyed by those who teach in good universities. "Academic freedom," as applied to higher education, is a contemporary term for the classical ideal of the right to teach and learn (Hofstadter and Metzger, 1955). Socrates, charged with impiety and the corruption of Athenian youth, defended himself by claiming that he and his students had the freedom to pursue truth. All wickedness, he argued, was due to ignorance. The freedom to teach and to learn would uncover knowledge, eliminate ignorance, and improve the society. His fellow citizens were not persuaded, and Socrates was sentenced to death. Academic freedom has fared better; though regularly battered, it has survived.

Although lacking a crisp, precise definition, academic freedom, as used in American higher education, typically refers to several related freedoms: (1) the freedom of professors to write, research, and teach in their field of special competence; (2) the freedom of universities to determine policies and practices unfettered by political restraints or other outside pressures; and (3) the freedom of students to learn.

Advocates argue that academic freedom ensures freedom of the mind for both students and scholars and therefore is essential to the pursuit of truth, the primary mission of higher education (Kirk, 1955; MacIver, 1955). The university should be a marketplace of competing ideas. Students should be exposed to a diversity of views, and the classroom should be free of restraint and open to the regular and robust exchange of opinions. The question is not about academic freedom in universities, but whether we should extend academic freedom to those who teach in elementary and secondary schools. The word *academy* originally referred to the garden where Plato taught, and academic freedom came to be associated with institutions of higher learning. Public schools are unlike universities, and public school teachers and students do not automatically have the same academic protection as their university counterparts. Some argue that the comparative youthfulness of the students and the nature of instruction demand that public school teachers be more accountable to the community for what they teach and how they teach it.

This narrow conception of academic freedom, as a right enjoyed only in higher education, is undergoing challenges from professional associations of teachers and other groups interested in public education (Kaplan and Schrecker, 1983).[2] The American Civil Liberties Union (ACLU), for example, objects to limiting academic freedom to university settings. The ACLU claims that academic freedom should extend to the public schools, which they describe as the "authentic academic community" for young people. "If each new generation is to acquire a feeling for civil liberties," the

ACLU argues, "it can do so only by having a chance to live in the midst of a community where the principles are continually exemplified" (*Academic Freedom in the Secondary Schools*, 1968, p. 4).

The courts have, on occasion, been highly supportive of academic freedom for public school teachers. Writing on *Wieman v. Updergraff* in 1952, Justices Frankfurter and Douglas argued that all teachers, from the primary grades to the university, share a special role in developing good citizens, and all teachers should have the academic freedom necessary to be exemplars of open-mindedness and free inquiry. Similarly, other courts have ruled that limiting academic freedom to postsecondary education would discriminate against students who do not attend college:

> To restrict the opportunity for involvement in an open forum for the free exchange of ideas to higher education would not only foster an unacceptable elitism, it would fail to complete the development of those not going to college, contrary to our constitutional commitment to equal opportunity. Effective citizenship in a participatory democracy must not be dependent upon advancement toward college degrees. Consequently, it would be inappropriate to conclude that academic freedom is required only in colleges and universities. *Cary v. Board of Education*, 427 F. Supp.945, 953, D.Colo. 1977, quoted in Rubin and Greenhouse, 1983, p.116)

The courts are not likely to settle the issue (O'Neill, 1984). The idea of extending academic freedom to public school teachers goes to the core of teaching and is properly a matter of

[2]Many national organizations are concerned with securing academic freedom for teachers in public schools. Students may wish to consult the following groups to ascertain their position on academic freedom: the American Association of School Libraries, the American Association of University Professors, the American Bar Association, the American Civil Liberties Union, the American Federation of Teachers, the American Historical Association, the American Library Association, the National Council for the Social Studies, the National Council of Teachers of English, and the National Education Association.

educational, not legal, policy. The issue raises a series of difficult questions that school boards, local communities, and teachers' organizations must address: Who should academic freedom protect? Is it a right that can be extended automatically to all public school teachers? Does academic freedom clash with the community's right to determine what to teach its children, and in what manner of instruction? Who decides what is an appropriate education for minor children? How do we best prepare our students for their roles as citizens? Can higher education continue to claim academic freedom as a special province reserved for university experts (Hook, 1953)? Or do universities ignore threats to academic freedom in public schools at their own peril (O'Neill, 1987)?

Chapter 15 presents competing perspectives on the issue of academic freedom for public school teachers and students. Position 1 encourages us to reserve academic freedom for researchers in universities, not extend it to teachers in public schools. Teachers in elementary and secondary schools, this position argues, need no freedoms beyond those the Constitution guarantees to all citizens. To give them more academic freedom could jeopardize their role as parental surrogates and political representatives of the society. Position 2 is more sympathetic to the empowerment of teachers. It defends academic freedom for public school teachers as a right essential to the search for knowledge and to the freedom of mind necessary for the development of democratic ideals.

## TEACHER UNIONS: DETRIMENTAL OR BENEFICIAL?

Teacher unions are here to stay. That much is clear. What is not yet clear is whether they will turn out to be beneficial, harmful, or merely irrelevant to the quality of education in American schools. (Finn, 1985, p. 331)

Are teacher unions necessary evils that demand accommodation in wage disputes? Are they potentially harmful to education, with the power to hijack the reform agendas of legislators and school administrators? Or are unions committed to working in a coalition—along with parents and administrators—that can reform schools and turn failing school districts around? The answers to these questions help define your position on the continuum of opinions about school reform.

The public is divided over the value of unions. A recent poll found that 27 percent of the respondents believe unions have improved schools; 26 percent believe unions have hurt schools; and 37 percent believe that teacher unions have made no difference (Rose and Gallup, 1998, p. 54). Before discussing the arguments in chapter 16, consider some of the background on teacher unions.

Teachers have been organized for well over one hundred years, but their earliest organizations were not really unions. The National Education Association (NEA), for example, was established in 1857 to represent the views of "practical" classroom teachers and administrators. Annual conventions of the NEA were not union meetings but settings for the exchange of ideas about teaching. Members typically avoided discussing how teachers could influence decisions about their work or wages. The NEA was less concerned with the personal welfare of classroom teachers than it was with advancing the profession of education. In its early years, the NEA was a male-dominated organization *for* teachers that was led by school superintendents, professors of education, and school principals (Wesley, 1957). As one critic of the NEA notes, the role of classroom teachers, especially women teachers, was "limited to listening" (Eaton, 1975, p. 10). Since the 1960s, the NEA has moved more aggressively to represent the views of all classroom teachers, advocating collective negotiations and encouraging its local affiliates to serve as bargaining agents for teachers.

Teacher unionism dates to the early twentieth century, when Chicago teachers organized to fight for better working conditions. In 1916, the American Federation of Teachers (AFT) was formed as an affiliate of the American Federation of Labor. Initially, the older NEA and the upstart AFT cooperated. The NEA focused on the professional and practical sides of teaching; the AFT concentrated on improving the economic aspects of teachers' lives (Engel, 1976). Over the years, local affiliates of the NEA and the AFT have become rivals in their efforts to become the teachers' bargaining agents.[3] More than 80 percent of U.S. teachers belong to either the NEA

or the AFT, and more than 60 percent work under a formal collective bargaining agreement. (In comparison, fewer than 15 percent of workers in private industry belong to labor unions.)

Today, teacher organizations often bear a greater resemblance to professional associations (for example, the American Bar Association or the American Medical Association) than to labor organizations (the International Ladies Garment Workers Union or the United Automobile Workers). However, the leaders of the old AFT identified with unionized workers in other industries. They believed that problems common to all workers could be solved through cooperation and collective action. They wanted teacher organizations to provide economic benefits for their members, and they argued that teacher unions could also assist labor by improving the education offered to working-class children. Despite numerous efforts to organize teachers and to revitalize education, including the development of a workers' college and special public schools for workers' children, membership in the AFT declined in the 1920s and remained flat throughout most of the 1930s. Teachers were reluctant to join unions, and most school administrators were openly hostile. In the 1920s, fearing worker radicalism and union activity, many school superintendents demanded that teachers, as a condition of employment, sign "yellow dog contracts," agreeing not to join a union.

The National Labor Relations Act (NLRA) of 1935 changed the status of unions by recognizing that workers in private industry had the right to bargain collectively. Most labor historians consider this legislation favorable

[3]Bargaining agents are the elected representatives of the teachers who negotiate on their behalf. These agents advocate for teachers on salary and working conditions, negotiating with the members or representatives of the board of education. (Sharp, 1993).

to unions.[4] In collective bargaining, employees, as a group, and their employers negotiate in good faith about wages and employment conditions (Lieberman and Moscow, 1966, p. 1). Employees are at a disadvantage when they bargain singly with employers, working alone against the power and resources at management's hand. Collective bargaining laws recognize that workers have the right to join together and elect a bargaining agent (a union) to negotiate with management. The NLRA required employers and unions to "meet at reasonable times and confer in good faith with respect to wages, hours, and other terms and conditions of employment."

Questions about its constitutionality clouded the early history of the NLRA. The Supreme Court eventually decided the issue, judging the act constitutional (*NLRB v. Jones and Laughlin Steel Company*, 1937). This was a major victory for organized labor, and it represented a great change in the thinking of the courts. Court rulings concerning the rights of workers to engage in collective negotiations can be traced to the Philadelphia Cordwainers case in the early part of the nineteenth century. In that case, the workers were found guilty of entering into a conspiracy (a union) to improve their wages. By the mid-nineteenth century,

courts no longer believed that those who advocated collective bargaining were involved in criminal conspiracies (*Commonwealth v. Hunt*, 1842), but unions and collective negotiations did not earn full legitimacy until the Supreme Court's 1937 decision.

The NLRA affects only workers in the private sector. It does not cover employees of federal, state, or local government, so this law did not guarantee collective bargaining for public school teachers. Schools are considered extensions of the state. School boards are, in a sense, state employers, and they are thus excluded from federal labor legislation. It has been left up to the states to regulate employment relations in public education. Following Congress's lead, the majority of state legislatures have taken action to recognize the rights of workers to organize and negotiate with employers. By the late 1990s, thirty-four states had laws legally protecting the rights of teachers to bargain collectively; nine states had laws making collective bargaining illegal; and six states were officially silent, neither denying or enabling collective bargaining, instead leaving the decision to local school districts (Lieberman, 1997, p. 48).

The organization of teachers in New York City in 1960 is considered a watershed for public school unions (Lieberman and Moscow, 1966, p. 35). The United Federation of Teachers (UFT), a local affiliate of the AFT, was made up of several New York City teacher organizations. The UFT asked the Board of Education to recognize the teachers' rights to bargain collectively and to conduct an election to determine which organization should represent them. The board was unsure

[4]Geoghegan (1991) argues that by bringing the federal government into union organization and labor-management negotiations, the NLRA was ultimately harmful to unions. He claims that by embracing the state, unions did themselves in. The short-lived government support for unions in the 1930s completely reversed by the 1980s, when anti-union sentiment contributed to their decline. Geoghegan argues that all labor laws should be repealed and that labor and management should simply go at each another.

how to implement collective bargaining, and it did not move swiftly. The unions accused the board of stalling, and on November 7, 1960, the UFT declared the first strike in the history of New York City education.

It was a brief but effective job action: The next day, the teachers were back in the classrooms. The board had agreed to hold elections and not to take reprisals against striking teachers. Union estimates put pickets at about 7,500, and it was claimed that another 15,000 teachers stayed home (Eaton, 1975, p. 165). The strike alerted the nation to the power of unions, and teachers began to recognize the advantages of collective negotiation as well as the power potential of the strike. Collective bargaining changed the relationship between classroom teachers and administrators. It promised teachers more pay, better job security, and an audible voice in education. As one labor historian puts it, "It essentially refined and broadened the concept of professionalism by assuring [teachers] more autonomy and less supervisory control" (Murphy, 1990, p. 209).

The New York City strike reverberated nationally. The results encouraged teachers, and it sent the two largest unions, the NEA and the AFT, scrambling for members. The NEA represents about 2 million teachers, about twice the number represented by the AFT. These organizations differ on specific issues. An examination of the views of each union can be found in the journal *The NEA Today* and the AFT's *American Teacher*. Regular columns by the AFT president appear in the *New York Times;* columns by the NEA president appear in the *Washington Post.*

Chapter 16 does not play out the debate between advocates of the NEA and supporters of the AFT, nor does it contain arguments about the morality or appropriateness of teacher strikes. The issue here is not whether teachers should or should not belong to professional work associations, but whether unions are good for the future of education. Position 1 argues that unions are undemocratic organizations that work against the best interests of pupils, parents, and teachers. Collective bargaining is not for the public good, nor will it contribute to school reform; it should be restricted if schools are to serve the children and the community. Position 2 argues that unions have had a positive effect on education, and that collective bargaining and union influence should extend beyond wages and hours to include matters of school policy and reform. This view holds that the success of future school improvement will be linked to the participation of unions in the reform agenda.

## *INCLUSION AND MAINSTREAMING: SPECIAL OR COMMON?*

One of the current issues facing schools across the United States is how to provide the most appropriate education for students who have special needs. Children who have particular mental or physical disabilities, are emotionally disturbed, or have other specific needs fall into this category. Sometimes the term *exceptional* is applied to this group of children in educational literature; usually, this term includes children identified as gifted and talented.

The main reason for trying to identify and evaluate children with special or exceptional needs is to provide them with the special educational assistance they need. For the physically disabled, that may mean special equipment such as magnification devices for the visually impaired. For learning disabled children, it may mean specially prepared teaching materials. For gifted and talented children, that may mean special artistic tutoring or advanced academic work.

Many conflicts arise over how to identify and evaluate special or exceptional needs. Exceptionality has always been an individual condition in human societies, and special education represents the institutional and educational programs which evolved during the eighteenth century to provide some assistance to those classified as exceptional (Winzer, 1993). The terms used to describe the exceptional child show changes in the public's view of such children. In earlier times, there was very little differentiation between various physical and mental disabilities; all were considered part of a single category. The "crippled," deaf, and mentally ill were grouped together. At the end of the eighteenth century, some differentiation began, with the "insane," the blind, and the "deaf and dumb" receiving the most attention.

Historically, special needs children were excluded from schools and often hidden away from public view. By the end of the nineteenth century in the United States, many states were establishing special schools for children with certain physical or mental disabilities, and the federal government was providing some support for this effort. The standard pattern for special needs children was separation from other children in school. The field of special education emerged and developed as a response to the in-

creasing social interest in educating these students. Starting in the 1960s, federal law provided grants to the states to expand and improve special education. In 1975, Congress passed the Education for All Handicapped Children Act, Public Law 94–142, which mandated equal opportunity for children with disabilities to a free and appropriate education, nondiscriminatory evaluation of children, education in the least restrictive environment, and accountability to parents of special needs children for their education. In the United States, the change in terms, and the changing social view, is illustrated by the 1886 Idiocy Act, the 1975 Education for All Handicapped Act (PL94–142), and the 1990 Americans With Disabilities Act (ADA).

There have been many efforts to define, measure, and educate children considered exceptional, yet debate continues. Categories of exceptionality currently include:

Blind/Visually Impaired

Deaf/Hearing Impaired

Orthopedically or Otherwise Health Impaired

Learning Disabled

Mentally Retarded

Gifted and Talented

Speech/Language Impaired

Emotionally Disturbed

Multiply Disabled

Others—for example, Autistic, Traumatic Brain Injured

(Ysseldyke and Algozzine, 1990; U.S. Office of Education, Office of Special Education Programs)

The major current issue about the education of children with special needs is the movement toward inclusion of these children into the regular classes and activities of the school. This issue incorporates many other issues related to how schools classify, evaluate, and educate exceptional children. In addition, it raises questions about teacher education and teacher practice, school economics and special funds for special education, tracking and other forms of student separation, dealing with disruptive students, and school decision making about the best education for each child.

After the passage of PL 94–142 in 1975, *mainstreaming* became a popular way to better integrate special needs children. Mainstreaming derived from the concept of the "least restrictive environment" found in the law. Children classified as special education students had a right to be in the least restrictive (or least different) environment; this meant they could attend general education schools and classes as long as they could learn in them. Many schools tried mainstreaming and met with both successes and failures. Problems revolved around the level of preparation and support regular education teachers received, limits on the extra support provided to assist in mainstreaming, and determining whether the children with special needs were able to maintain appropriate behavior and skills. Successes usually involved good school and teacher preparation, active parental participation, and individualization of instruction.

The current movement toward inclusion arose from mainstreaming. *Inclusion* brings the child with special needs fully into the regular school and classroom setting. It involves ed-ucating each disabled child, to the maximum extent it is appropriate, in the general classroom and school. The child's special needs are met through supportive services, curriculum modification, and assistance provided in the regular class. Teachers are specially prepared to educate special needs children, and regular and special education teachers work along with the parents of the child to prepare Individual Education Plans (IEP) for classified children. Inclusion gives the parents of children with special needs a significant level of participation in making educational decisions for the child. The intent is to stop separating students as much as possible. Under some circumstances, when the child's disabilities are particularly severe or restricting, the school may conduct a separate educational program. The basic principle of least restrictive environment, however, means that schools must consider students with special needs for placement in regular classes first. Only when compelling evidence shows that the student's needs can't be met in the regular classroom with extra support should the child receive separate instruction. Full inclusion is the idea that *all* students will be integrated into all facets of the regular classroom and school.

Chapter 17 presents two views of the contemporary debate over full inclusion. There are many possible sides to this issue, including obstinate advocacy and obstinate opposition. The views chapter 17 presents are more tempered. They offer divergent views of full inclusion policies and practices.

## SCHOOL VIOLENCE: SCHOOL OR SOCIAL RESPONSIBILITY?

One in five high school students now carries a firearm, a knife, a club, or some other weapon to school every, single day . . . Thirty-seven percent of students said they do not feel safe in schools. Sixty-three percent said they would learn more if they felt safer. Nearly 3 million crimes occur on or near school grounds each and every year. One-quarter of major urban school districts are forced to rely on metal detectors. Firearm violence kills an American child every three hours. (*Recess from Violence*, 1993, p. 2)

Violence predominates on television, often including large numbers of violent interactions per program . . . [Viewers], especially children, are "at risk" when they watch shows in which violence goes unpunished or the consequences of violence are not depicted. (Carter, 1996)

Violence and aggression have a long history in the United States. America was born of revolution. It has made heroes of frontier gun fighters and has celebrated wars and warriors. Americans have witnessed assassinations of national figures, racial lynchings, and riots by organized labor, farmers, and students. Until the 1930s, it was not possible to quantify the rate of violence, but since that time, the FBI's *Uniform Crime Reports* document a dramatic increase in violent crime, including murder, forcible rape, robbery, and aggravated assault. The murder rate in the United States is the highest in the industrialized world.

Violence has become one of the most troubling problems facing American educators. Schools, once safe havens from the outside world, now must contend with acts of violence at every grade level. With school violence on the increase, experts continue to debate its causes and how schools should handle violent students. Many teachers and criminologists argue that the time has come to crack down on the most violent offenders and expel them from school. They argue that the school's job is to teach academic subject matter to those who are at least marginally willing to cooperate. Others argue that educators are responsible for helping students with whatever problems they bring to school, even if it means expanding the role of the school into nonacademic areas.

In 1998, pollsters gathering information for the thirtieth annual Phi Delta Kappa/Gallup Poll asked people what they believed to be the greatest problems schools face. "Fighting/violence/gangs" appeared at the top of the list, followed by "lack of discipline/more control" (Rose and Gallup, 1998, p. 51). The same poll found that 63 percent of parents of public school students did not fear for the safety of their children at school. This statistic has remained relatively unchanged in the past twenty years (Rose and Gallup, 1998, p. 52).

Position 1 in chapter 18 argues that schools have an obligation to reduce school violence and that they already possess a range of effective strategies for doing so. Position 2 argues that it is not the school's job to protect the majority of students from the violent minority. The sole purpose of schools is academic: to pass on to succeeding generations the skills and abilities necessary for productive life. In this view, time spent on conflict resolution and violence management strategies is time stolen from teaching academic subjects. Students who cannot control their behavior or who are a threat to others should not be allowed to participate in the regular school program.

## PRIVATIZATION OF SCHOOLS: BOON OR BANE?

What are the reasons for the growth of the privatization movement? One is the allegedly greater efficiency of the private sector . . . In the context of privatization, however, "increased efficiency" is not just a fiscal concept. Instead, it should be viewed as a response to widespread dissatisfaction with government service . . . (Lieberman, 1989, p. 11)

School reformers fall into one of two general categories. The first group of reformers, well-represented in this book, find no fundamental problems with the basic governance structure of schools. They favor a tax-supported, state-run system of public education. Their proposed changes take the forms of granting teachers greater authority, reconfiguring the curriculum, or redefining the role schools play in the community. The second group of reformers rejects these approaches as useless tinkering with a fundamentally flawed mechanism. They argue that the way schools are governed needs to be changed, and that the public sector should retreat from the business of education.

Schools should be privatized; that is, many, if not all, of their essential services should be contracted out to private companies.

The term *privatization* means the transfer of activities from the public sector to the private. Essentially, the move to privatize arises from dissatisfaction with how the government delivers services. Public sector services are government-produced and -managed. For example, a city might deliver protection to its citizens by organizing its own police force, hiring officers, providing them with training, and promoting the good ones and firing the weak ones. Or the same city might choose instead to "buy" police services from a private business. The city might accept bids from competing companies, each explaining how they would offer police service to the city. The city would enter into a contractual agreement with the company that offered the most promising police protection at the most affordable rate. If the private company proved to be corrupt, inefficient, or too expensive, the city could fire and replace it.

Many people share the belief that government has become synonymous with waste and inefficiency and that the public would be better served if the government were to utilize more companies to provide services. State and municipal authorities, for example, have had a good deal of success in giving up their monopolies in certain areas—garbage collection and wastewater management, for example—and saving money through privatization (Clarke and Pitelis, 1993). Chapter 19 raises the question of whether schools should be privatized. What would they gain through privatization—and what would they lose?

The central question raised in this chapter is whether the public would be better served if the state gave up some or all of its monopoly over the control of education. Position 1 argues that public education has been a state-controlled monopoly for too long. Privatization would bring a greater range of choices to the public and encourage innovation in public education. Position 2 maintains that privatization is unlikely to deliver the efficiencies and increases in quality it promises and that it represents a threat to the social and democratic goals of public education.

## *References*

*Academic Freedom in the Secondary Schools.* (1968). New York: American Civil Liberties Union.

ARCHIBOLD, R. C. (1998). "Getting Tough on Teachers." *New York Times,* Section 4A (November 1, 1998), pp. 22–25, 30–31.

ARONOWITZ, S., AND GIROUX, H. A. (1985). *Education Under Siege: The Conservative, Liberal, and Radical Debate Over Schooling.* South Hadley, MA: Bergin & Garvey.

BOYER, E. L. (1983). *High School: A Report on Secondary Education in America.* New York: Harper and Row.

CARNEGIE FORUM ON EDUCATION AND THE ECONOMY. (1986). *A Nation Prepared: Teachers for the 21st Century.* Washington, DC: Carnegie Forum.

CARTER, B. (1996). "Report Becomes Weapon in Debate on Censoring TV Violence." *New York Times,* February 7, 1996. pp. 1–4) HTTP://www.NYTimes

CLARKE, T., AND PITELIS, C., EDITORS. (1993). *The Political Economy of Privatization.* New York: Routledge.

*Commonwealth v. Hunt.* (1842). Supreme Court of Massachusetts.

CORNFORD, F. M., EDITOR AND TRANSLATOR. (1968). *The Republic of Plato.* New York: Oxford University Press.

EATON, W. E. (1975). *The American Federation of Teachers, 1916–1961: A History of the Movement.* Carbondale: Southern Illinois University Press.

ENGEL, R. A. (1976). "Teacher Negotiation: History and Comment." In *Education and Collective Bargaining,* edited by E. M. Cresswell and M. J. Murphy. Berkeley, CA: McCutchan.

ETZIONI, A., EDITOR. (1969). *The Semi-Professions and Their Organization: Teachers, Nurses, Social Workers.* New York: Free Press.

FEIMAN-NEMSER, S., AND FLODEN, R. E. (1986). "The Cultures of Teaching." *In Handbook of Research on Teaching,* 3rd ed., edited by M. C. Wittrock. New York: Macmillan.

FINN, C. A. (1985). "Teacher Unions and School Quality: Potential Allies or Inevitable Foes? *"Phi Delta Kappan,* 66, 331–338.

GALLUP, A. (1984). The Gallup Poll of Teachers' Attitudes Toward the Public Schools. *Phi Delta Kappan 66,* 97–107.

GEOGHEGAN, T. (1991). *Which Side Are You On? Trying to Be for Labor When It's Flat on Its Back.* New York: Farrar, Strauss, and Giroux.

GOODLAD, J. I. (1984). *A Place Called School: Prospects for the Future.* New York: McGraw-Hill.

———. (1990). *Teachers for Our Nation's Schools.* San Francisco: Jossey-Bass.

HOFSTADTER, R. (1962). *Anti-Intellectualism in American Life.* New York: Random House.

HOFSTADTER, R., AND METZGER, W. P. (1955). *The Development of Academic Freedom in the United States.* New York: Columbia University Press.

HOOK, S. (1953). *Heresy, Yes—Conspiracy, No.* New York: John Day.

*Inegrity and the College Curriculum: A Report to the Academic Community.* (1985). Washington, DC: Association of American Colleges.

JACKSON, P. W. (1969). *Life in Classrooms.* New York: Holt, Rinehart and Winston.

JOHNSON, S. M. (1988.) "Unionism and Collective Bargaining in the Public Schools." In *Handbook of Research on Educational Administration,* edited by N. J. Boyan. New York: Longman.

JOYCE, B. (1991). The Doors to School Improvement. *Educational Leadership* 48, 59–62.

KAPLAN, C., AND SCHRECKER, E., EDITORS. (1983). *Regulating the Intellectuals: Perspectives on Academic Freedom in the 1980s.* New York: Praeger.

KIRK, R. (1955). *Academic Freedom: An Essay in Definition.* Chicago: Henry Regnery.

LIEBERMAN, M. (1989). *Privatization and Educational Choice.* New York: St. Martin's Press.

———. (1997). *The Teacher Unions: How the NEA and AFT Sabotage Reform and Hold Students, Parents, Teachers, and Taxpayers Hostage to Bureaucracy.* New York: The Free Press.

———, AND MOSCOW, M. H. (1966). *Collective Negotiations for Teachers: An Approach to School Administration.* Chicago: Rand McNally.

LORTIE, D. (1975). *Schoolteacher.* Chicago: University of Chicago Press.

MACIVER, R. M. (1955). *Academic Freedom in Our Time.* New York: Columbia University Press.

MURPHY, M. (1990). *Blackboard Unions: The AFT and the NEA, 1900–1980.* Ithaca: Cornell University Press.

NATIONAL COMMISSION ON EXCELLENCE IN EDUCATION. (1983). *A Nation at Risk: The Imperative for Educational Reform.* National Education Association. Washington, DC: U.S. Government Printing Office.

*NLRB v. Jones and Laughlin Steel Company.* (1937). 301 U.S. 1, 57 S.Ct. 615.

O'NEILL, R. M. (1984). "Freedom of Expression: Schools and Teachers in a Democracy." In *The Foundations of Education: Stasis and Change,* edited by F. P. Besag and J. L. Nelson. New York: Random House.

———. (1987). Higher Education's Responsibility. *Social Education, 51,* 435–437.

*Recess from Violence: Making Our Schools Safe.* (1993). Hearing Before the Subcommittee on Education, Arts, and Humanities of the Committee on Labor and Human Resources. U.S. Senate, 103rd Congress, First Session on S.1125, September 23, 1993. Washington, DC: US Government Printing Office.

ROSE, L. C. AND GALLUP, A. M. (1998). "The 30th Annual Phi Delta Kappa/Gallup Poll of the Public's Attitudes Toward the Public Schools." *Phi Delta Kappan, 80,* pp. 41–56.

RUBIN, D., AND GREENHOUSE, S. (1983). *The Rights of Teachers: The Basic ACLU Guide to a Teacher's Constitutional Rights.* Revised edition. New York: Bantam.

SHARP, W. L. (1993). *Collective Bargaining in the Public Schools.* Madison, WI: Brown and Benchmark.

SIKES, P. J., MEASOR, L., AND WOODS, P. (1985). *Teachers' Careers: Crises and Continuities.* Philadelphia: The Falmer Press.

SIZER, T. R. (1984). *Horace's Compromise: The Dilemma of the American High School.* Boston: Houghton Mifflin.

*Status of the American Public School Teacher: 1980–1981.* (1982). Washington, DC: National Education Association.

STUDY GROUP ON THE CONDITIONS OF EXCELLENCE IN AMERICAN HIGHER EDUCATION. (1984). In *Involvement in Learning: Realizing the Potential of*

*American Higher Education.* Washington, DC: National Institute of Education.

SWART, E. (1990). So, You Want to Be a "Professional"? *Phi Delta Kappan, 72,* 315–318.

VALENTINE, P. (1995). "Women's Working Worlds: A Case Study of a Female Organization." In *Women Leading in Education,* edited by D. M. Dunlap and P. A. Schmuck. Albany, NY: State University of New York Press.

WARREN, D. (1985). Learning from Experience: History and Teacher Education. *Educational Researcher 14,* 5–12.

WEISS, C. H. (1993). Shared Decision Making About What? A Comparison of Schools With and Without Teacher Participation. *Teachers College Record 95,* 69–92.

WESLEY, E. B. (1957). *NEA: The First Hundred Years.* New York: Harper and Brothers.

*Wieman v. Updergraff.* (1952). 244 U.S. 183.

WINZER, M. A. (1993). *The History of Special Education: From Isolation to Integration.* Washington, DC: Gallaudet University Press.

YSSELDYKE, J. E., AND ALGOZZINE, B. (1990). *Introduction to Special Education,* 2nd ed. Boston: Houghton Mifflin.

# CHAPTER 14

# School Leadership: Teacher-Directed or Administrator-Controlled?

## POSITION 1: FOR TEACHER-DIRECTED LEADERSHIP

Nineteenth-century authors have left us with terribly unflattering characterizations of school teachers. Consider, for example, Washington Irving's description of schoolmaster Ichabod Crane:

> The cognomen of Crane was not inapplicable to his person. He was tall, but exceedingly lank, with narrow shoulders, long arms and legs, hands that dangled a mile out of his sleeve, and his whole frame most loosely hung together. His head was small, and flat at top, with huge ears, large green glassy eyes, and a long snipe nose, so that it looked like a weather-cock, perched upon his spindle neck, to tell which way the wind blew. To see him striding along the profile of a hill on a windy day, with his clothes bagging and fluttering about him, one might have mistaken him for the genius of famine descending upon the earth, or some scarecrow eloped from a cornfield. (Irving, 1880, pp. 478–479)

Despite his appearance, Crane enjoyed a modest popularity with most members of the community. "By hook and by crook," Irving writes, "the worthy pedagogue got on tolerably enough, and was thought by all who understood nothing of the labor of headwork, to have a wonderfully easy life of it" (Irving, 1880, p. 482). To the younger and rougher men of the town, however, he was a social outcast and the object of ridicule. Crane's courtship with Katrina Van Tassel ended abruptly when his rival, Brom Bones, masquerading as a headless horseman, smashed a pumpkin on the schoolmaster's head and drove him out of town.

Charles Dickens's teacher, Thomas Gradgrind, is an even less sympathetic character than Ichabod Crane. Crane urged his students along the path of knowledge with the aid of a birch, but he was conscientious, not cruel, and he administered justice with discrimination. Gradgrind, however, was a callous and pedantic martinet who prepared his students for a world of the grimmest practicalities. In a chapter entitled "Murdering the Innocents," Dickens offers this description of his teaching:

"Girl number twenty," said Mr. Gradgrind, squarely pointing with his square forefinger, "I don't know that girl. Who is that girl?"

"Sissy Jupe, sir," explained number twenty, blushing, standing up, and curtsying.

"Sissy is not a name," said Mr. Gradgrind: "Don't call yourself Sissy. Call yourself Cecelia."

"It's father as calls me Sissy, sir," returned the young girl in a trembling voice, and with another curtsy.

"Then he has no business to do it," said Mr. Gradgrind. "Tell him he mustn't. Cecelia Jupe. Let me see. What is your father?"

"He belongs to the horse-riding, if you please, sir . . ."

"Very well, then. He is a veterinary surgeon, a farrier, and horse breaker. Give me your definition of a horse."

(Sissy Jupe thrown into the greatest alarm by this demand).

"Girl number twenty unable to define a horse!"

said Mr. Gradgrind, for the general behoof of all the little pitchers. "Girl number twenty possessed of no facts, in reference to one of the commonest of animals! Some boy's definition of a horse. Bitzer, yours . . ."

"Quadruped. Graminivorous. Forty teeth, namely twenty-four grinders, four eye-teeth, and twelve incisive. Sheds coat in the spring, in marshy countries, sheds hoofs too. Hoofs hard, but requiring to be shod with iron. Age known by marks in mouth . . ."

"Now, girl twenty," said Mr. Gradgrind, "you know what a horse is."

She curtsied again, and would have blushed deeper, if she could have blushed deeper than she had blushed all this time. (Dickens, 1854, pp. 1–4)

Dickens did not intend his portrayal of Gradgrind to be an assault on teachers; the novel is an indictment of the harsh factory system of nineteenth-century England and the schools that were all too willing to prepare students for work in them. However, Mr. Gradgrind is easy to dislike. Indifferent to his students' needs for esteem, insensitive to the imaginative side of childhood, and unaware of even the most rudimentary lessons from psychology, Gradgrind offers an unflattering image of public school teachers.

## *"Unmarriageable Women and Unsaleable Men"*

To a certain extent, Crane and Gradgrind represent the popular nineteenth-century image of school teachers, particularly male teachers. One historian notes that when Brom Bones smashed the pumpkin on Crane's head, "he was passing the symbolic judgment of the American male community on the old-time schoolmaster" (Hofstadter, 1962, pp. 315–316). During the last century, it was assumed that most of those who taught school would do so for only a short time. Women typically chose marriage and homemaking after a few years in the classroom. Ambitious men were expected to move from teaching to loftier, better-paying occupations. Classroom teaching was seldom the chosen lifetime work of the more able, and the way society treated teachers reflected their anticipated short-term commitment to the job. Teaching was considered as employment for workers who were "passing through" en route to more serious pursuits (Holmes Group, 1986, p. 32). Even Ichabod Crane abandoned teaching for a career in law.

Teaching was seen as a good short-term job, but most people disparaged it as a career choice, and those who chose to stay in the classroom for more than a few years often encountered social derision. In 1932, sociologist Willard Waller observed that teachers were not treated like other groups of workers. He noted that in small towns, unmarried teachers were expected to live in a teacherage— a special boardinghouse for schoolteachers—apart from other single adults who held nonteaching jobs. In barbershops and other male-dominated establishments, any exchange of ribald banter and off-color jokes would be suspended when a teacher entered. A male teacher was not accepted as "one of the boys." Waller also noted the popular prejudice against teachers that the wealthier and better-educated members of the community commonly held. "Teaching," he wrote, "is quite generally regarded as a failure belt . . . the refuge of unmarriageable women and unsaleable men" (Waller, 1932, p. 61).

By the latter half of the twentieth century, the nature of the teaching workforce had changed dramatically. Today, more women and men look at teaching not just as a job they pursue in their youth, but as a lifelong career. Those who work in public schools today must complete (in most states) five years of college education. Certification as a beginning teacher now requires at least a bachelor's degree with a strong general education component, specialized academic coursework, professional study, and practical experiences in schools. Many teachers have masters' degrees, and more than a few have doctorates. Today's teachers are unlike their nineteenth-century predecessors. They are well-educated and able, and they pursue teaching as a career, not as a short-term job. They are experts in the practical matters of teaching and learning, and they rightfully expect a greater voice in all matters of education, including school management and school reform.

## *Shared Decision Making Needed to Reform Schools*

Too many teachers have survived the challenges of teaching by finding comfort in the isolation of their classrooms . . . The current frustration and "job" dissatisfaction of many teachers are rooted in their lack of understanding of extra-classroom processes, from budgeting to scheduling. Of course the reverse is also true: Too many administrators lack background knowledge in instructional practices. (Carr, 1997, pp. 1, 4)

By the 1900s, a growing number of educational theorists and researchers had come to realize that improved education was most likely to be achieved by tapping the intellectual understandings and creative energies of classroom teachers (Barth, 1990; Schlechty, 1990; Smylie, 1994). The current school reform agenda aims at changing the governance structure of schools so that local teachers and administrators share the authority to make decisions about the students in their schools and the ways they are taught. Referred to as shared decision making (SDM) or school-based management (SBM), the reforms first proposed in the 1990s reflect the accumulated evidence about what makes schools effective in teaching children (Marsh et al., 1990; Hatry et al., 1994). SDM/SBM is designed to involve teachers in the decision-making process at the district level. Although the level of teacher involvement varies from district to district, teachers in general are beginning to participate more and more in decisions about curriculum, instruction, personnel, and educational policy. Schools are increasingly using teachers' talents, and teachers are more involved in selecting classroom materials, planning inservice workshops, designing evaluations, and assisting new teachers in mastering the art and science of teaching.

SDM/SBM is a promising grass-roots phenomenon that is harnessing the energy of teachers and administrators to reform schools on the local level. No longer are schools run from offices far removed from the classrooms where students learn. For the first time in many years, teacher authority is on the rise. Teachers' knowledge about students and about teaching is being transformed into educational policy. SDM/SBM involves more work for teachers; in addition to the demands of the classroom, they now contribute to the management and design of education. An expanded role in school management may not be right for all teachers, but those who choose to take on extra nonteaching tasks and participate in SDM/SBM do so because they believe it will result in better education for students. Teacher involvement in SDM/SBM cannot help but deliver better education.

The logic of the SDM/SBM reform impulse rests on several interrelated assumptions.

1. Teachers have a great store of practical knowledge about students, curriculum, and instruction. SDM/SBM is good for students. It puts control in the hands of the people who know education best: the classroom teachers.

2. Teachers must be treated as professionals in order to tap their talents, acknowledge their abilities, and improve their morale.

3. School reform has a greater likelihood for success when teachers are part of the decision-making process and identify personally with school outcomes.

4. SDM/SBM is essentially democratic and fair. It provides students with role models who have a sense of ownership in their work and the power to make the workplace better (Lieberman and Miller, 1990; Weiss, 1993).

5. Teaching will become an even more attractive job when teachers assume greater authority in directing the course of schooling. Increasing numbers of talented undergraduates will choose teaching as a career in direct proportion to the authority we give teachers to manage schools.

6. SDM/SBM is the final repudiation of the nineteenth-century view of teaching. Today's teachers are well-educated, well-trained, and fully capable of directing their working lives. SDM/SBM casts aside forever the view of teachers as social outcasts (Ichabod Crane) or martinets (Thomas Gradgrind). SDM/SBM recognizes that teachers are prepared and able to participate in the management of their careers.

## Power

> The school reform movement is replete with buzzwords such as "shared deci- sion making," "school-based management," and the "professionalization of teaching." Inherent in these concepts, but often overlooked in discussions of their implementation, is the issue of power. Power is a limited commodity in schools, and the established hierarchy places teachers in a low-power position, making it difficult for teacher leaders to be acknowledged as credible forces of change. (Troen and Boles, 1995, p. 371)

Over time, the education community has come to realize that school reform depends on giving teachers expanded roles and responsibilities in the school and the opportunity to direct change. Research evidence suggests that when teachers are given responsibility for school change, there is a greater likelihood that these changes will be positive and enduring (Roberts and Cawelti, 1984; Sarason, 1982). It is reasonable to predict that if schools are restructured so that teachers assume greater responsibility for essential school processes—from curriculum to staffing and assessment—students will receive an improved education. Common sense tells us that people work harder and feel better about their work when they have a personal investment in what they do and a sense of identifica- tion with the product of their efforts (Foster, 1991). Teachers are likely to work toward educational improvement in direct proportion to their involvement in school processes and decision making. The empowerment of teachers through SDM/SBM cannot help but pay dividends in improved education for students.

## POSITION 2: FOR ADMINISTRATOR-CONTROLLED SCHOOL LEADERSHIP

> The formal participation of teachers in decision making was not the main mechanism that led to change. Rather, in our sample, it was usually the arrival of a reform-minded principal or superintendent. . . . New ideas appear to come mostly from administrators. Administrators are the innovators because they have the resources and the time to learn about new ideas, the opportunities to communicate widely, and the authority to bring the proposals to the attention of the school . . . In most of the schools we studied, "empowered" teachers tend to use their power to slow the pace of change. (Weiss, 1993, pp. 80, 83, 89)

> Encouraging participation and sharing power do not mean a faculty needs to get together every time a decision is made. This in itself would be poor leader- ship! It means that procedures are established that provide the faculty with opportunities to have appropriate input on decisions that may be important to them . . . Most faculty do not want to be involved in decisions not affecting them, such as the technicalities of tasks remotely related to the classroom or the teacher's welfare. (Drake and Roe, 1999, pp. 122–123)

## Exercising Authority for the Good of Students

To consider restructuring schools and empowering teachers may be intellectu- ally pleasing, but it ignores the demands placed on schools, the authority vested in administrative offices, and the research on school reform. School leadership is not a struggle for control between administrators and teachers; it is the exercise of authority necessary to establish the most appropriate conditions for all children to learn.

"Authority" in this context means the legally designated exercise of responsibility. In public education, the state has given school administrators the authority to run schools and provide effective instruction (Abbott and Caracheo, 1988). We generally assume that those given authority will use it properly to produce desired ends. If individual school administrators fail to provide quality education, they should be replaced. If, over time, administrative authority is proved to be structurally unsound or unable to promote the conditions necessary for student learning, then the state can make changes in the authority structure of schools. However, research findings indicate no need for such changes. The solution for school problems, now and in the future, will most likely be realized through the leadership school principals and superintendents exercise.

Good management principles demand that, in large organizations, one person or one small group of people have the authority to direct corporate outcomes. It is part of the culture of American life to view management as accountable for the success or failure of the organization. Parents know that this is the pattern in government and industry, and they expect the same rules to apply to education. In schools, authority and responsibility rest with the administration. When parents have questions about academic achievement, school policy, or curriculum, they call the administrators. Parents demand accountability, and they expect school administrators to manage teachers and conduct the educational process for the good of the children.

Good schools could not exist without good teachers, but excellent teachers are not sufficient to provide good education. In the same way a winning baseball team is more than the sum of the athletic skills of the players, a good school is more than the total of the teachers' abilities. Someone has to direct and organize the efforts of the baseball team and the school so that the whole will be at least as good as the sum of its parts. Some person or group of people will always have to manage the operations of a school, measure their effectiveness, and chart its course. It is hard to manage and play simultaneously; each of these activities requires complete concentration and a separate set of skills. Although managing a baseball team is not a perfect metaphor for administering a school, both managers share a downside risk: When the team or the school is not doing well, critics often vent their frustrations on the most visible leader, demanding the replacement of the manager or the principal.

Unfortunately, all is not well with the schools, but before making changes in the authority structures of schools, consider the demands now placed on school administrators. School administration has become very complex. It was considerably less difficult to manage schools in the past—in 1910, for example, when only 9 percent of the population completed high school, or in 1950, when only 59 percent completed four years of high school. In those days, motivated, bright students with college aspirations and supportive parents made high schools far easier to administer (Murphy, 1991). Today, with three out of every four students remaining in school for twelve years, school administrators must oversee programs for students who in previous generations would have dropped out or been forced out of schools. Past administrators did not have to contend with drugs, AIDS, guns, or students with children of their own. Society has visited all of its failings on schools, yet now demands that all high school graduates meet higher academic standards and acquire marketable skills. More than ever before, schools need trained experts in the field of administrative leadership and educational policy who can bring out the best in teachers and ensure that the community is well served.

## Unbridled Teacher Power: A Threat to Community Control

> American education is awash in faddish innovations that regularly sweep through the profession like tropical storms: "whole-language reading," "constructivist math," "mixed-ability grouping," "multiculturalism," and so on. The faddishness gives the education system the appearance of ceaseless change. Yet few of these innovations improve academic performance. And nearly all of them are being undertaken within the organizational framework of a rigid, governmentalist monopoly . . . America's elected officials exert far greater leverage over their welfare, sanitation, and transportation services than over their public schools." (Finn, 1997, pp. 1–2)

In addition to managing the enterprise, public school administrators must guarantee that they are running the school in the best interests of the community. As Milton and Rose Friedman have pointed out, taxpayer support for public schooling in the United States was won on the promise that the local community would control education. Distrustful of the socialist philosophies that supported state-controlled education in Europe, Americans would support public schooling only if it were a part of a decentralized education system. The U.S. Constitution was designed to limit the role of the central government in education, and the states allowed local communities to control their schools. The schools were designed to be essentially democratic institutions, responsible to parents whose constant vigilance guaranteed the schools' service to community interests (Friedman and Friedman, 1979, pp. 154–155).

Over time, the power to run schools has shifted from the local communities to increasingly more centralized authorities. The city, county, state, and federal governments, combined with teacher militancy, have diminished community control over education. Effective administrators must preserve community control over important aspects of children's education, and they must assure parents that the schools are still the servants of the community. Parents and other citizens rightfully fear the encroachments of big government and organized labor. They have seen the diminution of their authority and the rise of unseen professionals and bureaucrats who control more and more aspects of their lives. Government has become at once more remote and more controlling. One of the last areas citizens typically exercise a measure of real control over is the public school system, and it is the people's right to control their schools; the schools in their neighborhood belong to them. Superintendents and principals must assure the community that education will not become the exclusive province of professional educators. Teachers already have a great deal of power. Giving teachers more power could only come at the expense of diminished parental control over education.

## Sacrificing Individual Freedom to Collective Power

In public education, "power" means the ability to either produce or resist instructional outcomes. School boards and state departments of education have the power to deliver new programs of instruction, but teachers have the power to disregard these initiatives by private noncompliance. Schools are not run by the brute force of administrators, and teachers and school administrators know that each teacher has a great deal of autonomy. When teachers close the doors to their classrooms, the control they have over learning outcomes is unmatched by anyone in the school system, including the superintendent and the board of education. Teachers can control what students learn through the ways they pace instruction, group students, determine levels of difficulty, and set criteria for assessment. Teaching is now a very loosely supervised profession; any change in school structure is likely to cost teachers their individual freedoms.

Classroom autonomy is among the key defining characteristics of the teacher's job, and one of the most closely protected. Teachers like the power to teach and to control instruction. Much to the frustration of administrators, attempts to diminish this autonomy—by introducing accountability measures or introducing new curricula, for example—often meet with resistance from teachers. For many teachers, the freedom to teach is among the most attractive aspects of the job. In the past, teachers have purchased this power over their classrooms by relinquishing influence at the school or district level (Corwin and Borman, 1988). The current demands for restructuring schools require that teachers have collective power to influence schools. Not only do such ideas run counter to tradition, but they also threaten teacher power in the classroom. If teachers became managers, they would have to relinquish the individual control they now enjoy over their own classrooms.

Cries for restructuring schools are insensitive to teachers' freedoms, and they ignore the contributions administrators make to education. Educational administration is the art and science of applying specialized academic knowledge to solve school problems. School administration requires the experience of a teacher, or at least a deep appreciation of the teacher's art; in addition, it demands a strong knowledge of human behavior, management theory, school law, and organizational leadership. Administrators should understand teaching from a teacher's point of view, but they must also be able to lead teachers and bring knowledge from administrative theory and research to bear on schools and on the problems of teaching and learning.

## The False Promise of Shared Decision Making

The public believes that effective administrators can change schools, and research evidence continues to document the successes of effective school leaders in improving the education of children (Immegart, 1988; Leithwood and Montgomery, 1982; Manassee, 1985; Weiss, 1993). The problem with schools is not that principals control them, and it is not likely that schools would improve if we handed control over to teachers. In the final analysis, administrators are responsible for the schools, and they must exert the leadership and accept the consequences for educational outcomes. Schools need effective leaders who can encourage learning, support and reward good teaching, and ensure that the school serves the community and follows all mandates.

Although there is strong evidence that effective principals are key to student learning, their potential in school reform is often underestimated. For too long, the image of the public school administrator was that of the rigid disciplinarian, a man who kept students in line with bluff and bluster, the retired coach who jollied the board of education with sports talk and assurances that everything was operating smoothly. Adopting management models borrowed from industry, public school administrators often emphasized the control of teachers rather than educational leadership.

Schools abandoned these conceptions of educational administration long ago. The image of the bullying, despotic principal exists largely in memory, a fiction recreated by special interest groups who would like to seize control of the schools. The stereotype fails to acknowledge the changed nature of educational administration. Effective administrative leadership continues to be the most essential ingredient in school reform (Murphy, 1991; Weiss, 1993). The conflicting expectations that the state, the community, the teachers, and the students exert on schools demand a specially trained group of managers. Without intelligent leadership from educational administrators, schools would be unlikely to meet any of their academic and social goals. Without trained, carefully selected administrators to lead educational reform, change becomes less likely and educational anarchy looms. The future success of public education depends, in large measure, on the ability of administrators to bring together the needs of the community with the special talents of classroom teachers.

No doubt you have heard that bringing teachers into the decision-making machinery of the schools will solve many school problems. At first glance, a changed role for teachers may sound appealing. Shared decision making promises to expand the supply of good ideas and bring frontline professionals into the conversations about school reform. However, even in schools that have tried to empower teachers, most new ideas still come from administrators. The research shows that shared decision making does not improve teacher morale, nor does it necessarily lead to school reform or improved learning (Weiss, 1993; Smylie, 1994).

It is up to administrators to lead school reform, though they are encouraged to include teachers in planning school reform. As one researcher notes:

> Despite the failure of [shared decision making] to live up to its hype, there is something intrinsically appealing about the notion that school administration derives its just powers from the consent of the governed, at least the adult governed. At a time when industry has moved toward greater worker participation in management, it seems fair that teachers, too, have a say in conditions that affect their work lives (Weiss, 1993, p. 87)

Good administrators will always recruit the most talented teachers to join in alliances for the improvement of the school, but there is insufficient evidence to warrant turning over total control of schools to teachers. Advocates of shared decision making seem to forget that teaching is a full-time, energy-draining job. To reserve part of a teacher's day to do administrative work means that teachers will have less time to teach. Schools are run for the benefit of the students, not the teachers. Research thus far does not support the claim that teacher management increases instructional effectiveness (Smylie, 1994). Unless shared decision making proves to be for the good of students, school leadership should remain in the hands of school administrators.

## For Discussion

1. Consider the following "1930s Rules for Teachers." Are any of these rules appropriate for today's teachers? If you were given the authority to construct a new set of six rules to govern the work of teachers, what rules would you write?

   1930s Rules for Teachers
   1. I promise to take a vital interest in all phases of Sunday-school work, donating my time, service, and money without stint for the uplift of the community.
   2. I promise to abstain from all dancing, immodest dressing, and other conduct unbecoming a teacher and a lady.
   3. I promise not to go out with any young men except insofar as it may be necessary to stimulate Sunday-school work.
   4. I promise not to fall in love, to become engaged, or secretly married. I promise not to encourage or tolerate the least familiarity on the part of my boy pupils.
   5. I promise to sleep at least eight hours a night, to eat carefully, and to take every precaution to keep in the best of health and spirits in order that I may better be able to render efficient service to my pupils.
   6. I promise to remember that I owe a duty to the townspeople who are paying my wages, that I owe respect to the school board and the Superintendent that hired me, and that I shall consider myself at all times the willing servant to the school board and the townspeople and that I shall cooperate with the town, the pupils, and the school.

2. This chapter presents two competing views of school organization. The first sees schools as rigid top-down bureaucracies and teachers as powerless workers with little influence. The second view sees schools as loosely organized and teachers as professionals with a great deal of autonomy and freedom in the classroom (Ingersoll, 1994). Which view of school organization do the teachers you know hold? Do the administrators in their schools share a similar perspective? If you can, interview several teachers to learn their views on school organization.

3. Spend a day with a school principal. Observe what he or she does. Interview the principal about the nature of the job, the range of problems

he or she confronts, and the demands on his or her time. What have you learned about the principal's role in school management that you did not know before?

## References

ABBOTT, M. G., AND CARACHEO, F. (1988). "Power, Authority, and Bureaucracy." In *Handbook of Research on Educational Administration,* edited by N. J. Boyan. New York: Longman.

BARTH, R. (1990). *Improving Schools from Within: Teachers, Parents, and Principals Can Make the Difference.* San Francisco: Jossey-Bass.

CARNEGIE FOUNDATION FOR THE ADVANCEMENT OF TEACHING. (1988). *Report Card.* Princeton, NJ: Carnegie Foundation.

CARR, D. A. (1997). "Collegial Leaders: Teachers Who Want More than Just a Job." *The Clearing House 5,* 1–5. (Lexis-Nexis)

CORWIN, R. G., AND BORMAN, K. M. (1988). "School as Workplace: Structural Constraints on Administration." In *Handbook of Research on Educational Administration,* edited by N. J. Boyan. New York: Longman.

DICKENS, C. (1854). *Hard Times, A Novel.* New York: Harper.

DRAKE, T. L., AND ROES, W. H. (1999). *The Principalship.* 5th ed. Upper Saddle River, NJ: Prentice-Hall.

FINN, C. A., JR. (1997). "Learning-Free Zones." *The Journal of American Citizenship Policy Review.* September/October, pp. 1–7. (Nexis-Lexis)

FOSTER, A. G. (1991). When Teachers Initiate Restructuring. *Educational Leadership 48,* 27–31.

FRIEDMAN, M., AND FRIEDMAN, R. (1979). *Free to Choose.* New York: Harcourt Brace Jovanovich.

HATRY, H. P., MORLEY, E., ASHFORD, B., AND WYATT, T. M. (1994). *Implementing School-Based Management: Insights into Decentralization from Science and Mathematics Departments.* Urban Institute Report 93–4. Washington, DC: The Urban Institute.

HOFSTADTER, R. (1962). *Anti-Intellectualism in American Life.* New York: Random House.

THE HOLMES GROUP. (1986). *Tomorrow's Teachers: A Report on the Holmes Group.* East Lansing, MI: Holmes Group.

IMMEGART, G. L. (1988). "Leadership and Leadership Behavior." In *Handbook of Research on Educational Administration,* edited by N. J. Boyan. New York: Longman.

INGERSOLL, R. M. (1994). Organizational Control in Secondary Schools. *Harvard Educational Review 64,* 150–172.

IRVING, W. (1880). *The Sketch Book.* New York: G. P. Putnam's Sons.

LEITHWOOD, K. A., AND MONTGOMERY, D. J. (1982). The Role of the Elementary School Principal in Program Improvement. *Review of Educational Research 52,* 309–339.

LIEBERMAN, A., AND MILLER, L. (1990). Restructuring Schools: What Matters and What Works. *Phi Delta Kappan 71,* 759–764.

MANASSEE, A. L. (1985). Improving Conditions for Principal Effectiveness: Policy Implications of Research. *Elementary School Journal 85,* 439–463.

MARSH, C., DAY, C., HANNAY, L., AND McCUTHEON, G. (1990). *Reconceptualizing School-Based Curriculum Development.* New York: The Falmer Press.

MURPHY, J. T. (1991). Superintendents as Saviors: From the Terminator to Pogo. *Phi Beta Kappan 72,* 507–513.

NATIONAL COMMISSION ON EXCELLENCE IN EDUCATION. (1983). *A Nationa at Risk: The Imperative for Educational Reform.* Washington, DC: U.S. Department of Education.

ROBERTS, A. D., AND CAWELTI, G. (1984). *Redefining General Education in the American High School.* Alexandria, VA: Association for Supervision and Curriculum Development.

SARASON, S. B. (1982). *The Culture of the School and the Problem of Change,* 2nd ed. Boston: Allyn and Bacon.

SCHLECHTY, P. S. (1990). *Schools for the 21st Century: Leadership Imperatives for Educational Reform.* San Francisco: Jossey-Bass.

SMYLIE, M. A. (1994). "Redesigning Teachers' Work: Connections to the Classroom." In *Review of Research in Education,* edited by L. Darling-Hammond. Washington, DC: American Educational Research Association.

TROEN, V., AND BOLES, K. C. (1995). "Leadership from the Classroom: Women Teachers as a Key to School Reform." In *Women Leading in Education,* edited by D. M. Dunlap and P. A. Schmuck. Albany, NY: State University of New York Press.

WALLER, W. (1932). *The Sociology of Teaching.* New York: John Wiley and Sons.

WEISS, C. H. (1993). Shared Decisions About What? A Comparison of Schools With and Without Teacher Participation. *Teachers College Record 95,* 69–92.

# CHAPTER 15

# Academic Freedom: Teacher Rights or Responsibility

## POSITION 1: FOR TEACHER RESPONSIBILITY

Teachers are the key to good education. They are also the key to poor education. When teachers are excellent, a school is excellent. But, as is widely known, many schools are not excellent, and many teachers are weak and ineffective. In fact, the great problems in U.S. education are largely due to teachers who should not be in classrooms. These teachers should be weeded out, but tenure laws and teacher unions protect the weakest and ensure poor educations for many of our children.

We do not have enough space in this essay to examine the many problems related to poor schools and poor teachers, but consider the enormous problem of poor teachers who are also zealots for causes that undermine American values. Worse even than weaknesses in teaching skill and knowledge are the weaknesses of zealotry—teachers eager to sell their beliefs to young people and irresponsible in their accountability to society. Pied Piper teachers are not weak in their beliefs and sales techniques, but they are weak in accepting their fundamental responsibility to society and its values; they fail to recognize the proper role of a teacher. Not only does tenure cover up poor teaching, it also protects socially dangerous teachers. They use the hollow claim of academic freedom to camouflage their activity.

Teachers are not immune to radical ideas, and they have a captive audience of immature minds. Oftentimes the academically weak teacher misunderstands the threats of anarchism, atheism, satanism, socialism, communism, and other extreme positions. They have a simplistic utopian view and want their students to adopt the same, so they impose their radical views on vulnerable young people. This denies the concept of education and threatens society. Nevertheless, state laws and unions protect teachers, no matter how radical and socially detrimental their concepts are. This protection, under tenure laws and the false cloak of academic freedom, allows miseducation in the schools.

Tenure laws make it almost impossible to rid schools of poor or zealous teachers. The false claim that academic freedom gives teachers the right to do what they wish does not take into account the real history of academic freedom for scientists and scholars. Nor does it reflect the social responsibilities attendant on teaching in public elementary and high schools. Because these young, most impressionable children must attend school by law, we must demand greater accountability from public school teachers than we do from teachers in colleges, where students are old enough to resist brainwashing.

Good teachers deserve respect and appreciation for their contributions to society. They deserve decent salaries and comfortable working conditions. They deserve the protection that the Bill of Rights gives to all U.S. citizens: freedom of speech, association, and assembly. No one would argue that good teachers should be treated like prisoners, without the freedom to express their creativity. Creativity that stimulates children to learn is one of the hallmarks of good teaching. Teachers do not, however, merit special treatment in regard to their freedom. Tenure should not protect them from losing their jobs for subverting students, for advocating radical ideas, for insubordination, or for proselytizing.

## Academic Freedom as License

Parading under the guise of academic freedom, this special treatment would give teachers license to engage in a variety of forms of educationally disruptive behavior. Forcing students to accept a teacher's view when that view does not coincide with community or family values is disruptive and unprofessional. Certainly, the teacher may have views that differ from community norms, but the classroom is not the place in which to express them. The pressures a teacher can exert on students are many; teachers should not use their positions to subvert parental ideas or to make students doubt basic values. Teachers should not have the freedom to preach radical ideas in schools.

A child brought up to revere the family, to believe in marriage, to support the United States, and to respect people in authority may find it traumatic when a teacher expresses approval of such activities as participating in homosexual acts, supporting abortion rights, espousing anti-Americanism, engaging in civil disobedience, or sexually using children (Leo, 1993). Teachers should not have the right to damage children in this manner. This is a form of child abuse, and when it happens, the teacher should be dismissed. Stretching the idea of academic freedom to protect such a teacher is an affront to the true meaning of academic freedom. The appropriate definition of academic freedom applies solely to the protection of university scholars as they research their specialties. It was never intended to cover schoolteachers and their students.

A license to teach is not a license to impose one's views on others. Corruption of the young is at the least a moral crime; it is ethically reprehensible. The majority of teachers accept this and discharge their duties with integrity and care. For them, teaching is a calling to instruct the young in the knowledge and values of the society. This represents the best in the profession and is a great support to the well-being of the community and nation. Unfortunately, some teachers do not subscribe to the values of their profession.

There are teachers who are caught in drug raids, who have cheated on their income tax returns, and who have committed robbery—but these are exceptions. Most teachers are not criminals. But when teachers do engage in criminal conduct, they are subject to criminal penalties and possible loss of employment. They do not receive special treatment. However, there is another form of crime, intellectual crime, that teachers may engage in under the guise of academic freedom. Intellectual crimes include ridiculing student or family values, advocating antisocial attitudes, indoctrinating children in secular humanism, and influencing students to think or act in opposition to parent and community norms. These crimes may have an even greater, more devastating effect on children and the society than legal transgressions because they tear at the moral fiber of the nation. Perpetrators should not have special protection. There is nothing academic about confusing and confounding children about their families and their society; teachers who commit such crimes deserve no consideration under the rubric of academic freedom. Distorting the minds of the young is misteaching and should be penalized.

Some schoolteachers and their unions want to open a large umbrella of academic freedom to cover anything a teacher does or says. Their claims to protection are not justified, but they make school administrators wary. Administrators do not want the American Civil Liberties Union or other local vigilante groups interfering in school affairs. Thus, radical teachers often get away with their preaching and mind-bending for years because the administration is afraid to reprimand them. Instead, the problem is hidden. Parents who protest are allowed to have their children transferred to other classes, but unsuspecting parents fall prey to these unprofessional classroom Fagins. It takes a courageous and persistent parent to thwart such a teacher. Often, public disclosure of the teacher's actions will arouse the community and force school officials to take action.

Radical teachers have also misused state tenure laws, which typically place excessive impediments to obstruct efforts to dismiss a teacher. As a result, very few school districts find it worthwhile to try to fire even the most incompetent teachers, and radical teachers recognize this. Tenured teacher firings are very rare; the radical teacher merely has to sit tight until tenure, and then anything is permissible.

Tenure laws create burdensome requirements that save teachers' jobs even when those teachers have demonstrated a lack of respect for parents, students, and community values. This is a travesty. We need to abolish or change these laws to make it easier to dismiss teachers who behave irresponsibly.

## Schools as Community and Family Agencies

Schools are not meant to be forums for teachers whose viewpoints differ sharply from those of the community. Instead, schools are intended to express and affirm community values. Malleable students are a captive audience; teachers must not have the right to impose contrary views on the young (McFarlane, 1994).

Teachers who abdicate their professional obligation to protect students from radical ideas deserve to lose their jobs. Responsible teachers recognize this; they understand that teachers deserve the general freedom of expression accorded all citizens under the Constitution, but not an additional license that would protect their jobs regardless of what they say in the classroom.

Teachers are an important resource in society. They have the power to shape the ideas and behaviors of young people. They also serve as agents of the community to assure the proper transmission of the common culture. Serious responsibilities fall on those who accept this role. Teachers derive their authority from the traditional presumption that they serve in place of the parent and as agents for the community, and thus they must respect and uphold parental rights and community sensibilities. Instruction that disrupts or erodes family and social values has no place in the schools and should result in teacher reprimand or dismissal. Academic freedom has sometimes been offered as a defense for teachers who deliberately challenge traditional values, but that is a smokescreen used to hide subversive and irresponsible teaching. Responsible teachers deserve freedom in teaching, but academic freedom and teacher freedom are different concepts.

We must bear two important considerations in mind in any discussion of academic and teacher freedom in the schools. First, academic freedom provides limited protection to university-level scholars who are experts in their specialized fields, and it is inappropriate to apply the concept to teachers below the college level. Second, freedom for teachers below the college level is not unlimited or unrestrained; it is necessarily related to traditional teacher responsibilities.

There is no doubt that, within the limits of responsibility, teachers deserve respect and some freedom to determine how to teach. That is, teacher freedom can be separated from academic freedom, which is intended to protect the rights of experts to present the results of their research. This separation does not denigrate teachers any more than it denigrates lawyers, doctors, and ministers as respected people who have no claim to special freedom in their work. Teacher freedom is protected by community traditions and the constitutional protection of free speech. Teachers do not need additional protections.

The U.S. Constitution's protections of free speech for all citizens are more than sufficient for teachers. Under the Constitution, any of us can say what we wish to say about the government, our employers, or the state of the world, provided it is not slanderous, imminently dangerous, or obscene. Obviously, we cannot say false things about someone without risking a libel suit, and we cannot yell "Fire!" in a crowded theater or "Bomb!" in an airport without risking arrest. Though we have the freedom to say them, we must also accept the consequences for our other statements. It would be absurd to expect an employer to keep an employee who made public statements that reflected negatively on the company. Can you imagine the president of IBM guaranteeing the job of a salesperson who wrote a letter that advocated the purchase of Apple computers, or who sent a memo to colleagues complaining about a supervisor?

Public expression of controversial views, as in letters to a newspaper editor, is a right in the United States. Teachers, of course, have the same right. But that does not mean that the teacher's job is safe, any more than the jobs of people employed by private firms who make controversial public statements.

Keeping a particular job regardless of one's actions is not a right the Constitution guarantees. Anyone who wishes to make public statements must recognize the risks involved. Teachers, more than most citizens, should be aware of the responsibilities surrounding public discourse. A teacher's inflammatory comments can lead to public outrage.

Schoolteachers should not expect job guarantees when they make negative comments about the schools, the community, or the nation. They also should not expect job protection when they teach children using propaganda or inaccurate or provocative material. Private schools can expect their teachers to uphold school and parent values because they have more latitude in dismissing unsatisfactory teachers. State tenure laws do not apply to them. Public schools are under some constraints because of those tenure laws, but they should be more aggressive in weeding out poor teachers. The public schools are public employers; the teachers are public employees. Each board of education has a responsibility to provide children with information, skills, a set of social values, and a moral code that strengthen the society. Teachers cannot abrogate that responsibility.

Further, school is compulsory for children. The students are a young and captive audience, subject to the whims and eccentricities of the teacher. They are much more impressionable than the typical adult and easy prey for a manipulative teacher. Yet, many teachers expect their jobs to be secure no matter what they say or do in public or in classrooms. They may call this academic freedom, but it represents not freedom but license.

## Academic Freedom as a Function of Academic Position

Academic freedom protects scholars who recognize the academic responsibilities inherent in it. Scholars who have developed expert knowledge in a subject field may conduct research that challenges accepted views: This is how we continue to refine knowledge. Academic freedom allows such scholars to publish or present their research without fear of losing their positions, but even these scholars have academic freedom only in those areas in which they have demonstrated expert knowledge. Academic freedom does not extend to everything they do or say. They have no greater freedom than any other citizen in areas outside their own expertise. An English professor who joins an activist group blocking traffic in an environmental protest has no claim to academic freedom for that activity—the professor is no different from any other citizen. The Constitution protects everyone's speech, but it does not and should not protect a faculty job. There is a difference between academic freedom and license, and no academic freedom should exist for those who indoctrinate others. Kirk (1955), Hook (1953), and Buckley (1951), provide philosophic grounds for limiting teacher freedom and denying indoctrination.

In specialized subject areas where a scholar has demonstrated expertise, he or she may need the protection of academic freedom to publish or present research results that differ from those of prior research. Some few public school teachers may have developed this expert knowledge and be conducting research, but this is not true for the vast majority. As philosopher Russell

Kirk has eloquently argued, not all subjects are equally deserving of academic freedom:

> The scholar and teacher deserve their high freedom because they are professors of the true arts and sciences—that is, because their disciplines are the fields of knowledge in which there ought always to be controversy and exploration; and their especial freedom of expression and speculation is their right only while they still argue and investigate. But if this body of learned men is trampled down by a multitude of technicians, adolescent-sitters, . . . and art-of-camp-cookery teachers (whose skills, however convenient to us, do not require a special freedom of mind for their conservation and growth) . . . then the whole order of scholars will sink into disrepute and discouragement. (Kirk, 1955, pp. 79, 80)

Unfortunately for teachers and scholars, the idea of academic freedom has been abused. Teacher unions and lawyers, attempting to save the jobs of teachers who are incompetent or who espouse antisocial propaganda, have clouded the positive idea of academic freedom. Academic freedom should not become a shield for incompetent, antisocial, or un-American teaching. Rather, relating the idea of teacher freedom to teacher responsibilities is a much sounder approach to the protection of teachers and the integrity of the society.

Law professor Stephen Goldstein (1976), in a well-reasoned article on this topic, argues that academic freedom is unsuited to elementary and secondary schools because of the age and immaturity of the students, the teacher's position of authority, the necessarily more highly structured curriculum, and the dominant role of the school in imparting social values. These factors cannot be easily dismissed. Elementary and secondary school teachers are different from university scholars in their training, their functions, their employment status, and their responsibilities. And the elementary and secondary schools have broad responsibilities to parents, the community, and the state that do not permit us to give license to teachers to do what they wish. Schools and teachers serve in capacities that require support for and advocacy of social and family values. Rhetoric about academic freedom does not diminish that significant responsibility.

## Responsibility and Power in Teaching

Teaching is one of the most influential positions in society. In terms of carrying values and ideas from generation to generation, teaching is next to parenting in its power. In some respects, the teacher exerts more influence on the views and values of children than parents do. Parents have great control over what their children see, hear, and do during the earliest years, but after the child starts school, the parent relinquishes increasing amounts of that influence to teachers.

Society gives teachers the authority to develop sound knowledge and values in children, and school is compulsory for that purpose. The child, being weaned from parental influence, looks to teachers for guidance. This is an important responsibility, one that merits serious consideration. Teachers bear duties to parents, to society, and to the child to provide a suitable education. They also have duties to the profession of teaching. Teachers and schools must recognize these multiple responsibilities.

All rights and freedoms are connected to responsibilities. Otherwise, where no social restraint exists, anarchy reigns. That is not freedom; it is a jungle without rules or ethics. Civilization demands both freedom and responsibility. Within that civilization, teachers' freedoms must be tied to their responsibilities, and their rights and freedoms are conditioned on their acceptance of those responsibilities. Teachers' freedoms are supported and limited by their responsibilities to parents, to society, to the child, and to the profession.

Parents have rights and obligations to their children, which teachers and schools must not undermine. The provision of food, clothing, and shelter is a parental obligation that another social institution takes over only when parents are incapable. Parents have moral obligations and rights, including instructing their children in determining right from wrong, good from bad. Parents must train their children in ethical conduct by providing them with a set of socially acceptable behaviors, including integrity, honesty, courtesy, and respect.

Parents also have many legal rights and obligations in regard to their children. They are expected to take good care of their children, and, under the law, they are given great latitude in providing that care. Parents are presumed to have the child's interests at heart. They are even permitted to exercise corporal punishment, more than any other person would be permitted to inflict upon a child, under the legal idea that the parent has broad responsibilities. At the root of laws regarding parents' rights and obligations is the idea that they are responsible for their children's upbringing, morality, and behaviors. Teachers act as surrogate parents in certain situations, and they should not deviate from the norms of the good parent in the good society.

## School as a Positive Parent Surrogate

The good society is made up of good families, and good schools are extensions of those families. This concept is quite different from the common idea that society is either the faceless government or just a collection of separate individuals. Social institutions confirm and sustain the family, even when specific families fail to live up to their responsibilities. Prisons, foster homes, mental institutions, orphanages, family welfare programs, reformatories, and court-mandated separations represent society's attempt to deal with these responsibilities when families fail. These institutions try to do a good job of surrogate parenting, but they are working with the results of a difficult situation. Such institutions can be considered negative because they exist to make up for problems in families and society.

Schools, however, are a positive social institution. They are specifically intended to encourage the development of children, extending the family influence to produce good citizens and good members of future families. Children are not put in schools as punishment, or as a way to make up for family irresponsibility. The schools exist to supplement and expand the good family and the good society. Schools, therefore, must continue the cultural heritage by passing on positive social and family values to the young.

## Teacher Responsibilities to Parents, Society, and Children

Schools, then, have a special obligation to be responsive to parents' concerns for their children. It is this reasoning that lies behind the legal concept that teachers act *in loco parentis,* or in place of the parent. That concept, which has deep social and legal roots, protects teachers in their handling of student discipline and evaluation. It also requires teachers to remain sensitive to parental interests. Parental rights and responsibilities extend until children reach adulthood. Parents do not usually consider their obligations as merely technical requirements; they have strong emotional commitments to their children that transcend legal and social expectations. Parents want, and expect, the best possible for their children.

Teachers, standing in place of the parents, take on similar responsibilities for the child's development and protection. Although teachers do not have the same innate responsibilities beyond providing a safe and healthy classroom environment, they do have moral, ethical, and legal duties. In addition, they have formal educational responsibilities: they must teach children the necessary knowledge and skills to get along in the society. Part of discharging these responsibilities is being responsive to parental concerns about the kinds of knowledge and values taught.

Teachers cannot have license to do anything they wish to students, physically or mentally. No one today would argue that teachers should be permitted to abuse children physically, although some teachers are permitted to exert limited physical control over children to maintain an educational environment. For example, teachers can require students to remain seated, to change seats, to be quiet, to go to the principal's office, or to line up for activities. Teachers are properly prohibited from such abusive activities as striking students or using electric cattle prods. Good teachers would never contemplate such malevolent behavior; it is outside the standards of professional conduct.

Mental abuse of students is equally abhorrent, but it is less easy to detect. The scars of mental abuse are not as obvious as those from physical damage. Mental abuse is no less harmful, however, to students, parents, or society. It can consist of vicious verbal personal attacks, indoctrination in antisocial values or behaviors, or manipulation of children's minds against parents or morality. Parents have a right to insist that teachers not subject their children to these tactics, but they are often unaware of them until after the damage has been done. Good teachers would not contemplate such misuse of their influential role in the lives of children; it would be unprofessional.

Parents have a right to monitor what schools are teaching to their children, to hold the school accountable for it, and to limit the potential for damage to their children.

## Teacher Responsibilities to the Society

The society, as well as parents, has a significant interest in the education of children. Schools were established to pass on the cultural heritage; to provide the skills, attitudes, and knowledge needed to produce good citizens; and to prepare children to meet their responsibilities in family, work, and social roles. Schools are social institutions, financed and regulated to fulfill social purposes.

Society has values, standards of behavior, and attitudes that the school must convey to children. These standards have evolved over a long period, and they represent our common culture. Society charges the school and the teachers to ensure that social standards, and the ideals these standards represent, are taught by example and by word.

Schools do not exist as entities separate from society, able to chart their own courses as though they had no social responsibilities. They were not intended to instruct students in antisocial, anti-American, or immoral ideas or behaviors, nor will society allow them to continue to do so.

Society trusts teachers to develop the young into positive, productive citizens. Those few teachers who use their position to attempt to destroy social values or create social dissension are violating that trust. Those who sow the seeds of negativism, nihilism, or cynicism are also violating that trust. Society has the right to restrict, condemn, or exclude from teaching those who harm its interests.

## Teacher Responsibilities to Children

The paramount responsibility of teachers is to their students—the future adult members of society. It is because students are immature and unformed that teachers must carefully exercise their influence and that teachers must temper their freedom with responsibility. Teachers hold great potential power over the lives of children, and the disparity in authority between teachers and students needs to weigh heavily in teacher decisions as to what to teach and how. The teacher derives power from maturity, physical size, and position. The child is vulnerable.

In forming and testing ideas, attitudes, and behaviors, the child looks to the teacher for direction. Children are naturally curious and positive, but they cannot yet fully discern between good and bad, proper and improper. Teachers have a responsibility to continue the moral and ethical education that good parents have begun. In addition, teachers need to help students develop habits of thinking that will help them gain knowledge of, and learn to appreciate, the language, history, science, and art of their society.

## Teacher Responsibilities to Their Profession

The profession of teaching has an extensive and illustrious history. It is based on the idea of service to children and to society. The teachers' code of ethics recognizes teacher responsibilities as singularly important. Teachers want to convey the cultural heritage to their students, along with a strong sense of social responsibility. Teachers can ask no less of themselves.

A basic responsibility of the teaching profession is to prepare young people for life in society. That includes teaching social values and knowledge to students, and the teacher's personal conduct should exemplify the society's ideals. The teaching profession recognizes both the needs of the child and the needs of society. Teachers have an obligation not to go beyond professional bounds, and to reject those who would tarnish the profession's reputation.

## POSITION 2: FOR INCREASED ACADEMIC FREEDOM

A society cannot be free when its schools are not. Ideas are the primary ingredients of democracy and education. The realm of ideas is protected by academic freedom. John Dewey (1936) noted over fifty years ago, "Since freedom of mind and freedom of expression are the root of all freedom, to deny freedom in education is a crime against democracy."

The need to lend strong support to academic freedom for schoolteachers and their students should seem obvious to anyone who supports a free society. The continuing development of American democracy requires that academic freedom be further expanded in schools for both students and teachers. Noddings (1999) points out that democratic education requires debate and discourse—only with teacher freedom can this happen.

One may wonder why this is a critical issue in education in the 2000s. Who could possibly be against academic freedom at this period in the United States? Unfortunately, narrow-minded, backward-looking people have increased their efforts to restrict schools and to impose censorship on students and teachers. The American Library Association's *Newsletter on Intellectual Freedom* reports on the variety of efforts in many states to censor, restrict, and constrain teachers and teaching materials. *Newsletter* issues published in the past five years have noted the following:

- Nobel Prize winner Toni Morrison's book, *Beloved*, won the Pulitzer Prize in 1987—but a school committee member in Madawaska, Maine, challenged its use in the schools because of some of its language. The challenger admitted he had not read the complete book.
- Parents in Oakley, California, want to remove John Steinbeck's *Of Mice and Men* from the schools because of racial epithets.
- The Florida Family Association, a self-identified Christian group, sent thousands of protests to school board chairs, homes, and churches in Largo, Florida, to urge the disbanding of a Gay and Straight Alliance student group at Largo High School.
- The Poetry Club at Medford, Massachusetts, High School was disbanded and reorganized after they hung a sign referring to the school as a red light district.
- School officials in Edison, New Jersey, removed Ray Bradbury's *The Martian Chronicles* from a school reading list because of a racial slur.
- Words about puberty and homosexuality were cut at the last minute from a school production of *A Chorus Line* in Huntington, New York; one student danced a part in silence.

Current infringements on teacher and student freedoms include the expansion of censorship from books and films to the Internet. Scare tactics created overkill in blocking access to many legitimate Internet sites. A 1999 report of the Censorware Project shows that Utah, for example, blocks access for all public schools and some libraries to such material as: The Declaration of Independence, The U.S. Constitution, the Bible, the Koran, all of Shakespeare's plays, and Sherlock Holmes ("Censored Internet Access in Utah Schools and Libraries," 1999).

Zealots on different sides of political, economic, and religious fences have tried to use the schools as agents to impose their views and values on the young. They don't want the schools to present opposing views or conflicting evidence, and they are against real critical thinking. That zealotry has increased the vulnerability of teachers who realize that good education requires dealing with controversial issues (Thelin, 1997).

The good teacher who is willing to examine controversial topics runs risks far beyond those suggested in high-sounding slogans about academic freedom. Ominous overt threats and subtle pressure from administrators, parents, special interest groups, and peers are likely to cool this teacher's ardor for freedom of ideas. The teacher who fulfills this basic educational responsibility may also encounter ostracism or ridicule. And teachers have been fired for doing what our society should expect all good teachers to do. All of these efforts are aimed at restricting the academic freedom of teachers and students and imposing censorship on the schools.

The American Library Association (ALA) *Newsletter on Intellectual Freedom* tracks censorship in schools and libraries, reports on news about censorship, and follows court cases related to censorship issues. The *Newsletter* is a depressing document to those who believe that an open democracy requires full academic freedom for teachers and students. Reports in the *Newsletter* show that censorship attempts have been launched in virtually every state over the past few years. Some states have numerous censorship attempts each year, and thousands of teachers and students are restricted by the actions of vigilante groups, school boards, and school administrators.

Studies confirm the fragile state of academic freedom in schools. Censorship of literature continues ("Censorship," 1990; Hymowitz, 1991; Flagg, 1992; Waldron, 1993; Simmons, 1991, 1994); school boards and administrators keep trying to expand their control over instructional material (Mesibov, 1991; Daly, 1991); and courts render inconsistent decisions on the protection of teacher freedoms (Mawdsley and Mawdsley, 1988; Turner-Egner, 1989; Melnick and Lillard, 1989; Sacken, 1989; Pico, 1990; "Censorship," 1990). With the continuing attacks and the vulnerability of teachers and schools to censorship and political restrictions, is it worth the effort to strive for academic freedom?

## The Essential Relationship of Academic Freedom to Democracy

Academic freedom is the right to "liberty of thought" claimed by teachers and students, including the right to "enjoy the freedom to study, to inquire, to speak . . . to communicate . . . ideas" (*Dictionary of the History of Ideas*, 1973, pp. 9, 10). The question of academic freedom must be examined from the perspective of a society that prizes freedom and self-governance, even when those ideals are not always evident in the everyday practice of the society. It is the ideals of a society that education best serves. The nature of the academy, at any level, interlinks with the goals of the society. A restrictive or totalitarian society demands a restrictive or totalitarian education system. A society that professes freedom should demand no less freedom for its schools (Rorty, 1994).

The defining quality of academic freedom is freedom in the search for knowledge. This freedom should not be limited to a small elite corps of "experts," but should extend to all students and teachers engaged in the quest for knowledge. In fact, the search for knowledge is not limited to experts, but is the primary purpose of schooling: Students must engage in the search. It is often students who recognize flaws in existing knowledge or who find new ways to understand. When only experts control knowledge, we risk conformity without challenges or conflicting opinions. We may not like challenges to ideas we find comfortable, but those challenges are the stuff of progress. Without challenges to comfortable superstitions, we would not have had scientific achievements leading to medical and technical progress. Without challenges to the idea of royalty or dictatorial governments, we would not have had the idea of democracy. Limiting the search for knowledge to a cadre of established experts is not in the interest of human progress.

One inescapable premise in a democracy is that the people are capable of governing themselves. That premise assumes that people can make knowledgeable decisions and can select intelligently from among alternative proposals. Education and the free exchange of ideas are fundamental to the premise. To think otherwise is to insult the essential condition of democracy.

The U.S. Supreme Court demonstrated its commitment to the principle of academic freedom in a 1967 decision, finding that a state law that demanded teachers take a loyalty oath was unconstitutional. The Court noted that academic freedom is a "transcendent value":

> Our nation is deeply committed to safeguarding academic freedom, which is of transcendent value to all of us and not merely to the teachers concerned. That freedom is, therefore, a special concern of the First Amendment, which does not tolerate laws that cast a pall of orthodoxy over the classroom . . . . The classroom is peculiarly the "marketplace of ideas." (*Keyishian v. Board of Regents*, 1967)

The democratic basis for academic freedom is part of that transcendent value. Democracy is now considered the most suitable way to organize U.S. society. We find that increasing numbers of countries and peoples throughout the world are embracing democracy as an ideal, but the definition of a democratic society is still evolving. Self-governance emerged as a set of contrary ideas, actually at odds with the prevailing concepts of government, and became a compelling vision of a better existence for the majority of people.

## Academic Freedom and a Free Society

Similarly, academic freedom has evolved and expanded from a narrow and limited definition to embrace both the general framework of schooling and the work of teachers. Differences in state laws and confusing court opinions have produced a mixed view of what specific actions are legally protected under the idea of academic freedom (O'Neil, 1981). The courts, however, have exhibited an expanding awareness of the need for academic freedom in schools.

Nothing remains static. Change is constant in society and in education. Ideas about society and schools arise, are tested, and are either expanded and improved or dropped. Democracy and academic freedom are evolving concepts. The basic principles are clear—for example, self-governance for democracy and enlightenment for academic freedom—but the practical definitions of these terms are under continuing development.

Propaganda and public deceit are practiced in all countries, including democracies, but citizens of a democracy are expected to have the right and the ability to question and examine propaganda and to expose those deceits. Dictatorial regimes do not need, and do not desire, the masses to have an education that enables them to question the information the government presents. Totalitarian states maintain their existence by using raw power and threats, by utilizing censorship and restriction, and by keeping the public ignorant. Governments in democracies can attempt the same maneuvers, but they run the risk of exposure and replacement. The more totalitarian the government, the more it uses threats, censorship, and denial of freedom in education. The more democratic the society, the less it employs threats, censorship, and restriction of education. This litmus test of a democracy is also a significant measure of academic freedom.

At the global level, a recent statement adopted by the International Federation of Library Associations and Institutions (IFLAI) holds that: "Human beings have a fundamental right to access to expressions of knowledge, creative thought, and intellectual activity, and to express their views publicly" (IFLAI Statement, 1999). Academic freedom is consistent with this position.

Because there has been a general misunderstanding of the central role schools play in a free society, teachers and students have often lived a peripheral existence in the United States. Teaching has been viewed as "women's work," and teachers as undeserving of the public trust to make wise decisions. States and communities impose restrictions on what teachers can teach and the methods of instruction they can use. School boards and administrators censor teachers and teaching materials for dealing with controversial topics. Students are virtually ignored, are treated as nonpersons, or are expected to exhibit blind obedience. These conditions raise questions about American society and the vitality of academic freedom. Academic freedom, the essence of the profession of teaching, has been insufficiently developed in our society and in the education of teachers.

## Educational Grounds for Academic Freedom

Where, if not in schools, will new generations be able to explore and test divergent ideas, new concepts, and challenges to propaganda? Students should be able to pursue intriguing possibilities under the guidance of free and knowledgeable teachers. Students can test ideas in schools with less serious risks of social condemnation or ostracism. In a setting where critical thinking is prized and nurtured, students and teachers can engage more fully in intellectual development. This is in society's best interests for two fundamental reasons: (1) new ideas from new generations are the basis of social progress, and (2) students who are not permitted to explore divergent ideas in school can be blinded to society's defects and imperfections and will be ill-equipped to participate as citizens in improving democracy.

There is no real threat to society when students examine controversial matters in school. Most young people encounter radical ideas in conversations with friends or in films, TV, and other media. In an educational setting, students can more fully consider opposing ideas, and they have the opportunity to criticize each view. The real threat to society is that students will *not* examine controversial material in schools, and that students will come to distrust education and society as places for the free exchange of ideas. Teachers and students need academic freedom to fulfill their educational mission in a free society. Daly and Roach (1990) call for a renewed commitment to academic freedom to pursue these social and educational ends.

The primary purpose of education is enlightenment. Although teaching can be conducted easily as simple indoctrination, with the teacher presenting material and students memorizing it without thought or criticism, that leads to an incomplete and defective education. Teaching can also be chaotic, with no sense of organization or purpose—this, too, is an incomplete and defective education. Neither of these approaches to teaching offers enlightenment. Education consists of ideas and challenges, increasingly sophisticated and complex. Indoctrination stunts the educational process, shrinking knowledge and constricting critical thinking. Chaotic schools confuse the educational process, mix important and trivial ideas, and muddle critical thinking. A sound education provides solid grounding in current knowledge and teaches students to challenge ideas in the process of critical thinking.

Education that provides ideas and challenges and stimulates increasingly sophisticated critical thinking is necessarily controversial. Some of the challenges will not be popular, and critical thinking may raise questions about ideas the community is comfortable or uncomfortable with. Teachers who fear political reprisal for providing a sound education find themselves in an anomolous situation. These teachers need protection from politically powerful groups, from vocal special interests, and from shifts in political views. Students also need protection from these forces, as well as from incompetent and indoctrinating teachers. Academic freedom for teachers and students is essential to education.

## The Center of the Profession

Academic freedom is at the heart of the teaching profession (Nelson, 1990). Professions are identified by the complex and purposeful nature of the work, the educational requirements for admission, and the commonly held social ethics and values. Medical professionals, for example, work to protect and improve health, have a specialized education in medical practice, and share a commitment to life. Attorneys work in the realm of law, have specialized training in the practice of law, and are dedicated to the value of justice. Teachers work to educate children, have subject knowledge and specialized education in teaching practice, and share a devotion to enlightenment.

In earlier times, when teachers were not required to have a college degree and their main role was to provide minimal literacy skills, they faced severe limitations on their freedom. With increasingly rigorous teacher credentialing regulations and improved professional study and practice, there are now no grounds for excessive restrictions on a teacher's work.

The nature of teachers' work and their shared devotion to enlightenment require a special freedom to explore new ideas in the quest for knowledge. This freedom deserves protection beyond that provided to all citizens under the constitutional guarantee of free speech. Unlike other citizens, teachers have a professional obligation to search for truth and to assist students in their search for truth (Zirkel, 1993). The practice of this profession and this obligation requires special protection from political or other interference. Teachers' jobs must not be at risk because they explore controversial material or consider ideas that are outside of the mainstream. That is part of the process of free and liberal education and is a basic condition of the teaching profession.

## Academic Freedom and Teacher Competency

The provision of academic freedom for teachers is not without limits or conditions. Not all persons certified to teach nor every action they take deserve the protection of academic freedom. The basic condition for academic freedom is teacher competence. Incompetent teachers should not receive that extra protection.

Teacher competence is a mix of knowledge, skill, and judgment. It includes knowledge of the material and of the students in class, professional skill in teaching, and considered professional judgment. Competence depends on more than just the accumulation of college credits or units of professional study; it includes a practical demonstration that the teacher can teach with knowledge, skill, and judgment. As in other professions, competence is measured by peers and supervisors, and it continues to be refined as a teacher gains experience. In teaching, initial competence is expected as the new teacher completes the teaching credential program. That program includes subject and professional study and practice teaching under supervision. According to the laws of various states, teachers serve several years under school supervision and are granted tenure if they are successful. This long test of actual teaching should be sufficient to establish competence. Incompetent teachers should not get tenure.

## Tenure and Academic Freedom

The main legal protection for academic freedom in the schools is state tenure law. Under tenure laws, teachers cannot be fired without cause. The tenured teacher who is threatened with firing has a right to such due process conditions as a fair hearing and specific allegations of the grounds for the firing that can be addressed in court. This protects tenured teachers from improper dismissal as a result of personality conflicts or politics. Grounds for dismissal, identified in the state law, often include moral turpitude, professional misconduct, and incompetence. The allegation must be clearly demonstrated and documented for the dismissal to be upheld. This is reasonable. It should be difficult to dismiss a tenured teacher who has demonstrated competence over a period of years. And teachers should not be dismissed on the basis of personal or political disagreements with administrators or others.

Nontenured probationary teachers also deserve the protection of academic freedom because they, too, are expected to engage in enlightening education. However, they do not have the same legal claims as tenured teachers. Tenured teachers serve on "indefinite" contracts that the school need not renew formally each year. Dismissal or nonrenewal of the probationary teacher's one-year contract can occur at the end of any given school term, often without specifying cause for dismissal. That leaves the nontenured teacher very vulnerable. Certainly, if the probationary teacher is not competent as a teacher, dismissal is appropriate. Dismissal for dealing with controversial topics in a competent manner should, however, be prohibited.

## Obstacles to Academic Freedom

The compelling reasons supporting academic freedom notwithstanding, historical, political, and economic pressures have often overwhelmed those reasons and have restricted teachers and students. American schools do not have an exemplary tradition in providing the academic freedom necessary to our democracy. Censorship, political restraint, and restrictions on freedom have a long and sordid history in the United States. Early schools, under religious domination, imposed moralistic requirements on teachers, firing them for impiety or for not exhibiting sufficient religious zeal. In the nineteenth century, the number of public schools increased rapidly, and many teachers had only limited education themselves; communities required strict conformity to social norms, and teachers could be dismissed for dating, dancing, drinking, visiting pool halls, or simply disagreeing with local officials.

In the first half of the twentieth century, political restraint and censorship replaced religious and moralistic restrictions on teachers (Pierce, 1933; Beale, 1936; Gellerman, 1938). College teachers often fared no better, and many suffered great indignities at the hands of college officials (Sinclair, 1922; Veblen, 1918/1957; Hofstadter and Metzger, 1955). As the twenty-first century emerges, it is clear that teachers have gained much in professional preparation and stature, but they are not yet free. Although teachers have more freedom now than when they were indentured servants in colonial times, significant threats to academic freedom continue to limit education and to place blinders on students.

A statement by the American Association of University Professors in support of academic freedom for precollege-level teachers identified a variety of political restraints imposed on such teachers (AAUP, 1986). The *Newsletter on Intellectual*

*Freedom* keeps track of the many cases of school and library censorship across the United States. There have always been large numbers of such cases in local communities, but since 1970, the frequency of reported censorship incidents has tripled. Moreover, estimates suggest that for each incident formally reported, about fifty other censoring activities go unreported (Jenkinson, 1985). The National Coalition Against Censorship, affiliated with dozens of professional and scholarly associations, formed recently because of this increase in censorship. Academic freedom remains a significant problem for U.S. teachers. Continuing vigilance is required because of the continuing threats to this freedom.

## The Censors and the Chill on Education

Topics that arouse the censors and others who want to control teachers vary over time and across locations. They also span both ends of the political spectrum. Socialism and communism were visible targets in the 1920s and again in the 1960s. They surfaced again in the early years of the Reagan administration. Sexual topics and profanity are constant targets of school censors. A more recent issue is the charge that schools teach secular humanism—a charge that teachers and materials are anti-God, immoral, antifamily, and anti-American. Among other current topics that stimulate people who want to stifle academic freedom are drugs, evolution, values clarification, economics, environmental issues, social activism, and the use of African American, feminist, or other minority literature (Jenkinson, 1990; Waldron, 1993; Japenga, 1994; Sipe, 1999). Internet censorship has extended the chilling effects to limit teachers, work. ("Censored Internet Access in Utah Schools and Libraries," 1999).

Censoring activities occur most frequently on the topics of sex, religion, race, patriotism, and economics. The materials that censors want taken out of the hands of teachers and students include classic writings by renowned authors, standard works that most educated people have read, and popular publications that are readily available on local newsstands or in public libraries, as well as some virtually unknown works that happen to arouse the ire of certain groups or individuals. Oftentimes, local censorship advocates have not read the whole book, but object to selected segments or parrot national organizations who object to ideas the books treat. Examples of books and other teaching materials that have been banned or challenged in recent years include such standard and popular works as:

*A Farewell to Arms*

*Anne Frank: Diary of a Young Girl*

*The Adventures of Huckleberry Finn*

*Beloved*

*Beowulf, a New Telling*

*Catch-22*

*The Catcher in the Rye*

*The Chocolate War*

*The Color Purple*

*Deliverance*

*From Here to Eternity*

*The Great Gatsby*

*Native Son*

*Of Mice and Men*

*The Pelican Brief*

*To Kill a Mockingbird*

*The Firm*

*The Hunt for Red October*

*I Know Why the Caged Bird Sings*

*My Friend Flicka*

*The Martian Chronicles*

*Sister Carrie*

*Slaughterhouse Five*

*The Sun Also Rises*

Other common targets for the censors include texts and reference works, such as:

*Focus on Algebra*

*Merriam-Webster Collegiate Dictionary*

*Human Anatomy and Physiology*

Some of the popular magazines censors want to ban include:

*Cosmopolitan*

*Editor and Publisher*

*National Enquirer*

*People*

*Playboy*

And films such as these continue to bring out the censors:

*1900*

*Glory*

*Lolita*

*Schindler's List*

*The Tin Drum*

(*Newsletter on Intellectual Freedom,* American Library Association, 1996, 1998, 2000; St. Charles, Illinois, Public Library Banned Books Week 1998 List; Foerstel, 1994)

Publicized censorship and restraint activities have a chilling effect on school boards, administrators, and even many teachers (Whitson, 1993). The mere fact that complaints might arise if a teacher touches on a controversial topic leads to fear and sinister implications. Administrators issue informal statements warning teachers not to use certain materials, and more experienced teachers suggest that their younger colleagues exercise extreme caution concerning anything remotely controversial. Daly (1991) found that few school districts had policies to protect teacher and student rights to academic freedom. As a result, there is an extraordinary amount of teacher self-censorship that denies to students and to society the full exploration of ideas. Many teachers avoid significant topics, or they neutralize and sterilize them to the point of student boredom. Academic freedom for teachers and students is not self-evident in the United States.

## The Free Society Requires Academic Freedom

Despite the history of weak protection of academic freedom and the often powerful political pressures brought to bear to stifle it, attaining freedom for teachers and students is worth the strenuous effort it demands. There are compelling democratic, educational, and professional grounds for expanding the protection of academic freedom to competent teachers and to all students. And there are important social reasons why the public should support academic freedom in public education. Academic freedom is more than a set of platitudes, state regulations, and court decisions. It should be a fundamental expectation of schools in a free society. Academic freedom is a central truth for the profession of teaching.

## For Discussion

1. Louis Menand (1996), distinguished Professor of English at the City University of New York, argues:

   Academic freedom is not simply a kind of bonus enjoyed by workers within the system, a philosophical luxury universities could function just as effectively, and much more efficiently, without. It is the key legitimating concept of the entire enterprise. Virtually every practice of academic life that we take for granted—from the practice of allowing departments to hire and fire their own members to the practice of not allowing the football coach to influence the quarterback's grade in math class—derives from it. (p. 4).

   a. Discuss whether this view of academic freedom at the university level is consistent with the principles and practices at the higher education institution you attend.

   b. Discuss why this view of academic freedom is or is not suited to teachers in precollegiate schools.

   c. What other implications for k–12 schooling does this concept of academic freedom convey?

2. Should there be any restrictions on what a teacher can discuss in class? What set of principles should govern the establishment of those limits? Should students have the same freedoms and limits? Is student age or teacher experience a significant factor in this determination?

3. Which, if any, of the following topics should be banned from schoolbooks or class discussion?

Explicit sexual material

Sexism

Racism

Fascism

Violence

Anti-American views

Socialism

Antireligious material

Inhuman treatment of people

Animal, child, or spouse abuse

What are the grounds for justifying censorship of any of these?

4. What role should teachers play in learning about and responding to efforts at censorship? Should the censors be censored?

## References

AMERICAN ASSOCIATION OF UNIVERSITY PROFESSORS (AAUP). (1986). *Liberty and Learning in the Schools.* Washington, DC: AAUP.

*Attacks on the Freedom to Learn.* (1985–1994). Washington, DC: People for the American Way.

BEALE, H. (1936). *Are American Teachers Free?* New York: Scribner's.

BUCKLEY, W. F. (1951). *God and Man at Yale.* Chicago: Regnery.

"Censored Internet Access in Utah Schools and Libraries." (1999). Report, Censorware Project. Online available at http://www.censorware.org. March 23.

"Censorship: A Continuing Problem." (1990). *English Journal* 79, 87–89.

CHENEY, L. (1992). "Telling the Truth." *Humanities* 13, 4–9.

DALY, J. K. (1991). "The Influence of Administrators on the Teaching of Social Studies." *Theory and Research in Social Education* 19, 267–283.

———, and Roach, P. B. (1990). "Reaffirming a Commitment to Academic Freedom." *Social Education* 54, 342–345.

DEWEY, J. (1936). "The Social Significance of Academic Freedom." *The Social Frontier* 2, 136.

*Dictionary of the History of Ideas.* (1973). I. Weiner, editor. New York: Scribners.

FLAGG, G. (1992). "'Snow White' is the Latest Title Under Attack in Schools." *American Libraries* 23, 359–361.

FOERSTEL, H. N. (1994). *Banned in the USA.* Westport, CN: Greenwood Press.

GELLERMAN, W. (1938). *The American Legion as Educator.* New York: Teachers College Press.

GOLDSTEIN, S. (1976). "The Asserted Right of Teachers to Determine What They Teach." *University of Pennsylvania Law Review* 124, 1, 293.

HENTOFF, N. (1991). "Saving Kids from Satan's Books." *The Progressive* 55, 14–16.

HOFSTADTER, R., AND METZGER, W. (1955). *The Development of Academic Freedom in the United States.* New York: Columbia University Press.

HOOK, S. (1953). *Heresy, Yes—Conspiracy, No.* New York: Day.

HYMOWITZ, K. S. (1991). "Babar the Racist." *The New Republic* 205, 12–14.

IFLAI STATEMENT (1999). "Libraries and Intellectual Freedom." International Federation of Library Associations and Institutions, The Hague, Netherlands. 25 March.

JAPENGA, A. (1994). "A Teacher at War." *Mother Jones* 19, 17.

JENKINSON, E. B. (1985). "Protecting Holden Caulfield and His Friends from the Censors." *English Journal* 74, 26–33.

———— (1990). "Child Abuse in the Hate Factory." In *Academic Freedom to Teach and to Learn*, edited by A. Ochoa. Washington, DC: National Education Association.

JONES, J. (1993). "Targets of the Right." *American School Boards Journal* 180, 22–29.

*Keyishian v. Board of Regents.* (1967). 385 U.S. 589.

KIRK, R. (1955). *Academic Freedom.* Chicago: Regnery.

LEO, J. (1993). "Pedophiles in the Schools." *U.S. News and World Report* 115, 37.

MAWDSLEY, R. D., AND MAWDSLEY, A. L. (1988). *Free Expression and Censorship: Public Policy and the Law.* Topeka, KS: National Organization on Legal Problems of Education.

McFARLANE, A. (1994). "Radical Educational Values." *America* 171, 10–13.

MELNICK, N., AND LILLARD, S. D. (1989). "Academic Freedom: A Delicate Balance." *Clearing House* 62, 275–277.

MENAND, L., EDITOR. (1996). *The Future of Academic Freedom.* Chicago: University of Chicago Press.

MESIBOV, L. L. (1991). "Teacher–Board of Education Conflicts Over Instructional Material." *School Law Bulletin* 22, 10–15.

NELSON, J. (1990). "The Significance of and Rationale for Academic Freedom." In *Academic Freedom to Teach and to Learn*, edited by A. Ochoa. Washington, DC: National Education Association.

*Newsletter on Intellectual Freedom.* (Bimonthly). Chicago: American Library Association.

NODDINGS, N. (1999). "Renewing Democracy in Schools." *Phi Delta Kappan* 80(8), 579–583.

O'NEIL, R. M. (1981). *Classrooms in the Crossfire.* Bloomington: Indiana University Press.

PICO, S. (1990). "An Introduction to Censorship." *School Media Quarterly* 18, 84–87.

PIERCE, B. (1933). *Citizens' Organizations and the Civic Training of Youth.* New York: Scribners.

RORTY, R. (1994). "Does Academic Freedom Have Philosophical Presuppositions?" *Academe* 80, 52–63.

SACKEN, D. M. (1989). "Rethinking Academic Freedom in the Public Schools." *Teachers College Record* 91, 235–255.

SIMMONS, J. (1991). "Censorship in the Schools: No End in Sight." *ALAN Review* 18, 6–8.

————, editor. (1994). *Censorship: A Threat to Reading, Learning, Thinking.* Newark, DE: International Reading Association.

SINCLAIR, U. (1922). *The Goose-Step.* Pasadena, CA: Sinclair.

———— (1923). *The Goslings.* Pasadena, CA: Sinclair.

SIPE, R. B. (1999). "Don't Confront Censors, Prepare for Them." *Education Digest* 64(6) Feb., 42–46.

*The Rights of Students.* 3rd ed. (1988). Washington, DC: American Civil Liberties Union.

THELIN, J. (1997). "Zealotry and Academic Freedom." *History of Education Quarterly* 37(3),338–420.

TURNER-EGNER, J. (1989). "Teachers' Discretion in Selecting Instructional Materials and Methods." *West's Education Law Reporter* 53, 365–379.

VEBLEN, T. (1918/1957). *The Higher Learning in America: Memorandum on the Conduct of Universities by Businessmen.* New York: Sagamore.

WALDRON, C. (1993). "White Teacher's Use of *Ebony* to Teach Tolerance at Texas School Ignites Uproar Among Parents." *Jet* 84, 10–16.

WHITSON, J. A. (1993). "After Hazelwood: The Role of School Officials in Conflicts over the Curriculum." *ALAN Review* 20, 2–6.

ZIRKEL, P. (1993). "Academic Freedom: Professional or Legal Right?" *Educational Leadership* 50, 42–43.

# CHAPTER 16

# Teacher Unions:
# Detrimental or Beneficial

## POSITION 1: TEACHER UNIONS ARE DETRIMENTAL

The rise of the Modern NEA [National Education Association] has exactly coincided with what critics have called the 1963–1980 "Great Decline" of the American education system. This decline notoriously affects performance (the proportion of all 17-year-olds scoring 700-plus verbal or math SATs fell by almost half; math has rebounded, verbal has never recovered . . .). The teachers' union has emerged as the major obstacle to school reform. . . . In its spare time the union fights attempts to limit taxes, to cut government spending and even to curb illegal immigration. Its agenda, in short, is more political than educational. (Brimelow and Spencer, 1995, p. 121)

Strikes, work slowdowns, and demeaning battles between teacher unions and school boards hinder rather than enhance education for the youth of the United States. With few exceptions, relationships between boards and unions are adversarial. Strikes and other less serious conflicts between boards and unions are never over the quality of education. Instead, they emanate from a "win what I want for myself, at any cost" mentality. (Streshly and DeMitchell, 1994, p. vii)

### Self-Serving Unsupported Claims

Officials of teacher unions say that when public monies are spent to improve working conditions for teachers, children are the ultimate beneficiaries. Their arguments are, no doubt, familiar to you: Public school students suffer because teachers are underpaid. Hard-working, devoted teachers deserve greater compensation. Unless teachers earn higher salaries, not only will the current crop of teachers become discouraged, but the brightest college graduates will not go into education. Union leaders similarly argue that teachers need greater power to remedy school problems. They claim that teachers will be more effective if they are allowed to join administrators in all areas of school management, including curriculum reform and the supervision and evaluation of teaching.

The logic in these examples is simple: What is good for teachers is good for children. If the public wants better education for its children, the public should support teacher unions in their efforts to improve education through increased remuneration and greater autonomy for teachers. Collective bargaining practices, picket lines, work stoppages (strikes), and the expansion of union control over schools should be considered beneficial to the community, parents, and students.

Convincing? Not really. Making schools good places for teachers does not serve the public interest. The public's interest in education is not measured in teachers' job satisfaction, but in the quality of learning provided to students.

Despite the rhetoric, it has not been demonstrated that teacher unions have a positive effect on student achievement or that increased teacher salaries improve education. More money for teachers does not translate into better schooling. Researchers find negligible differences in achievement between public school students in union and nonunion schools (Eberts and Stone, 1984). (In private schools, where teachers are typically not unionized and salaries are comparatively low, student achievement is high.) The unions do not make a positive difference in public schools.

How well do unions serve teachers? In fact, it is not possible to evaluate the impact unions have had on any specific school or on any single group of teachers or students. For example, we cannot know with any certainty how a group of unionized teachers would have fared economically over time had they not joined a union (Brimelow and Spencer, 1993). Perhaps they would have done better in salary negotiations or in their treatment by the board of education; perhaps not. There is no way to know. At best, we can only compare the gains of a specific group of teachers with average gains made by their colleagues across the state or nation. Therefore, it is not possible to conclude whether unionization has helped or harmed a specific group of teachers.

Similarly, there is no clear picture of the impact of compensation on teacher performance (Johnson, 1988; Stern, 1986). The public has been forced to accept the benefits of unionization on faith; scientific research does not support union arguments, which occasionally defy common sense. It is not likely, for example, that good teachers would suddenly become poor teachers if they lost union representation, and it is fatuous to assume that collective bargaining can improve the teaching skills of weak teachers.

## From Bread-and-Butter to Policy Issues

Despite the absence of hard data, unions claim they have improved teachers' salaries. They argue that the union-wage effect is in the neighborhood of 5 to 10 percent, not enough to make teachers wealthy, they admit, but enough to keep them paying their union dues and more than enough to encourage unions to extend their influence beyond bread-and-butter work issues. In the past, union efforts were typically limited to traditional labor concerns: wages and hours, working conditions, fringe benefits, grievance procedures, organization rights, and such specific work-related issues as extra pay for extra duty (coaching or directing school plays, for example). Over time, teacher unions began to demand a voice in policy issues, including curriculum reform, class size, disciplinary practices, textbook selection procedures, inservice training, teacher transfer policies, and personnel matters—including hiring and awarding tenure (Kerchner, 1986). Today, affiliates of both the NEA (National Education Association) and the AFT (American Federation of Teachers) want teachers to expand the scope of their activities and participate in discussions about education reform, political lobbying, and shared decision making. These demands go well beyond traditional bargaining agreements. Some union contracts have given teachers the right to make decisions about how schools spend money, how teachers teach, and how students are to learn. Under the familiar assumption that collective negotiations will create a better education for children, union leaders now argue that increased teacher participation in all the decision-making and managerial aspects will also reform schools.

Turning schools over to teachers distorts the authority structure. No matter how it is packaged, capitulating to demands to empower teachers destroys community control of education. In most communities, school board members are elected officials, voted into office on the basis of their personal qualifications and their educational platforms. They typically work long hours without pay to ensure delivery of an appropriate education to the children of their friends and neighbors. The school board appoints the superintendent of schools to implement local educational policies. On the recommendation of the superintendent, building principals are hired, a curriculum is developed, and teachers are recruited to implement the board's educational plan. School boards, as public employers, are given decision-making authority as a public trust, and teachers, who are not directly responsible to the electorate, should not be able to overturn this trust. If the board fails to deliver the education it has promised, the public can vote its members out of office, and the superintendent can be replaced.

The unions were not hired by the community, and they may not represent the most effective classroom teachers. They have no right to override the judgment of the community with their agenda. The unions are not suited to be district or school leaders, nor should they have leadership authority. Over the years, teacher unions have become stronger, and teachers have increased their political power. While teachers were winning, parents and the community were losing (Baird, 1984; Friedman and Friedman, 1979). If unions are allowed to bargain collectively about issues of policy and curriculum reform, schools will become less responsive to the community and more an agency of the unions. Responsibility for running schools should be entrusted only to those the voters have chosen. Collective bargaining must not steal the right of the community to control the education of its children.

Unfortunately, representatives of the NEA and AFT have been trained to regard local communities with disdain and to treat school boards as the enemy. In their pursuit of hegemony over the schools, unions have been willing to ignore the interests of the community, and unionized teachers, either willingly or through union coercion, have come to disregard the needs, aspirations, and futures of the children they teach (Braun, 1972; Brimelow and Spencer, 1993,

1995). Educational policy should not be a matter of union concern. The district, through its elected board and board-appointed administrators, is legally accountable to the public for the quality of education it provides. The unions have no such responsibility or authority, and they should defer to those who do.

## Apologizing for Bad Teachers

It is ironic that unions are demanding a greater role in school reform; given their record, we can argue that unions have caused more problems than they have solved. Unions have become apologists for teachers and an obstacle to school reform. On the one hand, unions love to praise the almost magical effect good teachers have on the lives of children. On the other hand, they fail to admit that weak teachers may be a cause of many of the schools' shortcomings. Everyone familiar with public schools knows that the quality of classroom instruction varies tremendously. Nestled among the great teachers, the good teachers, and the marginally adequate teachers are those who fail to convey enthusiasm for learning and, unfortunately, more than a few who have neither the personal qualities nor the skill and knowledge necessary to teach children. While the good teachers whet students' appetites for academic achievement, bad teachers kill interest, leave students with enormous gaps of information, and tarnish the reputation of the profession.

Unions talk about boosting teacher morale and teacher self-esteem, but they regularly oppose merit pay for good teachers. Some districts have proposed pay-for-performance plans that would reward unusually successful teachers—those who produce above-average learning gains in students—with higher raises, whereas those who evidence less success would earn lower-than-normal raises. Typically, teacher unions reject these plans, claiming that the plans are "not fair" or that the concept of a "good teacher" is too subjective to measure (Bradley, 1990; Lieberman, 1997). The public believes schools are designed to treat each child individually and to make judgments about those who should be rewarded and those who should fail. It suspects that schools would benefit if teachers were subject to similar judgments. Good teachers should reap the fruits of their individual talent; bad teachers should be fired.

In recent years, the popular press has not been kind to teachers. Stories of barely literate teachers and teachers who tyrannize students cause parents to recoil in horror. Although these accounts represent a tiny fraction of the nation's teachers, they are shocking, not only in their perversity but because the union consistently defends such poor and even dangerous teachers. In one case, a Chicago teacher punished bright students because they demanded more attention, and this made his work more difficult. His supervisors were alerted to the problem, but the teacher was not fired; under union rules, he could transfer to another school (Freedman, 1987). A special education teacher in New York City was arrested, convicted, and sent to prison for selling $7,000 worth of cocaine to a colleague. After five years of litigation and board of education expenditures of over $185,000, the teacher still had a job in the school system. He was even able to collect part of his teacher's salary while he was in prison (Dillon, 1994).

The public is generally sympathetic to teachers, but not to teacher unions, and it's not hard to understand why. Consider the example of a Florida typing teacher who had trouble controlling her class. When the students dismantled the equipment and threw books, she responded by throwing books back at them. When the building principal criticized her, she wrote a letter describing the "living flesh of my true hereditary genes and bones" and changing her name to "God" (Goldstein, 1998, p. 25). Because she was protected by union rules that restrict teacher dismissals, it took a year before this teacher could be removed from the classroom.

Trade unionists in education are hard put to account for the numbers of poor teachers in their ranks. Typically, they place the blame either on weak university programs in teacher education or on public school administrators. The sad fact remains that too many schools have teachers who are not able to do the work expected of them. Unfortunately, because of unions and tenure laws, even the poorest teachers will probably stay on the job until retirement. Left to their own devices, unions are unlikely to rid the profession of bad teachers. The job of the union is not to improve the teaching profession but to protect teachers. Given this goal, the unions can hardly refuse to fight dismissals, even when the teacher involved is obviously incompetent. As a result, it is nearly impossible to fire a tenured teacher. It is estimated that a typical school district nationwide would have to spend between $10,000 and $50,000 in legal fees to get rid of its worst teacher (Lieberman, 1985). In New York, it takes well over a year's time and costs the schools almost $195,000 to prosecute a single teacher accused of misconduct (Dillon, 1994). Between 1991 and 1997, only 44 of Illinois' 100,000 tenured public school teachers were dismissed for cause. In Florida only 0.02% of the tenured teachers are fired in a typical year (Goldstein, 1998).

Union opposition to culling incompetents from the classroom has forced school districts to decide whether to spend money on new books and programs or on litigation. In many states, union rules have brought administrative actions against ineffective teachers to an absolute halt (VanSciver, 1990). Unions cry for greater involvement in restructuring schools, but their opposition to pay-for-performance plans and their refusal to allow the dismissal of tenured but incompetent teachers cast great doubt on their potential contribution to reform. The public would be more supportive of unions if unions were as concerned about the quality of teaching as they are about protecting individual teachers.

## Resisting Change

Unions and teaching do not fit together gracefully. Unions are more appropriate for heavy industry, such as auto or steel production, where all workers perform similar tasks under much the same circumstances. The net effect of poor work or lazy workers is more destructive in teaching than it would be in factory occupations. One bad steel worker could make his or her coworkers' jobs more difficult, but he or she is unlikely to hurt the industry as a whole. An incompetent teacher who teaches dozens of children a year may have a much more harmful effect on many lives for many years.

Unions are educational anachronisms. They may have been necessary at one time, in the early days of public schooling, but they have become obstructionist opponents of change. Teachers should be treated individually, not collectively. Good teachers should be recognized for their professional competence and financially rewarded according to the quality their performance. Weak teachers should be helped or weeded out, and labor negotiations should not consume the energies of school teachers and administrators. If union contracts were limited to basic issues—wages, hours, and working conditions—school reform would not be forced to march to the lockstep cadence collective bargaining imposes. Given their record, teachers' unions should not be included in school reform.

Unions may argue it is coincidental that the rise of teacher unions in this country has been accompanied by rising education costs and declining standards of student performance. However, parents and other members of the community have every reason to be suspicious of the unions' potential for championing school reform. Teacher unions have consistently opposed higher standards, national assessments, vouchers, nonunion charter schools, tenure reform, and teacher accountability (Worth, 1998). Unions are tenacious in their defense of even the worst teachers, and their actions and political lobbying have become synonymous with educational mediocrity. To deal unions a hand in school reform would not be unlike hiring wolves to work as shepherds. The unions cannot be trusted to represent anything but the teachers' interests. That has been their historic mission, and they have served it well. The claim that they have reinvented themselves to serve the cause of school reform rings hollow. Until unions start talking about ridding the classroom of poor teachers and replacing life-time tenure with renewable short-term contracts, the public will not be convinced they are serious about reform. Unless unions demonstrate that they are on the side of the students as well as the teachers, they should be held at bay or they will hijack school reform.

## POSITION 2: TEACHER UNIONS ARE BENEFICIAL

There's a big lie being circulated that teacher unions are the main obstacles to education reform. This is nonsense. The people responsible for this lie don't care about evidence—in fact, evidence gets in the way of their anti-public-schools agenda. So the public needs to know that teachers and the unions they elect to represent them are working hard to make every American school a place where students can work and learn and parents can gladly send their children. (Feldman, 1998, p. 7)

Teachers care about teaching and learning. They know more about how children think and learn—and the conditions that promote thinking and learning—than do governors, business leaders, and most college professors. Why . . . is this voice of expertise not well articulated? And the answer kept coming back, "But teaching isn't organized that way." Collective bargaining legitimated teachers' economic interests, but it never recognized them as experts about learning. . . . If workers could organize around industrial life, why not organize around mental work? (Kerchner, Koppich, and Weeres, 1997, p. 7)

## Forcing Teachers to Unionize

In the early part of this century, teachers were trained to believe that sacrifice was the essence of their profession. Teachers worked long hours; their classes often numbered fifty or more students; their salaries were low; and schools were at times poorly heated, poorly ventilated, and unsanitary. Female teachers were not allowed to go out unescorted (except to attend church) or frequent places where liquor was served; and in many communities, when female teachers married, they were forced to resign from their jobs. In addition to living truncated social lives, teachers served at the whim of school boards, without any promise of tenure or health or retirement benefits. They were not considered worthy of participating in the book selection process and were excluded from the more substantive deliberations about curriculum.

As school systems developed into large bureaucratic organizations, conditions worsened. School principals became administrators. Once referred to as the "principal teacher" or the "main teacher," the head of a school became a manager who shared few of the problems of teachers and none of their perspective. Most of the new school administrators were male; most of the classroom teachers were female. Administrators regarded teachers as inferior workers who needed to be told what to do. The authority to run schools was vested in the men in the administrative offices, and teachers were not to challenge their authority. Over time, teachers came to realize that what they were being asked to give up in the name of professionalism was not good for them or their students, and that through collective action schools could be improved for everyone.

Teachers were never eager to join unions; they were forced to because the culture of administrative managers was at odds with the culture of working teachers (Jessup, 1978; Murphy, 1990; Urban, 1982). Teachers urged their colleagues to use unions and collective bargaining to improve their working conditions and to gain a voice in improving education. The following letter, typical of the calls for teachers to organize, was written in 1913:

> On the ground that teachers do the every-day work of teaching and understand the conditions necessary for better teaching, we propose the following principles for the new organizations: Teachers should have a voice and a vote in determination of educational policies. The granting of legislative opportunity to the teachers would inevitably contribute to the development of a strong professional spirit, and the intelligent use of their experience in the interest of the public. We advocate the adoption of a plan that will permit all teachers to have a share in the administration of the affairs of their own school. In no more practical way could teachers prepare themselves for training children for citizenship in democracy. . . . ("A Call to Organize," *American Teacher*, December 1913, p. 140, quoted in Eaton, 1975, pp. 13–14)

The decision to join the labor movement no doubt came hard to many teachers. Teachers tended to be politically conservative, first-generation college graduates who identified with management more than with labor (Aronowitz, 1973; Rosenthal, 1969). They belonged (and still belong) to a special category of white collar employees called "knowledge workers." Paid for what they know and how they use their knowledge to produce value, these workers, as a group, are highly individualistic, and difficult to unionize and organize into collective action (Kerchner, Koppich, and Weeres, 1997, p. 34). Strikes are anathema to most members of teacher unions (Rauth, 1990). The fact that the union movement has succeeded in recruiting teachers speaks well for unions; most teachers now belong to some sort of union, despite a decline in union membership in other fields and continued middle-class antipathy toward unions.

## Protecting Teachers' Rights

Unions have been good for classroom teachers. The research literature indicates unions have had a positive effect on teachers' working conditions. As a result of collective bargaining, teachers' salaries have increased, and teachers have gained protection against unreasonable treatment. Unlike earlier days, teachers cannot be dismissed simply because they consume alcohol or change their marital status. Unions have also been good for education. They have put the faculty squarely in the front ranks of the battle for better schools and better education for children. Unions have given faculty a collective voice in matters of curriculum and school policy.

Teacher unions have always attracted some bad press. Some of it is traditional antilabor rhetoric, and some of it is simply misinformed. No doubt you have heard that unions are to blame for declining student performance and that unions have hurt education by protecting weak teachers who deserve to be fired. This is not the case. In fact, it is mystifying when unions are blamed for protecting weak teachers. Before teachers are awarded tenure, they must graduate from state-approved teacher education programs, convince administrators to hire them, and survive an extended probationary period, typically from three to five years. Unions play virtually no part in any of these processes. Weak teachers may make it through this system, but they do so with no help from organized labor. Teacher unions are embarrassed by poor teachers, just as the American Bar Association and the American Medical Association are shamed by ineffective, corrupt, or lazy members in their ranks. No responsible union wants to protect incompetent workers.

In the mid-1990s, unions in several cities initiated a process to identify weak tenured teachers and refer them for help and possible dismissal. One union leader argues that peer review—the evaluation of teachers by other teachers—is an appropriate role for unions. He says this was one of the traditional functions of medieval guilds, the forerunners of modern day unions:

> Guilds began precisely *for* the regulation of practice. Middle management union people had bought the American legal model: not to judge but to defend. This kind of unconditional love and acceptance should be expected only from one's mother—not one's union. (Adam Urbanski, quoted in Birk, 1994, p. 10)

On the other hand, without union guarantees of due process, it is likely that many good teachers would be subject to dismissal for political or personal reasons. Therefore, unions protect all teachers' rights to a fair hearing when their jobs are at stake. Unions insist on protection of the due process rights of all teachers. Teachers should not be fired because of the arbitrary or capricious actions of administrators or members of the board of education. Unions recognize an obligation to stand behind teachers to make sure that any dismissal is the result of sufficient, demonstrable cause, not administrative whim, retribution, or discrimination. Union support guarantees fairness in the workplace.

You may have heard someone say, "Those who are good teachers have no need for tenure, and those who have need for tenure are not good teachers." This is dangerous rhetoric. Tenure is essential for the freedom to teach, and unions are steadfast in their support for teachers' right to tenure. Without the academic freedom tenure guarantees, teaching would be too chancy for all but the independently wealthy or the hopelessly foolish. Tenure is among the more misunderstood aspects of teaching. It is not designed to provide teachers with a sinecure, a lifetime job free from the threat of dismissal. Tenured teachers can be fired for incompetence, but they cannot be dismissed for being critical of school policy or for using an instructional approach the principal does not like. Tenure is essential to freedom of thought and action. It guarantees that teachers can use appropriate teaching methods and take reasonable academic positions in classrooms without fear of administrative reprisals. Tenure is the cornerstone of a merit system of employment. The unions' support for tenure helps to staff the nation's classrooms with practitioners secure in the knowledge that they are free to teach, governed by the norms of academic responsibility and unfettered by political constraints. It also assures the public that schools will remain forums dedicated to democratic processes and open inquiry.

## Extending Workplace Democracy

Most school boards now accept that teachers have the right to bargain over working conditions, but many remain unconvinced of the legitimacy of labor's voice in policy issues and matters of school reform. Some administrators argue that the traditional roles of school employees and employers must be preserved. Superintendents and principals should be the executives and managers, and teachers should be the workers; policymaking is the rightful province of the former, and implementation is the task of the latter. Administrators claim that policy should not be subject to the art of compromise, the democratic give-and-take of collective bargaining. Policymaking, they say, is not for teachers.

This is another flawed argument. Even if it were desirable to separate policy issues from teachers' work conditions, it is not possible. The concerns of teachers extend far beyond hours and wages. Classroom teachers are directly affected by a broad range of educational policy decisions. Restricting collective bargaining to bread-and-butter issues of working conditions, wages, and hours is based on a naive view of the ways in which schools function. Issues of school policy, from the adoption of a new basal series to the recruitment of a new building principal, influence every teacher's work. How could a teacher's work fail to be affected by changes in the materials he or she uses in class? Textbooks, curriculum packages, student assessment, the evaluation of teachers, and school disciplinary policies all affect the daily lives of teachers. Policies that regulate the school's organization are central to teaching and must be considered as the rightful province of collective negotiations. Children are better served when teachers have a voice in shaping policy and in making decisions about curriculum and personnel (Maeroff, 1988).

Unions have insisted that teachers be given a voice in school reform, but in doing so they are not depriving administrators of their authority. They are simply, in the best democratic sense, extending decision making to a broader constituency. Research suggests that workplace democracy has positive payoffs for schools. Collective bargaining about policy issues appears to produce a greater sense of professional efficacy in teachers; they feel better about their jobs, and they use their new authority to give more of themselves to the school (Johnson, 1988; Tuthill, 1990).

## Unions' Stake in Education Reform

Unions have opened the door to teacher decision making, and teachers have used this right to join with management to develop better schools. In education, labor and management are not necessarily adversaries; supporting the union does not automatically make teachers the enemies of administrators. No doubt, workers and management will always have different perspectives, but a negotiated contract can resolve these differences in outlook. The adversarial roles of union and management are giving way to more cooperative reform efforts that can better serve students.

Unions have always recognized their role in school reform, and they continue to insist that teachers have a collective voice in bringing about better schooling. Teachers' direct daily contact with students provides them with powerful data about which policies and programs work. Teachers know what schools need to do to improve schooling, and their unions want them to use their knowledge to solve school problems. Affiliates of the NEA and the AFT have been active in involving teachers in school reform movements (Rauth, 1990; Watts and McClure, 1990; Kerchner and Koppich, 1993). Unions realize that unless teaching becomes a better job for practitioners, it will be increasingly difficult to keep good teachers in the classroom. A sad fact of teaching is that too often the best teachers leave the field after only a few years. Lured by more lucrative careers or seduced into administration, where they can still effect change while earning better pay, many of the most able teachers look for ways out of the classroom soon after landing their first teaching jobs.

The teacher union in Rochester, New York, has been trying to keep teachers in the classroom by granting them more authority to run the schools. The union-conceived "career ladder plan" is designed to tap the knowledge of the best teachers. Senior teachers with at least ten years of teaching experience and five years in the district assume leadership functions in the school that combine administrative work with classroom instruction. The plan calls for selected teachers to spend half their time working in administrative or supervisory capacities and the other half teaching in the classroom. Their out-of-classroom work includes mentoring new teachers and developing and consulting on curriculum in specialty areas such as math, reading, and science. For their additional responsibility, and their eleven-month contracts, these lead teachers receive a 20 percent pay differential based on their regular salary. The Rochester teacher union has made it clear that they want teachers to work in a decision-making capacity in the schools. Teachers are no longer willing to be merely advisors. They will assume greater responsibility, but they want greater authority and a salary structure that reflects their new role in the schools. By the early 1990s, some Rochester teachers were earning salaries as high as $70,000, more than twice the national average.

The union model is designed to recognize exceptional teaching skills honed by years of experience. The most experienced teachers, like the most able surgeons and attorneys, should not only be the best paid; they should also be glad to take on the most challenging work. The president of the Rochester union wants his lead teachers to assume a "Clint Eastwood" attitude. They should say, "I'm a good teacher. I've seen it all. Give me any student or program that is the toughest challenge, and if I can't do it, it can't be done." Such attitudes put teachers where they belong: designing policy for, and participating in, the fight for better schooling. Unions and unionized teachers are the keys to the future of education. In the past, unions have used their collective bargaining power to improve schools and to make teaching a better job. Unions are eager to continue the education reform agenda; they want to use their power to improve the quality of teaching and learning.

In part, union interest in school reform is self-serving. Like everyone else, officials of teacher unions are aware of the criticisms directed at public schools. Unless schools regain public support, they will lose students to private and parochial schools and to voucher plans. Union support for school reform is genuine and harmonious with the long history of unionism: it's about job protection. As in other industries, the best way to protect jobs is through quality. American automobile plants will thrive and autoworkers will have secure jobs as long as American autoplants produce quality cars. Similarly, when teacher unions fight for better schools and better education, they are fighting for secure and rewarding jobs for teachers.

Union leaders also know that classroom teachers have the best and most up-to-date information about students and about the chances that a particular proposal will lead to successful school reform. Teachers have the practical classroom experience needed to determine which new reading or math programs are likely to be effective. A greater voice for teachers in curriculum reform will help schools.

Teachers also trust other teachers, and no one has the ability to help other teachers more than successful classroom practitioners. Every school has wonderfully successful teachers as well as teachers who need help in presenting information, encouraging the best work from students, or simply controlling the class. Classroom teachers are the best resource for helping colleagues improve their classroom skills and techniques. Teachers in the same building share common problems, knowledge of the local culture, and the intimacy of colleagues facing similar challenges. When good teachers help weaker teachers, everyone profits. Good teachers feel that their classroom skills are appreciated and utilized beyond the walls of their own rooms. Weaker teachers benefit from their colleagues' knowledge and know that immediate help is always available. Schools improve and students are better served.

When you think of teacher unions, try not to view them as organizations with narrow concerns and perspectives. Today's teacher unions are as dedicated to school reform and improved education as they are to serving teachers. In fact, they realize that the best way to serve teachers is to improve schools. The relationship between schools and unionized teachers is not unlike the new relationship forged between the United Auto Workers and the General Motors Saturn assembly plant. Both GM and the UAW recognized that to compete against foreign and domestic automakers in a fiercely competitive market, both sides needed to develop a new labor-management relationship (Kerchner, Koppich, and Weeres, 1997, p. 113). The old us-versus-them antagonism and secrecy has given way to a new and cooperative partnership. The goal is to make a better product.

Teacher unions argue that school problems are no less complex than automobile design and assembly problems. Without everyone pulling for better schools, reform agendas have little chance of success. GM and the UAW recognized that rules had to be rethought and new relationships forged. Teacher unions know that, too, and they are eager for school managers to join them.

## For Discussion

1. Assume that you are a tenured teacher attending a meeting with other teachers from your school district to decide whether or not to unionize. What arguments could you make to convince your colleagues to join a union? What arguments could you make to discourage them from joining?
2. Some authors make a distinction between older, "industrial-style teacher unionism" and the newer "union of professionals." Examine the contrasting sets of union mottos. Do they clearly reflect a change in the union position about work in schools? Can you add other sets of contrasting mottos?

| Industrial-Style Unions | Unions of Professionals |
|---|---|
| "Boards make policy, managers manage, teachers teach." | "All of us are smarter than any of us." |
| "It's us versus them." | "If you don't look good, we don't look good." |
| "Any grievant is right." | "The purpose of the union is not to defend its least competent members." |

(Kerchner and Koppich, 1993, p. 10)

3. The laws of many nations give teachers the right to strike. Teacher strikes are legal, for example, in Australia, Canada, France, Germany, Greece, Israel, Italy, Mexico, and Sweden. However, in the United States, only four states consider strikes by public employees legal (Hawaii, Montana, Oregon, and Pennsylvania). In all other states, strikes by public employees, including teachers, are illegal (Shanker, 1992, p. 287).

The strike is undeniably labor's most powerful weapon. What arguments can you offer to support the right of teachers to strike? What arguments would you use to deny teachers the right to strike?

4. In Japan, the *Nikkyoso* (Japan Teachers Union) enjoys general support from teachers, and the union plays a significant role in making decisions involving education policy matters and bread-and-butter job issues. Although the union takes strong positions, it does not use confrontational tactics. The Japanese traditionally dislike confrontation, preferring instead to make decisions based on consensual agreements between labor and management. The writings of Prince Shotuku Taishi (604 A.D.) reflect the Japanese cultural traditions of harmony and shared decision making:

> Decisions on important matters should not be made by one person alone. They should be discussed with many. But small matters are of less consequence. It is unnecessary to consult a number of people. It is only in the case of weighty affairs, when there is a suspicion that may miscarry, that one should arrange matters in concert with others, so as to arrive at the right conclusion.
>
> Harmony is to be valued, and an avoidance of wanton opposition to be honored. . . . When those high above are harmonious and those below friendly, and there is concord in the discussion of business, right views of things gain acceptance. Then what is there which cannot be accomplished? (quoted in Duke, 1986, pp. 30–32)

Compare the cultural values reflected in these quotes with American values concerning leadership and followership in the workplace. Do you think shared, harmonious decision making could become part of the culture in U.S. schools? What advantages or disadvantages would it offer?

## References

ARONOWITZ, S. (1973). *False Promises: The Shaping of American Working Class Consciousness*. New York: McGraw-Hill.

BAIRD, C. W. (1984). *Opportunity or Privilege: Labor Legislation in America*. Bowling Green, OH: Social Philosophy and Policy Center.

BIRK, L. (1994). "Intervention: A Few Teachers' Unions Take the Lead in Policing Their Own." *The Harvard Education Letter 10*, November/December, p. 10.

BRADLEY, A. (1990). "Rochester Teachers Reject 'Accountability' Contract." *Education Week*, October 3, p. 4.

———. (1991). "Administrators in Los Angeles Form a Bargaining Unit." *Education Week*, March 20, pp. 1, 16.

BRAUN, R. J. (1972). *Teachers and Power: The Story of the American Federation of Teachers*. New York: Simon & Schuster.

BRIMELOW, P., AND SPENCER, L. (1993). "The National Extortion Association." *Forbes 151*, July 7, pp. 72–84.

———. (1995). "Comeuppance." *Forbes 155*, February 13, pp. 121–127.

DILLON, S. (1994). "Teacher Tenure: Rights vs. Discipline." *The New York Times*, June 28, pp. 1, A15.

DUKE, B. (1986). *The Japanese School: Lessons for Industrial America*. New York: Praeger.

EATON, W. E. (1975). *The American Federation of Teachers, 1916–1961: A History of the Movement*. Carbondale: Southern Illinois University Press.

EBERTS, R. W., AND STONE, J. A. (1984). *The Effects of Collective Bargaining on American Education*. Lexington, MA: D.C. Heath.

FELDMAN, S. (1998). "The Big Lie," *New York Times*, June 7, p. 7.

FREEDMAN, M. (1987). *Difficulty of Firing Bad Teachers: Continuing Embarrassment for Schools. ENS Special Report.* Employers Negotiating Service, May 20, 1987.

FRIEDMAN, M., AND FRIEDMAN, R. (1979). *Free to Choose.* New York: Harcourt Brace Jovanovich.

GOLDSTEIN, A. (1998). "Ever Try to Flunk a Bad Teacher?" *Time,* July 20, p. 25.

JESSUP, D. K. (1978). "Teacher Unionization: A Reassessment of Rank and File Education." *Sociology of Education 51,* 44–55.

JOHNSON, S. M. (1988). "Unionism and Collective Bargaining in the Public Schools." In *Handbook of Research on Educational Administration,* edited by N. J. Boyan. New York: Longman.

KERCHNER, C. T. (1986). "Union-Made Teaching: Effects of Labor Relations." In *Review of Research in Education, vol. 13,* edited by E. Z. Rothkopf, pp. 317–349. Washington: American Educational Research Association.

KERCHNER, C. T., AND KOPPICH, J. E. (1993). *A Union of Professionals: Labor Relations and Educational Reform.* New York: Teachers College Press.

———— AND WEERES, J. G. (1997). *United Mind Workers: Unions and Teaching in the Knowledge Society.* San Francisco: Jossey-Bass.

LIEBERMAN, M. (1985). "Teacher Unions and Educational Quality: Folklore by Finn." *Phi Delta Kappan.* 66:341–343.

————. (1997). *The Teachers Unions: How the NEA and the AFT Sabotage Reform and Hold Students, Parents, Teachers, and Taxpayers Hostage to Bureaucracy.* New York: The Free Press.

————, AND MOSCOW, M. H. (1966). *Collective Negotiations for Teachers: An Approach to School Administration.* Chicago: Rand McNally.

MAEROFF, G. I. (1988). *The Empowerment of Teachers: Overcoming the Crisis of Confidence.* New York: Teachers College Press.

MURPHY, M. (1990). *Blackboard Unions: the AFT and the NEA, 1900–1980.* Ithaca, NY: Cornell University Press.

RAUTH, M. (1990). "Exploring Heresy in Collective Bargaining and School Restructuring." *Phi Delta Kappan 71,* 781–784.

RICHARDSON, J. (1994). "Two Indiana Suits Put Teachers and Union at Odds." *Education Week 14,* 1, 10.

ROSENTHAL, A. (1969). *Pedagogues and Power: Teacher Groups in School Politics.* Syracuse: Syracuse University Press.

SHANKER, A. (1992). "United States of America." In *Labor Relations in Education: An International Perspective,* edited by B. S. Cooper. Westport, CT: Greenwood Press.

STERN, D. (1986). "Compensation for Teachers." In *Review of Research in Education,* edited by E. Z. Rothkopf. Washington, DC: American Education Research Association.

STRESHLY, W. A., AND DEMITCHELL, T. A. (1994). *Teacher Unions and TQE: Building Quality Labor Relations.* Thousand Oaks, CA: Corwin.

TUTHILL, D. (1990). Expanding the Union Contract: One Teacher's Perspective. *Phi Delta Kappan 71,* 775–780.

URBAN, W. J. (1982). *Why Teachers Organized.* Detroit: Wayne State University Press.

VANSCIVER, J. H. (1990). Teacher Dismissals. *Phi Delta Kappan 72,* 318–319.

WATTS, G. D., AND MCCLURE, R. (1990). Expanding the Contract to Revolutionize School Reform. *Phi Delta Kappan 71,* 765–774.

WORTH, R. (1998). "Reforming the Teachers' Unions: What the Good Guys Have Accomplished—And What Remains to Be Done: Peer Review, Tenure Reform." *Washington Monthly,* 1–6, HTTP://web.Lexis-Nexis.com/universe.

# CHAPTER 17

# Inclusion and Mainstreaming: Special or Common Education

## POSITION 1: FOR FULL INCLUSION

Would you like to be excluded, hidden, or separated from other children in school? Would you like to be classified and labeled in a way that limited your participation? Would you want your child to be so treated?

That predicament has been the plight of "exceptional" children in U.S. society. They have been evaluated, classified, separated, and hidden in our schools. How can equality have any meaning when this happens?

Full inclusion of all children into school life is a fundamental principle in a free, democratic society. Full inclusion means that students who are classified "special" or "exceptional" because of individual physical or mental characteristics would not be isolated into separate schools, separate classes, or pull-out sessions. They would be full citizens and members of the school community, not only in regular classes but also as legitimate participants in the multiple activities of the school. Inclusion is consistent with fundamental principles of our society and with the law (Vargas, 1999). The United States should do no less than provide full inclusion.

Full inclusion expects far more of good education than merely adding classified students to general classes or mandating all students to run, climb, read, write, draw, or compute in only one way and at the same speed. Full inclusion assumes that schools should provide high-quality, individualized instruction, with well-prepared teachers, suitable and varied teaching materials, and appropriate schedules that support the idea that all students are capable of success. Thoughtful parents and serious educators recognize that the principle of full inclusion merely extends the democratic principle of quality education for all to include children with special needs. If we can attempt such an education for the majority of students, why not for all?

The concept of inclusion involves a set of school practices that Stainback, Stainback, and Jackson (1992) described:

1. All children are to be included in the educational and social lives of their schools and classrooms.
2. The basic goal is to not leave anyone out of school and classroom communities (thus, integration can be abandoned since no one has to go back to the mainstream).
3. The focus is on the support needs of all students and personnel.

Full inclusion does not mean that schools should bring in students with special needs only to insist on blind conformity to a single standard for all students; nor does it mean that nonconforming students should be ignored or mistreated in the "regular" schools. Rather, the concept of inclusion assumes that the individual needs of every student, whether classified "special" or not, must be seriously considered in order to provide a quality education. This assumption undergirds the idea of full inclusion for students who are "special" or "exceptional."

As a matter of human concern and fairness, we should not separate those who differ from the rest. In making the argument for inclusive schools that recognize the richness in human diversity, Cushner, McClelland, and Safford (2000) offer a philosophic and historic case for the inclusion of exceptional children:

> From its inception, a fundamental characteristic of American schooling has been its intended inclusiveness, across social boundaries, of gender, class, and—belatedly—race. Today, the term *inclusion* refers to the practice of including another group of students in regular classrooms, those with problems of health and/or physical, developmental, and emotional problems . . . Like societal inclusion, inclusive education implies fully shared participation of diverse individuals in common experiences. (pp. 161, 163)

## The Legal Basis for Full Inclusion

Over the past quarter-century, the U.S. Congress has clearly shown its intent that all children with disabilities be provided a free and appropriate education in the public schools. A series of modifications in supportive legislation, from 1975 to the present time, have improved the educational rights of children with disabilities and their families, leading to full inclusion as the next logical step. Turnbull and Turnbull (1998) defined this evolving policy as "Zero Reject" and noted that an important effect was *"to redefine the doctrine of equal educational opportunity* as it applies to children with disabilities and to establish different meanings of *equality* as it applies to people with and without disabilities" (p. 92; emphasis in original). Earlier laws relied on a concept of equality that meant equal access to different resources; children attended separate special education classes and schools. The newer laws assume that equal access means full access to regular resources—regular classes and schools, but with special support, to help students "more like than different from people without disabilities" (Turnbull and Turnbull, 1998, p. 93).

Clearly, the principle of inclusion goes well beyond the mainstreaming that has developed since the 1975 landmark federal legislation, the Education of All

Handicapped Children Act (Public Law 94–142). At the time Congress was considering the law, 1 million out of 8 million disabled children under age 21 were completely excluded from the U.S. public school system. They were "outcast children" (Dickman, 1985, p. 181). Mainstreaming grew out of an important clause of the law, offering the concept of the "least restrictive environment"; this meant that students with special needs who "demonstrate appropriate behavior and skills" should be in general classrooms rather than segregated programs. The law gave children with special needs the educational, emotional, and social advantages offered to other students. It also gave parents the right to be advocates in fashioning an appropriate education for their differently abled children.

Amendments and modifications to the 1975 law have included changes in the language—for example, replacing *handicapped* with *disabled* and renaming the law, calling it the 1990 Individuals with Disabilities Education Act (IDEA). Other important changes in the law have increased the expectations for mainstreaming and led toward full inclusion. The 1990 IDEA law requires that the school offer a set of placement options to meet the needs of students with disabilities, and that to the maximum extent appropriate, children with disabilities are to be educated with other children. Further, the law expects schools to provide supplementary aids and services for disabled children when needed; and it requires that any separate schooling or other removal of children with disabilities from the regular environment occur only when the child cannot learn in regular classes even with supplementary aids and services. This sets a high standard for schools to meet in order to exclude disabled students from regular classes.

Laws and court decisions are becoming more expansive in their recognition of the individual and social benefits of inclusion. *Mills v. Board of Education of the District of Columbia* (1972) produced a judgment in class-action litigation based on the foundational arguments of equal opportunity and due process. The judge in the *Mills* case decreed that children with physical or mental disabilities had a right to a suitable and free public education, and that lack of funds was not a defense for exclusion. Mainstreaming offered an interim process toward inclusion. The next obvious step is full inclusion for all students.

Parents have pursued full inclusion and have drawn increasing support from the courts. In a case about a New Jersey boy with severe disabilities, *Oberti v. Board of Education of the Borough of Clementon School District* (1993), a federal judge provided a ringing endorsement of full inclusion. The decision was based on the IDEA law and on other laws that guarantee disabled persons access to institutions that use federal funds.

## Democratic Purposes for Inclusion: The Civil Rights Case

At the center of education in a democracy are the concepts of equal opportunity and justice. Nothing defines a democracy more than the ideas that an educated populace can be self-governing and that citizens will be considered equal and will be treated with fairness. Democracy, by its very nature, requires all citizens to have the opportunity to be fully educated. Obviously, education cannot be reserved to a favored few. Nor can it be reserved for the favored majority who happen to be nondisabled. Equal opportunity and fairness underscore the idea of inclusion. There are many other important reasons for supporting the inclusion of special students in regular school classes and activities, but the fundamental premise of democracy expects no less.

Thomas Jefferson, in the Declaration of Independence, wrote: "We hold these truths to be self-evident, that all men are created equal; that they are endowed by their creator with certain inalienable rights, that among these are life, liberty, and the pursuit of happiness." This idea was basic to the U.S. Constitutional objectives of providing for justice, the blessings of liberty, and the general welfare. Should these not be the measure of life in the United States after two and a quarter centuries? Education is the primary means for realizing the great goals of the Declaration of Independence and the Constitution. Isolating special education students not only labels and stigmatizes them, it limits their full interaction with other people during their most formative years. This is clearly detrimental to these students, but it is also detrimental to the perceptions of nonexceptional students about life in the full society. Mainstreaming special education students into regular school classes is a giant step in the process of working toward full inclusion of these students into the life of the school.

In addition to the obvious educational value of allowing all students to participate fully in the schools, inclusion is also a civil rights issue. Discrimination against persons with disabilities has been legally outlawed in the United States. The 1990 Americans with Disabilities Act (ADA) barred such discrimination, just as other laws barred discrimination based on race, gender, or age.

Some institutions meet the access requirements of ADA on purely physical grounds, providing ramps and elevators as well as stairs and modifying doors and bathrooms. This minimal approach would be the equivalent of simply removing "White Only" signs after racial discrimination was ruled illegal and doing nothing more; it would still not deal with underlying and much more pervasive instances of institutional discrimination that restrict access and opportunity. In a larger context, education is a primary means of access to all of society's opportunities. Separate-but-equal education for African Americans was actually separate but not equal; similarly, separate special education is also separate but not equal.

There are many parallels between the way our society has treated minority children and the way it has treated disabled children in schools. One of the striking things about school-based classification of children into special education classes, programs, or schools is that students placed in the special category come disproportionately from minority ethnic and social class groups of society (Educational Testing Service, 1980; Heller et al., 1982; Anderson and Anderson, 1983; Brantlinger and Guskin, 1987). Obviously, this combination of class, race, and classification as disabled becomes a recipe for discrimination. Summarizing a substantial amount of research data gathered over twenty years, Wang (1990) notes that "Bias in assessment strategies, placement decisions, and referral rates are frequently cited as reasons that students from selected ethnic and social class status groups traditionally have been over-represented in special education" (p. 5). This parallel discrimination should be addressed as a civil rights issue on principle and a political issue in practice. Class and ethnicity have been used politically to limit the full participation of groups without wealth and power. Children with special needs have been subject to a similar political agenda that restricts access, opportunity, and fulfillment of the democratic ideal (Barton, 1988).

Exceptionality among individuals is a constant in human history. This condition of "abnormality" has historically been the basis for a variety of destructive actions by those in power, from infanticide to institutionalization. Winzer's (1993) comprehensive history of special education is based on a pertinent principle: "A society's treament of those who are weak and dependent is one critical indicator of its social progress. Social attitudes concerning the education and care of exceptional individuals reflect general cultural attitudes concerning the obligations of a society to its individual citizens" (p. 3). This, in the United States and in the civilized world, is a civil rights issue based on the most fundamental documents and foundational moral principles.

## Social Policy Considerations

Beyond the obvious civil rights concerns raised by separating special needs children from their peers in schools, there are other defects in this policy. As a matter of social policy, separation is inconsistent with the larger-scale interests of the United States. Sailor, Gerry, and Wilson (1991) note that U.S. social policy goals include:

- Maximizing economic, social, cultural, and political productivity of all citizens; maximizing the choices for personal freedom and independence (interdependence) of all citizens
- Assuring the integration and participation of all citizens within the social, economic, and political fabric of American communities
- Ensuring fairness and equity (justice) within the operation of the social, economic, and political institutions of the society
- Providing citizen access in governmental decision making to the smallest unit of government consistent with fairness and equity goals. (p. 180)

These broad social policy goals underlie the tenets of inclusion for special needs youth in all activities of society and its institutions. Obviously, schools are a central institution of all societies; full participation in the society requires full inclusion in the schools. Denying those rights to the disabled denies society the skills, the economic productivity, and the social and political values inherent in the full participation of individuals with disabilities. Institutionalization and separation are costly for society in both economic and human terms.

In the period before 1910, the United States had a pattern of institutionalizing children with disabilities in isolation from society. Families of these children hid them, provided private care, or sent them to institutions where they would live out their lives away from public view or participation. Changing public attitudes regarding our social responsibility for persons with disabilities, as well as a recognition of the general economic value in providing training for disadvantaged people, led to a variety of alterations in social policies and educational practices. This occurred at the same time as public schooling expanded in the early twentieth century. For the disabled, this meant segregation in separate schools and/or separate classes, teachers, and programs. The intent may have been benign, but this is inadequate as a social policy. Segregation may be better than complete exclusion, but it still offends a basic premise of a civilized society, offers little opportunity for participation in the full society, and reinforces the stigma associated with segregated schools, teachers, and programs. In current times, the stigma of separation has marginalized special education students and robbed society of their energies. Segregation does not match the social policy goals that Sailor, Gerry, and Wilson identified. We can and should do better.

## Social and Psychological Arguments for Inclusion

In addition to persuasive arguments based on fundamental democratic principles and on fair social policy in favor of full inclusion, social and personal psychology offer other important arguments for inclusion. Separation of exceptional children from the mainstream of children in schools has been recognized as traumatic for those separated, whether by race, gender, or abilities. In the landmark Supreme Court decision that declared racially segregated schools and the concept of "separate but equal" unconstitutional (*Brown v. Board of Education*, 1954), Chief Justice Earl Warren argued that separation in schools can cause children to "generate a feeling of inferiority as to . . . status in the community that may affect their hearts and minds in a way unlikely ever to be undone" (p. 493). Senator Lowell Weicker (1988) stated: "As a society, we have treated people with disabilities as inferiors and made them unwelcome in many activities and opportunities available to other Americans" (quoted in Stainback and Stainback, 1990, p. 7).

It is obvious that the perceptions of special needs children are strongly influenced by their separation. It goes beyond individual feelings of insecurity to the concept that the society values them less and prefers them out of sight. Ethnographic research done in a separate class of Trainable Mentally Handicapped students, identified as the Explorer group, illustrates this social ostracism. The Explorer group had been established in a regular school for over a year when researchers recorded these observations:

> There was little friendly contact between these young people and the regular student body. From what we had heard about Explorer, it sounded like what we called a "dump and hope" situation: someone had *dumped* the disabled students and an unmotivated teacher there, and then *hoped* that things would work out of their own accord. . . . Mr. _____, the class's special education teacher . . . said the district had transferred him against his will from another high school where he had taught students who were mildly retarded.

He felt unprepared to teach the students with more severe disabilities and doubted they could ever make friends with nondisabled peers. . . .

Classroom materials designed for young children, which stigmatize teenagers with disabilities by causing peers to view them as more incompetent than they really are (Bates, Morrow, Pancsofar, and Sedlak, 1984), were commonly used. . . . Worst of all, Mr. _____ and other staff (such as the school's speech therapist) seemed deliberately to convey their negative evaluations of the students' capabilities to the nondisabled kids. (Murray-Seegert, 1989, pp. 4, 5)

Other research confirms that children with special needs do better in both academic work and social adjustment in mainstreamed schools and in regular classes. Semmel, Gottlieb, and Robinson (1979) report that results from several studies showed that regular class placement was a factor in superior academic achievement among special students, and that special needs students did at least as well in academic work in regular classes as they had in special classes. In addition, Carlberg and Kavale (1980) found that the social adjustment of special needs youth was improved by mainstreaming into the life of the school. If social interaction improves for these students, while academic achievement improves or remains at least as high, then inclusion is a positive school practice. Wang, Reynolds, and Walberg (1990) report multiple studies which support inclusion.

Positive inclusion in schools depends upon collaborative efforts by regular and special education teachers, parents, and administrators. We must avoid the negative results that accrued from ill-prepared and poorly organized efforts at mainstreaming in the past. Teachers need to be prepared to work with special needs children in full inclusion schools. Villa, Thousand, and Chapple (1996) note that few teacher education programs prepare teachers for the new schools. This is a serious problem; teachers need more than a few lessons about handling diverse students. Teacher preparation programs should move quickly to integrate the most useful knowledge from special education research and practice and should emphasize special methods for dealing with a wide range of students and for individualizing lessons. In-service programs should provide intensive work to bring currently practicing teachers up to a standard of good teacher practice for all teachers of all students at all levels of school.

Not only are there serious detrimental consequences for the individual exceptional children who are placed in isolated or separated situations, but "average" children are likewise deprived of realistic social interaction and a more compassionate understanding of the lives of others. Additionally, the community as a whole suffers from the suspicion, distrust, and misunderstanding created by separation. The world's history of abusing, stigmatizing, and isolating the disabled illustrates that social consequence.

## A Depressing History of Discrimination, Isolation, and Separation of Disabled Persons

The United States and other nations have not always been forward-looking; social progress has often been halting and erratic. Our treatment of persons with disabilities historically derived from negative traditions and social attitudes toward "different" people in earlier societies. We have only recently introduced the basic documents and principles of justice and equality as criteria for the treatment of exceptional people.

There are few solid historical records of how disabled persons were treated prior to the eighteenth century. Fragmentary evidence shows that deformed children were left to die on hillsides in Sparta, that individuals who differed from the normal were abused, condemned, or destroyed in Roman times and after the Fall of Rome, and that many nations and religions of Europe used the disabled as scapegoats for disasters, witchery, and disorder, excluding them from religious organizations, identifying them as unfit for moral society, and denying them citizenship and civil rights (Winzer, 1993).

Earliest forms of discrimination and persecution were the result of ignorance and a questionable moral mentality. More recent discrimination has been partly based on a mistaken form of social Darwinism or scientism that presumes that the "survival of the fittest" permits the mistreatment of people with differences. This is an ethically defective view that those who survive are the best or most suitable in a society. Thomas Huxley (1897), in a famous essay, drew parallels between gardening and social organization in terms of a battle between a "state of nature" and a "state of art." He noted that gardeners intercede to assure nourishment, proper growing conditions, and weeding to provide a state of art, rather than simply letting natural selection take its course. He then writes of the ruthlessness and lack of ethics of an imagined administrator, who, under "purely scientific considerations," would systematically destroy the "hopelessly diseased, the infirm aged, the weak or deformed in body or mind, the excess of infants born" as the gardener might pull up defective or surplus plants to retain a state of art in the face of natural tendencies (pp. 21, 22). He concludes that "there is no hope that mere human beings will ever possess enough intelligence to select the fittest" (p. 34), and that the efforts of tyrants or mobs to screen "weak" individuals are morally corrupt, subject to self-interest, and unsuited to civilized society. No modern civilization would propose to torture disabled children to "rehabilitate" them, or to banish them from society to keep them hidden. Yet, isolation and separation in schools is a form of torture and exclusion.

## The "Exceptional" and the "Average"

The identification and measurement of exceptionality is a tradition in modern society, though it varies to some extent by nation and time period. In the United States at this time, exceptionality usually refers to observable or measurable differences in physical, mental, emotional, or other abilities. In school terms, exceptional children are those who differ from nonexceptional ones on the basis of their school achievement, for example, in reading, writing, listening, sitting attentively, seeing and hearing, and so on. Exceptionality in the United States has included both extremes of mental ability—the severely mentally or learning impaired and the gifted and talented. Both get special treatment and school support. The category of exceptional children also includes those who have a variety of measured physical differences from "average" children, including differences in sight, hearing, and use of limbs, but it does not include those students with extraordinary physical abilities. Similarly, only one end of the potential spectrum of emotional abilities is included in the exceptional category; only those labeled emotionally impaired. There are some problems, then, with consistency in the way we apply the definition of "exceptional."

The causes of exceptionality include genetics, at-birth disabilities, improper medical practice, disease, parental irresponsibility, accidents, and inadequate health care. These exceptionalities are not self-inflicted; they are often chance happenings, as in afflictions caused by accidents, birth defects, or childhood disease. Although exceptionality, in these terms, is relatively rare, it should not create a wall of separation from the rest of society; human variety is extraordinarily complex and incredibly wide-ranging. We have improved our measures, but the extent of human variability remains unknown. Further, the classifications themselves reflect cultural norms and prejudices.

The category of "disabled," "exceptional," or "handicapped" depends on the society, time period, and societal norms. Disability, according to Dickman (1985), is a deficit that occurs at birth or through disease or some other event, while handicaps are the secondary problems that occur because of discrimination, mistreatment, or help that is denied or delayed. The term *handicapped*, by this definition, represents a social problem of bias and discrimination, while *disability* is an individual problem. For another example, the category of "learning disabled," used widely in schools in the United States, varies significantly in the measures used to define it. The term is not used in developing nations, where certain forms of technological literacy are not as important, nor is it used much in the corporate world to define categories of people (Cushner, McClelland, and Safford, 2000).

Much of the dreary history of prejudice and discrimination against exceptional children has been based on a false sense of the meaning of "average," and on people's insecurities about their own abilities and talents. Those who differ are often labeled negatively in order to maintain the status of the favored. Although we often refer to an average, there may be no actual "average" person, in genetic traits, social characteristics, or preferred individual behavior. Who among us comes from a family of 2.3 children, an average family? How many are exactly average in height, weight, IQ, and shoe size? Do any of us always earn average grades or average test scores? Who wants an average marriage when over 50 percent end in divorce? There are many things each of us does far better or far worse than the average. Average also suggests dullness and conformity; richness comes from diversity. The idea of average is suitable as a broad guide for making tentative comparative judgments about many conditions like income, tax deductions, or sleep time needed each day. The idea of average can be informative and useful, but it should not be mindlessly used as a criterion to rank human qualities against. Exceptional children are exceptional when compared to certain measures of average, but all children differ from average in some respect.

## Meeting Potential Problems in Full Inclusion

Full inclusion of all children into the lives of schools is not an easy task (*NEA Today*, 1999). As is clear from the history of special education, many problems are associated with implementing full inclusion. Schools must address the fears of some parents, teachers, administrators, and community members by developing strong programs of information, discussion, preparation, and positive interaction. Special education teachers may fear losing their expert status and, perhaps, their jobs; regular teachers are concerned about their lack of preparation and, for some of them, about no longer being able to send annoying students to special education classes. Beyond ignorance and fears is a history of slowness and resistance in most school reform efforts. Thousand and Villa (1995) identify frequently cited causes of school intractability as: "(1) inadequate teacher preparation; (2) inappropriate organizational structures, policies, and procedures; (3) lack of attention to the cultural aspects of schooling; and (4) poor leadership" (p. 53).

These factors have a detrimental impact on efforts to develop full inclusion programs in schools. Clearly, we need to improve teacher education to better prepare teachers for educating diverse students and meeting individual student needs. Practicing regular education teachers also need assistance in changing their teaching practices and in working with special education teachers and parents on well-designed and implemented plans for individual students. We need to shake the lockstep curriculum, tracking, and teacher isolation common in the current school structure. This structure is not very good for regular classes; it is a major obstacle to full inclusion. We need to recognize that the school culture has been a long time in the making and that change is difficult for many people. We must seek involvement and support, providing high-quality assistance and incentives for improvement. And we must enlist the school leaders, faculty and administrators, in the process of full inclusion to develop strong leadership in implementing the best forms. Time, energy, and resources must be devoted to helping teachers become more collaborative and better oriented toward individual student needs, to helping administrators become more supportive and visionary, and to helping schools become more flexible.

We can learn from some of the mistakes made in trying to implement mainstreaming without thorough preparation. Mainstreaming has been a success in many schools and in the lives of many individual students who had previously been shunted to separate schools or classes. It has also been especially successful in alleviating the separation and isolation of special education students and in bringing their situation to light. The needs of these students and the previous inadequacies of the schools in meeting their needs are now part of the public discourse. Some of the most egregious problems and misperceptions that surrounded mainstreaming, however, remain.

There have been failures in mainstreaming in some schools, usually where students with special needs were dumped into existing classes without adequate support, without preparing school staff or community, or without considering the individual needs of all students. Some special needs students were not able to demonstrate "appropriate behavior and skills" under school guidelines, and these schools made little effort to make needed changes in program or personnel to ensure the student's success (Lombardi and Ludlow, 1996). Mainstreaming became popular in the schools in the 1980s, but many schools and teachers were unprepared for handling special needs and faltered, or were unnecessarily limited in their vision and operation. The most severely disabled students are still only mainstreamed in a few classes each day, usually classes such as art and physical education (*Education Week on the Web*, 1998).

Partly in recognition of the problems involved in mainstreaming, Congress amended the IDEA in 1997 (Public Law 105–17) with substantial changes required in developing the Individualized Education Plan (IEP). The new requirements increase the participation of general education teachers in planning for special needs students through membership on IEP teams and in the development of a student's IEP. In addition, schools must consider how the student's disability affects involvement and performance in the general curriculum of the school. These changes require general educators to become better informed and more actively involved in individualizing instruction for special needs children (*Teaching Exeptional Children*, 1998).

Inclusion, beyond mainstreaming, offers children with special needs the opportunity to be educated to "the maximum extent appropriate" (PL94–142) in "the school or classroom he or she would otherwise have attended if he or she did not have a disability" (Rogers, 1993). Mainstreaming is far preferable to ancient ideas for handling people with disabilities—infanticide, exile, exclusion, or hiding by separation. But inclusion offers a broad educational program even more consistent with a society based on democracy and ethics.

## Global Needs for Inclusive Education

Full inclusion is not a topic limited to the United States. It is estimated conservatively that moderate to severe disabilities affect 5.2 percent of the world population. This figure includes 7.7 percent of the populations of developed countries and 4.5 percent of the populations of less developed regions (Mittler, 1993); the total number of disabled persons was estimated to reach over 300 million as the 21st century starts. The disparity between the proportions of disabled persons in developed and less developed areas of the world reflects differences in the definitions of disabled, in health practices, and in governmental policies on reporting disabilities in different nations. Improvements in health practices throughout the world are expected to cause an increase in the proportion of disabled persons, since children who previously might have died at birth or in infancy will survive, but may have serious impairments (Mittler, et al., 1993).

In many nations, the integration of children with special needs into regular schools is a contemporary movement. For example, Italy has developed national policies for integration, the United Kingdom has established legislative policies that encourage local schools to integrate, and Austria provides model experimental projects to demonstrate the value of integration (Wedell, 1993). The United Nations has a history of concern for children, including children with disabilities; the 1959 Declaration of the Rights of the Child recognized the right of every child to develop to his or her full capacity. The UN Convention on the Rights of the Child (1989) affirmed the right to an education and, for disabled children, services which "shall be designed to ensure that the disabled child has effective access to and receives education, training, health care services, rehabilitation services, preparation for employment, and recreational opportunities in a manner conducive to the child's achieving *the fullest possible social integration and individual development* . . ." (article 23,3, emphasis added). The United States has, over the past several decades, met or surpassed the legislative expectations of international human rights documents in regard to disabled children. It is time for the United States to extend its commitments and embrace the full inclusion approach to educating disabled youth.

## Conclusion

The idea of fully including disabled children into the lives of school and society has been a long time coming. From a dismal period of exclusion, isolation, and separation, we moved to mainstreaming and limited inclusion. Now we should move forward to full inclusion. Strong arguments, from our basic principles as a free democracy to the positive effect inclusion would have on individuals and on society, support the wisdom of pursuing full inclusion.

We all have both individual and social needs and desires. We need food, clothing, and other necessary conditions of life. We want to be recognized for our individual merits and personalities. We want respect as individuals. We want our individual rights protected and we want the freedom to live without oppressive restriction. A democracy attempts to provide for these individual needs and wants by forging a generally understood social contract among its citizens. A sense of justice in such a society requires that all citizens have equal opportunity to build fulfilling lives in the society and the economy.

But we also have social needs, such as the opportunity for full participation in the larger society and the enjoyment of public resources and activities. With each of these sets of needs come some positive and some negative features. Sometimes individual personalities are offensive to others, and sometimes social participation is frustrating and difficult. These are not good reasons to exclude people from participation; to do so is patently undemocratic. We don't need, as individuals or as a society, forced separation and the stigmatizing that results. It is ethically and practically inconsistent to continue separating children with special needs from other children in our schools.

## POSITION 2: AGAINST FULL INCLUSION AND INTRUSIVE MAINSTREAMING

Fads and schools go hand in hand. The best place to find the newest fads in young people's language, music, dress, and manners is in a school—you'll find out what is or was cool, baaaaad, heavy, dork, and nerd, and you probably won't hear way out, groovy, swell, or twenty-three skiddoo. Not only are fads in popular culture highly noticeable in typical schools, but schools are the birthplace of many other types of fads, often as a response to calls for school or social reform. Unfortunately, many of these educational fads are poorly thought out and counterproductive.

Full inclusion appears to be one of the latest examples of education's susceptibility to fads and slogans. The damage that full inclusion policies and practices may create for the very children they claim to help can be significant. Full inclusion carries negative implications for schools, teachers, parents, children, and the community. Worse, the "proinclusionists" hide the inherent defects of inclusion behind noble-sounding slogans; they label opponents who speak against full inclusion as insensitive, inhumane, or undemocratic (Petch-Hogan and Haggard, 1999).

The mainstreaming movement, which thrust disabled children into classrooms without adequate preparation and with excessive expectations, elicited the same type of defensive rhetoric. Reasonable people who argued against large-scale mainstreaming have been chastised, pilloried, or ignored. Full inclusion has become another politically correct view, even though it would damage the effective special assistance programs our schools have spent years to develop and improve. As many experts (Kauffman and Hallahan, 1995) suggest, full inclusion is an illusion because general classrooms and schools will never be capable of meeting the needs of all special or exceptional students. These children require separate assistance and facilities to meet their needs. It is the child with special needs who most suffers from full inclusion.

Proponents of full inclusion advocate mandates, regardless of individual circumstances, school situations, or challenges to bureaucratic control. This limits the child with special needs by requiring his or her attendance in regular classes without the high-quality help available in a separate program. Typical special education programs provide specially trained teachers and paraprofessionals, smaller class sizes, adjusted curricula, and fairer competition. Such programs allow parents and teachers to jointly fashion an individualized program that maximizes the child's strengths and remediates areas of need. They are also able to access experts outside the school to assist the child with special needs in preparing for the transition from school to work life. Full inclusion limits nondisabled children by diverting time and energy from their teachers to meet the special needs of a few students and by sometimes disrupting their schoolwork when the behaviors of a child with special needs are inappropriate in a general classroom. Inclusion limits classroom teachers by requiring them to allot extra time, materials, and energy to children who need extra support, as well as requiring them to prepare and monitor individual education plans for each of these children. Finally, full inclusion limits the school's ability to make educational decisions in the best interests of individual students. Full inclusion is a form of social engineering that cannot fulfill what it promises without serious repercussions for children and schools.

# Laudable Goals, but Difficult Reality

The goal of inclusion may be laudable under some conditions and for some individuals. However, full inclusion for all students represents an ideal that does not mesh with day-to-day reality for large numbers of students. Blind adherence to the lofty idea of full inclusion can wreak havoc for children and schools. Many children are now participating successfully in effective special education classes and schools. Full inclusion is a threat to these children; they will be thrown into regular classes, subject to the vagaries of standardized education and general school funding. Zigler and Hall (1986) noted this problem in regard to excesses in the 1980s mainstreaming movement. This movement was based on the "normalization" principle, an idea that we should provide more "normal" school settings to socialize disabled children:

> Ironically, the very law that was designed to safeguard the options of handicapped children and their parents (the 1975 Education for All Handicapped Children Act) may, in the end, act to constrict their choices and result in disservice to the very children the legislators sought to help, by forcing schools to place them in programs that are not equipped to meet their needs. The normalization principle and the practice of mainstreaming may have deleterious effects on some children by denying them their right to be different. . . . Underlying the very idea of normalization is a push toward homogeneity, which is unfair to those children whose special needs may come to be viewed as unacceptable. (p. 2)

Full inclusion goes well beyond mainstreaming. As a result, it runs even greater risks of homogenizing our educational approach and causing a decline in special care and attention for children with exceptional needs. The political support for special programs and funds, support that took years to develop, will atrophy. Special education budgets will diminish. School administrators, with declining special education budgets, will be unlikely to champion the needs of this small and expensive proportion of their student populations. Regular class teachers, already overworked in large classes, will be unable to extend themselves even further for children who need more individualized help. Parents of nondisabled children may be sympathetic, but they are unlikely to support the diversion of general education funds, resources, and teacher time from the education of their own children.

We want as many disabled children as possible to be self-reliant, to be equipped for successful and productive lives, to participate constructively in the larger society, and to develop feelings of personal worth. We want no less for any child, but the child who is disabled needs special attention and support to reach these goals. One of the primary purposes of special education programs is to provide the setting and individualized attention these children need to develop self-reliance, success, productivity, and feelings of personal worth. These programs are jeopardized by the steamroller tactics of the full inclusionists.

Full inclusion is not needed in the schools. Thoughtfully involving certain children with special needs in regular school classes and activities, on an individual basis, offers benefits to the school and to the child. Careful inclusion, offered by a well-prepared school district to parents of children whose academic work is likely to be enhanced and whose behavior is not likely to disrupt the education of others, is a positive step—but should be rare if we are to preserve the benefits of special education.

Obviously, we already have careful inclusion in many good schools. Expert diagnosis, classification, parental involvement, individually developed special education programs, close evaluation of progress, and, for some, graduated access to regular classes have provided inclusion for individuals in many schools. These schools provide disabled children and their families with excellent resources, fine-tuned to the child's specific needs and carefully crafted to support the child's development. A focus on the child's highly individual needs and development is fundamental to this process.

## Treating Other Exceptional Children: The Gifted

Another interesting, real-life issue arises when we discuss full inclusion. Presumably, full inclusion would require schools to eliminate separate, special programs, forcing all exceptional students into regular classes in regular schools. Exceptions would occur only when the parents and school agree that the child cannot be educated in a regular class. But special school programs for exceptional children come in many varieties. Among them are the programs for gifted and talented children, honors programs, and tracking.

Gifted and talented programs, for example, are often separately organized, taught, and evaluated. As Clark (1996) notes in a comprehensive analysis of such programs: "Gifted and talented students have more complex needs than average and below average learners . . . if these needs are not met we now know that ability cannot be maintained; indeed, brain research tells us that ability will be lost . . . When no programs are available to this group of learners a disservice is done, not only to these students but to all of society, as our finest minds not only lack nurture, they are wasted" (p. 60).

In addition, we must recognize the political realities involved in efforts to end special programs for gifted, honors, or high-achieving students. These programs usually include children from the more powerful families in a community; these parents strongly support the programs; the programs demonstrate how special treatment makes a difference in student achievement; and the programs enhance the school's academic reputation. Under full inclusion, gifted and talented children would presumably be moved back into regular classes. Similarly, honors and remedial classes and tracking would be doomed. One-size-fits-all schooling, as full inclusion ideology proposes, is a prescription for mediocrity.

## Well-Deserved Special Treatment

It is easy to fling out high-sounding phrases about full inclusion and democracy. It is much more difficult to critically examine the potential consequences of a major change in the way we treat exceptional children in our schools. Inclusion of special needs children into regular schools and classes is an educational policy that needs critical assessment. Waving the flag of democracy may stir the faddists in education, but it will not hide the serious problems inherent in full inclusion.

Over history, children with disabilities have suffered; they have been reviled, ostracized, ridiculed, ignored, and destroyed. Some became members of circuses; some were hidden by their families; others were placed in ill-funded and ill-supervised institutions with no chance for improvement. The families of disabled children also suffered social malignment. And society lost the contributions it could have had from the many talents of people with disabilities.

Fortunately, society has made dramatic changes in the way it views the disabled. We now recognize that the special needs of these children require special treatment. We have developed schools and classes where exceptional children can find success and develop on their own terms in school and life. These programs offer a ray of hope to children who were ostracized and ignored in the past. Extra funding for special education provides more individualistic education, better prepared teachers, more appropriate teaching materials, superior facilities, and a setting better organized to help these children. Full inclusion could represent an effort to control school budgets by decreasing current special funding for special education and gifted and talented programs. Of course, it is cheaper to educate children with special needs in regular classes. But that would be an unwise and, in the long run, economically foolish move. Many special education schools and programs have been successful in preparing students to contribute to society. The actual proportion of exceptional children is very small, in the range of 5 percent nationally. That small number deserves special financing, special treatment, special teachers, and special programs to ensure they will become productive members of society.

Special education and exceptional programs offer important benefits to the child: a low student-teacher ratio for increased individualized instruction and attention; teachers especially trained to educate and develop the skills of exceptional students; experts organized into study teams to provide diagnosis, treatment, and evaluation of student development; homogeneous grouping to permit the teacher to concentrate on common needs and characteristics; more opportunity for student success among peers and more realistic competition in academics and/or athletics; funds for facilities, special equipment, and specially designed student learning materials; and increased student self-esteem from individual attention and by limiting negative interaction with non-disabled students. In addition, special education programs offer opportunity for remedial education that could return mildly disabled children to the regular program. These benefits continue to accrue to special education programs; they will be reduced with the advent of inclusion. Regular schools are unprepared to offer them in addition to their usual efforts, and initial extra funding will dry up or be absorbed into the ongoing operation of the schools.

## Full Inclusion and School Reality

Theoretically, inclusion could provide all the good things that special education now provides—special teachers, individualization, more self-esteem, but with the added benefit of allowing exceptional children to participate fully in the school program. Can any thoughtful observer of schools believe that this will really happen? Long-term experience with school reforms suggests that any immediate, positive effects of inclusion are likely to be overcome by the long-standing conformist standardization, bureaucracy, and funding requirements that make most schools dull and ineffective even for many regular students. The special needs child will be overlooked in these schools.

With children of all abilities and disabilities mixed in a class and school, the chance increases that the special needs of select students will be missed. The focus will shift away from giving special attention to individual children's strengths and disabilities and shift toward conforming to group standards imposed by state officials, meeting community expectations in test scores, or facing other accountability measures of group success. Large class size will make it difficult for the regular teacher to provide special assistance to exceptional children. Schools will not be able to fully control other students' disparaging or hurtful comments, and the exceptional children will again suffer. School funds will decrease to a common standard, without special funds for special children. Exceptional students require exceptional effort, but the schools will be stretched and will be unable to provide it.

In addition, the advocates of full inclusion are wrong when they argue that interaction with regular students in a regular program will benefit those who are disabled. A sorry history of taunting, labeling, ridicule, and exclusion by regular students is not likely to disappear because of some legislated program of interaction. There is no evidence that nondisabled children will suddenly develop appropriate classroom behavior when full inclusion takes place. Lectures and admonitions by school officials are not likely to make a dent in the problem, no matter how well-intentioned they are. Even if the majority of children are well behaved and nonprejudiced, it only takes a few to spoil the school setting for children with disabilities who have already been subjected to frequent stares and slights. School is tough enough for many regular students who happen to be different from the group. Life in many schools is not pleasant for children from poor families, children who stutter, children who are noticeably shorter or taller or more plump, children who are slower in speed or intellect, children from certain cultural backgrounds, and children who are not as gregarious or athletic or pretty as the leading cliques of students. School subcultures create cauldrons of despair for many students who are not accepted because of minor differences (Palonsky, 1975); consider the problem those with significant disabilities would face in regular schools.

## Classification and Myths

Many myths exist about the classification of children into separate special education programs. One myth is that classified students will be so unhappy or so ill-served by the programs that they will drop out. In fact, the national dropout rate for all students over age 14 is about 25 percent, but for students with disabilities the rate is only about 4 percent (Carlson and Parshall, 1996; U.S.

Department of Education, 1998). Another myth is that classification into special education is a one-way street, that those selected for special education never return to the regular program. In fact, the declassification rate of special education students is higher than their dropout rate; estimates of the declassification rate run from about 4 to 9 percent annually (Carlson and Parshall, 1996). A third, and most deleterious myth, is that classified children who are placed into separate special education programs are not challenged and are never able to make the school, social, and behavioral adjustments needed to fit into the regular school or into society. A significant study by Carlson and Parshall (1996) analyzed data about the approximately 7 percent of special education students who were declassified annually and placed into regular classes in Michigan over a five-year period. This study revealed two important bases for an argument against a one-size-fits-all full inclusion program:

1. Special education programs work, and students can achieve successful declassification; the vast majority of declassified children were well-adjusted in academic, social, and behavioral categories.
2. There is a continuing need for special attention for a minority of declassified children; about 11 percent of the declassified students needed extra care, and about 4 percent returned to special education classes.

On the one hand, it is remarkable that a sizable proportion of students in special education programs are able to join regular classes and be successful in terms of school, social, and behavioral criteria. On the other hand, the very small proportion of those who still need special care suggests we should keep separate programs available for those who, for whatever reasons, are better served in classified programs or are unable to make the necessary adjustments to the regular school. Carlson and Parshall's study noted that the poorest results from declassification efforts occurred for students who had emotional impairments. For those whose declassification was successful, Carlson and Parshall state: "Presumably, without special education services, these students would not have done as well in school as they did." (p. 98).

## Slogans and Myths: Equal Education

There are many slogans that our society expects caring people to support: Save the Whales, do unto others as you would have them do unto you, keep a stiff upper lip, free and equal education for everyone to the fullest possible extent. Saving the whales is more complicated than putting a bumper sticker on a car, boycotting fish, or voting for funds for oceanographic research. Treating others as you would like to be treated is a sound principle, but it is very difficult to translate into practice in the myriad daily involvements we confront. Stiff upper lips may be a good idea, but exactly what are they, and when are they not a good idea?

Unfortunately, the simplicity and moral righteousness of such slogans can be deceptive. Life's problems are complex; slogans ignore the complexity and offer a tantalizingly singular answer. Unfortunately, simplistic answers may make the problems worse. A bumper-sticker society may be unable to shift to being a thoughtful society. Making education a cornerstone of democracy is an excellent idea, but to make it work requires more than unsubstantiated claims and moral posturing.

The idea of free and open education, equally available to all with no differences in treatment or result, is an interesting utopian idea that is so far from reality it is painful. Yet, this is the basic concept underlying the current interest in inclusion. We don't yet have free and equal education, equal treatment, or equal results for the wide variety of students who attend "regular" public schools. It is unrealistic to believe that students shifted to meet inclusion goals will actually obtain equal access, treatment, or results. The "regular" classroom is a figment of ideological imagination; schools do not offer equality now.

Currently, even outside of separate special education classes, access to education differs along several dimensions. Tracking or ability-grouping students based on how they score on tests and how teachers evaluate them separates students for most of their school careers (Oakes, 1985; Urban and Waggoner, 1996; Spring, 1998). Schools in different communities offer differing advantages to their students as a result of funding differences that citizens vote on (Kozol, 1991). Because they need buildings and equipment, high school athletes are more costly to a school district than humanities students. The best athletes are selected for team membership; the poorest are not. Good readers are placed in one group and poor readers in another in elementary school classes. Not all students are admitted to college preparatory or honors classes. Advanced woodshop is limited to select students, as are advanced Latin and chemistry. Students who misbehave and disrupt others are separated in schools, and they may be denied access by suspension or expulsion. Remedial courses in math and literacy are limited to certain students.

Where a student happens to live is related to how well he or she will do in school and in gaining access to further education; higher-income communities have schools where students obtain higher standardized test scores and higher rates of college admission. Female students have less access to higher-level math and science classes than males. Minority students have less access to highly ranked colleges than majority students. When viewed on the basis of equality, these circumstances may not be ideal or even always supportable, but they are the reality of schooling in today's society. When we view these differences as means of providing the best education to those with the highest potential, they are more acceptable. Democracy does not require exact equality of condition. Also, the economic ideas behind capitalism, which have made this nation so successful, are inconsistent with mandated egalitarianism; capitalism requires that we reward competition and entrepreneurship.

Access to schooling controls the dimensions of equal treatment and results; if you can't get in or stay in school, you won't be accorded equal treatment or achieve equal results. Students who enjoy school, attend regularly, and complete assignments are more likely to get better grades and better recommendations from teachers and principals. Teachers' pets also earn better grades and references. After selecting out those who meet a set of minimum standards, the school band director still gives more solos to the better players than to the poorer ones. The best chess players and debaters get the best treatment on their respective teams.

## On the Fairness of Life

Life, as we know, is unfair. We see unfairness in human relations of all kinds, including those that take place in schools. We can't fix all unfairness, but we need to limit inappropriate discrimination and prejudice. Discrimination is inappropriate if it is based on criteria that are illogical, unethical, or lack a scientific basis. Discrimination is appropriate if it means separating existing individual differences to treat, protect, or nurture them. We discriminate among people by granting academic awards, among people with certain illnesses by treating them and protecting the society, and among animals by determining which are endangered and therefore deserving of special treatment. Prejudice means that we "prejudge" without knowledge; but making a judgment based on an understanding of available information is not prejudice. It is prejudice to claim, before ever tasting it, that broccoli tastes bad—but not to make the statement after tasting. Throughout life, we make judgments. Some may turn out to be wrong, but we can only try to use the best and most complete available information and reasoning to inform a judgment.

Fairness may sometimes mean providing different strokes for different folks if the criteria are sensible and consistent with social goals and individual interests. Putting all students into advanced Latin or into woodshop does not make sense; keeping disruptive or violent children in regular classes regardless of their behavior does not make sense; admitting all students to any college they desire does not make sense. We use criteria to limit those who can drive cars, handle food, practice medicine, cut and style hair, be convicted of a crime, or run for president. These limits are only unfair if they are abused, prejudicially applied, or not sensible.

One of the interesting ironies of the effort to establish full inclusion of exceptional children into regular schools is that many of its strongest advocates come from the special education network, and they do not want, themselves, to be integrated into "regular" departments or schools of teacher education. Surveys of leaders of schools of education across the United States in 1989 and 1994 found that almost three-fourths of them believed special education is best served by separating teacher education into general education and special education departments (Heller, 1996). One of the most frequent reasons given for the desirability of separation is the need to "identify with persons of equal interest, expertise, and common purpose" (p. 258). Another major reason was the increased status of or attention paid to special educators as a result of separation. Special education specialists do not want to be fully included in higher education for good reasons. Separate special education programs in the schools, when constructed properly, offer the same advantages to children with different needs.

Equality in a democracy does not mean total equality of condition. People differ in a wide variety of characteristics. While some people may prefer a system where all individuals are exactly the same, such a system never lasts. It is inconsistent with human nature. Our democratic society permits and encourages many practices of inequality. Sometimes these practices are designed to compensate for previous inequalities, such as racism or sexism. We develop programs to offer special treatment to those we think have been denied equal treatment in prior periods of time. Sometimes these practices are the result of natural human enterprise; competition provides different rewards for different achievements. Our economic system supports entrepreneurs, so those with the best or most popular ideas make the greatest gains. Sometimes practices of inequality are a result of the freedoms democracy provides. Citizens can vote and try to influence the votes of other citizens, but groups (corporations, unions, and other organizations) can combine to finance massive political or influence campaigns. These are unequal groups in size and economic clout, but we believe in the right to organize, express political opinions, and donate to causes we support.

Affirmative action programs, with their inflexible and destructive quota systems and their removal of merit considerations, have engendered strong criticism from all parts of the political spectrum. They are defended now mainly by a hard core of disciples. Similarly, the excessive and expensive busing imposed by court edicts shifted children from one school to another, but did not eliminate voluntary racial segregation in communities. If anything, busing exacerbated white flight to suburbs and private schools and caused a loss of faith in the public schools. Busing and forced integration in schools have certainly not altered basic racial prejudices or biases. Similarly, the main purposes of affirmative action and desegregation, to assure equal opportunity under the Constitution, have been subverted by legislative zealotry and bureaucratic manipulation. Reasonable people from all sides decry prejudice, bias, hate crimes, and discrimination based on stereotypes—but they do not want government to mandate actions on matters that should be left to individual choice. That is a difficult line to draw, but it is important to do so in a democracy.

## Legislation, Courts, and Problems
## Caused by Full Inclusion

Full inclusion of children with disabilities into regular classes runs some of the same risks of arousing overzealous legislation and activist court interpretation. Legislated mainstreaming has created significant problems—for schools, for teachers, for both disabled and nondisabled children, and for communities. Court interpretations of the laws threaten to leave mainstreaming in another social engineering predicament akin to those associated with affirmative action and busing. Extending mainstreaming to full inclusion promises to cause even more complicated problems and more bureaucratic and bungling answers. A recent court case, *Oberti v. Board of Education of Clementon (NJ) School District* (1993), illustrates a number of problems associated with the practice of mainstreaming, the laws governing it, and court interpretations:

The case involves an 8-year-old child with Downs syndrome that impaired his intellectual functioning and ability to communicate. The school district, after testing and review by specialists, determined that the child's educational interests would be best served by placing him in a developmental kindergarten class in the morning to observe and socialize with peer children, but that his academic work would be done in a separate special class in the afternoon. During the morning class, the child exhibited serious behavioral problems, including repeated toilet accidents, temper tantrums, crawling and hiding under furniture, and hitting and spitting on other children in the class. Also, the child repeatedly hit the teacher and the teacher's aide.

Obviously, he was disruptive in the class and the frustrated teacher sought help from the district Child Study Team. The Individual Education Plan required under the IDEA law and used for the original placement did not cover ways to handle his behavioral problems. Interestingly, the child did not exhibit disruptive behavior in the separate afternoon special education class. After study, the district wanted to place the child in a completely separate program, but the parents refused. After a hearing, there was an agreement that the child would be placed in a separate program for one year. In that year, his behavior improved and he made academic progress. When the parents found, however, that the district did not plan to place him back into "regular" classes the following year, they objected and another hearing occurred before an administrative law judge. The judge agreed with the district that the separate special education class was the "least restrictive environment" under the IDEA law, that the child's misbehavior in the developmental kindergarten class was extensive, and that there was no meaningful educational benefit from that class. Unsatisfied, the parents then went to court, getting an expert witness professor from Wisconsin who claimed that the child could be in regular classes, provided there were supplementary aids and special support, such as:

1. Modify the existing regular curriculum for this student;
2. Modify this child's program to provide for meeting a different set of criteria for performance;
3. Use "parallel" instruction—the child would be in the classroom, but would have separate activities;
4. Remove the child for instruction in certain special areas.

The district's expert witness, a professor from a nearby college, claimed that the child could not benefit from placement in a regular class, his behavior could not be managed, the teacher could not communicate with him because of his communication problems, and that the curriculum could not be modified enough to meet this child's needs without compromising its integrity. Other witnesses, including people who had worked with the child in other public school and Catholic school settings, testified that he had very disruptive behavior, including hitting, throwing things, and running away.

This judge, citing the IDEA law, held that the district had the burden of proof and that they had failed to meet the law's requirement for mainstreaming. (*Oberti v. Board of Education*, 1993)

This case suggests a series of problems for schools, parents, communities, and children under the idea of mainstreaming. The court directed that a disruptive and misbehaving child is to attend regular classes, where his actions are likely to be detrimental to the academic work of the other students and to the ongoing work of the teacher. The disabled child's schoolwork, apparently satisfactory in separate special education classes, suffered significantly in the regular placement, even on a part-time basis; yet under the court's order, he would now be in regular classes full time. Presumably, the child's misbehavior related to the situation in the first regular class assignment, where he may have gotten less teacher attention and more ridicule or ostracism from the other children. Is it going to help the child now to attend regular classes full time? The child's parents may feel better that their child is in regular classes, but how will the child progress? The parents of the nondisabled children do not have the same right to refuse placement, to require formal hearings on details they don't like, or to protest in court when their children are subjected to a significantly modified curriculum or class disruption. School rules established for all children to provide order and safety are placed in jeopardy by a court order that makes the school ultrasensitive to the parents of a single student. How much is too much disruption or violence?

A number of classroom issues are raised by the suggestion of the expert witness from Wisconsin to mainstream with supplementary activities and support. Teachers work hard on a school curriculum and finding ways to teach it; how are they to modify that curriculum adequately for one severely disabled student without compromising the integrity of the curriculum as a whole? It may be educationally sound to educate each child individually in his or her own class, but how can a teacher do so for 25 children all day—or over 100 students changing hourly in a secondary school? Is it equal and fair treatment if the teacher gives very special treatment to one disabled child, designing different activities and individual levels of performance, but does not do so for each of the other children? If the special needs child has "parallel" instruction provided in class and is removed from the class for certain special instruction, how does that differ in substance from a separate special education program? Although the child is in a regular class, he is to be separated for much of his work, and he may even become more of a target for other children because of his differential treatment.

## Conclusion

Assuming that the goal of inclusive school policies is to attempt to bring disabled children into the mainstream of American life, it is not reasonable to obstinately oppose the basic idea of inclusion. The ideal, however, is far removed from the reality of life. Not only is the idea of inclusion unrealistic, given the obvious diversity among people and resources in the world, it is also just a bad idea at this time. It is a bad idea because it is harmful to the children who are now well-served in separate special programs, because it hides an ideology of social engineering, because it debases individual initiative and freedom, and because it magnifies and enhances the value of conformity. This is not the ideal of equality of opportunity.

Excessive mainstreaming caught schools unprepared, frustrated good teachers, diminished special services provided to individual children, and created confusion in the schools. Well-prepared schools, specially trained teachers, clear guidelines for diagnosis and education, smaller classes, special materials to enhance learning, and a setting conducive to the best education now exist in many places: special education and gifted and talented programs offer these advantages. Full inclusion would overturn these in favor of a mandate for standardization and chaos beyond what occurred in the excessive mainstreaming programs.

Schools vary significantly across the United States, within each state, and in the world. It is impossible to define a "regular" school or classroom. Is a one-room school in rural Nevada "regular?" What about an urban school in Manhattan, or a suburban school in Beverly Hills? There are some common patterns in schools, but much current schooling occurs with separate groups of students. The Bronx High School of Science, vocational-technical high schools, tracking programs, honors programs, remedial courses, basic and advanced courses, reading groups, and selection for music and athletic programs illustrate the common practice of educating certain students separately for particular reasons. Full inclusion threatens these efforts to provide the best individual education for different students.

## For Discussion

1. Identify the best arguments for and against full inclusion. Analyze the evidence presented for each of them. What kinds of research would be needed to provide that evidence? What research is currently available on these matters?

2. Current U.S. Department of Education data show that the annual rate of growth in the number of children ages 3 to 21 who receive special education (over 3 percent) continues to exceed the annual rate of growth in the general population between ages 3 and 21 (about 1 percent). The proportion of children evaluated as gifted and talented is about 3 percent of the student population. What reasons would explain an increase in the proportion of children needing special education? What difference should this increase mean for school decisions on full inclusion? How should gifted and talented programs be treated?

3. How should the movement toward mainstreaming and full inclusion influence teacher education programs?

4. Table 17.1 shows five-year trends in the number of children classified under federal categories to define disabled children under IDEA law.
   a. What does the table suggest about the definitions of disability?
   b. What would account for large changes in the numbers of classified children in different categories?
   c. What changes do you think schools would need to make to provide for full inclusion of these children?

### TABLE 17.1 Five-Year Trends in Disability Classification Under IDEA

|  | 1990–1991 | 1994–1995 | Percent Change |
|---|---|---|---|
| Speech/Language Disabilities | 987,000 | 1,024,000 | 3.6 |
| Specific Learning Disabilities | 2,144,000 | 2,514,000 | 17.3 |
| Mental Retardation | 551,000 | 570,000 | 3.5 |
| Seriously Emotional Disturbances | 391,000 | 428,000 | 9.6 |
| Multiple Disabilities | 97,000 | 90,000 | −8.2 |
| Hearing Impairment | 59,000 | 65,000 | 10.7 |
| Orthopedic Impairment | 49,000 | 61,000 | 22.8 |
| Other Health Impairment | 56,000 | 106,000 | 89. |
| Visual Impairment | 24,000 | 25,000 | .5 |
| Autism | * | 23,000 | * |
| Deaf and Blind | 1,500 | 1,300 | −12.7 |
| Traumatic Brain Injury | * | 7,200 | * |
| All Disabilities Total |  |  | 12.7 |

*Data not available, categories added 1991–1992; autism cases in 1991–1992 were 5,000; Traumatic Brain Injury cases in 1991–1992 were 2,500. (*Source:* U.S. Department of Education, Office of Special Education Program; numbers rounded.)

## References

ALLAIN, V. A., AND PETTUS, A. (1998). *Teaching Diverse Students: Preparing with Cases.* Bloomington, IN: Phi Delta Kappan Educational Foundation.

ANDERSON, G. R., AND ANDERSON, S. K. (1983). "The Exceptional Native American." In *The Politics of Special Education* (1988), edited by L. Barton. London: Falmer Press.

BARTON, L. (1988). *The Politics of Special Education Needs.* London: Falmer Press.

BRANTLINGER, E. A., AND GUSKIN, S. L. (1987). "Ethnocultural and Social Psychological Effects on Learning Characteristics of Handicapped Children." In *Handbook of Special Education,* edited by M. C. Wang, et al., vol 1. Oxford: Pergamon.

*Brown v. Board of Education of Topeka, Kansas.* (1954). 347 U.S. 483.

CARLBERG, C. AND KAVALE, K. (1980). "The Efficacy of Special Versus Regular Class Placement for Exceptional Children: A Meta-Analysis." *Journal of Special Education* 14, 295–309.

CARLSON, E., AND PARSHALL, L. (1996). "Academic, Social, and Behavioral Adjustment for Students Declassified from Special Education." *Exceptional Education* 63(1): 89–100.

CLARK, B. (1996). "The Need for a Range of Program Options for Gifted and Talented Students." In *Controversial Issues Confronting Special Education,* edited by W. and S. Stainback. 2nd ed. Boston: Allyn and Bacon.

CUSHNER, K., MCCLELLAND, A., AND SAFFORD, P. (2000). *Human Diversity in Education.* 3rd ed. New York: McGraw-Hill.

DAY, J., AND BORKOWSKI, J., EDITORS. (1987) *Intelligence and Exceptionality.* Norwood, NJ: Ablex Publishers.

DICKMAN, I. (1985). *One Miracle at a Time.* New York: Simon & Schuster.

*Education Week on the Web.* (1998). "Inclusion." Washington, DC: Editorial Projects in Education. www.edweek.org.

EDUCATIONAL TESTING SERVICE. (1980). "New Vistas in Special Education." *Focus* 8, 1–20.

GLIEDMAN, J., AND ROTH, W. (1980). *The Unexpected Minority: Handicapped Children in America.* New York: Harcourt, Brace Jovanovich.

GOLAN, L. (1995). *Reading Between the Lips: A Totally Deaf Man Makes It in the Mainstream.* Chicago: Bonus Books.

HELLER, H. W. (1996). "A Rationale for Departmentalization of Special Education." In *Controversial Issues Confronting Special Education,* edited by W. and S. Stainback. 2nd ed. Boston: Allyn and Bacon.

HELLER, K. A., HOLTZMAN, W. H., AND MESSICK, S., EDITORS. (1982). *Placing Children in Special Education: A Strategy for Equity.* Washington, DC: National Academy of Sciences Press.

HOFFA, H., AND MORGAN, G. (1990). *Yes You Can: A Helpbook for the Physically Disabled.* New York: Pharos Books.

HUXLEY, T. (1897). *Evolution and Ethics, and Other Essays.* New York: D. Appleton.

KAUFFMAN, J., AND HALLAHAN, D., EDITORS. (1995). *The Illusion of Full Inclusion.* Austin, TX: Pro-Ed.

KAVALE, K. A., AND FORNESS, S. R. (1995). *The Nature of Learning Disabilities.* Mahwah, NJ: Lawrence Erlbaum.

KIRK, S., AND GALLAGHER, J. (1986). *Educating Exceptional Children.* Boston: Houghton Mifflin.

KLEINFIELD, S. (1979). *The Hidden Minority: America's Handicapped.* Boston: Little, Brown.

KOZOL, J. (1991). *Savage Inequalities.* New York: Crown Publishers.

LIPSKY, D. K., AND GARTNER, A. (1996). "Inclusion, School Restructuring, and the Remaking of American Society." *Harvard Education Review* 66(4), 762–796.

LOMBARDI, T. P. (1994). *Responsible Inclusion of Students with Disabilities.* Fastback 373. Bloomington, IN: Phi Delta Kappa Educational Foundation.

LOMBARDI, T. P., AND LUDLOW, B. L. (1996). *Trends Shaping the Future of Special Education.* Bloomington, IN: Phi Delta Kappa Educational Foundation.

MEISEL, C. J., EDITOR. (1986). *Mainstreaming Handicapped Children.* Hillsdale, NJ: Lawrence Erlbaum.

*Mills v. Board of Education of the District of Columbia.* (1972). 348 F. Supp.866.

MITTLER, P., BROUILLETTE, R., AND HARRIS D., EDITORS. (1993). *Special Needs Education.* World Yearbook of Education. London: Kogan Page.

MURRAY-SEEGERT, C. (1989). *Nasty Girls, Thugs, and Humans Like Us: Social Relations Between Severely Disabled and Nondisabled Students in High School.* Baltimore: Paul H. Brookes.

*NEA Today.* (1999). "Inclusion Confusion." 17(8), 4. May 1.

OAKES, J. (1985). *Keeping Track: How Schools Structure Inequality.* New Haven, CT: Yale University Press.

*Oberti v. Board of Education of the Borough of Clementon, NJ, School District.* (1993). 995 f.2d 1204 (3rd Cir. 1993).

PALONSKY, S. (1975). "Hempies and Squeaks, Truckers and Cruisers: A Participant-Observer Investigation in a City High School." *Educational Administration Quarterly* 2:86–103.

PETCH-HOGAN, B., AND HAGGARD, D. (1999). "The Inclusion Debate Continues." *Educational Forum* 35(3), 128–40.

ROGERS, J. (1993). "The Inclusion Revolution." *Phi Delta Kappa Research Bulletin* no. 11, 1–6.

SAILOR, W., GERRY. M., AND WILSON, W. C. (1991). "Policy Implications of Emergent Full Inclusion Models." In *Handbook of Special Education: Research and Practice,* vol 4. edited by M. C. Wang, et al. Oxford: Pergamon.

SEMMEL, M. I., GOTTLIEB, J., AND ROBINSON, N. M. (1979). "Mainstreaming." *Review of Research in Education 7*, 223–279.

SPRING, J. (1998). *American Education.* 8th ed. New York: McGraw-Hill.

STAINBACK, W., AND STAINBACK S. (1990). *Support Networks for Inclusive Schooling.* Baltimore: Paul H. Brookes.

———— (1992). *Controversial Issues Confronting Special Education.* Needham Heights, MA: Allyn and Bacon.

STAINBACK, S., STAINBACK, W., AND JACKSON, H. J. (1992) "Toward Inclusive Classrooms." In *Curriculum Considerations in Inclusive Classrooms,* edited by S. and W. Stainback. Baltimore: Paul H. Brookes.

*Teaching Exceptional Children.* (1998). "Changes in IDEA Support." 30(6), 50+.

THOUSAND, J. S., AND VILLA, R. A. (1995). "Managing Complex Change Toward Inclusive Schooling." In *Creating an Inclusive School,* edited by R. A. Villa and J. S. Thousand. Alexandria, VA: Association for Supervision and Curriculum Development.

TURNBULL, H. R., AND TURNBULL, A. P. (1998). *Free Appropriate Public Education: The Law and Children with Disabilities.* 5th ed. Denver: Love Publishing.

UNITED NATIONS CONVENTION ON THE RIGHTS OF THE CHILD. (1989). New York: United Nations.

URBAN, W., AND WAGGONER, J. (1996). *American Education: A History.* New York: McGraw-Hill.

VARGAS, S. R. L. (1999). "Democracy and Inclusion." *Maryland Law Review* 58(1), 150–79.

VILLA, R. A., THOUSAND, J. S., AND CHAPPLE, J. W. (1996). "Preparing Teachers to Support Inclusion." *Theory Into Practice* 35(1), Winter.

VENN, J. (1994). *Assessment of Students with Special Needs.* New York: Macmillan.

WANG, M. C. (1990). "Learning Characteristics of Students with Special Needs." In *Special Education: Research and Practice,* edited by M. C. Wang et al. Oxford: Pergamon.

WANG, M. C., REYNOLDS, M. C., AND WALBERG, H., EDITORS. (1991). *Handbook of Special Education: Research and Practice.* Oxford: Pergamon.

————, EDITORS. (1990). *Special Education: Research and Practice.* Oxford, Pergamon.

WEDELL, K. (1993). "Varieties of School Integration." In *Special Needs Education,* edited by P. Mittler et al. World Yearbook of Education. London: Kogan Page.

WESTMAN, J. C. (1990). *Handbook of Learning Disabilities.* Needham Heights, MA: Allyn and Bacon.

WILLIAMS, P. (1991). *The Special Education Handbook.* Milton Keynes England: Open University Press.

WINZER, M. A. (1993). *The History of Special Education: From Isolation to Integration.* Washington, DC: Gallaudet University Press.

YSSELDYKE, J. E., AND ALGOZZINE, B. (1990). *Introduction to Special Education.* 2nd ed. Boston: Houghton Mifflin.

ZIGLER, E., AND HALL, N. (1986). "Mainstreaming and the Philosophy of Normalization." In *Mainstreaming Handicapped Children,* edited by C. J. Meisel. Hillsdale, NJ: Lawrence Erlbaum.

# CHAPTER 18

# *School Violence: School or Social Responsibility*

## *POSITION 1: SCHOOLS CAN CURB VIOLENCE AND EDUCATE*

I believe that school is primarily a social institution. Education being a social process, the school is simply that form of community life in which all of those agencies are concentrated that will be most effective in bringing the child to share in the inherited resources of the race, and to use his own powers for social ends . . . I believe that education, therefore, is a process of living and not a preparation for future living. (Dewey, 1897, "My Pedagogic Creed," reprinted in Dworkin, 1959, p. 22)

We didn't call ourselves gangs. We called ourselves clubs or *clicas.* In the back lot of the local elementary school, about a year after Tino's death, five of us gathered in the grass and created a club—"The Impersonations" . . . It was something to belong to—something that was ours. We weren't in the Boy Scouts, in sports teams, or camping groups. The Impersonations is how we wove something out of the threads of nothing. (Rodriguez, 1993, p. 41)

John Dewey helped define the contemporary relationship between Americans and their public schools. Schools are extensions of the community in this country, he argued. When social problems overwhelm the community's resources, schools are expected to lend their strength and assistance. Schools share in the burden of caring for the community's children and for equipping them with the skills and habits necessary to survive and succeed. Schools take the highest ideals of the community and translate them into academic and social problems for all children. As Dewey wrote, "What the best and wisest parent wants for his own child, that must the community want for all its children" (Dworkin, 1959, p. 54).

Dewey recognized that social conditions constantly change and that schools always have to adjust to new demands placed on communities. In a speech delivered in 1899, he said, "It is useless to bemoan the departure of the good old days of children's modesty, reverence, and implicit obedience, if we expect merely by bemoaning and by exhortation to bring them back. It is radical conditions which have changed, and only an equally radical change in education suffices" (Dworkin, 1959, p. 37).

In the late nineteenth century, the industrial revolution had upset the traditional structure of the community and the nature of work. As a result, families had changed, and they were not able to carry out the full range of their former functions. Schools were pressed into service to expand their role, to go beyond providing instruction in reading and arithmetic and help children adjust to the "radical conditions" of the day. Helping children adjust to the problems of a new industrial economy imposed a great burden on public education. Helping children understand and overcome the radical conditions of the twenty-first century may require even greater effort, but it is not a problem schools can shirk. The community's problems are always the school's problems.

## The Violent Community

Violence is among the most "radical conditions" now confronting the nation and its school-age children. Violence increasingly affects the daily lives of children, and violence-prevention and aggression-management programs have become part of the curriculum in schools. As one teacher notes:

> Five years ago, I noticed the topics at teachers' convention had begun shifting from curriculum matters to coping skills. Workshop sessions had cute names and suggested strategies for redirecting aggression, signing good-behavior contracts, and letting the group decide the consequences of inappropriate behavior. As the years passed, session names became a little more serious and so did the topics—"coping skills" became "survival skills." Now, sessions like "Legal Rights of Teachers," "Sex Harassment in the Schools," "Dealing with Violent Students," and "Gang Signs and Symbols" get more attention than ever before. (Mahaffey, 1994, p. 82)

American society is violent. It has been violent for a long time, and violence currently presents unprecedented dangers to school-age children. Films, music videos, and television in the United States are the most violent in the world (Derksen and Strasburger, 1996). Messages about aggressive behavior enter the world of children no matter how hard families may try to screen them out. These messages flow not only from children's direct experiences, but also from news reports, film, music, and advertising. War toys line the shelves of stores; cartoon heroes destroy cartoon villains on television and in films; music videos hint darkly at anger and destruction; and computer games allow interactive simulations of murder and mayhem.

Television brings a steady volume of vicarious violence into living rooms. Over 97 percent of U.S. households have at least one television set, and it is estimated that young children watch an average of four hours of television a day. Each year, they are likely to watch passively, and typically without adults present, acts of violence at unprecedented levels. The typical child in the United

States will see an estimated 8,000 murders and 100,000 acts of televised violence before the end of elementary school (*TV Violence*, 1993) and another 100,000 hours before the end of high school. Does this make children more violent? Does viewing televised violence desensitize them to real-world violence or encourage a distorted view of the world? It's hard to know with certainty how viewing violence affects children, but some authorities believe we are raising a generation of children unlike any other. The media expose them to more aggressive acts than children saw in the past, and "they are taken away from other things they could be doing, should be doing, and have been doing for generations before the advent of television—like playing, interacting with other children, and participating in family and community life" (Carlsson-Paige and Levin, 1990, p. 10). While the schools alone cannot overcome the problem of violence, they are central in the struggle to protect children and to teach them that physical aggression is not the preferred solution to problems.

Violence inevitably flows from the community into the children's daily lives (Dill and Haberman, 1995; Levine, 1996; Moore and Anderson, 1995). Many children suffer nightmares stemming from the violence in their lives. Increasing numbers of students report that they do not feel safe in their schools (Harris, 1994). Ronald Stephens, executive director for the National Schools Safety Center, testifying before a Congressional subcommittee, remarked, "Literally, our children are dying to come to school . . . A lot of former fistfights are being replaced by gunfights; the former fire drills are being replaced by crisis drills, and even by the new drive-by shooting drills" (*Recess from Violence*, 1993, p. 37). Although violence is more prevalent in urban areas and among the poor and minorities, no one in any neighborhood is immune, as the April 1999 shootings of twelve students and a teacher in a suburban Littleton, Colorado, high school demonstrated. School violence affects young women as well as young men and children as young as ten (Goldstein, Harootunian, and Conoley, 1994). "No matter where you are, parents want their students to be safe and secure . . . that might even precede a quality education . . . Anyone who thinks they are not vulnerable is really naive" (Michael Durso, principal of Springbrook High School in Washington, D.C., quoted in U.S. Department of Health, Education, and Welfare, 1997).

While the overall rate for violent crimes has been declining, the rate among school-age children is on the rise. Adolescents experience the highest victimization rate in crimes involving a handgun; the victimization rate for persons 16 to 19 years of age was seventeen times the rate for those 65 and older (U.S. Department of Justice, 1994, p. 5). Crime and victimization rates are highest among urban minorities. Statistics indicate that "the lifetime risk of being murdered is about 32 per 1,000 for black males and 18 per 1,000 for native Americans. By contrast, it is 6 per 1,000 for white males and 3 per 1,000 for white females" (Roth, 1994, p. 2). Teachers, especially those in schools serving predominantly low-income and minority children, report steady increases in violence. Overall, it appears that more children are exposed to higher levels of violence in their lives than ever before, and more children are demonstrating more aggressive behaviors in school than earlier generations of children. Reports of increasing childhood aggression are especially troublesome considering the research that links a child's inability to manage aggression with violent behavior in adulthood (Caspi et al., 1994; Goldstein, Harootunian, and Conoley, 1994; Reiss and Roth, 1993).

## Schools and Violence

More than half of all public schools in America report one or more incidents of serious crime or violence during a school year, and the problem is worse for middle schools and high schools than for elementary schools. In the 1996–1997 academic year, for example, 74 percent of middle schools and 77 percent of high schools reported one or more violent incidents, compared to 45 percent of elementary schools (U.S. Department of Health, Education, and Welfare, 1997).

The bad news is easy to report. The statistics are alarming: violence is increasing; too many children feel unsafe in schools; many schools have to invest in metal detectors and guards instead of books and field trips. The good news is harder to quantify, but it should be reassuring: School programs can make a difference in preventing childhood aggressive behavior and future adult violence (Bodine and Crawford, 1998; *Recess from Violence*, 1993; Reiss and Roth, 1993).

Violent behavior is one of the most frequently studied social phenomena of our day. The social and behavioral sciences have learned a lot about violence, and we have every reason to assume that schools can successfully stem the tide of violent behavior and protect children and society from the violent among us. Research indicates that certain factors predispose children toward violent behavior. Children who are at-risk for violence typically "bring to school a pattern of behavior that makes it difficult for them to establish trust, autonomy, and social competence" (Wallach, 1993, p. 4). The factors most often found in this pattern include: (1) excessive viewing of violence on television; (2) repeated examples of bullying behavior; (3) evidence of poor parenting, such as abuse, neglect, or lack of parental nurturing; (4) history of harsh or erratic discipline at home; and (5) inability to develop friendships in school (Reiss and Roth, 1993, pp. 7–8). These are, of course, only statistical correlates of violent behavior. Not all rough and uncontrolled kindergartners become violent middle school students. However, children who exhibit several of these factors are at-risk for committing later violence.

Schools have been developing a wide range of programs to prevent or manage the problem of violent behavior. Some programs focus on the physical aspects of the school, such as installing better lighting and metal detectors. Other programs integrate control of aggression into the curriculum (Bodine and Crawford, 1998; Goldstein, Harootunian, and Conoley, 1993).

In addition to establishing school-based programs, policymakers are now debating the role that schools should play in contending with violence in the larger community. For example, it is well known that children of abusive parents often use excessive physical punishment in disciplining their own children. One policy under consideration would require the parents of aggressive, potentially disruptive children to attend school-sponsored parenting classes. Another outreach proposal would encourage pregnant women who grew up in physically abusive homes to take school-run parenting classes (Reiss and Roth, 1993).

The best violence prevention programs use the academic power of the schools to support the community. The problem is complex, and there are no simple solutions. To solve the problem of school violence, children must learn how to understand and control their anger and practice using nonviolent problem-solving techniques. Schools can help students manage their aggression by teaching alternatives to violence through violence-prevention curricula.[1]

## Violence-Prevention Curricula

Consider a few violence-prevention strategies suggested by national organizations. We present them as illustrative examples rather than prescriptive remedies. Many schools are now using schoolwide conflict resolution approaches, teaching children to handle their own disputes and to assume responsibility for helping other children find peaceful resolutions to their disagreements. These programs are disarmingly simple and effective. First, children are taught that conflicts are inevitable, and that in most disputes, both sides are apt to believe that they and they alone are in the right. Conflict resolutions approaches, such as those the National Education Association recommends, encourage students to listen to each other and take responsibility for ensuring that they resolve conflicts by conversation and negotiation rather than by physical means.

In a conflict resolution program, when a playground dispute occurs, an older child, trained by the teachers, asks both parties to tell their sides of the story. Certain ground rules are decided beforehand: no yelling, no cursing, no interrupting, no put downs of the other person. The older student, acting as a conflict manager, seeks to guide the disputants to solve their own problems. If they cannot, the conflict manager tries to help. A teacher or administrator is always available. The goal is to provide a caring community in which all children feel safe, where they can resolve their problems, and where everyone is responsible for others' well-being. Caring communities teach children to handle problems without resorting to violence (Bodine and Crawford, 1998; Brendtro and Long, 1995). By practicing mediation techniques, participants also learn to be good communicators and thoughtful problem solvers. One student trained as a mediator said that the program "informed me on how to be a better listener and taught me how to help other people solve their problems." Another participant said, "I got a chance to understand people and the ethics of helping people solve problems" (Morse and Andrea, 1994, p. 82).

Secondary school students are encouraged to use role-playing strategies to examine critical incidents in their lives. The goal is to have students see how simple, commonplace events can escalate into violence. In the following example, written by eighth-grade students, one young woman taunts another:

---

[1]Schools are now experimenting with hundreds of new curricular interventions designed to reduce violence. You may want to examine some examples in your community or check national sources. Information from the National Schools Safety Center is available on the Internet at http://www.nsscl.org. NSSC is a nonprofit organization, established by presidential directive in 1984, and is charged with promoting violence-free and crime-free schools. NSSC serves as a clearinghouse for current information on school safety and violence-prevention planning.

"I heard that she was at the movies with your boyfriend last night. All over him."

"I wouldn't take it," adds another girl.

"She doesn't need your boyfriend. What was she doing with him anyhow?"

The young women simulate pushing and shoving. They break off from the simulation with self-conscious laughter, recognizing, perhaps, that in real life the angry words they scripted all too often escalate into real acts of violence. The classroom teacher applauds the students' effort, and the class examines what has taken place. A rumor was spread; it led to an exchange of words; verbal accusations threatened to become physical. In real life, it could easily have resulted in injury. How could this have been avoided? The teacher asks. What did others do to make the situation worse? What could they have done to help? (*Violence in the Schools*, 1993).

For too many children, violence is a way of life. School programs can help students find alternatives to violence. According to Rodney Hammond, an authority on school violence, "The most effective violence-prevention interventions tend to be very structured programs that focus on teaching the behaviors that tend to prevent the development of violent coping strategies and that work intensively with youth over a sustained period of time." He adds, "Slogan campaigns and scare tactics simply do not work" (*Recess from Violence*, 1993, p. 41).

Violence-prevention curricula are new and their successes have not been carefully evaluated or scientifically assessed. However, the evidence collected thus far supports the effectiveness of conflict resolution programs and other violence-prevention interventions in teaching students to manage conflicts through nonviolent means (Bodine and Crawford, 1998). Even more convincing is the observable difference these curricula bring to schools. As one school administrator notes, "It makes a difference in my school, and I have a reduction of 10 percent in some problems. These materials are OK by me, and I don't need researchers to say it works" (Lawton, 1994, p. 10).

Every school should adopt an appropriate set of strategies for preventing and managing violence in the lives of students. Nonviolence can be an important curriculum strand running through the social studies, language arts, and other subject areas. School programs for reducing overly aggressive behavior show great promise, but for many children they may not be sufficient. Teaching students mediation skills, for example, is not likely to erase completely the violent patterns already established in the lives of many children. These young people need greater, more intensive support than teachers alone can provide. Violence is a learned response, and because it is learned, it can be unlearned (Noguera, 1995; Sautter, 1995). Schools, working with social service agencies and psychologists, can replace antisocial behaviors with prosocial behaviors and provide positive role models for children.

The absence of appropriate parental supervision is a strong predictor of trouble with school discipline. Once thought of as a problem confined to the poor, lack of supervision and the absence of positive role models are now recognized as much broader problems. Students from all social classes need sources of support other than the family. Colleges and universities help by matching volunteer mentors with at-risk students. The mentors act as role models, older brothers or sisters, and surrogate parents. They help with homework and teach study skills. They are models of problem solvers who do not resort to violence and examples of success who have not succumbed to the temptations of crime. Above all, they offer at-risk children a caring, thoughtful person in their lives. Their presence cannot be underestimated. Children at-risk for violence have had too few positive role models in their lives. Schools and teachers can help. Research indicates that "the involvement of just one caring adult can make all the difference in the life of an at-risk youth" (Sautter, 1995, p. K8). How much should schools give? How hard should teachers try? William Ayers suggests an interesting standard. He asks:

> Is it good enough for my child? That's the standard we might approach when we think of justice for kids. The question cannot be about some abstract child, every child, the mob of children. That turns other people's children into things—objectifies them—and makes throwing them onto the garbage heap not merely possible, but quite likely. To ask, is it good enough for my child?—not, is it a perfect arrangement for my child?—is to begin to set limits of acceptability. (Ayers, 1997, p. 188)

Schools cannot curb violence by themselves, but working with other agencies, they can reach out to potentially troubled young people in the community, provide support, and offer a real promise of a less turbulent future. Schools can also reach out to new mothers in the community, especially pregnant teenagers and others who are at risk of providing poor role models, and teach them the skills they need to pass on to their children. Schools can join with social welfare agencies to help families learn to resolve social conflicts without violence. The process is likely to be slow and expensive, but if it does not begin in the schools, the future social and personal costs are likely to be tremendous. These children and their problems will not go away or get better by themselves. To paraphrase John Dewey, what the best and wisest parents in the community want for their children should be made available to all children through the power of the schools. Schooling is about living today, not preparation for living in the future. Schools must teach students how to deal with the problems they confront in their daily lives and help them find nonviolent ways to resolve these conflicts. For schools to do less is to betray the social responsibility the schools have to improve community life.

## POSITION 2: SCHOOLS MUST ELIMINATE VIOLENCE IN ORDER TO EDUCATE

Federal agencies are now making millions of dollars available for "conflict resolution" classes, for creating "safe haven" rooms in schools, and for "peer mediation" programs. Getting a federal grant has become simple: just start your own conflict resolution program . . . Statistics can be trotted out to "prove" that these violence-prevention classes and other cognitive approaches have culminated in a decrease in fighting and physical violence . . . Older students, said to be peer mediators, "trained in conflict resolution" by conflict resolution teachers, ask younger bellicose students if they can agree not to bother one another, not to call one another's mother obscene names, not to insult one another. If they "feel comfortable" with such an agreement, they shake hands, congratulations are extended all around—and the fight resumes the next time they look at one another. (Devine, 1996, pp. 161–166)

We assign a great many things to schools that they cannot do, and we do a weak job of enlisting others in their missions . . . When they are effective . . . schools can do a good job of imparting cognitive learning to children: history, chemistry, literature, and so on. But they are not powerful enough instruments that we should expect them to prevent adolescent pregnancy, to redistribute income, to stop drug abuse, to halt the spread of AIDS, and more . . . Spreading their efforts across too many fronts may also leave them effective on none. (Finn, 1993, p. 25)

U.S. schools began with modest academic goals: teach children to read and write. Over the years, schools enhanced their curricula to include academic instruction in content as well as skills. The argument in this section is simple, direct, and straightforward: Schools should teach academic content in the most compelling and academically legitimate ways possible. This is the job schools are entrusted with, and this is what teachers are trained to do. Without academic skills, students are at a disadvantage. They will not be able to compete for places in the best colleges. They will not be able to earn scholarships, and they will not be able to land good jobs and launch promising careers. Schooling is primarily about teaching and learning academic subject matter and the mastery of skills necessary for success in life. We will further argue that (1) violence in schools is an overstated problem; (2) violence-prevention curricula are of questionable value; and (3) schools should not do the job of welfare agencies, police, or social psychologists.

## Decline of Family Values

To argue that these are not normal times would be to belabor the obvious. The family is in disarray, and family values are all but lost to many Americans. Thirty percent of all children are born to single mothers. The problem is even greater in some minority populations. For example, in the African American community, 70 percent of all births are to mothers out of wedlock, and the number of unmarried African American women bearing children increased from 215,000 in 1970 to 415,000 in 1996 (Holmes, 1998). Too many youngsters have no one to teach them family values. Too many children show up at the doors of the nation's schools with only a vague sense of right and wrong, no self-discipline, and a limited ability to get along with other children. Increasing numbers of today's youth claim that the counterculture or gang life offers the sense of belonging, worth, and purpose they lack within their families.

Children do not show up for the first day of kindergarten as blank slates: Their early lives have etched upon them complex habits and predispositions. Some children are ready to begin school; their parents have invested tremendous amounts of time and energy in them. These children are self-controlled. They demonstrate mastery over their emotions, an enthusiasm for learning, and respect for the authority of the teacher. Others are not ready for school. Victims of poor parenting or no parenting at all, they come to school with insufficient preparation for the academic side of school and inadequate control over their own behavior. Teachers spot them quickly. They are overly impulsive, physically aggressive, and uncooperative. They are not likely to do well in school, and they threaten the education and well-being of other children. Psychologists predict that "undercontrolled" 3-year-old children will tend to lean toward delinquency when they enter adolescence (Caspi et al., 1994, p. 188).

We are not trying to alarm you. Only a small fraction of students exhibit aggressive behaviors or other traits that predict adult violence. In fact, we think that school violence is an overstated problem. Potentially violent students represent only 1 percent of the children who enter school, and the rate of violence in school has not changed significantly in twenty years. In 1998, the Website of the National Center for Education Statistics (http://www.nces.ed.gov) listed a study conducted by the University of Michigan's Survey Research Center. This study indicates that school-crime victimization rates between 1976 and 1996 saw little change, except for a slight increase in the number of students reporting threats of violence. Theft of property was the most commonly reported crime during this period, followed by deliberate damage to property.

Despite widespread publicity depicting schools as dangerous places, rife with crime and violence, the conclusion drawn from school reports of violence suggests that widespread school violence may be more of a media creation than a serious school problem. After reviewing the research literature on school crime, Lawrence (1998) argues that "It is difficult to conclude that schools are violent places, when data indicate that on average 99 percent of students are free from attack in a month's time." (p. 29)

For the moment, at least, it is fair to argue that schools are no more dangerous than they have been in the past two decades, and that teaching is among the nation's safest professions. In 1998, the Bureau of Justice released a study of violence in the workplace from 1992 through 1996. Police officers hold the nation's riskiest job; 306 of every 1,000 officers were attacked or threatened during the period of the study. The rate for junior high/middle school teachers was 57 per 1,000. Special education teachers were attacked or threatened with violence at a rate of 41 per 1,000, and elementary school teachers experienced these problems at a rate of 16 per 1,000 over the four-year period (Sniffen, 1998). The majority of students teachers identify as "problems" are described as such for reasons other than the potential to do physical harm to others or themselves.[2]

Schools are generally safe places, but problem students do exist. What responsibilities do schools have to teach the distracting handful of children who are not able to control their aggression? This is a difficult question. None of us wants to appear callous or indifferent to children, but schools are not social welfare agencies. Teachers are not social workers or psychiatrists. They are educators trained to teach children reading, math, social studies, and other important skills. It is not reasonable to expect schools and teachers to function as therapists. Violence-prevention curricula sound noble and high-minded, but they are a diversion from the schools' academic mission and are of doubtful benefit. In 1997, after reviewing 70 federally funded programs with a total of $2.4 billion in funds aimed at reducing school violence and substance abuse, the General Accounting Office concluded that these programs had not demonstrated their worth:

> Insufficient information exists on the programs' performance. Although we identified some promising approaches for preventing substance abuse and violence, our work suggests that additional research is needed to further test these approaches' effectiveness and their applicability to different populations in varied settings. (U.S. General Accounting Office, 1997, p. 85)

---

[2]Brophy and McCaslin list twelve types of "problem" elementary-school-age students examined in the research literature:

1. *Failure-syndrome-exhibiting:* These children believe they cannot do schoolwork. They often avoid work or give up easily, expecting to fail and saying "I can't do it."
2. *Perfectionistic:* These children are unusually anxious about making mistakes. They have unrealistically high self-images, and they are never satisfied with their performance. They often hold back from class participation unless they are very sure of themselves.
3. *Underachieving/Alienated:* These children do the minimum to get by. They do not value or enjoy school work.
4. *Low achieving:* These students have difficulty with schoolwork even when they are willing to try. Their problem is low potential or lack of readiness.
5. *Hostile-aggressive:* These students express hostility through direct, intense behaviors. They intimidate and threaten other students, are easily angered, and may hit and push other students or destroy property.
6. *Passive-aggressive:* These students indirectly express their opposition and resistance to the teacher. They disrupt classrooms surreptitiously and exhibit subtle noncompliance.
7. *Defiant:* These children want to have their own way. They may resist the teacher verbally, saying, "You can't make me," or "You can't tell me what to do." They resist nonverbally, as well, by posturing, frowning, and sometimes by being physically violent toward the teacher.
8. *Hyperactive:* These children squirm, wiggle, jiggle, and show excessive and almost constant movement. They are often out of their seats and bothering other children.
9. *Distractable:* These children have very short attention spans. They are unable to sustain attention and concentration.
10. *Immature:* These children have poorly developed self-control, social skills, and emotional stability.
11. *Peer-rejected:* These children are often forced to work and play alone, although they seek acceptance by other students.
12. *Shy/withdrawn:* These children avoid personal interaction with other classmates. They are quiet and do not call attention to themselves. (Brophy and McCaslin, 1992, pp. 62–63)

Today a small group of problem students is attracting a disproportionate share of curriculum attention and federal and state dollars. The education of the majority of cooperative students is being held ransom by an unruly minority.

## Who Are the Potentially Violent?

We know who is likely to commit crimes, the early experiences that lead to violent behavior, and the personal and family traits that tend to protect children from becoming violent adults. Unfortunately, research has not yet developed a strong knowledge base about the causes of violent behavior and the effectiveness of violence-prevention programs (Reiss and Roth, 1993). No one knows how to prevent potentially violent children from becoming violent adults. Schools now embracing one violence-management curriculum or another are doing so without adequate evidence of its effectiveness. In most cases, these programs are likely to be a waste of taxpayers' money. Many of the causes of violence are not within the schools' control (Weishew and Peng, 1993). Violent children become violent adults, and if children have not learned to control their aggression by the time they come to school, it may not be possible for them to disentangle the patterns of violence that took shape in their early years.

In a perfect world, all children would come to school free from violent tendencies. If it were in our power, we would have all children raised in loving, drug-free, nurturing homes. They would all bond with an adult who dispenses love freely and teaches them that they belong to someone and someone belongs to them. The children's earliest experiences would have shown them that disagreements are part of life, but discord can be settled through calm discussions rather than rancor or violence. We would like all children to have high IQs. We would like them all to have parents who are literate adults, free from alcohol and drug addiction, who study books about child rearing and read stories to their children. We would like all children to have limits on their television viewing. We would like all these things and more, but social policies cannot create them. Too many children are born to single mothers who are unprepared for the task or unable to give them what they need to be successful in life. Drug addiction, crime, and poverty are beyond the control of the schools. Short of taking children out of undesirable home situations and having substitute parents raise them, there is little schools can do but accept increasing numbers of unprepared and potentially disruptive students.

Although public schools must work with all students, they do not have to mix the disruptive and the potentially violent with other students; nor do they have to encourage violent students to stay in school until graduation. Students who arrive at school ready to learn should be introduced to a rigorous and sound academic education. It is the academic side of school that will matter to them in life. Children come to school to improve their academic skills and increase their store of intellectual capital—the knowledge needed to be successful in life. As Hirsch notes, "Sociologists have shown that intellectual capital (i.e., knowledge) operates in almost every sphere of modern society to determine social class, success or failure in school, and even psychological and physical health" (1996, p. 19). Students are disadvantaged by too small a share of intellectual capital, and they need to start early and move quickly in securing as much of it as they can. The vast majority of students do not need special curriculum treatments to teach them how to get along with others, settle disputes without violence, or manage aggression. They need academic content to succeed in life, and that's what schools should deliver.

Conflict-resolution curricula distract students from academic pursuits and send students an undesirable, if unintended, message: "We expect school to be violent, so let's talk about it" (Devine, 1996, p. 165). Violence is not a way of life for most children, and schools should treat it as something unacceptable. Directing conflict-management programs to all students, rather than at the violent minority, sends a negative message that violence is a normal part of life and everyone must learn to manage it or otherwise cope with it.

## Schools and Violence

Let's look at what we know about potentially violent children and what schools can reasonably do about them.

Overly aggressive children should be identified in kindergarten and trained to work on anger control. Although a school cannot replace the family, it can provide some of the supports found in the homes of self-controlled, high-achieving students. For example, school discipline policies should incorporate the reward-and-punishment systems successfully used by middle-class parents. Students should learn that appropriate behavior earns teacher praise and special privileges, while inappropriate behavior results in the loss of praise and privilege. Aggressive children who have been exposed to a great deal of violence on television could be made aware of the prosocial models the medium offers (for example, "Mr. Rogers"). This would be reasonable, inexpensive, and not too intrusive on the privacy rights of students or their parents.

No one believes that schools alone can solve problems of violence (Lawton, 1994). The influences of early family experiences are pervasive (Caspi et al., 1994). Unfortunately, schools may not be able to correct the courses children from chaotic family environments take. Research provides little encouragement that school interventions successfully prevent violence, and the research may simply be conforming public knowledge. A Gallup poll of the public's attitude toward the public schools asked respondents to rate the importance of various factors as causes of school violence. Listed in order of frequency, the public rated the following factors as "very important" (Elam, Rose, and Gallup, 1994, p. 44):

1. Increased use of drug and alcohol among school-age youth
2. Growth of youth gangs
3. Easy availability of weapons
4. Breakdown in the American family
5. Lack of school authority to discipline
6. Increased portrayal of violence in the media
7. Inability of school staff to resolve conflicts between students

Note that the first six responses are beyond the school's control. It is not until number five that schools are even mentioned. The public recognizes that society has visited many of its problems on the schools, including the vexing problem of school violence. However, the public is not convinced that solutions to the problem lie within the schools' power. Asked to rate various measures for their potential effectiveness in reducing violence, 88 percent of the respondents listed "stronger penalties for possession of weapons by students" first. At the bottom of the list, mentioned by 51 percent and 45 percent of respondents, respectively, were, "courses offered by the public schools in how to be a good parent," and "conflict education for students" (Elam, Rose, and Gallup, 1994, p. 44).

Of course, schools should try to help all students, but they should not impede the progress of the well-behaved. It is reasonable for schools to try every measure to help young children adapt to school and school discipline. But let's face it, some children will never adjust to the academic demands and the self-discipline required for academic success. According to U.S. Justice Department statistics, about 6 percent of adolescents are responsible for two-thirds of violent crimes committed by juveniles (Bodine and Crawford, 1998, p. 6). This tiny percentage of students should not be such a huge focus of school attention and such a constant drain on school budgets. If these students have not learned to control themselves by early adolescence, schools should waste no more time or money on them.

## Alternative Schools

Educators have long recognized that alternatives to public school are sometimes necessary to serve special populations of students—teenage mothers, for example, or the physically disabled. The one-size-fits-all model of the comprehensive public high school does not serve everyone equally well, and some students resent the conformity and order of traditional education. Many educators now recognize that the structure of traditional high schools may contribute to the problem of school violence. Students unaccustomed to the impersonal rules governing school behavior and the emphasis schools place on quiet compliance may lash out at teachers and other students (Epp and Watkinson, 1997; Lawrence, 1998).

Sometimes housed within the regular school building, and sometimes in separate facilities of their own, alternative schools are designed for students who, because of any number of problems—academic, behavioral, or social—are not able to learn well in a traditional environment. These schools have become widely accepted and popular among students. They offer specially designed curricula, more individual attention, and specialized vocational programs.

Alternative schools are likely to be less formal than traditional schools, and they typically offer a lower student-to-teacher ratio. The record indicates that these schools have gone a long way toward ameliorating the anonymity and isolation students experience in traditional schools. Many formerly disruptive students behave better when they work in a small, supportive setting. They are able to find a niche that eluded them in traditional schools (McPartland et al., 1997).

Alternative schools can be very effective, and they should be viewed as the first treatment for disruptive students who have not been helped by special curricular treatment in regular schools and classes. Unfortunately, although alternative schools try to accommodate students with a wide range of problems, they do not work for everyone. In fact, they may not work well for many of the most disruptive students (Lawrence, 1998). The same students that caused problems in traditional schools often continue to present problems when they transfer to alternative schools. For these students, more dramatic interventions are in order.

## *Shock Camps*

"I realized I was wrong . . . I thought I wasn't hurting nobody just because I was selling drugs. [I thought] if I don't sell it, somebody else is going to sell it. But I was wrong. I was hurting people's families . . . I realized it was bad." [Reynaldo] emersed himself in drug treatment sessions and came to terms with his own addiction; he studied and took the GED exam. Now, on the eve of his graduation from boot camp, he talks of going to college and finding a job. (Anderson, 1998, p. 121)

The primary mission of the Thunderbird Youth Academy is to effect the socialization of "at-risk youth" by elevating their academic level, improving their self-esteem, pride, and confidence levels and teaching them basic life skills essential to successfully competing in their work place and managing a healthy family environment . . . The academy operates within a "Quasi Military" environment utilizing military assets, doctrine, and principles wherever practical. The overriding question being addressed during the pilot phase is . . . can the problem of disenfranchised high school dropouts and their impact on society be effectively and economically addressed by an in-place National Guard force structure. (The Oklahoma Youth Challenge Program History and Goals, 1998)

What should we do with undisciplined, troubled adolescents? Educators are considering a different sort of schooling for violent or potentially dangerous youths (Portner, 1994; Newman, 1995). Although at first glance our recommendation might seem draconian, for violent students, shock camps offer promising alternatives to public and alternative schools. Based on a military model, these programs emphasize discipline in order to "shock" participants toward a better path. Currently, shock camps operate in twenty-seven states for the treatment of criminal offenders, and over a thousand camps have opened in the last several years to serve youths who seem to be heading for violence and criminality.

Shock camps have a lot to offer young people. For the first time in their lives, young men and women learn to lead orderly and regimented lives. As one writer describes it, shock camp residents at one facility "get up at dawn for calisthenics and run a mile, work all morning at a lumberyard, attend afternoon counseling and academic sessions, partake of all meals in silence, speak only when spoken to, and endure more physical training before lights out at nine" (Yen, 1994, p. 10).

Do these programs work? It may be too early to determine the effectiveness of shock-camps as they seek to instill appropriate values and self-discipline in their graduates. Some studies indicate that young people graduating from shock camps have a recidivism rate of 50 percent—that is, half of all shock camp graduates return to crime. Obviously, shock camps are less than perfect, but compare their success rate to the 70 percent recidivism rate for all violent youths (Sautter, 1995). Shock camps show promise. They protect the majority of students by removing the violent minority, and the camps don't burden schools with tasks they are not suited for. Shock camps for the disruptive are certainly less agreeable than regular public schools, and they should be. Students need to know that schools will not tolerate violence and that repeated antisocial behaviors will guarantee them a life far less pleasant than life at school.

We have argued that schools should embrace all students equally when they first begin school. Special curriculum interventions—the so-called conflict- and dispute-resolution curricula—should be reserved exclusively for students who demonstrate behaviors associated with violence in adults (for example, physical aggression and lack of self-control). Schools should use every technique at their disposal to curb disruptive behavior and bring the unruly child back into the fold. However, by middle school, students who impede the learning process or who threaten the welfare of other children should be considered as candidates for alternative schools. As we have noted, these alternative schools have amassed a sound, though not perfect, record for educating the disaffected. For the small handful of very disruptive students who are unable to cooperate in an alternative school, shock camps are a sensible last resort.

You may well ask whether expelling problem students from the public school system is likely to increase their inclination toward further violence and criminality. It's hard to know. Research indicates that future dropouts have high levels of criminal behavior while in school, but some evidence indicates that after these students drop out of school, they may have less trouble with the law (Herrnstein and Murray, 1994). As we have argued, schools often add to the problems of young people. Many students who do not succeed academically feel frustrated. Others feel confined by school rules and the abrasiveness of school crowding (Lawrence, 1998; Noguera, 1995; Sautter, 1995). Some students may learn better in another environment, and schools should find places for such students. Schools are academic institutions designed to teach cognitive skills. Students who cannot learn to play by the rules of civilized behavior—to exercise self-discipline, order, and respect for others—ultimately have no place in school.

## For Discussion

1. One writer argues that it's not TV that causes violence among children, and that society finds it easier to blame TV for promoting violence than to confront the real causes of crime: poverty, drug abuse, and other social conditions. He writes:

Youths in different parts of the United States are exposed to the same media but display drastically different violence levels. TV violence does not account for the fact that the murder rate among black teens in Washington, D.C., is twenty-five times higher than that of white teens living a few Metro stops away. It doesn't explain why, nationally, murder doubled among nonwhite and Latino youth over the last decade, but declined among white Anglo teens. Furthermore, contrary to the TV brainwashing theory, Anglo 16-year-olds have lower violent-crime rates than black 60-year-olds, Latino 40-year-olds, and Anglo 30-year-olds. Men, women, whites, Latinos, blacks, Asians, teens, young adults, middle agers, senior citizens in Fresno County—California's poorest urban areas—display murder and violent-crime rates double those of their counterparts in Ventura County—the state's richest. (Males, 1997, p. 2)

Do you find these arguments persuasive? What role do the media play in promoting violence—or, at least, making it appear a normal and acceptable part of life?

2. The National Association for the Education of Young Children wants to regulate television programming aimed at young children "to limit media exposure to violence and restrict practices that market violence through the linkup of media, toys, and licensed products" (*NAEYC*, 1993, p. 82). Media representatives argue that such regulation would amount to censorship and a violation of the First Amendment's guarantee to freedom of the press. They argue that "violence on the home screen *follows* the violence in our lives"; it does not *cause* violence (*TV Violence*, 1993, p. 281).

   Which position do you support? If you support the NAEYC point of view, would you favor regulations that limit children's exposure to video games that encourage aggressive behavior? What about music videos that suggest danger and violence?

3. Consider the following checklist posted on the National School Safety Center's Internet site for "identifying potentially dangerous students who may become campus assassins" (July 21, 1998):

**Assessment Tool for Predicting Violent Juvenile Behavior**

1. _____ Has a history of tantrums and uncontrollable angry outbursts.
2. _____ Characteristically resorts to name calling, cursing, or abusive language.
3. _____ Habitually makes violent threats when angry.
4. _____ Has previously brought a weapon to school.
5. _____ Has a background of serious disciplinary problems at school and in the community.
6. _____ Has a background of drug, alcohol, or other substance abuse or dependency.
7. _____ Is on the fringe of his/her peer group with few or no close friends.

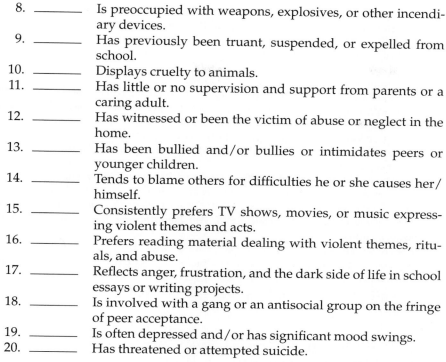

8. _____ Is preoccupied with weapons, explosives, or other incendiary devices.

9. _____ Has previously been truant, suspended, or expelled from school.

10. _____ Displays cruelty to animals.

11. _____ Has little or no supervision and support from parents or a caring adult.

12. _____ Has witnessed or been the victim of abuse or neglect in the home.

13. _____ Has been bullied and/or bullies or intimidates peers or younger children.

14. _____ Tends to blame others for difficulties he or she causes her/himself.

15. _____ Consistently prefers TV shows, movies, or music expressing violent themes and acts.

16. _____ Prefers reading material dealing with violent themes, rituals, and abuse.

17. _____ Reflects anger, frustration, and the dark side of life in school essays or writing projects.

18. _____ Is involved with a gang or an antisocial group on the fringe of peer acceptance.

19. _____ Is often depressed and/or has significant mood swings.

20. _____ Has threatened or attempted suicide.

Each affirmative answer is worth five points. NSSC says that each youngster with a score between 5 and 20 points is potentially at risk for juvenile misbehavior. A youngster scoring between 25 and 50 points is at risk and needs a significant amount of support and mentoring. A youngster with 55 or more points is at serious risk of harm to himself and/or others. If you identify students in the last category, NSSC advises seeking support from law enforcement, social and health services, family court, and other youth-serving professionals.

What is your opinion of the usefulness of this assessment tool? Should this tool, or one similar to it, be used to evaluate all students? What should be done with students who fall into the first two categories?

4. The National Association for the Education of Young Children argues against the use of corporal punishment in schools. It argues that the "use of corporal punishment in such situations teaches children that physical solutions to problems are acceptable for adults and that aggression is an appropriate way to control the behavior of other people. The institutional use of corporal punishment should never be condoned" (*NAEYC,* 1993, p. 83).

What policies concerning corporal punishment exist in your state and in your local school district? What are your personal views about corporal punishment as a form of discipline? If some parents approve of the teacher's use of physical punishment and prefer that their children be disciplined in this manner, should the teacher accede to the parent's wishes?

## *References*

ANDERSON, D. C. (1998). *Sensible Justice: Alternatives to Prison.* New York: The New Press.

AYERS, W. (1997). *A Kind and Just Parent: The Children of Juvenile Court.* Boston: Beacon Press.

BODINE, R. J., AND CRAWFORD, D. K. (1998). *The Handbook of Conflict Resolution Education: A Guide to Building Quality Programs in Schools.* San Francisco: Jossey-Bass.

BRENDTRO, L., AND LONG, N. (1995). "Breaking the Cycle of Conflict." *Educational Leadership 52,* 52–56.

BROPHY, J., AND McCASLIN, M. (1992). "Teachers' Reports of How They Perceive and Cope with Problem Students." *The Elementary School Journal 99* (1), 3–68.

CARLSSON-PAIGE, N., AND LEVIN, N. (1990). *Who's Calling the Shots? How to Respond Effectively to Children's Fascination with War Play and War Toys.* Philadelphia: New Society Publishers.

CASPI, A., ET AL. (1994). "Are Some People Crime-Prone?" *Criminology 32,* 163–196.

DERKSEN, D. J., AND STRASBURGER, V. C. (1996). "Media and Television Violence: Effects on Violence, Aggression, and Anti-Social Behavior in Children." In *Schools, Violence, and Society,* edited by A. M. Hoffman. Westport, CT: Praeger.

DEVINE, J. (1996). *Maximum Security.* Chicago: University of Chicago Press.

DILL, V. S., AND HABERMAN, M. (1995). "Building a Gentler School." *Educational Leadership 52,* 69–71.

DWORKIN, M. S. (1959). *Dewey on Education.* New York: Teachers College.

ELAM, S. M., ROSE, L. C., AND GALLUP, A. M. (1994). "The 26th Annual Phi Delta Kappa/Gallup Poll of the Public's Attitude Toward the Public Schools." *Phi Delta Kappa 76,* 41–64.

EPP, J. R., AND WATKINSON, A. M. (1997). *Systemic Violence in Education: Broken Promise.* Albany, NY: State University of New York.

FINN, C. E., JR. (1993). Whither Education Reform? In *Making Schools Work,* edited by C. L. Fagnano and K. N. Hughes. Boulder, CO: Westview Press.

GOLDSTEIN, A. P., HAROOTUNIAN, B., AND CONOLEY, J. C. (1994). *Student Aggression: Prevention, Management, and Replacement Training.* New York: Guilford.

HARRIS, LOUIS, AND ASSOCIATES. (1993). *Violence in America's Public Schools.* New York: Metropolitan Life Insurance Company.

———. (1994). *Violence in America's Public Schools: The Family Perspective.* New York: Metropolitan Life Insurance Company.

HERRNSTEIN, R. J., AND MURRAY, C. (1994). *The Bell Curve: Intelligence and Class Structure in American Life.* New York: Free Press.

HIRSCH, E. D., JR. (1996). *The Schools We Need and Why We Don't Have Them.* New York: Doubleday.

HOLMES, S. A. (1998). "Black Couples are Favoring Small Families." *New York Times,* July 21. http://www.NYTimes.com.

LAWRENCE, R. (1998). *School Crime and Juvenile Justice.* New York: Oxford University Press.

LAWTON, M. (1994). "Violence-Prevention Curricula: What Works Best?" *Education Week,* November 9, pp. 1, 10–11.

LEVINE, M. (1996). *Viewing Violence: How Media Violence Affects Your Child's and Adolescent's Development.* Garden City, NY: Doubleday.

MAHAFFEY, F. (1994). "Eliminate Violence in the Classroom." *Utne Reader,* January/February, pp. 82–83.

MALES, M. (1997). "Who Us? Stop Blaming the Kids and TV for Crime and Substance Abuse." *The Progressive,* October, pp. 1–5. (Internet)

MCPARTLAND, J., JORDAN, W., LEGERS, N., AND BALFANZ, R. (1997). "Finding Safety in Small Numbers." *Educational Leadership 55,* 14–17.

MOORE, M., AND ANDERSON, J. W. (1995). "War's Young Victims." *Washington Post National Weekly Edition,* May 8–14, pp. 6–7.

MORSE, P. A., AND ANDREA, R. (1994). "Peer Mediation in the Schools: Teaching Conflict Resolution Techniques to Students." *NASSP Bulletin 78,* 75–82.

*NAEYC Position Statement on Violence in the Lives of Children.* (1993). *Young Children 48,* 80–85.

NEWMAN, M. (1995). "Disciplinary Schools Planned for Students Carrying Weapons." *New York Times,* March 8, pp. 1, B4.

NOGUERA, P. A. (1995). "Preventing and Producing Violence: A Critical Analysis of Responses to School Violence." *Harvard Educational Review 65,* 189–212.

*The Oklahoma Youth Challenge Program History and Goals.* (1998). http://www.tya.onenet.net/history.htm.

PORTNER, J. (1994). "A New Breed of School for Troubled Youths." *Education Week 13,* 30–31.

*Recess from Violence: Making Our Schools Safe.* (1993). Hearings Before the Subcommittee on Education, Arts, and Humanities of the Committee on Labor and Human Resources. U.S. Senate, One Hundred Third Congress, First Session on S.1125 (September 23) Washington: U.S. Government Printing Office.

REISS, A. J., JR., AND ROTH, J. A. (1993). *Understanding and Preventing Violence.* Washington, DC: National Academy Press.

RODRIGUEZ, L. J. (1993). *Always Running, La Vida Loca: Gang Days in L.A.* Willimantic, CT: Curbstone.

ROTH, J. A. (1994). *Understanding and Preventing Violence.* Washington, DC: National Institute of Justice.

SAUTTER, C. R. (1995). "Standing Up to Violence." *Phi Delta Kappan 76,* K1–K12.

SNIFFEN, M. J. (1998). "Pinpointing Dangerous Professions." Associated Press, July 27. http://biz.yahoo.com.

*TV Violence.* (1993). *CQ Researcher 3,* 268–288, March 26. Washington, DC: Congressional Quarterly.

U.S. DEPARTMENT OF HEALTH, EDUCATION, AND WELFARE. (1997). *Violent Schools—Safe Schools: The Safe Schools Survey Report of the Congress.* Washington, DC: HEW.

U.S. DEPARTMENT OF JUSTICE. (1994). "Firearms and Crimes of Violence: Selected Findings from National Statistical Series," February 1994 MCJ-146844. Washington, DC: Department of Justice.

U.S. GENERAL ACCOUNTING OFFICE. (1997). "Substance Abuse and Violence Prevention." Testimony before the Subcommittee on Oversight and Investigations, Committee on Education and the Workforce House of Representatives. Washington, DC: General Accounting Office.

*Violence in Schools.* (1992). *CQ Researcher 2,* 785–808, September 11. Washington, DC: Congressional Quarterly.

*Violence in the Schools.* (1993). National Education Association Video, Teacher TV Episode #15. West Haven, CT: National Education Association.

WALLACH, L. B. (1993). "Helping Children Cope with Violence." *Young Children 48,* 4–11.

WEISHEW, N. L., AND PENG, S. S. (1993). "Variables Predicting Students' Problem Behaviors." *Journal of Educational Research 87,* 5–17.

YEN, M. (1994). "A Shock that Seldom Jolts." *The Washington Post National Weekly Edition,* November 28–December 4, pp. 10–11.

# CHAPTER 19

# Privatization of Schools: Boon or Bane

## POSITION 1: PUBLIC SCHOOLS SHOULD BE PRIVATIZED

One of the most interesting innovations sweeping across the world is privatization. Privatization means changing public services once operated by governmental agencies to private operations, cutting tax costs and government bloat and inefficiency. Public education is one of the most tax costly, bloated, and inefficient enterprises of government. Thus, schools are a prime candidate for privatization.

As democracy and capitalism increase across the globe, privatization will continue to be a strong movement in public life during the twenty-first century. Government-run operations show weaknesses that private enterprise can overcome. The concept of privatization is consistent with the tradition and evolution of market-based economics and private enterprise that have made the United States a model for other nations. Worldwide, leaders recognize private enterprise as the key vehicle for improving the lives of citizens while making government more efficient with available funds and resources. Nations from many geographic areas and differing economic traditions, including Spain, the Phillipines, Nepal, Ukraine, Canada, Austria, Australia, Indonesia, and India, are moving toward private operation of a variety of public services. The United States is actually lagging behind other nations in this global movement.

### What Can Privatization Provide for Schools?

Schools are among the social institutions increasingly undergoing privatization in many nations. England and New Zealand provide excellent examples of this process; the public in each of these nations recognizes the value of private enterprise in more effectively and efficiently operating schools.

Any market-driven enterprise must be flexible and diverse enough to stack up against global competitors. This idea applies to schools as well. There are a variety of ways to privatize the public schools with significant improvements in services and efficiency. Private operation of the schools, undertaken in any of a number of structures, can allow schools to shift easily to meet changing conditions.

## A Variety of Approaches to School Privatization: Charter Schools to Food Operations

There are several forms of privatization in schools, from completely privatizing operations to making a limited number of functions privately operated. In public-private partnerships, the school board hires private managers to run the public schools under a five-year contract that includes specified performance standards and allows the board to fire the managers with ninety days' notice. Although complete privatization offers some distinct advantages, allowing districts to hold private managers accountable for student learning, it is also possible to identify limited segments of current school operations that private contractors could handle to the benefit of students and taxpayers.

Some public schools now contract for selected services that are too costly or too cumbersome to handle under public control. School boards have been providing education since we established the idea of public education, but now they are becoming purchasers of educational services provided by private enterprise. Many school districts contract with computer corporations for payroll and accounting services. Others have found that contracting with popular fast-food companies, such as McDonalds and Pizza Hut, to provide school lunch service is more cost-effective, more acceptable to students, and sometimes more nutritious than the standard school cafeteria food.

Private contracts for specific services, from the provision of food to managing all school operations, have proved their value to students, school officials, and taxpayers. Piecemeal privatization of school services has been working well for years in many schools. Now private operation of individual schools, and even entire city school districts, is developing. Charter school programs, in which the state grants specific charters to groups to organize or take over schools, are now legal in many states.

The Massachusetts charter school law allows profit-making companies to apply for charters. The Edison Project, developed by business entrepreneur Chris Whittle, recently won three charters to operate public schools in Massachusetts as part of its original plan to establish up to 200 public, but for-profit, schools nationwide. Whittle's Channel One, the privately sponsored television channel for schools, has been operating successfully in a number of school districts—another example of the privatization of schools. The Edison Project has over 50 schools under its management, with low costs and good results (*Denver Post*, 1999).

There are many examples of privatizing parts of school operations, such as custodial, bus, or cafeteria services. There are also examples of privatization of individual schools, such as charter schools and the contracts given to Educational

Alternatives Inc. (EAI), a private firm headquartered in Minneapolis, to operate individual schools in Baltimore and in southern Florida. But no city had completely privatized its schools until Hartford, Connecticut, took that step in 1994. Educational management organizations, like HMOs for medical care, are emerging to improve schools. Sylvan Learning Systems, Nobel Learning Communities, and Knowledge Universe are current examples of private management of education. The 21st century should see expansion of school privatization from 13 percent in 2000 to 25 percent by 2020.

In complete privatization, a private organization takes charge of the schooling operation under rigorous contracts with the local board of education to guarantee performance or face dismissal. Included in complete privatization would be such activities as:

Managing the school(s)

Hiring, organizing, and evaluating the teaching and support staff

Developing the curriculum and purchasing teaching materials

Providing in-service assistance to teachers

Evaluating student learning

Communicating with parents and the community

Setting up the school's physical plant and facilities

Providing custodial and ancillary maintenance

Arranging for health and food services

Accounting, budget development and analysis, and school financing

Clearly, any of these individual items are also excellent candidates for partial privatization of school operations.

## *Reasons for the Privatization of American Public Schools*

### 1. Improving Schools for Our Children

The most important reason to involve private enterprise in schools is to benefit our children. Our primary resource deserves the best schools we can provide. Both students and parents appreciate well-run schools where success is the motivating purpose. When educational results make communities ashamed of their schools, children and parents are understandably reluctant to support or take pleasure in them. The faceless bureaucracy created for government-operated schools not only overwhelms local budgets, but it also does not respond to complaints. Private enterprise could not survive with that approach; its success is linked to ever-increasing efficiency and customer satisfaction.

Privatization also increases accountability, making school staffs responsible for meeting performance standards for the benefit of children. Accountability, a keystone of private enterprise, offers a way to clearly identify problems and to reward good performance in schools. Instead of weak and vague educational jargon that hides poor school practices, private enterprise sets specific goals and measures how well schools meet them. Schools that work will be rewarded; those that don't will be changed or closed.

The Edison Project, an innovative approach to school privatization, contracts with public schools to operate them without an increase in costs, but with better results and, in addition, making a profit. The Edison purposes are clear and direct: "to offer the best education in the world," "to welcome all students," and "to operate at an affordable price" ("An Invitation to Public School Partnership: Executive Summary," the Edison Project, undated). This puts the focus on student achievement. The Edison Project includes strict performance conditions in its contracts, which can be terminated on short notice if results are not satisfactory. What public school operation gives the public the same guarantee? Educational Alternatives Inc. (EAI), another major private contractor for public school operations, also puts performance conditions in its contracts and focuses on improving student work.

## 2. Breaking the Public School Monopoly

A second reason for privatizing schools is to break the monopoly public education has had in the United States. This will offer democratic choices to parents who are concerned about their children's educations but have always had to send them to state-specified schools. School choice is certainly in the best interest of children and their parents, but it also forces schools to compete in order to attract students and the financial support they need.

The public schools have established a monopoly over taxpayer-supported education in the United States. Law professor John Coons (1987) describes the U.S. education system as a "state-run monopoly" rather than a system of public schools. He argues that these state-run schools strip families of the authority to choose their children's schools by limiting them to local public school boundaries. Public schools have no competition, and their access to public funds to educate children is legally protected. The comparatively few private and parochial schools in the nation are currently prohibited from receiving taxpayer money. As a result, they serve a different and more selective clientele than their public counterparts; they don't compete for the taxpayer dollar. Without competition, the public schools have developed into self-protective havens where performance is not a high priority.

The public schools have had a monopoly for far too long, and they have suffered from the lack of competition. They have institutional hardening of the arteries, bloated and inefficient operations, and slow bureaucratic response to public concerns. These schools have little reason to provide better public service, increase their efficiency, require higher standards, or eliminate layers of bureaucracy. Privatization offers a way to bring customer satisfaction and state-of-the-art efficiency to such schools without the self-serving bureaucracy. Of course, the public schools do not welcome the idea of privatization, and their unions continue to fight it (Shanker, 1994a, 1994b).

## 3. Increasing Productivity

Third, privatizing will increase productivity in the public schools, a place where productivity has not changed for a century. In most public school districts, the schools are operated in much the same manner as they were when our grandparents were students. Private industry could not operate in this manner without suffering financial collapse. Expensive, labor-intensive public schools with inflated administrations sap local and state finances. Improvements in technology and communications have revolutionized U.S. business and provided manifold increases in productivity, but there has been virtually no change in the public schools. Computers and other forms of high technology speed up all forms of industry, but the schools, even with lots of computers, continue to take the same costly approach. Improved productivity is necessary in the modern world; no nation can afford the luxury of wasting time and resources. Improved productivity is consistent with the best thinking in economics and the best use of public money. Anderson (1998) notes that most school administrators come through the ranks of education and lack the business background and discipline needed to develop and implement sound strategic planning, efficient resource allocations, monitoring and accountability control, and effective management in schools. That may explain their lack of interest in improving productivity in the schools.

Public schools exemplify the wasteful public agency where productivity has declined while costs have escalated. In high-cost, high-maintenance buildings, students attend classes about six hours a day for about one-half of the calendar year. Teachers still teach about twenty-five students per hour in separate classrooms using multiple copies of costly printed textbooks, similar to the way in which teachers taught at the beginning of the twentieth century. Those teachers, no matter how good or bad they are, are paid according to a standard scale, earning from about $25,000 to $60,000 per year for only nine months' employment. The one-size-fits-all teacher pay scale depends on seniority, not on how well each teacher teaches or how well students learn. Excellent teachers receive the same pay as poor teachers, just because they have the same number of years of service. This compromises good teachers and forces many of them away from teaching as a career.

## 4. Meeting Global Competition

There is no doubt that schools exert great influence on the future of the United States and its role in the global marketplace. International competition requires the United States to remain on the cutting edge of innovation or suffer future decline. If the public schools are not up to the task, we need to find other ways to continue to improve the nation's status. This is one strong reason to move toward privatization of the schools. The obvious necessity of assuring America's place as a world leader and correcting long-term performance problems in public education underscores the point that privatization of schools is an idea whose time has come. The resounding collapse of the Soviet Union illustrated defects in economic structures that depend on government operation. Now we are in a race to see which nation will provide leadership in private development.

In an increasingly competitive global environment, the United States must maintain its leadership. To continue providing expensive and plodding public services in the face of increasingly efficient private operations throughout the rest of the industrialized world puts us at a severe disadvantage. Our nation deserves better. Further, the burden taxpayers bear as a result of inefficient government management of services has become excessive, while actual services decline. The privatization of public services promises significant benefits in worldwide competition and offers lower taxes, customer-focused service, and greater efficiency.

## Revitalizing the Public Sector: Improving Schools

Privatization is a valid idea for any public sector enterprise that has become stagnant. The purpose of a public agency is to provide needed services where private enterprise has been unable to do so. This does not mean that public agencies, once established, must always continue. The standard we must measure all public enterprises against is whether the quality of service they afford is the best we can get for the price we pay. If public agencies don't measure up against their counterparts in the private sector, we should replace them. That is the essence of privatization. Public agencies often outlive their purposes and become an inefficient drain on public funds. They become complacent and bloated, protected from the marketplace. As Denis Doyle (1994), a senior fellow at the Hudson Institute, argues:

> While it is the business of the public to provide public service, the question before us should be, Does government need to own and operate the means of production to see that the service is provided wisely and well? To which our answer must be, "Only rarely and in special circumstances." (p. 130)

Doyle submits that police departments and the issuance of currency must remain in public hands, but that construction of public roads, buildings, and bridges can be performed (and already is) mainly by private contractors, as are trash collection and maintenance in many cities. Further, contracting out for services is just good business for many public agencies. In particular, Doyle singles out public schools as places where entrepreneurship is clearly needed to provide innovation and confront unproductive and conformist traditions. He points out that "the uniformity of the school system, once thought to be a virtue, is clearly a liability in the modern era" (p 129).

Public schools are key examples of a public agency that deserves constant critical review for the quality of its service and its public costs. The schools consume more taxes than any other agency in local communities, and they also account for the largest part of most state budgets. That favored financial position should have made U.S. schools the best in the world, but we all know this is not the case. The evidence shows that public schools spend increasing amounts of taxpayer money while becoming more and more mediocre. We must reverse the direction of this downward spiral. Privatizing schools is one strong alternative to the spend-and-decline model we have seen in education during the latter half of the twentieth century.

Historically, we could argue, the public schools made a contribution to the development of our nation by providing access to education for many people and offering basic literacy and Americanization to immigrant children. There is certainly good reason to continue to provide mass education for all students in this modern and globally competitive age, but there is no reason that the government must own and operate the schools. The government school is an anachronism of a bygone period, held over because of romantic ideas about tradition. It is one holdover we will look back on one day and wonder why it lasted so long and cost so much to maintain. Government schools have come to represent high costs, low efficiency, and bureaucratic layering. It is time to shake up the bureaucrats and consider innovative ways to improve our schools at less cost. Privatization offers just that to schooling.

## Obstacles to Privatization of Schools

Obviously, lack of knowledge and public apathy are serious obstacles to any innovation. These obstacles can be corrected through a public information and education program. When people understand that, for less cost, they can have better service and more accountability, they quickly become supporters of the shift to private operation. Other, more difficult, obstacles remain.

Public employee labor unions have been lobbying extensively against privatization of public services. The teacher unions have been particularly active in opposing school privatization. Teacher unions are among the largest, best financed, and most active organizations in state legislatures. Many state legislators admit that they fear the power of the teacher unions. The teacher unions' self-serving approach to restricting privatization has not been to the unions' credit. Teacher unions have actually filed suit against school vouchers in Milwaukee, against school management contracts in Baltimore, Hartford, Connecticut and Wilkinsburg, Pennsylvania, and against school janitorial contracts in California (Eggers and O'Leary, 1996).

Government bureaucracies can also present obstacles to private enterprise, since bureaucracies may lose some of their power over key decisions. Under charter school laws in many states, charter schools are not subject to some of the bureaucratic regulations that have kept the public school establishment so entrenched. They may establish evaluations that hold teachers accountable without worrying about tenure requirements, develop a curriculum without contending with state mandates, and organize classes and provide instruction without meeting some of the trivial specifications that have petrified public education. The public education bureaucracy has built a massive fortress of regulations, with personnel required to draft, monitor, and alter each segment. Deregulation is a fearful event to some agency bureaucrats whose influence and positions are in jeopardy.

## Privatization Is in America's Interest

President Reagan established the President's Commission on Privatization to explore the separation between public and private delivery of goods and services and to recommend the transfer of selected public services to the private sector. The commission's report, *Privatization: Toward More Effective Government* (1988), expressed a concern about government-operated services:

> The American people have often complained of the intrusiveness of federal programs, of inadequate performance, and of excessive expenditure . . . government should consider turning to the creative talents and ingenuity in the private sector to provide, whenever possible and appropriate, better answers to present and future challenges. (p. xi)

The report identified the essential ways to privatize as (1) selling off government assets, (2) contracting work out to private companies, and (3) providing vouchers to purchase private services. In a long and well-documented presentation that used testimony from some of the United States' most eminent scholars, the commission noted its primary interest in "the American consumer who is in need . . . of education; of loans for school, home, farm, or business; of transportation; of health care; of other social services" (p. xi). Obviously, members of the commission considered education one of the most significant public services, and one seriously in need of improvement.

With regard to education, the commission found that:

> The recent record of educational achievement has fallen far short of the basic goals that Americans set for their schools. . . . Despite substantial public spending on education—at all levels of government—the nation's schools were not producing commensurate results—educational report cards have turned the 1980s into a decade of dissatisfaction with schools. (*Privatization*, 1988, p. 85)

The commission's report showed that taxpayer spending on public schools doubled during the prior two decades, but educational results have been far less impressive than we would expect from that level of public financial support. For comparison, expenditures per student in private education are about two-thirds the per-student costs of public education. Although the nation spends heavily on public schools, average SAT test scores declined in the 1980s. These scores have only haltingly started to increase, and a massive infusion of tax dollars over the past decades has not been shown to have any effect on them. The National Assessment of Educational Progress (NAEP) and other tests of basic skills also show that U.S. students perform poorly. In the international arena, comparative studies of test scores show that U.S. students rank at the bottom among industrialized democracies (Finn, 1995; Mandel, et al. 1995). Public schools are not improving by following the patterns of the past. Pumping more taxpayer money into those schools is not likely to alter their long-term deficiencies. Emily Feistritzer (1987) reported several years ago that there is no apparent correlation between education spending and student achievement. At no additional cost, privatization can improve schools, increase teacher motivation, and enhance student learning.

Clearly, the decline in U.S. education as school costs were rapidly increasing was of great concern to the commission. Public schooling is one of the areas we can improve by applying expertise in management, cost control, and performance. Schools are a public service that the creative talents of the private sector can help.

## Privatization and the Public School Crisis

The most significant commission recommendations for reforming education involve providing school choice, giving parents vouchers for use at private schools, and allowing private schools to participate in other federal programs. While these are important ideas that we should pursue, they may be insufficient to stem the decline in public education. Although the commission was accurate in its assessment of problems in public schools and its determination that significant change was needed, it did not go far enough in its recommendations for privatizing schools. There are many reasons to seriously question the continuation of public education as it is presently organized and operated (Geiger, 1995).

Schools are a lockstep system, out of touch with contemporary business management. Current school management follows an archaic and costly pattern, under regulations the education establishment set up early in this century. Many small schools have separate administrations and budgets for providing essentially the same services. New Jersey, for example, has more than 600 separate school districts. In some states, even tiny schools are mandated to employ a school principal, and often a superintendent and other staff. In large districts, multiple, well-paid school administrative officers never teach a student and seldom visit the district's schools. The organizational structures of schools are more similar to those of inefficient early factories than they are to the structures of modern corporations.

Public schools are managed through an old-fashioned system that relies on politics to get more tax money, elaborate and expensive lobbying efforts in state legislatures to improve teacher salaries and keep teacher unions in power, and coziness with state education agencies to maintain the status quo. Increasing state regulation only serves to further bloat school administrations. And all this is practiced without any accountability. The failings of public schools are revealed in the low test scores of U.S. students as compared with those of other nations, in the discourteous behavior of students, and in low public esteem.

The schools are mired in bureaucracy and self-protective traditional thinking. They are not efficient institutions. Instead of attempting to keep costs down while improving quality, a standard that business sets, schools simply obtain increased tax funds without improving productivity. They continue to be shelters for inefficient public employment.

There are numerous places to increase productivity in this antiquated system of education. The school day and school year are expensive links to our agricultural past. Most industrialized nations keep students in school for longer days and for more days of the year, which is part of the reason why we do not compare well in student achievement. The traditional form of small-group instruction, with one well-paid teacher for each class of twenty-five students, does not take advantage of striking advances in communication technology or flexible management. It increases school staff, but does not add to student learning. Interactive computers linked with major libraries and scholars would make better use of limited resources. The lack of salary recognition for teachers who increase student achievement limits teachers' motivation to seek more innovative and efficient ways to prepare students. Similarly, administrators with make-work jobs or infrequent contact with the classroom are not likely to be enthusiastic about improving their productivity. The inertia of low productivity is built into the current public schools; private enterprise offers a fresh approach.

## The Privatization Movement: A Global Context

Schools are not the only public agency that could be improved by privatization. In fact, a worldwide privatization movement is already in progress, rapidly improving services in many other areas, such as transportation and communication. Schools are an important part of this movement, and the effort to privatize them should be viewed in the larger context.

The global political economy has changed since the end of the Cold War, as the world increasingly recognizes the values inherent in free market enterprise. Privatization is a concept in keeping with the realization that communism and socialism are defective political systems. Communism robs people of their individuality, and socialism robs them of their personal motivation. The former communist and socialist nations of the old Soviet bloc realize that privatization of wasteful and bureaucratic state-owned industries is the only way to improve their economies and the lives of their people.

As the Soviet Union collapsed in the late 1980s and early 1990s, the Russian and other former communist governments tried to embrace capitalistic economics by replacing public ownership with privately held and operated businesses. This experiment has been slow and difficult because of the many years of communist rule and the serious economic decline state socialism caused. Economic analyses (Earle, Frydman, and Rapaczynski, 1993; van Brabant, 1992; Vickers and Yarrow, 1991) describe the difficulties such nations as Hungary, Poland, Czechoslovakia, and Russia encountered in their massive efforts to restructure a failed system, but economists generally recognize the need to privatize in order to compete in the global market. Earle, Frydman, and Rapaczynski, for example, note:

> After decades of experience with malfunctioning command economies and unsuccessful attempts to improve their performance through moderate "market socialist" reforms, the countries of Eastern Europe and the former Soviet Union are struggling to radically transform their economic systems. (p. 1)

In addition, members of Russia's old ruling Communist Party have attempted to undermine and destabilize the shift toward capitalism. If the Russian people can persist in their short-term sacrifices, they will be far better off than they were under communism. Had Russia pursued more complete privatization more quickly, it would now be stronger and more economically competitive. In 1990, formerly communist East Germany had almost 14,000 state-owned businesses, and just four years later, the number was fewer than 150 (Protzman, 1994). Private enterprise and marketplace competition are replacing inefficient government-controlled business enterprises.

Other nations are engaging in massive privatization of publicly owned industries. Several South American countries are privatizing telephone companies and airlines, as well as mineral development. Great Britain, suffering under Labour Party governments and socialistic economics for several decades, more recently privatized many publicly owned and operated industries. The British economy has improved significantly as a result. Privatization is an idea taking hold for industries in many nations. Water and wasteland treatment, for example, are 100 percent privatized in England, while the United States has only privatized about 15 percent.

The competition that is a hallmark of private enterprise requires efficient operation and consumer satisfaction—two elements lacking in government monopolies. Under privatization, it is possible to maintain and improve public services while cutting taxes. In addition, private enterprise is built on the human desire to succeed and to get credit for succeeding. This is a system that motivates people to achieve more and that rewards those who show improved work. No wonder the process of privatization is sweeping the world, creating increased global competition.

The key to continued world leadership is to constantly search for better ways to do things. We should not be content with old structures and the myths that support them if those structures are no longer efficient. Just as an old car must be replaced when it costs more to repair it than it is worth, we need to review some social agencies to see if they are as efficient as possible alternatives. It may be romantic to keep an old car, but it may not be wise economically. Similarly, public agencies may not be efficient and effective in their delivery of services.

Schools are basic to the national interest and to international competition. America's leadership depends on top-quality, well-educated people; that is, successful students from achievement-driven schools. The talents and vision of such people are limited by cookie-cutter schools that offer less than the most current and efficient approaches to education. The private sector of the U.S. economy, which demands innovation and efficiency in order to survive, offers an avenue for reshaping U.S. schools to meet the demands of global competition in the twenty-first century. For many good reasons, privatization of schools is the wave of the twenty-first century.

## POSITION 2: PUBLIC SCHOOLS SHOULD BE PUBLIC

The idea that private operation of public services is superior is a socially destructive myth. Schrag (1999) points out that "the pattern in our society is toward withdrawal from community into private, gated enclaves with private security, private recreational facilities, private everything, even as the public facilities deteriorate" (p. B–11). Social destruction results from the self-serving myth, promoted in the corporate world and corporate-oriented mass media, that private enterprise offers superior services. There is no solid evidence. The media uncritically report on charter schools as innovations to improve education, but a vast, two-and-a-half-year study by researchers at UCLA found little support for this claim; charter schools neither fulfill their promises nor improve student achievement (Magee and Leopold, 1998). Privatizing schools is not improvement or progress, just another avenue for private wealth to gain more control of our society.

Striking examples of improvements and declines in the quality of human life can be attributed to both private and public enterprise; neither has an automatic superiority in economic, ethical, or social terms. In addition to the lack of clear supportive evidence about the extraordinary claims of privatization advocates, questions arise about the ideology of privatization and its consequences for society.

Inherent in the privatization mythology is the presumption that if something makes a profit, it must be good for us. How can a democracy sustain the idea that greed offers more to a society than social responsibility? Privatization encourages privateering over the public good. Privatizing public schools is another example of this mythology, backed by a siren song of lower costs and better scores. Significantly, the issue shifts attention from the fundamental social purposes of public education in a democracy. While this shift may serve the purpose of those who advocate privatization, basic social purposes must be the centerpoint of any substantial debate over privatization.

In a capitalistic democracy, some activities fit private enterprise and some deserve public operation and oversight. *Savage Inequalities* (Kozol, 1991) documents how underfinanced public schools in poor areas make a mockery of democratic ideals. Jonathan Kozol, in an interview reported in *Selling Out Our Schools* (*Rethinking Schools*, 1998), finds no evidence that "a competitive free market, unrestricted, without a strong counterpoise within the public sector will ever dispense decent medical care, sanitation, transportation, or education to the people" (p. 1).

A major test of that balance lies in the fundamental social purposes of an activity. Thus, we can measure the public and private operation of schools against the broad social purposes of schooling. Any debate over privatizing the public schools should focus on whether public or private control is more likely to move us toward fulfilling those purposes.

The clamor to privatize and a long-term campaign to demonize public schools stifle the debate on social purposes (Troy, 1999). The necessary long-range social perspective is lacking in the pressure to privatize schools (Hunter and Brown, 1995). Shortsighted goals of achieving higher test scores and saving money are insufficient reasons for privatizing, even if private schools would assure these results. The privatization myth magnifies the social and economic problems that have plagued public schools for over a century, while it hides the significant historical defects of private enterprise.

Despite a century-long tradition of excellent public service in difficult social and financial conditions, public schools have been subjected to a relentlessly negative campaign during the past two decades. The history of private enterprise—with its questionable ethics, cavalier treatment of employees and the public, financial manipulation of the political process, and declarations of bankruptcy when in trouble—goes unmentioned in mass media reporting and public discourse on privatization. Much of the support for privatization of public schools revolves around shallow advertising that capitalizes on negative images of public schools, unsupported claims of potential cost savings, and a paternalistic aura that corporations know best. The evidence does not support the claims. A Brookings Institute study of privatization in public schools, especially big city schools, found that most arguments for school privatization are based on wishful thinking (Ascher, Fruchter, and Berne, 1996).

The rush to privatization demands a serious look at rationales, practices, and potentials. In certain situations and under strict public regulation, it may be reasonable to provide some aspects of public services, such as food service in school lunchrooms, through private contracts. But wholesale privatizing is an extremely hazardous approach to dealing with public services. In areas as important to the future of society as education, privatizing may destroy the soul of democratic life.

To address the lacks in long-range perspective and in maintaining a balanced view, we present two major points: (1) Public schools serve significant public purposes, and (2) privatization is being championed under a number of myths that hide its unpleasant characteristics. Our conclusion: that public schools must not be sacrificed to private profiteering.

## Privatizing and the Democratic Purpose of Public Education

To be self-governing, a democracy requires a well-informed, active, and free populace. The primary ideals of democracy in the United States include justice, equality, and freedom. Within those high social ideals, the overriding purpose of public education is to prepare students for active and knowledgeable participation in society. In schools, that preparation involves the development of language facility, social knowledge, ethical conduct, and sound critical thinking—all in the context of the accumulated wisdom of the arts and sciences. Standardized test scores, of course, reveal relatively little about this significant curriculum or about the social purposes public schools serve. Further, these instructional topics, and the related extracurricular life of the school, are baseless without the root purpose of improving civilization by focusing on ensuring and expanding justice, equality, and freedom. To lose sight of that grand democratic ideal by working to trim costs and raise test scores is to undercut the fabric of American society.

This relationship between a democratic society and the need for publicly operated schools has been widely recognized throughout history. Aristotle (1988), the first Western political philosopher, clearly recognized the need to provide schooling for all citizens to preserve a democracy. Jefferson (1939) understood the close relation between a democracy's requirement for knowledgeable citizens and its provision of common schooling. Among the most compelling statements for public education in a democratic society is John Dewey's *Democracy and Education* (1916). In recent years, leading political theorists have reiterated the significance of public education to democracy (Gutmann, 1987).

The goals of improving justice, equality, and freedom are central to the idea of a public school, but not to private enterprise. Clearly, we have a long way to go in public education to meet these high standards; minorities and women have not had equal opportunities or freedom in schools. But we are improving significantly in this area, and we continue to pursue those goals in public education. Privatizing, with its attendant emphasis on cutting costs and improving test scores, is less likely to expand opportunities for the weakest or most disadvantaged. When you take seriously the need to educate the whole society, and not merely the elite, you improve society—but you probably won't increase average test scores or cut the school budget.

In addition to making strong efforts to improve justice and equality, schools allow the freedom of inquiry needed to fulfill the claim of democracy. Education for knowledgeable self-governance liberates us from ignorance, including the ignorance perpetuated by propaganda and censorship. Public education for all citizens, then, requires student and teacher freedom of inquiry and critical thinking about social problems. But free, critical study of social problems may not be a goal in corporation-operated schools. The open examination of controversial topics, necessary in democratic society, may conflict with corporate agendas in an ethos in which business knows best.

Not only has the common schools tradition in the United States been a keystone of democratic society by offering individuals the opportunity to develop the skills and knowledge needed to self-govern, but schools have also provided a community-centered service responsible to the community in a variety of ways. Privatization threatens that tradition. Dayton and Glickman (1994) point clearly to one aspect of the threat:

> A fundamental problem with the privatization movement is that it views public education as merely another individual entitlement and ignores the vital public interests served by common public schools. Public education is democratically controlled by the elected representatives of the People. Ultimately it is the People who decide how public education funds are expended. Privatization systems use public funds, but limit public control. Allowing private control of public funds circumvents the democratic control and interests of the People. (p. 82)

A significant question regarding the privatization of public schools is whether private management is likely to view justice, equality, and freedom as the schools' most important purposes. Public education may have some difficult problems, but its purposes are clear and positive. Can the private sector be trusted to foster these democratic ideals?

## Recent Examples of School Privatization: Reasons for Resistance

The two most prominent efforts to privatize public schools in the United States have already been fraying at the edges and engaging in questionable practices that should arouse the public's skepticism about the whole process (Toch, 1995; Saks, 1995; Schrag, 1999; CUPE Report, 1998).

## The Edison Project

The Edison Project, the most widely advertised effort to take over and profit from the operation of public schools, was established by Christopher Whittle in 1991. Whittle, a strong advocate of free market economics, was known for comments that were "unbelievably hostile to the public school world" (*New York*, 1994, p. 53).

Using Whittle's funds for startup, with the expectation that investors would seize the new money-making opportunity, the Edison Project began by proposing to build new schools. That idea changed quickly to an effort to contract for the complete operation of existing public schools. Whittle had predicted that the Edison Project would be operating 200 private schools by 1996, and would be educating 2 million children by the year 2010. He also pledged to personally finance the education of 100 "Whittle Scholars" for a year at the University of Tennessee (*New Yorker*, 1994). The widely publicized project now appears unable to meet any of its initial projections. Edison reportedly was operating twelve for-profit schools at the end of the twentieth century, with a record of high teacher turnover because of organizational disarray, lack of materials and support, and other related problems (CUPE Report, 1998).

In 1992, Whittle persuaded Benno Schmidt, then president of Yale University, to become the Edison Project's chief executive officer, reportedly "in exchange for equity in the new company and a salary that insiders estimate at around 1 million dollars" (*New York*, 1994. p. 53). The *New York Times* (Applebome, 1994) reported Schmidt's salary at $800,000, but whichever figure is accurate, Schmidt's move from one of education's highest paid positions as Yale president (with a salary in the range of $150,000) to private enterprise certainly profited him. A $1 million executive salary is twenty-five times the average public school teacher's salary of about $40,000 and nearly seven times the salary of the highest-paid public school administrators of about $150,000. How can privatization, with such huge executive salaries, bring cost savings to taxpayers without cutting instructional support?

Taxpayer financing has not adequately provided the good salaries and working conditions those who serve in public education deserve, but money is not the primary motivation for their commitment to social improvement. Taxpayers get a bargain when good teachers agree to stay in public education. Providing million-dollar salaries to private school executives, while proposing to lower the costs of school operation, suggests mirrors-and-smoke accounting or major cuts in the most direct services to students. Privatization means even lower pay and higher workloads for teachers and counselors, increased savings on textbooks and materials, cutting or elimination of other services, and higher salaries for executives. This corporate model—excessively paid executives over exploited workers vulnerable to the executive's budget cuts—benefits an elite few, but does not benefit society in general.

There should be no confusion about who is going to pay executive salaries after private corporations take over the public schools: The formula calls for public funds. Can private business show how to better finance schools with public funds, make a profit, and preserve educational quality? The financial management of Whittle's corporation may provide a perspective. By 1994, Whittle Communications had reached a state of financial collapse. *The New Yorker* magazine (1994) featured a long story detailing this collapse under the title "Grand Illusion," and subtitled with the line, "But the biggest surprise may be that it took so long for anyone to know that things had gone so wrong" (p. 63). The story described Whittle's reputation on Madison Avenue as a "legendary salesman" and one whose "most striking quality may be his charm" (p. 63).

Whittle had earlier established Channel One, a private television channel that "gave" TV equipment to schools on the condition that students be required to watch the channel and its commercials daily. Needing capital to try to save his other ventures, Whittle sold Channel One to K–III Communications. K–III owns *Seventeen* magazine and the *Weekly Reader,* a school newspaper, and is itself under the control of the same corporate body that controls RJR Nabisco. That relationship raised some concerns about corporate interests and influence when the *Weekly Reader* carried a story on "smokers' rights" (*Wall Street Journal,* 1994). But the larger concern is about the broad effort to commercialize public education.

The Edison Project's financial difficulties illustrate some of the defects inherent in the privatization scheme. Venture capital, with its high risks and potentially high rewards for a few, is not the best model for organizing public schools in a democracy. Public schooling's long-term goals of providing knowledge and encouraging ethical conduct based on justice, equality, and freedom are socially constructive. Are those goals best served by people known as legendary salespeople hostile to public schools? A public education system based on charm and advertising is inconsistent with the democratic purposes of education. The potential damage to youth and to the society is too great.

## Another Privatization Experiment

The second most visible effort to privatize public schools involves Educational Alternatives, Inc., or EAI, founded in 1986. That organization obtained the first contract for the private operation of an entire public school district—the Hartford, Connecticut schools. The controversial decision was described as the result of a city "torn between a desperate plight and a radical plan" (*Time,* 1994, p. 48). Hartford's schools suffered from problems similar to those of many urban districts: neglect, intensified social problems, and the high costs of maintaining old schools and senior staffs. Per-student expenditures were higher, at about $9,000, than those of the average district in the state, but student test scores were low and the dropout rate high. The board of education chose EAI to undertake a five-year contract to pay the bills, shape the curriculum, train the teachers, and then keep whatever money was left in the public school budget, about $200 million per year, as profit.

One question the *Time* article posed was, "What will be the driving motive: Improving schools or improving EAI's bottom line?" (p. 49). In a commentary raising questions about the Hartford deal with EAI, Judith Glazer

(1994) suggested that "American education is for sale" to "profit-making companies whose bottom line is not education but the strength of their financial performance for their stockholders" (p. 44). Glazer makes a strong point that if Hartford's school problems had become so dire, the public should have held the state governor, state legislature, city council, and local school board accountable for neglecting their duty to provide quality public schools.

EAI's record in school privatization is sketchy. In 1992, the corporation obtained a $135 million contract to take over a few schools in Baltimore. EAI agreed to improve instruction and to make school operations more efficient, with any unspent funds going to the company as profit. Judson (1994) reports that the school district uses its public budget to pay EAI the city's average amount per student, or about $6,000. In fact, most non-EAI schools actually receive less than the average total student expenditure because the costs of maintaining the central district offices are figured into the averages, but are not counted against EAI's budget. Thus, EAI actually gets about $1 million more per school per year than other schools.

EAI improved physical facilities at the schools, but spent "more than the average amount of money" and "had not begun to deliver on its promise, that private enterprise can do a better job for less in running big-city public schools" (Judson, 1994, p. A13). Albert Shanker (1994b) stated that EAI changed some arrangements after the agreement, putting special education students in regular classrooms and then replacing special education teachers with "interns," recent college graduates paid $7 per hour with no benefits.

EAI initially reported that scores in EAI schools in Baltimore had increased considerably, but an examination of the scores by the *Minneapolis Star-Tribune* found that EAI had inflated the data (Leslie, 1994). EAI later acknowledged its error; data show that standardized test scores in the EAI schools have actually gone down (Judson, 1994). After this was publicized, the eight schools used to make comparative evaluations with EAI schools were changed by dropping the three non-EAI schools at which students did very well (Shanker, 1994a). This change should make EAI school test scores look better, but not because of improved education. Surprisingly, for all the fanfare about business's hard-nosed accountability for performance in private enterprise, the Baltimore contract does not set any performance standards for EAI to meet (Judson, 1994), and the comparative evaluation program has been compromised.

By 1996, EAI had lost both contracts, Hartford and Baltimore. An AFT report on the Baltimore school project showed that EAI had a profit of $2.6 million, that teacher morale had declined, and that there was no improvment in student test scores. The salary of the CEO of EAI was reported in 1996 to be $325, 000, with an additional $193,000 in stock options (CUPE Report, 1998).

## Privatization and Private Enterprise

The stories of the Edison Project and EAI are cautionary tales for those considering the privatization of public education. Another example comes from Canada, where Alberta is rethinking its charter schools. The largest one in

Calgary closed, leaving large unpaid bills and frustrated parents—apparently, no one monitored the money (Sheppard, 1998).

In the areas where private enterprise is supposed to afford the best leadership (efficiency, financial acuity, accountability, and performance), these private ventures do not measure up. Instead, evidence of financial manipulation, wastage and inefficiency, and insufficient public accountability crops up. Further, private enterprise has offered no demonstration that instruction was actually improved and at a lower cost when private groups take over. The public should be very suspicious when these corporations report the results of their work or their financial positions. The social purposes of public education, of course, are not addressed in these examples. Where is the concern for justice, equality, and freedom?

Private entrepreneurship is one of the values American society holds dear. We prize the brave individuals who risk their financial security to bring new ideas and products to the public marketplace. Thomas Edison and Alexander Graham Bell are considered heroes who endured sacrifices and hard work to emerge as successful inventors and businessmen. Private entrepreneurs encourage innovation, experimentation, and development. This is often to the advantage of the society, as well as to the economy. But private entrepreneurship is also marked by unethical and illegal practices, including fraud and scams, graft and corruption, "Let the buyer beware" as a common corporate philosophy, and irresponsible pollution of the environment. The robber baron mentality permeates much of private enterprise, where payoffs and hidden conspiracies for fixing prices or controlling the market are simply ways of doing business. The primary value is personal greed. In these ways, private enterprise has shown little regard for social responsibility.

Some of the practices of private enterprise, and their eroding effect on public servants, were at the root of President Eisenhower's warnings about military-industry entanglements long before public disclosures of military spending made the United States an object of international ridicule: The military was purchasing $2,000 screwdrivers and $500 toilet seats under Pentagon contracts with private industry. Incompetent private operation and lack of adequate governmental regulation have cost taxpayers billions in government bailouts of Chrysler, Lockheed, and the savings and loan associations. Yet, private enterprise maintains an aura of respectability that implies it is better than public operations.

## Exposing the Myths of Privatization

Clever packaging in a period when people distrust government and are concerned about rising taxes has made privatization popular. There are, however, several presumptions that privatization is based on, and they are simply false or at least seriously questionable. The popular media have not challenged these presumptions. They are the myths of private enterprise, and they deserve to be fully examined before the public purse is opened even wider to private operations.

Myths about privatization include the ideas that privatization is:

- efficient, so it can save tax money while providing quality services.
- market-driven, so it is responsive to the consumer.
- performance-based, rewarding the productive and cutting out the incompetent.
- a success as a worldwide movement.

## Efficiency

Efficiency is the main claim of private enterprise. It is almost an article of faith, but the claim collapses under scrutiny.

Efficiency is a means, not a goal; the mere act of being efficient is inadequate as a rationale for social policy. There has to be a purpose for striving to make human activities efficient. In a democratic society that respects the environment and aspires to equity for its members, efficiency can be a worthwhile pursuit, but effectiveness is more important. The efficient use of resources, human and other, should aim to preserve and improve the environment. That is a worthy goal, and efficiency is an appropriate means to reach it; but environmental improvement by efficiency is not in the interests of many industries. Efficient operation of social services should have the purpose of improving the lot of society as a whole, not just of one class of people. That statement of purpose suggests the kind of social benefits efficiency should supply. We must ask, would the efficiency improve civilization by increasing justice, equality, freedom, and life for the common citizen?

Against this measure, the superficial type of efficiency of the private sector is found wanting. The profit motive defines efficiency as a cost-saving way to increase corporate income. Saving time by requiring dangerous shortcuts may appear to be efficient, but may simply be foolhardy. Efficient slaughter of wild animals, once a pastime of the wealthy and a business enterprise, sped the endangerment of many species. Wild animal wall trophies and exotic meat dishes are not worth the price of those forms of efficiency.

Efficient manufacturing has created toxic waste, workplace accidents, worker health problems, overproduction, and waste. The actual social costs of this type of efficiency are seldom calculated. The environmental and human costs of industrial efficiency are hidden in the search for profit. In addition, the public often subsidizes the private sector through corporation-friendly policies on taxes and the use of natural resources.

A related concern is whether the captains of industry are themselves efficient and productive. Do they seem to practice what they preach for the public sector? Are their homes, cars, boats, and planes evidence of efficiency? Do they lead lives that model efficiency and social improvement? Although it is possible to find examples of wealthy, powerful people who make significant contributions to the improvement of society and who strive for efficient and productive lives, that is not the standard. Lives of excessive consumption and waste, with little obvious concern for the general quality of life in society, is the more typical example. Large homes, expensive cars, servants, yachts, exclusive clubs, private planes, and legal and financial assistance to take advantage of tax loopholes typify those who gain the most from private enterprise. These are not the accoutrements normally found among public school educators, whose lives are devoted to public service. Conspicuous consumption is a characteristic of private enterprise, not of public employment.

### Market-Driven and Consumer-Responsive

Another myth is that the private sector must be superior because it has to compete in the open marketplace and please its customers. However, it should be clear that there is no free and open market in the current economy. The marketplace itself is a myth. Price-fixing, monopolistic trusts, special interest legislation, weak regulatory agencies, and other corporation-protective practices skew the market to benefit the biggest corporations and the most politically adept businesspeople. Lobbying, graft, buyouts, control of the regulating authorities, and an "old boys' network" combine to deny newcomers equal opportunity in the marketplace. Most corporate strategies aim to gain control of the market to keep others out, not to encourage free competition. When that doesn't work well, corporations appeal to the government for special treatment or subsidies, or they undergo bankruptcy, which hurts small investors but leaves the executives wealthy. The free market does not exist.

Consumer responsiveness is another figment of the imagination. Marketing to increase consumerism is a high priority in the private sector, but the primary purpose is to increase profits, not to please customers. Enticing consumers to buy things they do not need is one of the purposes of advertising. Making consumers believe they are getting a good deal is the sales force's job. But making sure that manufacturers provide complete information, fully back up warranties, don't mislead customers, and meet safety requirements is the government's job through laws, consumer affairs departments, and the courts. Consumer protection and satisfaction is a public concern, fostered by decades of consumer manipulation. Every consumer has experienced traumatic confrontations with corporations; they make errors, furnish poor-quality goods or services, are unwilling to correct or replace items, use bait-and-switch tactics, provide weak warranties, list conditions of sale in unreadable fine print on contracts, and inflate credit charges. Private enterprise is ill-suited to truly satisfy consumers. Too many businesses have a record of enticement, profit, and resistance to customer complaints once a sale has been made.

### The Performance-Based Corporation, Rewarding Merit, and Cutting Incompetence Myths

One of the most interesting myths about private enterprise is that it is rigorous about performance, expecting increased productivity and eliminating incompetence. But performance, in business terms, is merely selling more products at less cost with more profit. This goal has nothing to do with quality. Presumably, performance-based systems would not reward underperformance, but the business news is filled with stories of CEOs whose corporations underperform, but who still receive large salary increases and bonuses. Nor does the myth of the performance-based corporation square with the ideas most people have about corporate life: Incompetence occurs regularly and at high levels, office politics is more important than the quality of work, and you can't challenge higher-level decisions even when these decisions are obviously wrong.

If U.S. businesses are so committed to performance, why was there a decline in its quality of manufacture and share of the world marketplace? Why are corporation stockholder meetings a façade to cover the actions of a small group of board members, while good ideas from ordinary stockholders are essentially excluded? Why is the business of consumer advocate offices increasing, and why don't corporations encourage strong consumer protection laws? Why are the most meritorious employees often forgotten, while the connected earn quick promotions? These and other points suggest that performance is not always the corporation's focus, and is not a major principle in big business.

### The Successful Worldwide Movement Myth

The vaunted privatization of public services in many nations has been unraveling. Britain's problems with the privatization of public services illustrate public loss for private gain. After World War II, Britain moved to public ownership of many enterprises to provide better accessibility to education, health care, and social services. Fifteen years of the Thatcher and Major governments produced privatization, and public services found themselves under assault.

Ellingsen (1994a) examined this privatization program and found: "Britain's passion for privatization has produced no payoff for the public . . . the public is starting to realize not only that the sell-offs have made millionaires of those who run former state enterprises, but have cost consumers something like $9 billion" (p. 21). The minister responsible for most of the privatization, Lord Parkinson, admitted after retiring that auctioning public businesses had not gone as planned; private shareholders did well, but the customers did not. British Telecom, auctioned in 1984, had embarrassingly high profits, while customers paid about $1 billion more than necessary. Water authorities, after privatization, saw their profits soar, while "customers are paying an extra $640 million for service that, as yet, has not fundamentally improved" (p. 21).

As a result of privatization, London Electricity executives saw their salaries rise from averages well below those in the private sector—from $2 million to over $4 million annually for each of the twelve top officers. One executive retired on a $3 million pension, about $200,000 per month for each month he was in the privatized corporation. Under privatization, British Gas doubled the chief executive's salary to more than $1 million. Public utilities were sold at excessively low prices that allowed quick profits, and executive income was linked to those profits in a charade claim of performance—all essentially at taxpayer expense. Some government ministers left public service to become members of the boards of the newly privatized companies (Ellingsen, 1994a). The greed of privatization has transformed the benevolent post-World War II British welfare state into a nation plagued by increased separation between the social classes, illegal child labor, hidden sweatshops, and crime and drugs (Ellingsen, 1994b).

Australia's experience with privatization also was problematic. Although studies concluded that a Sydney harbor tunnel was not economically viable, a private firm was proposed as a cost-saving approach to build and operate one. After two years of private operation, taxpayers have learned they will pick up a previously unreported tab of $4 billion to cover extra expenses during the thirty-year life of the private contract. Following that disclosure, alarms were sounded about other privatization efforts because of secrecy, hidden costs, and lack of scrutiny of private contracts for public services, such as building and operating hospitals, prisons, airports, railroads, and water services ("Why Parlt [Parliament] Must Scrutinize Projects with Private Sector," 1994; "Auditor Criticises Secrecy on Public Works Contracts," 1994; "Public Funds, Public Works," 1994). The public services employees' organization warned that a proposed bill to privatize state utilities (gas, electricity, and water) could lead to the destruction of the public sector without adequate protection for consumers or public funds or the provision of quality service ("Competition May Kill Utilities: ACTU," 1994).

Citizens of other nations have also suffered under privatization. In Eastern Europe and the former Soviet Union, privatization created high unemployment, extraordinary inflation, pyramid schemes that enriched a few and caused financial disaster for many, and social unrest (van Brabant, 1992; Earle, Frydman, and Rapaczynski, 1993).

These myths of privatization should become part of the public debate before we take irretrievable actions to dismantle the public schools.

## Ideology or Sound Thinking?

After studying the economics of public service privatization for over six years, Sclar (1994) dismissed the claim that it would save money while improving services. He found this promise to be ideological hype, a starkly conservative agenda unsupported by research or practice. Sclar suggests that real competition in the global marketplace will require an improved public infrastructure, not its decimation by privatization. Undercutting public services, increasing in actual total costs, and raking in windfalls for the well-connected do not offer a quality of life that encourages global leadership. Sclar concludes: "Finally, it is the public sector that is the dispenser of social justice. It is difficult to envision America sustaining itself as a progressive democracy with that role impaired" (p. 336).

In a system of democratic capitalism, where the relationship between the public and private sectors is delicate, there are many tensions. Private enterprise has some virtues and advocates, but it creates severe economic disparity among people and carries a history of exploitation. Similarly, public enterprise offers virtues and has supporters, but it creates tax burdens and itself to bureaucratic bungling. Each sector serves different needs of individuals and of the society at large. Increasing the proportion controlled by the private sector comes at a cost to the public. For a democracy, the cost of privatizing public education is too high.

## For Discussion

1. Table 19.1 shows categories and examples of government services that are candidates for privatization.
   a. What are the advantages and disadvantages of privatization in regard to each of the examples?
   b. What criteria should be used to determine the advantages and disadvantages?
   c. How do these criteria fit a discussion of privatizing schools?
   d. Who should be empowered to make the decisions about privatization?

**TABLE 19.1  Government services and privatization.**

| Category of Service | Example Activities for Privatization |
| --- | --- |
| Defense | military support, training |
| Health | public hospitals, FDA operations |
| Transportation | airports, Amtrack, FA, urban mass transit |
| Recreation | parks service, public land development |
| Justice | crime control, prisons |
| Communication | public radio, monitoring airwaves |
| Taxes | collection enforcement, IRS audits |

2. Shanker (1994b) noted that a public-private venture called "performance contracting" was started during the Nixon administration to save the public schools. The idea was for private firms to contract to improve student test scores in specific subjects. The result, says Shanker, was scandalous: repetitive test taking, or drill teaching of answers to test questions, because the companies were good at marketing, but knew little about education. If we are to privatize the public schools, what conditions should be established or regulated?

3. The Government Accounting Office (1996) found five studies conducted between 1991 and 1996 that compared public and private prisons in California, Texas, Washington, Tennessee, and New Mexico on the criteria of operational costs and quality of service provided. The GAO drew no conclusions from these studies because they found little or no differences in operational costs or in quality of service provided. How does this report support public or private operation of prisons?

4. The Milwaukee parental choice program, a voucherlike plan that uses state funds for sending a small group of children from poor families to private schools, has been evaluated in three independent studies. The evidence shows that parents in the privatization program are more satisfied with school than are those who are not in the program, but the evidence also shows that there is no difference between public and private schools in actual student achievement. What could account for these findings? What implications can we draw from the evidence? What does this say about privatization?

5. Discuss the following proposition: Even if it costs more to better educate children under private operations, this would clearly show the public the need to better finance schools. Either way, it benefits education.

## References

ANDERSON, C. (1998). "Schools Need Privatization Lesson." *North County* (CA) *Times,* November 28, pp. A–14.

APPLEBOME, P. (1994). "A Venture on the Brink: Do Education and Profits Mix?" *The New York Times,* October 30, p. 28.

ARISTOTLE. (1988). *The Politics,* edited by S. Everson. Cambridge, England: Cambridge University Press.

ASCHER, C., FRUCHTER, N., AND BERNE, R. (1996). *Hard Lessons: Public Schools and Privatization.* Washington, DC: Brookings Institute Press.

"Auditor Criticises Secrecy on Public Works Contracts." (1994). *Sydney Morning Herald,* October 18, p. 1.

BRETT, C. (1994). "Education in No-Zone Land: The Price of Free-Market Learning." *North & South* 102, 75–88.

"Competition May Kill Utilities: ACTU." (1994). *Sydney Morning Herald,* October 29, p. 39.

COONS, J. (1988). "Testimony, Hearings on Educational Choice. December 22," Cited in *Privatization: Toward More Effective Government.* Washington, DC: U.S. Government Printing Office.

CUPE REPORT (1998). Canadian Union of Public Employees. www.cupe.ca

Dayton, J., and Glickman, C. D. (1994). "American Constitutional Democracy: Implications for Public School Curriculum Development." *Peabody Journal of Education* 69, 62–80.

*Denver Post.* (1999). "Education Creeps Toward Privatization." Feb. 21, Sect. 1, p. 1.

DEWEY, J. (1916). *Democracy and Education.* New York: Macmillan.

DOYLE, D. (1994). "The Role of Private Sector Management in Public Education." *Phi Delta Kappan* 76, 128–132.

EARLE, J., FRYDMAN, R., AND RAPACZYNSKI, A. (1993). *Privatization in the Transition to a Market Economy.* New York: St. Martin's Press.

*Education Week.* (1994). "Even as Whittle Falls on Hard Times, Edison Model Leaves Wichita Hopeful." *Education Week* 14 (11), 12, 13.

*Education Week.* (1994). "The New Politics of Education: School Districts for Sale." Commentary. *Education Week* 14:44+.

EGGERS, W. AND O'LEARY, J. (1996) "Union Confederates." *American Spectator.* March.

ELLINGSEN, P. (1994a). "Making Profit in Private." *Sydney Morning Herald,* November 26, p. 21.

——— (1994b). "Rule Britannia—A Nation of Despair." *Sydney Morning Herald,* October 29, p. 28.

FEISTRITZER, E. (1987). "Public vs. Private: Biggest Difference Is Not the Students." *The Wall Street Journal,* December 1, p. 36.

FINN, C. (1995). "The School," *Commentary.* 99:6–10.

GEIGER, P. E. (1995). "Representation and Privatization." *American School and University,* 67, 28–30.

GIBBS, N. (1994). "Schools for Profit." *Time,* October 17, pp. 48–49.

GLAZER, J. (1994). "The New Politics of Education: Schools For Sale." *Education Week* 14, 44–ff.

Government Accounting Office. (1996). "Private and Public Prisons: Studies Comparing Operational Costs and/or Quality of Service." Report GCD-96-158. Report to the Subcommittee on Crime, Committee on the Judiciary, House of Representatives. Washington, DC: August.

GUTMANN, A. (1987). *Democratic Education.* Princeton: Princeton University Press.

HUNTER, R. C., AND BROWN, F. EDITORS. (1995). "Privatization in Public Education." *Education and Urban Society,* 27:107–228.

JEFFERSON, T. (1939). *Democracy.* New York: Greenwood Press.

JUDSON, G. (1994). "Hartford Hires Group to Run School System." *The New York Times,* October 4, pp. B1, B6.

KOZOL, J. (1991) *Savage Inequalities: Children in America's Schools.* New York: Crown.

LESLIE, C. (1994). "Taking Public Schools Private." *Newsweek,* June 20, p. 7.

MAGEE, M., AND LEOPOLD, L. S. (1998)."Study Finds Charter Schools Succeed No More than Others." *San Diego Union-Tribune.* December 4, pp. A-1, 15.

MANDEL, M., ET AL. (1995). "Will Schools Ever Get Better?" *Business Week,* April 17, pp. 64–68.

*New York.* (1994). "Has Benno Schmidt Learned His Lesson?" October 31, pp. 49–59.

*New Yorker.* (1994). "Grand Illusion." October 31, pp. 64–81.

*Privatization: Toward More Effective Government.* (1988). Report of the President's Commission on Privatization. Washington, DC: U.S. Government Printing Office.

PROTZMAN, F. (1994). "East Nearly Privatized, Germans Argue the Cost." *The New York Times,* August 12, pp. D1, D2.

"Public Funds, Public Works." (1994). *Sydney Morning Herald,* October 18, p. 18.

*Rethinking Schools.* (1998). "The Market Is Not the Answer: An Interview with Jonathan Kozol." www. rethinkingschools.org.

SAKS, J. B. (1995). "Scrutinizing Edison." *American School Boards Journal* 183, 20–24.

SCHMIDT, P. (1994). "Hartford Hires E.A.I. to Run Entire District." *Education Week,* 14:1, 14.

SCHRAG, P. (1999). "Private Affluence and Public Squalor." *San Diego Union-Tribune* 8(8) Jan. 8, B11.

SCLAR, E. (1994). "Public-Service Privatization: Ideology or Economics?" *Dissent,* Summer, pp. 329–336.

SHAFER, G. (1999). "The Myth of Competition and the Case Against School Choice." *The Humanist* 59(2), 15+.

SHANKER, A. (1994a). "Barnum Was Right." *The New York Times,* October 23, p. E7.

———. (1994b). "A History Lesson." *The New York Times,* March 6, p. E7.

SHEPPARD, R. (1998). "A School Failure." *MacLeans* 111, 52–53.

*Time.* (1994). "Schools for Profit." October 17, pp. 48–49.

TOCH, T. (1995). "Taking Public Schools Private: A Setback." *US News and World Report* 117, 74.

TROY, F. (1999). "The Myth of a Failed Public School System." *Church and State* Jan., pp. 17–20.

"Tunnel Payout Climbs to $4 billion." (1994). *Sydney Morning Herald,* October 17, p. 3.

VAN BRABANT, J. V. (1992). *Privatizing Eastern Europe.* International Studies in Economics and Econometrics, No. 24. Boston: Kluwer Academic Press.

VICKERS, J., AND YARROW, G. (1991). "Economic Perspectives on Privatization." *Journal of Economic Perspectives* 2, 111–132.

*Wall Street Journal.* (1994). "A KKR Vehicle Finds Profit and Education a Rich But Uneasy Mix." October 12, pp. A11, A12.

"WHY PARLT [PARLIAMENT] MUST SCRUTINIZE PROJECTS WITH PRIVATE SECTOR." (1994). *Sydney Morning Herald,* October 18, p. 19.

# Index